Content Standards Grades 5–8

● Science as Inquiry

Content Standard A: As a result of their activities in grades 5–8, all students should develop

- Abilities necessary to do scientific inquiry
- Understandings about scientific inquiry

● Physical Science

Content Standard B: As a result of their activities in grades 5–8, all students should develop an understanding of

- Properties and changes of properties in matter
- Transfer of energy
- Motion and forces

● Life Science

Content Standard C: As a result of their activities in grades 5–8, all students should develop an understanding of

- Structure and function in living systems
- Population and ecosystems
- Reproduction and heredity
- Diversity and adaptations of organisms
- Regulation and behavior

● Earth and Space Sciences

Content Standard D: As a result of their activities in grades 5–8, all students should develop an understanding of

- Structure of the earth system
- Earth in the solar system
- Earth's history

● Science and Technology

Content Standard E: As a result of the activities in grades 5–8, all students should develop an understanding of

- Abilities of technological design
- Understanding about science and technology

● Science in Personal and Social Perspectives

Content Standard F: As a result of the activities in grades 5–8, all students should develop an understanding of

- Personal health
- Risks and benefits
- Populations, resources, and environments
- Changes in environments
- Natural hazards
- Science and technology in society

● History and Nature Of Science

Content Standard G: As a result of the activities in grades 5–8, all students should develop an understanding of

- Science as a human endeavor
- History of science
- Nature of science

Teaching Children
Science
A Discovery Approach

seventh edition

Joseph Abruscato

Retired, University of Vermont

Donald A. DeRosa

Boston University

ALLYN & BACON

Boston • New York • San Francisco
Mexico City • Montreal • Toronto • London • Madrid • Munich • Paris
Hong Kong • Singapore • Tokyo • Cape Town • Sydney

For my daughters, Anne Marie and Elizabeth
Like a gentle breeze on a warm summer day, you refresh my spirit and bring me joy! —J. A.

To my family for their love, inspiration, and support. —D. D.

Series Editor: Kelly Villella Canton
Series Editorial Assistant: Annalea Manalili
Senior Marketing Manager: Darcy Betts Prybella
Production Editor: Annette Joseph
Editorial Production Service: Dee Josephson/Nesbitt Graphics
Composition Buyer: Linda Cox
Manufacturing Buyer: Megan Cochran
Electronic Composition: Nesbitt Graphics
Interior Design: Denise Hoffman
Photo Researcher: Annie Pickert
Cover Designer: Susan Paradise

For related titles and support materials, visit our online catalog at www.pearsonhighered.com.

Between the time website information is gathered and then published, it is not unusual for some sites to have closed. Also, the transcription of URLs can result in typographical errors. The publisher would appreciate notification where these errors occur so that they may be corrected in subsequent editions.

Library of Congress Cataloging-in-Publication Data

Abruscato, Joseph.
  Teaching children science : a discovery approach / Joseph Abruscato, Donald A. DeRosa. — 7th ed.
    p. cm.
  Includes bibliographical references and index.
  ISBN 0-13-715677-4 (978-0-13-715677-1)
  1. Science—Study and teaching (Elementary)   I. DeRosa, Donald A. II. Title.

  LB1585.A29 2010
  372.3'5— dc22

                                                          2009000637

Printed in the United States of America
10 9 8 7 6 5 4 3   EB 13 12 11 10

Credits appear on page 450, which constitutes an extension of the copyright page.

Allyn & Bacon
is an imprint of

www.pearsonhighered.com

ISBN-10: 0-13-715677-4
ISBN-13: 978-0-13-715677-1

Brief Contents

Contents

2 Constructing Knowledge and Discovering Meaning   25

How can I help children learn science?

3 The Inquiry Process Skills   41

How can I help children use the inquiry process skills to make discoveries?

4 Planning and Managing   57

How can I plan and manage inquiry-based,
discovery-focused units and lessons?

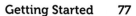

5   Strategies and QuickChecks   77

*How can I effectively use cooperative learning, questioning
and wait-time strategies, active listening, demonstrations,
and textbooks in my classroom?*

8 Using Technology to Enhance Science Learning   131

What comes first, content or technology?

9 Adapting the Science Curriculum   141

How can I adapt the science curriculum for children from diverse cultural backgrounds, children with special needs, and children with special gifts?

Part Two　　The Earth/Space Sciences　　161

10　Earth's Surface, Atmosphere, and Weather　　167

Content

11 The Cosmos   181

Content

12 Earth/Space Science Lesson Ideas   195

Putting the Content into Action

15 Life Sciences Lesson Ideas 281

Putting the Content into Action

Part Four   The Physical Sciences   337

Preface

As with previous editions, this edition of *Teaching Children Science* benefits from the wonderful insights and suggestions of readers like you. Education, and especially teaching about teaching, is always a work in progress. Textbooks have always been a two-edged sword for me. On the one hand they provide a springboard for ideas, on the other they can be pedantic and boring to read. Traditionally, *Teaching Children Science* has striven to be conversational, engaging, and practical. Hopefully it is one of those textbooks that you will keep in your library and refer to for years to come. As was the case with prior editions, there are six major reasons for the continued success of this book:

1. *Flexibility.* This single volume contains information about the three essential components of teacher preparation: science methods, science content, and science activities for children. In using this book, instructors and students alike can hone in on particular components and draw upon others as needed or desired.

2. *An inviting, engaging, and motivating style.* This is an upbeat book whose solid content is delivered in a way that makes it actually enjoyable to read. I *still* have negative feelings about the ponderous, unreadable, lifeless education methods texts that I used as a student and that still exist today. Many education texts are so massive and unmotivating. School classrooms need to be exciting, engaging places, and that won't happen if teachers use books whose heft and style inadvertently have the opposite effect.

3. *An inquiry-based and discovery-focused message.* This book presents a consistent and clear message about the type of learning experiences that teachers need to create. Namely, children learn best in classrooms in which they make discoveries (with the teacher's strong guidance) using inquiry-based approaches.

4. *A constructivist approach.* There is little question that we create much of our own reality. One way of looking at how we integrate life experiences into our mental processes is provided by the theory of constructivism. When applied in the classroom, this theory guides teachers in thinking about what they are doing to help children get beyond scientific misconceptions and acquire more appropriate knowledge, skills, and values. Constructivism is used as a guiding principle throughout the book.

5. *A wealth of information.* As noted earlier, this book provides the three essential components for teacher preparation: methods, content, and activities. Part One, which includes the first nine chapters of the book, provides the basic "how-to-do-it" information for teaching science. Additional content information specific to teaching about topics in the earth/space, life, and physical sciences is provided in Chapters 10, 11, 13, 14, 16, and 17, respectively. As educators, we are challenged not only to understand science, but to help naïve learners grasp foundational scientific concepts that they can build upon as they grow intellectually. Chapters subtitled "Putting the Content into Action" follow the content chapters. These chapters (Chapters 12, 15, and 18) are designed to help us, as educators, create learning experiences that help students construct the fundamental concepts of science that will provide a strong foundation on the path to scientific literacy. It's all here. Seek and you will find!

NSES

6. *References to standards.* "If you don't know where you're going, you'll end up some-place else." All of us who teach children science need some direction, and the best current direction is provided by the National Science Education Standards (NSES). As described later in this Preface, the NSES are addressed at relevant points throughout the book and tied to every demonstration and activity. Project 2061, an initiative sponsored by the American Association for the Advancement of Science (AAAS) that provides resources for the advancement of science, mathematics, and technology, is also addressed in the text through a series of boxes.

Project 2061

Implications for Your Inquiry-Based, Discovery-Focused Classroom

To develop an inquiry-based, discovery-focused classroom, you'll need to draw on a wide range of resources. One resource that may prove useful is the curriculum development effort known as *Project 2061*. Developed by scientists and educators, and with the sponsorship of the American Association for the Advancement of Science, this project is intended to help reform K–12 science, mathematics, and technology education. Its basic reference document, *Science for All Americans*, offers recommendations called *benchmarks* in many areas, which will be important to you as you plan and teach.

Project 2061 has twelve benchmarks that you may wish to study in some detail:

- The nature of science
- The nature of mathematics
- The nature of technology
- The physical setting
- The living environment
- The human organism
- Human society
- The designed world
- The mathematical world
- Historical perspectives
- Common themes
- Habits of mind

To find helpful information about any of these benchmarks, visit the Project 2061 website at www.project2061.org/.

How This Book Is Organized

Part One: Strategies and Techniques

Again, the first nine chapters of this book deal with major topics that will shape what you teach, how you teach, and how you interact with children. To help focus your reading and discussion in these chapters, keep in mind that each has a consistent format that includes these components:

- *Text:* A discussion of specific content-related topics
- *Reality Check:* A thought-provoking challenge for you to complete individually or as a member of a cooperative learning group
- *Summary:* A review of the main ideas in the chapter
- *Going Further:* Learning activities that you may do on your own or in a cooperative learning group
- *Print Resources for Discovery Learning:* A list of books and articles that will help extend your study of the chapter's main points
- *Electronic resources:* Weblinks, videos, and animations available on MyEducationLab.

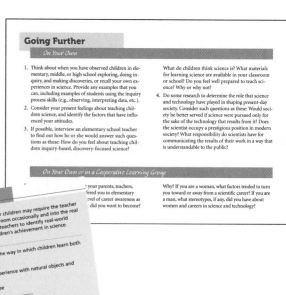

Going Further

On Your Own

1. Think about when you have observed children in elementary, middle, or high school exploring, doing inquiry, and making discoveries, or recall your own experiences in science. Provide any examples that you can, including examples of students using the inquiry process skills (e.g., observing, interpreting data, etc.).

2. Consider your present feelings about teaching children science, and identify the factors that have influenced your attitudes.

3. If possible, interview an elementary school teacher to find out how he or she would answer such questions as these: How do you feel about teaching children inquiry-based, discovery-focused science?

What do children think science is? What materials for learning science are available in your classroom or school? Do you feel well prepared to teach science? Why or why not?

4. Do some research to determine the role that science and technology have played in shaping present-day society. Consider such questions as these: Would society be better served if science were pursued only for the sake of the technology that results from it? Does the scientist occupy a prestigious position in modern society? What responsibility do scientists have for communicating the results of their work in a way that is understandable to the public?

On Your Own or in a Cooperative Learning Group

[...] your parents, teachers, [...] fered you in elementary [...] vel of career awareness as [...] did you want to become?

Why? If you are a woman, what factors tended to turn you toward or away from a scientific career? If you are a man, what stereotypes, if any, did you have about women and careers in science and technology?

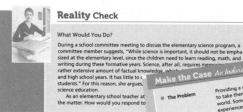

Reality Check

What Would You Do?

During a school committee meeting to discuss the elementary science program, a committee member suggests, "While science is important, it should not be emphasized at the elementary level, since the children need to learn reading, math, and writing during these formative years. Science, after all, requires memori[...] rather extensive amount of factual knowledge, which [...] and high school years. It has little to [...] students." For this reason, she argues, [...] science education.

As an elementary school teacher at [...] the matter. How would you respond to [...]

Make the Case *An Individual or Group Challenge*

● **The Problem**

Providing a rich learning environment for children may require the teacher to take them out of the traditional classroom occasionally and into the real world. Sometimes, it is difficult for new teachers to identify real-world experiences that will really improve children's achievement in science.

● **Assess Your Prior Knowledge and Beliefs**

What do you presently believe about the way in which children learn both in and out of the classroom?

1. Children learn best from direct experience with natural objects and phenomena.

_____ agree   _____ disagree

Your evidence: _____

2. Hands-on science experiences automatically reinforce children's learning.

_____ agree   _____ disagree

Your evidence: _____

3. A child's prior knowledge and beliefs should be assessed before new experiences are introduced to ensure that the experiences will be meaningful.

_____ agree   _____ disagree

Your evidence: _____

4. Children have few misconceptions about the natural world

Parts Two Through Four: Methods, Content, and Activities for Teaching Science and Technology Units

Each part opens with an introduction that provides background information about the field of science at hand: the earth/space sciences (Part Two), the life sciences (Part Three), or the physical sciences (Part Four). In each part, a section called *History and Nature* looks at careers in science, key events in the development of the field, and the lives of real women and men who helped shape that development. Another section called *Personal and Social Implications* (topics emphasized in the NSES) reviews issues of personal and community health as well as the hazards, risks, and benefits that go along with scientific development. A final section, *Technology: Its Nature and Impact,* discusses and illustrates specific developments and considers the long-term implications of technology for our world.

Following each content section, you will find chapters that integrate the unit and lesson planning strategies addressed in Part One. These chapters provide starter ideas and inquiry questions along with suggested activities, WebQuests demonstrations, in-class learning centers, bulletin boards, field trips, and cooperative learning projects. Every activity is correlated to one or more of the NSES. Although the lesson ideas suggest motivations and activities, it is up to you to mold them into engagements and explorations that create learning experiences rich in content for your students. New to this edition are sample lessons accompanying each planning chapter that illustrate how the lesson ideas and activities might be developed into an entire lesson.

For the Teacher's Desk

The materials in this section are provided as a resource for your use now and in the future. The first part, *Your Classroom Enrichment Handbook,* includes guidelines for obtaining materials, ensuring safety, curriculum planning, and finding source materials, among other things. A section provides position statements from the National Science Teachers Association (NSTA) on these subjects: women in science education; multicultural science education; substance use and abuse; and science competitions. The second part, *Your Science Source Address Book,* provides contact information in these areas: Free and Inexpensive Materials; The "Wish Book" Companies; Bilingual Child Resources; Special-Needs Resources; Science Teachers Associations; and NASA Teacher Resource Centers. All of this information has been reviewed and updated for this new edition.

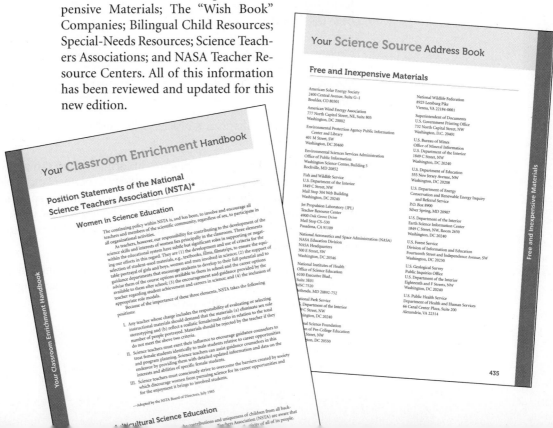

New to This Edition

There has been growing interest in understanding how people learn, bolstered by an increasingly deeper understanding of how the brain processes information. This edition addresses a practical framework for teaching children thinking strategies for seeking scientific explanations. It strives to present practical classroom applications from the growing body of knowledge on how people learn that elementary school teachers can incorporate effectively into their teaching methods and strategies.

- Chapters 1 and 2 take a deeper look at the meaning of inquiry so we might teach inquiry more effectively. Inquiry is described in the context of a progression of mental modeling: Descriptive models require us to be active observers, integrating prior knowledge and new observations in our explanations. Explanatory models are built on the foundation of good descriptive models, which give rise to hypotheses and predictions. Experimental models provide a systematic method to acquire meaningful data that support or fail to support hypotheses.

- Chapter 3 takes a deeper look at the science process skills in the context of the progression of inquiry. It also introduces a 5E instructional strategy as a framework for planning inquiry-based units and lessons. The 5E approach is based on engagement, exploration, explanation, elaboration, and evaluation.

- In Chapter 4 you will find a revised outline for planning lessons, highlighting the importance of identifying the content to be taught. Most of us need to review scientific concepts and are often faced with teaching concepts that we have long ago forgotten or never quite learned. This chapter guides you through the process of analyzing the content, identifying what to teach and what not to teach. In-depth examples of lesson plans that can be used as templates are included in Chapter 4 and throughout Part Two in the chapters subtitled "Putting the Content into Action."

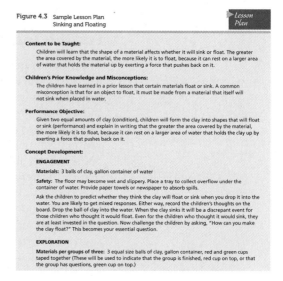

Figure 4.3   Sample Lesson Plan
Sinking and Floating

Content to be Taught:
Children will learn that the shape of a material affects whether it will sink or float. The greater the area covered by the material, the more likely it is to float, because it can rest on a larger area of water that holds the material up by exerting a force that pushes back on it.

Children's Prior Knowledge and Misconceptions:
The children have learned in a prior lesson that certain materials float or sink. A common misconception is that for an object to float, it must be made from a material that itself will not sink when placed in water.

Performance Objective:
Given two equal amounts of clay (condition), children will form the clay into shapes that will float or sink (performance) and explain in writing that the greater the area covered by the material, the more likely it is to float, because it can rest on a larger area of water that holds the clay up by exerting a force that pushes back on it.

Concept Development:
ENGAGEMENT

Materials: 3 balls of clay, gallon container of water

Safety: The floor may become wet and slippery. Place a tray to collect overflow under the container of water. Provide paper towels or newspaper to absorb spills.

Ask the children to predict whether they think the clay will float or sink when you drop it into the water. You are likely to get mixed responses. Either way, record the children's thoughts on the board. Drop the ball of clay into the water. When the clay sinks it will be a discrepant event for those children who thought it would float. Even for the children who thought it would sink, they are at least invested in the question. Now challenge the children by asking, "How can you make the clay float?" This becomes your essential question.

EXPLORATION

Materials per groups of three: 3 equal size balls of clay, gallon container, red and green cups taped together (These will be used to indicate that the group is finished, red cup on top, or that the group has questions, green cup on top.)

- Chapter 5 includes a discussion of science kits and their use in the elementary science classroom.

- Chapter 6 has been reorganized in terms of formative and summative assessment and connects assessment strategies more closely to performance objectives introduced in Chapter 4. Prompts, rubrics, probes, performance, and authentic assessment are addressed in depth with examples of each. Practical guides for designing assessment are provided as well as in-depth discussion about constructing rubrics and scoring guides.

- Although the previous editions addressed strategies for using art, music, and physical education to teach science, Chapter 7 in this edition encourages teaching the science of art, music, and physical education.

- Chapter 8, "Using Technology to Enhance Science Learning," is *new* to this edition. In it you will find strategies for using technology to support inquiry through real-time data collection, authentic science experiences, simulations, webquests, information gathering, tutorials and games, ask a scientist, and the use of interactive whiteboards. Sample webquests based on the 5E approach, introduced in Chapter 4, are introduced in this chapter.

- Chapter 9 recognizes the growing emphasis on inclusion of all students in the elementary science classroom and the challenges inclusion places on curriculum and instruction. Differentiated learning and universal design for learning (UDL) offer helpful perspectives and strategies for effectively addressing the challenges of inclusion. Consequently, they are two important new topics that have been added to "Adapting the Science Curriculum," accompanied by a discussion of the range of learning disabilities as well as strategies for teaching gifted learners.

- Part Two has been reorganized. Content chapters for the earth and space sciences, life sciences, and physical sciences are each followed by "Putting the Content into Action." As with previous editions, these chapters include starter ideas along with suggested activities, webquests, demonstrations, in-class learning centers, bulletin boards, field trips, and cooperative learning projects. You will also notice the inclusion of essential questions that accompany starter ideas to guide inquiry.

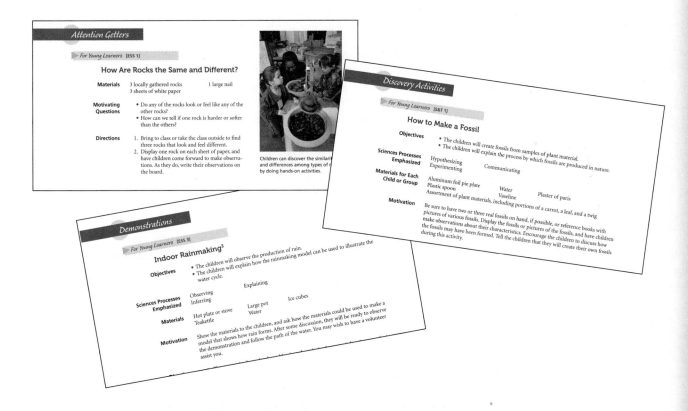

I have often been told that it is helpful to see examples of lesson plans that exemplify the strategies and philosophies put forth in Part One of the text. Therefore, fully developed lessons for each of the big content ideas in Parts Two, Three, and Four have been included as examples to inspire the development of your own lesson plans.

By now, you are intimately familiar with the content and organization of this seventh edition of *Teaching Children Science,* and I hope you are eager to dive into it! Use it now, during your teacher preparation, as a textbook and then later, in your years as a teacher, as a trusted and valued resource. You may also find useful another book I wrote for pre- and in-service teachers called *Whizbangers and Wonderments: Science Activities for Young People* (also published by Allyn and Bacon).

Finally, let me say once again, as has been stated in the prefaces to previous editions of *Teaching Children Science,* that the order of the words in the title of this book is purposeful. *We* are teaching children science. It's not the other way around!

Supplements

- **Instructor's Manual/Test Bank** provides concrete suggestions to help instructors fully utilize the text and MyEducationLab. Each chapter contains chapter objectives, key terms and concepts, and discussion and activity suggestions as well as a comprehensive test bank. This resource is available for download by logging on to the Instructor Resource Center from the Pearson Higher Ed catalog (www.pearsonhighered .com/educator.) Please contact your local Pearson representative if you need assistance downloading this guide.

- **PowerPoint Presentation** offers slides for each chapter outlining key concepts and including select figures and tables. This resource is available for download by logging on to the Instructor Resource Center from the Pearson Higher Ed catalog (www.pearsonhighered.com/educator.) Please contact your local Pearson representative if you need assistance downloading this guide.

(www.myeducationlab.com <http://www.myeducationlab.com>)
This research-based learning resource brings teaching to life. Through authentic in-class video footage, simulations, examples of authentic teacher and student work, lesson plans and more, MyEducationLab prepares teacher candidates for their careers by affording opportunities for observation and reflection through a series of assignable application activities.

About the New Co-Author

Dr. DeRosa has worked in the field of science education for twenty-four years as a classroom teacher and teacher educator. He is a member of the Department of Curriculum and Teaching at the Boston University School of Education, where he teaches methods in elementary science education. He serves as the director of CityLab, a biotechnology-learning laboratory for teachers and students at the Boston University School of Medicine. His research interests focus on the development of effective methods to teach scientific thinking. He has co-authored several curriculum supplements in biotechnology, frequently conducts workshops on inquiry-based science teaching for in-service teachers, and has consulted in the development of biotechnology programs throughout the United States.

Acknowledgments

Although this book has only two authors, many people have shaped its content, directly and indirectly. We would like to thank our many colleagues for their continued support and encouragement, including Lowell J. Bethel at the University of Texas; Jack Hassard at Georgia State University; Russell Agne, Susan Baker, and Joyce Morris at the University of Vermont; Rod Peturson of the Windsor Schools, Ontario, Canada; Marlene Nachbar Hapai at the University of Hawaii, Manoa; William Ritz at California State University, Long Beach; and Larry Schaeffer at Syracuse University.

In addition, we would like to thank those individuals who reviewed this edition for Pearson Allyn & Bacon for the valuable suggestions they offered: Anna R. Bergstrom, Texas Lutheran University; Mildred E. Berry, Florida Memorial University; Kim Trask Brown, University of North Carolina–Asheville; Jim Dawson, Rochester College; Dawn Parker, Texas A&M University; Margaret Pope, Mississippi State University; Susan Stratton, SUNY Cortland; and Norma H. Twombley, Johnson State College. And I would like, once again, to thank the reviewers and survey respondents from previous editions: Stan Chu, Bank Street College of Education; Thomas W. Giles, Cumberland College; Steve Gregorich, California State University, Sacramento; Tom Howick, University of Southern Maine; William Hughes, Ashland University; Raymond Jobin, Keene State College; Archibald Sia, California State University, Northridge; Rene Stofflett, University of Illinois; Barbara Kasten, Trinity College; Bonnie Kotvis, Alverno College; Margaret Mason, William Woods College; J. Philip McLaren, Eastern Nazarene College; Lucy J. Orfan, Kean College of New Jersey (now Kean University); and Harold Roberts, Hendrix College.

Finally, we would like to thank Dee Josephson and Michael Goodman for their attention to the details of the book.

D. D.

part **one**

Strategies and Techniques

The whoosh and locomotive roar of a powerful tornado, tossing about cars and flattening houses; the careful maneuvering of a brightly colored lady bug, making its way through branches and leaves, touching, smelling, and tasting all in its path; and the first dark, belching breaths of a volcano coming to life after being dormant—all are parts of the natural world in which we live.

Wanting to make sense of that world is a powerful drive that leads us humans to inquire, to discover, and ultimately, to understand. And to empower children to be able to inquire, discover, and understand—not just now but throughout their lives—is the greatest challenge we teachers face. To teach children *science* is to meet that challenge head on.

Part One of this book will help prepare you to meet that challenge. To be sure, there is *much* to know! First of all, you need to know your children. How do children learn, and what can you do to enhance their learning? How can you help them learn the inquiry process skills and construct their own scientific knowledge?

You also need to know what to teach and how to teach it. What are the recommendations of the National Science Education Standards (NSES) and other curriculum guideposts that your school district or state might have? How can you plan meaningful lessons and units and manage an inquiry-based classroom? How can you make good use of the valuable resources of the Internet? How can you integrate science with other subject areas? What specific strategies and techniques will help you foster discovery learning? And what can you do to adapt science activities for children who come from diverse cultural backgrounds and who have special needs and abilities?

Finally, you need to know how and when to assess children's progress in meaningful ways. What are the different approaches to assessment, and how successful are they? Again, what does the NSES recommend? How can children best show what they have learned in terms of both understanding and inquiry?

The chapters in Part One (Chapters 1–9) will answer these questions and more, and, in completing them, you will build a foundation of general knowledge about teaching children science. Once that foundation is firmly in place, you can add the specific knowledge and skills related to the earth/space, life, and physical sciences, which are the subjects of the chapters in Parts Two, Three, and Four, respectively.

Yes, it's a lot to learn! And I encourage you to learn it well, so that you will get off to a good start as a teacher. Mastering this information is essential to developing your own approach to teaching children science.

The truth is, becoming an OK teacher isn't too difficult. But becoming a truly excellent teacher—one who broadens children's horizons, gives them a knowledge base upon which they can build, and raises their hopes and dreams to unexpected heights—takes focus and determination. *That's* what you and I will be working toward throughout this book!

chapter 1

Inquiry: The Path, Discovery: The Destination

Inquiry is not just teaching science, but using science to teach thinking.

▶ Getting Started

A man lives on the twelfth floor of an apartment building. Every morning he takes the elevator down to the lobby and leaves the building. In the evening, he gets into the elevator, and, if there is someone else in the elevator—or if it was raining that day—he goes back to his floor directly. Otherwise, he goes to the tenth floor and walks up two flights of stairs to his apartment.[1]

Can you explain why the man sometimes takes the elevator directly to the twelfth floor while at other times he takes it to the tenth floor and walks two flights? You may have seen this puzzle or similar ones, known as lateral thinking puzzles, which challenge us to think creatively outside the box. What does this have to do with science?

Science seeks explanations to our everyday questions and offers us strategies for thinking of what to do when we do not have the answer. Consider how you tried to solve the puzzle. Did your mind go blank? Were you wondering where to begin? Did you know what questions to ask? Science teaching means teaching children how to think and figure out what to do when they do not have the answer. Science thinking skills are the tools of discovery. By teaching your students how to seek explanations, you will lead them onto a path of exploration where they will no longer be restricted by memorizing what others have discovered, but they will use their skills to make their own discoveries and keep pace with an ever-changing world.

As elementary school teachers, you provide the most important link to start the children on the path to discovery. This chapter is about understanding the practical thinking strategies and skills that you can teach your students to embark on this journey. We will revisit the puzzle later in the chapter.

A Chance to Touch Tomorrow

All of the flowers
Of all of the future
Are in the seeds of today
—Source unknown

As you awake and start your new day, I'd like you to think of these three short lines as your gentle alarm. I want them to remind you of the enormous potential that lies in the hearts and minds of children. You are their temporary mindstretcher and caretaker. You are the overseer of the seeds and the creator of the rich soil that will nurture these seeds of new tomorrows to grow. *What* and *how* you teach children will race ahead of you to a time you will never know. The responsibility is enormous. It will take dedication, energy, and the unwavering belief that what you do and how you do it will actually change lives.

What and *how* you teach will touch tomorrow. *You* will touch tomorrow.

Turning Your Teaching Fears into Hope

Now I might be wrong, but my guess is that you are not *that* confident about teaching children science. You may fear that science will be difficult for children to understand and that it will provoke questions that will be hard for you to answer. You may also think that science time will be a period of utter chaos and confusion, as liquids bubble out of beakers and chemicals flash, pop, and bang.

It is my hope that most of you have had wonderful experiences in science and that you will share the challenge of seeking explanations and the thrill of discovery with your students. On the other hand, perhaps your encounters with science have emphasized the memorization of myriad facts and formulas rather than the journey of exploration and discovery that is science. Imagine that children on a Little League team or in a dance troupe are given books to study about the rules, history, and techniques of baseball or dance and practices consist of discussion, reviews, and videos of "real" baseball games or dance recitals. How many of those children do you think will learn to understand and love the game of baseball or the art of the dance? What are the chances that any of them will pursue a career in baseball or ballet? The answer is likely none of them. Most parents expect that the children will take a bat, ball, and glove to the playing field or dance shoes and leotard to the studio and experience the excitement of the game or the movement of the dance.

All too often, science is taught by giving students a textbook, showing them a movie, and telling them the "facts," which they are expected to dutifully recite on tests. In this book, you will learn to help children experience the dynamics and challenges of science through active participation in the processes of science. With your help, elementary school students will enjoy successes as well as failures, but along the way they will acquire new skills, gain confidence, and discover new and deeper understandings of the world and their place in it.

You are embarking on a journey to become not only a coach but also a player on the field of science. The ensuing chapters will explain ways to "show" instead of "tell." You will learn to model sound scientific thinking and strategies for seeking explanations. The most important skill that you teach your students will be the ability to know what to do when they do not have the answer. Scientific thinking is not only good science, it is good thinking. During this journey, you will overcome your fears, expand your hopes, and fulfill your dreams of becoming an elementary science teacher as you experience the thrill of scientific discovery that you can share with your students. Let's begin the journey by considering the children who will be in your classroom.

Your Children: Curious, Aspiring Scientists Who Need Guidance and Direction

Children love to touch! At least, most children do. They also like to look at things, to smell them, to move them about, and to twist and turn them. Children want to know how things work, and, like squirrels, they sometimes horde papers, science materials, and wildlife in their desks for more detailed inspection later.

At the heart of science is this natural human desire to explore the world that is directly reachable as well as those worlds that are hard to reach. The children in your classroom are, in this respect, very much like scientists. In fact, some would say that *they* are more like scientists than are teenagers or even college students!

However, do not assume children are adult scientists in small bodies. Curiosity is a wonderful attribute and precursor of scientific thinking, but in order to truly become scientific thinkers, children must develop habits of mind that go beyond their natural curiosity. Scientific inquiry requires careful, active observations of the details and connections of systems and events that we encounter, which often go unnoticed by casual observers. As the famous physicist Richard Feynman once said, "The first principle is that you must not fool yourself and you are the easiest person to fool."[2] Your elementary school children will tend to have boundless energy and curiosity. Your job will be to make sure that you deliver a curriculum that capitalizes on both and encourages them to become active observers and scientific thinkers.

By providing children with hands-on experiences, you will help them correct faulty knowledge, add new knowledge, and create accurate conceptions about the natural world.

Shaping Young Minds: A Wonderful and Awe-Inspiring Opportunity

As elementary school teachers, you will be entrusted by parents with the responsibility of developing the most important organ in the individual, the brain. The title of a book written by James Zull, *The Art of Changing the Brain*, aptly suggests the magnitude of the career you have chosen. As a teacher, you will be responsible for shaping thousands of young brains. You will actually influence the creation of synapses and neural networks associated with thinking and reasoning. As the gatekeepers of learning, you can start children on the path to a lifetime of discovery by teaching them the thinking skills they need to explore the unknown.

The Developing Brain

The child's brain is not simply a small adult brain. It is undergoing important stages of development. The brain is equipped with an abundance of neurons (specialized brain cells) at birth. As one learns, the connections among neurons (synapses) increase, and the ability of brain cells to transmit signals improves (myelination). The experiences you provide children can stimulate and strengthen connections among brain cells that reinforce learning. Unused synapses are pruned, whereas useful synapses are reinforced and developed. As elementary school teachers, you work with children at a time when their brains are undergoing significant developments that will last a lifetime. Although you do not need to become a cognitive neuroscientist to be a good teacher, you do need to become aware of fundamental ways in which the developing brain processes information.

What Is Scientific Thinking? A Look at Some Masters

Great thinkers such as Einstein, Galileo, and da Vinci had the ability to create detailed mental models. We all create mental models to some extent. When we can "see" or "picture" a situation in our minds, we can often understand and explain it better. Expressions such as, "I see what you mean" or "It is like . . ." suggest this tendency to create mental models. Great thinkers have the extraordinary ability to create and keep complex mental models of a system in their minds and imagine what would happen when different elements in the models interact in novel ways. For example, Einstein could imagine what would happen when someone rode a beam of light, and da Vinci could imagine the miracle of flight. As educators, we need to teach our students the cognitive skills necessary to create mental models and to create a culture of thinking in which these cognitive skills become habits of mind. Habits of mind take years to develop; they cannot be covered in a lesson or two. The habits of good, scientific thinking must become a conscious part of the culture of learning; children need to be made aware of their thinking strategies when they are thinking scientifically.

What Does Scientific Thinking Look Like?

Scientific thinking is a process of asking questions and seeking explanations. In order to teach scientific thinking, it is helpful to identify a framework for scientific thinking that is practical and teachable. One such framework consisting of three primary modeling steps: descriptive modeling, explanatory modeling, and experimental modeling, referred to as the progression of inquiry, provides the foundation for instructional strategies. The three stages will be addressed more fully in Chapter 3.[3]

Descriptive Modeling   Before trying to explain a mystery, we have to be able to describe what we know about the mystery. Most of early elementary school is spent on developing observational skills to make good descriptive models. It is no small accomplishment to be an active observer when one encounters a completely novel phenomenon. Good scientists recognize the distinction between looking and observing. The observational skills that you teach your students will differ only with respect to levels of sophistication and technology from the skills used by experienced scientists. Scientists who use electron microscopes to measure distances in angstroms ask the same descriptive questions as first graders who use rulers to measure distances in centimeters.

Explanatory Modeling   The descriptive model reveals connections and relationships that suggest explanations. Explanations yield hypotheses, or proposed relationships, that may be tested.

Experimental Modeling   Experimental models test predictions that are based on hypotheses. Designing a good experiment requires a prediction that can be tested, the use of independent, dependent, and controlled variables as well as the construction of a controlled experiment. These terms are explained in Chapter 3. The experiment usually leads to new observations, which yield deeper insights that modify the descriptive model, deepen the explanatory model, and lead to more experimentation. Science is a dynamic, ongoing process (Figure 1.1).

Developing Positive Affect   For many teachers, a lesson about a caterpillar becoming a butterfly will only be about a caterpillar and a butterfly. But the same lesson in the hands of a master teacher—a great teacher, an extraordinary teacher, a truly gifted teacher—will be an experience in which the children are thunderstruck with the realization that *one living thing has become a completely different living thing right before their eyes.*

The day of that lesson will be one on which those children's lives will be changed forever. They will leave school filled with a sense of wonder that was sparked by the thrill of discovering brand-new knowledge that is as extraordinary as anything they will see on television. They will want to know more—curious about what may lie around the corner. They will also leave with new attitudes, values, and a confidence in their ability to learn that will shape who they are and who they will become.

This change in attitudes and values signals the development of *positive affect.* The science experiences you deliver to children will do much to create positive affect about science, school, and the wonders of the natural world. It is the classroom environment that will help children grow toward the positive goals presented so beautifully in Dorothy Law Nolte's "Children Learn What They Live" (see Figure 1.2, page 9).

Developing Psychomotor Skills   You might not think of your classroom as a place where children learn to coordinate what their minds *will* with what their bodies *perform*—but it is. Children need to develop gross motor abilities as well as fine motor skills, and well-planned science experiences can help them do so.

Gross motor skills can be developed through inquiry-based activities such as assembling and using simple machines, hoeing and raking a class vegetable garden, and carefully shaping sand on a table to make various land forms. Examples of experiences that develop *fine motor skills* include cutting out leaf shapes with scissors, drawing charts and graphs, and sorting seeds on the basis of physical characteristics. So, in addition to gaining knowledge and understanding and developing positive affect, science time can be a time to improve a child's physical skills.

Figure 1.1

The Progression of Inquiry

Source: Adapted with permission from P. Bergethon, (1999). *The Path to Science Literacy: From Brain to Mind to Literacy.* Holliston, MA: Symmetry Learning Systems, 16–17.

Developing Responsible Citizens   When your children look at you during science time, they aren't thinking about issues such as raising taxes to pay for a park's underground sprinkler system or what impact the new factory under construction in town may have on worldwide CO_2 emissions and global warming trends. However, at some time in their lives, they will be concerned about societal issues. And to be responsible citizens, they will need to address such issues with wisdom—wisdom based on a foundation of knowledge constructed many years earlier. Perhaps some of that knowledge will be gained in your classroom.

Figure 1.2
A child's environment has a powerful impact on his or her affective development.

Children Learn What They Live

By Dorothy Law Nolte

If children live with criticism, they learn to condemn.

If children live with hostility, they learn to fight.

If children live with fear, they learn to be apprehensive.

If children live with pity, they learn to feel sorry for themselves.

If children live with ridicule, they learn to feel shy.

If children live with jealousy, they learn to feel envy.

If children live with shame, they learn to feel guilty.

If children live with encouragement, they learn to be confident.

If children live with tolerance, they learn patience.

If children live with praise, they learn appreciation.

If children live with acceptance, they learn to love.

If children live with approval, they learn to like themselves.

If children live with recognition, they learn it is good to have a goal.

If children live with sharing, they learn generosity.

If children live with honesty, they learn truthfulness.

If children live with fairness, they learn justice.

If children live with kindness and consideration, they learn respect.

If children live with security, they learn to have faith in themselves and in those about them.

If children live with friendliness, they learn the world is a nice place in which to live.

If you live with serenity, your child will live with peace of mind.

With what is your child living?

With your guidance, children will learn that real inquiry requires gathering evidence before reaching a conclusion. Hopefully, learning to gather knowledge systematically and to reach carefully thought out conclusions will be skills they apply as they confront societal issues in the future. If you do your job, then today's children will make positive contributions to the civic decision-making processes that will lead to a better life for us all.

Scientific Literacy: Your Science Teaching Will Create It

Add *STS* to the list of acronyms you carry in your brain. It stands for *science, technology, and society*, a catchphrase that represents what average citizens should know about two things that affect them and their society constantly: science and technology. In short, STS is related to creating citizens who are scientifically literate.

NSES

To create citizens who understand the implications of developments in science and technology is an enormous task. But the task for you, as a teacher, is more specific and reachable: teaching children to become scientifically literate.

To help you in this effort, the National Science Education Standards (NSES) identify what it means to be scientifically literate and suggest what should be taught at various grade levels to reach this goal. The NSES list the following goals for members of a scientifically literate society:

- Experience the richness and excitement of knowing about and understanding the natural world;

- Use appropriate scientific processes and principles in making personal decisions;

- Engage intelligently in public discourse and debate about matters of scientific and technological concern; and

- Increase their economic productivity through the use of the knowledge, understanding, and skills of the scientifically literate person in their careers.*

Note that while the NSES provide a guide to grade-level appropriate content and insights about how the content should be taught, it is ultimately your responsibility as the classroom teacher to make decisions about the teaching strategies that are suitable for your students.

Later in this book (in Chapters 4, 10, 13, and 16), you will learn what content the NSES suggest for your classroom. You will discover that much of the content suggested has, as its focus, the creation of citizens who have a good understanding of new developments in science and technology and what implications those developments have for their lives.

Gender and Equity Issues: Your Science Teaching Will Help Resolve Them

> The scientist is a brain. He spends his days indoors, sitting in a laboratory, pouring things from one test tube into another. . . . He can only eat, breathe, and sleep science. . . . He has no social life, no other intellectual interests, no hobbies or relaxations. . . . He is always reading a book. He brings home work and also brings home creepy things.[4]

Although students made these observations almost 50 years ago, their attitudes reflect, to a large degree, the views of society today. The students' choice of pronoun does not seem to reflect the purposeful use of *he* for *she* but rather the strength of the stereotype of the scientist as male.

One of my favorite classroom activities is to ask each student to draw a picture of a scientist at work (see Figure 1.3). In most cases the scientist is depicted as a bespectacled, old, white male with a slightly mad glint in his eyes, having a very bad hair day. While it may seem amusing, the real harm of this stereotype lies in the fact that it may discourage young females, minorities, and students with disabilities from considering science or science-related careers and foster the notion that they are not expected to succeed in

---

*Reprinted with permission from *National Science Education Standards*© 1996 by the National Academy of Sciences, courtesy of the National Academies Press, Washington, D.C.

Figure 1.3   A sampling of "Draw a Scientist" illustrations by elementary students

science. Hopefully, you will be a classroom leader who is able to create an environment that helps to overcome these stereotypes.

The science classroom can also provide you with a wonderful opportunity to assist children from cultural minorities and for whom English is not their home language. When children are encouraged to explore phenomena that are real to them, to learn and use inquiry skills, and ultimately to make their own discoveries, the power of these experiences will do much to integrate *all* children into the task at hand.

Just think of how fortunate you are to teach children science, a subject whose natural allure for children will draw them into learning experiences irrespective of gender, language, and cultural barriers. By having a classroom that respects cultural and linguistic diversity and addresses gender inequities, you can make a real difference in the lives of children. That's right! *You* can and will make a difference.

Science: What Is It, Really?

Science seeks explanations of the natural world. It consists of the following components:

- A systematic quest for explanations
- The dynamic body of knowledge generated through a systematic quest for explanations

Unfortunately, science is often associated only with the body of knowledge, which is tantamount to skipping the movie and watching only the final scene. The ending does not make sense if you do not know the plot. When science is presented as only facts and answers, it ceases being science. Anyone with access to a computer can find information. Science involves the process of generating information. Science teaches us what to do when we do not have the answer. It is a systematic search with a variety of strategies that results in a dynamic body of scientific knowledge. For example, Pluto is no longer considered a planet, the earth is no longer considered flat, and limitations of Newtonian physics have been accepted. The scientific body of knowledge is not static.

As an elementary school science teacher, you will teach process skills, values, and attitudes associated with seeking scientific explanations as well as the body of knowledge that constitutes current scientific explanations of natural phenomena. (See Table 1.1, page 12.)

Table 1.1   Examples of science as a body of knowledge, as a process, and values associated with science

Body of Knowledge	
• Energy can change form.	• For every action, there is an equal and opposite reaction.
• Matter can change form.	• Like poles of magnets repel each other.
• The total amount of matter and energy in the universe never changes.	• Unlike poles of magnets attract each other.

Inquiry Process Skills		
• Descriptive modeling	• Explanatory modeling	• Experimental modeling
Questioning	Questioning	Questioning
Observing	Hypothesizing	Predicting
Enumerating	Inferring	Identifying variables
Classifying	Interpreting data	Controlling variables
Measuring	Communicating	Controlling experiments
Comparing		Communicating
Communicating		

Values and Attitudes Associated with Scientific Inquiry	
• Skepticism	• Cooperation
• Criticism	• Persistence
Ability to criticize	• Freedom to think originally
Acceptance of criticism	• Organization

The Nature of Science

The American Association for the Advancement of Science (AAAS) suggests that there are particular ways of observing, thinking, experimenting, and validating that reflect how science tends to differ from other modes of knowing. These particular attributes contribute to what is referred to as the nature of science. AAAS suggests the following attributes associated with the nature of science:

- The Scientific World View
    - The world is understandable.
    - Scientific ideas are subject to change.
    - Scientific knowledge is durable (scientists tend to modify rather than reject existing ideas).
    - Science cannot provide complete answers to all questions.

- Scientific Inquiry

  Science demands evidence.

  Science is a blend of logic and imagination.

  Science explains and predicts.

  Scientists try to identify and avoid bias.

  Science is not authoritarian.

- The Scientific Enterprise

  Science is a complex social activity.

  Science is organized into content disciplines and is conducted in various institutions.

  There are generally accepted ethical principles in the conduct of science.

  Scientists participate in public affairs both as specialists and as citizens.*

Your Attitude Makes a Difference

If, as a teacher, you emphasize only the facts of science, children will learn that science is an accumulation of factual knowledge. However, if you emphasize the process of science, children will learn that science is a way of seeking explanations. A well-rounded student understands science as both a process and a body of knowledge. Children will enter your classes with their own perceptions of science formed through experiences outside of school, at home, and through the media. Figure 1.4 offers the ideas of some fourth graders about science. As their teacher, you will have a significant impact on their understanding and attitude about what science is and how science is done. It is not only what you teach, but also your attitude toward science that will impact students.

Consider Renee, a third-grade teacher, on bus duty early one spring morning greeting and directing the children as they clamor off the buses. Mary, a curious third grader, can hardly contain her excitement as she runs up to Renee with a plastic container teeming with wriggling worms she and her mother found while planting a garden. Mary grabs a handful of worms to show Renee, who contorts her face into a disgusted grimace exclaiming, "Yuk . . . get those things away from me. Mary, I don't like worms. Please, I hope you are not thinking about bringing them into my classroom." Mary's smile vanishes as

Reality Check

What Would You Do?

During a school committee meeting to discuss the elementary science program, a committee member suggests, "While science is important, it should not be emphasized at the elementary level, since the children need to learn reading, math, and writing during these formative years. Science, after all, requires memorization of a rather extensive amount of factual knowledge, which should be saved for the middle and high school years. It has little to offer developing minds of elementary school students." For this reason, she argues, minimal time should be allotted to elementary science education.

As an elementary school teacher at the meeting, you are asked your opinion on the matter. How would you respond to this school committee member's suggestion?

*American Association for the Advancement of Science (1989). *Science for All Americans.* New York: Oxford University Press. Reprinted with permission

Figure 1.4
A few fourth-grade children offer their definitions of science.

"Science is a class that we go to and learn about important things we have to know. I think science is the funnest class I've ever been to." —*Jennifer*

"Science is . . . I think that science is neat, fun. It is interesting you learn all kinds of neat stuff." —*Renee*

"Science is fun and it can be really hard to do. It is very hard to do some of the worksheets." —*Mark*

"Science is . . . Alot of fun we study Whales. We work in books and get more homework but science is fun learning experiment. We make maps and we blow them up." —*Alan*

"Science is the explanation for the way the things on Earth work." —*Nico*

"Science is important to me. I will be an vet or animal scientist. I love science and when I'm sad or up set I try to be scietific and it cheers me up. It makes me happy when I make a dedution. Once I start trying to think up the answer to a problem and I won't I mean won't stop even for eating and sleeping even reading! So I love science a lot." —*Mary Catherine*

"Science is important to me couse we have alot of pages we have to do. I think it is easy to do." —*Robbie*

"Science is fun. I liked it when we used salt and flour to mold a map. Salt and flour is sticky. I like science." —*Erik*

she walks quietly to the grassy area next to the school and dumps the worms on the soft ground.

Although this scenario may seem somewhat exaggerated, similar scenes have taken place in school yards and classrooms. Mary did not learn anything about worms or their role in the ecosystem of the garden. Much worse, Mary may take home the lesson that adult, educated women should not like worms or be curious about such things one finds in nature. As you may have concluded from the drawings done of scientists on page 11, research using the Draw a Scientist task (DAST) reveals that children in the United States generally think of scientists as white males, most often involved in work in a laboratory.[5] Teachers need to promote images of scientists that reflect a diversity of gender and race, so all students have the opportunity to envision themselves as scientists.

Science as a Set of Values

Although there are many values you can emphasize as you help children experience science processes and learn content, there are six that you will find particularly useful:

1. Truth
2. Freedom
3. Skepticism
4. Order
5. Originality
6. Communication

Because science seeks to make sense out of our natural world, it has as its most basic value the search for *truth* based on evidence. The scientist seeks to discover not what should be but what *is*. The high value placed on truth applies not only to the discovery of facts, concepts, and principles but also to the recording and reporting of such knowledge.

The search for truth relies on another important value: *freedom*. Real science can only occur when a scientist is able to operate in an environment that provides him or her with the freedom to follow paths wherever they lead. Fortunately, free societies rarely limit the work of scientists. Freedom to follow pathways also means the freedom to risk thinking independently and creatively. As educators, we must provide opportunities for students to think while taking care to think with, not for, students. We must foster the development of foundational thinking strategies so that children can take advantage of the freedom to think afforded them in our open society. A successful free society depends on the ability of its citizens to make informed decisions.

Skepticism—the unwillingness to accept many things at face value—moves scientists to ask difficult questions about the natural world, society, and even each other. Scientists value *skepticism,* and skepticism sometimes causes nonscientists to doubt the results of scientific enterprise. In an article entitled "Uh-Oh, Here Comes the Mailman," James Gleick, a well-known science writer, describes excerpts from some of the letters he has received:

> Here is a lengthy single-spaced essay (painstakingly tied up with what looks like tooth floss) titled "Chaos and Rays." Apparently, one of these rays "impregnates the chaos" and "fructifies the forces."

> A Canadian reader has discovered (he encloses the calculations) that all spheres, including the Earth, are 20 percent larger than geometers have thought—"Perhaps the reason missiles keep crashing short of their course."[6]

While Professor Gleick may smile at these letters, he also makes this observation:

> It's hard to remember, but it's surely true, that the instinct bubbling to the surface in these letters is the same instinct driving real scientists. There is a human curiosity about nature, a desire to peer through the chaos and find the order.[7]

There is, then, an underlying *order* to the processes and content of science. In their search for truth, scientists gather information and then organize it. It is this order that allows scientists to discover patterns in the natural world. Children need to develop this ability to organize information, which is why you will be helping them learn how to organize and keep track of their observations.

For all its order, however, science also values *originality*. Although some may view science as a linear activity—one in which people plod along, acquiring more and more detailed explanations of phenomena—in reality, science is fueled by original ideas and creative thinking. It is this kind of thinking that leads to discoveries.

Children love to talk with each other; so do scientists. The talk of scientists includes reports, articles, speeches, and lectures, as well as casual conversations. The ability to communicate results is vital if knowledge is to grow. Without extensive *communication,* progress would be greatly limited.

As a teacher, you will need to help children understand that science is more than a collection of facts and a group of processes. Science is a human activity that has as its framework a set of values that are important in day-to-day life.

Technology and Engineering: They Are Changing Your Life and Their Lives

Go to **MyEducationLab**, select the topic Technology, watch the video entitled "Technology," and complete the question that accompanies it.

What do these terms have in common: prescription drugs, hip-replacement surgery, instant hair dye, solar panels, fuel cells, soft contact lenses, electric cars, CAT scans, X-ray treatment for cancer, and ramen noodles (noodle-like material that can be reconstituted through the addition of tap water)? The answer, of course, is *technology*. They all are products or procedures that apply science to the solution of human problems—real or imagined.

Today, one of the most immediate technological challenges concerns climate change and the rising costs of fossil fuels, which have created a need to seek alternative methods to generate energy. Green buildings that take advantage of wind, solar, geothermal, and even human energy are emerging at an increasingly rapid pace. These technologies integrate earth science, energy transfer and conversion, simple machines, and biology in meaningful and relevant contexts. In your role as elementary school teachers, you will have a tremendous opportunity to lay the foundation of energy literacy for generations of young people who may become engineers, architects, and designers that make pivotal decisions about life style changes that will affect our planet and its inhabitants for years to come.

One of your obligations in teaching children science is to pay attention to how technology-based products and procedures work. You will find this goal referred to in any list of curriculum objectives as *technological design*. The NSES point out that children should be able to do these things:

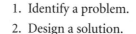

1. Identify a problem.
2. Design a solution.
3. Implement their solution.
4. Critically examine how well their solution worked.
5. Communicate with others about their design and the strengths and weaknesses of their solution.[8]

How might teaching about technological design be translated into your own real-world classroom? Children could design any of the following:

1. A dog-walking machine
2. A machine for removing and sorting garbage and trash from lunch trays
3. A solar oven to cook s'mores
4. A backpack with a self-contained umbrella that automatically opens during a rainstorm

Advances in technology enable us to convert renewable energies such as wind into electricity.

The point is that new and emerging technology impacts virtually every minute of a child's day. In order for children to lead lives in which technology is used intelligently, with minimal negative side effects, they need to understand what technology is, how new products and procedures are designed, what resources are needed, and what deleterious consequences may occur, such as allergic reactions, environmental pollution, and safety hazards. Students need to fully understand the larger impact of new technologies within the context of how those technologies affect their communities—and themselves.

Discovery: Your Destination

"How do we know what we know?"

It certainly seems like a simple question when you look at it. I could even develop a rather complicated answer for it, if I was so disposed—but I won't! I suggest that we know what we know because we have made discoveries, and we have made those discoveries through inquiry. You made discoveries yesterday, you will make discoveries today, and you will make discoveries tomorrow. In fact, you are making discoveries as you read the printed words on these pages.

Discovery, which is part of the subtitle of this book (*A Discovery Approach*), is the journey on which you will lead your students to deeper understanding of the natural world. It is our discoveries that make us what we are. They underlie what we think, feel, and do.

Now the question is, How do you make those discoveries? Although there are many paths to discovery, this book is based on the path called *inquiry*. In fact, the paths of inquiry are different for bakers, accountants, cosmetologists, auto mechanics, and

Make the Case *An Individual or Group Challenge*

The Problem	The children in your classroom may be unaware of the many ways in which science and technology affect their daily lives.

Assess Your Prior Knowledge and Beliefs

To what extent are each of the following aspects of your life affected by science and technology?

Health	very little	little	somewhat	a great deal
Safety	very little	little	somewhat	a great deal
Nutrition	very little	little	somewhat	a great deal
Personal security	very little	little	somewhat	a great deal
Communication	very little	little	somewhat	a great deal
Transportation	very little	little	somewhat	a great deal
Recreation	very little	little	somewhat	a great deal

The Challenge	Your principal has asked you to give a five-minute talk at the next meeting of the Parents/Teachers Organization to encourage parents to cultivate their children's interest in science and technology. Identify five key points you would make in your presentation.

shepherds. We will focus on the way *scientists* inquire because we want children to make their science-related discoveries in the same way that real scientists do. (Shepherds may do it very differently.)

Inquiry: The Path Children Will Take toward Discovery

"Do chickens have teeth?"

"Why does a light bulb get hot?"

"Why are there holes in cheese?"

"Why can't we send the new baby back?"

Go to **MyEducationLab,** select the topic Inquiry, watch the video entitled "Inquiry Learning," and complete the questions that accompany it.

Questions, questions, and more questions! Asking questions is what makes we humans what we are. We seem to have a genetic urge to make sense of our surroundings, and this constant questioning is our most powerful tool. When you teach science, that is the tool all children will bring to you—the urge to question their surroundings—and so it will provide the foundation for much of your teaching.

Science seeks explanations, which are sought through a process of inquiry. You are already familiar with the progression of inquiry: descriptive modeling, explanatory modeling, and experimental modeling. These are helpful theoretical categories, but they mean little unless the theory can be translated meaningfully in the classroom.

Inquiry is about asking questions, but the challenge is to know what questions to ask. How often have you been in a new situation and heard, "If you have any questions, just ask," and you do not know where to begin. Peter Bergethon suggests the following set of fundamental questions that provide us with direction when we don't know where to begin:[9]

- What are the elements of the system?
- What are the properties of the elements?
- What is the context or background space of the system?
- What are the rules of interaction (connections) among the elements?
- What are the emergent properties (characteristics) of the system?

These questions guide our initial observations and enable inquirers to be active observers. Often during class, teachers ask students to make observations without teaching them how to observe. They just expect them to look. But looking is not the same as observing. When we look at things we are passive and wait for something to happen; when we observe, we become active participants. The fundamental questions of inquiry guide observation. They provide a starting point to organize our thoughts. Let's use the puzzler at the beginning of the chapter as an example of how to use the fundamental questions of inquiry. Recall the puzzle:

A man lives on the twelfth floor of an apartment building. Every morning he takes the elevator down to the lobby and leaves the building. In the evening, he gets into the elevator, and, if there is someone else in the elevator—or if it was raining that day—he goes back to his floor directly. Otherwise, he goes to the tenth floor and walks up two flights of stairs to his apartment.[10]

The first inclination of most people is to attempt to answer the question right away. Scientific thinking requires us to take a systematic approach, beginning with a descriptive model. In other words, we need to get our minds around the event to understand what we are dealing with before we attempt an explanation. We begin by describing the situation using the fundamental questions of inquiry:

- What are the elements?

   Man, elevator, floors, stairs, apartment, someone else, elevator, rain

- What are the properties of the elements?

   At least 12 floors, 2 flights of stairs

- What is the background space?

   Time (morning, evening), apartment building

- Rules of interaction

   Man goes down 12 floors in the elevator

   Man goes up to the tenth floor in the elevator

   Man walks up two flights of stairs

   Man goes to the twelfth floor directly from the lobby if it is raining outside or if there is someone else in the elevator with him.

- Emergent properties

   Man moves between the lobby and his apartment

At this point, you probably do not have enough information to explain the man's behavior. Much like a detective solving a mystery, your systematic analysis of the situation enables you to ask meaningful questions to deepen your descriptive model. Let's imagine the scene as it unfolds based on our descriptive model and our prior knowledge. Our knowledge of elevators suggests that there must be a panel of buttons on the wall. The rules of interaction between the man and the elevator suggest that the doors open, he steps into the elevator, and pushes the lobby button on the panel. Doing so brings him to the lobby. In the evening, the process is repeated. Except this time we know that he presses the tenth floor button if he is alone, travels to the tenth floor where he exits the elevator, and walks two flights to the twelfth floor. As we continue to run the model in our minds, we imagine the situation with someone else in the elevator. In this situation, someone has to push the twelfth floor button, and the man travels to the twelfth floor where he exits. When it is raining, the man can be alone and press the twelfth floor button to travel directly to the twelfth floor.

Reality Check

To build habits of mind associated with descriptive modeling, begin each class with an entrance activity. Project pictures of familiar scenes and ask students to describe the scene as they enter the classroom. Review the descriptions in terms of the fundamental questions of inquiry. After a few classes, students expect to find a picture and immediately create their descriptive models. As the weeks progress, exchange the familiar pictures with unfamiliar pictures (microscopic images, pond life, ecosystems, molecules), items, or even lateral thinking puzzles and ask students to develop descriptive models. Doing so consistently over a period of time develops habits of mind associated with observation strategies for creating descriptive models as a first step to inquiry.

Do you have an explanation yet? Go to the end of the chapter, p. 24, for the solution. Don't worry if you did not arrive at the correct explanation. Although identifying the best explanation is the desired outcome, it is the process that is important in this example. That is why science inquiry is called re-search, and not simply search; we must seek answers and retry to seek them again. Hopefully you realize that a scientific approach is a strategy that keeps you moving toward a better explanation.

National, State, and Local Standards: They Will Light Your Way

Go to **MyEducationLab**, select the topic Lesson and Unit Planning, watch the simulation entitled "Content Standards," and complete the questions that accompany it.

NSES

Have you ever dreamt that you were lost in a forest and had no idea of how to get out? You may remember such a dream as an overpowering nightmare from which you awoke filled with dread and hopelessness.

The thought of teaching children science may be similarly overwhelming, but it should not leave you feeling hopeless. You should feel uplifted! In the bad dream, you were alone. In the real world of teaching children science, you are not. Many people have spent their entire professional lives developing goals, objectives, procedures, and materials for science teaching. You will have access to the fruits of all of their labor. For now, think about just one aspect of all of this: the goals and objectives of your science teaching.

Again, you will not have to invent them all yourself! A group of scientists and educators have created the *National Science Education Standards (NSES)*, which outline suggested science content by grade level. (You may recall that we discussed the NSES with respect to technology earlier in the chapter.) The NSES are readily available to you in print form and on the Internet, and an important portion of those standards related to the content you should be teaching or at least considering is reprinted inside the front cover of this book.

Project 2061

Implications for Your Inquiry-Based, Discovery-Focused Classroom

To develop an inquiry-based, discovery-focused classroom, you'll need to draw on a wide range of resources. One resource that may prove useful is the curriculum development effort known as *Project 2061*. Developed by scientists and educators, and with the sponsorship of the American Association for the Advancement of Science, this project is intended to help reform K–12 science, mathematics, and technology education. Its basic reference document, *Science for All Americans*, offers recommendations called *benchmarks* in many areas, which will be important to you as you plan and teach.

Project 2061 has twelve benchmarks that you may wish to study in some detail:

- The nature of science
- The nature of mathematics
- The nature of technology
- The physical setting
- The living environment
- The human organism
- Human society
- The designed world
- The mathematical world
- Historical perspectives
- Common themes
- Habits of mind

To find helpful information about any of these benchmarks, visit the Project 2061 website at **www.project2061.org/**.

Although the NSES are like the lighthouse that points to the final destination, they do not set the course. It is up to you and your district or department team to determine how the students will reach the standards. Rest assured that the NSES are only some of many guides available to help determine what to teach. Individual states, provinces, and local communities also have developed standards and curriculum maps. Sometimes called frameworks, they provide varying degrees of guidance in the forms of content, teaching, and sample lessons. Additionally, there is an abundance of resources available through the Internet. In the information age, your biggest challenge will not be to create original science lessons as much as it will be to recognize and choose effective, inquiry-based science lessons. No two classes and teachers are exactly alike; therefore, you will need to adapt and revise each lesson to best fit your teaching style and the needs of the children in your class.

Rest assured that you are not lost and alone in the forest. The path you will take as you lead children to discovery is well marked. You will have many resources as you guide children to explore, inquire, and discover. You are definitely not alone. Sleep well, and then awake and seize the day!

Yes, You Can Do It! Science for All Children, Every Day in Every Way

Go to **MyEducationLab**, select the topic Cross-Curricular Connections, watch the video entitled "Emerging Curriculum Built on Children's Interests" and complete the questions that accompany it.

This book is full of resources that will help you create wonderful classroom experiences for children—experiences in which they explore, inquire, and discover. In Part One of this book (which includes this and the next eight chapters), you will learn basic science-teaching methods that will also help you create that wonderful classroom! And beyond Part One, you will find three very specific parts of the book that deal with teaching the earth/space sciences, the life sciences, and the physical sciences. In the chapters in those parts, you will find unit and lesson "starter ideas," activities and demonstrations, and even basic science content for your reference as you prepare to teach children science.

I am confident that you will be successful if you are motivated to use your talent to its fullest and the available resources to the maximum. If you do, each day in your classroom will be a day when every child has the opportunity to explore, inquire, and discover. So, get started on your journey to discover how children actually learn science.

Summary

You will be teaching children not only science but also strategies for thinking and knowing what to do when they do not have the answer by creating a classroom environment that embraces and directs children's natural curiosity. You will guide children to develop habits of mind necessary to be active and curious observers, to seek explanations based on evidence, and to systematically test explanations through experimentation. In doing so, your students will use and develop inquiry process skills, positive attitudes toward science, and abilities to do science.

Science is both a body of knowledge about the natural world and a systematic way of gathering knowledge. In other words, it is a *product* (an organized set of facts, concepts, and principles) as well as a *process* (a method of obtaining and extending that knowledge). Technology is the application of that knowledge or the systematic ways of getting knowledge to solve human problems.

The general approaches for teaching science that you will use in the classroom will be guided by an understanding of the mental modeling inherent in the progression of inquiry: description, explanation, and experimentation. These three components of the progression of inquiry provide a simple framework that supports instructional strategies. Five fundamental questions of inquiry provide a structure for beginning inquiry:

1. What are the elements of the system being studied?
2. What are the properties of the elements?
3. What is the background space or context of the system?
4. What are the rules of interaction among the elements in the system?
5. What are the emergent properties of the system?

The challenges of teaching children science will require you to use a variety of resources, including units and lessons that you plan yourself, science resource books, and the Internet. Know that you are not alone in your quest for effective science teaching strategies. Organizations such as the National Academy of Sciences (National Science Education Standards) and the American Association for the Advancement of Science (Project 2061) as well as local science standards and frameworks will also be your guide as you plan learning experiences in which children learn to seek explanations through inquiry and discovery.

Going Further

On Your Own

1. Think about when you have observed children in elementary, middle, or high school exploring, doing inquiry, and making discoveries, or recall your own experiences in science. Provide any examples that you can, including examples of students using the inquiry process skills (e.g., observing, interpreting data, etc.).

2. Consider your present feelings about teaching children science, and identify the factors that have influenced your attitudes.

3. If possible, interview an elementary school teacher to find out how he or she would answer such questions as these: How do you feel about teaching children inquiry-based, discovery-focused science?

What do children think science is? What materials for learning science are available in your classroom or school? Do you feel well prepared to teach science? Why or why not?

4. Do some research to determine the role that science and technology have played in shaping present-day society. Consider such questions as these: Would society be better served if science were pursued only for the sake of the technology that results from it? Does the scientist occupy a prestigious position in modern society? What responsibility do scientists have for communicating the results of their work in a way that is understandable to the public?

On Your Own or in a Cooperative Learning Group

5. Discuss the role models that your parents, teachers, textbooks, and the media offered you in elementary school. Can you recall your level of career awareness as an elementary student? What did you want to become?

Why? If you are a woman, what factors tended to turn you toward or away from a scientific career? If you are a man, what stereotypes, if any, did you have about women and careers in science and technology?

Resources for Discovery Learning

Internet Resources

 To access these helpful websites, go to **MyEducationLab,** select Resources, and then Web Links. To learn more, click on the following links and you will easily be directed to each website.

- **AAAS Project 2061: Benchmarks for Science Literacy:**
  www.project2061.org/default_flash.htm

- **Inquiry and the National Science Education Standards:**
  http://books.nap.edu/html/inquiry_addendum/

- **Kids Draw a Scientist; Perceptions of Scientists:**
  http://science.easternblotnet/?p=52

- **National Science Education Standards:**
  www.nap.edu/openbook.php?record_id=4962

- **National Science Teachers Association:**
  www.nsta.org/

- **NetLinkd (NSES and AAAS 2061 Relationship):**
  www.sciencenetlinks.org./benchmarks.htm

- **Project 2061 Overview:**
  www.project2061.org/

Print Resources

Suggested Readings

Bodzin, Alec, and Mike Gehringer. "Breaking Science Stereotypes." *Science and Children* 25, no. 5 (January 2001): 36–41.

Coverdale, Gregory. "Science Is for the Birds: Promoting Standards-Based Learning through Backyard Birdwatching." *Science Scope* 26, no. 4 (January 2003): 32–37.

Davis, Elizabeth A., and Fitzpatrick, Doug. "It's All the News: Critiquing Evidence and Claims." *Science Scope* 25, no. 5 (February 2002): 32–37.

Demers, Chris. "Analyzing the Standards." *Science and Children* 37, no. 4 (January 2000): 22–25.

Dillon, Nancy. "Sowing the Seeds of the Standards." *Science and Children* 37, no. 4 (January 2000): 18–21.

Ferrell, Kathy. "Keeping the Joy in Teaching." *Science Scope* 24, no. 6 (March 2001): 50–52.

Fitzner, Kenneth. "Issues-Oriented Science." *Science Scope* 25, no. 6 (March 2002): 16–18.

Goodnough, Karen. "Humble Advice for New Science Teachers." *Science Scope* 23, no.6 (March 2000): 20–24.

Houtz, Lynne E., and Quinn, Thomas H. "Give Me Some Skin: A Hands-On Science Activity Integrating Racial Sensitivity." *Science Scope* 26, no. 5 (February 2003): 18–22.

Jesky-Smith, Romaine. "Me, Teach Science." *Science and Children* 39, no. 6 (March 2002): 26–30.

Kelly, Catherine A. "Reaching the Standards." *Science and Children* 37, no. 4 (January 2000): 30–32.

Koenig, Maureen. "Debating Real-World Issues." *Science Scope* 24, no. 5 (February 2001): 18–24.

Lee, Suzie. "Achieving Gender Equity in Middle School Science Classrooms." *Science Scope* 26, no. 5 (February 2003): 42–43.

Lightbody, Mary. "Countering Gender Bias in the Media." *Science Scope* 25, no. 6 (March 2002): 40–42.

Lowery, Lawrence F. (Ed.). *NSTA Pathways to the Science Standards: Guidelines for Moving the Vision into Practice.* Arlington, VA: National Science Teachers Association, 1997.

Lucking, Robert A., and Christmann, Edwin P. "Tech Trek: Technology in the Classroom." *Science Scope* 26, no. 4 (January 2003): 54–57.

McDuffie, Thomas E., Jr. "Scientists—Geeks and Nerds." *Science and Children* 38, no. 8 (May 2001): 16–19.

National Research Council. *National Science Education Standards.* Washington, DC: National Academy Press, 1996.

Ostlund, Karen, and Mercier, Sheryl. *Rising to the Challenge of the National Science Education Standards: Grades 4–8.* Arlington, VA: National Science Teachers Association, 1996.

Ostlund, Karen, and Mercier, Sheryl. *Rising to the Challenge of the National Science Education Standards: Grades K–6.* Arlington, VA: National Science Teachers Association, 1999.

Timmerman, Barbara. "Keeping Science Current." *Science Scope* 25, no. 6 (March 2002): 12–15.

Notes

1. *Brain Food.* www.rinkworks.com/brainfood/p/latreal1.shtml (accessed 02-10-08).
2. Thinkexist.com. http://thinkexist.com/quotes/richard_feynman/ (Richard Feynman was a theoretical physicist 1918–1988).
3. P. Bergethon, *Introducing Your Students to the Scientific Method* (Holliston, MA: Symmetry Learning Systems, 1999).
4. M. Mead and R. Metraux, "Image of the Scientist among High School Students," *Science* 126, no. 3270 (August 30, 1957): 384–390.
5. C. R. Barman, K. L. Ostlund, C.C. Gatto, M. Halferty, "Fifth Grade Students' Perceptions About Scientists and How They Study and Use Science." 1997 AETS Conference Papers and Summaries of Presentations, 1998.
6. James Gleick, "Uh-Oh, Here Comes the Mailman," *The New York Times Review of Books* 4 (March 1990): 32.
7. Ibid.
8. Based on Lawrence F. Lowery (ed.), *NSTA Pathways to the Science Standards: Guidelines for Moving the Vision into Practice* (Arlington, VA: National Science Teachers Association, 1997), p. 84.
9. P. Bergethon, *Learning the Language of Patterns* (Holliston, MA: Symmetry Learning Systems, 1999).
10. *Brain Food.* www.rinkworks.com/brainfood/p/latreal1.shtml (accessed 02-10-08).

▶ **Answer to Elevator Puzzler:** You may be able to infer (a science process skill) that the man is not capable of pressing the twelfth floor button when he is alone. However, someone else can press it for him when other people are in the elevator. When it is raining, he can push the twelfth floor button with an umbrella. You now have an explanatory model. You can hypothesize that the man is too short to reach the twelfth floor button on the elevator panel.

Note that the hypothesis is a proposed relationship that suggests a rationale behind the explanation. Finally, you would need to observe the man in the elevator to reject or fail to reject your hypothesis. This is an experimental model. If you find out that the man is indeed too short to reach the buttons on the panel, then you fail to reject your explanation and hypothesis. If the evidence does not support your explanation, then you reject your explanation or hypothesis.

chapter 2

Constructing Knowledge and Discovering Meaning

How can I help children learn science?

▶ **Getting Started**

Suppose one of your fourth-grade students wonders aloud, "Why can't it be summer every day of the year? Summer is such a wonderful time of year!" Before you provide your student with the explanation of why the seasons change, take a moment to think about your response . . .

Consider that graduates were asked to explain the reason for the seasons during commencement at Harvard University in 1987.[1] You may be surprised to learn that twenty-one out of twenty-three graduates got it wrong. The most common answer was that the seasons are caused by the distance of the Earth from the sun, a common misconception. It is possible that several of the students were once taught the correct reason for the seasons at some point in their academic careers, but because it is difficult to let go of explanations, they clung to this common misconception. If so, did they really learn the reason for the seasons the first time around?

So what is learning, really? Learning is the result of deepening or changing our mental models to more accurately describe and explain a phenomenon. It is usable

knowledge that can be recognized and applied (transferred) in a novel context. According to the National Research Council, "Experts' knowledge is connected and organized around important concepts (e.g., Newton's second law of motion); it is 'conditionalized' to specify the contexts in which it is applicable; it supports understanding and transfer (to other contexts) rather than only the ability to remember."[2] Understanding change requires us to deepen our understanding by modifying our existing knowledge. To truly understand the reason for the seasons, one first needs to understand the warming effects of indirect light opposed to direct light on a given surface area, and the interaction of sunlight on a planet tilted at approximately 23 degrees as it revolves around the sun. Then one can begin to understand that indirect light warms the earth less in the winter than in the summer.

Learning doesn't happen only for children, and it doesn't happen only in school. Learning is an ongoing process, in which the learner integrates new knowledge with previous knowledge and discovers new ways of thinking, acting, and feeling. We are *always* constructing new meanings in this way. I am always learning, you are always learning, and right now, somewhere a child is learning that it doesn't matter whether a corn seed is planted upside down or rightside up. That child is learning that in the proper environment, new shoots, like young children, grow toward the light.

Traditional Views about How Children Learn Science

There are two traditional and very broad ways of thinking about how children learn. One is known as *behavioral theory,* and the other is known as *cognitive theory.* If you wish to be successful in teaching children science, you will need to use elements of both and integrate these ideas with *constructivism:* a modern view of learning that you will learn about later in this chapter.

Project 2061

Implications for Helping Children Construct Knowledge and Discover Meaning

Project 2061 addresses the thinking skills you may wish to consider as you teach children science. Namely, they are outlined in the benchmark "Habits of mind":

- Values and attitudes
- Computation and estimation
- Manipulation and observation
- Communication skills
- Critical-response skills

Note that the item "Critical-response skills" is intended to help children separate sense from nonsense, which is crucial to helping them become scientifically literate citizens.

You'll find specific benchmarks (or recommendations) for the skills of most interest to you at the Project 2061 website: **www.project2061.org/.**

Behavioral Theory

The behavioral approach suggests that what a child does, and consequently what a child learns, depends on what happens as a result of the child's behavior. From this perspective, your job as a teacher is to create a classroom in which good things happen when children work with science materials, interact with one another in cooperative group work, and complete science projects. If children enjoy these experiences, receive praise from peers and the teacher, and are successful, they will be learning and developing a positive attitude. In order to have more experiences and receive more praise, they will continue to work hard.

From the behavioral perspective, the teacher's job is to create a science-learning environment in which certain behaviors and the acquisition of knowledge, concepts, and skills are increased and reinforced. *Tangible reinforcers* include receiving good grades, winning certificates and prizes in science fairs, earning points for free time, earning the privilege of taking care of the classroom animals for a week, and so forth. *Intangible reinforcers* include recognition of good work and praise from the teacher and the child's peers and parents. Figure 2.1 offers a list of some practical applications of behavioral principles.

Cognitive Theory

Cognitive theorists believe that what children learn depends on their mental processes and what they perceive about the world around them. In other words, learning depends on how children think and how their perceptions and thought patterns interact.

To understand the cognitivist view, try this: Look at the drawing on the left. What does it look like? Now ask other people to look at the drawing. What do they believe it is? If you ask a few people, you will soon discover that people perceive the world differently and that their solutions to questions depend on what they see and how they think.

Figure 2.1   You can find many ways to apply behavioral principles in your science classroom.

Practical Applications

Behavioral Principles for Your Science Classroom

1. *Reinforce positive behavior.*

   EXAMPLES
   - Praise children when they complete projects well.
   - Tell children who do a particularly good job of cleaning up after a messy science activity that you appreciate their efforts.

2. *Reinforce effort.*

   EXAMPLES
   - Thank children for trying to answer questions during class discussions.
   - Praise children whose behavior improves with each field trip.

3. *After a behavior has been established, reinforce the behavior at irregular intervals.*

   EXAMPLES
   - Surprise the class with special visitors or field trips during particularly challenging units.
   - Take individual photographs of children at work on long-term (multiweek) science projects, and present them unannounced at various times during the project.

According to cognitive learning theorists, a teacher should try to understand what a child perceives and how a child thinks and then plan experiences that will capitalize on these.

Many learning theories have evolved from cognitivism. In the sections that follow, you will read about two of the most important of these theories.

Piaget's Theories   Jean Piaget spent his professional life searching for an understanding of how children view the world and make sense of it. His work led him to propose that children progress through stages of cognitive development. The list that follows gives the stages and a few examples of the characteristics of each stage:

1. *Sensorimotor knowledge (0 to 2 years).* Objects and people exist only if the child can see, feel, hear, touch, or taste their presence. Anything outside the child's perceptual field does not exist.

2. *Preoperational (representational) knowledge (2 to 7 years).* The ability to use symbols begins. Although the child is still focused on the "here and now" early in this stage, the child can use language to refer to objects and events that are not in his or her perceptual field. The child has difficulty understanding that objects have multiple properties. For instance, he or she is not completely aware that a block of wood has color, weight, height, and depth all at once. Concepts of space and time are difficult to grasp. The child does not *conserve* attributes such as mass, weight, and number. For example, the child views a drink placed in a tall, narrow glass as more than the same amount of drink placed in a short, wide glass.

3. *Concrete operations (7 to 11 years).* The child can group objects into classes and arrange the objects in a class into some appropriate order. The child understands that mass, weight, volume, area, and length are conserved. The child has some difficulty isolating the variables in a situation and determining their relationships. The concepts of space and time become clearer.

4. *Formal operations (12 years through adulthood).* The child is able to think in abstract terms, is able to isolate the variables in a situation, and is able to understand their relationship to one another. The child's ability to solve complex verbal and mathematical problems emerges as a consequence of being able to manipulate the meanings represented by symbols.

Giving students opportunities to deepen their understanding through discovery is essential to constructing new knowledge.

Bruner's Theories   Jerome Bruner's research reveals that teachers need to provide children with experiences to help them discover underlying ideas, concepts, and patterns. Bruner is a proponent of *inductive* thinking, or going from the specific to the general. You are using inductive thinking when you get an idea from one experience that you use in another situation. Bruner believes that children are able to grasp any concept, provided it is approached in a manner appropriate for their particular grade level. Therefore, teachers should encourage children to handle increasingly complex challenges.

Constructivism: A Modern View of How Children Learn Science

What Is Constructivism?

Constructivism is a theory of human learning that is rooted in cognitive psychology and, to a lesser extent, behavioral psychology. It provides modern science teachers invaluable guidance. In fact, if you grasp the essential principles of constructivism, you will find it much easier to answer the two questions that will always be running through your mind as you approach a topic: *What should I teach?* and *How should I teach?*

Three Constructivist Principles to Guide Your Planning and Teaching

Go to **MyEducationLab**, select the topic Teaching Strategies, watch the video entitled "Constructivist Classrooms," and complete the question that accompanies it.

Three fundamental principles underlie the theory of constructivism:

1. *Naive conceptions.* A person never really knows the world as it is. Each person constructs beliefs about what is real.
2. *Assimilation.* Students try to reconcile new experiences and data with their present understanding so that the new data support and deepen but do not change their fundamental mental model.
3. *Accommodation.* Students cannot reconcile new experiences and data with their present understanding and they have to change their mental model to logically explain the experience.

Naive Conceptions   The first of these three principles is very important to teachers. Your experience with children probably has already taught you that not everything a child believes or knows is true. For example, Tom may believe that sweaters keep him warm because sweaters are warm. Uncle Harry, who lives with Tom's family, has told him many times to wear a warm sweater on a cool day. The belief that a sweater is warm is an example of a *naive conception*: an idea that does not fit reality when its validity is checked. Children and adults have many naive conceptions, and it is extremely difficult for a teacher to help a child construct new understandings if the child's naive conceptions filter out new experiences.

Assimilating and Accommodating New Learnings   Much of teaching is really re-teaching and challenging mental models with discrepant events, which leads to assimilation or accommodation. Different, but complementary to one another, these last two principles both address ways in which a child tries to fit new ideas into those already in place. Suppose, for example, that Eddie enters class believing Earth is flat, based on his daily encounters with a seemingly flat world, and is taught that Earth is round. In order to reconcile his prior belief that Earth is flat with the new information that Earth is round, he creates a mental model of a pancake shaped Earth that fits both with his prior understanding of a flat Earth and with the new information that Earth is round. Cognitive psychologists use a term to describe this situation: *assimilation*.

Inquiry requires children to be active observers of the world around them.

Suppose, however, that Eddie learns that ships sailing over the horizon do not fall off the edge of Earth or that if one sails far enough west, he ends up back in the east! When challenged to explain this phenomenon, he cannot reconcile it with his current mental model of a flat Earth. He is faced with the choice of either having to reject the evidence, or *accommodate* his mental model to one of a spherical Earth. Assimilation and accommodation are not mutually exclusive. They often complement each other in the learning process.

Constructivism focuses on the interplay between what the child already knows and the experiences the teacher provides. The conceptions and naive conceptions that the child has before an experiment make a very real difference in what the child will learn. Figure 2.2 identifies some practical applications of constructivism.

Figure 2.2   Practical strategies for identifying prior knowledge

Constructivism for Your Science Classroom

1. Prior to a lesson or unit, ask your students what they think and believe about a topic, and organize their input with a simple graphic organizer on a piece of newsprint that can be kept in the class for the duration of the unit. Label one column, "What we know" (to assess prior knowledge), and the other column, "What we want to learn" (to initiate the inquiry process). Enter the children's initial thoughts, and then add a third column labeled, "What we learned" to be completed by the class over the course of the unit.

2. Develop some true/false questions about the topic. Children's responses will give you a sense of their prior knowledge. Example:

    a. Water can move rocks. T/F

    b. Rocks never change. T/F

    c. All rocks are the same. T/F

    d. Some rocks can float. T/F

3. The Internet is also another way to get an idea of children's common prior knowledge or misconceptions before you prepare a lesson. There are several sites available through most search engines or go to MyEducationLab for more links.

4. Probe prior knowledge with an authentic experience. For example, if the unit topic was weathering and erosion, you might want to show them a rock with evidence of weathering or take them out on the school grounds where there is a good example of weathering and erosion. Point out evidence that you know is the result of weathering and erosion (i.e., rock outcropping with cracks and splits and smaller rocks at the base). Wonder out loud how the smaller rocks got there, and ask the students for their explanations.

Contributions of Neuroscience

Developments in the technology of cognitive neuroscience provide windows into the workings of the human brain like never before. Teachers in the twenty-first century will need to become increasingly familiar with ways in which the brain processes information to understand the implications for learning. Educators need to know how to interpret, critically assess, and appropriately implement the emerging research on the neuroscience of thinking and learning.

Ways to Support Your Constructivist Teaching

The NSE Standards

Here is a question for you: Do you know what *rebar* is? Oh, you don't. Before I reveal its meaning, you must answer another question: Have you ever thought of becoming a construction worker instead of a science teacher? Perhaps you haven't.

Surprisingly, teaching children science has elements of the construction industry in it. For one thing, you want to build a foundation that will give your children the knowledge, skills, and attitudes to keep them interested and constantly learning about science and technology. Without that foundation, children will find it difficult, if not impossible, to add new layers of learning.

That's where rebar comes in. It is a thick strand of steel that runs within the concrete slabs of a foundation. You probably have seen rebar sticking out from chunks of broken concrete. The rebar strengthens the concrete so that the foundation is durable and can stand the test of time.

The specific science content identified in the National Science Education Standards (NSES) is our teaching "rebar." Content from the standards must cross and recross the plans you create and the lessons you teach. That content will strengthen the foundation on which children will construct knowledge and discover meaning.

Let's be more specific about how the NSES will support and reinforce your constructivist teaching. I'll discuss this support within the three guiding principles of constructivism presented earlier in this section:

1. **Naive conceptions.** *A person never really knows the world as it is. Each person constructs beliefs about what is real.*

   The most basic support for this principle comes from the existence of the NSES themselves. Since we finally have science standards, you, as a teacher, have something against which to compare students' prior knowledge and beliefs. If you listen carefully to children, you'll hear some amazing things about how they think the world works. Unfortunately, some of those beliefs are simply wrong!

   What you need to do is first carefully study the standards to ascertain within which standard children's inaccurate knowledge and misconceptions lie. Then, you can take guidance from the chapters of this book and other resources to properly address the deficiencies.

   Here are two examples:

   A child says: "I think that the moon followed us when my mom walked me to Janet's house for a sleepover."

   This misconception can be dealt with by providing content and experiences related to Earth and Space Sciences Standards ESS 2 and ESS 3—"Objects in the sky" and "Changes in earth and sky."

   A child says: "My dad said Becky caught a cold because she played outside without her jacket on."

   This misconception can be dealt with by providing content and experiences related to Science in Personal and Social Perspectives Standard SPSP 1—"Personal health."

Make the Case *An Individual or Group Challenge*

● **The Problem**

Providing a rich learning environment for children may require the teacher to take them out of the traditional classroom occasionally and into the real world. Sometimes, it is difficult for new teachers to identify real-world experiences that will really improve children's achievement in science.

● **Assess Your Prior Knowledge and Beliefs**

What do you presently believe about the way in which children learn both in and out of the classroom?

1. Children learn best from direct experience with natural objects and phenomena.

   _____ agree   _____ disagree

   Your evidence: _____

2. Hands-on science experiences automatically reinforce children's learning.

   _____ agree   _____ disagree

   Your evidence: _____

3. A child's prior knowledge and beliefs should be assessed before new experiences are introduced to ensure that the experiences will be meaningful.

   _____ agree   _____ disagree

   Your evidence: _____

4. Children have few misconceptions about the natural world.

   _____ agree   _____ disagree

   Your evidence: _____

5. For highly able children, it probably makes little difference whether direct or hands-on instruction is used in the classroom.

   _____ agree   _____ disagree

   Your evidence: _____

6. Because children progress through identifiable stages of development, teachers should provide experiences that fit only the stage of development indicated by the children's age.

   _____ agree   _____ disagree

   Your reasoning: _____

● **The Challenge**

Integrate your knowledge of how children learn into one paragraph that will provide a rationale for taking the children to locations beyond the school grounds. Your intention is to use this paragraph in a letter you will send (with your principal's permission) to community leaders who may be willing to donate funds for this curriculum enrichment project.

2. **Assimilation.** *Students try to reconcile new experiences and data with their present understanding so that the new data support and deepen, but do not change their fundamental mental model.*

The NSES clearly state that children should have the ability both to do scientific inquiry and to understand scientific inquiry (see Content Standard A). By creating science unit and lesson plans for children that are consistent with the methods advocated in this book, you will be infusing the curriculum with discovery experiences and activities that are based on careful inquiry. Children will learn to confront the differences between what they believe and what they discover with their own senses. Your challenge is to teach them that firsthand, personally gathered knowledge must override incorrect beliefs.

Here are two examples:

A young child might say: "Magnets pull on everything."

This misconception can be countered and replaced by having children actually do magnet activities in which they make discoveries to the contrary.

An older child might say: "It's starting to get hot. Earth must be getting closer to the sun."

This misconception can be countered by doing an activity in which children use models to discover that the inclination of Earth as it proceeds in orbit varies the surface area upon which a given amount of sunlight falls. In other words, when Earth is in a position in orbit in which the Northern Hemisphere is inclined away from the sun, a given amount of sunlight is spread over a larger surface area and people in the Northern Hemisphere have winter. The warming of Earth doesn't have much to do with how close Earth is to the sun.

3. **Accommodation.** *Students cannot reconcile new experiences and data with their present understanding, and they have to change their mental model to logically explain the experience.*

By helping children learn about *and* practice the scientific methods of inquiry—as expressed in the Science and Technology Standards S&T 2 and S&T 5, "Understanding about science and technology," and in History and Nature of Science Standards HNS 1 and HNS 2, "Science as a human endeavor"—children will learn that some ways of getting knowledge are better than others.

Children's lives and future success will be greatly enhanced if they learn to appreciate the importance of stating hypotheses, gathering information systematically, and withholding the drawing of conclusions until all the facts are in. If you emphasize the nature of careful scientific inquiry as children make discoveries, they will construct new and more complete understandings about the world in which they live.

Reality Check

As you begin a unit on light, you place an apple on the table and ask the children to write down whether they think that they would still be able to see the apple if the room was completely dark, (with no light present at all) and to explain their answer. After reading some of the answers, you realize that some children believe that they could see the apple because the light goes from their eyes to the apple. Explain how the children might use assimilation, accommodation, or a combination of both to change their mental model.

Gardner's Multiple Intelligences

If you intend to create a discovery-focused, inquiry-based classroom, in which children construct knowledge and discover meaning, you will need to consider a "raw material" that is more important than any aquarium, ant colony, or microscope in the room. That raw material is the intelligence of children.

Introductory psychology books tell us that intelligence is measured by IQ tests, which is a less than satisfying answer. At the very minimum, *intelligence* relates to a capacity to learn as well as an ability to apply that learning. It is usually reported as a number called an *intelligence quotient,* or *IQ.* Someone of normal or average intelligence has an IQ of 100.

How will knowing that number for each of your students help you create a classroom in which all children can construct knowledge and discover meaning? For instance, would knowing that Maria has an IQ of 135 and Ricky has an IQ of 110 change how you teach Maria and Ricky? Probably not. In fact, this traditional way of measuring and reporting a child's theoretical capacity to learn will be of little help as you plan science experiences that are responsive to individual differences.

Gardner's Original Theory   Howard Gardner has suggested a radically new way of thinking about intelligence. Early in his work, he discovered seven different intelligences that he believes each of us has to various degrees:

1. Logical-mathematical
2. Linguistic
3. Musical
4. Spatial
5. Bodily-kinesthetic
6. Interpersonal
7. Intrapersonal[3]

According to Gardner's theory, each child can be viewed as having a greater or lesser capacity to learn in each specific area. This means, in turn, that you as a teacher can focus on particular intelligences as you create science-learning experiences. You can teach to each child's strengths and find appropriate ways to help him or her grow in weak areas.

Gardner's Addition: Naturalist Intelligence   In more recent years, Gardner's work has led to what he describes as *naturalist intelligence:* the ability to discern subtle characteristics and patterns and then easily group objects or events in appropriate categories.[4]

As a science teacher, the possibility that this intelligence exists could be very important, since you might be able to identify how much individuals are "science prone" based on their measured naturalist intelligence. Knowing this could help you adjust your teaching to build on the abilities of children who have strong naturalist intelligence and to develop ways to be more responsive to children who have a more modest level of naturalist intelligence. Adjustments might include providing some children with more sophisticated observation and classification challenges and others with more time to complete work that requires high levels of naturalist intelligence. Making adjustments like these is at the heart of constructivist teaching, as doing so helps you capitalize on the wide range of intelligences a child might have.

See Figure 2.3 for a few real-world examples of how you can help children grow in all eight of Gardner's multiple intelligences.

Figure 2.3 Gardner's theory of multiple intelligences has implications and many practical applications for providing a variety of learning experiences in the classroom.

Practical Applications

Gardner's Theory of Multiple Intelligences for Your Science Classroom

1. *Logical-mathematical*

   EXAMPLES
   - Emphasize the underlying patterns children observe in science activities.
   - Have children list the steps they undertook in an activity and what they thought at each step.

2. *Linguistic*

   EXAMPLES
   - Emphasize writing down predictions, observations, and so on in science journals and the importance of using appropriate descriptive words and new terminology.
   - Encourage children to maintain their own science dictionaries, which will include new science terms and drawings to illustrate word meanings.

3. *Musical*

   EXAMPLES
   - Whenever possible, use vocal and instrumental music selections to accompany the introduction of new concepts. For example, use songs related to the seasons when carrying out a unit on climate.
   - When teaching a unit on sound, emphasize the connections to music, such as the effect of changing the thickness of a string or the length of the air column of an instrument.

4. *Spatial*

   EXAMPLE
   - Have children express what they have learned through drawings and models.

5. *Bodily-kinesthetic*

   EXAMPLES
   - Encourage children to use equipment that builds upon coordination skills, such as the microscope, balance, and hand lens.
   - Wherever possible, have children demonstrate new learnings through movement and dance. For example, children might create a dance to illustrate the expansion of a balloon resulting from increasing the energy of motion of the molecules contained within it.

6. *Interpersonal*

   EXAMPLES
   - Have children create simulated television advertising on issues investigated in class, such as the environment or proper nutrition.
   - When doing cooperative group work, provide time for children to process how well their group has worked on a science project.

7. *Intrapersonal*

   EXAMPLE
   - Provide opportunities for children to informally assess their interest in science, how well they are learning, and how they feel about matters related to science and technology.

8. *Naturalist*

   EXAMPLE
   - Early in the school year, give children sets of natural objects or pictures of natural objects or events they have not previously seen (e.g., rocks, leaves, pictures of various cloud types). Then ask them to observe and group members of each set.

Be careful not to interpret Gardner's intelligences as exclusive domains. Most students will possess each intelligence to a degree. Some students may be more adept at processing information in a particular domain.

Go to **MyEducationLab**, select the topic Diverse Learners, watch the simulation entitled "Providing Instructional Supports: Facilitating Mastery of New Skills," and complete the questions that accompany it.

● Alternative Learning Styles

Think about what's the best way for you to learn. Is it enough to read the material and perhaps highlight key points here and there? Do you take notes, as well? Or does your best learning come from discussing the ideas with others or from doing a project or activity? And what about the person sitting next to you in a class? Does he or she learn in the same way that you do?

Constructivism is based on the idea that we are unique as a result of our different life experiences and that these experiences result in our individual knowledge and beliefs. It is these differences in knowledge and beliefs that make us different from one another. And because we are all fundamentally different in this sense, we will all learn differently, too. We have individual *learning styles*. And for you, as a science teacher, the implications of this are enormous.

One of your greatest challenges will be creating a classroom atmosphere and learning experiences that optimize learning for children with a diversity of learning abilities. It is not unusual for classrooms to have students with emotional, physical, and cognitive disabilities, gifted talents, or English language barriers. Differentiated learning and Universal Design for Learning (UDL) provide important teaching strategies that address the range of learning styles often encountered in a classroom.

Differentiated instruction acknowledges that all children do not learn alike and that instruction should provide several options for learning. Teachers need to create flexible, yet focused learning experiences that recognize the diversity of learning approaches.

UDL is an approach to teaching that facilitates differentiated instruction. It is similar in its approach to universal design in architecture by integrating structures everyone can use. Curb cuts and ramps that benefit wheelchair users are equally accessible by ambulatory people. Likewise, graphic organizers, visual displays, and vocabulary lists benefit all students, not just those with reading challenges. UDL is based on the following three general strategies:

Multiple means of representation: provide learners various ways of acquiring information and knowledge

Multiple means of expression: provide learners alternatives for demonstrating what they know and learn

Multiple means of engagement: pique learners' interests, challenge them appropriately, and motivate them to learn

Differentiated learning and UDL will play an integral role in lesson plans and strategies developed in Chapter 9.

If you are an experienced teacher who has attended many in-service workshops or courses or you are a preservice teacher who has had a variety of courses concerning how to teach, you may have heard and learned about learning styles. This is an interesting area of study because so many experts have their own ideas about the learning styles that people may have. Some expound about convergent and divergent thinkers; some emphasize the idea that some people prefer concrete experiences and others prefer abstract discussions of ideas and principles; some suggest that people can be grouped on the basis of whether they respond quickly (impulsive) or think first and talk or act later (reflective). See Figure 2.4 for some practical applications of this theory.

Figure 2.4   An understanding of individual learning styles can help you prepare science experiences that all children can learn from and enjoy.

Practical Applications

Learning Styles for Your Science Classroom

1. *It is likely that children prefer to learn in different ways.*

   EXAMPLE   • Study curriculum materials to ascertain whether they will accommodate differences in learning styles, and then develop some alternative teaching techniques. For example, if children are expected to name and describe the functions of the organs of the digestive system, study the unit carefully and try to come up with two or three different ways for children to learn this information.

2. *You can tell a great deal about how children learn by observing how they deal with new learning experiences.*

   EXAMPLE   • Early in the year, provide activities that include studying a section in a reference book, doing hands-on activities, doing library research, and working with a computer program. Observe how various children approach each task and their relative success with each.

3. *Provide a range of experiences in the classroom so that all children have opportunities to put their preferred learning styles to use as often as possible.*

   EXAMPLE   • Think about the extent to which the activities for each unit are the same or different in terms of what children actually do, and consider how you could build in variations in approach. For example, suppose you realize that all the activities for a unit on sound require the children to do the activity first, observe phenomena, and then report results. To accommodate children who have trouble with this approach, adapt a few of the activities early in the unit, so that children have the option of reading and talking about a concept before beginning an activity.

4. *Familiarize yourself with the needs of your students.*

   EXAMPLE   • Review Individualized Education Plans and speak with guidance counselors or previous teachers. Are there students in your class for whom English is a second language? Do any of the students have physical disabilities such as hearing or visual impairments? Are there children with learning disabilities among your students?

5. *Study the curriculum materials to ascertain whether they will accommodate a variety of learning options. Look for ways that you can incorporate multiple means of representation, expression, and engagement.*

   EXAMPLE   • As an engagement exercise, you plan to have students distinguish the sounds of mystery objects in a drop box, but this will be difficult for the hearing impaired students. Therefore, you could place the drop box on an improvised drum made out of a box with a balloon stretched across the top. All students can put their fingertips on the drumhead and feel the vibrations of different objects when they are dropped. This tactile experience not only benefits the hearing impaired students but also introduces all students to the role of vibrations in sound and sets the foundation for inquiries about frequency and pitch.

Summary

Constructivism, a useful theory about how children learn, has evolved from classical learning theories such as behaviorism and cognitivism. Constructivism recognizes that individuals enter a learning situation with prior knowledge and that individuals modify or change their view of the world (mental models) through assimilation and/or accommodation. Learning is the acquisition of usable knowledge that can be recognized and applied (transferred) in a novel context. The challenge for you as a teacher is to help children replace naive conceptions or lack of knowledge about the natural world by constructing more accurate and complete understandings.

Additional interesting insights about teaching and learning come from the NSES and from the idea that each of us has a preferred style of learning. Children come to our classrooms with a wide range of abilities. The more options available for learning experiences that challenge and deepen mental models the more likely children will encounter rich learning experiences that connect with their learning styles. Differentiated instruction and UDL are two approaches that help us optimize learning for children with a diversity of learning styles.

Going Further

On Your Own

1. Informally assess the extent to which you can apply your knowledge of the NSES, UDL, and learning styles to support constructivist teaching in an actual science classroom. Do this by interviewing a primary-, elementary-, or middle-grade teacher to determine what factors he or she believes affect how well a child learns science and what types of science experiences happen in the classroom. Gather as much information as you can without guiding the interview toward any of the ideas from this chapter. After the interview, make a list that summarizes the key points made by the teacher. Categorize the items with respect to their relevance to constructivism, the standards, multiple intelligences, and learning styles. (Be mindful of preserving the confidentiality of your interviewee in any summary report you prepare.)

2. Interview a school principal to determine what he or she believes are the key factors that affect the quality of science instruction in the school. After the interview, prepare a chart that relates key phrases from the interview to the major ideas of this chapter.

3. Based on your personal experiences as a student or teacher, to what extent are behavioral principles applied when children have science experiences? Provide as many firsthand examples as you can.

4. Based on your personal experiences as a student or teacher, to what extent are cognitivist principles applied when children have science experiences? Provide as many firsthand examples as you can.

5. Based on your personal experiences as a student in science classrooms, would you say that you have a preferred style of learning that leads to success in such environments? If you would, identify the factors that contribute to your preference.

On Your Own or in a Cooperative Learning Group

6. Have each member of the group interview at least one child to find out about his or her knowledge or beliefs about a key concept from the life, earth/space, or physical sciences and technology. In the course of each interview, be sure to encourage the child to respond to questions that might reveal some naive conceptions. Use questions such as these: Why doesn't the moon fall to the earth? Are whales fish? Does the sun move across the sky? Is a sweater warm?

7. As a group, reflect on the difference between *assimilation* and *accommodation*. Have group members identify one or two naive conceptions that they once had about the life, earth/space, or physical sciences and technology. Have individuals indicate whether it was difficult or easy for them to revise these conceptions when they learned facts to the contrary or had direct experiences that produced results in conflict with their conceptions. Based on this group work, prepare a list of implications for teachers who wish to create science classroom environments in which children have experiences that reveal naive conceptions and lead to new learnings.

Resources for Discovery Learning

Internet Resources

 To access these helpful websites, go to **MyEducationLab,** select Resources, and then Web Links. To learn more, click on the following link and you will easily be directed to the website.

- **North Central Regional Educational Laboratory:** www.ncrel.org/sdrs/areas/issues/content/cntareas/science/sc500.htm

- **Science Myths** www.amasci.com/miscon/miscon.html

Print Resources

Suggested Readings

Aram, Roberta J., and Bradshaw, Brenda. "How Do Children Know What They Know?" *Science and Children* 39, no. 2 (October 2001): 28–33.

Association for Supervision and Curriculum Development. "The Science of Learning [special section]." *Educational Leadership* 58, no. 3 (November 2000): 8–78.

Avraamidou, L., et. al. "Giving Priority to Evidence in Science Teaching: A First-Year Elementary Teacher's Specialized Practices and Knowledge." *Journal of Research in Science Teaching* 42 (November 2005): 965–986.

Bransford, Jon, Cocking, Rodney, and Brown, Ann. *How People Learn: Brain, Mind, Experience, and School.* Washington, DC: National Academy Press, 2000.

Buck, Gloria A., and Meduna, Patricia. "Exploring Alternative Conceptions." *Science Scope* 25, no. 1 (September 2001): 41–45.

Burris, S., et. al. "The Language of Learning Styles." *Techniques* (Association for Career and Technical Education) 83, no. 2 (February 2008): 44–48.

Farenga, Stephen J., et al. "Balancing the Equity Equation: The Importance of Experience and Culture in Science Learning." *Science Scope* 26, no. 5 (February 2003): 12–15.

Fetters, Marcia, et al. "Making Science Accessible: Strategies to Meet the Needs of a Diverse Student Population." *Science Scope* 26, no. 5 (February 2003): 26–29.

Flores, M. M. "Universal Design in Elementary and Middle School." *Childhood Education* 84, no. 4 (Summer 2008).

Frazier, Richard. "Rethinking Models." *Science Scope* 26, no. 4 (January 2003): 29–33.

Kang, N. H. "Elementary Teachers' Epistemological and Ontological Understanding of Teaching for Conceptual Learning." *Journal of Research in Science Teaching* 44, no. 9 (November 2007): 1292–1317.

Levy, H. M. "Meeting the Needs of All Students through Differentiated Instruction: Helping Every Child Reach and Exceed Standards." *The Clearing House* 81, no. 4 (March/April 2008): 161–164.

Otero, V. K., et al. "Preservice Elementary Teachers' Views of Their Students' Prior Knowledge of Science." *Journal of Research in Science Teaching* 45, no. 4 (April 2008): 497–523.

Pusey, Douglas. "Accessible Reading Assignments." *Science Scope* 26, no. 5 (February 2003): 44–46.

Science Scope 26, no. 4 (January 2003). (Entire issue emphasizes how to address misconceptions about science.)

Searson, Robert, and Dunn, Rita. "The Learning-Style Teaching Model." *Science and Children* 38, no. 5 (February 2001): 22–26.

Van Klaveren, Karen, et al. "How Do Your Students Learn?" *Science Scope* 25 no. 7 (April 2002): 24–29.

Yilmaz, K. "Constructivism: Its Theoretical Underpinnings, Variations, and Implications for Classroom Instruction." *Educational Horizons* 86, no. 3 (Spring 2008): 161–172.

Notes

1. M. H. Schneps and P. M. Sadler, *A Private Universe* (Harvard-Smithsonian Center for Astrophysics: Pyramid Films, 1988).
2. John D. Bransford, Ann L. Brown, and Rodney R. Cocking, editors. *How People Learn: Brain, Mind, Experience.* (Washington, D.C.: National Academy Press, 1999).
3. Thomas Armstrong, *Multiple Intelligences in the Classroom* (Washington, DC: Association for Supervision and Curriculum Development, 1994), pp. 2–3.
4. Kathy Checkley, "The first seven . . . and the eighth: A conversation with Howard Gardner," *Educational Leadership* 55, no. 1 (September 1997): 8, 9.

chapter 3

The Inquiry Process Skills

How can I help children use the inquiry process skills to make discoveries?

▶ Getting Started

Her lips are starting to swell and crack under the broiling desert sun. Hot dry air has been relentlessly attacking since daybreak. She stops for a moment, lifts the bandana covering her mouth and nose, and shakes out her stringy hair. Incredibly, with that headshake, something catches her attention. To her left, a tiny, gray fossil bone fragment sticks out from the soil. The last gust of wind must have revealed it. Now she doesn't feel the sun or the heat or the dust at all! Her full attention is focused on the fragment.

A series of images flashes through her mind as she compares what she can tell about this fragment to what she already knows. Her mental pictures are of dinosaur skeletons, and none has the anatomical structure into which this tiny bone would fit. It is a toe bone, for sure—but one she has never seen before. Her heart starts to race at the thought of this.

From her grimy tool pack, she carefully pulls several tiny dental picks and small brushes and gently works away the material around the bone. With each gentle poke and sweep of the brush, she grasps more clearly what has just been revealed to her eyes

alone: A brand-new dinosaur has stuck its toe into her world and ours. Her careful observation has led to an extraordinary discovery.

She will draw the fossil, photograph it, plot its location, and then ever so slowly search the surrounding area for more fragments. Eventually, she will pull from the reluctant earth a creature that so far has only been imagined. A wonderful discovery has been made—and she made it!

Discovery: The Destination

When we discover, we find or gain knowledge, usually for the first time. And while the act of discovery may only take an instant, getting there can take a long, long time.

When we teach science with the focus on discovery, we prepare children to make their personal discoveries with our strong guidance. We give them their very own "tool packs." And with any luck at all, they will those tools in a variety of contexts all through their lives. Only a few children will find brand-new dinosaurs, but all of them will use the tools of scientific inquiry to unearth the facts and develop the concepts, principles, attitudes, and values that will help them lead full and productive lives.

It's now time to focus on how you can make discovery learning a central feature of every class you teach. First, we'll look at a formal definition of *discovery learning* that will give direction to the science units and lessons you plan and teach.

What Is Discovery?

"Discovery simply means coming to know something you didn't know before."

Discovery learning happens when a child uncovers new information or gleans new insight about how to approach a problem or task and then completes the task or solves the problem on her or his own. It is an individual and personal experience. *Classrooms don't discover; individual children do.*

More important than uncovering new information, discovery learning is obtaining new ways to find answers. Discovery seeks explanations based primarily on observation and description. Discovery and inquiry are closely related; however, Leslie Trowbridge and Roger Bybee make an important distinction between discovery and inquiry. "Discovery occurs when an individual is mainly involved in using his mental processes to mediate (or discover) some concept or principle."[1] True inquiry goes beyond discovery to seek verification through identifying questions and designing thoughtful investigations based on hypotheses, predictions, experimentation, data collection, and analysis.[2] As an elementary school teacher, you will emphasize discovery skills as a foundation for inquiry.

How Do I Teach So Discovery Learning Happens?

To teach for discovery learning, you must, wherever possible, provide hands-on, mind-stretching experiences that will enable children to use their knowledge and skills to make discoveries. Your challenge is to provide the physical and intellectual context that ensures that these new discoveries are related to what learning has come before and to what learning will follow. Discovery learning does not happen in a vacuum. It is connected to the past and to the future. It is your job to be sure that these connections are made.

Your role as teacher goes beyond providing students with the opportunity to discover; you must also teach them how to discover. Your charge is to craft interactive learning experiences that guide students to develop the intellectual and physical tools necessary to seek explanations.

Is Discovery Time Really "Circus Time"?

OK, it's true: Some science classrooms *do* become accidental "circuses." It happens from time to time when teachers make the naive assumption that if they just provide a super-rich context of science "stuff," then good things will automatically happen. Well, sometimes they do, and sometimes they don't.

There is nothing accidental about good teaching. Teaching discovery does not happen by simply providing an engaging activity and hoping children will learn something of value. Avoid the temptation to let the activity drive the learning. It is not productive to build a model of a volcano as a fun activity without carefully building it around a lesson about convection and pressure. Select activities carefully and use them as experiences to develop the targeted learning objectives.

Inquiry: The Path

By now, you should understand that the point of your science experiences with children is to foster discovery learning. Remember to think of discovery learning as a *destination*.

You must also be firm in your conviction that discovery learning does not happen by accident. It must be clearly guided—by you. In fact, some educators use the term *guided discovery* to describe learning experiences for children.

The obvious question at this point (which I really hope is running through your mind) is, How do I guide children so they really get on the path of discovery and then actually make their own discoveries? Recall from earlier chapters that that path is *inquiry*.

What Is Inquiry?

Within the current educational scene, the term *inquiry* has far too many definitions, and that's unfortunate. I will explain it as clearly as I can, beginning with this straightforward definition:

> *Inquiry is the careful and systematic method of asking questions and seeking explanations.*

To further enhance your understanding of the term, let me share this detailed definition proposed by the National Science Education Standards (NSES):

> Scientific inquiry refers to the diverse ways in which scientists study the natural world and propose explanations based on the evidence derived from their work. Inquiry also refers to the activities of students in which they develop knowledge and understanding of scientific ideas, as well as an understanding of how scientists study the natural world.[3]

As a teacher, you will use inquiry to teach science as well as teach students to inquire. You should have a fairly clear understanding of what discoveries will be made and how to guide children's inquiry in fruitful ways. The information in the following section will help you with that.

Examples of Inquiry Methods

In describing *inquiry* in further detail, the NSES give examples of activities that children or scientists would do if they were engaged in inquiry:

1. Making observations
2. Posing questions
3. Examining books and other sources of information to see what is already known

4. Planning investigations
5. Reviewing what is already known based on experimental evidence
6. Using tools to gather, analyze, and interpret data
7. Proposing answers, explanations, and predictions and communicating the results
8. Identifying assumptions, using critical and logical thinking, and considering alternative explanations[4]

This is an overwhelming range of activities! Fortunately, over the years, these ideas have been transformed into much more useful forms. Educators have identified the specific classroom skills that children need in order to actively participate in the activities listed above. They are commonly called the *inquiry process skills* or *skills of inquiry*.

A little later in this chapter, we will learn what these skills are. (See the section titled "The Inquiry Process Skills," on pages 46–53.) But for now, I want to turn your attention to a topic that will help you grasp how to incorporate discovery-focused, inquiry-based science in your classroom. Educators have devised a way for you to think about this "big picture" in a simple and effective way. It's called the *learning cycle*.

The Learning Cycle

Go to **MyEducationLab**, select the topic Inquiry, watch the video entitled "The Learning Cycle," and complete the question that accompanies it.

A Framework for Teaching Inquiry: The 5E Instructional Strategy

Learning cycles are models of how people encounter and acquire new knowledge. They provide a framework for the educator to design effective learning experiences. Over the years, there have been several variations on the learning cycle. We will use one in this book that is commonly used among science educators to frame the inquiry-based, discovery learning that is characteristic of science education. It consists of five phases commonly referred to as the 5E's: Engagement, Exploration, Explanation, Elaboration, and Evaluation.[5,6] See Table 3.1.

Engagement   Engagement piques children's interest, solicits prior knowledge, and establishes focus usually in the form of an essential question. The essential question will anchor the lesson as it progresses. Often the engagement presents children with a discrepant event that challenges their perception of the world and encourages them to raise questions, which are the foundations of inquiry. It is during the engagement that children construct their initial descriptive model.

Go to **MyEducationLab**, select the topic Earth and Space Science, and read the lesson plan entitled "How Can You Measure How Fast the Wind Blows?" "How Does the Wind Speed Vary with Location and Time?" for an example of Engage, Explore, and Explain.

Exploration   Exploration provides opportunities for children to encounter new information necessary to answer the essential question. The new information should challenge the children's mental models and lead to assimilation or accommodation resulting in a deeper mental model that more accurately explains the phenomenon. Exploration activities are student centered. They may be in the form of information gathering, experimentation, or how-to activities. Stations, interactive demonstrations, and experimentation are just some of the methods that may be used during the exploration. It is not unusual for children to experience some cognitive dissonance during the exploration as their prior knowledge is challenged.

Explanation   Explanation is an opportunity for the children to express what they have discovered during the exploration. You may be tempted to explain what the children should have learned rather than listening to what the children learned. However, if the exploration is effective, children should make connections that answer the essential

Go to **MyEducationLab**, select the topic Inquiry, watch the video entitled "Explanation," and complete the question that accompanies it.

question. If the children express misconceptions, you must correct them by challenging the children's incorrect mental model in light of new data. This is the phase at which an explanatory model is constructed.

Elaboration   Elaboration is a time for children to apply, exercise, and transfer their newly acquired knowledge. Often the elaboration challenges children to recognize the application of their new understanding in a different context, reinforcing and deepening their understanding of the new information.

Evaluation   Evaluation is both formative and summative. Formative evaluation occurs throughout the learning experience to inform teachers and children about their progress. The teacher receives feedback through a variety of message checks about

Table 3.1   Summary of the 5E instructional model as it relates to the progression of inquiry

Phase	Instructional Goals	Learning Goals
Engagement	Create discrepant events Encourage children to express prior knowledge Prompt Question Process children's responses Listen	Develop a descriptive model Express prior knowledge Generate questions
Exploration	Orchestrate learning experiences for students to encounter new knowledge and deepen descriptive models Question Coach	Deepen descriptive model Employ experimental model Encounter new knowledge through observation, experimentation, manipulation Make connections Generate, collect, record data
Explanation	Restate essential question Process student responses Reinforce correct responses Correct misconceptions	Create an explanatory model Articulate response to essential question Correct misconceptions
Elaboration	Create challenges for students to apply and transfer newly acquired knowledge	Reinforce explanatory model Apply new knowledge in a novel context
Evaluation	Collect student feedback through message checks Identify specific benchmarks to gauge student progress toward concept attainment Modify lesson in response to student feedback Create summative assessments to evaluate individual student learning	Demonstrate mastery of new knowledge at the nominal, descriptive, and explanatory levels of understanding (see Chapter 6)

Go to **My EducationLab**, select the topic Inquiry, watch the video entitled "Evaluation," and complete the question that accompanies it.

whether children are making progress toward the learning objectives, while children receive feedback to reinforce or redirect them on the right track. Summative assessment usually occurs at the end of a unit to inform the teacher that the children are learning what the teacher intended to teach. See Chapter 6 for a more in depth look at evaluation and assessment.

It is not necessary to use all the phases of the 5E instructional model in each lesson. For example, the first lesson in a unit may be engagement, while the following three unit lessons may be explorations, and the fifth lesson an explanation. The 5E instructional strategy will be used as a framework for creating lessons and units throughout this text.

The Inquiry Process Skills

Recall that science is about the process of seeking explanations through a progression of inquiry: descriptive modeling, explanatory modeling, and experimental modeling. The 5E instructional strategy is a framework for designing lessons during which children experience this progression to deepen their understanding of science content and process. In doing so, they will develop and reinforce a range of important process skills associated with the progression of inquiry listed in Table 3.1. In the following section, I discuss specific inquiry process skills in the context of the progression of inquiry.

● Inquiry Process Skills Used to Create Descriptive Models

Go to **MyEducationLab**, select the topic Inquiry, and read the lesson plan entitled "How Can You Improve Your Inquiry Skills?"

Process skills can be closely associated with the phases of the progression of inquiry. We begin with the inquiry skills commonly associated with descriptive modeling.

- Observing
- Using space/time relationships
- Using numbers
- Questioning

Project 2061

Implications for Including the Inquiry Process Skills in Your Teaching

Project 2061 has a very strong emphasis on teaching inquiry process skills to students. It suggests that teachers should help students look at the world in a more scientific or objective manner, that students should be actively involved in exploration, and that everyone should be aware that scientific exploration is an important enterprise of modern society. Project 2061 addresses these three areas within the benchmark "The nature of science":

- The scientific world view
- Scientific inquiry
- The scientific enterprise

To find specific recommendations for each area, visit the Project 2061 website at **www.project2061.org/.**

- Classifying
- Measuring
- Communicating

Observing

▶ *What Does It Mean?*

Observing means using the senses to obtain information, or *data,* about objects and events. It is the most basic process of science. Casual observations spark almost every inquiry we make about our environment. Organized observations form the basis for more structured investigations. Acquiring the ability to make careful observations will create a foundation for making inferences or hypotheses that can be tested by further observations.

Careful, organized observations require the observer to take an active role. It is easy to confuse active observation with passive looking. The active observer uses five fundamental questions of inquiry proposed by Peter Bergethon:[7]

- What are the elements of the system?
- What are the properties of the elements?
- What is the context or background space of the system?
- What are the rules of interaction among the elements?
- What are the emergent properties of the system?

Sample Activity

Children can observe that different animals have very different solutions to the problem of getting from place to place. By directly observing animals outdoors or displayed in the classroom, children can describe whether each animal walks, swims, or flies. You may wish to challenge children to identify animals that can do all three—for example, ducks.

Observing is the most basic of all the inquiry process skills.

Using the Inquiry Process Skills to Create a Descriptive Model of a Butterfly

Table 3.2 illustrates how the fundamental questions of inquiry may be used to generate a simple descriptive model of a butterfly. Note how the descriptive model facilitates other inquiry process skills such as **enumeration** (number of legs) and **ordination** (head is above the thorax). **Questioning** is inherent in the fundamental questions of inquiry. Although these are general questions that apply to any system, construction of the descriptive model inevitably leads to more system-specific questions: "Why do some butterflies have brightly colored wings while others have very plainly colored wings?" "How do butterflies eat?" and so on. These questions can be selected and used by the teacher to address learning objectives. In fact, as the teacher, you will deliberately craft the engagement experience to pique curiosity around the questions that you want to address. **Measuring** is simply an application of technology to deepen the accuracy of the descriptive model. Children can measure the length of the head, thorax, and abdomen, the height of the wings, or the overall length and height of the butterfly. When several descriptive models of butterflies are collected, children can compare and **classify** the butterflies according to elements and properties. Children may use **space/time relationships,** noting that the butterflies move among similar types of flowers and are most active at certain times of day. Lastly, children need to **communicate** their models, which can be achieved through a variety of modalities such as writing, drawing, verbalizing, or simulating. Note the dependency of a good descriptive model on the implementation of inquiry process skills.

Using Space/Time Relationships

▶ What Does It Mean?

All objects occupy a place in space. The inquiry skill *using space/time relationships* involves the ability to discern and describe directions, spatial arrangements, motion and speed, symmetry, and rate of change.

Sample Activity

Provide each child or group of children with a small metal mirror (metal instead of glass as a safety precaution) and half an apple or a pear made by a lengthwise cut through the fruit. Ask children to discover if the right and left sides of the half are symmetrical. They can put the mirror lengthwise down the middle of the fruit section to see if they can observe the image of a complete fruit.

Using Numbers

▶ What Does It Mean?

We need numbers to manipulate measurements, order objects, and classify objects. The amount of time spent on the activities devoted to *using numbers* should depend largely on the school's mathematics program. It is important for children to realize that the ability to use numbers is also a fundamental process of science.

Sample Activity

Help young children learn to compare sets with the use of natural objects such as rocks. Place a collection of rocks on a table. Pick out a set of six rocks, and ask various children to come to the collection and make a set containing one more element

Table 3.2   Description of a butterfly—based on the fundamental questions of inquiry

Elements	Properties	Background space	Rules of interaction	Emergent properties
• Legs ⟶	• 4 long, 2 short, black	• Light (sunlight?) seemingly outside, on a plant	• Legs and wings attached to thorax	• Colorful
• Antennae ⟶	• Black 2, long		• Head in front of thorax	• Still
• Wings ⟶	• Yellow, black, blue, curved, 2 wings		• Abdomen behind thorax	• Fragile
• Head ⟶	• Black, round, round proboscis		• Butterfly on leaf	
• Thorax ⟶	• Red, black, larger than head			
• Abdomen ⟶	• Yellow, black dots, 8 segments			

than your set. Encourage children to use language such as the following to describe their set: "My set has seven, which is more than your set of six rocks." Do this with other sets of rocks.

Classifying

▶ *What Does It Mean?*

Classifying is the process scientists use to impose order on collections of objects or events. Classification schemes are used in science and other disciplines to identify objects or events and to show similarities, differences, and interrelationships.

Sample Activity

Ask children to bring pictures of plants and animals to school. Use the pictures from all the children to develop entries for a classification system.

Measuring

▶ *What Does It Mean?*

Measuring is the way observations are quantified. Skill in measuring requires, not only the ability to use measuring instruments properly, but also the ability to carry out calculations with these instruments. The process involves judgment about which instrument to use and when approximate rather than precise measurements are acceptable. Children can learn to measure length, area, volume, mass, temperature, force, and speed as they work on this process skill.

Sample Activity

Have children estimate the linear dimensions of classroom objects using centimeters, decimeters, or meters, and then use metersticks to measure the objects.

Communicating

▶ *What Does It Mean?*

Clear, precise communication is essential to all human endeavors and fundamental to all scientific work, which makes *communicating* skills valuable. Scientists communicate orally, with written words, and through the use of diagrams, maps, graphs, mathematical equations, and other visual demonstrations.

Sample Activity

Display a small animal such as a gerbil, hamster, or water snail. Ask children to write descriptions of the organism, emphasizing the need to include details such as size, shape, color, texture, and method of locomotion.

● Inquiry Process Skills Used to Create an Explanatory Model

- Inferring
- Hypothesizing

Inferring

▶ *What Does It Mean?*

Inferring is using logic to make assumptions from what we observe and question. The ability to distinguish between an observation and an inference is fundamental to clear thinking. An observation is an experience that is obtained through the senses. An inference is an assumption based on an observation. Consider the observation that butterflies are often found on flowering plants. One might infer that butterflies use the flowers as a source of food.

Sample Activity

Take children on a mini–field trip to a tree on school property, and have them prepare a list of observations about the ground at the base of the tree, the tree bark, and the leaves. Ask children to make inferences from their observations about the animals that may live in or near the tree (e.g., birds, insects, squirrels).

Hypotheses and Predictions

▶ *What Do They Mean?*

Hypotheses are often confused with predictions. A hypothesis, which begins with an explanatory model, is a proposed relationship put forth to explain a phenomenon. One might hypothesize that butterflies prefer yellow flowers. The *prediction* is the basis for an experiment. A prediction based on our hypothesis would be that if butterflies are presented with yellow flowers and white flowers, then the butterflies will land on the yellow flowers.

Sample Activity

Fill one plastic bag with cold air and one with hot air. (Use a hair dryer on low heat, being careful not to touch the bag with the hair dryer.) Ask your students to explain why the bag with hot air floated to the ceiling. They could hypothesize that hot air is lighter (less dense) than cold air. Ask them to make a testable prediction based on the hypothesis. For example, if we fill two equal size bags with hot air and cold air, the bag with hot air will weigh less.

Inquiry Process Skills Used to Create an Experimental Model

Experiments test predictions. A good experiment should test one variable and keep all other conditions the same. Failure to do so results in confusion about what variable caused the results.

Good experiments employ the following inquiry process skills:

- Predicting
- Identifying variables
    - Independent
    - Dependent
    - Controlled
- Designing experimental controls

Predicting

▶ *What Does It Mean?*

A *prediction* is a specific forecast of a future observation or event. Predictions are based on observations, measurements, and inferences about relationships between observed variables. A prediction that is not based on observation is only a guess. Accurate predictions result from careful observations and precise measurements.

Sample Activity

Have children construct a questionnaire about breakfast cereal preference and gather data from all the classrooms in the school except one. Have students analyze their data and make a prediction about the outcome of the survey of the children in the last room before polling those children.

Identifying Variables Variables are factors that can make a difference in an investigation. Experimental design consists of one independent variable, one dependent variable, and several controlled variables.

1. **Independent variable**

   The *independent variable* is the variable being tested. It is the variable that the experimenter manipulates or changes. For example, if one were to follow through with an experiment to test the hypothesis that butterflies prefer yellow flowers, the independent variable is the color of the flowers.

2. **Dependent variable**

   The *dependent variable* is the change that is measured. It changes in response to the independent variable. In our example, the dependent variable would be the number of butterflies that are attracted to the yellow flower.

3. **Controlled variables**

   For an experiment to be informative it must measure the effects of just one variable. Therefore, the only variables that change are the independent and dependent variables. All the other factors that could change must be kept the same or *controlled*. Referring to the sample experiment, the same butterflies and types of flowers should be used under the same conditions such as location, lighting, time of day, and temperature.

4. Experimental control

The *experimental control* is a parallel experiment that is usually done to determine whether the independent variable is responsible for the observed effect. In the control, the factor being tested is not applied. In this case, one would replace the yellow flowers with white flowers to determine whether the butterflies display a preference for the substituted flowers.

Sample Activity

Ask children whether bread will last longer (not become moldy) if it is kept at 4°C rather than at room temperature. Design an experiment by leaving one piece of bread in a plastic bag on a counter and one piece of bread in a plastic bag in a refrigerator at 4°C. Record the room temperature. Count the number of days until each piece of bread becomes moldy. The independent variable is temperature. The dependent variable is the time for the bread to become moldy. The controlled variables are bread from the same loaf, same size of bread pieces, same size and type of plastic bag, and the same handling procedures. The controlled experiment is bread stored at room temperature.

Experimenting encompasses all of the basic and integrated inquiry process skills.

Interpreting Data

▶ *What Does It Mean?*

The process of *interpreting data* involves making predictions, inferences, and hypotheses from the data collected in an investigation. We are constantly interpreting data when we read weather maps, watch the news on television, and look at photographs in newspapers and magazines. Students should have had previous experience in observing, classifying, and measuring before the process of interpreting data is approached.

Sample Activity

Ask the students to interpret the data in the graph below, of the distance from the starting point a person on a bike is over a time period of 15 seconds.

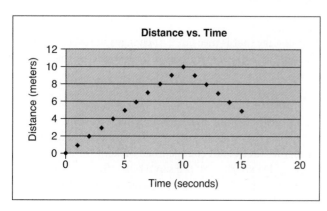

How far away from the starting point was the bike after 5 seconds? 10 seconds? 15 seconds?

How fast was the bike traveling expressed as meters per second during the first 10 seconds?

Describe what took place after 10 seconds.

Defining Operationally

▶ *What Does It Mean?*

When students use the *defining operationally* process, they define terms in the context of their own experiences. That is, they work with a definition instead of memorizing it. A definition that limits the number of things to be considered and is experiential is more useful than one that encompasses all possible variations that might be encountered. In the physical sciences, an operational definition is based on what is done and what is observed. In the biological sciences, an operational definition is often descriptive.

Sample Activity

Have students invent operational definitions for plant parts based on the functions of the parts they observe. For example, part of an operational definition for a *stem* is that "water moves up it." This definition might be derived by observing that a carnation stem placed in colored water serves to conduct the coloring to the petals. Part of the operational definition for a *bud* might include a reference to it as a site where students have observed a flower or a leaf emerge.

Make the Case *An Individual or Group Challenge*

● **The Problem**

Children in discovery-focused, inquiry-based classrooms may become so involved in their explorations that they spend too much time *doing* and too little time *thinking*.

● **Assess Your Prior Knowledge and Beliefs**

What are your present beliefs about each of the following?

1. Before engaging in an activity, children should establish a hypothesis.

    _____ agree   _____ disagree

    Your reasoning: _____

2. Even if there is an official recorder, all the children in a group should record their personal observations.

    _____ agree   _____ disagree

    Your reasoning: _____

3. As long as children have hands-on, inquiry-based experiences, they will learn the inquiry process skills.

    _____ agree   _____ disagree

    Your reasoning: _____

● **The Challenge**

Your state or province has awarded you a $500 grant for a single discovery-focused science project that involves a simulation of life in a space colony on Mars. At the end of the year, you must write a report describing what the children have learned. Describe how you would incorporate the children's mastery of the basic inquiry process skills as central elements of your report.

Summary

The science knowledge, concepts, skills, attitudes, and values that are the fabric of your curriculum are all the result of discoveries made over many years of scientific inquiry. One important approach to teaching children science is to create a classroom environment in which they make their own discoveries through careful inquiry about various aspects of the natural world.

Although there are many ways to foster discovery-focused, inquiry-based learning in the science classroom, one important strategy involves the five stage learning cycle, called the 5E's, that consists of engaging, exploring, explaining, elaborating, and evaluating. These stages can be the framework for both units and lesson plans to foster the discovery and construction of new knowledge. As children progress through these stages,

Reality Check

Watch the teaching video "Animal Behavior" on MyEducationLab. Use the chart below to identify the use of the inquiry process skills by students. To access the video, go to MyEducationLab, select the topic Life and Environmental Science, and watch the video entitled "Animal Behavior."

Inquiry process skills	Frequency count as ₦	Comments
Observing		
Using space/time relationships		
Using numbers		
Questioning		
Classifying		
Measuring		
Communicating		
Predicting		
Identifying variables		
Independent		
Dependent		
Controlled		
Designing experimental controls		
Inferring		
Hypothesizing		

Watch the same video to identify evidence for each of the stages of the 5E instructional strategy.

they become actively involved in the progression of inquiry and a variety of science processes skills used in developing descriptive, explanatory, and experimental models. Use the 5E's as a guide to plan your science inquiry units and lessons. Look for the application of the inquiry process skills as evidence that children are inquiring in your science classroom.

Going Further

On Your Own

1. This chapter described a five-stage learning cycle that can be useful as you think about fostering discovery learning in the classroom. Pick a science topic that you might teach a group of children, and provide examples of specific things you might do to involve students in each stage of the cycle.

2. Some of the inquiry process skills discussed in this chapter are also used in the nonscience portions of the elementary/middle school curriculum (e.g., social studies, language arts, and so on). Select three inquiry process skills, and discuss how each might be used to integrate at least one other subject with science.

3. This chapter discussed the importance of using the inquiry process skills in doing hands-on science. What potential is there for an elementary- or middle-grade teacher to teach some of these skills through classroom demonstrations? Explain your response.

4. Some resistance to including the inquiry process skills comes from teachers who have not had much personal experience with science activities or experiments in college. To what extent did your college-level experience include opportunities to utilize the inquiry process skills?

On Your Own or in a Cooperative Learning Group

5. How might a week of classroom time (30 minutes per day) early in the school year be used to teach children in primary, elementary, or middle school that science is a way of doing things as well as an organizational collection of facts, concepts, and principles? Illustrate your idea with specific examples.

Resources for Discovery Learning

Internet Resources

 To access these helpful websites, go to **MyEducationLab,** select Resources, and then Web Links. To learn more, click on the following links and you will easily be directed to each website.

- **Constructivism and the Five E's:**
  www.miamisci.org/ph/lpintro5e.html

- **Eisenhower National Clearinghouse: The Ohio State University:**
  www.enc.org/

- **Exploratorium Institute for Inquiry:**
  www.exploratorium.edu/IFI/resources/websites.html

- **Science Education Projects Funded by the National Science Foundation:**
  http://watt.enc.org/nsf.html

- **The Science Learning Network:**
  www.sln.org/

- **Professional Development Summer Opportunities for Teachers: NSF-Funded Projects:**
  www.ehr.nsf.gov/her/esie/teso/

- **Project 2061: American Association for the Advancement of Science:**
  www.project2061.org/

Print Resources

Suggested Readings

Barman, Charles. *A Procedure for Helping Prospective Elementary Teachers Integrate the Learning Cycle into Science Textbooks.* Monograph 4. Arlington, VA: Council for Elementary Science International, an affiliate of the National Science Teachers Association, n.d.

Bybee, R. W., Taylor, J. A., Gardner, A., Van Scotter, P., Powell, J. C., Westbrook, A, and Landes, N. *The BSCS 5E Instructional Model: Origins, Effectiveness, and Applications Executive Summary.* Colorado Springs, CO: BSCS, 2006.

Colburn, Alan. "An Inquiry Primer." *Science Scope* 23, no. 6 (March 2000): 42–44.

Delisle, Robert. *How to Use Problem Based Learning in the Classroom.* Alexandria, VA: Association for Supervision and Curriculum Development, 1997.

Denniston, Erin. "What a Puzzle!" *Science and Children* 39, no. 8 (May 2002): 14–18.

Hall, Sue, and Hall, Dori. "Packing Peanut Properties." *Science and Children* 39, no. 5 (February 2002): 31–35.

Hammrich, Penny L., and Fadigan, Kathleen. "Investigations in the Science of Sports." *Science Scope* 26, no. 5 (February 2003): 30–35.

Hanuscin, D. L., et al. "Learning to Observe and Infer." *Science and Children* 45, no. 6 (February 2008): 56–57.

Inquiry and the National Science Education Standards: A Guide for Teaching and Learning. Center for Science, Mathematics, and Engineering Education (CSMEE), National Research Council. Washington, D.C.: National Academy Press, 2000.

Koschmann, Mark, and Shepardson, Dan. "A Pond Investigation." *Science and Children* 39, no. 8 (May 2002): 20–23.

McWilliams, Susan. "Journey into the Five Senses." *Science and Children* 40, no. 5 (February 2003): 38–43.

Morrison, J. A. "Individual **Inquiry** Investigations in an **Elementary Science** Methods Course." *Journal of Science Teacher Education* 19, no. 2 (April 2008): 117–134.

Pathways to the Science Standards: Elementary School Edition. Arlington VA: NSTA Press, 2000.

Pine, J., et al. "Students' Learning of Inquiry in 'Inquiry' Curricula." *Phi Delta Kappan* 88, no. 4 (December 2006): 308–313.

Shaw, Mike. "A Dastardly Density Deed." *Science Scope* 26, no. 4 (January 2003): 18–21.

Sitzman, Daniel. "Bread Making: Classic Biotechnology and Experimental Design." *Science Scope* 26, no. 4 (January 2003): 27–31.

Thompson, R., et al. "Investigating Minerals: Promoting Integrated Inquiry." *Science Activities* 44, no. 2 (Summer 2007): 56–60.

Thompson, S. L. "Inquiry in the Life Sciences: The Plant-in-a-Jar as a Catalyst for Learning." *Science Activities* 43, no. 4 (Winter 2007): 27–33.

Waffler, Elizabeth Sumner. "Inspired Inquiry." *Science and Children* 38, no. 4 (January 2001): 28–31.

Wittrock, Cathy A., and Barrow, Lloyd H. "Blow-by-Blow Inquiry." *Science and Children* 37, no. 5 (February 2000): 34–38.

Notes

1. L. W. Trowbridge and R. W. Bybee, *Becoming a Secondary School Science Teacher* 4th ed. (Columbus, OH: Merrill Publishing Co., 1986), p. 182.
2. Ibid., pp. 182–183.
3. National Research Council, *National Science Education Standards* (Washington, DC: National Academy Press, 1996), p. 23.
4. Ibid.
5. R. W. Bybee, et al. (2006). *The BSCS 5E Instructional Model: Origins, Effectiveness, and Applications.* (BSCS: Colorado Springs, CO).
6. You may encounter variations on the 5E model, such as the 6E model, which adds "e-search" representing explicit technology integration.
7. P. Bergethon, *Learning the Language of Patterns* (Holliston, MA: Symmetry Learning Systems, 1999).

chapter 4

Planning and Managing

How can I plan and manage inquiry-based, discovery-focused units and lessons?

▶ Getting Started

Children are beginning to gather in the school yard. Family and parents of the youngest children give a final hug and wave good-bye, pausing just out of sight only to peek back around the corner for one last look at their children as they begin the first day of school. Friendly teachers greet the younger children, who make their way tentatively into the school yard. The older children run without hesitation onto the playground, greeting classmates and immediately starting a spirited game of tag.

Suddenly, I am standing all alone in the classroom, the walls are bare and my plan book is empty. A wave of panic slowly begins to creep over me. In an instant the children are somehow sitting at their desks. Twenty-four little faces look up at me with great expectations. I have nothing to offer them.

Several teachers have had similar dreams just before the start of a new school year. Although this chapter may not prevent such dreams, it will help you plan inquiry-based science lessons in advance so waking will be much more pleasant.

Curriculum, Unit Planning, and Lesson Planning—How Are They Different?

Sometimes the terms "curriculum," "unit," and "lesson" are used interchangeably, but they differ primarily in scope. Curricula are made up of a sequence of units and lessons that address a primary subject. Third-grade science or fourth-grade social studies are two examples of curricula. Units address subtopics within a curriculum, such as a unit on life cycles or the forces that shape the earth. Lessons address topics within a unit and target specific learning objectives. Describing the four stages of the butterfly life cycle or discovering how simple machines work are examples of lesson topics. As you read on, you will gain a deeper understanding of each term.

The Scope of the Science Curriculum

Imagine observing a tiny gnat walking across a pebble as lightning flashes in the sky. How does each component of this scene fit into the area of knowledge we call *science?* The gnat is understood through biology, the science of living things. The origin and characteristics of the pebble are understood through the earth/space sciences. The energy of the lightning flash and the atoms and molecules that make up the gnat and the pebble are understood

Good planning will result in dynamic and effective learning adventures for your students.

through the physical sciences. Each component of the scene represents one part of the *scope,* or breadth of content, of science.

The scope of the curriculum refers to the range and depth of content while the sequence of the curriculum refers to the order in which the content will be addressed. The scope of science illustrated in the brief example of the gnat, pebble, and lightning reminds us that science is an integration of earth/space, life, and physical sciences.

The *earth/space sciences* represent our knowledge of the origins of the universe and of our Earth in particular. They include astronomy, geology, meteorology, and other areas of study. The earth/space science topics commonly taught in elementary school include the following:

1. The stars, sun, and planets
2. The soil, rocks, and mountains
3. The weather

The *life sciences* include botany, zoology, and ecology. These disciplines are usually represented in the elementary science curriculum as the following topics:

1. The study of plants
2. The study of animals
3. The study of the relationship between plants and animals
4. The study of the relationship between living things and the environment

The *physical sciences* include physics and chemistry. Physics is concerned with the relationship between matter and energy. Chemistry is concerned with the manner through which various types of matter combine and change. In the elementary school, the following topics would be considered part of the physical sciences component of a science curriculum:

1. The study of matter and energy
2. The study of the chemical changes that matter undergoes

Technology and engineering represent the application of scientific principles by humans to solve problems. Content Standard E of the National Science Education Standards (NSES) suggests that elementary students develop:

- Abilities of technological design
- Understanding about science and technology
- Abilities to distinguish between natural objects and objects made by humans[1]

Children should learn how to use principles of science to design solutions to problems and make useful things. This may involve modeling, such as building a bridge out of toothpicks, or the actual design and construction of a solar oven. Just as inquiry is fundamental to the discovery in science, the engineering design process is fundamental to problem solving and creativity in technology.

The National Science Education Standards: Implications for Appropriate Scope

The NSES were developed by the National Academy of Sciences in 1996 to guide state and local school communities toward the appropriate content, professional development, and general teaching strategies for science education. As such, they provide a wonderful reference to the "big picture" of effective science education and lend credibility to decisions based on the principles and guidelines. Most often states will interpret the NSES to create science standards relevant to the needs of the region. In turn, local school districts will further refine state standards to address the needs and resources of the community. It is up to you, the teacher, to ultimately translate the district's vision into positive and effective learning experiences for your students. This chapter will help you plan such a learning experience. The area of the standards that will probably be of most interest to you will be that dealing with what you should be teaching. If you wish to teach content that is sensitive to the NSES recommendations, then its scope should at least range across the following eight topics, or *standards:*

1. Unifying concepts and processes in science
2. Science as inquiry
3. Physical science
4. Life science
5. Earth and space sciences
6. Science and technology
7. Science in personal and social perspectives
8. History and nature of science[2]

The first standard—"Unifying concepts and processes in science"—identifies broad science concepts that are needed to tie the other content areas together:

1. Systems, order, and organization
2. Evidence, models, and explanation
3. Change, constancy, and measurement
4. Evolution and equilibrium
5. Form and function[3]

If you presently lack a strong science content background, you will need to study the explanations and examples of these unifying concepts presented in the full NSES report.

The second standard—"Science as inquiry"—essentially states that children should be expected to ask questions about objects, organisms, and events; plan and carry out investigations; gather data; explain what they have learned; and communicate what they have learned. Teachers are expected to help children understand that scientists continually engage in these aspects of inquiry themselves.[4]

Standards 3 through 8 are more straightforward than the first two. Study Figure 4.1 (pages 61–63) to get a clear picture of the intended scope for units and lessons based on the NSES. Also use this figure as a reference as you consider the appropriate sequence of topics for children. As you use these lists, however, please bear in mind that they are *recommendations* and should be treated as such.

Figure 4.1 The National Science Education Standards, Grades K—8

Unifying Concepts and Processes

Standard: As a result of activities in grades K–12, all students should develop understandings and abilities aligned with the following concepts and processes.

Systems, order, and organization

Evidence, models, and explanation

Constancy, change, and measurement

Evolution and equilibrium

Form and function

Content Standards Grades K–4

SCIENCE AS INQUIRY*

Content Standard A: As a result of activities in grades K–4, all students should develop

- Abilities necessary to do scientific inquiry
- Understanding about scientific inquiry

PHYSICAL SCIENCE [PS]*

Content Standard B: As a result of the activities in grades K–4, all students should develop an understanding of

- Properties of objects and materials [PS 1]
- Position and motion of objects [PS 2]
- Light, heat, electricity, and magnetism [PS 3]

LIFE SCIENCE [LS]

Content Standard C: As a result of the activities in grades K–4, all students should develop an understanding of

- The characteristics of organisms [LS 1]
- Life cycles of organisms [LS 2]
- Organisms and environments [LS 3]

EARTH AND SPACE SCIENCES [ESS]

Content Standard D: As a result of the activities in grades K–4, all students should develop an understanding of
- Properties of earth materials [ESS 1]
- Objects in the sky [ESS 2]
- Changes in earth and sky [ESS 3]

SCIENCE AND TECHNOLOGY [S&T]

Content Standard E: As a result of the activities in grades K–4, all students should develop an understanding of

- Abilities of technological design [S&T 1]
- Understanding about science and technology [S&T 2]
- Ability to distinguish between natural objects and objects made by humans [S&T 3]

*This general standard is the foundation of all the NSES. Since it is emphasized in all *Teaching Children Science* activities, it is not identified for each experience.

**All the bracketed symbols to the right of the standards were prepared for this book by this author.

(continued)

Figure 4.1 The National Science Education Standards, Grades K—8 (continued)

SCIENCE IN PERSONAL AND SOCIAL PERSPECTIVES [SPSP]

Content Standard F: As a result of the activities in grades K–4, all students should develop an understanding of

- Personal health [SPSP 1]
- Characteristics and changes in populations [SPSP 2]
- Types of resources [SPSP 3]
- Changes in environments [SPSP 4]
- Science and technology in local challenges [SPSP 5]

HISTORY AND NATURE OF SCIENCE [HNS]

Content Standard G: As a result of the activities in grades K–4, all students should develop an understanding of

- Science as a human endeavor [HNS 1]

Content Standards Grades 5–8

SCIENCE AS INQUIRY

Content Standard A: As a result of their activities in grades 5–8, all students should develop

- Abilities necessary to do scientific inquiry
- Understandings about scientific inquiry

PHYSICAL SCIENCE [PS]

Content Standard B: As a result of their activities in grades 5–8, all students should develop an understanding of

- Properties and changes of properties in matter [PS 4]
- Motion and forces [PS 5]
- Transfer of energy [PS 6]

LIFE SCIENCE [LS]

Content Standard C: As a result of their activities in grades 5–8, all students should develop an understanding of

- Structure and function in living systems [LS 4]
- Reproduction and heredity [LS 5]
- Regulation and behavior [LS 6]
- Population and ecosystems [LS 7]
- Diversity and adaptations of organisms [LS 8]

EARTH AND SPACE SCIENCES [ESS]

Content Standard D: As a result of their activities in grades 5–8, all students should develop an understanding of

- Structure of the earth system [ESS 4]
- Earth's history [ESS 5]
- Earth in the solar system [ESS 6]

Figure 4.1 The National Science Education Standards,
Grades K—8 (continued)

SCIENCE AND TECHNOLOGY [S&T]

Content Standard E: As a result of the activities in grades 5–8, all students should develop an understanding of

- Abilities of technological design [S&T 4]
- Understanding about science and technology [S&T 5]

SCIENCE IN PERSONAL AND SOCIAL PERSPECTIVES [SPSP]

Content Standard F: As a result of the activities in grades 5–8, all students should develop an understanding of

- Personal health [SPSP 6]
- Populations, resources, and environments [SPSP 7]
- Natural hazards [SPSP 8]
- Risks and benefits [SPSP 9]
- Changes in environments [SPSP 10]
- Science and technology in society [SPSP 11]

HISTORY AND NATURE OF SCIENCE [HNS]

Content Standard G: As a result of the activities in grades 5–8, all students should develop an understanding of

- Science as a human endeavor [HNS 2]
- Nature of science [HNS 3]
- History of science [HNS 4]

The Sequence of the Science Curriculum

A knowledge of the scope of science will help you decide what topics can be reasonably included within the body of science experiences you present to children. However, one important question still remains: In what order should these topics be presented? For example, should children learn about the earth they live on before they learn about the structure and function of their bodies, or should the sequence be reversed?

The NSES: Implications for Appropriate Sequence

One of the very best ways of starting a spirited discussion in a teachers' meeting is to say something like, "The butterfly life cycle is too complicated for second-graders." If you are silly enough to make such a statement, you should be prepared to immediately weave your own protective chrysalis!

Too often, interested parties tell us that first-graders should learn X, second-graders should learn Y, and so on. That approach is much too specific and assumes that children in certain grades are homogeneous in terms of their present knowledge of science as well as their interest and ability to pursue science concepts. They are not. What children are able to do at a given grade level largely depends on the particular children, the teacher, and the resources available.

The NSES take a more sensible and flexible approach to recommending the sequence in which science topics should be introduced. They identify the recommended content for grades K–4 and 5–8, as shown in Figure 4.1.

Determining the Sequence of Your Curriculum

There is no definitive answer to the question of sequence. However, these four guidelines may help you consider the place of science in a child's school experience:

1. Research suggests that learning is optimized when the content is relevant and meaningful for the learner.[5] Any decision you make should favor those topics that will generate the most learner involvement and interest.

2. As a general rule, organize learning experiences from the child outward. That is, select experiences that relate first to the child and then to the science content. In teaching electricity, for example, have children consider how they use electricity before they study its source.

3. In general, when deciding to expose children to a concept that can be considered concretely or abstractly, use the concrete approach first.

4. The sequence of topics should be logically connected. There are many possible connections among topics. For example, when teaching a unit about the water cycle, one might choose to begin the unit with principles of evaporation and condensation. Alternatively, the big idea of the water cycle could be introduced first and explained more deeply in subsequent lessons about evaporation and condensation. However you choose to sequence the content, the connections among topics should make sense.

Unit Planning

What Makes a Good Unit Plan?

When full-time teachers lack a sense of the "big picture," their students have, in effect, a substitute teacher every day of the school year. Each school day that children have learning experiences that are not part of any larger context is a day that relates neither to the past nor to the future.

Children need appropriate learning experiences in school—activities that will reflect their teacher's concern with goals and that will involve them cognitively, affectively, and

Project 2061

Implications for Your Planning and Managing

Clearly, Project 2061 tells you much about what you *should* teach, but it also provides some direction about *how* you should go about it. It draws on research about how children learn as well as what methods effective teachers tend to use with children. This latter area is referred to as *craft knowledge.*

Project 2061 presents its recommendations for what you should actually do in the classroom in the benchmark "Effective learning and teaching." There are two key ideas within this benchmark:

- Principles of learning
- Teaching science, mathematics, and technology

You'll find specific recommendations for these ideas at the Project 2061 website: **www.project2061.org/.**

Figure 4.2
A science unit may have many components, but each component has a specific purpose.

Component	Purpose
• Rationale	• Helps you think through the reasons for doing a unit on a particular topic
• Performance objectives	• Help you focus on the intended outcomes of the unit
• Content to be taught*	• Clearly identifies and specifies the content children are intended to learn in the unit
• Content outline (for teachers)	• Helps you review the content that will provide the foundation for the learning experience
• Daily lesson plans*	• Help you think through learning activities and their relationship to engagement, exploration, and concept explanation
• Materials list	• Helps you make certain that you have all the materials needed for science activities that occur in daily lessons
• Audiovisual materials and list	• Help you make certain that you have such tools as computer hardware and software, videotapes, and other required equipment
• Accommodations	• Identifies accommodations and modifications necessary to provide the least restrictive and most accessible learning experience for the children in your class
• Assessment strategies	• Help you consider informal and formal ways to assess the extent to which children have achieved cognitive, psychomotor, and affective growth during the unit

*Considered in greater detail later in this chapter

physically. To accomplish this, teachers must plan their science units. Unit plans can take a variety of forms. The list of possible components in Figure 4.2 may prove useful when you develop your own unit plans.

The Role of Textbooks in Unit Planning

Many schools use textbooks or curriculum guides as organizing elements for the curriculum. With some creative planning on your part, such materials can offer a starting point for the development of meaningful science experiences for children. After diagnosing student needs and interests, you can use a portion of a textbook or curriculum guide as a basis for a unit plan. Indeed, the teacher's editions of many recent science textbooks can be important planning resources. Many contain lists of concepts to show scope and sequence; lists of emphasized inquiry process skills; ideas for beginning units and lessons; lesson plans; lists of science materials needed; science content for the teacher; lesson enrichment ideas; bulletin board and field trip ideas; lists of related children's books and websites; and computer software and audiovisual aids.

Although a teacher's edition can be an important resource, it is not a recipe book and should not be used in place of your own planning. After all, you are the one who best knows the needs of the children in your class.

Lesson Planning

"Be very, very careful what you put into that head, because you will never, ever get it out."
—Cardinal Wolsey (1475 ?-1530)

What Makes a Good Lesson Plan?

If you were to lock three teachers in a room and ask them (under pain of losing their parking spaces) to reach a consensus about the best format for a lesson plan, you would probably end up with four formats (and three teachers walking to school). The fact is, there are many approaches to lesson planning, and it is difficult to know in advance which one will work best for you.

Developing a Good Lesson Plan Using Six Elements

Go to **MyEducationLab**, select the topic Earth and Space Science, watch the video entitled "Properties of Air: Pressure," and complete the questions that accompany it.

The lesson plan outline discussed here includes major elements to be considered in your lesson planning. Your department or district will likely have variations that you should incorporate as well. Hopefully this discussion will help you develop effective and engaging lessons.

Although developing lesson plans can be daunting at first, the payoffs are well worth the effort. Good lesson plans result in focused, dynamic learning experiences wherein children are thoughtful and engaged. Well-thought-out lesson plans also facilitate good classroom management, which maximizes student time on learning and minimizes disorder and discipline issues. Be that as it may, you need a starting point for lesson planning. The following six key elements—enhanced with additional components suggested by veteran teachers, school administrators, and others—will serve you well. Creating a targeted learning experience is similar to writing a play with a thought-provoking engagement to set the plot, development of the plot, and a culminating scene that ties the story together. To better visualize each element of a lesson plan, we will walk through a sample lesson plan, "Sinking and Floating," in Figure 4.3.

Element 1: Content to be Taught: Identify What You Intend to Teach

Although identifying the content to be taught may be an obvious first step of lesson planning, it is often taken for granted. Be very clear about what you intend to teach. If you are unclear about what you want the children to learn at the start, then your lesson will become increasingly more difficult to plan. It is like trying to button your shirt. If you miss the first button, then all the buttons are off.

Most likely you will be developing lessons from a unit based on a topic in the science standards. Let's use an example from the NSES Earth and Space Sciences for grades K–4, Content Standard B: As a result of the activities in grades K–4, all students should develop an understanding of properties of objects and materials.[6]

Let's try to outline the content for the sinking and floating example. Information is easily accessible through the Internet, making it relatively easy to create a content outline. If you use Internet sites, be sure to use reputable sources for your content outline such as university or nationally recognized sources. Cross-check references if in doubt. An example of a content outline is given in Figure 4.4. Note that the content outline is for you, the teacher. You will need to decide the depth of content to teach depending on the children's abilities. The underlying concept for this lesson is buoyancy, quite a difficult concept for students to get their minds around, let alone third-graders. Although you may not teach the complete story of buoyancy to third-graders, you can provide an encounter with the idea that lays a foundation so that they are prepared to develop a deeper understanding of buoyancy in later years.

Figure 4.3 Sample Lesson Plan:
Sinking and Floating

Lesson Plan

Content to Be Taught:

Children will learn that the shape of a material affects whether it will sink or float. The greater the area covered by the material, the more likely it is to float, because it can rest on a larger area of water that holds the material up by exerting a force that pushes back on it.

Children's Prior Knowledge and Misconceptions:

The children have learned in a prior lesson that certain materials float or sink. A common misconception is that for an object to float, it must be made from a material that itself will not sink when placed in water.

Performance Objective:

Given two equal amounts of clay (condition), children will form the clay into shapes that will float or sink and explain in writing (performance) that the greater the area covered by the material, the more likely it is to float, because it can rest on a larger area of water that holds the clay up by exerting a force that pushes back on it (criteria).

Concept Development:

ENGAGEMENT

Materials: 3 balls of clay, gallon container of water

Safety: The floor may become wet and slippery. Place a tray to collect overflow under the container of water. Provide paper towels or newspaper to absorb spills.

Ask the children to predict whether they think the clay will float or sink when you drop it into the water. You are likely to get mixed responses. Either way, record the children's thoughts on the board. Drop the ball of clay into the water. When the clay sinks it will be a discrepant event for those children who thought it would float. Even for the children who thought it would sink, they are at least invested in the question. Now challenge the children by asking, "How can you make the clay float?" This becomes your essential question.

EXPLORATION

Materials per groups of three: 3 equal size balls of clay, gallon container, red and green cups taped together (These will be used to indicate that the group is finished, red cup on top, or that the group has questions, green cup on top.)

Procedure: Each child should have a science notebook.[7]

Part I: Ask each child to record in their science notebooks what they need to do to the clay to make it float.

Part II: Arrange children in groups of three. Instruct the children to discuss among the members of their group how they could make the clay float. Tell the children to record any questions or wonderments (use the thought stem, "I wonder . . .) in their science notebook. When they finish, tell them to turn the red/green cups so red is on top, indicating that the group is finished and ready for Part III. The teacher will bring instructions for Part III to each group.

Part III: Tell the children to use the clay and container of water to test their ideas. Let each person take a turn doing a test. Instruct the children to draw a picture of their design and explain in writing why they think the clay did or did not float. All entries are to be written in their science notebooks.

(continued)

Figure 4.3   Sample Lesson Plan:
Sinking and Floating (continued)

Lesson Plan

EXPLANATION

Ask the children, "Did anyone succeed in making the clay float?"

Process responses: Create two spaces on a table in the front of the room, label one *floaters* and one *sinkers*. Have children bring the clay models that they made to the table and group them according to floaters or sinkers. If they all have floaters, be prepared with a few shapes that will sink and place them along with the original ball of clay in the sinker group.

Individual reflection: Ask each child to create a descriptive model of floaters and sinkers; be sure they include the observed interactions of the clay with the water. Then have them write an explanation in their science notebook describing why they think the floaters floated, and the sinkers sank.

Pairing and sharing: Have the children share their ideas with a partner.

Then lead a discussion of the children's ideas in class. Prompts might include:

What do the floaters have in common?

How are the floaters different from the ball of clay that sank?

Why do you think the shape makes a difference?

What advice would you give to someone who wanted to make a ship out of steel?

Summarize: Demonstrate and reinforce the concepts that the greater the area covered by the material, the more likely it is to float, because it can rest on a larger area of water that holds the clay up by exerting a force that pushes back on it.

ELABORATION

Ask the children to explain how a ship made of steel can float.

EVALUATION

> **Instructions:**
> 1. *You will be given two bricks of clay that are the same size.*
> 2. *Form one brick of clay into a shape that you think will sink.*
> 3. *Form the other ball of clay into a shape that you think will float.*
> 4. *Draw a picture of each design in the space below.*
> 5. *Write an explanation that describes why your designs sink or float.*

Shape of clay that will sink

Shape of clay that will float

Figure 4.3   Sample Lesson Plan:
            Sinking and Floating (continued)

Lesson Plan

Explain:
I think the clay will sink
because . . .

_____
_____
_____
_____

Explain:
I think the clay will float
because . . .

_____
_____
_____
_____

Accommodations::

Accommodations for this example include reading the instructions with children who are English language learners and providing the option of answering orally in addition to writing the answer. Children with visual impairments will benefit from the tactile nature of the investigation. Large print instructions will also help. One possible modification would be requiring the children to identify the clay shape that is likely to float, rather than explain the properties of the shape that contribute to floating.

Gifted learners can be challenged to explore the concept of density. Give them a thin square of metal about 2 cm x 2 cm and about 1 cm thick. Note that the dimensions make it relatively easy to determine the volume (Length x Width x Height). You want the metal square to sink in water. Give them an equal size of a material that is less dense and will float, such as styrofoam. Ask them why equal volumes and area of styrofoam float and the metal sinks. Let the children try to explain the properties. Guide them to determine the volume and mass of each item, and recognize the mass per unit volume differs. Then have them compare it to the same mass per unit volume of water. Identify these ratios as densities. Provide a chart of substances and their densities relative to the density of water and ask the children to determine which items will float in water.

Element 2: Prior Knowledge: Describe Common Misconceptions about the Topic   No child is a blank slate. They have ideas about the world based on their prior experiences. Sometimes these ideas are accurate, but more often they are incomplete or tainted with misconceptions. Therefore, consider what you can reasonably assume about their knowledge of the subject and common misconceptions. This will become easier with experience and the longer you work with the children in your class. You can also access information on the Internet about common misconceptions (cf. links to misconceptions at MyEducationLab). In the sinking-floating example, it can be assumed that in previous lessons children have learned that certain materials float or sink. A common misconception about floating and sinking is that for an object to float, it must be made from a material that itself will not sink when placed in water.

Element 3: Performance Objectives   Performance objectives provide a clear statement of the behaviors that the children will exhibit to demonstrate their learning. The only way to assess learning is through their observable behaviors and performances. There must also be criteria associated with behaviors and performances to indicate satisfactory learning.

Performance objectives consist of three components: a condition for learning, an observable performance to indicate learning, and criteria to rate the level of performance.[8] Clear performance objectives will make it easier to assess the children's understanding at the end of the lesson using performance assessments.

Figure 4.4
Sample of a teacher's content outline

1. *An object will float if it displaces a mass of liquid equal to the object's mass.*
2. *The shape of an object affects the mass of liquid that it can displace.*
   a. The greater the volume of the object, the more liquid it can displace.
   b. The lower the volume of the object, the less liquid it can displace.
3. *Example:* clay ball and clay canoe
   a. A clay ball will sink in water because its volume does not displace its mass in water.
   b. A clay canoe will float in water because it does displace its mass in water.

It often helps to reorganize the content to identify the important connections and contexts that need to be taught. This reorganization of content helps put the content in a logical framework for thinking about and teaching the content. It will also be useful to determine assessment strategies.

1. *Identify the elements*
   1.1. Water
   1.2. Objects that float or sink
2. *Properties of the elements*
   2.1. Shape
   2.2. Weight (mass)
3. *Identify the rules of interaction among the elements*
   3.1. Objects float if they displace (push away) a mass of liquid that is the same as the mass of the object.
   3.2. Objects sink if they displace (push away) a mass of liquid that is less than the mass of the object.
   3.3. Shape is a factor that determines how much liquid an object can displace.
       3.3.1. Shapes that take up more volume can displace more water
4. *Emergent properties*
   4.1. The shape of a material can determine whether it sinks or floats.
   4.2. Example
       4.2.1. A ball of clay will sink, but a canoe shape displaces more water relative to its weight (mass) and will float.

Element 4: Concept Development Safety: Concept development describes the presentation of the lesson to the students. Include safety notes throughout the lesson as reminders of necessary safety precautions. Read more on safety in the classroom in the section entitled "For the Teacher's Desk."

▶ *Engagement*

Recall from Chapter 2 that effective learning occurs when the context is meaningful. As with any good movie or novel, the writer must engage the attention of the audience quickly. As an elementary school teacher, you will find that the window of opportunity to capture and hold the children's attention usually closes quite quickly. You need to craft an engagement that not only piques the children's curiosity but also establishes a central question that creates a desire and need for deeper inquiry.

There are three main types of inquiry questions: information gathering, addressing the general question, "I wonder what happens when . . . ?" Such as, "I wonder what stages a caterpillar goes through to become a butterfly?" or "What phases does the moon go through over the course of a month?" Questions can be experimental, asking, "I wonder what would happen if . . . ?" As in, "I wonder what would happen if we put the plants in the closet?" Lastly, questions could address "How to do it" as in, "How can I build a better bridge?"

Discrepant events are counterintuitive experiences that pique curiosity and a desire to seek an explanation. They grab our attention and interest because the outcome is usually the opposite of what is expected. An example of a discrepant event is given in Figure 4.5.

▶ *Exploration*

Recall from Chapter 2 that exploration provides an opportunity for children to encounter and reflect on new content. Whatever strategy one chooses for the exploration, it should enable the children to be active participants in the learning experience such as describing changes, manipulating variables, or designing solutions. Exploration is the concept development stage during which a variety of teaching methods that you have been learning can be employed.

▶ *Explanation*

The explanation follows the natural flow of the inquiry lesson. It is tempting to simply tell the children the answer at this point. It is best to provide an opportunity for the children to communicate their explanation first, so they can make logical connections on their own. The explanation may be expressed in writing, through a diagram, orally, or kinesthetically using a simulation. You can reinforce their correct answers and challenge inaccuracies through questioning and concept attainment methods. It is at this point that you can become more didactic to explain the answer. Direct teaching during the explanation stage is meaningful because the children will have a genuine investment in the question and consequently will be more eager and receptive to the explanation.

▶ *Elaboration*

Elaboration challenges the children to deepen and reinforce what they have learned by applying the concept in a similar context.

Figure 4.5
Discrepant Event:
The Ping Pong Ball
and the Funnel

Present the children with a Ping-Pong ball and funnel. Put the Ping-Pong ball in the funnel with the stem pointing down. Ask the children to predict what will happen to the Ping-Pong ball when someone blows through the stem into the funnel. Most often children will predict that the ball will be pushed out of the funnel. In fact, the ball will remain in the funnel, no matter how hard you blow.
Explanation: Air exiting the stem into the funnel must travel faster to get around the ball. The fast-moving air around the bottom of the ball creates an area of lower pressure relative to the slower air movement above the ball, resulting in a higher pressure area above the ball, which pushes the ball down and keeps it in the funnel. This is an example of the Bernoulli effect.

Element 5: Evaluation (Assessment)
"Did the children learn what you thought you taught?" Assessment is the opportunity to rejoice in the fruits of your labor. After all, you have worked hard to design and execute a learning experience for the children in your class that is thought provoking and productive.

There are several strategies for assessment that probe children's understandings and abilities at a variety of levels: nominal, descriptive, and explanatory. A more detailed description of these levels and assessment strategies will be addressed in Chapter 6.

Element 6: Accommodations
Accommodations are designed to provide all the children with the least restrictive environment for learning experiences. For example, teaching English language learners may require you to post word banks or provide supplemental instructions with illustrations and diagrams. Large print and seating near the front of the room may assist children with visual impairments. Accommodations usually benefit all children. Universal Design for Learning is a teaching strategy that facilitates learning for all children. It is based on the following:

Multiple means of representation to give learners various ways of acquiring information and knowledge

Multiple means of expression to provide learners alternatives for demonstrating what they know, and

Multiple means of engagement to tap into learners' interests, challenge them appropriately, and motivate them to learn

Modifications differ from accommodations in that they alter curricular content by raising or lowering the performance expectations. Examples consist of more challenging work for gifted children or lower expectations for mentally disabled children.

Chapter 9 addresses accommodations in more detail.

Reality Check

One of my favorite activities in elementary school was making "Oobleck," a simple mixture of two parts cornstarch to one part water. It is a material that seems to have the properties of both a solid and a liquid. Perhaps your fourth-graders will enjoy it, too. But as a teacher, you recognize that although an activity may be fun there should be some benefit to learning in the activity. You do a quick Internet search and find the following explanation of Oobleck:

> When enough pressure is applied, the Oobleck acts like a solid. When little or no pressure is applied, it acts like a liquid. This is a result of long chains called *polymers* (*poly* = many, *mer* = part) that form when cornstarch is added to water. Anytime a polymer is added to a liquid, it slows down the reaction time of the liquid and makes it harder for the liquid to move. Cornstarch is a polymer that slows down the movement of water. If pressure is applied quickly, the cornstarch polymer gets tangled up and acts like a solid. If pressure is applied slowly, the polymers don't get as tangled, making the Oobleck act more like a liquid.[9]

Based on your knowledge of national and local science standards, what content could you justify teaching to your fourth-graders based on this activity?

Classroom Organization and Management

Go to **MyEducationLab,** select the topic Classroom and Community Resources, watch the video entitled "Using Centers 1," and complete the questions that accompany it.

I'm not going to provide an elaborate treatise on maintaining appropriate classroom behavior. The fact is, I have seen more *teachers* produce discipline problems than I have seen *children* cause them. If you are able to maintain appropriate behavior when you teach social studies, reading, math, or any other subject, you will be able to do so when you teach science. If you have problems with classroom control, science activities will neither solve your problems nor make them worse. Even so, you can take some steps that will help things go more smoothly for everyone. Appropriate classroom behavior is not hard to achieve; it just requires attention to a few common-sense matters.

Distributing Materials

The attack of a school of piranha on a drowning monkey is a model of tranquility when compared with a group of 20 children trying to acquire a magnet from a tote tray containing 10 of them.

In order to distribute materials effectively, you need to devise techniques that are appropriate for your setting. In some settings, for example, two or three children can distribute materials to all the groups. Another technique is to have one child from each group come forward to acquire needed materials. Regardless of the procedure you employ, try to avoid having all the children get what they need simultaneously.

Providing Work Space

"Please make him (her) stop bugging us, or I will wring his (her) neck."

This is a rather common classroom request (threat) among children involved in science activities. One way to diminish this type of problem is to give your learning groups some work space. This may be difficult if you have a small room, but you should try anyway. Movable bookcases, room dividers, and similar objects should be pressed into service to give groups of children semiprivate work spaces. Because science activities provide ample opportunities for social interaction among group members, there is little need for groups to interact with one another. Such contact is often counterproductive.

The most important element of a science work space is a flat surface. If you have the opportunity to select furniture for your classroom, choose tables and chairs rather than conventional desks. The typical classroom desk for children is designed for *writing*, not for doing science activities. If your classroom has desks with slanted tops, you will need to acquire tables, build your own tables, or use the floor as the place for science activities. Some teachers find that the inflexibility presented by traditional desks can be overcome by placing tables along the periphery of the room. Students can then carry out their science activities on the tables and use their desks during other instructional activities.

Providing Clear Directions

"I didn't know what I was supposed to do with the ice cubes, so I put them down her back."

Children (and adults) seem to get into trouble when they don't understand what they are supposed to be doing. So, it should come as no surprise that problems arise in the classroom when children don't understand what your expectations are. If you learn to announce these expectations clearly and simply, you will find that misbehaviors decrease.

If the science activity the children are going to do requires procedures or materials they are unfamiliar with, you will need to model the use of these materials or procedures (except, of course, when the objective of the activity is the discovery of how to use them). *Children who do not know how to read a meterstick will use it as a baseball bat or sword rather than as a device for making linear measurements.* By taking a few minutes to teach children how to use materials and equipment properly, you can make the process of discovery more pleasant—for you and for them.

Summary

The success of an inquiry-based, discovery-focused classroom depends on your abilities to both plan and manage. The science curriculum for children typically consists of a number of learning units. Unit plans are long-term plans for science experiences that focus on particular topics. Daily lesson plans are single components of unit plans. This chapter suggests six elements in the lesson planning process and offers an example of each in the context of a complete lesson plan. Of course there are other lesson plan formats, but this will serve as a framework from which to begin the planning process. There will be several more examples of lesson plans in Part Two of this book. Hopefully, you will use this framework to create your own approach to planning lessons.

A classroom in which students carry out science activities as part of group work undoubtedly will face some classroom management challenges. Teachers can use various techniques to ensure that science time is rich in appropriate learning opportunities yet manageable, as well.

Going Further

On Your Own

1. How you plan for teaching will probably depend to a great extent upon your general outlook on the nature of teaching and how children learn. To bring these perceptions into focus, respond to each of the following statements:
   a. Careful planning is consistent with how I carry out the activities in my life.
   b. Planning can restrict flexibility.
   c. I never had a teacher who planned.
   d. Children will learn regardless of how much teachers plan.

2. Review the sample lesson plan in this chapter. Then select a science topic appropriate for the grade level you are interested in and develop a lesson plan. If possible, teach the lesson to a group of children or peers who role-play children. Assess the extent to which your lesson relates to the 5E learning cycle.

3. Sketch your vision of the ideal classroom in which to teach science. Label the special areas in your classroom. Note, in particular, the location and arrangement of classroom seating and work space. What advantage does your ideal classroom have over a conventional elementary school classroom? How could you use your ideas for classroom organization in a conventional classroom?

On Your Own or in a Cooperative Learning Group

4. Brainstorm a discrepant event to engage children in each of the following science topics. Write a performance objective for each activity. Be sure to include a condition, measurable performance, and criteria for scoring.
   a. Indoor Gardening
   b. Animals with Pouches
   c. The Changes in the Seasons
   d. Earthquakes
   e. Friction

5. Role-play a job interview between a school principal and a teaching candidate for either a self-contained classroom or a departmentalized school. During the interview, the "principal" should ask about the following:
   a. The teacher's awareness of the NSES
   b. The science content and experiences appropriate for children at that grade
   c. The planning style the prospective teacher would use
   d. The management strategies the teacher would use
   e. Ideas the teacher has for giving children opportunities to explore
   f. Alternate techniques the teacher could use to introduce a concept
   g. Ideas that the teacher has for helping children apply concepts to new situations

Resources for Discovery Learning

Internet Resources

 To access these helpful websites, go to **MyEducationLab,** select Resources, and then Web Links. To learn more, click on the following link and you will easily be directed to each website.

- **Discovery Education:**
  http://school.discoveryeducation.com/

- **Discrepant Events Best Teaching Practices:**
  www.agpa.uakron.edu/k12/best_practices/discrepant_events.html

- **The Drinking Happy Bird University of Virginia Physics Department:**
  http://galileo.phys.virginia.edu/outreach/8thGradeSOL/Evaporation.htm

- **National Science Digital Library:**
  http://nsdl.org/

- **NyeLabs:**
  www.billnye.com

- **Science NetLinks:**
  www.sciencenetlinks.com

Print Resources

Suggested Readings

Ansberry, Karen Rohrich and Morgan, Emily. *Picture Perfect Science Lessons: Using Children's Books to Guide Inquiry.* Arlington, VA: NSTA Press, 2005.

Avraamidou, L., et al. "Giving Priority to Evidence in Science Teaching: A First-Year Elementary Teacher's Specialized Practices and Knowledge." *Journal of Research in Science Teaching* 42, no. 9 (November 2005): 965–986.

Cummings, Carol. *Winning Strategies for Classroom Management.* Alexandria, VA: Association for Supervision and Curriculum Development, 2000.

Fetters, Marcia, et al. "Making Science Accessible: Strategies to Meet the Needs of a Diverse Population." *Science Scope* 26, no. 5 (February 2003): 26–29.

Giacalone, Valerie. "How to Plan, Survive, and Even Enjoy an Overnight Field Trip with 200 Students." *Science Scope* 26, no. 4 (January 2003): 22–26.

Gooden, Kelly. "Parents Come to Class." *Science and Children* 40, no. 4 (January 2003): 22–25.

Ledoux, M., et al. "A Constructivist Approach in the Interdisciplinary Instruction of Science and Language Arts Methods." *Teaching Education (Columbia, S.C.)* 15, no. 4 (December 2004): 385–399.

Marble, S. "Inquiring into Teaching: Lesson Study in Elementary Science Methods." *Journal of Science Teacher Education* 18, no. 6 (December 2007): 935–953.

Melber, Leah M. "Tap Into Informal Science Learning." *Science Scope* 23, no. 6 (March 2000): 28–31.

Molledo, Magdalena. "The Resourceful Teacher." *Science Scope* 24, no. 6 (March 2001): 46–48.

Morrison, J. A., et al. "Using Science Trade Books To Support Inquiry in the Elementary Classroom." *Childhood Education* 84, no. 4 (Summer 2008): 204–208.

Redmond, Alan. "Science in the Summer." *Science Scope,* 24 no. 4 (January 2000): 28–33.

Roy, Ken. "Safety Is for Everyone." *Science Scope* 26, no. 5 (February 2003): 16–17.

Silverman, E., et al. "Cheep, Chirp, Twitter, & Whistle." *Science and Children* 44, no. 5 (February 2007): 20–25.

Sussman, Beverly. "Making Your Science Program Work." *Science Scope* 23, no. 6 (March 2000): 26–27.

Sutton, Kimberly Kode. "Curriculum Compacting." *Science Scope* 24, no. 4 (January 2000): 22–27.

Notes

1. *National Science Education Standards* (Washington, D.C. National Academies Press, 1996). Courtesy of National Academies Press.

2. National Research Council, *National Science Education Standards* (Washington, DC: National Academy Press, 1996), p. 6. Courtesy of National Academies Press.

3. Ibid., 104.

4. Ibid., 103.

5. James Zull, *The Art of Changing the Brain* (Sterling, VA: Stylus Publishing LLC, 2002).

6. National Research Council, *National Science Education Standards* (Washington, DC: National Academy Press, 1996).

7. More on science notebooks in Chapter 6: Assessment.

8. Robert F. Mager, *Preparing Instructional Objectives: A Critical Tool in the Development of Effective Instruction* (Atlanta, GA: The Center for Effective Performance, 1997).

9. Paul D. Reed, Polymers and You (CIBT-RTC October 2005). http://cibt.bio.cornell.edu/programs/archive/0510rtc/Polymers.pdf.

chapter 5

Strategies and QuickChecks

How can I effectively use cooperative learning, questioning and wait-time strategies, active listening, demonstrations, and textbooks in my classroom?

▶ **Getting Started**

My greatest challenge as a teacher is to refrain from telling my students everything—far more than they want to know. This problem seems to be a highly contagious ailment that can be transmitted from professor to student. I have reached this conclusion because I find that teachers in grades K–8 tell their students too much—usually more than the children really want to be told. A favorite story of mine concerns a first-grade child who asks a teacher to explain nuclear fusion. The teacher replies, "Why don't you ask your mother? She is a nuclear physicist." The child replies, "I don't want to know *that* much about it."

Perhaps it is just human nature to tell people more than they really want to know. In my case, it happens when I get excited about the content I am sharing; I want everyone to get the information quickly. When I work in science classrooms, I try to restrain

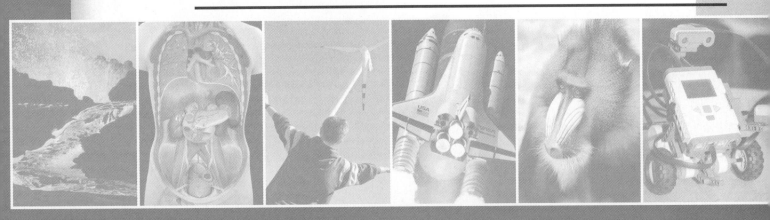

myself from talking so much because I know that I will enjoy watching children discover something special on their own, and I know that will happen only if I talk less. That smile or screech of excitement from a child who makes a discovery is powerful medicine that stops my wagging tongue.

How can we do more real science with children? Perhaps the first step is to talk less and to use more creative strategies that help children learn on their own—with our guidance, to be sure, but not with so much guidance that the smiles and screeches are lost.

Cooperative Learning Strategies

Go to **MyEducationLab**, select the topic Laboratory and Demonstrations, watch the video entitled "Cooperative Learning," and complete the questions that accompany it.

Each stage of the learning cycle can be enriched by the use of well-planned group work. One promising approach to improving the quality of group work is the use of *cooperative learning groups,* which consist of children who are, in fact, working *together* on a project. That is to say, they are supportive of one another and accountable for both their individual learning as well as the learning of every other person in their group.

Creating and Using Cooperative Learning Groups

Cooperative learning groups have very special characteristics that distinguish them from traditional classroom learning groups. Figure 5.1 makes a point-by-point comparison of nine of those characteristics, clearly contrasting these two approaches to group work.

In fact, these characteristics of cooperative learning groups emerge from three more fundamental elements, or strategies, of cooperative learning. If you can incorporate these strategies into your work with children before, during, and even after group work, you will increase the chances for successful group work. Here is a brief discussion of each:

1. *Teach for positive interdependence.* Help all members of each group understand that their success depends on the extent to which they agree on goals, objectives, and the roles each member is expected to carry out. They also need to agree in advance on an acceptable way to share available resources and information.

The success of a cooperative learning group depends on the success of each of its members.

Figure 5.1
What are the differences between a cooperative learning group and a traditional learning group?

Cooperative Learning Group	Traditional Learning Group
• Positive interdependence	• No interdependence
• Individual accountability	• No individual accountability
• Heterogeneous	• Homogeneous
• Shared leadership	• One appointed leader
• Shared responsibility for each other	• Responsibility only for self
• Task and maintenance emphasized	• Only task emphasized
• Social skills directly taught	• Social skills assumed and ignored
• Teacher observes and intervenes	• Teacher ignores group functioning
• Groups process their effectiveness	• No group processing

2. *Teach for individual accountability.* Help all members of each group understand that they are accountable not only for their own learning and behavior but also for helping other group members learn and work productively.

3. *Teach interpersonal and small-group skills.* If you expect children to work together and display appropriate group process skills, you will have to take the time to teach them those skills. Before group work, discuss group process skills such as sharing leadership, praising good work done by others, and active listening. Also teach children how to analyze how well the group process itself is going and how to modify the process to improve it.

▶ *Do It! Use the Cooperative Learning QuickCheck*

Figure 5.2 is a tool that you can use as you guide group work in your own classroom or as you observe another teacher's groups at work. Simply observe a group or a number of groups at work for a period of time, and use the points in the QuickCheck to help you determine the true nature of the group work that's occurring. You should check off (✓) each cooperative learning behavior that you observe. Think about whether you are observing a cooperative or a traditional learning group. Then use the results of your observation for guidance when you create and oversee future cooperative group work during science time.

Questioning Strategies

Go to **MyEducationLab**, select the topic Questioning Strategies, watch the video entitled "Questioning," and complete the question that accompanies it.

Every now and then, I visit a classroom that makes me feel like I've entered a time machine and been transported back to the days of the Spanish Inquisition. At those times, I feel like I'm an observer in an interrogation room—not a classroom. Questions, questions, and more questions!

Asking children a reasonable number of purposeful questions can be a helpful strategy. But too often, what I hear are rapid-fire questions that simply require recall and not much actual thought. In fact, sometimes children don't even have a chance to think about the possible answers before the next question is put forth.

Figure 5.2   Use this checklist to determine the level of cooperative learning in science group work.

Quick Check

Cooperative Learning QuickCheck

1. Does the group display *positive interdependence?*

    _____ Group members agree on general goals.

    _____ Group members agree on specific objectives.

    _____ Group members agree on roles for each group member.

    _____ Group members are sharing resources.

    _____ Group members each have a role that is integral to the completion of the task.

2. Does the group display *individual accountability?*

    _____ Group members try to keep the group on task.

    _____ Group members help one another complete tasks.

    _____ Group members try to keep their resource materials organized.

3. Does the group demonstrate *interpersonal and group process skills?*

    _____ Leadership is being shared among group members.

    _____ Group members praise each other.

    _____ Group members actively listen to one another.

    _____ Group members say and do things that keep the group moving ahead.

• Improving the Questions You Ask

Educational researchers have long been concerned about the quantity and quality of teacher questions. As a teacher, you have found or will soon find that it takes self-discipline to ask questions that actually stimulate thought and move children along the road to inquiry-based, discovery-focused learning.

Fortunately, you can take some practical steps to ensure that the time you spend probing what children actually know will be well spent. To begin, gather data about what you presently do in terms of question asking. You can do this by videotaping or audiotaping lessons or parts of lessons you teach to children or to peers. Then classify the types of questions you ask. One system for classifying questions has as its foundation the six cognitive levels—knowledge, comprehension, application, analysis, synthesis, and evaluation.

After carefully studying these six cognitive levels, Orlich and others proposed a more simplified three-category system for classifying questions.[1] The three categories of questions are as follows:

1. *Convergent questions* get children to think in ways that focus on basic knowledge or comprehension.

    Examples

    How did the yeast help our dough rise?

    What did the three-horned dinosaur eat?

    How was the plant cell different from the animal cell?

    How many planets orbit the sun?

2. *Divergent questions* get children to think about a number of alternative answers.

Examples

What are some ideas about what caused the dinosaurs to become extinct?

If you were a prey animal in the jungle, what could you do to keep safe from predators?

What are some ways we could reduce the amount of water and electricity wasted in our school?

3. *Evaluative questions* get students to offer a judgment based on some criteria.

Examples

If a power plant was going to be built next to your house, which one type of energy would you want it to generate?

If you could pick only three foods to take on a week-long camping trip, what would they be?

Where would be the safest place to be during an earthquake?

▶ *Do It! Use the Questioning QuickCheck*

I have used these three categories in creating a Questioning QuickCheck (see Figure 5.3). By counting the number of each type of question asked, you can analyze the tapes

Figure 5.3   Use this form to count questions by type during a live or recorded teaching episode.

Questioning QuickCheck

Date of episode _____   Start time _____   End time _____

Observe

1. *Convergent questions* get children to think in ways that focus on basic knowledge or comprehension.
   Tally of questions asked:

2. *Divergent questions* get children to think about a number of alternative answers.
   Tally of questions asked:

3. *Evaluative questions* get students to offer a judgment based on some criteria.
   Tally of questions asked:

Evaluate

1. How long did you observe, listen to, or watch the teaching episode? _____

2. How many of each type of question were asked?
   Convergent _____
   Divergent _____
   Evaluative _____

3. What was the total number of questions asked? _____

that you make of your own teaching or as you observe others teach. Clearly, to create an inquiry-based, discovery-focused classroom, a balance must be reached among the types of questions you ask. Using the Questioning QuickCheck will help you start that process.

Wait-Time/Think-Time Strategies

Have you ever heard of *wait-time* or *think-time?* Unfortunately, teachers' questioning behavior tends to follow a certain pattern: We ask a question, receive a response from a child, and then *immediately* react to the response and ask another question. The generally too-short gap between our question and the child's answer is known as wait-time or think-time. Experts tell us that that time is usually just two or three seconds long, if that. Regardless, it is too brief for the children to actually think deeply about one question before hearing its answer or yet another question.

Allowing More Time

Allowing a very short wait-time/think-time turns your classroom into a game show of sorts, in which you are trying to catch the children and indirectly embarrass them. By increasing wait-time or think-time, you can produce some very positive results. In particular, by allowing more time between questions, you can change a traditional classroom into a richer environment for inquiry-based, discovery-focused learning.

Researchers Tobin and Capie, in building on the previous work of Mary Bud Rowe, describe the following benefits of increasing wait-time beyond three seconds:

1. The length of student responses increased.
2. The number of unsolicited but appropriate responses increased.
3. Failure to respond decreased.
4. Confidence, as reflected by a decrease in the number of inflected responses, increased.
5. The incidence of speculative responses increased.
6. The incidence of child-child comparisons of data increased.
7. The incidence of evidence-inference statements increased.
8. The incidence of questions asked by students increased.
9. There was an increase in the incidence of responses emanating from students rated by the teacher as relatively slow learners.
10. The variety in the type of verbal behavior of students increased.[2]

The pause provided by a sufficient wait-time seems to refresh and improve the learning process. Make a real attempt to slow down the pace of questioning in your classroom.

▶ Do It! Use the Wait-Time/Think-Time QuickCheck

The QuickCheck in Figure 5.4 lists a variety of strategies you can use in the classroom to improve your own wait-time/think-time.[3] Check off (✓) the strategies as you try them, and make note of which ones seem especially effective using an asterisk (*).

Figure 5.4 Use the strategies in this checklist to slow down the pace of questioning.

Quick Check

Wait-Time/Think-Time QuickCheck

1. *To improve wait-time/think-time:*

   _____ Prompt the children to think about the answer before answering.

   _____ Mentally count off five seconds after you ask a question.

   _____ As you wait, look around the room to observe any signs of confusion about the question.

   _____ If the child's answer is appropriate, praise him or her and then count off another five seconds mentally before asking another question.

2. *If the children don't respond:*

   _____ Ask the childen if they would like you to ask the question in a different way.

   _____ Repeat the question with some modifications.

   _____ If possible, represent the question graphically on a chalkboard, whiteboard, or transparency.

   _____ Try to ask a simpler form of the question.

   _____ Ask if anyone in the class can rephrase the question for you.

   _____ Ask if part of the question is too difficult, and modify it accordingly.

   _____ Use the think-pair-share technique. After the children have reflected individually, ask them to share their ideas with their neighbor and then report to the class.

3. *If the children do respond appropriately:*

   _____ Liberally praise the responding child or children.

   _____ Ask the child to elaborate on his or her answer.

4. *If the children offer a partial response:*

   _____ Focus on the adequacy of the answer and capitalize on it (for instance, by asking "Can anyone help Jamie's answer?")

   _____ Praise the act of responding, perhaps by saying "That was a very good try, Jamie."

Active Listening Strategies

"For the third time, you draw the food chain arrows so the arrow heads point to the living things that receive the energy. Why do I keep seeing people draw the arrows from the killer whale to the seal? Was anyone listening when we talked about the food chain?"

It's very frustrating when you suddenly realize that your students are not listening to you, their classmates, or even visiting speakers as intently as you might wish. To help them improve on this skill during science time, focus on the idea of *active listening,* which is the conscious effort to focus one's attention on what people are saying as they are saying it. This is an important life skill that children need to master—and *you* may need a little work on it yourself! (I am relatively easily distracted, since I find everything around me quite interesting, so I need to work on active listening, also!)

● Increasing Active Listening

You can take some practical steps to increase active listening in your classroom:

1. *Restructure the physical setting to minimize distractions.* A classroom in which children are involved in hands-on activities will not be as quiet as a library. As you speak, there will be the bubbling sounds of the fish tank, the background noise of shifting chairs and desks, and so on. The first step in providing an environment in which active listening can occur is to compensate for background noise. Do this by having the children speak louder when asking or answering questions, by moving classroom furniture so that everyone can see the speaker, and by having the children look directly at and speak directly to the group or person they are addressing.

2. *Have children listen for key science words.* One way to keep their attention on the speaker is to listen for words such as *up, down, under,* and *above* that signal what is to follow. You will need to teach the children to use such terms as *observe, classify, graph, measure,* and *predict* and then to reinforce the use of these words through your praise. On a regular basis after a child has spoken or you have spoken, ask a question such as "Did you hear any key words when Emilio told us about last night's storm?" By teaching the children to listen for key words and what follows them, you and they will hear more of what is actually being said.

3. *Have children create questions for the speaker.* Challenge them to become such good listeners that you and they will be able to ask the speaker a question that uses some of his or her own words and ideas. For example, if Nadine is reporting the results of her group's work on rock classifying to the full class, ask the class at the end of the report if they have any questions for Nadine or her group. By doing this, you will help the children realize that they should be so attentive to the speaker that they can later ask good questions about what was said.

Figure 5.5   Use this checklist to apply specific strategies for improving the quality of listening in the science classroom.

Quick Check

Active Listening QuickCheck

_____ 1. Move the classroom furniture as needed so everyone can see the speaker.

_____ 2. Remind the children to look directly at and speak directly to the speaker.

_____ 3. Encourage children who are asking or answering questions to speak loudly enough for everyone to hear.

_____ 4. Remind the children to listen for signal words that the speaker uses, such as *up, down, under,* and *above.*

_____ 5. Remind the children to listen for key science words that the speaker uses, such as *observe, classify, measure,* and *predict.*

_____ 6. Challenge the children to come up with questions for the speaker that use some of his or her own words and ideas.

_____ 7. Model how to summarize what a speaker has said by restating or rephrasing what the children say.

_____ 8. Have the children practice summarizing or restating what the speaker has said.

4. *Practice summarizing what the speaker has said.* When children speak or ask questions, listen so attentively that you can restate in summary form what they said. To do this, you have to use the natural gaps in a speaker's speech patterns to mentally summarize the key ideas as they emerge. Model this by occasionally restating or rephrasing a child's question in a shorter form and then checking with him or her to see if you have captured the point or question.

▶ *Do It! Use the Active Listening QuickCheck*

You can apply these four guidelines to a real classroom setting by using Figure 5.5, the Active Listening QuickCheck. It provides some very specific steps you can take to increase active listening. Check off (✓) each strategy as you try it.

Demonstrations

"Do it again!"

This exclamation should bring joy to your heart after you do a science demonstration for children. These three little words send a clear message that you have made contact with a child's mind.

● Presenting a Good Science Demonstration

In recent years, I have observed fewer and fewer demonstrations in elementary science classrooms. It seems that a long-overdue emphasis on having *children* do activities has taken an important job away from the *teacher:* showing children phenomena they cannot efficiently, effectively, or *safely* discover for themselves. Because it has enormous potential for focusing

Science demonstrations have enormous potential for focusing children's attention on specific phenomena.

attention on a given phenomenon, the science demonstration can be an important tool for promoting inquiry in children. A demonstration can raise many questions for children, which can then be addressed in greater detail by individual science activities.

Of course, demonstrations can be misused in the classroom. They should never replace children's involvement in science activities, and they should not be used solely to reproduce phenomena that children have already read about. Instead, demonstrations should be used to intensify children's curiosity about a unit to be studied; to clarify the confusion that may result from attaining contrary results by children who have carried out identical science activities; and to tie together various types of learning at the end of a unit. Be sure to consider safety precautions and maintain a safety zone for the students when using hot liquids or potentially hazardous materials.

Make the demonstration interactive. Although you may be manipulating equipment and materials, actively involve the children in the thought process of the demonstration. Ask them to make predictions, to seek explanations, and to make suggestions about how you might proceed with the demonstration. Interactive demonstrations provide a great opportunity for you to model thinking.

▶ *Do It! Use the Demonstration QuickCheck*

The chapters in Part Two of this book include elementary school demonstrations for the life, physical, and earth/space sciences. Other sources of science demonstrations are provided in the resources at the end of this book. Bear in mind that by using larger equipment or materials, you can transform virtually any science activity into a demonstration you feel the children should experience as a class.

A number of considerations must be made in order to present an effective demonstration. Use Figure 5.6, the Demonstration QuickCheck, to assess the effectiveness of the science demonstrations that you or others do. Check off (✓) each item that applies.

Figure 5.6   Use this checklist to evaluate a science demonstration for children that you observe or perform.

Quick Check

Demonstration QuickCheck

_____ 1. The teacher began the demonstration promptly; the children didn't have to wait an excessive amount of time while the teacher got prepared.

_____ 2. The demonstration was essentially simple and straightforward, not elaborate and complex.

_____ 3. All the children in the class could observe the demonstration.

_____ 4. It seemed as if the teacher had pretested the demonstration; there was no evidence that this was the first time it had been tried—for example, missing equipment, confusion in the sequence of steps.

_____ 5. The teacher was able to create a bit of drama by presenting purposely puzzling situations or outcomes that were unexpected to the children.

_____ 6. The demonstration did not endanger the health or safety of the children.

_____ 7. The demonstration seemed to fit the topic under study.

_____ 8. The demonstration was appropriately introduced, carried out, and concluded.

_____ 9. The children had an opportunity to ask questions, make statements, and give reactions.

_____10. The demonstration provided a significant learning experience for the children.

Make the Case *An Individual or Group Challenge*

● **The Problem**

A large class may make so many demands on a teacher's time and attention that some children who have a special aptitude for science may go unnoticed.

● **Assess Your Prior Knowledge and Beliefs**

Based on your personal experiences, comment on how much each of the following may increase the likelihood of a teacher's recognizing children with a special aptitude for science:

1. The group leader shares the results of a science activity with the class as a whole.

   _____

2. The teacher leads a discussion about a field trip the class has recently taken.

   _____

3. The teacher asks questions that will reveal the children's knowledge of a topic.

   _____

4. The teacher discusses the results of a demonstration.

   _____

5. The teacher helps a cooperative learning group summarize its findings.

   _____

6. The teacher praises a group that has completed its science activity before other groups.

   _____

7. The teacher asks groups to select their own leaders.

   _____

● **The Challenge**

It has become clear that you must find some way to reach those children who are not working to their full potential in science. You have decided to teach a few students in higher grades some basic questioning and cooperative group skills and then use these students as assistants. You have already decided to call the project "Science Buddies." What factors should you consider in the early stages of planning for this project?

Science Textbooks

The year was 1489. The city was Florence, Italy. A young man, just 14 years old, was walking through the work yard next to a cathedral that was being built. He came upon an enormous old block of poorly shaped marble resting in the weeds, which was called "The Giant" by marble workers and sculptors. Many had tried to make some use of it and failed. "It had lain for 35 years in the cathedral's work yard, an awesome ghostly reminder to all young sculptors of the challenge of their craft."[4]

Twelve years later, the same man rediscovered and very carefully studied the sleeping, malformed Giant. Now, at 26, he saw something in the marble that only he could release. That something would become known as *David*, and the man who stripped away the excess marble to reveal perhaps the most extraordinary sculpture known to humankind was Michelangelo. Within the imperfect, he saw what few others could see: potential.

Using Textbooks as Resources

Your science classroom will be filled with imperfect resources: computers with Internet access that may lock up just as your children reach the best part of your research assignment, stacks of videotapes of nature adventures that really don't fit your curriculum, and bookshelves of textbooks that seem far too dull for your active children. You can spend a great deal of time wishing that you had better resources, but doing so will make no difference at all.

Science textbooks, bought with taxpayer money and intended as useful resources, will probably be flawed in one way or another. Their limitations will be obvious to all, but their potential will be unseen by many. Jones tells us that "U.S. textbooks are about twice the size of textbooks in other countries, and this is one situation where bigger is definitely not better."[5] She goes on to cite another expert who comments on the fact that textbooks seem unfocused, repetitive, and lacking coherence.

Although modern textbooks have definite weaknesses, they also contain some resources that you, a discovery-oriented teacher, can make good use of—*if* you are creative. They contain science content written at particular grade levels and provide many hands-on science activities. In addition, they usually come with teacher's guides that include enrichment ideas.

The activities in a textbook series, of course, reflect a particular scope and sequence of science content. If you have the freedom and the desire to create your own science curriculum, the textbook can still be quite useful. By omitting some of the structure present in the textbook's directions to the children, you can modify the activities so that they place more emphasis on discovery learning.

Textbooks are typically divided into a number of *units*, or groups of chapters. If you look over the units and the teacher's guide that accompanies the book, you will find many helpful teaching ideas. You will also find that many of the suggestions can be applied to learning units that you devise on your own. Many teacher's guides for textbooks provide bulletin board ideas, suggestions for field trips, lists of audiovisual materials, lists of children's books, and other helpful information that you can use to enrich your learning units.

In sum, you should consider these criteria in determining the usefulness of a certain textbook:

1. Content
2. Reading level
3. Approach to instruction
4. Physical characteristics
5. Availability of supplemental materials

Figure 5.7   Use this checklist to assess the quality of science textbooks available for children at your grade level.

Quick Check

Textbook Quality QuickCheck

1. *Content*
   _____ Does the content easily correlate with National Science Education Standards, state standards, and local standards?
   _____ Are the inquiry process skills emphasized?
   _____ Are there unit, chapter, section, and lesson objectives, and are they clearly written?
   _____ Is the content accurate and up-to-date?
   _____ Are the units, chapters, sections, and lessons logically organized?
   _____ Are distinctions made between *fact* and *theory?*
   _____ Are connections made between science and technology and personal/social perspectives?
   _____ Are the accomplishments of women, individuals from diverse cultural backgrounds, and individuals with special challenges included?
   _____ Do the end-of-unit, -chapter, or -section questions go beyond simple recall?
   _____ Is the content relevant to students' daily lives?

2. *Reading Level*
   _____ Is the reading level appropriate for the intended grade level?
   _____ Will the material engage student interest?
   _____ Is new vocabulary clearly introduced and defined?
   _____ Is there a glossary?

3. *Approach to Instruction*
   _____ Does the book appropriately relate the reading of science content to inquiry-based, discovery-focused activities?
   _____ Can the science activities be done with readily available, inexpensive materials and equipment?
   _____ Are there suggestions for follow-up activities that students could carry out on the Internet, at home, or as special long-term projects?

4. *Physical Characteristics*
   _____ Does the book look interesting from the view of students at your grade level?
   _____ Is the size and font of the print appropriate for students at your grade level?
   _____ Are the photographs and artwork clear, purposeful, and engaging?
   _____ Are the charts and graphs labeled well, and do they clarify the text?
   _____ Is there an appropriate mix of photos and art representing females, males, students with challenges, and students from diverse cultural backgrounds?

5. *Availability of Supplemental Materials*
   _____ Does the teacher's guide (teacher's edition) seem useful in terms of providing help in planning lessons and units?
   _____ Are any of the following available?
      _____ Transparencies
      _____ Lab books, workbooks, or other student materials
      _____ Assessment materials
      _____ Videos/CD-ROMS
      _____ Related software
      _____ Correlated science materials and equipment kits

Textbooks can provide you and your children a general structure for science content and experiences, ensuring continuity both during a single school year and from year to year within a school. Keep in mind, however, that the extent to which textbooks lead to discovery learning will, in the final analysis, depend on you.

▶ *Do It! Use the Textbook Quality QuickCheck*

If you have access to a collection of modern textbooks that are used in an elementary or middle school, you will likely find it very useful to systematically analyze a few of them, using the five criteria just listed. Doing so will reveal a great deal to you about the content that is commonly taught at particular grade levels as well as the quality of textbook resources that teachers might use. Use Figure 5.7, the Textbook Quality QuickCheck (page 89), to guide your efforts, checking off (✓) each criterion that applies. You may wish to add additional criteria to the checklist as you put it to use.

Science Kits

You are likely to teach at a school that uses any one of several prepared science curriculum kits consisting of a series of modules comprised of equipment and materials with supportive student worksheets and teacher guides. Science kits often provide background for teachers, inquiry-based activities, assessments, and ideas for integration across disciplines.

Integration of the kits into your science class requires proper professional development and support from people who have used the kits in their classroom. It takes an initial investment of time and energy to become familiar with a kit's layout and approach. Kits, like textbooks, are not designed (or should not be designed) to be teacher-proof. Rather, they provide a framework that a good teacher will modify to fit his or her teaching style and students' needs.

Using Science Kits Effectively in your Classroom

Keep It Simple   If it is your first time using the kit, begin with one module, preferably one on a topic with which you feel comfortable and that you enjoy. Once you get a feel for the teaching progression and layout of the module, other modules will be easier to implement.

Familiarize Yourself with the Kit   Spend some time unpacking the kit and reading through the manual to be sure the materials are sufficient and the progression of inquiry makes sense. Jones identifies material management and time management among the common challenges that teachers using kits encounter.[6] Therefore, familiarize yourself with the activities on your own prior to using them in class. Often kits go unused because some of the consumable materials are missing, therefore check and restock the kits after each use. Most consumables can be located and replenished easily (i.e., cotton balls, rice, tongue depressors).

Use the Kit as a Guide   Teaching science inquiry can be challenging if you are not comfortable with the science content or with the student-centered and sometimes chaotic dynamic of discovery learning. Science kits can be a welcome guide to keep you anchored the first time you teach a unit. Research suggests that science kits, by providing focus and structure, help teachers overcome the initial apprehension of teaching inquiry.[7]

Modify the Kit to Fit Your Needs   You don't have to do everything in the kit. Use the elements of the kit that suit your purpose without compromising the integrity and intellectual honesty of the lesson. As you become more familiar with the kit and its options, you will find yourself adapting it to fit your needs.

▶ *Do It! Use the Science Kit QuickCheck*

Science kits can provide a foundation for rich learning experiences. Good kits can introduce you to new teaching strategies as well as provide the basis for dynamic learning experiences for your students. Use the Kit QuickCheck in Figure 5.8 to assess science kits. Check off (✓) each criterion that applies.

Figure 5.8   Use this checklist to assess science kits.

Science Kit QuickCheck

1. Content
_____ What science topics does the kit address?
_____ Is the content appropriate for the grade level?
_____ Does the content address the NSES or the local standards?
_____ Is the content accurate and up to date?
_____ Is there a content background for teachers?
_____ Is it clear and informative?

2. Process
_____ Does the recommended teaching strategy include engagement and exploration activities?
_____ Do the activities connect meaningfully with the science content?
_____ Do the activities support inquiry?
_____ Is there evidence that students will use science process skills to create descriptive, explanatory, or experimental models?
_____ Are both formative and summative assessment strategies included?
_____ Are the student guides clear?
_____ Does the kit reflect principles of universal design for learning (see Chapter 9), providing multiple means of engagement, representation, and expression?
_____ Are there enrichment activities?
_____ Are there suggestions for interdisciplinary connections, e.g., to math and language arts?
_____ Is safety addressed? Are Material Data Safety Sheets provided as needed?

3. Materials
_____ Are the materials and equipment complete?
_____ Is the equipment in good working order?
_____ Are consumables inexpensive and easy to replenish?

Summary

Classroom teachers can use a variety of strategies to teach children science in an effective yet creative way. Cooperative learning groups can be used as an important part of any learning environment that encourages discovery learning. Teachers' use of questioning and wait-time strategies, ability to teach children to become active listeners, inclusion of science demonstrations along with hands-on activities, and creative use of textbooks and science kits can all serve to enhance and enrich the learning environment.

Going Further

On Your Own

1. Reflect upon the science activities you experienced in elementary school:
   a. Specifically, what activities do you remember? Why do you think you remember them?
   b. If you do remember activities, were they carried out by individual children or by groups? What do you think motivated the teacher's decision in this respect?
   c. While the activities were underway, were there any specific problems with work space, classroom behavior, or the availability of science materials? If so, what?
   d. Would you say that your teacher or teachers encouraged discovery learning?

2. Select a chapter from a conventional elementary school science textbook that contains some science activities. Develop a strategy for using the activities and text materials as the basis for a group of discovery-based lessons. How does your strategy compare with the more conventional use of chapters in science textbooks? Would your approach offer any cooperative learning possibilities?

3. How could you use some of the ideas in this chapter to create an ideal curriculum for children at the grade level you are most interested in? Be specific and focus upon the following:
   a. The content you would stress
   b. The concepts you would stress
   c. How the curriculum would reflect the teaching style you would use
   d. The use of cooperative learning groups
   e. The use of teacher demonstrations and hands-on student activities
   f. The use of effective questioning and wait-time strategies
   g. The use of textbooks as resources
   h. The use of science kits as resources

On Your Own or in a Cooperative Learning Group

4. With others, role-play the best and worst science demonstrations you have ever observed. What factors contributed to the quality (or lack thereof) of each? If you are doing this activity by yourself, respond in writing.

5. Select a topic commonly covered in elementary school science, and create five questions the teacher could use to help children make discoveries in this field of study. Also try to think of a demonstration that the teacher could use to raise questions among the children that might lead to discoveries.

6. Formulate a position on each of the following statements. You may wish to have a minidebate in which various members of the group adopt extreme positions.
   a. Discovery learning uses up valuable classroom time.
   b. Textbooks cannot be used with inquiry-based techniques.
   c. By asking questions, you can slow down a child's thought processes.

Resources for Discovery Learning

Internet Resources

 To access these helpful websites, go to **MyEducationLab,** select Resources, and then Web Links. To learn more, click on the following links and you will easily be directed to the websites.

- **Curricular Companions:**
  www.keystone.fi.edu/matrix1.shtml

- **The Cooperative Learning Center at the: University of Minnesota**
  www.co-operation.org

Print Resources

Suggested Readings

Brune, Jeff. "Take It Outside!" *Science and Children* 39 no. 7 (April 2002): 29–33.

Corder, Greg, and Reed, Darren. "It's Raining Micrometeorites." *Science Scope* 26, no. 5 (February 2003): 23–25.

Fones, Shelly White. "Engaging Science." *Science Scope* 23, no. 6 (March 2000): 32–36.

Freedman, Michael. "Using Effective Demonstrations in the Classroom." *Science and Children* 38, no. 1 (September 2000): 52–55.

Galus, Pamela. "Reactions to Atomic Structure." *Science Scope* 26, no. 4 (January 2003): 38–41.

Irwin, Leslie, et al. "Science Centers for All." *Science and Children* 40, no. 5 (February 2003): 35–37.

Jones, M. T., et al. "Implementing Inquiry Kit Curriculum: Obstacles, Adaptations, and Practical Knowledge Development in Two Middle School Science Teachers." *Science Education* 91, no. 3 (May 2007): 492–513.

Kelly, Janet, et al. "Science Adventures at the Local Museum." *Science and Children* 39, no. 7 (April 2002): 46–48.

Krutchinsky, Rick, and Harris, William. "Super Science Saturday." *Science and Children* 40, no. 4 (January 2003): 26–28.

MacKenzie, Ann Haley. "Brain Busters, Mind Games & Science Chats." *Science Scope* 24, no. 6 (March 2001): 54–58.

Reeve, Stephen L. "Beyond the Textbook." *Science Scope* 25, no. 6 (March 2002): 4–6.

Souvignier, Elmar, and Kronenberger, Julia. "Cooperative Learning in Third Graders' Jigsaw Groups for Mathematics and Science with and without Questioning Training." *The British Journal of Educational Psychology* 77, no. 4 (December 2007): 755–771.

Stivers, Louise. "Discovering Trees: Not Just a Walk in the Park!" *Science and Children* 39, no. 7 (April 2002): 38–41.

Notes

1. Donald Orlich et al., *Teaching Strategies: A Guide to Better Instruction* (Lexington, MA: D. C. Heath, 1994), pp. 186–193.
2. Kenneth G. Tobin and William Capie, *Wait-Time and Learning in Science* (Burlington, NC: Carolina Biological Supply, n.d.), p. 2.
3. I drew ideas for the Wait-Time/Think-Time QuickCheck from a variety of sources that you may find of interest, including Robert J. Stahl (1995), "Using 'Think-Time' and 'Wait-Time' in the Classroom" (ERIC Digest no. ED370885); it can be found on the Internet at <www.ed.gov/databases/ERIC_Digests/ed370885.html>. Another useful source, which focused on college teaching assistants, is "Teaching Tips for TAs: WAIT-TIME" (June 14, 2000), published by the Office of Instructional Consultation, University of California, Santa Barbara, and located on the Internet at <www.id.ucsb.edu/IC/TA/ta.html>.
4. Robert Coughlan, *The World of Michelangelo* (New York: Time, 1966), p. 85.

5. Rebecca Jones, "Solving Problems in Math and Science Education," *The American School Board Journal* 185, no. 7 (July 1998): 18.

6. M. T. Jones, et al., "Implementing Inquiry Kit Curriculum: Obstacles, Adaptations, and Practical Knowledge Development in Two Middle School Science Teachers," *Science Education* 91, no. 3 (May 2007): 492–513.

7. Ibid, p. 509.

chapter 6

Assessment of Understanding and Inquiry

A good teacher asks, "How am I doing?"
A great teacher asks, "How are my students doing?"

▶ **Getting Started**

> *"What d'ja git?"*
> *"She gave me a C!"*

Would overhearing this exchange between two students—after you've taught a unit that took three weeks to plan and far too many afternoons shopping at discount stores for inexpensive activity materials—get your attention? And would it sting just a bit?

It would and should for two reasons. First of all, it would tell you that the end-of-unit test probably didn't assess whether your children actually learned some science. Second, it would tell you that your children have the extraordinary idea that

the teacher *gives* a grade. Notice the phrasing *She gave*. Does that imply, even slightly, that the student's grade was *earned*?

In this chapter, you will learn about a range of assessment techniques that will help you discover whether your children are actually learning science. Carefully studying these materials will help you create a classroom in which the children are more concerned about what they *learned* and less concerned about the gifts they think you give!

Two Approaches to Assessment: Formative and Summative

I do not recall where or when I heard the statement, "*A good teacher asks, 'How am I doing?' A great teacher asks, 'How are my students doing?'*" But a truly outstanding teacher should ask both questions. Formative and summative assessments are two approaches that help us focus on these two, very important aspects.

Formative assessment occurs during instruction to let us know whether the children are on the pathway to learning the intended content. It serves as a check on the execution of the lesson plan, answering the questions, "Are the children doing what you intended them to do?" and "Are there signs that the children are constructing the understanding and developing the concepts that you targeted for learning?" If the children are on track to learning, then you can continue the lesson as planned. If feedback from your formative assessment indicates that the children are not on track, then it is not too late for you to revise and adjust the lesson accordingly. A lesson plan is just that, a plan. The saying that even the best plans go astray is all too true when teaching. Formative assessment keeps you from being surprised when plans falter and provide you with time to adjust and salvage the lesson. In this respect, formative assessment addresses how you are doing as well as how your students are doing.

Summative assessment occurs after the intended learning has taken place. It answers the questions, "What did the students learn? Did they learn what I thought I taught?" It is a culminating activity during which students demonstrate their understanding of the content or skills that you intended to teach. Summative assessments are usually used for purposes of placement, grading, accountability, and informing parents and future teachers about student performance.

Teachers often ask me for a list of formative and summative assessment tools. Unfortunately, it is not that easy. Although some assessment tools are usually associated with one of the two approaches, often the methodologies overlap. Whether an assessment is formative or summative depends on how you choose to use the data.

I will resist the urge to classify any assessment methodology as strictly formative or summative. Throughout this chapter, we will consider several assessment methodologies and evaluate the strengths and weaknesses of each. It will be up to you choose the appropriate assessment strategies for your purposes.

The design of good assessment tools is made easier by stating clearly and concisely the content to be taught and establishing good performance objectives. You will be reminded to refer to both of these components in your lesson plan as you develop assessments.

A Brief Comment on Performance Assessment and Authentic Assessment

Performance assessment and authentic assessment have very similar meanings. Performance assessment is a measure of assessment based on authentic tasks such as activities, exercises, or problems that require students to show what they can do.[1] Authentic assessments

Descriptions of Formative and Summative Assessment as Described by the National Research Council[2]

Formative assessment refers to assessments that provide information to students and teachers that is used to improve teaching and learning. These are often informal and ongoing, though they need not be. Data from summative assessments can be used in a formative way.

Summative assessment refers to the cumulative assessments, usually occurring at the end of a unit or topic coverage, that intend to capture what a student has learned or the quality of the learning, and judge performance against some standards. Although we often think of summative assessments as traditional objective tests, this need not be the case. For example, summative assessments could follow from an accumulation of evidence collected over time, as in a collection of student work.

present students with real-world challenges that require them to apply their relevant skills and knowledge.[3] The assessment strategies used for each type of assessment are often interchangeable. I consider authentic assessments a type of performance assessment, and consequently will address performance assessments in general. Let's begin by looking to the National Research Council as our guide.

The National Science Education Standards (NSES) Approach to Assessment

The NSES recommend assessing children in two broad areas: understanding and inquiry. *Understanding* means what you would expect it to mean—whether children comprehend the science ideas you are teaching. *Inquiry* focuses on whether children have the ability to actually seek their own explanations. The following sections will further clarify the intent of the standards as well as provide some practical examples.

Assessment Strategies

Go to **MyEducationLab**, select the topic Assessment, watch the video entitled "Ongoing Assessment: Assessing Knowledge and Understanding," and complete the questions that accompany it.

Prompt and Rubric   Basic to the NSES approach to assessment is the use of prompts and rubrics. A *prompt* is a question or group of questions that includes a statement about a task to be done along with directions on how to do it. A *scoring rubric* (pronounced "roo-brick") is used to describe the criteria that should be used when assessing a child's performance.[4] Let's look at examples of the use of prompts and scoring rubrics in the classroom.

▶ Example of a Prompt and Rubric

Topic: Sound (for grades 1–3)

Content to be assessed: Sounds are caused by vibrations.

Performance objective: Given a drum, pencil, and rice, students will hit the drum with the pencil and explain orally that sound is produced by vibrations.

Prompt: "This little drum is made by stretching plastic wrap over a jar. I'd like you to tap the drum with the eraser, look at the plastic, and tell me what you see and what you hear. Then sprinkle some rice grains on the plastic and look at it as you tap it again."

Questions:

1. What do you observe when you hit the drum with an eraser?
2. What do you think causes sound?

Rubric:

3	2	1
Student's description of what was observed includes the plastic moves up and down, the vibration causes sound	Student's description includes a response with one correct observation	No response is given or incorrect responses are given

You could use this prompt and rubric as a formative assessment if it was administered during the lesson or as a summative assessment after the lesson.

Reality Check

Write a prompt and scoring rubric for the following content to be assessed:

Content: Energy from the sun is converted to food by plants. Animals such as mice and rabbits eat the plants to get their food. Animals such as snakes and hawks eat mice and rabbits. When living things die, they are broken down by organisms such as bacteria and fungi and returned to the soil where they can be used again by plants. When elements of the food chain are removed, the organisms that depend on them have to find other food sources or die.

Performance Objective: Given a food web diagram, students will explain what will occur if the mice are removed from the food web. The students will score at least satisfactory on the rubric that you will create. (Go to Rubrics and Scoring Guides on page 109 if you need help.)

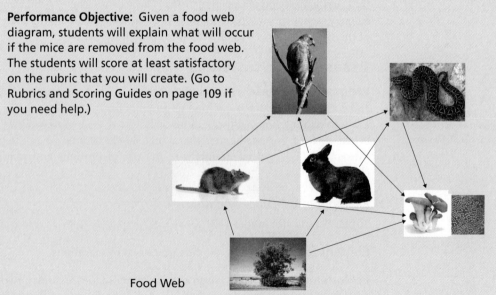

Food Web

Go to **MyEducationLab**, select the topic Inquiry, watch the video entitled "Evaluation," and complete the question that accompanies it.

● Performance Assessment

Inquiry is a central component of the [National Science Education] *Standards*. It involves developing descriptive models, explanatory models, and experimental models using science process skills such as asking questions, planning, designing and conducting experiments, analyzing and interpreting data, and drawing conclusions.[5] Your young students may be able to do all or part of the inquiry process on their own. You will need to assess the degree to which your students can carry out the process of inquiry, keeping in mind that the inquiry can be measured on a continuum from being highly directed to completely open ended. The more the students initiate questioning, exploration, data collection, data analysis, and conclusions on their own, the less directed the inquiry.

Because inquiry is a process, assessing students' ability to do inquiry frequently takes place over an extended time. Atkin, Black, and Coffey in *Classroom Assessment in the National Science Education Standards* suggest that, "The best way to support inquiry is to obtain information about students while they are actually engaged in science investigations with a view toward helping them develop their understandings of both subject matter and procedure."[6] Performance assessment strategies lend themselves to evaluation of students' abilities to inquire. Note that a collection of data from several assessment instruments over time will provide you with a good idea of what students can do with respect to inquiry.

As their name implies, performance assessments are based on observations of students as they demonstrate a specific task or problem-solving skill. They are usually evaluated using a rubric or scoring guide. The evaluator collects data about the student's procedures and conclusions through direct observation of behavior, written records such as notes, worksheets, lab reports, or products such as posters, role plays, and recordings.

▶ *Example of a Performance Assessment*

Topic: Light and plants (for young learners)

Engagement: What will happen if Mrs. Riley's plants are kept in the closet without light instead of in sunlight on the window sill?

Exploration: I will give each group two plants. You have one week to find out what will happen to the plants if they are kept in a closet without light. Use the following questions to guide your investigation:

1. Make a prediction that you can test.
2. Describe how you will test your prediction.
3. Carry out your test.
4. Make observations of your plants each day and record your observations in your science notebook, using words and drawings.
5. At the end of your test, state your results.

Explanation: Students will describe whether their evidence supports their prediction or does not support their prediction.

Scoring guide:

Performance	Criteria	Potential score	Student score
Prediction	Prediction is testable	1	
Test of prediction	Implies treatment	1	
	Implies control	1	
	Identifies observables (color, height . . .)	1	
Daily observations	Makes daily entries	1	
	Uses words to describe observables	1	
	Uses drawings to describe observables	1	
	Observations are accurate	1	
Results	Results are consistent with observations	1	
Explanation	Students relate that the presence of light is necessary for Mrs. Riley's plants to live	1	
Total score		10	

Portfolios

A *portfolio* is an organized collection of a person's work that shows the very best that he or she can do. Although each piece placed in a portfolio can be assessed with respect to the degree to which the student achieved specific unit objectives, the portfolio as a whole will illustrate the child's progress.

You can learn a great deal by observing a child at work.

You may be wondering what specific examples of a child's science work should go in a science portfolio. Here are some products that could be included:

- Written observations and science reports
- Drawings, charts, and graphs that are the products of hands-on, discovery-focused activities
- Thank-you letters to resource people who have visited the classroom (e.g., beekeepers, veterinarians, health care providers)
- Reaction pieces, such as prepared written responses to science software, videos, discovery experiences, field trips, and websites
- Media products, such as student-produced science work in audio, video, or digital form

● Anecdotal Records

Name: Jimmy Green   *Age: 8*
Grade: 2   *Date: May 5*

This week Jimmy's group, the Science Stars, which was responsible for taking care of the aquarium, found a dead guppy. Jimmy volunteered to bury it in the school lawn. He told the group, "Even though it's dead, it'll help the grass grow."

A teacher's brief notes about a child's behavior can reveal a great deal about what the child has or has not learned. The notes, called *anecdotal records,* can help you assess how well individual children are doing. They can be particularly helpful when you wish to reflect upon and assess how well individual children are mastering inquiry process skills or developing desirable attitudes and values.

● Affective Development Checklists

"Boy, do I hate science!"

If you heard one of your students say this, what would you conclude about his or her affective development? Your only basis for assessing changes in *affect* is your observation of the affect-laden behaviors students exhibit. Their comments, smiles, frowns, in-class behavior, and out-of-class behavior reveal a great deal about how much they are developing favorable attitudes toward science and your teaching.

Figure 6.1 presents a list of behaviors that you may wish to draw on to create your own affective development checklist. Add your personal observations of student behaviors to create a more comprehensive list.

Figure 6.1   Draw from these behaviors to create an affective development checklist.

- Makes drawings and diagrams of science-related objects and events
- Is curious about new objects, organisms, and materials added to the classroom
- Talks about surprising things he or she notices in the environment
- Spends free time at the in-class science learning center
- Questions but is tolerant of the ideas of others
- Enters science fairs and school science expositions
- Brings science-related magazine pictures to class
- Checks science-related books out of the class or school library
- Reads science fiction
- Collects natural objects as a hobby
- Comments on science-related programs seen on TV
- Comments on science-related films
- Asks for class field trips to museums, planetariums, and so on
- Invents things
- Builds models
- Asks questions about science-related news stories
- Asks to do more science activities
- Asks to make or fix science equipment
- Volunteers to carry out demonstrations
- Asks to work on science-related bulletin boards
- Asks to distribute materials and equipment for activities
- Questions superstitions
- Asks to take care of classroom animals or plants

Science Conferences with Children

The words we speak tell a great deal about what we know and how we feel. The quickest and possibly most reliable way to find out if children in a discovery-oriented classroom are learning is to give them an opportunity to talk to you. If you learn to listen carefully and gently probe around the edges of a child's talk, you will discover whether he or she has grasped the real meaning of a food web, has had anything to do with creating the group's drawings showing the movement of the continents, or is becoming increasingly curious about the natural world.

Science Notebooks

Have you ever watched a child fish around in his or her desk to locate a bologna-stained sheet of paper that contains yesterday's science notes? Some teachers have found that a journal or notebook devoted only to science can be a great asset for children as well as a useful tool for assessing how well individual students are doing. I have noticed an increase in the use of science notebooks in elementary school science classes during the past few years. While it may seem like semantics, science notebooks can be distinguished from science journals in that science notebooks allow for more reflection and less structure than science journals typically do. Children are encouraged to include not only formal investigative elements, such as procedures, data, and results, but also their questions, predictions, reflections, and to express their feelings about science. Most importantly, notebooks provide a place for students to record new concepts they have learned or want to learn. Figures 6.2a and 6.2b show examples of entries in science notebooks. Here are some suggestions for implementing the use of science notebooks:

1. At the start of the year, ask each child to obtain a notebook he or she will devote exclusively to science. You may also wish to have the children construct their own science notebooks.

Figure 6.2   Examples of science notebook entries

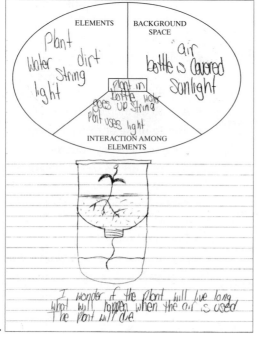

a.

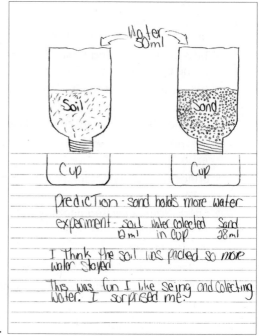

b.

2. Encourage the children to design covers for their science notebooks. One way to do this is to have a general discussion about the major themes or units they will do during the year.

3. Encourage children to write in their notebooks each day, and provide time for them to do so. Offer some guiding questions, such as "What did you do? What did you learn? How do you feel about what you have learned?"

4. Schedule time at the end of each teaching unit for children to discuss some of the things they have written.

5. Consider using the science notebooks during parent-teacher conferences. Also consider putting the notebooks on display for Parents' Night or Back-to-School Night.

Probes

Probes are similar to prompts and rubrics, but designed more specifically to uncover whether a student understands a particular rule of interaction that you targeted in the lesson. *Probes* include a simple question that seeks a two-part answer. The first part usually involves lower order thinking skills such as identification or naming. The second part of the probe requires students to demonstrate higher order thinking by stating rules of relationship between or among elements.

▶ *Example*

Is it a physical change or a chemical change?

The list below involves situations that cause changes in materials. Put a P next to the situations in which the materials in italics undergo a physical change and a C next to the situations in which the materials in italics undergo a chemical change.

_____*Ice cream* melts in the sun

_____*Wood* is cut to make sawdust

_____A *car* rusts

_____*Wood* is burned in a fire

_____*Water* evaporates from a pan

_____An *egg* is fried

Explain your thinking. Describe in writing a "rule" to decide if something undergoes a physical or chemical change.

Children's Self-Assessment

As teachers, we may forget that children naturally reflect on how well they do in each activity that is a part of their science experience. And so it should seem logical to capitalize on self-reflection when you incorporate assessment into your classroom.

There are many ways to stimulate children's self-assessment. For example, before the children begin to write in their science notebooks, you might say, "So far this month, you have worked on two projects. One was building a flashlight, and the other was using a flashlight and mirrors to study how light behaves. What did you learn in each project?" The children's responses will represent their efforts to assess what they have done. This is important information to you as a teacher.

● Concept Mapping

Go to **MyEducationLab**, select the topic Lesson and Unit Planning, watch the videos entitled "Concept Mapping" and "Concept Mapping 2," and complete the questions that accompany them.

A family is seated around the dinner table. The dad passes a bowl of reconstituted instant mashed potatoes to his son and asks, "So, what did you learn in science today?" The child responds, "Nuthin."

How can this be? That child spent the entire day in a lovely, pastel-walled classroom overflowing with books and science materials, was taught by knowledgeable and motivated teachers, had access to a variety of resources (including four or five computers with Internet access), took an around-the-school-yard nature field trip with his class, and also attended a special all-school assembly with Dr. Science, who performed demonstrations that flashed, popped, and banged. Yet the child answered his dad's question with "Nuthin." What went wrong?

The answer is simple: The child doesn't really know what he learned. By that, I mean that the child has had no opportunity to make what he learned *explicit.* He probably learned many things today, but he has not brought them to the forefront of his consciousness and tied them all together. Consequently, both the child and his dad finish their meal thinking that the day was as bland as those mashed potatoes.

One way to help a child assess self-learning is to have him or her make a concept map after an inquiry-based experience. You can even use a concept map as a personal unit-planning device. Even so, I am presenting it here as an assessment tool, so you can see what children have learned in a concrete way. They will literally draw you a picture!

A *concept map* is a diagram that represents knowledge by identifying basic concepts and topics and showing how these items are related. Such a map is created using these two symbols:

1. *Node*—A shape (typically a circle or oval) that contains a word or phrase to represent the item of content knowledge.

2. *Link*—A line with an arrowhead at one or both ends that's used to connect the nodes and to show the relationship between them. A single arrowhead indicates that one node leads to or is part of another. A double arrowhead indicates that nodes are reciprocal or mutually supportive of each other.

Figure 6.3   This concept map represents what one child learned in a school yard field trip to observe types of living things.

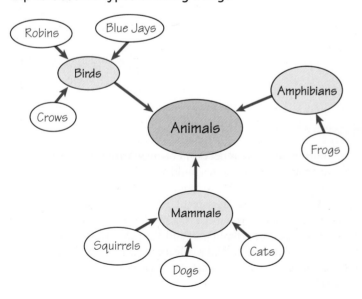

Figure 6.3 shows the concept map a child drew after going on a school yard field trip to observe types of living things in the environment. Starting with "Animals" in the center of the page, the child branched out to classes of animals, such as "Mammals" and "Birds," and then became even more specific by noting types of animals within each class, such as "Dogs" and "Squirrels" under "Mammals." Note that all of the arrows point the same way: back to "Animals."

By studying a child's concept map, you can assess what he or she has really learned during an experience and how he or she has tied specific pieces of knowledge together. The child will benefit from creating the map because he or she will make what might have been abstract or general more concrete and specific. As a result, the child will have a much fuller knowledge of what was learned—and it won't seem like "Nuthin"!

Traditional Assessment Techniques

● End-of-Chapter Homework

". . . and then do numbers 1 through 5 on the last page."

Does this bring back a few classroom memories? Giving children an end-of-chapter homework assignment is a common way for teachers to discover whether the children remember what they have read. When you make such an assignment, you believe that children will read the chapter first and then answer the questions. Perhaps in elementary and middle school, you read your science chapters before you did your homework. If so, I congratulate you! If you didn't, this is a good opportunity to consider what traditional end-of-chapter homework does and doesn't accomplish.

▶ *What Does It Accomplish?*

An end-of-chapter assignment tells the children that you are serious about the content you are teaching. It forces them to look at and, if you are fortunate, read text material, if only to find answers to the questions they have been assigned. This type of assignment provides you with one small indicator of how serious a child is about his or her schooling. The actual appearance of a textbook in the home also tells parents that the child is doing something in science class. Finally, homework assignments that are *not* done provide you with a reason for talking with a child and the child's parents about his or her effort.

▶ *What Doesn't It Accomplish?*

End-of-chapter homework does not tell you much about what children know, and it doesn't tell you if they like science. Completed homework seldom reveals any understanding of information beyond the recall level of the cognitive domain. End-of-chapter homework will probably not pique children's interest to the point that they will want to learn more about the topic.

Using End-of-Chapter Homework Effectively   Before making the assignment, talk with children about the purpose of the homework and the reading they have done. Use statements such as "You know this first chapter on living things told us about the differences between living and nonliving things. The questions at the end will help you find out if you remember and understand some of the big ideas." After this introduction, give children a few minutes of class time to begin the assignment. Doing so will increase the probability that children will do the homework and possibly make the experience somewhat more meaningful to them.

● Quizzes

Do you still live in fear of the "pop" quiz? Does your heart flutter a bit just hearing the term *quiz*? Quizzes are a part of the classroom assessment process from elementary school through graduate school, and their effect on students seems to remain rather constant. A quiz takes little time and is usually used as a quick assessment of whether students remember or understand factual information or concepts.

▶ *What Do They Accomplish?*

Quizzes tell teachers whether children can think fast and have a sufficient command of writing to get their responses on paper before time is up. They are easy to grade and provide a snapshot of the student's recall of information. They also serve to keep children "on their toes," but they should not divert teachers from the science experiences that should be taking place in the classroom.

▶ *What Don't They Accomplish?*

Quizzes do not tell teachers much about in-depth understanding. Children's lack of success on quizzes may not reveal a deficit in knowledge or understanding but rather a deficit in being able to express themselves quickly.

Using Quizzes More Effectively   Quizzes should be used in moderation. If you wish to find out whether children are learning, giving a quiz now and then that is focused on the important ideas of a science unit can provide some information about student progress. Doing so can also help you discover that you need to modify your teaching or help a particular child before a unit is completed.

Tests

Given the large numbers of children in most classrooms, most teacher-developed tests are composed of short-answer questions and some multiple-choice items. At the end of the test, there may be a few so-called essay questions. In inquiry-based classrooms, teachers who use tests are likely to include some questions dealing with how science activities were conducted and what was learned from them.

▶ *What Do They Accomplish?*

Test results tell children, parents, and you how well the children answered the questions that were asked. Test results give children a way to assess their own progress and a way to compare themselves to others. They give you a neat and tidy way to get information to use for grading. They also tell you which children in the class are good test takers. That information is important if you want to teach children skills that will be useful in later life.

If you create a test with questions that discover more than children's recall abilities, you may get more useful information. The test results may reveal whether children understood concepts, were able to apply what was learned, and were able to analyze the science phenomena studied. If, however, the test consists solely of recall questions, only the children's memory will be assessed.

Traditional assessment may not reflect all of the learning that occurs in a discovery-based science classroom.

▶ *What Don't They Accomplish?*

Tests tell you only what children know and understand about the particular questions you asked. Very few tests assess how well children can express their thoughts. Questions that elicit this information are challenging to create, require many minutes for children to complete, and demand that the teacher spend a considerable amount of time outside class carefully reading each response, reflecting on the work, offering written feedback, and assigning grades.

Tests probably do little to motivate children to think about science as an interesting subject area or to increase their career awareness. Nor does success on science tests indicate that children like science, are interested in science, will engage in free reading about science topics, will watch televised science programs, or even will become interested observers of the natural world.

Using Tests More Effectively   As you prepare a test, try to cross-reference each item to one of the cognitive, affective, or psychomotor objectives of the teaching unit. By doing this, you can measure student progress over all of the unit's objectives. To help you assess student achievement on the objectives of the unit and the quality of the questions you have asked, after the test, prepare a chart on which you will record the number of children who answer each question correctly.

Library Reports

Can you recall going to the school library or media center to do research on a topic for a science report? Perhaps you remember poring through encyclopedias and other reference books to find information on such topics as whales, volcanoes, tornadoes, and rockets. A great deal can be learned through library work that is related to the science experiences that occur in the classroom.

▶ *What Do They Accomplish?*

Science library reports are common assignments in elementary and middle school and provide students with information and ideas that can round out what they have learned through hands-on activities, demonstrations, and class discussions. Library reports can lead children to think about topics and questions that were not considered during class. They can also help improve a child's grade for a marking period by making up for low quiz or test grades.

▶ *What Don't They Accomplish?*

When used in the traditional manner, library reports do little to extend and enrich the basic knowledge, skills, and attitudes emphasized in a discovery-focused classroom. They do not present children with an opportunity to touch science materials or to move through the full learning cycle. In the best circumstances, library reports tell you whether children can look up information in reference books and summarize what they have learned.

Using Library Reports More Effectively   In order for library reports to be meaningful, they should engage children in a quest that resolves some issue or problem. Therefore, if the children are engaged in inquiry-based science experiences related to the life cycle of insects, you might say, "I would like you to do work in the learning center that will help you answer the question 'Why don't we ever see baby butterflies?'" This type of assignment captures the same curiosity that you are hoping to capitalize on with hands-on discovery science. Children should be going to the library or learning center to learn how to use books and media as *tools* that are as essential to the pursuit of science as microscopes and metersticks.

Activity Write-Ups

How will you know that children are learning, fitting new learnings into previous knowledge, and constructing new meanings? You can discover this by observing them, by listening to them, and by reading what they have written in their activity write-ups.

▶ *What Do They Accomplish?*

Having children synthesize and share what they have learned in activity write-ups tells them that you believe thinking, talking, and writing about what they have experienced is important. Listening to a child's observations of water droplets forming on an ice-filled glass or reading a list of written observations gives you valuable information about the learning that is occurring in your classroom.

▶ *What Don't They Accomplish?*

A variety of problems can arise when you use activity write-ups. The most obvious one is that a child may have completed an activity successfully but not be a good writer. Under these circumstances, a poor report may tell you more about his or her language arts abilities than science abilities. If you rely only on activity write-ups, children with language difficulties will be unable to express what they have learned.

By necessity, the activity write-up is a very brief sketch of the work the child has done. While it will tell you a good deal about the results of a child's experimentation, it will tell you little about all the experiences he or she may have had as the activity was carried out.

Using Activity Write-Ups Effectively   When you look at or listen to a child's activity write-up, you need to be able to assess whether the efforts reflect the child's or the group's work on the activity. To help you make this assessment, take some time to explain to the children the importance of clearly identifying all the group members involved in preparing the report.

Another component of assessing the quality of a write-up is determining whether an incomplete report shows a lack of effort on the child's part or a limitation in his or her ability to use language. The only way to make this distinction is to ask the child clarifying questions.

Go to **MyEducationLab**, select the topic Assessment, watch the video entitled "Standardized Tests," and complete the questions that accompany it.

● Standardized Tests

If you walk down a school hallway and notice that it is strangely quiet, that the children are seated quietly at their desks, and that the public address system is not blaring messages, chances are the children are taking a standardized test. For some reason, standardized tests create a time of palpable quiet and anxiety.

In addition to the usual battery of IQ tests and personality inventories, some school districts have children take achievement tests in a variety of subjects. If you teach in a school that requires a standardized science achievement test, you may find that *you* are more concerned about the results than the children are.

▶ *What Do They Accomplish?*

A standardized achievement test in science compares how much the children in your class know compared to children nationwide, as reflected in norms. If the children in your class do well, it may make you feel very successful. If they do poorly, you may feel obliged to rethink what and how you are teaching. The results provide teachers, administrators, and members of the community with an opportunity to compare the success of their children to that of children around the country.

▶ *What Don't They Accomplish?*

If you have been teaching science using a hands-on, discovery-focused approach, you may have good reason to be anxious when the children in your class are expected to display a command of the basic subject matter on a standardized test. After all, teaching science in a hands-on fashion may not provide the background in science knowledge that children from more traditional textbook-oriented classrooms have. On the other hand, the children in your class will probably have acquired many inquiry process skills and have developed a favorable attitude toward science. Standardized achievement tests will not reveal your success in helping children grasp central science concepts through hands-on experimentation.

Using Standardized Achievement Tests More Effectively   First, help children understand that the results of a standardized test will not measure all that they have learned. If, for example, your class has carried out a hands-on unit on the use and waste of water in your school, explain to the children that they should not expect to see questions about it on the test. Point out that some of the science units they have studied have given them a lot of information that will not be measured. Emphasize that they should not feel bad if many of the things they have learned are not on the test.

Also, take some class time before the test to teach basic standardized test-taking strategies. The children likely will take many standardized tests while they are students and when they pursue employment. Investing time and energy to improve test-taking skills may annoy you because of your own feelings about testing, but it may help children become more successful test takers.

Rubrics and Scoring Guides

Go to **MyEducationLab**, select the topic Assessment, watch the video entitled "Forms of Assessment," and complete the questions that accompany it.

Most of the assessment strategies presented to this point are fine for collecting data in the form of student outcomes. Frankly, collecting student work is relatively easy compared to analyzing student outcomes and making judgments about a student's performance. For each assessment strategy, you will need to make a tool to analyze the outcomes. Most often you will use an answer key or a rubric.

Answer keys are helpful when clearly defined answers are required. The students either name the parts of a flower or they don't. Rubrics, on the other hand, provide a guide for you to evaluate less structured and more open-ended responses typical of students seeking to provide explanations. They are often helpful when assessing process rather than factual content. There are two basic forms of rubric: analytical and holistic. Analytical rubrics specify performances for each criterion. They provide more detail about a student's performance. Holistic rubrics provide a general assessment based on all the criteria at once. They do not disaggregate performance on each criterion and are better for quick evaluations of student work.

I rewrote the rubric used earlier for Mrs. Riley's plants using all three forms. Note that rubrics all include criteria, performance for criteria, and a rating scale. They differ by degrees of specificity.

Analytical List: Lists desired performance for each criterion

Criteria	Performance	Potential score	Student score
Prediction	Prediction is testable	1	
Test of prediction	Implies treatment	1	
	Implies control	1	
	Identifies observables (color, height . . .)	1	
Daily observations	Makes daily entries	1	
	Uses words to describe observables	1	
	Uses drawings to describe observables	1	
	Observations are accurate	1	
Results	Results are consistent with observations	1	
Explanation	Students relate that the presence of light is necessary for Mrs. Riley's plants to live	1	
Total possible score		10	

Analytical Continuum: Specifies levels of performance for each criterion

Criteria	Meets criteria 3 pts	Satisfactory 2 pts	Needs improvement 1 pt
Prediction	Clearly stated, testable	Stated but not clearly testable	Difficult to discern prediction
Test of prediction	Demonstrates experimental model: Clearly implies treatment Experimental control Variable control Identifies observables (color, height . . .)	Implies treatment Suggests an awareness of controls but does not clearly discern variables or observables	Does not suggest an awareness of an experimental model
Daily observations	Evidence of descriptive modeling, addresses elements, rules of interaction, and background space Makes comprehensive daily entries Uses drawings to describe observables Observations are accurate	Makes daily observations Observations are generally accurate Intermittently supported by text or drawings Moderate evidence of descriptive modeling	Sporadic entries Little or no evidence of descriptive modeling
Results	Results are consistent with observations	Results exhibit some inconsistencies with observations	Results are inconsistent with observations
Explanation	Explanatory model based on descriptive model	Explanatory model partially based on descriptive modeling	Explanatory model is unrelated to descriptive model
	Students relate that the presence of light is necessary for Mrs. Riley's plants to live	Students relate light to plant growth in general without expressing cause and effect related to Mrs. Riley's plants	Students demonstrate no awareness of the relationship of light to plant growth
Total possible score	15		

Holistic Rubric: Does not list specific levels of performance for each criterion. It provides a general assessment based on overall criteria

Meets criteria
- Makes a clear and testable prediction
- Designs a solid experiment with appropriate controls and variables
- Records accurate and informative daily observations
- Results are consistent with observations
- Explanation is consistent with observations

Satisfactory
- Prediction is stated but not testable
- Experimental design has most of the controls and variables
- Observations are fairly consistent and descriptive
- Results are mostly consistent
- Explanation relates light to plant growth

Needs improvement
- Prediction is difficult to discern
- Demonstrates little awareness of experimental design
- Exhibits minimal descriptive modeling
- Results are largely inconsistent with observations
- Does not articulate a connection between plant growth and light

Reality Check

It is your first parent conference night. You are well prepared, having displayed student work for the parents, being sure to include a sample from every child in your class. You have portfolios for each student as well as their grades on all the assignments to date. Although you look forward to meeting the parents of your students, you are also a bit anxious. It will be easy to report to the parents of the students who are doing well, but what do you say to the parents of the children who seem to be struggling? You are particularly concerned about explaining Amanda's performance in science to her parents. You search for a way to describe her performance in a manner that will be informative and constructive. While reviewing Amanda's portfolio, you realize that she has done well on matching and fill in the blank sections of probes and that she is often but not always able to link ideas on concept maps and diagrams, but she does not perform well on performance assessments that require her to generate explanations. Based on the following guide, what can you tell Amanda's parents about the level of understanding exhibited by Amanda?

Level of understanding	Assessment strategies	Comments
Nominal	Matching Fill in blank Vocabulary quiz	Demonstrates ability to identify and associate elements and concepts Answers often memorized No indication of deep understanding
Descriptive	Concept map Diagram Essay Poster Lab report Activity write up	Demonstrates ability to express rules of interaction/connections among elements
Explanatory	Performance assessment Lab practical Model Simulation	Demonstrates ability to propose an explanation or demonstrate ability based on the rules of interaction among the elements of the system

Sample response: Amanda does well identifying scientific terms and recognizing most of the main concepts. Her concept maps and diagrams demonstrate that she is able to recognize the fundamental relationships and main connections among most of the science concepts. She is off to a good start. The next step for Amanda is to use her ability to create good descriptive models and recognize important connections to generate responses to open-ended questions more independently. I will continue to help her make the transition to this higher level of mastery by providing her with opportunities to use her concept maps, which she does quite well, as a guide to generate answers to open-ended questions. You can support her in this at home by suggesting that she make a concept map when she is working on a response to an open-ended question and help her use the concept map by pointing out connections that lead to an explanation. We should see her progress in her responses to open-response questions on standardized testing this spring.

Summary

A teacher asks, "Did I teach you that?"

Now comes the real challenge: How do you create a meaningful assessment system that will tell whether your students understand the science content and can conduct inquiry?

Use as your foundation the major approaches to assessment discussed in this chapter. Then consider your curriculum—specific units you teach or observe being taught. With that material in mind, try to answer the question, "What is the ideal way to assess whether children are understanding and inquiring successfully?" Certainly, the answer must lie in your clever integration of assessment strategies plus your familiarity with what you teach.

Assessment lets you know the impact of the many hours spent planning and agonizing to get a lesson or unit just right. Good assessment begins with the identification of clear and concise content to be taught and an awareness of the student behaviors and outcomes that you will measure to indicate learning. Remember there is no one-size-fits-all assessment strategy. Use a variety of traditional and performance assessments to meet your needs. For example, suppose a child does poorly on a quiz but evidence from formative assessments such as science notebooks and probes suggests that the child is more proficient than the quiz suggests. You can follow up the quiz with a student conference to gain better insights about the child's understanding and level of mastery. Use the guide in Figure 6.4 to help you plan your assessment. Many other questions will also likely come to mind as you reflect on the results you acquired by using the guide.

The "bottom line" for assessment is that you need to use a variety of measures because you will have a variety of students in terms of achievement levels, aptitudes, and attitudes. If you are able to assess students' performance well and then use that information gathered sensibly, your students will become better students and you, of course, will become an even better teacher.

Figure 6.4 Use the guide to help you plan your assessment.

- Know what you intend to teach
    Look to the content to be taught for guidance

- Decide which of your assessments will be formative or summative
    On the path to learning (formative)
    Mastery of content (summative)

- Know which student performances indicate learning
    Look to your performance objectives for guidance
    Be sure that the criteria are measurable

- Choose assessment strategies that meet your needs

- Develop a rubric that you can use to analyze student outcomes

Going Further

On Your Own

1. Imagine that you are an elementary- or middle-grade science teacher who has just received a $1,000 grant to improve the strategies and techniques used to assess children in science. What would you spend the money on? Explain your rationale.

2. Select a science topic you might teach to children at a grade level of your choice. For that topic, suggest a specific subject for an age-appropriate, inquiry-based project. Then briefly describe how you would apply the strategies suggested by the NSES to determine whether the children were successful in completing the project.

On Your Own or in a Cooperative Learning Group

3. Create a poster listing five techniques children should use to prepare for a traditional science unit test. Highlight techniques that you or members of your group learned through direct experience as students.

4. Imagine that you and some other teachers have decided to give a Back-to-School Night presentation that will provide the rationale for using science portfolios in place of traditional assessment techniques. Prepare a PowerPoint presentation that you could use as part of the presentation.

5. On a sheet of newsprint, have your group identify one science topic at a grade level of interest. Under that topic, list three or four "content points" that children should understand by the time the unit has been completed. Show that you can implement the techniques suggested by the NSES for gauging how well children understand the content points. Identify a prompt and a scoring rubric that a teacher could implement to assess understanding.

Resources for Discovery Learning

Internet Resources

 To access these helpful websites, go to **MyEducationLab**, select Resources, and then Web Links. To learn more, click on the following links and you will easily be directed to each website.

- **Association for Supervision and Curriculum Development:**
  www.ascd.org/portal/site/ascd

- **Authentic Assessment Toolbox:**
  http://jonathan.mueller.faculty.noctrl.edu/toolbox/index.htm

- **Science Notebooks in K12 Classrooms:**
  www.sciencenotebooks.org/

- **Trends in International Mathematics and Science Study:**
  nces.ed.gov/timss

- **Programs for International Student Assessment**
  www.nces.ed.gov.surveys/pisa

Print Resources

Suggested Readings

Barton, James, and Collins, Angelo. *Portfolio Assessment.* White Plains, NY: Dale Seymour, 1997.

Brown, Janet Harley, and Shavelson, Richard. *Assessing Hands-On Science.* Thousand Oaks, CA: Corwin Press, 1996.

Classroom Assessment in the National Science Education Standards. Washington, D.C. National Academy of Science, 2001.

Coray, Gail. "Rubrics Made Simple." *Science Scope* 23, no. 6 (March 2000): 38–49.

Craven, John A., and Hogan, Tracy. *Science Scope* 25, no. 1 (September 2001): 36–40.

Davis, Elizabeth A., and Kirkpatrick, Doug. "It's All the News: Critiquing Evidence and Claims. *Science Scope* 25, no. 5 (February 2002): 32–37.

Demers, Chris. "Beyond Paper-and-Pencil Assessments." *Science and Children* 38, no. 2 (October 2000): 24–29, 60.

Eberle, F. et al. "Formative Assessment Probes." *Science and Children* 45, no. 5 (January 2008): 50–54.

Enger, Sandra, and Yager, Robert. *Assessing Student Understanding in Science.* Thousand Oaks, CA: Corwin Press, 2001.

Franklin, John. "Assessing Assessment." *Curriculum Update* (Spring 2002): 1–8.

Gandal, Matthew, and McGiffert, Laura. "The Power of Testing." *Educational Leadership* 60, no. 5 (February 2003): 39–42.

Goodnough, Karen, and Long, Robin. "Mind Mapping: A Graphic Organizer for the Pedagogical Toolbox." *Science Scope* 25, no. 8 (May 2002): 20–24.

Guskey, Thomas R. "How Classroom Assessments Improve Learning." *Educational Leadership* 60, no. 5 (February 2003): 6–11.

Jabot, M., et al. "Mental Models of Elementary and Middle School Students in Analyzing Simple Battery and Bulb Circuits." *School Science and Mathematics* 107, no. 1 (January 2007): 371–381.

Neill, Monty. "The Dangers of Testing." *Educational Leadership* 60, no. 5 (February 2003): 43–45.

Olson, Joanne K., and Cox-Peterson, Anne M. "An Authentic Science Conference." *Science and Children* 38, no. 6 (March 2001): 40–45.

Otero, V. K., et al. "Preservice Elementary Teachers' Views of Their Students' Prior Knowledge of Science." *Journal of Research in Science Teaching* 45, no. 4 (April 2008): 497–523.

Pelligrino, James W. "Knowing What Students Know." *Issues in Science and Technology* 19, no. 2 (Winter 2002–2003): 48–52.

Sclafani, Susan. "No Child Left Behind." *Issues in Science and Technology* 19, no. 2 (Winter 2002–2003): 43–47.

Shepardson, Daniel P., and Britsch, Susan J. "Analyzing Children's Science Journals." *Science and Children* 38, no. 3 (November/December 2000): 29–33.

Smith, Deborah C., and Wesley, Ann. "Teaching for Understanding." *Science and Children* 38, no. 1 (September 2000): 36–41.

Stavy, Ruth, and Tirosh, Dina. *How Students (Mis-) Understand Science and Mathematics.* New York: Teachers College Press, 2000.

Stearns, Carole, and Courtney, Rosalea. "Designing Assessments with the Standards." *Science and Children* 37, no. 4 (January 2000): 51–55.

Sunda, Ruth. "Thinking about Thinking—What Makes a Good Question?" *Learning & Leading with Technology* 30, no. 5 (February 2003): 10–15.

Varelas, Maria, et al. "Examining Language to Capture Scientific Understandings." *Science and Children* 38, no. 7 (April 2001): 26–29.

Ward, Robin E., and Wandersee, James. "Roundhouse Diagrams." *Science Scope* 24, no. 4 (January 2000): 17–27.

Waters, M., et al. "Science Rocks! A Performance Assessment for Earth Science." *Science Activities* 45, no. 1 (Spring 2008): 23–28.

Notes

1. Association for Supervision and Curriculum Development. www.ascd.org/portal/site/ascd (accessed 05-26-08).
2. J. Myron Atkin, Paul Black, and Janet Coffey, eds. *Classroom Assessment in the National Science Education Standards.* (Washington, D.C.: National Academy of Science 2001), p. 25. Reprinted with permission from the National Academics Press, Copyright © 2001, National Academy of Sciences.
3. Funderstanding. www.funderstanding.com/index.html (accessed 05-26-08).
4. For a detailed discussion of the use of prompts and scoring rubrics, see National Research Council, *National Science Education Standards* (Washington, DC: National Academy Press, 1996), pp. 91–98.
5. J. Myron Atkin, Paul Black, and Janet Coffey, eds. *Classroom Assessment in the National Science Education Standards* (Washington, D.C.: National Academy of Science, 2001) p. 60.
6. Ibid., p. 25.

chapter 7

Integrating Science

*How can I integrate inquiry-based science
with other subjects in a child's school day?*

▶ **Getting Started**

Sarah was excited to finally have her own classroom. As a student teacher she always felt
like a guest, no matter how gracious an effort her cooperating teacher made to help
Sarah feel welcome. Sarah knew and the students knew that it really was not her class.
Today she had a totally different feeling as she entered the school as a full-fledged faculty
member. There were still several weeks remaining before the first class, but she wanted to
begin planning the curriculum and preparing the room for that first day in September.
As she entered the room she noticed a vase of flowers on the desk. She was very lucky to
have such a thoughtful mentor teacher. This was going to be a wonderful year. Next to
the vase lay the district curriculum frameworks. Her mentor teacher suggested that she
familiarize herself with the frameworks before planning the curriculum. The document
seemed awfully thick as Sarah lifted it and began to read through it. An hour later, her
initial excitement dampened, Sarah wondered how she was ever going to cover all the
content. There were standards for language arts, history and social science, mathematics,
science, as well as health, art, and English language proficiency. Sarah knew that each
subject was not a separate entity, at least not in real life, and that she had to integrate the

content not only to cover it, but also to enrich the learning experience for her students. However, integration is easier said than done. She was going to need some help.

The good news for Sarah and all teachers is that human knowledge is interconnected. In fact, the same strategies for discovery and inquiry used in science apply across disciplines. The historian seeking to explain the causes of the American Revolution would ask about the key issues, how they are related, their contexts, and how they merged to create conditions ripe for a revolution. The literary agent reviewing a book might ask about the characters, how they are related, and how the time period or social context come together to form the plot. These are nothing more than versions of the more general fundamental questions of inquiry: What are the elements, rules of interaction, and background space that lead to the emergent properties of the system? This way of thinking connects learning in different domains to a common process of inquiry and discovery.

As you plan science units, remember that science experiences can draw together a variety of subjects, acting as a kind of "superglue" that connects the learning in a range of areas and shows how human knowledge and experience fit together to form a larger, more meaningful whole. So let's consider some practical things you can do to integrate science with other subjects.

Go to **MyEducationLab**, select the topic Cross-Curricular Connections, watch the video entitled "Integration," and complete the question that accompanies it.

Project 2061

Implications for Integrating Science across the Subject Areas

Project 2061 provides strong guidance for integrating science with mathematics and technology, using particular themes. And you can use these themes to find ways of integrating science with other subjects in the curriculum (something that Project 2061 does not do directly).

Here are the themes that Project 2061 provides for tying together science, mathematics, and technology:

- Systems
- Models
- Constancy and change
- Scale

Using "Systems" as a theme, for example, you would teach children that a whole object, event, or interaction is made of parts, that those parts relate to each other, and that those parts affect the whole. Using the theme of "Models," you would teach that models are either real things or ideas that are used as tools to understand the world. The theme of "Constancy and change" addresses those ideas and discoveries that have withstood the test of time along with the nature of change and how small changes can have large effects. Finally, in teaching the theme of "Scale," you would help children see that things that differ from one another in terms of size, weight, or any other variable may also behave differently.

Specific recommendations for implementing these four themes are available at the Project 2061 website: **www.project2061.org/.**

Science and the Language Arts

"That cloud looks like a pregnant polar bear."

Children have a natural inclination to react to the world around them, and they absorb information from what they see, hear, taste, and touch as well as what they read. They can also respond in many ways, talking, writing, and drawing about what they absorb. Like scientists, children develop a repertoire of specific reading and writing process skills that enable them to carefully observe and react to what they experience through their senses. The next few sections will describe techniques you can use to help children expand both their science and their language arts abilities.

Selecting Trade Books That Stimulate Inquiry and Discovery

Do you love books? I certainly hope so! One feature of your classroom should be an extensive collection of books that motivate children to think and engage in inquiry-based, discovery-focused science.

Trade books are volumes distributed by commercial publishers that do just that. They are not textbooks. Instead, they present about scientific adventures, the lives of scientists, science careers, and provide factual material about stars, planets, dolphins, the rain forest, and much more.

How can you select the best possible trade books for your children? Try using the following criteria, which were suggested by a distinguished panel of teachers and other science educators:

- The book has a substantial amount of science content.
- The information presented is clear, accurate, and up-to-date.
- Theories and facts are clearly distinguished.
- Facts are not oversimplified so as to make the information misleading.
- Generalizations are supported by facts, and significant facts are not left out.
- The book does not contain gender, ethnic, or socioeconomic bias.[1]

I won't provide you with a list of recommended science trade books, because so many new ones appear each month. Instead, I'll direct you to two excellent and easily accessible sources that *will* provide you lists of the very best modern trade books for children and youths:

1. An annual article in *Science and Children* whose title is always "Outstanding Science Trade Books for Students K–12"
2. The Internet site www.nsta.org, where you may select the feature "NSTA Recommends"

Three Integrating Techniques

As the children entered the classroom on Monday morning, their exclamations could be heard the length of the hallway. "Wow!" "What happened here?" "It's beautiful!"

Over the weekend, their fourth-grade teacher had transformed the classroom into a tropical rain forest. The children knew that this was going to be no ordinary day. But their teacher was no ordinary teacher.[2]

Indeed, any teacher who finds creative ways to cross subject matter barriers using language arts as the bridge is special. You can be such a teacher if you focus on actively finding techniques to tie science and language arts together. Rakow and Vasquez, who described the fourth-grade teacher in the preceding excerpt, suggest three ways to do this:

1. *Literature-based integration* is simply the use of modern nonfiction science books, such as the trade books just discussed, to help children acquire science-related information. Additionally, for those children who might benefit from getting science information through a story line, many fictional books by authors such as Eric Carle and Tomie dePaola have science information and concepts threaded through them.

2. *Theme-based integration* is instruction in which a major theme or concept becomes the foundation for a learning unit that cuts across subject lines. Think in creative ways as you identify a theme such as "Ecosystems," "Space Neighbors" for astronomy, or "Animals with Pouches" for the life sciences.

3. *Project-based integration* involves children in actually carrying out a long-term activity in which they investigate a real-world problem. Here are a few examples of science-related projects that provide excellent opportunities to tie language arts development to science content:
   - Discovering the amount of paper wasted each day in a classroom or school and communicating ideas to others that will help solve the problem
   - Discovering how much water is wasted at school water fountains each day or week and communicating ideas to others that will help stop the waste
   - Discovering how well school hot lunch offerings and student choices match proper nutrition guidelines and communicating ideas to others that will help children choose better lunches[3]

Science-related projects provide excellent opportunities for integrating the language arts.

Weaving It All Together with Language Arts

Class time overflows with children dictating stories, chanting, singing, speaking, writing, constructing "big books," and the like. These experiences help children develop and improve their language arts skills.

Language arts teaching strategies can be easily adapted to enrich and extend children's science experiences. Writing stories about butterflies and rockets, making "big books" about insects, and writing and singing songs about saving the earth's natural resources are activities that involve children in a variety of science topics and help develop their language arts skills.

I hope that you will create appropriate ways to develop each component of the language arts through science. In the sections that follow, you will find some very specific ways to achieve a science/language arts synergy.

Extending the Basics: Vocabulary, Comprehension, and Writing

Using Descriptive Modeling to Build Vocabulary   Someday, somewhere, some child will come up to you, look you straight in the eye, and ask with a giggle, "What grows down while growing up?" And you will enjoy not only the joke but also what telling it has to say about that child's ability to use language.

Unfortunately, for many children, words and their meanings are *not* sources of jokes and riddles. For these children, words are mysterious combinations of ink marks that make little sense and create little pleasure. If you are not alert to the need to teach and reinforce reading skill development, the printed page of a science book can serve as a source of frustration for a child with limited vocabulary skills.

Reality Check

When developing theme-based science units, avoid broad topics such as, "The Rain Forest," or the "Oceans of the World." Rather, identify a science concept and essential question that will serve as the focus of inquiry, such as "Rain forests and oceans: How can they both be ecosystems?" This theme develops the concept of ecosystems, rather than the rain forest or ocean as entities in and of themselves. Most of your students will live neither in the rain forest nor the ocean, but all will live in an ecosystem.

Below are broad topics for theme-based integration. Rewrite each with an essential question that reflects a science concept.

Theme	Essential question
Volcanoes	
Adaptation	
Minerals	
Earthquakes	
The solar system	
Life cycles	

Descriptive modeling provides a meaningful context for children to use words and consequently build their vocabulary. Here are some specific strategies that you can use to help children broaden their vocabulary through descriptive modeling:

1. Provide a list of descriptive terms that children can use while developing their descriptive models.

2. Post new science words and their definition as they emerge in class on a piece of newsprint or poster board to create word banks. Keep the word banks posted in the room for children to refer to during the unit.

3. Look through science trade books and elementary science textbooks before the children work with them *to identify terms that may be too difficult to learn from the context,* and then preteach those words.

4. *Pronounce science vocabulary words with children* before they reach them in their science materials.

5. *Have each child develop a personal word card file* that lists and defines each new science word. Each card should include the word, the sentence in which the word was found, a phonetic respelling of the word, and, if appropriate, a drawing or diagram showing the object or concept that the word defines.

Comprehension   The quest to seek explanations makes science a compelling backdrop for comprehension. If children are engaged and invested in finding an answer, then they will be more motivated to read for understanding.

You can help children build their comprehension skills in science by focusing their attention on prereading experiences. Before the children begin reading a specific text, trade book, or Internet article, focus your discussion of the material around three magic words:

1. *What?* When you distribute trade books, text material, or resource material on a science topic, take the time to discuss exactly what you expect the children to do with it. Describe how much time they will have and what they are expected to produce as a result of the reading.

2. *Why?* Take the time to explain to children why they are going to do the assignment. Do your best to describe how it will relate to work they have done before and work that will follow.

3. *How?* Describe how you expect children to learn from the material they are reading. You might say something like this: "Here are some topics you can use to organize the information you get about the planets from your reading: What is the planet's size compared to Earth? What is the surface like? How long is a day on the planet? Why don't you list them in your science notebook before you start reading. That way, you will have a specific place to put the information that you find in the book."

Writing

> *Writing is like talking to your best friend.* —Eric, a first-grader
>
> *Writing is a dance in the sun.* —Christi Ann, a second-grader
>
> *Writing is meeting the person in me I never knew.* —Mike, a seventh-grader[4]

This excerpt from *Reading and Learning to Read* tells a lot about the power you give children when you help them learn how to move their thoughts to a page. Science classrooms that provide children with opportunities to explore the natural world are places that provoke thought and thus create an unending array of possibilities for communication through the powerful medium of the written word. When you are teaching science, you are offering the possibility of many "dances in the sun."

You are quite fortunate when you teach children science because the breadth of content, processes, and affect that you teach is well matched by the range of writing forms that elementary school children need to practice. In *Language Arts: Learning Processes and Teaching Practices,* Temple and Gillet suggest that there are six basic writing forms:

Description	Expression	Persuasion
Exposition	Narration	Poetry[5]

Here are some examples of how you can help children develop their abilities with each writing form. I am sure that you can suggest many others.[6]

- *Description.* Have the children describe in detail an animal they observe on a class trip to a zoo.
- *Exposition.* Have the children explain how to make a flashlight lamp light using just one battery, one wire, and one bulb.
- *Expression.* Have the children write thank-you letters to a park ranger who visited the class to talk about protecting the natural environment.
- *Narration.* Have the children write stories about an incident in the life of a young girl who decides to be the first astronaut to set foot on the planet Mars.
- *Persuasion.* Have the children write scripts for a children's television commercial that will convince others to eat more green, leafy vegetables.
- *Poetry.* Have the children observe and draw a seashell and then write poems that use at least three of the observations they made about the shell.

Science and Mathematics

"Whose mine is it?" asked Milo, stepping around two of the loaded wagons.

"BY THE FOUR MILLION EIGHT HUNDRED AND TWENTY-SEVEN THOUSAND SIX HUNDRED AND FIFTY-NINE HAIRS ON MY HEAD, IT'S MINE, OF COURSE," bellowed a voice from across the cavern. And striding toward them came a figure who could only have been the Mathemagician.

He was dressed in a long flowing robe covered entirely with complex mathematical equations and a tall pointed cap that made him look very wise. In his left hand he carried a long staff with a pencil point at one end and a large rubber eraser at the other.[7]

This excerpt from *The Phantom Tollbooth* comes from the part of the book in which Milo, the watchdog Tock, and the Dodecahedron are about to find out where numbers come from.

"So that's where they come from," said Milo, looking in awe at the glittering collection of numbers. He returned them to the Dodecahedron as carefully as possible but, as he did, one dropped to the floor with a smash and broke in two. The Humbug winced and Milo looked terribly concerned.

"Oh, don't worry about that," said the Mathemagician as he scooped up the pieces. "We use the broken ones for fractions."[8]

The journey of Milo and his friends to the numbers mine has always struck me as an excellent frame of reference for both understanding the difficulties children may have with mathematics and helping them overcome those difficulties. Some children view numbers as squiggly lines on paper that have no basis in reality. For all they know, numbers come from number mines! Although there are many aspects of elementary school mathematics that can be reinforced, extended, and enriched as children do science, three are particularly important: computational skills; data collection and expression; and logical reasoning.[9]

● Computational Skills

Figure 7.1 provides examples of various ways in which computational skills can be practiced and put to real work during science. As you look over the figure, see if you can think of other ways to have children work on computation as they carry out science activities and projects.

● Data Collection and Expression

Zing! Another rubber band flies across the science classroom. Is this a sign of unmotivated students in an undisciplined classroom? Not this time. This otherwise unruly behavior is actually part of a hands-on activity that teaches students the basics of graphing and experimental design.[10]

Although I definitely don't suggest this particular activity for either brand-new or veteran teachers with limited classroom management skills, I share it with you to focus attention on what a creative science teacher can do to build a child's science/math skills. Even though shooting rubber bands will not be your first choice as an activity to use when your school principal is observing your magnificent teaching talents, it does provide a good data-collection and data-expression experience. Notice the true sophistication of the activity:

In this experiment the independent (or manipulated) variable is the width of the rubber bands and the dependent (or responding) variable is the distance they fly. Does the width of a rubber band affect the distance it travels? Ask students to write a prediction using an if-then sentence format that states how the independent variable will affect the dependent variable. Once they have constructed a prediction, let the rubber bands fly![11]

Figure 7.1
A variety of science activities can be done to improve math computational skills.

Computational Skill	Science-Teaching Example
• Counting	Determine the number of pieces of litter on the school lawn.
• Addition	Keep track of the number of birds that visit a feeder.
• Subtraction	Measure children's heights at the beginning and end of the year and calculate growth.
• Multiplication	Estimate the number of birds in a flock on the school lawn by first counting a small group and then multiplying by the number of groups.
• Division	Do a school survey of animals in classrooms, and find the average number in each.
• Working with fractions	Place half a collection of seeds in moist soil and half in dry soil, and compare their relative growth.
• Working with decimals and percentages	Study the list of ingredients and the nutrition chart on a box of sweetened cereal, and figure out what part of the weight of the cereal is sugar.

Even if you are not quite ready (or will never be ready) to extend science through rubber band shooting, you can do equally interesting, if not equally exciting, activities that lead to data collection and expression. For example, you can have the children observe changes in the level of water in an open container. Begin by having a child place a mark on the container to show the present water level. The children can then mark the level each day for several days. At the end of the time, the children can measure the distance from the first mark to the new marks and make graphs to show the changes.

Can very young children express data through graphs and charts? They certainly can! By cutting paper strips that represent the distance from the water level to the original mark in the preceding example, the measurement for each day can be recorded. The paper strips can then be placed in sequence to produce a rudimentary graph of changes in water level.

Make the Case *An Individual or Group Challenge*

The Problem

As a result of their school and real-world experiences, children may conclude that science is an isolated and complex branch of human knowledge.

Assess Your Prior Knowledge and Beliefs

Check your beliefs and knowledge about the following:

1. Children in the elementary grades learn that science is separate and different from other subjects.

   strongly disagree   disagree   agree   strongly agree

2. Children in the elementary grades learn that science is difficult.

   strongly disagree   disagree   agree   strongly agree

3. In the middle grades, children experience science as a separate subject.

   strongly disagree   disagree   agree   strongly agree

4. In the middle grades, children learn that science is a difficult subject.

   strongly disagree   disagree   agree   strongly agree

5. Science activities in most elementary- and middle-grade textbooks and resource books connect science to other school subjects.

   strongly disagree   disagree   agree   strongly agree

The Challenge

Before being interviewed for a teaching position, you review the science curriculum and notice that it includes sample science activities. At the end of each activity is the side heading "Connections," which suggests how to relate the activity to other subjects. During the interview, the interviewer tells you, "We are so excited about our new curriculum. It is really interdisciplinary. I think you've had a chance to look it over. What do you think of it?" How would you respond?

Following the data-gathering process, the children can be led through a discussion of the lengths of their paper strips. Their understanding of math concepts can be probed and developed with questions such as these:

1. Can you explain why the strips are different lengths?
2. How much longer is the longest strip than the shortest?
3. How do the changes shown by your strips compare with those shown by other children's strips?

Logical Reasoning

An important goal of mathematics education for children is to develop an understanding of the logical structure of mathematics. In practice, this means a child is able to look at collections of items and make statements about them and the outcomes of grouping and regrouping them. This is the mathematics of sets and subsets, open sentences, and the commutative, associative, and distributive properties. Science experiences can provide children with opportunities to put their understanding of mathematical concepts to work. You could, for example, have the children in your class do these activities:

1. Group collections of plants into sets and subsets.
2. Devise a system for classifying organisms into the set of all plants and the set of all animals.
3. Identify the similarities and differences of various elements of the set of all birds and fish.
4. Use a list of characteristics to determine whether an organism is part of such subsets as fish, birds, and reptiles.

Science and the Social Studies

"After analyzing what kind of garbage was in and around the creek (like grocery carts, litter, and car tires), the students agreed that the source of the trash was from various people and places. When the students had decided who was responsible, it was more difficult for them to decide who should help with their cleanup. How could they ask people in the apartments to come clean up the creek safely and without offending them?"[12]

Social studies and science can easily be integrated, because societal problems, in many cases, lend themselves to real-life inquiry-based experiences for children. The outdoor experience just described shows how challenging children with meaningful projects can tie together science and social studies. And in doing so, it can raise important issues about individual and societal attitudes and values.

Attitude and value development is an important dimension of social studies that can easily be integrated with science. Children who learn that questions of values cut across content areas are more apt to appreciate the significance of such topics. Here is a sampling of the types of questions you can use to stimulate attitude- and value-based science discussions and to generate ideas for activities and projects that relate science and social studies:

1. Should animals be kept in zoos?
2. Should cities and towns have animal control officers?

Figure 7.2
Many social studies topics can be extended through science activities.

Social Studies Topic	Related Science Concept
• The natural resources of a country	The sun as the original energy source in the solar system
	The protection of air and water resources
	The use of alternative energy sources
• The history and development of a country or part of the world	Contributions made by specific scientists and inventors
• The employment of North Americans in diverse occupations	Career awareness for occupations in science and technology
• The structure of the family and other social groups; the interaction of group members	The effect of improved technology on providing increased leisure time
• The production, transportation, and consumption of goods and services	The improvement of the quality and quantity of agricultural products through selective breeding and food preservation technology

3. Should a factory that provides many jobs for people but also pollutes the town's air and water be closed down?

4. Should people be required to wear seat belts?

5. Should commercials for sugar-sweetened cereals be shown during Saturday morning children's shows?

As with any science lesson or unit, clearly identify the targeted scientific content to be taught. If you prepare a science unit on pollution, consider the science behind the pollution. For example, if you choose a lesson on oil pollution, address the effect of oil on the capacity for bird feathers to repel water or on the density of oil compared to water. When children address legal and social issues such as whether there should be offshore oil drilling, encourage them to use reasoning based on the science rather than pure emotion.

Also see Figure 7.2, which shows how a number of social studies topics can be extended through related science content. Integrating these two content areas will help children realize the science/social studies connection.

Science and Art

Recently, I began to plan a unit on the human body. In an art unit that I had done a few years ago, the class used fabric crayons to make a wall mural for display in the hall. So I decided to use these crayons to make ourselves walking, anatomically correct models of the digestive and respiratory systems.[13]

Jackie Moore, the teacher who came up with this clever idea, goes on to explain that first she had each child bring in a white, cotton-blend T-shirt. The fabric crayons were

Figure 7.3
These sample activities integrate art and science.

- *Tree Stump Rubbings:* Place paper on a smooth, recently cut tree stump, and rub the paper with a pencil. Follow-up activities may include discussions about climatic changes, as reflected in changes in the annual ring pattern, and how to find the age of the tree.

- *Leaf Rubbings:* Place paper over a variety of leaves, and rub the paper with the side of a crayon. Follow-up activities can include observation of leaf veins in the print and discussion of the variety of leaves found or defects in leaf surfaces as a result of insect activity.

- *Native Crafts:* Use natural objects to make sculptures, including mobiles or stabiles, and pictures. Examples include stone people, acorn people, apple-head dolls, fruit and vegetable prints, dried flowers, and shell sculptures.

- *Sand Painting:* After studying the origin and characteristics of sand, dye the sand to use in sand paintings. This can be integrated with social studies, since it is an activity that comes from the heritage of native North Americans.

- *Moving Sculpture:* Build simple circuits to operate sculptures that have moving parts as well as blinking lights.

used to draw the systems and organ labels on paper, and the drawings were then ironed on the shirts. She describes the culminating activity this way:

> To show off our beautiful bodies all my 125 students wore their shirts on the same day. Quite a sight to behold! Interestingly enough, the students do better on questions dealing with these two systems than on any of the other systems that we study.[14]

This activity shows how you can easily encourage children to use art with science and thereby help them see the relationship between art and science. There are many other activities that you can use to accomplish this. Use those described in Figure 7.3 to get you started on developing your own strategies for relating science and art.

Science and Music

Music has become so much a part of our daily lives that we are sometimes oblivious to it, but the children that you teach are not. Even very young children are able to hum, dance, whistle, and sing a multitude of breakfast cereal commercials and know some of the words and phrases of the most popular songs on MTV. Music has had a profound impact upon our culture, and we should be able to take advantage of its ability to attract and hold a child's attention when we teach science.

Hapai and Burton have prepared a helpful resource book called *BugPlay* that offers many strategies for integrating one common science topic—insects—with the rest of the school curriculum. One of my favorite songs from this book, and a favorite of children for obvious reasons, is "Cock-a-Roaches."[15]

Another strategy for relating music and science is to locate music that was composed to express feelings about topics that you are covering in science. For example, if you teach the four seasons, you can fill your classroom with selections from Vivaldi's Concerto in F Minor, op. 8, no. 4, "Winter," from *The Four Seasons.*

Science and Health and Physical Education

The sun is shining. Feel its warm glow on your seed bodies. Now it's raining . . . a gentle rain. You are beginning to grow ever so slowly. Feel your sides enlarge. What are you growing into? A dandelion? A flower? A blade of grass? A young sapling? Feel your arms and fingers stretch into leaves, petals, or branches. S-T-R-E-T-C-H. Reach for the sky. Reach for the sun. Now there's a wind, a gentle breeze. Now there's a rainstorm. Move as a flower, plant, or tree would move in a rainstorm. Now the sun is peeking out from behind a cloud. Fill your body with its wonderful warmth. Breathe in the air . . . in and out . . . in and out.[16]

Wouldn't doing this activity be a nice way to review some of the concepts taught in a unit on green plants while helping a child develop his or her motor skills? The concepts that underlie physical education activities for children are clearly related to many of the topics of elementary school science.

The physical education component of a child's day focuses on such matters as engaging in recreational activities that may be carried out over a lifetime, improving general health, and developing strength and coordination through a variety of movement activities. Thus, much of what is done during a modern physical education class actually is related to common science vocabulary terms, such as *time*, *space*, and *force*. Whether children become aware of this relationship is certainly a debatable question.

To build your own bridge between physical education and science, you need to establish a working relationship with your school's physical education teacher. If you teach in a self-contained classroom, strive to develop each curriculum—science and physical education—in a way that emphasizes and extends the concepts common to both.

Reality Check

Choose one or all of the integration challenges below:

1. During art the children mix magenta, yellow, and cyan paint to get a variety of colors. Some of the children, who are in the school musical, have noticed that different colored lights are used to make different colors on stage. But they noticed that the stage lights are colored red, green, and blue rather than magenta, yellow, and cyan like the paint in art class. They are confused and ask you why the stage lights don't mix the same colors as the paint. How can you use the children's curiosity to integrate science and art? Hint: go to www.omsi.edu/visit/tech/colormix.cfm.

2. How would you integrate a social studies unit on the Pilgrims with a science unit on the weather?

3. The children are having a kick ball tournament in physical education class. There is a controversy brewing about how much air to put in the ball. Some argue that the harder the ball, the farther it will go. Others argue that ball will travel farther if it is softer. How can you take advantage of this disagreement to deepen the children's science content and or process knowledge?

Teaching the Science of Art, Music, and Physical Education

Although the previous sections addressed strategies for using art, music, and physical education to teach science, also consider the perspective of teaching the science of art, music, and physical education. Art, music, and physical activity have a wealth of scientific principles embedded within them. For example, what makes color? How can the stage lighting in a play make a red dress look black? Prisms, rainbows, chromatography, reflection, absorption, spectrum, and primary colors are all associated with learning the science of color. The same idea applies to music, which of course is sound consisting of vibrations, frequency, and intensity.

Summary

Inquiry and discovery are at the heart of science experiences for children and can also serve as the "glue" that ties together various subjects during the school day. Science experiences offer many opportunities to build and extend language skills. Math experiences for children—including computation, data collection and expression, and logical reasoning—can be easily tied to science work, as can activities in subjects such as social studies, art, music, health, and physical education. There is great potential for the teacher who is willing to invest the energy to integrate science across disciplines. Consider not only teaching science using art, language arts, math, social studies, and physical education, but also teaching fundamental concepts of science inherent in these subjects.

Going Further

On Your Own

1. Identify a reading or language arts activity that you could have children do when they are learning about each of these topics:
   a. The seasons
   b. Sound energy
   c. Endangered animal species
   d. Rocks and minerals
   e. The role of technology in their lives

   For each activity, suggest whether you would do it at the beginning, middle, or end of a unit of study.

2. What special techniques might you use to help poor readers read science materials successfully? How could you help children with writing problems improve their written communication skills while they learn science? Be specific in your responses, citing techniques that could be used with a wide variety of science content.

3. Can you recall a science experience that you had as an elementary school child that integrated at least one other content field? If you can't recall such an experience, try to recall a science activity that could have been related to another content field with minimal teacher effort. What benefits could result from such an integrated activity?

4. The study of current events can provide many opportunities to relate science and social studies. Identify a recent news story that had a significant scientific or technologic dimension. For this current event, describe a scientific principle that you could teach and a series of classroom activities that would provide children with experiences that highlight the relationship of science and social studies.

5. Select a topic in science that could be used as a theme in a variety of subject areas. If you are working with a group, have each person play the role of the teacher of a specific subject in a departmentalized elementary or middle school. Discuss how a group of teachers at the same grade level might plan a teaching unit that integrates the subject areas. (If you are doing this on your own, prepare a written statement that highlights possible comments each teacher might make.)

6. Interview a teacher who works in a self-contained classroom. During the interview, determine the following:
   a. The major science topics emphasized during the year
   b. The science processes that are emphasized

   c. The extent to which the topics are enriched as a result of his or her efforts to relate other subjects to science

7. Interview a teacher in a departmentalized elementary or middle school. During your discussion, determine the following:
   a. The major topics and processes emphasized during the year
   b. The approximate length of a science class
   c. Whether other teachers at the grade level are aware of the topics dealt with in the science curriculum
   d. Whether all the teachers at the grade level ever work together to plan and teach units with interdisciplinary themes

Resources for Discovery Learning

Internet Resources

To access these helpful websites, go to **MyEducationLab,** select Resources, and then Web Links. To learn more, click on the following link and you will easily be directed to the website.

- **Association for Supervision and Curriculum Development:**
  www.ascd.org/portal/site/ascd

- **NSTA Position Statement: Science/Technology/Society: A New Effort for Providing Appropriate Science for All**
  www.NSTA.org/about/positions/sts.aspx

Print Resources

Suggested Readings

Akerson, Valerie. "Teaching Science When Your Principal Says 'Teach Language Arts.'" *Science and Children* 38, no. 7 (April 2001): 42–47.

Ansberry, Karen R., and Morgan, Emily. *Picture Perfect Science Lessons: Using Children's Books to Guide Inquiry.* Arlington, VA: NSTA Press, 2005.

Barman, Charles, et al. "Assessing Students' Ideas about Plants." *Science and Children* 40, no. 1 (September 2002): 25–29.

Burns, John E., and Price, Jack. "Diving into Literature, Mathematics, and Science." *Science Scope* 26, no. 1 (September 2002): 15–17.

Butzow, John, and Butzow, Carol. *Science through Children's Literature.* Engelwood, CO: Libraries Unlimited, 2000.

Fioranelli, Debra. "Recycling into Art." *Science and Children* 38, no. 2 (October 2000): 30–33.

Freedman, Robin Lee Harris. *Science and Writing Connections.* White Plains, NY: Dale Seymour, 1999.

Keena, Kelly, and Basile, Carole G. "An Environmental Journey." *Science and Children* 39, no. 8 (May 2002): 30–35.

Kupfer, Joseph H. "Engaging Nature Aesthetically." *Journal of Aesthetic Education* 37, no. 1 (Spring 2003): 77–89.

Lee, Michele, Lostoski, Maria, and Williams, Kathy. "Diving into a Schoolwide Science Theme." *Science and Children* 38, no. 1 (September 2000): 31–35.

Minton, Sandra. "Using Movement to Teach Academics: An Outline for Success." *Journal of Physical Education, Recreation and Dance* 74, no. 2 (February 2003): 36–40.

Mixing It Up: Integrated, Interdisciplinary, Intriguing Science in the Elementary Classroom. Arlington, VA: NSTA Press, 2003.

Morris, R. V. "Social Studies around the Blacksmith's Forge: Interdisciplinary Teaching and Learning." *The Social Studies (Washington, D.C.)* 98, no. 3 (May/June 2007): 99–103.

National Science Teachers Association (NSTA), Children's Book Council Joint Book Review Panel. "Outstanding Science Trade Books for Students K–12." *Science and Children* 39, no. 6 (March 2002): 31–38.

Nikitina, Svetlana. "Movement Class as an Integrative Experience: Academic, Cognitive, and Social Effects." *Journal of Aesthetic Education* 37, no. 1 (Spring 2003): 54–63.

Rogers, M. A. P., et al. "Connecting With Other Disciplines." *Science and Children* 44, no. 6 (February 2007): 58–59.

Shaw, E. L., et al. "From Boxed Lunch to Learning Boxes: An Interdisciplinary Approach." *Science Activities* 42, no. 3 (Fall 2005): 16–25.

Silverman, E., et al. "Cheep, Chirp, Twitter, & Whistle." *Science and Children* 44, no. 6 (February 2007): 20–25.

Terrell, Arlene G. "Leaders, Readers, and Science." *Science and Children* 39, no. 1 (September 2001): 28–33.

Young, Rich, Virmani, Jyotika, and Kusek, Kristen M. "Creative Writing and the Water Cycle." *Science Scope* 25, no. 1 (September 2001): 30–35.

Notes

1. National Science Teachers Association (NSTA), Children's Book Council Joint Book Review Panel, "Outstanding Science Trade Books for Students K–12," *Science and Children* 39, no. 6 (March 2002): 33.
2. Steven J. Rakow and Jo Anne Vasquez, "Integrated Instruction: A Trio of Strategies," *Science and Children* 35, no. 6 (March 1998): 18.
3. Ibid., 19.
4. Jo Anne L. Vacca, Richard T. Vacca, and Mary K. Gove, *Reading and Learning to Read* (Boston: Little Brown, rpt. 1991), p. 127.
5. Charles Temple and Jean Wallace Gillet, *Language Arts: Learning Processes and Teaching Practices* (Glenview, IL: Scott, Foresman, 1989), p. 231.
6. You may wish to refer to the presentation of a sample unit on space exploration, which shows a detailed integration of the language arts with a science topic, in Susan I. Barcher, *Teaching Language Arts: An Integrated Approach* (New York: West, 1994), pp. 351–367.
7. From *The Phantom Tollbooth* by Norman Juster, copyright © 1961 and renewed 1989 by Norton Juster. Used by permission of Random House Children's Books, a division of Random House, Inc.
8. Ibid., 180.
9. AIMS Activities that Integrate Math and Science and GEMS (Great Explorations in Math and Science) are two interesting curriculum development projects involved in the preparation of teaching materials that cut across the traditional boundaries of mathematics and science. To receive overviews of available integrated activities from these projects, write to AIMS Education Foundation, P.O. Box 8120, Fresno, CA 93747, and GEMS, Lawrence Hall of Science, University of California, Berkeley, CA 94720.
10. Richard J. Rezba, Ronald N. Glese, and Julia H. Cothron, "Graphing Is a Snap," *Science Scope* 21, no. 4 (January 1998): 20.
11. Ibid.
12. Kelly Keena and Carole G. Basile, "An Environmental Journey," *Science and Children* 39, no. 8 (May 2002): 32.
13. Jackie Moore, "Iron-On Respiratory System," *Science and Children* 28, no. 1 (September 1990): 36.
14. Ibid.
15. From *BugPlay*, © 1990 Addison-Wesley Publishing Co., Menlo Park, CA.
16. Milton E. Polsky, "Straight from the Arts," *Instructor* 99, no. 7 (March 1990): 57.

chapter 8

Using Technology to Enhance Science Learning

What comes first, content or technology?

▶ Getting Started

And now please welcome President Abraham Lincoln.

Good morning. Just a second while I get this connection to work. Do I press this button here? Function-F7? No, that's not right. Hmmm. Maybe I'll have to reboot. Hold on a minute. Um, my name is Abe Lincoln and I'm your president. While we're waiting, I want to thank Judge David Wills, chairman of the committee supervising the dedication of the Gettysburg cemetery. It's great to be here, Dave, and you and the committee are doing a great job. Gee, sometimes this new **technology** does have glitches, but **we couldn't live without it, could we?** Oh—is it ready? OK, here we go (http://norvig.com/Gettysburg/).[1]

Go to http://norvig.com/Gettysburg/ to see the PowerPoint presentation Lincoln might have made had the technology been available in 1863. Having seen the Power-Point presentation, do you think this Gettysburg Address would have had the same enduring effect to honor the men and women who fought in the battle as Lincoln's original speech? Hardly. The point of course is that technology for its own sake

has just as much potential to destroy the message as it does to enhance it. Although technology has wonderful potential for education, it must be used in the service of education and not simply because it is available. Sometimes drawing a graph with paper and pencil is a much more powerful learning tool than creating an Excel spreadsheet. Above all remember that you, the teacher, will always be more important than the technology.

This may seem like an ominous beginning for a chapter on the use of technology in the science classroom, but it is meant to put the use of technology in perspective. Used properly, technology has much to offer to the enrichment of science education. Technology can be a powerful educational tool, the potential of which we will explore in this chapter.

What Does Technology Really Mean?

Before beginning the chapter, we need to clarify what is meant by technology. Most often technology is thought of in the context of computer use in the classroom. However, educational technology has been around much longer than computers. Instructional technology consists of the tools used to enhance learning. In science, technology has always played a pivotal role by enabling scientists to deepen their descriptive models through the development of increasingly refined instruments that allow them to see the world more clearly. From a simple magnifying glass to the Hubble telescope, technology has expanded our ability to understand the world and the universe. This chapter will address the interface of computer technology with science education to advance the children's understandings of scientific process, concepts, and skills. Note that assistive technologies designed specifically to assist students with learning disabilities will be addressed in Chapter 9.

Technology: Why Use It?

In general, technology is familiar to children; it is fun and here to stay. I recognize that you may be teaching children who do not have access to computers at home. However, they will need to be users of technology in the twenty-first century, which is a reason to use technology appropriately in your classroom.

Technology can be engaging. It provides a window to a variety of virtual experiences that pique curiosity and can be used to inspire questions. It has the power to connect children with a community of learners, including peers as well as experts in the fields of science. Roblyer (p. 18) notes that technology enhances instructional methods by providing immediate feedback, visual demonstrations, and self-paced learning.[2]

As science educators, we recognize that science consists of both systematic processes and the collective explanations generated by the community of scientists using those processes. Computer technology assists science by providing tools that enhance inquiry through data collection, calculation, analysis, storage, and retrieval. It also provides dynamic modeling through simulations as well as dialogue and information gathering. Evidence suggests that technology enables the development of higher order thinking skills when students use technology to problem solve.[3] Keep in mind that as children use technology to explore scientific concepts, they are also improving their technological skills that are essential for the information age of the 21st century.

Figure 8.1   Questions for Judging the Credibility of an Educational Website

- Is it hosted by a reputable science or education organization? i.e., college, university, or government agency?

- If it is not hosted by known credible institutions, does the site reference credible institutions?

- Is the information presented consistent and valid with your understanding of the topic?

  If you suspect the validity of the information provided on the site, can you cross-reference the information with known reliable sources?

- Is it a safe website for children?

  Does it provide links to questionable sites with inappropriate themes?

  Does it solicit information from students? If so, what information?

- What does it have to offer educationally?

  Does it provide solely nominal information such as definitions and descriptions?

  Is it supported by graphics that clarify ideas?

  Is the text well written and developmentally appropriate for your students?

  Does the site provide opportunities for the children to interact with knowledge?

- Interactive simulations?

  Does the site provide opportunities for children to manipulate variables or discover how to do something?

  Does the simulation invite students to think about choices? Does it challenge them to use higher-level thinking skills?

Information Gathering

Go to **MyEducationLab**, select the topic Technology, watch the video entitled "Technology," and complete the question that accompanies it.

The Internet offers a seemingly infinite source of information. The challenge is to find good, manageable sources of information. Although there are many good sites run by individuals, I suggest using government websites such as NASA (www.nasa.gov) or the United States Geological Survey (www.usgs.gov). These sites frequently have sections dedicated to science education that include lesson plans, simulations, and links to other reputable sources. Other reliable sources include academic institutions such as universities and colleges, as well as museums and science centers such as the Boston Museum of Science (www.mos.org) and the Exploratorium (www.exploratorium.org). Figure 8.1 lists questions to consider when evaluating the educational value of a website.

Science WebQuests

You can incorporate information gathering into an inquiry experience for students using WebQuests. WebQuests engage students by creating a need to gather, analyze, and synthesize information that addresses a specific problem or challenge. A WebQuest should not generate a list of factoids that are simply copied from a website, nor should a WebQuest merely direct students to visit websites. WebQuests should actively involve students with content at the websites. Bernie Dodge, at San Diego State University, pioneered the development of WebQuests. You can find examples and templates for creating WebQuests at The WebQuest Page www.webquest.org/index.php.

Although there are several suggested templates for creating WebQuests, I find it helpful to follow the same 5E instructional strategy used in this book. The exploration uses the Internet as a tool to encounter new knowledge through information/data gathering, simulations, or virtual experimentation. The steps in the formation of a WebQuest are outlined below, followed by an example in Figure 8.2.

1. *Engage:* Set the context, pique interest, provide background information, and identify the challenge

2. *Explore:* Guide the students to websites where they encounter new information and interact with new knowledge

   a. The exploration can be guided using hyperlinks embedded in a procedure using software such as PowerPoint, Inspiration, or similar software.

   b. Or, the exploration can be presented in text format as exemplified in Figure 8.1

3. *Explain:* Provide students with an opportunity to articulate their responses to the challenge. Consider requiring the use of presentation software as an explanation tool

4. *Elaborate:* Provide an opportunity to transfer or apply the new knowledge

5. *Evaluate:* Assess the degree to which the students met the criteria of the learning objectives

Ask a Scientist

There are several online sites where children can ask a scientist for advice or for the answer to a puzzling question. This is helpful especially after the children have worked with a concept and generated meaningful questions. It is not helpful for children to use Ask a Scientist as a first resort. Wait until they have tried to seek an explanation and use Ask a Scientist sites for clarification. By asking someone, presumably an expert, there is the added motivation to develop a coherent, well-articulated question. Evidence suggests that children are much more motivated to express themselves well when they know other people outside the classroom will see their work.[4] Keep in mind that most scientists who respond on these sites are volunteers. It is unlikely that they will be able to address every question, and some of the more routine questions will be found in the FAQs. Therefore, be sure the students put some time into developing their questions to utilize this resource effectively. Suggest the following guidelines to students for preparing Ask a Scientist questions:

- Do your best to research the topic in the library or on the Internet. Check the FAQ section of the site if there is one. You may find others have asked the same or a similar question.

- Tell the scientist what you have learned in your basic research. Include your grade level in your e-mail.

- Don't be surprised if scientists give suggestions about how to discover an answer rather than answer your question directly. They are trying to help you learn how to inquire.

- Reply to the scientists who answered your question to thank them and let them know you received their responses. You may have a follow-up question.

Ask a Scientist links can be found on MyEducationLab.

Figure 8.2   Sample WebQuest

Engagement:

You are going camping with family and friends in the Grand Canyon in June after school gets out. The trip involves hiking several miles over the course of seven days. You need to pack as lightly as possible. Rather than take a camping stove and bottles of gas (wood for burning is scarce) you and your friend think that you can build a solar oven to do your cooking. Do you think this is a good idea? Explain your decision based on how solar ovens function and the properties of the Grand Canyon. To answer these questions, you will need to learn more about the Grand Canyon and how solar ovens work.

Exploration:

1. Go to http://solarcookers.org/basics/how.html to learn about how solar ovens work.

    a. Find the four principles of solar ovens. Record them in your science notebooks. (Upper elementary school students can go to http://tamaradwyer.com/solcook/phys_sci.html for a detailed description of the solar oven science.)

2. Based on your understanding of how solar ovens work, **explain** whether you think the Grand Canyon is a good place to use solar ovens.

    a. Go to weather-2-travel.com/climate-guides/index.php?destination=grand-canyon-az and www.thetrain.com/grandcanyon/climate/. Use the climate data that you find to support your answer. Record your answer in your science notebook.

3. Based on your understanding of how solar ovens work, draw a picture in your science notebook of what your solar oven might look like. Describe how each part of your solar oven would work. Remember to consider the four principles of solar ovens in your picture and explanation.

Explanation:

1. Do you think it is a good idea to try to use solar ovens during your camping trip in the Grand Canyon? Explain your decision based on what you learned about the function of solar ovens and the properties of the Grand Canyon in June.

    a. Discuss this in your group. Ask one person from each group to share the group's opinion. The other members in the group must be prepared to support the opinion with evidence.

2. Share your solar oven drawings with your group members. Combine your ideas to draw, on a poster board or PowerPoint presentation, your group's design for a solar oven.

Elaboration:

Go to www.solarnow.org/pizzabx.htm and use the directions as a guide to make a solar oven. You can change the directions if you think you can make a better solar oven than the one suggested. Try to make your solar oven reach a temperature of 100°F (38°C).

Evaluation:

1. Give each student a diagram of a solar oven with each part labeled. Ask them to describe in writing the function of each labeled part in the solar oven.

2. Bring their solar ovens outside on a sunny day and place a thermometer in each solar oven. Challenge the students to get the temperature of their solar ovens to 100°F (38°C), using only solar energy.

Figure 8.3
Computer probe
interface

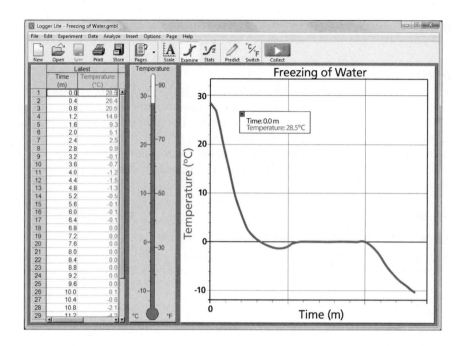

● Real-Time Data Collection

Computer Probe Interfaces   The science classroom in particular benefits from interfaces between computers and sensors that can collect a range of data such as motion, temperature, speed, distance, blood pressure, and a host of other observables. The software accompanying the probes allows students to visualize their own data immediately and manipulate variables to deepen their understanding of complex concepts and relationships. (See Figure 8.3.) As an example, students can graph and compare the rate of temperature change in their solar ovens or see the relationship between distance and time using a motion detector to track a rolling ball. The probes are simple to use and usually plug into the USB ports on both Mac and PC computers.

Digital Microscopes   Microscope interfaces with the computer are particularly helpful for projecting real-time micro images on a screen using an LCD projector. Like the probes, the microscopes come with software that makes it easy to project images up to 200X magnification, although I rarely need above 60X (Figure 8.4). Some software allows you to record video or still images and even time lapse events. Digital microscopes are particularly helpful for assuring that the entire class is looking at the same micro image when developing a particular concept.

Figure 8.4   Fire ant magnified

Virtual Imaging   Tools such as telescopes and microscopes extend our senses and abilities to make observations and construct descriptive models. Online tools enable children to see far out into the galaxy or peer into the often bizarre world of the microcosm. Other tools allow children to extend their abilities to make connections among a host of variables and imagine what properties emerge when they all interact at a unique time and place. These tools provide windows to new perspectives on the world and universe. One relatively new site is the World Wide Telescope, created by Microsoft (www.worldwidetelescope.org). "The WorldWide Telescope (WWT) is a Web 2.0 visualization software environment that enables a computer to function as a virtual telescope—bringing together imagery from the best ground and space-based telescopes in the world for a seamless exploration of the universe."[5] You will need to download supporting software from the site to use the World Wide Telescope. The directions are clear and downloading is relatively easy. When you succeed, you will have a portal into the galaxies to explore with your students.

Authentic Science Experiences

There are several Internet sites that provide students opportunities to be involved in authentic research. Authentic research involves students in collecting, sharing, and analyzing data associated with real-world investigations. The questions and data collection methods are usually determined by the organization hosting the site. Students participate in some form of data collection or investigation and share their data and conclusions with peers virtually on the Internet. Participation on these sites will require time on your part to enroll your class and become familiar with the logistics and procedures. Like anything else, it gets easier after you have done it once. Some sites require that teachers participate in a workshop in order to have total access to the sites.

The Global Learning and Observations to Benefit the Environment (GLOBE, www.globe.gov) is one example of an authentic learning site. Be prepared to spend some time becoming familiar with the site and all it has to offer to you and your students. In some respects, it is a one-stop site for integrating computer technology into your science curriculum. It enables your class to participate in environmental studies at the appropriate developmental level with school children of all ages from around the world. It is authentic in the respect that students can be directly involved in asking questions, collecting data, accessing data, analyzing data, and submitting data online for the GLOBE community to share. Inquiry-based guides and assessment tools are available as well as simulations that can be used to deepen students' descriptive models and allow them to manipulate variables to seek explanations. Teachers need to attend special workshops in order to fully participate in the program.

Tutorials and Games

Tutorials and games can be valuable for reviews and self-paced learning. Games like hangman, crossword puzzles, etc., are useful for reviews but usually do not inspire higher-level thinking. Tutorials provide young children with self-paced learning like www.edheads.org/activities/simple-machines/index.htm. Others help students associate properties with concepts such as simple circuits. See, for example, www.deltamicro.co.uk/primary_online/circuits.html.

Simulations

Computers and the Internet enable children to extend their mental models. Great thinkers such as Einstein, da Vinci, and Galileo are thought to have had the ability to imagine the interaction of several variables at once and how they all come together to explain a phenomenon. Most of us can do this to some extent, but computers enhance our ability to create models and predict the interactions among many variables. The weather is a good example of how several rules of interaction come together at a given time and place. Computer models greatly enhance our ability to predict the weather by predicting the interactions among these multiple variables.

Simulations allow students to manipulate variables and see how the interactions among variables change the system. They help students understand complex relationships such as speed and distance or succession in ecosystems. Simulations are also helpful because they allow students to visualize phenomena that would be inaccessible or otherwise dangerous, such as launching rockets or mixing chemicals. Lastly, they allow students to deepen their descriptive models, formulate hypotheses, make predictions, design experiments to test their predictions, and revise their explanations, thereby completing the progression of inquiry. There are several simulations available on the Internet. Registration and a fee are required for some, but there is often a free trial period. Many sites, such as Explorelearning (www .explorescience.com/), include assessments and lesson plan supplements that accompany the simulations.

Using Technology to Communicate Results

An essential element of science is peer review. Science advances through sharing insights and discoveries that other scientists build upon. Teaching students to communicate their ideas, discoveries, and questions is an integral component of science education. Presentation software such as PowerPoint provides students with tools to present their results and data. Simple line graphs, bar graphs, and pie charts can be constructed using programs such as Excel. Digital cameras are wonderful tools for recording images that can be printed or displayed electronically. I encourage students to record changes throughout the seasons of a particular tree or ecosystem with digital cameras. One caution with graphic presentations such as PowerPoint is the tendency to spend more time on design than substance. There are so many options available with respect to fonts, colors, and animations that students can easily spend most of their time deciding on design elements rather than thinking about the substance of the presentation. Therefore, I urge you to set limits by restricting the range of fonts, colors, and design elements that students can use in a report. This is not an unrealistic requirement because scientists frequently follow rigid guidelines for publishing and presenting at conferences.

Interactive Whiteboards

Computer-generated presentations offer great graphics and images, but it is difficult to spontaneously add a student's insights and observations to the presentation during the class. It is at those times that I long for good old overhead projectors with clear acetate film that I can write on to incorporate class responses in real time. Interactive whiteboards provide a much needed bridge between static presentations and the real-time ebb and flow of the classroom. As the term implies, interactive whiteboards enable various modes of instructional technology to be seamlessly integrated into class lectures and demonstrations. Whiteboards enable the user, teacher or student, to control the computer from the whiteboard rather than using a keyboard or mouse. Touching the whiteboard is the equivalent of clicking on the object with the mouse. Writing tablets allow notes to be made directly on the white board, saved, and distributed electronically or in print. Interactive whiteboards bridge the gap between prescribed presentations and real-time student-teacher interactions.

Interactive whiteboards provide several benefits for teachers and pupils. Whiteboards are similar to other presentation tools insofar as teachers can prepare graphics, text, and media files in advance. Software for whiteboards continues to grow, enabling teachers to incorporate a variety of media into their whiteboard presentations. The greatest benefit may be in the opportunity for students to receive immediate feedback while working on activities at the board. The appropriate software provides feedback that allows them to take risks and test ideas that they can immediately revise and develop in real time to deepen their understanding.[6]

Summary

Instructional technology as used in this chapter refers to the use of computers and the Internet as tools to enhance science education. Both provide rich opportunities to deepen children's understanding of science and the processes of science. The Internet provides a portal into vast stores of information and data collection techniques that advance descriptive models and simulations to run virtual experiments and enrich explanatory models. Authentic learning experiences via the Internet enable students to participate in meaningful data collection and motivate them to a higher level of accountability through interaction with a community of peers and scientists. Students can dialogue with members of the scientific community through Ask a Scientist sites and have access to cutting edge images and data through sites such as the World Wide Telescope. Probes and microscopes that interface with computers allow students immediate access to data supporting discoveries and construction of knowledge. Interactive whiteboards provide a teaching tool that integrates the tools of technology in a seamless and effective manner in the classroom.

All this technology is wonderful, but it is only as effective as the teacher who uses it wisely to serve the goals of learning and not simply because the technology is available. Using technology effectively for learning takes time and effort. Used appropriately, technology can unlock exciting and fruitful learning opportunities for you and your students. Even if you are uncertain about your ability to incorporate technology meaningfully in the classroom, don't be afraid to try it. As Napoleon Hill (1883–1970) said, "Don't wait. The time will never be just right." But do remember, as with any powerful technology, it must be used judiciously. Often a sketchpad and a pencil are all the technology needed to discover the wonders of the world.

Going Further

On Your Own

1. Choose a topic from the National Science Education Standards. Design a WebQuest for students for the topic.

2. Identify the major classroom management problems you feel might result from having technology in the classroom. Briefly describe what preventative steps a teacher might take to minimize such problems.

3. At the beginning of the chapter, the point was made that technology should serve education rather than drive education. Create a set of guidelines for determining when it is appropriate to use technology for science education.

On Your Own or in a Cooperative Learning Group

4. Try to achieve consensus among your group members as you prepare one response to each of the following questions:

   a. What are the long-term benefits of having a classroom in which children are able to link to the outside world through computer networking?

b. What are the negatives for children and teachers who use this networking capability?

5. Visit an elementary school science class and note whether and how any of the technologies mentioned in this chapter are integrated into the science learning experience. Describe how the technologies were beneficial or not beneficial to the learning experience.

6. Interview practicing elementary school teachers about their views on the use of technology to teach science.

7. Imagine that you are writing a technology grant for your elementary school. Describe the rationale you would provide to justify the use of technology in the science classroom and how you intend to use technology to enrich the science curriculum.

Resources for Discovery Learning

Internet Resources

 To access these helpful websites, go to **MyEducationLab,** select Resources, and then Web Links. To learn more, click on the following links and you will easily be directed to each website

- **Ask a Scientist:**
  www.askascientist.com

- **Bugscope:**
  http://bugscope.beckman.uiuc.edu/

- **Cornell University Library:**
  www.library.cornell.edu/olinuris/ref/webcrit.html and www.library.cornell.edu/okuref/research/webeval.html

- **Explore eLearning:**
  www.explorescience.com/

- **Howard Hughes Medical Institute (HHMI):**
  www.hhmi.org/askscientist/

- **NASA Kids Club:**
  www.nasa.gov/audience/forkids/kidsclub/flash/index.html

- **The Noon Day Project:**
  www.k12science.org/noonday/

- **Project RoadKill:**
  http://roadkill.edutel.com

- **Square of Life:**
  www.ciese.org/curriculum/squareproj/proj_inst.htm

- **TeAchnology:**
  www.teach-nology.com/web_tools/web_quest

- **Topmarks Educational Search Engine: Primary Interactive Whiteboard Resources:**
  www.topmarks.co.uk/Interactive.aspx?s=science

- **US Department of Energy:**
  www.newton.dep.anl.gov/aasinfo.htm

- **WebQuest.org:**
  http://webquest.org/index.php

- **Wonderful World of Weather:**
  www.k12science.org/curriculum/weatherproj/index.html

Notes

1. Peter Norvig. http://norvig.com/Gettysburg. Reprinted with permission.
2. M. D. Roblyer, *Integrating Educational Technology into Teaching* (Upper Saddle River, NJ: Pearson, 2007.)
3. Research by the Center for Applied Research in Educational Technology (CARET, http://caret.iste.org/).
4. M. Cohen, & M. Reil. "The Effect of Distant Audiences on Children's Writing." *American Educational Research Journal* 26, no. 2 (summer, 1989): 143–159.
5. World Wide Telescope. www.worldwidetelescope.org. accessed 05-24-08.
6. *Getting the Most from Your Interactive Whiteboard: A Guide for Primary Schools.* Millburn Hill Road, Science Park: Coventry, UK British Educational Communications and Technology Agency (Becta), 2004, pp. 10–11.

chapter 9

Adapting the Science Curriculum

How can I adapt the science curriculum for children from diverse cultural backgrounds, children with special needs, and children with special gifts and talents?

▶ **Getting Started**

You notice that Donny rarely interacts with the other students in the classroom. He prefers to keep to himself and read even during recess and group work. Lauren excels at anything hands-on, yet she can't seem to sit still during quiet reading times and is a distraction for other students. Carla, your straight A student, often looks bored during class. It does not seem as though you can challenge her enough. Francis is reading two levels below grade level, and Julia's Individualized Education Plan (IEP) requires modifications to the curriculum. Meanwhile, there are five other students for whom you need to make accommodations. How do you meet the needs of all these children in the same class?

This chapter will help you prepare science learning experiences for all children in your class. I hope it will prepare you to say to every child who enters your classroom, "Hello, I am glad you are going to be in my class. This is the place where *everyone* learns."

The "Digital Divide": A Cautionary Tale

A classroom computer that's connected to the Internet is a special "window on the world." It can bring children the images of young hawks being fed and raised, cavorting rain forest animals, and a dolphin giving birth. Children who don't have this "window"—due to the fact that they attend underfunded schools or live in homes that lack the resources or inclination to own a computer—see none of these virtual real-world wonders.

As you study this chapter, which focuses on the unique needs of special children, keep in mind that not all children have access to the technology that will bring these wonders and other advantages to their lives—now or in the years ahead. And when these children encounter one more thing that divides them from the larger society, they may become more removed, more distant, and even alienated from their schooling.

As you teach *all* children through the medium of science, try to bring to bear as much technology as your school has to offer. If you can help children cross the "digital divide," you will be doing much to broaden their self-confidence, their career aspirations, and ultimately their horizons.

Children from Diverse Cultural Backgrounds

● Getting Science Reading Materials for Non-English Speakers

Las Cremalleras Tienen Dientes Y Otras Preguntas Sobre Inventos

If English is your only language, you must really be puzzled by the above quote! Even if you have studied the language used, my guess is that you only partially understand it.

I will give you the translation later in this section, but for now, I want you to think about what it's like for a non-English-speaking child, likely new to the United States, to see books and headings that look as forbidding as the quote above looks to *you*. Add to this language confusion the idea that the quote probably has something to do with science, a potentially difficult subject, and you should more fully appreciate the challenge that science time must be for non-English speakers as well as their teachers.

In a perfect world, all teachers would be fluent in at least one other language. But unless you were fortunate enough to be raised in a bilingual home, the odds of your being able to communicate effectively with a newly immigrated non-English-speaking child are slim, at best. Even if you are fluent in a second language, the odds are still not in your favor (or more importantly, the child's), since that language may not be Spanish, Cantonese or Mandarin Chinese, Bosnian, Laotian, Cambodian, or Vietnamese—the home languages of many new arrivals to the United States.

Your success in helping non-English-speaking children learn science and expand their abilities with English will depend in part on whether you can bring to your classroom resources in other languages. However, these resources are meant to serve as a bridge to the ultimate goal of science and English-language proficiency. Children should be gradually weaned from their dependency on translations.

One way to find such materials is to contact community groups that represent speakers of various languages and find out what science resources might be borrowed from scientifically literate community members. Another strategy is to contact a local university to see if undergraduate or graduate students studying a given language would be available to make translations from English. Finally, if you are a world traveler, you might consider visiting one or more of the countries represented by your students. During your visit, you may be able to acquire resource materials that can be put to good use in your classroom.

Are you still curious about the quote presented at the start of this section? It's the title of a book for children that, roughly translated from Spanish, reads, *I Wonder Why Zippers Have Teeth and Other Questions about Inventions*. It is one of many Spanish language science books available from the Center for the Study of Books in Spanish for Children, which maintains a database of thousands of titles with brief descriptions. (See the Notes at the end of the chapter for the center's Internet address.)[1]

Isabel Schon, an expert in the use of books for children in Spanish, makes the following point about the availability of books in Spanish. But I think what she says can be applied to books in other languages as well:

> Encouraging young Spanish speakers into the world of science is becoming easier every day. The ever-increasing number of high-quality, informative, and appealing books being published in Spanish make the observation, identification, description, experimental investigation, and/or theoretical explanation of phenomena much more rewarding.[2]

● Reinforcing Reading and Language Arts Skills

Hands-on, discovery-based science experiences can be great confidence builders for children from diverse cultural backgrounds, even if their present reading and language arts skills in English are weak. Your challenge as a teacher is to remember that you can use a child's success in science as a starting point to build a positive attitude toward school. Let's take a unit on weather as an example. Here are some very specific ways to extend the unit to the areas of reading and language arts, which can be applied to any science unit:

1. Use daily weather observations by students to create a language experience chart. You may have learned this technique in reading and language arts methods courses or workshops. To make such a chart, transcribe the children's oral observations onto a large sheet of paper, and have them read and discuss the material.

2. Have cooperative learning groups make model weather instruments and maintain their own language experience charts. You or a child with advanced writing abilities can transcribe the observations to the chart.

3. Expect children to make labels for the parts of their model weather instruments.

4. Expect children to keep personal logs of their daily weather observations, and occasionally read to them from their logs.

5. Have children record their individual weather reports on audiocassette tape or videotape.

6. Read or have one of the children read weather-related passages from children's books.

7. Encourage children to cut out weather-related headlines from a daily newspaper, and read them to the class.

8. Using suggestions from the class, write short poems about weather on chartpaper.

9. Have the children create dictionaries of weather terms, including pronounciation hints and drawings.

10. Have the children create a school weather report and present it on the school public address system every morning.

These techniques will be most effective if they are rooted in your belief that children from diverse cultural backgrounds who have language difficulties need every possible opportunity to practice the skills of reading, speaking, and writing. Two other techniques are especially helpful for children who are not fluent in English in the classroom: peer tutoring and parent/classroom connections.

Organizing Peer Tutoring

The key to success in peer tutoring lies in the selection of the tutors. Ideally, tutors are good students who are fluent in both languages, who understand the content you are teaching, and who possess those special personal characteristics that permit them to function as positive, supportive tutors.

Peer tutors also need some help from teachers. If possible, you should provide them with materials that display and explain science concepts in the child's native language as well as in English. If you happen to be fluent in the native languages of the children in your classes, you may wish to prepare alternative materials similar to those shown in Figure 9.1.[3] Children who speak only English may enjoy the challenge of trying to explain what the foreign terms on such diagrams mean.

Fostering Parent/Classroom Science Connections

Science time can be a learning experience that fully and appropriately involves the parents of children from diverse cultural backgrounds. Reaching out to these parents is well worth the effort, even though time and energy are at a premium for modern parents and teachers. You may need the assistance of someone who is fluent in the child's home language to use the following ideas:

1. Send a letter to parents at the beginning of the year explaining what science time for students will be like. Write the letters in English and in the children's home languages, and send both copies to parents.

2. Send home a monthly science newsletter in the children's home languages that includes examples of students' work.

3. Call five parents a week to make contact for future communication.

4. Invite parents to school for a Science Open House, and invite school professionals who speak the home languages to be present.

5. Prepare home study science activity sheets in children's home languages.

6. Send a letter to parents asking for volunteers to accompany the class on field trips or to come to class when science activities are done. If you are not fluent in children's home languages, having a helper who can communicate in more than one language can be a boon.

For additional ideas on how to meet the special needs of minority and bilingual children in the classroom, contact one

Figure 9.1 With a little effort, you should be able to find drawings that are labeled in children's native languages.

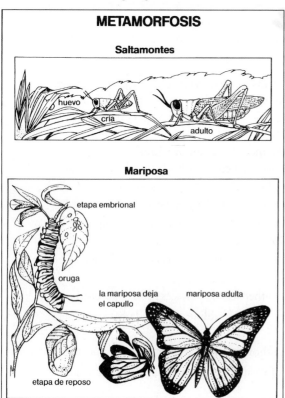

of the bilingual educational multifunctional support/resource centers listed in the For the Teacher's Desk section at the end of this book. As you review the listing, notice that the resource centers provide services for specific geographic regions.

Children with Special Needs

Go to **MyEducationLab**, select the topic Students with Special Needs, watch the simulation entitled "Assessing the General Education Curriculum," and complete the questions that accompany it.

Perhaps we, as teachers, should take a vow with respect to children who have impairments—namely, that we will not give these children additional challenges while they are in our care. My language may seem a bit strong, but it is possible to put these children at even greater risk when we make *content* adjustments when we should be making *methodology* adjustments. Children with disabilities need to learn the same things as other children, but they may need to learn these things in different ways or at different rates. Every child needs opportunities to explore, to inquire and acquire knowledge and skills, and to discover and apply what he or she has learned.

The Inclusion Challenge

The 1975 Education for All Handicapped Children Act (P.L. 94–142), renamed in 1991 the Individuals with Disabilities Education Act (IDEA) requires a free and appropriate education with related services for each child in the least restrictive environment possible. In response, some children with special needs have been moved from traditional special education or resource rooms to regular classrooms in a practice known as *inclusion* or *mainstreaming*. Although educating these children in classrooms with their agemates may seem like a good idea, actually doing it can be a difficult, intense process. In too many

Make the Case *An Individual or Group Challenge*

The Problem	Because technological innovations occur so rapidly these days, it is difficult for teachers to select the best classroom technology for children with impairments.
Assess Your Prior Knowledge and Beliefs	Based on your personal experience in science classrooms, assess your present knowledge about the classroom devices that could help you achieve the fullest possible participation of children with these impairments:

    1. Hearing_____

    2. Visual_____

    3. Orthopedic_____

The Challenge	Four engineers have formed a company to design and manufacture instructional equipment for children with impairments. They have asked you to suggest ideas for new devices or for improvements in existing devices that would assist these children in a hands-on, discovery-based classroom. What will you suggest?

All children—including those with special needs—need opportunities to explore, acquire knowledge and skills, and apply what they have learned.

cases, it's assumed that the physical placement alone is enough and that good things will automatically happen for everyone involved. It isn't quite that easy, however, especially in a science program designed to provide appropriate inquiry-based experiences for everyone. The strategies discussed in the next few sections will help you ensure that every child who is *physically* included in your classroom will be *educationally* included as well.

The Range of Disabilities

Disability is a term that encompasses a variety of physical and cognitive needs. It includes learning disabilities such as dyslexia, emotional or behavioral issues including attention deficit disorder, and physical disabilities that limit mobility or sensory perception. The literature includes English language barriers as disabilities as well. It is well beyond the scope of this text to address each disability separately. However, there are guiding principles that can inform your curriculum design and teaching to make your classroom a rich learning environment for all students.

Guiding Principles for Inclusion: Differentiated Instruction and Universal Design for Learning

Differentiated Instruction

Clearly not all students learn in the same manner. A one-size-fits-all approach to teaching and learning simply does not suffice to provide all students with opportunities to reach their fullest potential. Differentiated learning recognizes that students benefit when they have multiple options for learning. Consequently, teachers are challenged to be flexible in their approach to teaching the same content using a wide variety of teaching strategies to accommodate children with different learning modalities and needs based on cognitive, emotional, and physical abilities. Admittedly, this is quite an overwhelming charge. There is often, though not always, only one teacher for a classroom of students. Even with the assistance of others in your classroom, you still need to plan in order to differentiate instruction. Have no illusions that this is easy, but it is a worthy and attainable goal. One approach to assist you in planning for and providing differentiated learning is a strategy called Universal Design for Learning (UDL).

Go to **MyEducationLab**, select the topic Technology, watch the video entitled "Lesson on Birds," and complete the questions that accompany it.

Universal Design for Learning

UDL has its roots in architectural design strategies that include access to buildings for people with disabilities. Briefly stated, rather than create separate ramps for wheelchair users, UDL incorporates the ramps as the main access for all users. It has been found that ramps and similar accommodations such as curb cuts and audio signals at crosswalks benefit all users, not just those with disabilities.

The same approach applied to curricula and teaching strategies results in a flexible classroom environment that accommodates a wide range of learners. UDL incorporates multiple learning modalities, including visual, auditory, kinesthetic, and tactile, to provide access to learning for a variety of student needs relating to learning styles, cultural backgrounds, languages, and disabilities. There are three guiding principles to UDL:

- Provide multiple means of engagement.
- Provide multiple means of representation (and/or participation).
- Provide multiple means of expression.

Note that the principles of UDL coincide nicely with the 5E instructional strategy. Engagement is apparent, whereas exploration requires representation of concepts, and explanation calls for multiple means of expression.

The science classroom/lab affords several opportunities to implement these three principles. Each principle requires you to consider a variety of ways that students with different learning styles can access learning experiences. Adapting your curriculum to the principles of UDL can be a liberating experience that gives you license to think creatively. For example, to teach the properties of sound to students who are hearing impaired you could have them feel vibrations representing frequency and intensity through different media. But don't make this a separate activity for the hearing impaired; incorporate it into the lesson for the entire class. The wonderful outcome of UDL is that a variety of access points to the curriculum will benefit all students.

Some general strategies for each principle are given in the Figure 9.2. The value of UDL is in using a variety of strategies to access the same learning experience. For example, you may choose to engage students by putting two tomato plants on the table—one that is full of foliage, erect, and bright green, the other that has few leaves, limp, and pale green—and ask why the plants are different. At the same time, you can post the question on the board. Project a closeup of the plants on a screen using a live video projection (or prepared photos from a digital camera, which are easy to upload) and/or handout pictures of the two plants. Ask the children to prepare a descriptive model using a think-pair-share strategy. Post a word bank of descriptors on the board with pictures next to the descriptors. Let the children touch the plants to feel differences as well. Note that students with visual impairments benefit from close-up views of the plants provided by photos, video, and feeling the plants. Hearing-impaired students can rely on text and peer sharing, while English language learners benefit from word banks supplemented by pictures as well as think-pair-share strategies.

Figure 9.2   Strategies for UDL

1. Multiple means of engagement
   - Read aloud
   - Read with the text projected on the board
   - Supplement text with pictures, graphics, and video, audio
   - Music related to topic
   - Simulation
   - Role play (i.e., students role-play water molecules during phase changes)

2. Multiple means of representation and participation
   Representation
   - Word bank posted in classroom
   - Ideas bank posted in classroom
   - Electronic version of the text (varying text sizes, read aloud with text-to-speech)
   - CD-ROM or online encyclopedia with images and spoken text
   - Music for reflection time
   - Links to foreign language websites on the subject
   - Printed and electronic concept map with images, text, and hyperlinks
   - e-text outline of lecture content with main ideas highlighted
   - Tool to translate words or connected text into other languages
   - Graphic highlighting of important ideas (on screen or on paper)
   - Digital photograph collection
   - Concept maps
   - Time lines

   Participation
   - Cooperative groups with assigned tasks complementary to abilities
   - Stations
   - Role plays
   - Manipulatives

3. Multiple means of expression
   - Writing
   - Discussion
   - Role play
   - PowerPoint
   - Poster
   - Concept map
   - Play
   - Song
   - Art

Science also involves laboratory investigations at the bench as well as in the field. Making these inquiry experiences available to a range of abilities can be enhanced by resourcefulness and technology. Not all students will be able to collect pond samples, for example, but they can decide where to take the samples and work with a partner who can collect the samples for them.

Technology provides unique access to data collection and analysis. Examples include:

- Meters and probes with audible readout (e.g., enabling a light probe to emit a tone that increases in pitch proportionally to changes in light intensity)
- Talking thermometers, balances, and calculators; laboratory glassware with raised numbers
- Electronic note takers and portable word processors
- Digital voice recorders
- Adequate lighting and magnification
- Digital cameras[4]

Accommodations and Modifications

These terms are used to describe the general strategies that support inclusion in classroom practice. These strategies differ significantly in the type of support we provide for students with disabilities and the expectations we have for students with disabilities.

- **Accommodations**

  Services or support provided to help a student fully access the subject matter and instruction as well as to validly demonstrate what he or she knows. An accommodation *does not change the content* of instruction nor the performance expectations.

- **Modifications**

  Curriculum modifications made when a student either is taught something different from the rest of the class or is taught the same information but at a different level of complexity. A modification *does change the content* of instruction and the performance expectations.[5]

Reality Check

You have initiated an outdoor education program at your school. Your fourth-grade class has decided to integrate their history unit about the Pilgrims with science by planting a Three Sisters Garden of corn, beans, and squash. One of your performance objectives is for the students to gather descriptive information about the life cycle of plants over the course of the project. You organize the class of fifteen students into five groups of three. The class consists of seven boys and eight girls. Two of the boys have been diagnosed with attention deficit hyperactivity disorder. One girl is legally blind, another girl has a learning disability and is reading at the first-grade level, and one girl is an English language learner. Identify two strategies to differentiate learning for this class using the principles of universal design.

Teamwork Is Essential

Most of us are not qualified to identify a learning disability, although years of experience working with children will make you sensitive to the practical implications of processing problems. One of the most important steps you can take to effectively include students with disabilities in your classroom is to work with the special education team. Leverage their expertise and experience to understand the needs of the child and the strategies that best serve the student. Communicate your observations about the student(s) in your classroom and seek the team's advice. Consult the child's IEP to identify the accommodations and/or modifications that are mandated by the plan. Work with paraprofessionals if they are present in the classroom for particular students. Invite them to discuss the needs of the child with whom they are working and seek their input about the child's attitude and performance. They may have insights from working closely with the child that they can share. Also speak with the child's guardians to better understand the needs of the child in your classroom. Use all the resources available to you in order to create the optimal learning environment for all your students.

Science Experiences for Children with Visual Impairments

Children with visual impairments don't need to be placed in special classrooms. A visual impairment affects only the *manner* through which knowledge enters a child's mind; it should not, in any way, affect the *nature* of the knowledge you select for the curriculum. (I am, of course, using *knowledge* in its broadest sense to include skills, attitudes, values, and so forth.)

But if you do not modify the curriculum, then what do you do? The answer is straightforward. You modify equipment, materials, and experiences that are visually based by incorporating the use of touch, hearing, and smell.

Science Reading Materials One convenient approach to delivering printed science information to children with visual problems is to have sighted students with good oral-reading skills audiotape books, chapter sections, newspaper stories, and other printed materials. This can be an ongoing class project, in which children take turns preparing instructional materials. Another strategy is to have the school purchase large-type books, talking books, and braille books (if your children have braille reading skills). (See the Notes at the end of the chapter for major sources of such materials.)[6]

An outcome of The Individuals with Disabilities Education Act was the establishment of the National Instructional Materials Access Center. It makes the conversion of print instructional materials in specialized formats such as braille, audio, or digital texts available to distributors. Resources such as the Louis Database of Accessible Materials (www.aph.org/louis/index.html) enable you to search for available instructional print materials for the vision impaired.

Science Activities and Equipment Some children with visual impairments have a degree of residual vision; that is, they may be able to distinguish light areas from dark areas and to differentiate shapes. To capitalize on these abilities, speak with the child, the child's parents, and perhaps the child's physician (with parental permission, of course) to get ideas about how to modify equipment for him or her.

A small digital recorder can be an important addition to your classroom equipment. It can take the place of a notebook by permitting the child to record the results of science experiences. The recording procedure will also help the child understand that you are holding him or her as accountable as the other students for taking and maintaining notes. Also consider the increasing availability of voice recognition software to assist children with disabilities that make writing challenging.

Look for ways to provide appropriate tactile experiences for children with visual impairments. I have used interlocking snap beads to represent DNA molecules. Each shape represented a different nucleotide. Staples or liquid glue can be used to raise the print of graphs or diagrams. The AAAS (1991) recommends the use of technology to facilitate observations and data collection such as talking thermometers, timers, and calculators.[7] Familiarize visually impaired students with the location of emergency exits, eye washes, and emergency showers with respect to their work space.

Here is a challenge for you: How would you have a child with a visual impairment observe a fish in an aquarium? Because aquarium fish usually are not noisy creatures and are tucked in water, which is itself encased in glass or plastic, this problem may seem insurmountable—but it isn't. If you place within the aquarium a slightly smaller plastic aquarium that has holes drilled in it, the child will be able to lift and tip the inner aquarium until most of the water drains into the larger aquarium. The fish will become trapped in the water that remains at the bottom of the inner aquarium. Use caution handling the fish. As any good fisherman knows, do not touch the fish with dry fingers. Be sure the child's hands are wet with the water in which the fish is kept. Encourage the child to treat the fish gently and to stroke it along the grain of the scales. Alternatively, use an anatomically correct model or professionally mounted fish for the child to touch in order to get a sense of the fish's external structure.

As the aquarium question illustrates, the real challenge to a child's learning may be the difficulty the teacher has in finding a way around or through a seemingly insurmountable problem. You are not completely on your own, however, as you think through these problems. Through research in specialized catalogs and your personal contacts with special education personnel, you will discover that adapted equipment is available to help children and adults with visual impairments measure such variables as elapsed time, length, volume, mass, and weight.

There should be an "eleventh commandment" for teachers who work with children who have visual impairments: Do not be meek in your demeanor as you go forth to make requests for special adapted materials and equipment. Your efforts to accommodate the special needs of children will be rewarded in many ways. The children will learn, and their peers will gain important knowledge and attitudes about people who may seem different but, in fact, are not.

Science Experiences for Children with Hearing Impairments

Mainstreamed children with hearing impairments range from those who do not require a hearing aid to those who have no hearing. Some of these children will be skilled lip readers, some will be adept at sign language, and some will have neither of these skills.

Children who have hearing impairments can benefit greatly from the multisensory, hands-on approach to science used in any discovery-oriented classroom. Your principal challenge will be helping these children participate fully in the experiences. Written or pictorial directions for activities and assignments, directions on task cards, and even acting out the steps of an activity will prove helpful. In the upper-elementary grades and in the middle grades, you may wish to have children take turns taking notes from your oral presentations and sharing them with students who have hearing impairments.

The child with a hearing impairment should have an unobstructed view of you and the location where you carry out demonstrations. This will allow the child to search for visual cues to supplement any information that you transmit orally. As you carry out demonstrations, explain content, and give directions, try to position your head so that the child can read your lip movements and facial expressions. You may want to remind the child's classmates to do the same.

Children with hearing impairments benefit greatly from participating in multisensory, hands-on science activities.

When working with a child who has a hearing impairment, be careful not to form an opinion about his or her intellectual abilities based only upon listening to his or her speech. The inability to articulate properly results from not having a model for the spoken words and does not indicate intellectual ability. By encouraging the child's oral responses, you will provide him or her with an opportunity to build self-confidence and practice articulation.

Science Experiences for Children with Physical Impairments

Physical impairments may range from mild to severe and differ widely in origin. Some physical challenges may result from accidents and diseases, and some may be congenital. As a science teacher, your concern should focus on the specific problems that the child may have as the class does hands-on activities. Think about whether the child has problems grasping objects, moving, stopping, or remaining steady. Also keep in mind the space needed for children with crutches, the room required for a wheelchair to navigate, and the access available at some field trip sites.

As you consider these matters, you may find that you have to make accommodations in the classroom for a child with a physical challenge or adaptations to the science materials and equipment that he or she will use. For example, you may need to arrange seating so that a child in a wheelchair has ready access to all parts of the room. Or you may need to be sure that a child who has a problem moving quickly has a work space that is close to the distribution point for science materials. Of course, the accommodations needed will vary with each child.

A child's physical challenge can provide a growth experience for the classroom if you capitalize on the opportunities it provides for building a sense of community among all the children. By helping children interact positively with *all* their peers, you not only help the child with a physical impairment but also the entire class.

Science Experiences for Children with Emotional Problems

Some children display emotional behaviors that interfere with their ability to function well academically or with their personal and social development in the classroom. These children may have little self-confidence, be frightened easily, be depressed, be disobedient or defiant, or simply spend their time daydreaming. The child with emotional problems acts the way he or she does for a reason. Unfortunately, the reason may have eluded even the most skilled school psychologist or psychiatrist.

The causes for the behavior you observe will probably lie outside your ability to remediate. However, the science activities you offer can serve an important therapeutic function. They can enable the child to manipulate and control variables and thus give him or her a unique opportunity to operate in responsible ways. This often benefits all children as well as those with attention deficit disorders to remain stimulated.

The 5E instructional strategy is designed to engage students in thought-provoking hands-on activities. If children can find success through such activities, they will gain self-confidence and pride in accomplishment. You may not be able to remedy children's basic emotional problems, but you can create an environment that can enhance feelings of self-worth.

As a teacher of science in a regular classroom, you should help your students welcome and encourage any child with emotional problems who joins the class for the day or a portion of the day. Remember, children with emotional problems need ever-increasing contact with children who display appropriate behaviors. Some teachers may be concerned that the rest of a class will learn inappropriate behaviors from a mainstreamed child with emotional problems. If this occurs, it may be that the teacher has been unable to create a total classroom environment that values and affirms productive and appropriate social behaviors.

Learning Disabilities

Learning disabilities (LD) are neurologically based processing problems. These processing problems can interfere with learning basic skills such as reading, writing, or math. They can also interfere with higher-level skills such as organization, time planning, and abstract reasoning. The types of LD are identified by the specific processing problem. They might relate to getting information into the brain (Input), making sense of this information (Organization), storing and later retrieving this information (Memory), or getting this information back out (Output). Thus, the specific types of processing problems that result in LD might be in one or more of these four areas.[8] Work closely with the special-education team and keep in mind the principles of differentiated learning and UDL as you address the LD needs of students in your class.

Children with Special Gifts and Talents

Many of the children in our schools have extraordinary intellectual abilities, and many have other abilities that are far more advanced than those of their agemates. In fact, it is estimated that between 3% and 5% of the school-age population fits this definition. How can you tell which children have special abilities? The following definition may help:

> Children capable of high performance, including those with demonstrated achievements or ability in any one or more of these areas—general intellectual ability, specific academic aptitude, creative or productive thinking, leadership ability, visual and performing arts, or psychomotor ability.[9]

Also keep in mind that gifted and talented children may come from diverse cultural backgrounds or they may have impairments, as discussed in previous sections of this chapter. Think of your classroom as a garden in which each gifted and talented child can blossom. Science can provide these children with unique opportunities to design and carry out explorations of their environment. Because gifted and talented children may move very quickly through the planned learning experiences you provide for your class, the challenge is to keep them growing and blossoming. You will need to find ways to extend and enrich your science activities so that these children do not become bored.

The National Association for Gifted Children recommends that an effective approach to programming for gifted learners should be seen as a combination of three elements: accelerative approaches, in which instruction is matched to the competence level of students; enrichment approaches, in which opportunities for the investigation of supplementary material are given; and individualization, in which instruction is matched specifically to the learner's achievement, abilities, and interests.[10]

Acceleration often refers to specialized courses or grade skipping, both of which are probably beyond the scope of your responsibilities as a classroom teacher. However, you can enrich and individualize instruction in your classroom using differentiated instruction that addresses gifted and talented students.

Day-to-Day Enrichment Activities

Here are some enrichment activities you may wish to use even if your school has a standard science curriculum or a specific set of textbooks or other resource materials:

1. Get single copies of advanced levels of the materials for each child you think will benefit from such materials or activities.

2. Each time the class begins a new unit of work, have conferences with your gifted children to identify enrichment readings and activities for them to work on in the course of the unit and establish a schedule of follow-up conferences.

3. Develop strategies that will enable these children to share their readings and related experiences with the rest of the class.

4. In general, expect these children to participate fully in all regular activities, but try to put their special gifts and talents to use as they go beyond the basic curriculum.

Challenge Projects

Gifted and talented children are a special joy to teach because many are able to function with considerable independence in the classroom. This capacity for independent, self-directed work is well suited to long-term science projects. I call such activities *challenge projects*. Here are a few examples:

Can You Make:
> A sundial and use it as a clock?
>
> A model wind-speed indicator?
>
> A water filter using sand and pebbles that will clean up muddy water?
>
> A compound machine from a group of simple machines?
>
> A working model of a liquid-based fire extinguisher?
>
> A simple battery-operated electric motor?
>
> A balance that really works?
>
> A clay contour map of the school grounds?

All challenge projects should begin with a teacher/student conference that focuses on the child's interest in and capacity to undertake various projects.

Integrate the enrichment activities and challenge projects into the curriculum. Avoid activities that are add-ons or busy work. Rather, make the learning experience one that genuinely deepens understanding, and make it optional yet available to all students. For example, suppose you were teaching a lesson on heat exchange using the freezing of water as an example. Provide an option for all students to calculate the latent heat of ice using the relationship expressed as

Heat gained by ice + Heat gained by water from melted ice =
Heat lost by container + Heat lost by water

$$m_i L_i \quad + \quad m_{wi} c_w \Delta T \quad = \quad m_c c_c \Delta T \quad + \quad m_w c_w \Delta T$$

where m = mass, i = ice, w = water, wi = water from melted ice, c = container.

Solve for L to get the latent heat of ice.

Provide resources for the students to investigate the kinetic molecular theory.

Responding to the special needs of gifted and talented children will provide you with many opportunities to stretch your own intellectual and imaginative abilities. You will find helping these children to reach their full potential is an extremely enjoyable part of teaching.

Summary

Teachers need to know how to use and provide access to the latest classroom technology so that special-needs children are not limited in their progress as a result of the "digital divide." Science time should be seen as an opportunity for all children to practice their reading and language development skills. Inquiry-based, discovery-focused activities, and the stimuli such activities provide, can help children from diverse cultural backgrounds increase their language skills as they learn science.

Children with special needs—whether visual or physical impairments, hearing problems, or emotional problems—must participate as fully as possible in the science activities that take place in the classroom. Your response to their special needs requires both an understanding of the unique challenges they offer and the ability to develop a variety of ways to make the curriculum accessible to them.

Gifted and talented children also have special needs. The science curriculum for these children should include various enrichment activities, challenge projects, and other opportunities to use their unique talents and abilities.

Use the principles of UDL to guide differentiated instruction as you plan the appropriate accommodations to your curriculum and teaching. Work with members of the special education team to provide meaningful and effective inclusion for all students in your class.

Going Further

On Your Own

1. If you have a disability or were an ELL in elementary school, comment on any special challenges you had to overcome to be a successful student in science class. If you feel that there were no such challenges, note whether this was due to special circumstances, such as a particularly responsible and encouraging teacher, parental support, and so on. If you do not have a disability or were not an ELL in elementary school, interview someone who is and record his or her responses to these questions.

2. How serious is the problem of science career awareness for children from diverse cultural backgrounds? Would broader media coverage of minority-group members in scientific fields counterbalance the

underrepresentation of such individuals in curricular materials? What do you see as the teacher's role in building scientific career awareness?

3. Identify a science activity you would do with children, and then describe how you would adapt it to the needs of a child with a visual or hearing impairment.

4. Write a sample letter that you could use to establish communication among yourself, a scientist living in the community, and a gifted child with a strong interest in science. In the letter, highlight the benefits that both the child and the scientist would enjoy.

5. Use the principles of UDL to develop an inquiry-based learning experience for a fifth-grade class of 20 students. The class consists of one student with a hearing impairment, one student with a learning disability, and two gifted students. The IEP for the LD student recommends the following strategies and accommodations:
    Repeat and clarify directions.
    Preview and review vocabulary.

Use a multimodal approach with audio and visual supplements. Always relate classroom activities to timetable and agenda.

6. Role-play the following situations with your group. When you are done, discuss each situation:
    a. A parent/teacher conference regarding a gifted child whose parent is dissatisfied with your response to the child's special abilities. This parent is particularly concerned about accelerating the child's learning in both science and mathematics.
    b. Same as in "a," except the child has a hearing or visual impairment.
    c. A conference in which the teacher encourages the parents of a child with a physical impairment to allow the child to participate in a field trip to a water treatment plant.

If you are doing this activity by yourself, write a brief description of what might take place in each of these three conferences.

Resources for Discovery Learning

Internet Resources

 To access these helpful websites, go to **MyEducationLab,** select Resources, and then Web Links. To learn more, click on the following links and you will easily be directed to each website

- **CAST Teaching Every Student:**
  www.cast.org/teachingeverystudent/

- **Center for Applied Special Technology:**
  www.cast.org/research/udl/index.html

- **Differentiated Instruction:**
  www.frsd.k12.nj.us/rfmslibrarylab/di/differentiated_instruction.htm

- **Learning Disabilities Association of America:**
  www.ldanatl.org/aboutld/teachers/index.asp

- **National Association for Gifted Children:**
  www.nagc.org/

Print Resources

Suggested Readings

Allan, Alson. "The Minority Student Achievement Network." *Educational Leadership* 60, no. 5 (December 2002/January 2003): 76–78.

Bernstein, Leonard, et al. *African and African-American Women of Science.* Saddle Brook, NJ: Peoples Publishing Group, 1998.

Bernstein, Leonard, et al. *Latino Women of Science.* Saddle Brook, NJ: Peoples Publishing Group, 1998.

Bernstein, Leonard, et al. *Multicultural Women of Science.* Saddle Brook, NJ: Peoples Publishing Group, 1996.

Buck, Gayle A. "Teaching Science to English-as-Second-Language Learners." *Science and Children* 38, no. 3 (November/December 2000): 38–41.

Burgstahler, S. *Universal Design of Instruction (UDI): Definition, Principles, and Examples.* Seattle: DO-IT, University of Washington, 2008.

Carolan, J., et al. "Differentiation: Lessons from Master Teachers." *Educational Leardership* 64, no. 5 (February 2007): 44–47.

Cassano, Paul, and Antol, Rayna A. "Integration and Integrity." *Science Scope* 24, no. 7 (April 2001): 18–21.

Cawley, John F., Foley, Teresa E., Miller, James. "Science and Students with Mild Disabilities Principles of Universal Design." *Intervention in School and Clinic* 38A, no. 3 (January 2003): 160–171.

Curriculum Access and Universal Design for Learning. ERIC/OSEP Digest #E586 ERIC Clearinghouse on Disabilities and Gifted Education **ERIC Identifier:** ED437767 **Publication Date:** 1999-12-00 **Author:** Orkwis, Raymond

Delisle, J. R. "For gifted students, full inclusion is a partial solution." *Educational Leadership* 57, no. 3 (November 1999): 80–83.

Farenga, Stephen J., et al. "Rocketing into Adaptive Inquiry." *Science Scope* 25, no. 4 (January 2002): 34–39.

Fetters, Marcia, Pickard, Dawn M., and Pyle, Eric. "Making Science Accessible: Strategies to Meet the Needs of a Diverse Student Population." *Science Scope* 26, no. 5 (February 2003): 26–29.

Flores, M. M. "Universal Design in Elementary and Middle School." *Childhood Education* 84, no. 4 (Summer 2008): 224–229.

Garrett, Michael Tlanusta, et al. "Open Hands, Open Hearts: Working with Native Youth in the Schools." *Intervention in School and Clinic* 38, no. 4 (March 2003): 225–235.

Gooden, Kelly. "Parents Come to Class." *Science and Children* 40, no. 4 (January 2003): 22–25.

Hall, T. (2002). *Differentiated instruction*. Wakefield, MA: National Center on Accessing the General Curriculum. Retrieved [insert date] from http://www.cast .org/publications/ncac/ncac_diffinstruc.html

Hehir, T. "The Changing Role of Intervention for Children with Disabilities." *Principal (Reston, Va.)* 85, no. 2 (November/December 2005): 22–25.

Hehir, Thomas. "Confronting Ableism." *Educational Leadership* 64, no. 5 (Feb 2007): 8–14.

Hrabowski, Freeman A., III. "Raising Minority Achievement in Science and Math." *Educational Leadership* 60, no. 5 (December 2002/January 2003): 44–48.

Krutchinsky, Rich, and Harris, William. "Super Science Saturday." *Science and Children* 40, no. 4 (January 2003): 26–28.

Lord, Thomas R., and Clausen-May, Tandi. "Giving Spatial Perception Our Full Attention." *Science and Children* 39, no. 5 (February 2002): 22–25.

Nitzberg, Joel, and Sparrow, Judith. "Parent Outreach Success." *Science and Children* 39, no. 3 (November/ December 2001): 36–40.

Pemberton, Jane B. "Integrated Processing: A Strategy for Working Out Unknown Words." *Intervention in School and Clinic* 38, no. 4 (March 2003): 247–250.

Rolon, Carmen A. "Educating Latino Students." *Educational Leadership* 60, no. 5 (December 2002/ January 2003): 40–43.

Schon, Isabel. "Libros de Ciencias en Espanol." *Science and Children* 37, no. 6 (March 2000): 26–29.

Schon, Isabel. "Libros de Ciencias en Espanol." *Science and Children* 38, no. 6 (March 2001): 23–26.

Schon, Isabel. "Libros de Ciencias en Espanol." *Science and Children* 39, no. 6 (March 2002): 22–25.

Talanquer, Vicente, and Sarmiento, Griselda. "One Foot = One Cenxocoalli: Measuring in the Pre-Hispanic World." *Science Scope* 25, no. 7 (April 2002): 12–15.

The Templeton National Report on Acceleration. *A Nation Deceived: How Schools Hold Back America's Brightest Students*. Vol. I. Edited by Nicholas Colangelo, Susan G. Assouline, Miraca U. M. Gross. 2004. The Connie Belin & Jacqueline N. Blank International Center for Gifted Education and Talent Development. Iowa City: Iowa.

The Templeton National Report on Acceleration. *A Nation Deceived: How Schools Hold Back America's Brightest Students*. Vol. II. Edited by Nicholas Colangelo, Susan G. Assouline, Miraca U. M. Gross. 2004. The Connie Belin & Jacqueline N. Blank International Center for Gifted Education and Talent Development. Iowa City: Iowa.

Williams, Gregory J., and Leon Reisberg. "Successful Inclusion." *Intervention in School and Clinic* 38, no. 4 (March 2003): 205–210.

Winebrenner, S. "Gifted students need an education, too." *Educational Leadership* 58, no. 1 (September 2000): 52–56.

Notes

1. You may reach the Center for the Study of Books in Spanish for Children at www.csusm.edu/campus.centers/csb.
2. Isabel Schon, "Libros de Ciencias en Espanol," *Science and Children* 35, no. 6 (March 1998): 30.
3. Many major publishers of educational materials prepare direct translations of some or all of their elementary- and middle-grade science books. I extend my thanks to Holt, Rinehart and Winston for their permission to reproduce Figure 9.1, which first appeared in J. Abruscato et al., *Ciencia de Holt*, Grade 5 Teacher's Guide (New York: Holt, Rinehart and Winston, 1985), p. TM10.
4. From Cynthia Curry, Libby Cohen, and Nancy Lightbody. "Universal Design in Science Learning." *The Science Teacher* 73, no. 3 (March 2006): 32–37.

5. Lauren Katzman (personal communication, April 15, 2007).

6. Sources of materials, such as large-type books, talking books, and braille books are the American Printing House for the Blind (Box 6085, 1839 Frankfort Avenue, Louisville, Kentucky 40206) and The Lighthouse for the Blind and Visually Impaired (1155 Mission Street, San Francisco, California 94103).

7. American Association for the Advancement of Science. "Laboratories and Classrooms in Science and Engineering." (Washington, DC: 1991) [ED 373 997].

8. Learning Disabilities Association of America. Types of Disabilities. www.ldanatl.org/aboutld/teachers/understanding/types.asp. Downloaded (06-03-08).

9. Dorothy Sisk, *What If Your Child Is Gifted?* (Washington, DC: Office of the Gifted and Talented, U.S. Office of Education, n.d.).

10. National Association for Gifted Children. www.nagc.org/. (accessed 06-03-08).

Science Content
to Discovery Lessons

Parts Two, Three, and Four provide an overview of content in the earth and space sciences, life sciences, and physical sciences. Following each content chapter you will find a chapter entitled, "Putting the Content into Action," which integrates the unit and lesson planning strategies addressed in Part One. Each planning chapter includes specific content starter ideas for units and lessons along with activities in the forms of attention getters, discovery activities, and demonstrations. The lesson ideas suggest activities that you can mold into engagements and explorations to create discovery-based learning experiences rich in content for your students. New to this edition are complete sample lessons accompanying each content area that illustrate how the lesson ideas and activities could be developed into an entire lesson.

part **two**

The Earth/Space Sciences

▶ **History and Nature of the Earth/Space Sciences**

Tonight, and every night, *you* have the chance to see a wondrous puzzle exactly as generations of humans before you have seen it. Tiny objects will begin to emerge, gleaming and glimmering, and darkness will envelop everything around you. This great and glorious puzzle is the night sky.

Trying to make sense of what lies above us is a mark of our humanity. Likewise, the mysteries of the earth below make us wonder. We ask "What?" and "How?" and "Why?"

These are the same questions that guide what earth and space scientists do. They search for answers to the puzzles of our world, so we will eventually understand what really lies above and below. The earth/space sciences include the fields of astronomy, geology, oceanography, meteorology, and astronomy. Each requires people who wonder.

Careers in the Earth/Space Sciences

Many career paths exist for those women and men who have the required motivation, knowledge, and skills to formally explore the sky above and the earth below. Here are a few of the wide range of possibilities:

● *Geologist.* I love to tease my geologist friends by calling them "rock watchers." Of course, they tell me with great gusto that they do much more than watch rocks—and of course, they do. Geology includes the study of the origin of the earth, the history of the earth, and the external and internal structure and movements of the earth.

- *Oceanographer.* Not all oceanographers spend the day scuba diving in warm tropical waters, but some do! In fact, the work done by oceanographers takes them to oceans all over the world. That work might involve study of the characteristics of the seafloor, the ocean water itself, and the forms of life in, on, and under the ocean.

- *Meteorologist.* The constantly smiling and sometimes overly excited weather people you watch on local news shows may be meteorologists or newscasters acting as if they are meteorologists. A real meteorologist has taken courses dealing with atmospheric phenomena and how various weather systems affect life on earth.

- *Astronomer.* If you've looked at the night sky and been enthralled by the amazing display of objects above your head, you have taken the first step that all astronomers take: to think beyond the boundaries of Earth and its atmosphere. Modern astronomers have excellent backgrounds in physics and mathematics as well as considerable computer expertise.

Key Events in the Understanding of the Earth/Space Sciences

610–425 B.C.E.	Philosophers Anaximander, Pythagoras, Xenophanes, and Herodotus propose that fossils found inland once lived in the sea.
140	Ptolemy incorrectly concludes that the earth is at the center of the solar system.
1797–1726	James Hutton concludes that processes that were constantly occurring—such as erosion, deposition, earthquakes, and volcanic eruptions—produced the rocks of Scotland. These ideas are the foundation for the principle of uniformitarianism, which suggests that landforms developed over long periods of time through the actions of slow geological processes such as erosion and weathering.
1781	William Herschel discovers the planet Uranus, the first such discovery since ancient times.
1804	Georges Cuvier studies fossils found around Paris and suggests that they are thousands of centuries old. This meant that the earth was much older than people thought at the time.
1820–1821	Mary Anning excavates the world's first fossil plesiosaur.
1830	Charles Lyell publishes *Principles of Geology*, a book that Charles Darwin took along on his explorations.
1847	Maria Mitchell, an American astronomer and professor, discovers a comet whose path took it near the star Polaris.
1856	The first recognized fossil human, a Neanderthal, is discovered in Düsseldorf, Germany.
1912	Alfred Wegener proposes the theory of continental drift, suggesting that the individual continents were once part of one supercontinent.
1957	The Soviet Union launches *Sputnik,* the earth's first artificial space satellite.
1969	American astronaut Neil Armstrong walks on the surface of the moon.
1969	The American *Apollo* missions bring rocks home from the moon to the earth.
1971	Stephen Hawking poses the hypothesis that primordial black holes might have been created in the Big Bang: a theorized explosion that marked the origin of the universe billions of years ago.
1974	Stephen Hawking applies quantum field theory to black hole spacetime and shows that black holes radiate mass/energy that may result in their evaporation.

1980   Alan Guth proposes the inflationary Big Bang universe, which suggests that the universe expanded at a rate that kept doubling for a brief period of time after the Big Bang.

1980   Louis W. Alvarez, Walter Alvarez, Frank Asaro, and Helen V. Michel publish their asteroid impact theory of dinosaur extinction in *Science Magazine*.

1981   The United States launches the first space shuttle: the *Columbia.*

1990   The Hubble Space Telescope is placed in orbit; after its optical systems are improved, it sends back extraordinary pictures of the universe.

1990   The COBE (Cosmic Background Explorer) satellite transmits data that indicate that the background radiation of the universe is what would be expected if the universe originated in a manner consistent with the Big Bang theory.

1991   The Chicxulub Crater is discovered in the Yucatán Peninsula, supporting the asteroid impact theory first suggested in 1980.

1993   J. William Schopf publishes a description of the oldest fossils known to science: 3.5 billion-year-old microfossils from the Apex Basalt in Australia.

1995   Michael Mayor and Didier Queloz identify the first planet outside our solar system.

1997   The Mars probe *Sojourner* lands and transmits pictures of the planet's surface to Earth.

1998   The moon probe *Lunar Prospector* sends back data that indicate that some water in the form of ice lies beneath its surface.

1998   Construction begins on the *International Space Station.*

2001   The *Mars Global Surveyor* probe completes its primary mapping study of the Martian surface and reveals that there once was and now may be liquid water near the surface.

2004   The rovers *Spirit* and *Opportunity* land on Mars and begin sending back images and data of the red planet. On March 2, 2004, NASA announced that the rovers had confirmed liquid water once flowed on Mars.

2008   The orbiter spacecraft *Messenger* begins sending back a complete picture of Mercury, shedding light on its geological history.

Women and Men Who Have Shaped the Development of the Earth/Space Sciences

PTOLEMY (about 85–165 AD) was an astronomer, mathematician, and geographer. He proposed that the earth was at the center of the universe and that the other heavenly bodies—such as the sun and planets—moved in orbits around it. He was, of course, incorrect.

TYCHO BRAHE (1546–1601), a Danish astronomer, gathered data that were eventually used to predict the motion and orbits of the planets. These data quashed any remaining support for the Ptolemaic, or Earth-centered, view of the universe.

SOPHIA BRAHE (1556–1643), the younger sister of Tycho Brahe, gathered and contributed data used to predict planetary orbits. In addition to her astronomical work, she was also a well-known horticulturalist and historian.

NICOLAUS COPERNICUS (1473–1543) was a mathematician, physician, lawyer, and perhaps priest who became known for suggesting that the sun was at rest in the center of the universe. This is now know as the heliocentric theory.

GALILEO GALILEI (1564–1642) is credited with many discoveries related to the motion of the pendulum, the construction of compasses and telescopes, and observations of the satellites of Jupiter and the phases of Venus. He espoused Copernicus's view that the planets revolved around the sun and was accused of being a heretic.

ISAAC NEWTON (1642–1727) provided the foundation for modern physics and mathematics. His studies of the natural world led to the development of the law of inertia, the law of action and reaction, and the relationship of force to the acceleration of a mass. He proposed the universal law of gravitation and is credited as being the co-inventor of calculus.

CAROLINE LUCRETIA HERSCHEL (1750–1848) and her brother William gathered data on astronomical objects. After William's death, Caroline completed their work on the creation of astronomy data sources, which were called *catalogs.*

MARY ANNING (1799–1847), a self-taught paleontologist, became known for excavating the fossil remains of an icthyosaurus, a plesisaur, and a pterodactyl.

MARIA MITCHELL (1818–1889), an American astronomer, discovered a comet whose path took it near the star Polaris; she was also known for her analysis of sunspots.

CHARLES D. WALCOTT (1850–1927) was a geologist and paleontologist who made a number of discoveries related to ancient animal and plant life. The most important of these was his study of the Middle Cambrian Burgess Shale, which had an extraordinary range of fossils.

ANDRIJA MOHOROVICIC (1857–1936), a Croatian geologist and meteorologist, made extraordinary discoveries related to weather and seismology. The Mohorovicic discontinuity, the boundary between the crust and the mantle of the earth, was eventually named in his honor.

ALBERT EINSTEIN (1879–1955) was a German-born physicist whose special theory of relativity and general theory of relativity provided the basis for much of what is known about the nature of time, space, and matter.

ALFRED WEGENER (1880–1930) was trained in astronomy but pursued meteorology as his profession. Curiously, he eventually became world famous for work in yet another field: geology. He first proposed the theory of plate tectonics, which is the foundation for modern ideas about continental drift.

CHARLES FRANCIS RICHTER (1900–1985) carried out work on the classification of earthquakes based on energy release. The Richter scale was developed from his careful analysis of data acquired at the Caltech Seismological Laboratory.

LUIS ALVAREZ (1911–1988) received the Nobel Prize for physics in 1968 for his study of subatomic particles. He became even more famous for his study of a thin, clay layer under the earth's surface that contains large amounts of iridium. This discovery lent support to the theory that dinosaur extinction was caused by an asteroid crashing into the earth and releasing the iridium-containing material.

WALTER ALVAREZ (1940–), the son of Luis Alvarez, discovered a thin, clay layer of soil that had high concentrations of iridium and also marked the end of the Cretaceous period and the dinosaurs. This research gave credence to the asteroid impact theory as the explanation for dinosaur extinction.

VERA COOPER RUBIN (1928–) has studied the orbital velocities of hydrogen clouds, and her results support the belief that there are large amounts of dark matter in the universe. (Dark matter is matter that cannot be seen or measured directly.)

STEPHEN HAWKING (1942–), an English physicist, has emerged as one of the most inventive scientific geniuses since Einstein. His theories about black holes and the origin of the universe guide what today's cosmologists explore. His ideas may ultimately provide physicists with a grand unified theory: one equation that will encompass all of the other equations that describe interactions in the universe.

▶ Personal and Social Implications of the Earth/Space Sciences

The quality of the air we breathe and the water we drink, the safety of the structures in which we work and live, and the protection of our natural resources can all be influenced by knowledge gained through the earth/space sciences. This knowledge affects us as individuals and as members of the communities in which we live.

Personal and Community Health

The work done in the earth/space sciences affects our well-being in many ways. For instance, geologists gather information about the quality of agricultural soils and the safety of recreational areas such as ski slopes and reservoirs formed behind earthen dams. The safety of our transportation system, including roads, tunnels, and bridge supports, all depends on geologists' knowledge of the rocks and rock layers underneath them.

We count on the forecasting capabilities of meteorologists to tell us how to dress for personal comfort and to provide us with a timeline for the pending arrival of violent weather. And the knowledge of the night skies provided by astronomers permits us to navigate the earth safely and even guides farmers and fishermen in their food production efforts.

Hazards, Risks, and Benefits

Today, earthquakes, volcanic eruptions, violent weather, tsunamis, and the like can all be forecast using the predictive capacities of the earth/space sciences. Given these predictions, individuals and societies can make important health- and safety-related decisions, often saving lives. In the developed nations of the world, personal housing, civic structures, and commercial buildings are all built to withstand disasters of all kinds.

▶ Earth/Space Science Technology: Its Nature and Impact

The women and men who explore the earth/space sciences solve the mysteries of nature by observing, poking at, and prodding it with *technology.* That technology is sometimes as simple as a compass and sometimes as complex as a radiotelescope. Whether simple or complex, the technology used by earth/space scientists is always designed for a very specific purpose.

The Design of Earth/Space Science Technology

Astronomy, geology, meteorology, oceanography, and the other subdisciplines of the earth/space sciences depend on *instrumentation:* radiotelescopes that "listen" to the stars, seismographs that reveal movements within the earth, weather instruments that gather data about the atmosphere, and underwater microphones that track migration patterns of sea life. All of these instruments are designed to meet the following criteria:

1. The problem addressed with the technology has been clearly specified and is one for which data can be expected to be obtained.

2. The technology itself can reliably gather, display, and transmit data.

3. The data gathered are presented in a manner that can be easily interpreted.

4. The device or instrument provides researchers with constant feedback about the accuracy of the data being represented, errors that may have occurred in the gathering and processing of the data, and suggestions for troubleshooting malfunctions.

Examples of Earth/Space Science Technology

A variety of instruments are used to gather information about the earth, the oceans, the atmosphere, and outer space:

Hand lenses (magnifying glasses)   Seismographs
Microscopes   The global position system (GPS)
Optical telescopes   Weather maps
Radiotelescopes   Anemometers
The Hubble Space Telescope   Barometers
High-resolution cameras   Thermometers
Satellites   Scuba equipment
The orbiting space station   Bathyscaphe (self-propelled underwater
Radar   observatory)
Sonar   Computers

Long-Term Implications of Earth/Space Science Technology

Earth/space scientists seek to provide answers to basic questions about the earth—our home. Some of the data they acquire will eventually be used to improve our quality of life in ways large and small. However, earth/space scientists generally do not focus on the immediate application of new knowledge and skills to human problems. That is the work of engineers and technicians.

Engineers, who search for solutions to human problems, understand that their work has real limitations. For instance, their solutions are usually temporary, because the frontiers of scientific knowledge are constantly expanding. Their solutions may also be too be costly and carry risks. For example, the use of movement-sensitive underwater microphones may disrupt whale migration patterns.

Some technological solutions may even have harmful consequences. For example, an imperfect or malfunctioning earthquake or tsunami warning device might produce information that causes people to panic—triggering the hording of food and water and producing evacuation problems—when there was really no cause for alarm in the first place. So, not all technological solutions are successful.

chapter 10

Earth's Surface, Atmosphere, and Weather

Content

Spaceship Earth: What Is It Made Of?

You don't have to hitch a ride on the next space shuttle to treat yourself to a high-speed space adventure. You are having one right now! All living things—including you and me—are passengers on the most elaborate and marvelous spaceship that will ever hurl through space and time. It's the top-of-the-line luxury model, fully equipped with water, oxygen, and abundant food. And best of all, each and every seat has a fantastic view!

We can become so comfortable riding along on *Spaceship Earth* (otherwise known as the "third rock from the sun") that we take its very existence and nature for granted. If you take the time to learn more about the earth, you will discover that it's just as fascinating as the moon, planets, stars, and mysteries that lie at the far reaches of the universe.

● The Earth Beneath Your Feet

The earth, our personal spaceship, is full of surprises. One of the most extraordinary findings actually comes from the common misconception that we're walking around on some enormous, solid ball of rock. In fact, the earth is a giant, layered sphere made of

Go to **MyEducationLab**, select Resources, and then Web Links. Then select "United States Geological Survey."

materials that are as different as oil and water and rock and diamonds. Even more surprising is that at the center of the earth lies something completely unexpected—a liquid.

To understand the makeup of the earth, we need to figuratively peel off layers and work our way to its center. The first layer is a thin shell that ranges from 11 kilometers (about 7 miles) to 32 kilometers (about 20 miles) in thickness. This crust is thought to be divided into seven major sections called *crustal plates.* These plates are interesting for many reasons, including the fact that they are slowly moving and carrying oceans and continents along with them.

Under this first layer, we find the *mantle,* which is about 2,870 kilometers (1,780 miles) deep. Figure 10.1 shows the crust and the mantle. Earthquake waves move faster in the upper mantle than in the crust. Knowing the rates at which earthquake waves travel through the different layers gives geologists important clues about the nature of the rock layers themselves.

Under the mantle, we find the *core.* Although no one is exactly sure of its composition, we do have an important clue: The fact that the earth has a magnetic field strong enough to turn a compass needle is evidence that a mass of molten metal exists at the center. The movement of this hot liquid metal, which is likely a mixture of iron and nickel, may create electric currents that produce the magnetic field.

● Gradual Changes in the Earth's Surface

If you look outside your window, you may see mountains, prairies, a desert, a lake, or maybe just other buildings. Whatever the case, the view you see creates an illusion—an illusion of permanence. In fact, all of our surroundings are in the process of gradual change, including the walls of the buildings you may see. More startling yet is the idea that even the enormous continents are in constant motion.

Most geologists now believe that all the continents were once joined into a single, large land mass. Alfred Wegener, who proposed this theory in 1912, named this land mass *Pangaea.* He believed that it broke apart and the pieces slowly drifted to where they are now. They are still moving but only very slowly at rates of between 1 and 5 centimeters per year. Australia and Africa are moving northward, so some time in the next 50 million years, Australia may strike Asia and Africa may strike Europe. Wegener's theory seems correct

Figure 10.1   The upper mantle between Hawaii and California

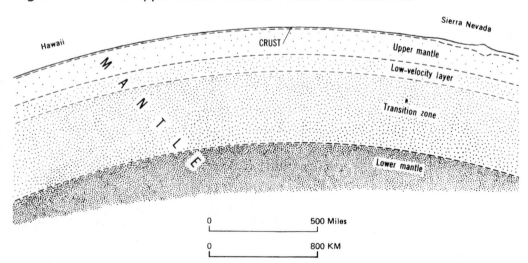

because geologists have discovered similar rock structures on the west coast of Africa and the east coast of South America. This similarity, along with the discovery of similar fossils in both locations, is strong evidence that the two continents were once part of the same land mass.

Continental drift is not the only cause of change in the earth's surface. External forces, such as weathering and erosion, constantly wear down the surface, and internal forces, which come from heat and pressure, push rock layers upward and sideways to form mountains and cause plate movement.

In order to keep track of when these various changes happened during the earth's history, scientists have created a geologic time scale. The largest division in the scale is the *era*. Each era is named for the type of life that existed then. Here are the four eras of geologic time and the approximate beginning of each:

Precambrian era	4,500,000,000 years ago
Paleozoic era	600,000,000 years ago
Mesozoic era	225,000,000 years ago
Cenozoic era	70,000,000 years ago

Table 10.1 gives an overview some of the most important characteristics of each era.

Table 10.1   The four eras

Era	Living Things Present	General Characteristics
Precambrian: 4,500,000,000 years ago	Single-celled and multicelled life appear.	This era represents about 90% of all geologic time. The earliest rocks on Earth are found in Precambrian deposits. They are about 4.5 billion years old.
Paleozoic: 600,000,000 years ago	The first land plants, reptiles, fish, spiders, and insects appear.	This was a time of great change. Sheets of ice covered much of the land in the Southern Hemisphere. Seas and oceans formed in the Northern Hemisphere. In time, much of the ice melted and land masses emerged from the oceans.
Mesozoic: 225,000,000 years ago	The first mammals, frogs, flowering plants, and dinosaurs appear. The dinosaurs also become extinct.	The Appalachian Mountains, Rocky Mountains, and Sierra Nevada Mountains were all formed. Great seas in the middle of North America disappeared, and these areas formed plains. The levels of the oceans dropped, and the climate became colder.
Cenozoic: 70,000,000 years ago	Mammals flourish, including humans, dogs, horses, and cattle.	Movement of the seven crustal plates pushed up mountains and increased earthquakes and volcanic activity. Glaciers from both polar regions spread out toward the equator. At one point, glaciers covered North America between the Appalachian Mountains and the northern Rocky Mountains. Eventually, the glaciers receded into south central Canada.

● **Violent Changes in the Earth's Surface**

If you stood between the railroad tracks in front of a freight train moving only 1 mile (less than 2 kilometers) an hour, you would gradually learn that powerful forces can have great consequences even though they are acting slowly. The same is true for the movement of crustal plates discussed earlier in this chapter. Violent changes happen where the plates meet, pushing and slowly grinding against one another.

Earthquakes   Imagine being sound asleep and being awakened by the feeling that your house was rocking back and forth. If you have actually had this experience, you know that this is what it's like to be in an earthquake.

This probably isn't news to you if you live in California, one part of North America where seismographs record a great deal of activity from the movement of plates. In western California, the Pacific plate is moving northwest and rubbing against the North American plate—the plate that North America rides on. Figure 10.2 shows the location of the San Andreas fault, which runs from northern to southern California. This figure also shows the dates of major earthquakes in California and areas where rock layers are very slowly being pushed out of position.

Volcanoes   On August 24, in the year 79, the apparently extinct volcano Vesuvius suddenly exploded, destroying the cities of Pompeii and Herculaneum.[1] Vesuvius had been quiet for hundreds of years, its surface and crater were green and vine covered, and no one expected the explosion. Yet in a few hours, volcanic ash and dust buried the two cities so thoroughly that their ruins were not uncovered for more than 1,600 years!

Molten rock below the surface of the earth that rises in volcanic vents is known as *magma*, but after it erupts from a volcano, it is called *lava*. It is red hot when it pours out

Figure 10.2
This map shows the San Andreas fault system and other geological faults in California.

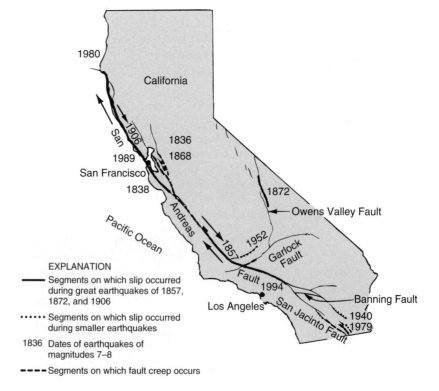

of the vent, but it slowly changes to dark red, gray, or black as it cools. If lava erupts in large volumes, it flows over the surface of the earth. Generally, very hot lava is fluid, like hot tar, whereas cooler lava flows more slowly, like thick honey.

All lava that comes to the surface of the earth contains dissolved gas. If the lava is a thin fluid, the gas escapes easily. But if the lava is thick and pasty, the gas escapes with explosive violence. The gas in lava may be compared with the gas in a bottle of soda pop. If you put your thumb over the top of the bottle and shake it, the gas separates from the liquid and forms bubbles. When you remove your thumb, there is a miniature explosion of gas and liquid. The gas in lava behaves in somewhat the same way; it causes the terrible explosions that throw out great masses of solid rock as well as lava, dust, and ashes.

The violent separation of gas from lava may produce rock froth, called *pumice*. Some of this froth is so light that it floats on water. In many eruptions, the froth is broken into small fragments that are hurled high into the air in the form of volcanic ash (gray), cinders (red or black), and dust.

● The Earth's Land Surface

Rocks   A rock can be much more than what it seems at first glance. Indeed, rocks provide us with many of the things that make possible an enjoyable and productive life. From rocks come the soils that nourish plants; the minerals we use for nutrients, fertilizer, adornment, and raw materials for manufacture; and, of course, the special stones that skip across the surface of a quiet pond on a hot summer day.

Igneous rocks are formed from the heating or cooling of melted materials in the earth (see Figure 10.3). The word *igneous* comes from a Latin word meaning "coming from fire." Igneous rocks on land are exposed to the elements of the hydrosphere and atmosphere. Water, wind, and temperature changes cause the chemical and physical breakdown of igneous rocks, a process known as *weathering*. The particles and pieces removed by weathering are moved from place to place by the wind, water, and, in some cases, glaciers. This movement results in *erosion*, or the wearing away of the land. Many of the particles and pieces are washed into streams and rivers and eventually transported to the oceans. Thus, matter that was originally inland igneous rock is washed up in layers at the water's edge to form beaches or, more commonly, settles in layers on the ocean floor.

Particles of rock transported to the oceans are called *sediment*. Over a long time, layers of sediment may become pressed together, eventually becoming *sedimentary rocks* (see Figure 10.4). Sedimentary rocks are formed from particles that were originally part of any other type of rock, from chemical reactions that occur in the ocean and result in small crystals, and from organic matter.

Figure 10.3
Igneous rocks are the result of volcanic activity.

Figure 10.4
Sedimentary rocks are formed in layers.

When rocks are heated or pressed together for a long time, they can change. Rocks that have undergone this process are known as *metamorphic rocks* (see Figure 10.5). Fashioned deep within the earth, metamorphic rocks are formed from igneous or sedimentary rocks. The term *metamorphic* comes from Greek words meaning "change" and "form."

Minerals   Rocks are combinations of *minerals,* naturally occurring chemical elements or compounds. Gold, silver, and platinum, for example, are well known and highly valued minerals found in rocks. Many mineral compounds include oxygen and another element found in abundance in the earth's crust: silicon. These compounds are known as *silicates.* Quartz, feldspar, and mica are all examples of silicates. Quartz consists of one silicon atom for every two oxygen atoms. Because its atoms are tightly joined, it is a very hard mineral. Feldspar commonly contains aluminum-oxygen and silicon-oxygen combinations of atoms. In some feldspars, however, sodium, calcium, or potassium replaces the aluminum. Feldspar is a softer mineral than quartz. Mica has an atomic pattern that causes it to be easily separated into thin sheets. Biotite and muscovite are two minerals that are micas.

Ores (which are useful metals) and gems (which are crystals that have an unusual color and the ability to reflect light from their many faces, or facets) are also minerals, but they are not silicates. Other nonsilicate minerals are calcite, gypsum, halite, and fluorite. Sulfur, gold, and graphite are nonsilicate minerals that are elements. An *element* is a substance composed of just one type of atom.

Scientists are able to identify the minerals that make up rocks by performing laboratory tests. Each mineral has a variety of identifying characteristics, including color; streak (the color it leaves when it is rubbed against a piece of porcelain); luster (the property of reflecting, bending, or absorbing light); the form of its crystals; cleavage and fracture (how it splits or breaks apart); relative weight; and hardness (how easily it can be scratched). Figure 10.6 shows the hardnesses of common minerals as determined by a measuring system known as *Mohs' hardness scale.* As you can see from these charts, if you know the Mohs' scale for some common materials, you can determine the hardness of another mineral by scratching it with the materials.

Figure 10.5
Metamorphic rocks are the result of pressure, heat, and chemical action.

Figure 10.6 These charts illustrate the Mohs' hardness scale and the relative positions of some common materials in it.

Some Common Materials and Their Relative Positions in the Hardness Scale

Hardness	Common Material	Comment
about 2.5	Fingernail	Will scratch gypsum with difficulty but will not scratch calcite.
about 3	Copper	Scratches calcite; will also be scratched by calcite.
about 5 to 5.5	Glass	With difficulty scratches apatite; also scratched by apatite.
about 5.5 to 6	Knife blade	Will scratch feldspar with difficulty.
about 7	File	Will scratch quartz with difficulty.
about 9	Silicon carbide	With difficulty scratches corundum; also scratched by corundum.

Mohs' Hardness Scale

Hardness	Mineral
1	Talc
2	Gypsum
3	Calcite
4	Fluorite
5	Apatite
6	Feldspar
7	Quartz
8	Topaz
9	Corundum
10	Diamond

Explanation: A given mineral will scratch those minerals above it in the table and will be scratched by those below it.

In addition to the common characteristics noted in the previous paragraph, a mineral may display some special properties, such as magnetism (being attracted to a magnet); fluorescence (glowing under ultraviolet light); phosphorescence (glowing after an ultraviolet light that has been shining on it is turned off); and radioactivity (giving off rays that can be detected by a Geiger counter).

Fossils The earth today contains billions of living things that display amazing variety in both appearance and behavior. However, life as we know it has changed a great deal over the 5 billion years in which the earth has existed. For example, dinosaurs once lived in Utah, great mammoths lived in Canada, and swampy forests once stretched across parts of Pennsylvania and Illinois. We know this, even though none of these things exist anymore, because we have found evidence of their existence in the form of fossils.

Fossils are created in a variety of ways. Because dead plants and animals usually decay quite rapidly, only the harder parts of their bodies are preserved. These parts are fossilized as a result of the presence of water containing mineral matter that replaces the hard portions of the animal. This explains why teeth, shells, bones, and woody tissues are all commonly found fossils. If plant or animal remains are covered by a protective material soon after death, the likelihood of fossilization increases. For example, the remains of creatures that live in the water fall to the bottom of the lake or seafloor, where soft mud and sand may bury them. Fossils that form in such environ-

Figure 10.7 This reconstruction of an American mastodon becoming entrapped in a La Brea tar pit captures the anguish of that moment in time. Fossilized remains found in the La Brea tar pits have provided a great deal of information about early life on North America.

ments are preserved in sedimentary rocks. Some fossils are found in the form of molds or casts. For example, seashells buried in mud and sand may eventually dissolve in the water. The cavity that is left may preserve the outline of the shell and its surface. Minerals from groundwater may settle in this mold and eventually form a cast of the original shell.

Fossils are seldom found in igneous rocks, because the process by which such rocks are formed would tend to destroy any remains of living things. However, wind-blown ash from volcanic activity may settle on animal or plant material and provide a protective covering that increases the likelihood of fossilization. Yellowstone National Park in Wyoming contains fossilized remains of forests that were covered by volcanic ash and dust.

Some unfossilized remains of plants and animals that lived millions of years ago have been found. At least one mammoth has been discovered preserved in ice. Natural mummies have also been found. Amber, a fossilized plant resin, has served as the final resting place for a variety of small plants and animals, and tar pits have been the source of beautifully preserved animal bones. The La Brea tar pits in the Los Angeles area are probably the best-known source of information about the plants and animals that lived thousands of years ago. Apparently, the animals became stuck in these natural tar pools. The tar has acted as a preservative and has provided scientists with excellent specimens of plant and animal life (see Figure 10.7).

Fossils of the earliest humanlike creatures have been found in Africa and are approximately 2 to 3 million years old. Modern humans—that is, creatures that would appear to us to be very much like ourselves—have probably existed for about 100,000 years. Our present physical and mental capabilities make us a species with an enormous capacity to both adapt to diverse environments and change environments to fit our needs.

Dinosaurs Few members of the parade of life that has marched across the earth offer as much fascination to children and adults as the dinosaur. The dinosaur was an air-breathing animal that could be as small as a chicken or as large as a whale. Body forms varied considerably from species to species: Some dinosaurs walked on two feet, others on four; some had horns, others had talons, and still others had large teeth. Some dinosaurs were meat eaters, and others were vegetarians.

Tyrannosaurus was a dinosaur that reached a length of 14 meters (about 46 feet), weighed more than an elephant, had teeth that were 8 to 15 centimeters (about 3 to 6 inches) long, huge feet, powerful claws, and relatively small, grasping "animal hands." It spent most of its time on land, moved about on two legs, and was a meat eater.

Apatosaurus, a large amphibian, was probably a vegetarian. It walked on four legs and had a very large and long neck. Fossil evidence of an apatosaurus more than 21 meters (about 69 feet) long has been found in Colorado.

Stegosaurus was about 6.5 meters (21 feet) long, moved about on four limbs, and had a small head and brain and a large, curved, armor-plated back. The armor consisted of a double row of upstanding plates over the full arch of the back and two or more spikes on a powerful tail. The spikes on the tail were an effective weapon for warding off attackers. Although its brain was small, stegosaurus had a large nerve center in its pelvis that controlled the muscles of the tail and the rear legs.

Triceratops was one of a group of horned dinosaurs. Its huge head was approximately one-third its entire length. On its head were one small horn and two large ones. Its bony crest apparently protected its neck. This dinosaur was 7 meters (about 22 feet) long and was a vegetarian.

Fossil evidence reveals that the peak of the dinosaurs' development occurred near the end of the Cretaceous period in the Mesozoic era. However, no one is sure why the dinosaurs became extinct. Some scientists have suggested that a catastrophe such as an earthquake, volcano, or sunlight-blocking cloud resulting from a comet strike killed the dinosaurs. However, this theory does not explain why *only* the dinosaurs were destroyed, while other life forms survived. Scientists have also conjectured that the apatosaurus and its vegetarian relatives eventually became extinct because their huge bulk made it difficult for them to move to new environments as changes occurred in their natural habitat, but this does not explain the extinction of all the dinosaurs. Changes in climate may have changed the vegetable and animal life upon which dinosaurs fed, but there were places where such climatic changes did not occur, so some species of dinosaurs should have survived. Perhaps one of the children you teach will someday develop a theory that explains the extinction of the dinosaur satisfactorily.

The Earth's Oceans

When we look at the ocean, we see nothing but water. Imagine for a moment that the water disappeared. What would you expect the floor of the ocean to look like?

The Ocean Floor　　With the water gone, you would see gently sloping areas, known as *continental shelves*, along the edges of the continents. These areas extend outward to a region of ocean floor that slopes steeply to a flatter part of the ocean floor called the *abyssal plain*. Not all continents have a gradually sloping continental shelf. In some places, the shelf extends hundreds of kilometers; in other places, the coastline drops immediately into deep water.

The continental shelf receives the sediment carried by rivers from the land surface. The material covering it is called the *continental deposit*. The edges of the continental shelf mark the beginning of a steeply sloping region known as the *continental slope*. The continental slope extends until it reaches the ocean floor, which is lined with ridges known as *midocean ridges*. Between the ridges lie the *abyssal plains*. The ridge that rises from the Atlantic Ocean floor is called the *Mid-Atlantic Ridge*. The islands known as the Azores are the peaks of the Mid-Atlantic Ridge that have risen above the water. Although there are ridges in the ocean floor beneath the Pacific Ocean, they are not as tall as the Mid-Atlantic Ridge.

The ridges on the ocean floor are made by molten rock from deep within the earth pushing upward and slowly spreading out to the east and west. Thus, the ridges indicate places where the ocean floor is actually expanding. The movement of continents away from these areas is known as *continental drift*. Because the earth is not becoming larger, there must be an explanation for what happens as new land is created at the ridges and pushed outward. The explanation can be found in *ocean trenches*. At other places on the ocean floor the earth's crust is being pushed downward, creating large trenches. Ocean trenches are the most striking feature of the Pacific Ocean floor. The trenches are thousands of kilometers long and hundreds of kilometers wide.

Ocean Currents   Throughout history, sailors have used their knowledge of the locations of ocean currents to move from place to place quickly and to avoid sailing against currents. But what causes the currents in the first place? The explanation must begin with sunlight. The equatorial regions of the earth receive more sunlight than other places on the planet's surface. Because they do, the oceans in the equatorial regions absorb an enormous amount of energy and become warm. The warmed waters have a tendency to move, and it is this moving of ocean water away from the equator that results in the major ocean currents. The earth's rotation turns these currents clockwise in the Northern Hemisphere and counterclockwise in the Southern Hemisphere. Along the eastern coast of North America, a powerful current called the *Gulf Stream* carries warm waters from the equator northward and then eastward toward England.

Although many people are familiar with the major ocean currents at the water's surface, few people realize that there are currents far beneath the surface. There is, for example, a deep current that flows out of the Mediterranean under the surface current that flows into the Mediterranean at the Straits of Gibraltar. It is said that ancient sailors familiar with this unseen current sometimes took advantage of it by putting weighted sails *into* the deep water.

Seasonal changes in the strength, direction, and temperature of currents produce a variety of effects. Fish dependent on the movement of currents to carry food to the area of the ocean in which they live may perish if the current changes. Variations in the temperature of a current can affect the hatching of fish eggs. These effects impact humans because humans depend on the ocean's resources.

Ocean Resources   The oceans of our planet are a source of food, minerals, water, and perhaps, if we discover how to convert ocean movements into a usable form, energy. The challenge we face is to harvest the ocean's resources without diminishing their richness.

The living resources of the ocean begin with *phytoplankton*—tiny, one-celled plants that carry out photosynthesis. Their capturing of sunlight is the first step in creating the food chains and webs found in the oceans. Phytoplankton serve as food for microscopic animals known as *zooplankton*. Zooplankton are then eaten by larger organisms, and these organisms are eaten by still larger organisms. Thus, the energy originally received by the phytoplankton is passed along through the ocean food chains and webs (see Figure 10.8).

Figure 10.8   If you examine this ocean food chain closely, you will discover how the energy consumed by phytoplankton eventually sustains life for the shark.

The food chains and webs of the oceans can be thought of as a vast repository of protein-rich foods, and many modern technologies are used to locate and acquire fish, mollusks, and crustaceans for human consumption. Hopefully, international agreements concerning overfishing and water pollution control measures will permit future generations to benefit from these food resources.

The adage "Water, water everywhere and not a drop to drink" may have been true once with respect to salty seawater, but it is not true any longer. One important ocean resource is the water itself. Modern desalinization plants make it possible for communities that do not have access to freshwater to get it from saltwater. This is accomplished by evaporating seawater, which yields freshwater as vapor. The water vapor then condenses to form liquid water, which can be used for drinking, farming, or industrial uses. Sodium chloride and other substances are left behind as solids. The process is somewhat costly in terms of the energy required to evaporate seawater; however, as the technology improves and becomes more efficient, more of the earth's population will get its freshwater from seawater.

The ocean is a vast resource for humankind. With technological advances and a sensitivity to maintaining the quality of the water in the earth's oceans, humans will no doubt find and use other valuable ocean resources.

The Earth's Atmosphere and Weather

Go to **MyEducationLab**, select the topic Earth and Space Science, watch the video entitled "Properties of Air Pressure," and complete the questions that accompany it.

The thin layer of air surrounding the earth—the *atmosphere*—changes continuously. When we use the term *weather*, we are describing the condition of the atmosphere at a given time. That condition may be hot, cold, windy, dry, wet, sunny, or cloudy. The term *climate* is used to describe the total effect of the day-to-day changes in the atmosphere.

Because the earth receives almost all its heat energy from the sun, we can say the sun is the principal cause for changes in the weather. Heat energy from the sun causes the air to warm and move upward, water to evaporate into the atmosphere, and the flow of air parallel to the earth, which we call *wind*. These changes play a part in determining the extent and type of *precipitation* (rain, snow, hail, sleet) that reaches the earth's surface.

Scientists who study the weather and predict weather changes are called *meteorologists*. Every country has meteorologists who gather weather data from a variety of sources, summarize it, record it using various symbols on a weather map, and then make predictions.

Water in the Atmosphere

The percentage a meteorologist finds when the amount of moisture in the air is compared to the amount of moisture the air could hold at a particular temperature is known as the *relative humidity*. When the relative humidity is high, the air contains a great amount of moisture and the evaporation of perspiration is slow, which makes us feel uncomfortably warm. When the temperature in the air drops to a certain point, the air can no longer hold the water vapor in it. The air at this temperature is *saturated*. The temperature at which a given body of air becomes saturated is called the *dew point*. As air rises in the atmosphere, it cools. When the rising air is cooled to its dew point, condensation may occur. Drops of water form when enough molecules of water vapor accumulate around and become attached to a particle of dust in the atmosphere. Billions of tiny droplets of water form a cloud.

There are two ways in which water exists in the atmosphere: as clouds and as precipitation. Table 10.2 gives an overview of the characteristics of cloud and precipitation types.

Violent Weather

The earth is not always a peaceful place, and the same is true of its atmosphere. Under the right conditions, violent weather—including thunderstorms, tornadoes, winter storms, and hurricanes—can have a great impact on the surface of the earth and all of the life on it! Table 10.3 describes some common violent weather phenomena.

Table 10.2   Water in the atmosphere

Water Form	Characteristics
Clouds	*Low clouds* include fog, stratus, stratocumulus, cumulus, and cumulonimbus. Their bases range from the surface up to 1,900 meters (about 6,200 feet). These clouds are usually made up entirely of water droplets and are extremely dense.
	Middle clouds include both altocumulus and altostratus. The average heights of their bases range from 1,980 to 7,000 meters (about 6,500 to 23,000 feet). They are usually made of water droplets, ice crystals, or both and vary considerably in density.
	High clouds are cirrus, cirrocumulus, and cirrostratus. Their bases are generally above 5,030 meters (about 16,500 feet). They are always made of ice crystals and vary greatly in density.
	Cumulonimbus clouds are in a category by themselves. They may reach from the lowest to the highest atmospheric levels. During their life cycle, they may produce many of the other cloud types.
Precipitation	*Dew* is condensed water vapor that has formed tiny water droplets on cool objects.
	Frost forms when water vapor changes directly into ice crystals.
	Rain is condensed water vapor that falls as a liquid.
	Snowflakes are usually six-sided crystals formed by the direct change of water to a solid.
	Hail is round, hard pellets of ice associated with a thunderstorm. Hail pellets are concentric layers of ice formed as a result of the movement of the pellets in vertical cycles through thunderclouds.
	Sleet is small particles of clear ice that were originally raindrops. It results from raindrops passing through a layer of cold air.

Tomorrow's Weather

Because changes in the conditions of the atmosphere (the weather) tend to move in regular patterns above the earth's surface, the weather we will experience tomorrow will likely be much the same as the weather someplace else today. As a result, the most important tool that the weather forecaster has is the *weather map*. He or she studies the most recent weather map and tries to predict both the strength of the disturbances observed and their path. The forecaster also studies the map to see where and how new disturbances are being formed.

Meteorologists in North America know that in the middle latitudes, the upper air moves from west to east. Storms tend to enter from the west, pass across the middle of the continent, and move toward the North Atlantic. Thus, the weather that is likely to affect a local area is predicted on the basis of the larger-scale weather movement depicted on a weather map. The map is created by first recording symbols representing the data gathered at weather stations—pressure, temperature, humidity, wind direction, wind velocity, and cloud types.

Meteorologists use a variety of instruments to collect this data. The pressure of the air above us is measured with a *barometer*. The *wind vane* is used to determine the direction of the wind at the earth's surface. Wind speed is measured with an *anemometer*, an instrument consisting of a set of cups mounted so that they can easily be rotated by the wind. The amount of moisture in the air is determined by a *hygrometer*. The amount of moisture that reaches the ground as precipitation is measured by *rain and snow gauges*.

Table 10.3 Violent weather phenomena

Phenomenon	Characteristics
Thunderstorm	Upward and downward air movements (convection) produce a thunderstorm. Denser air sinks and warmer, less dense air rapidly rises. The down draft produces winds and heavy rain or hail. Some thunderstorms even produce tornadoes.
	Thunder is produced by the explosive expansion of air heated by a lightning bolt. The lightning is seen before the thunder is heard. The distance from lightning in miles can be estimated by counting the time in seconds between seeing lightning and hearing thunder and then dividing by 5.
	Lightning is caused by the movement of charged particles in a thunderstorm that produces electric fields. These cause currents (lightning) to flow within a cloud, from cloud to cloud, from cloud to ground, and in some cases, from ground to cloud.
Tornado	This short-lived storm has high-speed winds that rotate counterclockwise. These winds may appear as a funnel attached to a thundercloud, which can pick up and move dust and debris if it nears or touches the ground.
Snowstorm	A storm in which snow falls for several hours without letting up.
Freezing rain, freezing drizzle, and ice storm	Freezing rain or freezing drizzle occurs when the surface temperature is below 0°C (32°F). The rain falls as a liquid but freezes in an ice glaze on objects. If the glaze is thick, it's called an ice storm.
Cold wave	A time period in which the temperature falls far below normal.
Hurricane	A violent rain and wind storm that gets energy from the heat of seawater. The quiet core, or eye, is surrounded by blowing winds. The thunderclouds of a hurricane sometimes cause tornadoes.

The characteristics of the air high above the earth are commonly determined by the use of *radiosondes*. These are miniature radio transmitters to which are attached a variety of weather instruments. Radiosondes are carried aloft by balloons or small rockets. Data gathered by the instruments are transmitted back to earth by the radio transmitter.

In recent years, *weather satellites* have greatly improved the accuracy of weather forecasts. Their photographs of the clouds over the earth's surface reveal a great deal about weather phenomena. Such satellite photography, when used with information about air temperature, atmospheric pressure, and humidity, is of great assistance to meteorologists as they develop their weather forecasts for a particular area.

Summary Outline

I. The earth consists of various layers; the outermost layer is the crust, which is divided into seven crustal plates.

   A. The crust of the earth has undergone numerous gradual and violent changes during the earth's history.

   B. The land surface of the earth is composed of a variety of rocks, minerals, and soils.

   C. Fossil evidence of life forms that have existed in various periods of the earth's history has been found.

     D. The ocean floor has many features, including the continental shelf, continental slope, and ocean ridges.

     E. Ocean currents are the result of the sun warming the water and the earth's rotation.

     F. Humankind depends on the oceans as a source of food and other natural resources.

II. The atmosphere is a thin layer of constantly moving air that surrounds the earth.

     A. Water vapor in the atmosphere sometimes condenses to form clouds.

     B. Some water vapor in the atmosphere condenses and falls to earth as precipitation.

     C. Thunderstorms, tornadoes, winter storms, and hurricanes are examples of violent weather phenomena.

     D. Barometers, anemometers, and hygrometers are some of the instruments used to measure weather phenomena.

     E. Using information from these instruments and weather maps, scientists are able to make short-term and long-term weather forecasts.

Note

1. The discussion of volcanoes was excerpted with minor modifications from *Volcanoes*, a pamphlet prepared by the U.S. Geological Survey, U.S. Department of the Interior. This pamphlet is available for purchase from the Superintendent of Documents, Government Printing Office, Washington, DC 20402.

chapter 11

The Cosmos

Content

Are We Alone?

Are we all alone in the vastness of space?
Are other planets in orbit around distant stars?

Although we still don't have an answer to the first question, we do have an answer to the second. Humankind has made an extraordinary discovery: There *are* planets around other stars!

Powerful telescopes, the careful study of light spectra from stars, advanced computer software, new techniques for studying the wobbles in the movements of stars (an important clue for the presence of a planet), and diligent work by astronomers have revealed that there are stars in the evening sky that do have planets. The names of three of them are 51 Pegasi in the Pegasus constellation, 70 Virginis in the Virgo constellation, and 47 Ursae Majoris in the Big Dipper. Even more amazing, a family of planets has been discovered orbiting Upsilon Andromedae, a star similar to our sun and 44 light-years away.

So, now we know that planets may be far more common in the universe than we would have ever believed. But where does that leave us? Will we *ever* get the answer to that first question: *Are we alone?* Perhaps, but as we use powerful radiotelescopes to search the sky for signals sent by intelligent life, we can also pursue other questions that are just as interesting. For instance: How did the universe come into existence? When did the universe come into existence? What is the real meaning of *time?* and Did time exist before the universe came into being? There are even more mind-wrenching questions, such as whether universes parallel to ours exist or whether matter that enters a black hole can pop out somewhere else in our universe or another universe—if there are other universes.

All of these questions bring us very close to the edge of what people call *science fiction*, yet each day, real-live and very respectable scientists search for the answers. These esoteric questions, as well as those focused more closely on our planet and solar system, will eventually produce answers. We are moving closer and closer to the time when we'll finally be able to answer the question, *Are we alone?*

What Is the Universe and How Was It Formed?

The universe is all of the matter, energy, and space that exists. But how did this matter, energy, and space begin? Scientific debate over how the universe began seems to be endless. One important theory, known as the *Big Bang theory,* suggests that the universe had a definite beginning. According to the theory, approximately 8 to 20 billion years ago, the universe was created as a result of a fiery explosion. Astronomical observations that reveal all galaxies have been moving apart from one another at enormous speeds and other evidence supports this theory. By reasoning backward from the present outward movement of galaxies, we can assume that all the matter of the universe was once packed together.

The theory of a cosmic explosion is also supported by a discovery made in 1965 by Arno Penzias and Robert Wilson of the Bell Laboratories. Penzias and Wilson discovered and measured the strength of faint radiation that came from every direction in the sky. The entire universe seems to be immersed in this radiation. Measurements of the strengths and forms of radiation coincide with the strengths and forms that would have resulted from an enormous explosion occurring billions of years ago.

Maps of the sky made from data gathered by the *Cosmic Background Explorer* (COBE) satellite show slight differences in the background radiation discovered by Penzias and Wilson. Advocates of the Big Bang theory claim the data are exactly what a scientist would predict if the universe began with a Big Bang.

Although the Big Bang theory offers many explanations for astronomical phenomena, some recent discoveries have strongly challenged it. Observational studies of galaxies by Dr. Margaret J. Geller and Dr. H. P. Huchra of the Harvard–Smithsonian Center for Astrophysics and others have found some organized patterns of galaxies. However, according to the Big Bang theory, these patterns or structures, including an enormous chain of galaxies about 500 billion light-years across and known as the *Great Wall,* should not exist because galaxies should be homogeneously distributed.

Perhaps future studies will be able to explain the organized pattern of galaxies within the confines of the Big Bang theory. On the other hand, future studies may provide data that suggest alternate theories that better explain the nature of the universe we observe today.

● Magnetars

A new type of star has been discovered, and we know of its existence because, for one brief moment, it affected our environment. Called a *magnetar,* it is believed to be a neutron star that has a magnetic field billions of times more powerful than the earth's magnetic field. A neutron star is a remnant of a collapsed star and is extremely dense. The forces that form a neutron star are so powerful that the original star's protons and electrons were compressed together to form neutrons.

Some scientists have thought for awhile that this strange type of star existed, but there was no proof until recently, when an intense pulse of x-rays and gamma rays entered our solar system and set off detectors on spacecraft orbiting our earth and surveying other planets. The intensity of the radiation was powerful enough to cause some spacecraft to automatically shut down their instruments to prevent them from being damaged. Fortunately, the radiation didn't penetrate our atmosphere any further than a distance of 48 kilometers (about 30 miles) from our planet's surface. The burst of radiation probably occurred when something caused the magnetic field around the magnetar to become rearranged. No real harm was done, except to disappoint those scientists who were confident that magnetars didn't exist in the first place.

Quasars, Pulsars, and Black Holes

Magnetars aren't the only fascinating objects in the universe. There are faint blue celestial objects that are thought to be the most distant and luminous objects in the universe. There are rotating neutron stars thought to be remnants of *supernovas,* exploding stars that at peak intensity can outshine their galaxies. Astronomers have even found evidence that some stars have collapsed, forming such a powerful gravitational field that no light or any other radiation can escape. These objects, known as *black holes,* along with quasars and pulsars, raise many interesting questions about the universe in which we exist.

Table 11.1 gives a brief summary of the characteristics of quasars, pulsars, and black holes.

Galaxies

Within the universe are billions of clusters of stars, known as *galaxies.* Each galaxy contains hundreds of millions of stars, clouds of dust, and gas. Galaxies themselves are thought to be parts of clusters of other galaxies and nebulae, which are huge bodies of dust and gas (see Figure 11.1).

The galaxy of stars that contains our sun is known as the *Milky Way.* The stars in the Milky Way are so far from one another that measurement in kilometers (or miles) would be impossible to imagine. As a result, astronomers use a measuring unit called the *light-year.* A light-year represents the distance that light travels in one year. Light travels 299,792 kilometers (about 186,000 miles) in just one second, so one light-year represents a distance of 9,450,000,000,000 kilometers (about 6,000,000,000,000 miles).

Table 11.1   Characteristics of quasars, pulsars, and black holes

Object	Characteristics
Quasar	The name *quasar* comes from the term *quasi-stellar objects.* Quasars are extremely bright objects in the universe that shine with an intensity that's much more powerful than that of hundreds of galaxies. Their energy seems to come from gas and the remnants of stars spiraling into black holes. Quasars are thought to be at the centers of galaxies. Quasars are some of the oldest objects in the universe and are billions of light-years from Earth.
Pulsar	A pulsar is a dense, rapidly spinning remnant of a supernova explosion. (A supernova is the explosive end to the life of a massive star.) The pulsar consists solely of neutrons and produces intense magnetic fields that sweep across space like lighthouse beacons. When the first pulsar was discovered, its extremely regular rate of pulsing was thought to be a signal from another intelligent civilization.
Black hole	Black holes cannot be seen, but their presence is detected by studying the behavior of objects near them. Black holes are often thought of as vacuums that take in all that is around them, but that is not completely true. Some black holes emit radiation as matter is drawn in. Observable X-rays and radio waves are then emitted. A black hole is formed by the collapse of an old star into an extremely dense state surrounded by a powerful gravitational field. It is thought that some black holes may contain the masses of millions or billions of stars. These supermassive black holes may begin as ordinary black holes and over a long period of time take in the masses of large numbers of surrounding stars. Another theory is that they were formed during the Big Bang.

Figure 11.1 The Andromeda Spiral Galaxy, which is visible as a faint patch in the constellation Andromeda, is about 2 million light-years from Earth.

Astronomers have estimated that the Milky Way is tens of thousands of light-years in length and one-eighth that distance in width. Their evidence seems to indicate that our galaxy has a spiral shape. The closest star to our sun, Alpha Centauri, is more than four light-years away. The distance from the Milky Way to the nearest galaxy is 1,500,000 light-years.

Constellations

Constellations are groups of stars that seem to form specific patterns when viewed from Earth. Ages ago, people on Earth looked up at the night sky and saw that the stars that make up the Milky Way seemed to be organized into patterns. Each area of the sky containing such a pattern was identified as a constellation, and all the stars within the pattern were considered to be part of it. Many constellations were given names from mythology. Others were named for their apparent resemblance to familiar animals and objects. At present, there are 88 named constellations.

The easiest constellations to recognize are the polar constellations, those groups of stars located around the North Star (Polaris). To locate the North Star, find the constellation known as the Big Dipper. By sighting along an imaginary line between the two stars at the rim of the Big Dipper, you should be able to locate the North Star.

Our Solar System

Go to **MyEducationLab**, select Resources, and then Web Links. Then select "Solar System Exploration."

Our sun, the planets revolving around it, and associated clouds and bodies of matter make up what we call the *solar system,* which scientists believe was formed about 4.5 billion years ago. The sun's gravitational pull is the dominant force in the solar system, and the sun itself is the most massive part of the solar system.

Our Sun, a Star

With all of the new solar data pouring in from spacecraft, the sun is proving to be a more complex star[1] than we ever realized. Of course, the answers to many of our questions may be hidden in the data now on hand. Most scientists seem to agree on how the sun was born and how it will die. They have even calculated how much longer it has to live: 5 billion years as a normal, or main-sequence, star.

Astronomers believe that the sun and planets were formed from an enormous contracting cloud of dust and gas. All parts of this cloud did not move uniformly. Some parts formed local condensations that eventually became our planets, moons, comets, and asteroids. Gradually, the main cloud became spherical. Gravitational contraction increased its temperature. Eventually, the core temperature rose to a point at which the cloud's hydrogen nuclei began to fuse. Nuclear energy then produced enough outward pressure of heated gas to balance the inward force of gravity and maintain the sun as a glowing star. This process is believed to have begun about 5 billion years ago.

About 5 billion years from now, the sun will have depleted the hydrogen fuel in its core. Its thermonuclear reactions will then move outward where unused hydrogen exists. At the same time, the tremendous nuclear heat at the sun's core will also move outward, expanding the sun by as much as 60 times. As the sun cools by expansion, its surface color will become a deep red. It will then be a *red giant*—not a main-sequence star. Looming across much of our sky, it will boil off our water and air and incinerate any remnants of life.

When the sun exhausts its hydrogen fuel, it will no longer be able to withstand gravitational contraction. Eventually, it will shrink to a *white dwarf,* no bigger than the earth but so dense that a piece the size of a sugar cube would weigh thousands of kilograms. Eventually, after billions of years, our sun will cool and dim to a *black cinder*. Only then will eternal night fall upon the solar system.

The Moon

Earth has a single natural satellite: the moon. The first human footsteps on the moon were made by American astronauts, who explored its dusty surface in 1969. Six two-man crews brought back a collection of rocks and soil weighing 382 kilograms (842 pounds) and consisting of more than 2,000 separate samples.

Rocks collected from the lunar highlands date from 4.0 to 4.3 billion years ago. The first few million years of the moon's existence were so violent that little trace of this period remains. As a molten outer layer gradually cooled and solidified into different kinds of rock, the moon was bombarded by huge asteroids and smaller objects. Some of the asteroids were the size of Rhode Island or Delaware, and their collisions with the moon created huge basins hundreds of kilometers across.

The catastrophic bombardment died away about 4 billion years ago, leaving the lunar highlands covered with huge overlapping craters and a deep layer of shattered and broken rock (see Figure 11.2). Heat produced by the decay of radioactive elements began to melt the inside of the moon at depths of about 200 kilometers (124 miles) below its surface. Then, from 3.1 to 3.8 billion years ago, great floods of lava rose from inside the moon and poured over its surface, filling the large impact basins to form the dark parts of the moon, called *maria,* or seas. Surprisingly, recent analysis of data from the moon has revealed the presence of water trapped as ice at its polar regions.

Figure 11.2 This lunar landscape photo was transmitted to Earth by a Surveyor spacecraft.

The Planets

Eight planets, including Earth, revolve around the sun. Three of these planets—Mercury, Venus, and Mars—resemble Earth in size, density, and chemical composition. The other four—Jupiter, Saturn, Uranus, and Neptune—are larger and have thick, gaseous atmospheres (see Figure 11.3).

In 2006 the International Astronomical Union redefined the definition of the term planet as a celestial body that (a) is in orbit around the Sun, (b) has sufficient mass for its self-gravity to overcome rigid body forces so that it assumes a hydrostatic equilibrium (nearly round) shape, and (c) has cleared the neighborhood around its orbit.[2] Cleared the neighborhood means that the planet is the dominant gravitational force and that any other bodies of similar size in the area of the planet are under its gravitational influence.

Figure 11.3
The relative sizes of the planets

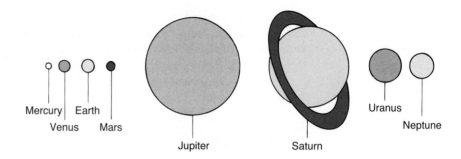

The moon is an example of a body under the gravitational force of Earth. Hence the moon is not a planet, whereas Earth is a planet. Under the new definition Pluto has lost its status as a planet and is now considered a dwarf planet. A dwarf planet needs to meet the same first two criteria as a planet except that it has not cleared the neighborhood around its orbit, and it is not a satellite. To make matters more complicated, as of June 11, 2008, Pluto became a special type of dwarf planet called a "plutoid."[3] Plutoids are Pluto-like dwarf planets.

It's important to be aware of the key physical characteristics of each planet in our solar system, the nature of any atmosphere that exists, and the kind and number of satellites it has. Table 11.2 provides a considerable amount of detail for each planet, including its distance from the sun, diameter, rotation period, and so on. And the following sections detail some of the key characteristics of each planet.

Mercury   This is a small, heavily cratered, rocky planet. Dried gullies on and in the surface may indicate the presence of streams and seas millions of years ago. There is possibly water under the surface now. In fact, scientists are reasonably sure they have found water under Mercury's north and south poles. Mercury has a very thin atmosphere that's composed of carbon dioxide and small amounts of nitrogen. No natural satellites orbit this planet.

Venus   The planet's surface is covered with lava flows from ancient volcanoes, quake faults, and impact craters. One of the lava-filled basins is larger than the continental United States. There is even one volcano that is taller than Mt. Everest. The atmosphere is a poisonous mixture of carbon dioxide and sulfuric acid. Thick clouds hide the Venusian surface. No natural satellites orbit Venus.

Earth   Earth is known as the "blue planet," because most of its surface is covered with water. The land masses on Earth, or continents, have mountains, deserts, forests, and plains. The crust of Earth is active with earthquakes and volcanoes, which are found at various locations. Ancient craters on Earth's surface—for instance, in places such as Arizona and in the Gulf of Mexico—indicate that it has been struck by asteroids over its history.

Earth's atmosphere contains oxygen, nitrogen, carbon dioxide, and other gases. There is also an ozone layer, which protects living things from solar ultraviolet radiation, and clouds, which are part of Earth's water cycle. Earth has one natural satellite: the moon.

Go to **MyEducationLab**, select Resources, and then Web Links. Then select "Mars Exploration Program."

Mars   A tiny, toy-like robotic vehicle called *Sojourner* was sent to Mars in 1977 (see Figure 11.4). It successfully traveled over a small portion of the Martian surface and sent back pictures to Earth. Although *Sojourner* showed us some Martian rocks, our telescopes and other instruments have provided a larger view of the Martian landscape. The surface has dried gulleys, which may indicate that Mars had running water and streams at one time. Additionally, geological features resembling shorelines, gorges, riverbeds, and islands have also been observed. Finally, Mars has polar ice caps, which likely consist of water. Following up on the

Table 11.2 Characteristics of the planets

Characteristic	Mercury	Venus	Earth	Mars	Jupiter	Saturn	Uranus	Neptune
1. *Mean distance from Sun (millions of kilometers)*	57.9	108.2	149.6	227.9	778.3	1,427	2,871	4,497
2. *Period of revolution*	88 days	224.7 days	365.3 days	687 days	11.86 years	29.46 years	84 years	165 years
3. *Equatorial diameter (kilometers)*	4,880	12,100	12,756	6,794	143,200	120,000	51,800	49,528
4. *Atmosphere (main components)*	Virtually none	Carbon Dioxide	Nitrogen Oxygen	Carbon Dioxide	Hydrogen Helium	Hydrogen Helium	Helium Hydrogen Methane	Hydrogen Helium Methane
5. *Moons*	0	0	1	2	47	30+	20+	8
6. *Rings*	0	0	0	0	3	1,000 (?)	11	4
7. *Inclination of orbit to ecliptic*	7°	3.4°	0°	1.9°	1.3°	2.5°	0.8°	1.8°
8. *Eccentricity of orbit*	.206	.007	.017	.093	.048	.056	.046	.009
9. *Rotation period*	59 days	243 days retrograde	23 hours 56 min.	24 hours 37 min.	9 hours 55 min.	10 hours 40 min.	17.2 hours retrograde	16 hours 7 min.
10. *Inclination of axis**	Near 0°	177.2°	23° 27'	25° 12'	3° 5'	26° 44'	97° 55'	28° 48'

*Inclinations greater than 90° imply retrograde rotation.

Figure 11.4 Sojourner on the surface of Mars

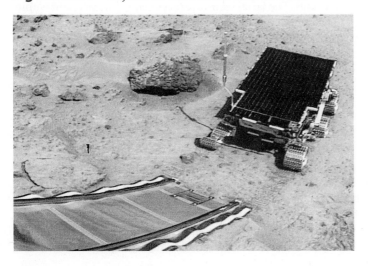

Sojourner mission, the *Phoenix Mars Lander* arrived on the planet May 25, 2008. One of its main objectives was to collect and test surface samples for evidence of liquid water on the planet. The second objective was to search for evidence of a habitable zone that could support life at the microbial level. Analysis of the data was underway at the time of this publication. Go to http://phoenix.lpl.arizona.edu for updates of the *Phoenix Mars Lander* mission.

The Martian atmosphere, like that of Venus, is composed primarily of carbon dioxide with small amounts of nitrogen, oxygen, and argon. The small amount of water vapor in the air condenses to form clouds along the slopes of volcanoes. Some fog even forms in Martian valleys. Mars has two

Figure 11.5   This photomontage of Saturn and its rings and moons was created by an artist who juxtaposed a series of photographs transmitted by the Voyager spacecraft.

moons—Phobos and Deimos—and each has a heavily cratered surface.

Jupiter   This planet, the largest in our solar system, has an atmosphere that is mostly hydrogen and helium whirling above a ball of liquid hydrogen. Jupiter's extraordinarily large atmosphere includes the Great Red Spot: a giant storm that is at least three times the size of Earth.

A number of natural satellites travel around Jupiter. The four largest are Ganymede, Callisto, Io, and Europa, and two of next largest are Amalthea and Himalia. The moon Europa has a deep ocean of liquid water under an icy crust.

Saturn   This planet seems to have no solid surface and is composed of hydrogen gas. The sixth planet from the sun, Saturn is known for its intricate ring system. The rings are made of ice and rock particles, which vary in size from being as small as dust to as large as boulders. The rings appear to be held in their respective orbits by the gravitational attraction of the planet and its satellites (see Figure 11.5).

Saturn has at least 30 moons. Titan is the largest, and the next six in size are Rhea, Iapetus, Dione, Tethys, Enceladus, and Mimas. The moon Titan has an atmosphere rich in nitrogen, as did Earth's atmosphere in its early days. Consequently, this moon holds great interest to scientists searching for extraterrestrial life.

Uranus   This, the third-largest planet in our solar system, rotates on its side! It has no solid surface, although it may have a small, silicate-rich core. The atmosphere of Uranus contains hydrogen, helium, water, ammonia, and methane. The blue-green color of the planet is due to the presence of methane gas above the cloud layers. Astronomers have detected a system of faint rings around the planet. Uranus has over 20 moons. Five of the largest are Miranda, Titania, Oberon, Umbriel, and Ariel.

Neptune   This gaseous planet is composed of hydrogen, helium, and methane, and these gases are thought to surround an Earth-sized liquid core. Like Uranus, there is sufficient methane on Neptune to give it a slightly bluish color. Winds in the atmosphere of Neptune are the fastest anywhere. They are three times stronger than any winds on Earth and nine times more powerful than the winds of Jupiter.

Neptune has several faint rings. The farthest ring has been named Adams, and within it are arcs named Liberty, Equality, and Fraternity. The moons of Neptune include Naiad, Thalassa, Despina, Galatea, Larissa, Proteus, Triton, and Nereid. The largest of these moons, Triton, travels in an orbit opposite to the planet's rotation direction. This means that Triton is continually getting closer to the planet and will crash into it in about 10 to 100 million years!

Meteors

Meteors are masses of stone and iron from space that sometimes strike Earth. Some meteors have a mass of less than one gram; others have masses of thousands of kilograms. Although many meteors enter Earth's atmosphere, few reach the planet's surface. Most are simply burned up by the friction they produce as they move through the atmosphere. Some meteors are so large that parts of them remain after their journey through the atmosphere. If they reach Earth's surface, they are known as *meteorites*. Scientists have various theories about the origin of meteorites. Most think they originated in our solar system, perhaps from the band of planet-like objects between the orbits of Mars and Jupiter.

● Comets

Comets are heavenly bodies surrounding the solar system. They move in large orbits; occasionally, a comet may be pulled from its normal orbit and move toward the sun. Comets are thought to be composed of solidified ammonia, carbon dioxide, and ice. The solid portion of a comet is known as its *head*. The comet's *tail* is formed by the evaporation of solidified matter by energy from the sun. The tail of a comet always points away from the sun. Although comets do not produce light themselves, energy from the sun causes the material in their heads and tails to give off light.

● Asteroids

Between the orbits of Mars and Jupiter lies a belt of objects that are smaller than any of the planets. These objects are called *asteroids*. Scientists are not sure how the asteroids were formed. Some believe they are the remnants of a planet that once existed between Mars and Jupiter. Others think they are leftovers from the materials that combined to form Mars and Jupiter.

Some asteroids leave their orbits and cross the paths of planets or moons. Craters observed on the moon and on Mars are probably the result of collisions with asteroids. Some craters on Earth can be explained most easily as the results of collisions with asteroids millions of years ago.

Exploring Space: The First Steps

The development of powerful rockets has made possible the exploration of outer space. (An explanation of the scientific principles involved in rocket propulsion may be found in Chapter 17.) The first step toward space exploration began in earnest in 1957 with the Soviet Union's launch of the first artificial space satellite: *Sputnik I.*

On August 17, 1958, the United States attempted its first launch of a rocket to the moon. Intended to place an artificial satellite in orbit around the moon, this mission was a failure. On July 2, 1959, the Soviet Union fired a rocket that went into orbit around the sun. A later rocket in the launch series was sent past the moon and transmitted pictures from its far side, but humans did not visit the moon until July 20, 1969, when Neil Armstrong stepped upon its surface. This was one of the many outcomes of the *Apollo* space exploration program, which witnessed visits on the moon's surface by 12 astronauts in all from 1969 to 1972. To date, however, the moon is the only place in space that humans have visited.

Four years earlier, in 1965, both American and Soviet unmanned spacecraft had flown by Mars and taken pictures of its surface. In 1971, *Mariner 9* was placed in orbit about that planet. The pictures it transmitted to Earth showed a surface that looked as if it had been sculptured by intensive flooding millions of years ago. Curiosity about another planet—Mercury—led to the launch of *Mariner 10*, which flew within 720 kilometers (about 450 miles) of the planet in 1974. Television cameras and scientific instruments sent back information concerning temperature, solar wind, and the planet's surface.

Since that time, various spacecraft have been used to explore Venus and other planets. American *Mariner* and Soviet *Venera* rockets both have reached the Venusian atmosphere and transmitted information. *Venera IX* and *X* landed on the surface of Venus in 1975. A year later, in 1976, more detailed information about the surface of Mars was gathered by the spacecraft *Viking 1* and *2,* which dropped small instrument packages to the surface. As stated previously, the *Phoenix Mars Lander* touched down on Mars May 25, 2008, to search for evidence of liquid water having once existed on the planet and for evidence of habitable zones for microbial life.

The first American spacecraft to orbit Venus was *Pioneer Venus I,* which reached the Venusian atmosphere on December 5, 1978. A few days later, *Pioneer Venus 2* discharged five probes toward the planet's surface. Each transmitted important information about the Venusian atmosphere before being destroyed by the planet's heat. Soviet *Venera* spacecraft parachuted instrument packages to the surface of Venus in 1978. These landers sent information to orbiting spacecraft, which reflected it to Earth.

Space Probes

Voyager 1 and *2* are rocket probes launched in 1977 to observe phenomena on Jupiter, Saturn, Uranus, and Neptune. It is hoped that one or both of these probes will be able to reach the edges of our solar system and beyond. At present, the probes are sending back an enormous amount of data about the outer planets. Data gathered by *Voyager 2*'s flyby of Uranus in 1986 provided extremely sharp pictures of its major satellite. Updates on the journeys of Voyager 1 and 2 can be found at http://voyager.jpl.nasa.gov/

If they are not destroyed, the *Voyager* spacecraft will escape the solar system at a speed of 62,000 kilometers (about 38,700 miles) per hour. On board each spacecraft are a phonograph record, sound-reproduction equipment, and playing instructions. The records include music, spoken languages, and common sounds from nature. Also included is a plaque that shows pictures of humans and describes, in scientific symbols, Earth, its location, and its people. The *Voyager* spacecraft will reach the first star in their interstellar voyage in about 40,000 years. Perhaps someone or something will interrupt them before then and learn about our planet and its people from the information, equipment, and pictures on board.

The *Magellan* spacecraft was deployed by the space shuttle *Atlantis*. Its interplanetary journey includes a careful study of Venus. *Magellan's* onboard instruments, which include radar imaging systems, have transmitted rather spectacular images of the Venusian surface. Early radar images include that shown in Figure 11.6, which shows 75 kilometer (46 mile) long valleys that have been nicknamed "Gumby" by photoanalysts.

The Hubble Space Telescope

The Hubble Space Telescope (HST) was deployed from a space shuttle launched on April 24, 1990, and just one month later, on May 20, humans saw the first pictures transmitted from the telescope. The HST was designed to gather the sharpest pictures ever of astronomical objects (see Figure 11.7). Unfortunately, defects in one of the Hubble's mirrors limited its effectiveness. To correct this problem as well as upgrade related equipment, astronauts from the space shuttle *Endeavor* carried out the most complicated space repairs ever attempted. They secured the HST in the shuttle cargo bay, replaced its solar panels, installed a device to correct the mirror defects, replaced gyroscopes (instruments that sense the telescope's orientation in space), replaced one of its cameras, and released the upgraded HST into orbit. The Hubble Space Telescope is continually repaired and upgraded and is now able to detect stars that are 13 billion or more light-years away.

Figure 11.6
This Magellan radar image of Venus shows a set of valleys nicknamed "Gumby."

Figure 11.7
Compare these photographs of the nearest starburst spiral galaxy, NGC-35. The image on the left was taken with a land-based telescope. The detailed area shown on the right is an image by the Hubble Space Telescope (HST). The HST's high resolution allowed astronomers to quantify complex structures in the starburst core of the galaxy for the first time.

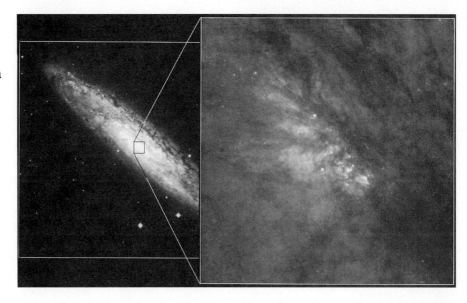

● The Space Shuttle

The American space shuttle[4] continues to offer great potential in the exploration of outer space because of its ability to carry scientists and its great maneuverability. It can orbit Earth like a spacecraft and land like an airplane. The shuttle is designed to carry heavy loads into orbit around Earth. Other launch vehicles have done this, but unlike these vehicles, which can be used only once, each space shuttle orbiter can be reused more than 100 times (see Figure 11.8).

The shuttle permits the checkout and repair of satellites in orbit and the return of satellites to Earth for repairs that cannot be done in space. Thus, the shuttle makes possible considerable savings in spacecraft costs. The types of satellites that the shuttle can orbit and maintain include those involved in environmental protection, navigation, energy, weather forecasting, fishing, farming, mapping, and oceanography.

Principal Components   The space shuttle has three main units: the *orbiter*, the *external tank*, and two solid rocket *boosters*. The orbiter is the crew- and payload-carrying unit of the shuttle system. It is 37 meters (122 feet) long, has a wingspan of 24 meters (79 feet), and without fuel weighs about 68,000 kilograms (150,000 pounds). It is about the size and weight of a DC-9 commercial airplane.

The orbiter can transport a payload of 29,500 kilograms (65,000 pounds). It carries its cargo in a cavernous payload bay 18.3 meters (60 feet) long and 4.6 meters (15 feet) in diameter. The bay is flexible enough to provide accommodations for unmanned spacecraft in a variety of shapes and for fully equipped scientific laboratories.

The orbiter's three main liquid rocket engines are fed propellants from the external tank, which is 47 meters (154 feet) long and 8.7 meters (28.6 feet) in diameter. At liftoff, the tank holds 703,000 kilograms (1,550,000 pounds) of propellants, consisting of liquid hydrogen (fuel) and liquid oxygen (oxidizer). The hydrogen and oxygen are in separate pressurized compartments of the tank. The external tank is the only part of the shuttle system that is not reusable.

A Typical Shuttle Mission   In a typical shuttle mission, lasting from 7 to 30 days, the orbiter's main engines and the booster ignite simultaneously to rocket the shuttle from the launch pad. Launches are made from the John F. Kennedy Space Center in Florida for east-west orbits and from Vandenberg Air Force Base in California for north-south orbits.

Figure 11.8   A successful shuttle launch

At a predetermined point, the two solid rocket boosters separate from the orbiter and parachute to the sea, where they are recovered for reuse. The orbiter continues into space, jettisoning its external propellant tank just before orbiting. The external tank enters the atmosphere and breaks up over a remote ocean area.

The orbiter then proceeds on its mission in space. When its work is completed, the crew directs the orbiter on a flight path that will take it back to the Earth's atmosphere. Various rocket systems are used to slow its speed and adjust its direction. Previous spacecraft followed a direct path from space to the predetermined landing area. The orbiter is quite different. It can maneuver from the right to the left of its entry path a distance of about 2,035 kilometers (about 1,265 miles). The orbiter has the capability of landing like an airplane at Kennedy Space Center or Vandenberg Air Force Base. Its landing speed is about 335 kilometers (about 208 miles) per hour.

Successes and Tragedies   The NASA space shuttle program has enjoyed many successes during its 20-plus years. Its first success was in April 1981, when the orbiter *Columbia* carried out a two-day mission that proved the shuttle could put a spacecraft in orbit and return safely. Missions that followed included the deployment of satellites, scientific explorations, the deployment of the Hubble Space Telescope, and flights to assist in the building and servicing of the *International Space Station*.

These successes have not been without human costs, however. On January 28, 1986, the orbiter *Challenger* exploded just 73 seconds after liftoff. This accident took the lives of all seven crew members, including the first teacher-astronaut, Christa McAuliffe. On February 1, 2003, the space shuttle *Columbia* suffered a catastrophe on re-entry into the earth's atmosphere. Again, all seven crew members were killed. Each of these tragedies was followed by an intense investigation in order to determine the cause and to hopefully prevent a similar event from happening in the future. To be sure, the exploration of space will continue and the mysteries of the universe will continue to be revealed.

Exploring Space: The Next Steps

The X-37: A Starting Place

"May we have your attention please? Those preparing to board the X-37 for an orbital Earth flight should kindly unfasten their seat belts and proceed to hatch #9. The X-37 is in the cargo bay and now prepared for boarding. Please check under your seat and in the luggage compartment above your head for any personal items you may have brought onboard the shuttle. Have your boarding pass available for the flight attendant at hatch #9. Enjoy your '21-Day Eye-on-the-Earth Excursion.' We'll see you on the ground."

At some point in your life, or in the lives of the children you teach, ordinary people will view wondrous Earth from space with their own eyes. It's difficult to predict when and how it will happen, but research to develop cost-effective ways to achieve orbital flight is well underway. Through contracts with private companies, NASA is now exploring the design of spacecraft that will reduce the cost of putting 1 pound (about 2.2 kilograms) of payload into space from $10,000 to $1,000. That means that space travel may be in your future!

The space vehicle in your future will have some of the same characteristics as the *X-37*, an experimental test vehicle (see Figure 11.9). Known as a "spaceplane," the *X-37* is intended to be ferried to Earth's orbit by a shuttle, to remain in Earth's orbit, and then to land on its own on a conventional airport runway. In the years ahead, new versions of the *X-37* will be developed and tested. Perhaps some will even have solar panels that can be used to power the craft in orbit. For now, building a reusable passenger-carrying spaceplane poses an enormous challenge. But one thing is certain: Testing will continue and sometime, somewhere, in some yet undesigned spaceplane, a tourist will be awakened by "May we have your attention please . . ."

The International Space Station: A Rest Stop on the Road to Mars?

High above our heads, men and women are at work in and on the *International Space Station.* This space laboratory is permanently orbiting Earth at a distance of 200 miles (323 kilometers). As you read these words, scientists in the space station are conducting an intensive study of how the human body and other biological systems respond to prolonged time in space. They are also at work constructing additional internal and external parts for the space station using twenty-first-century materials and techniques adapted for use in space.

The *International Space Station* is a cooperative venture of a number of countries. Each is making its own unique contribution to this, the largest cooperative scientific and engineering effort in human history. When it is complete, the space station will contain facilities for biotechnology, fluids and combustion, a space station furnace, gravitational biology, centrifuge, and human research.

Crews are continually onboard the space station and busily at work. The United States and Russia have delivered people, equipment, and supplies to the station, including materials created by other nations. Additionally, unmanned rockets have been used as "freighters" to carry equipment and supplies to the *International Space Station.* So, the science fiction of our childhood has become today's reality: We have space "ferries"!

Given this, we can only wonder what humankind will accomplish next, as today's science fiction frontier becomes tomorrow's rest stop on our journey to Mars and beyond!

Figure 11.9
The X-37 advanced technology flight demonstrator will operate in both the orbital and re-entry phases of flight.

Summary Outline

I. The universe is all the matter, energy, and space that exist.

    A. Recent discoveries of patterns of galaxies pose a challenge to the Big Bang theory.

    B. In recent years, scientists have discovered and begun studies of extraordinary astronomical phenomena, such as magnetars, quasars, pulsars, and black holes.

II. The solar system consists of the sun, its eight planets, and associated clouds of matter, including meteors, comets, and asteroids.

    A. The sun is a star that will use up its supply of hydrogen and come to the end of its existence in about 5 billion years.

    B. The moon, which is a satellite of Earth, is airless and lifeless.

    C. The eight planets that circle the sun are Mercury, Venus, Earth, Mars, Jupiter, Saturn, Uranus, and Neptune.

III. Powerful rockets have enabled humans to explore outer space in a variety of ways.

    A. Manned and unmanned space probes have explored space since 1957.

    B. The space shuttle is a space vehicle that can return to Earth and be reused in subsequent space journeys.

    C. The *X-37* will serve as the prototype for a spaceplane.

    D. The *International Space Station* will be a permanently orbiting scientific laboratory. It may also serve as a launching pad for the human exploration of Mars.

Notes

1. The discussion of the sun was excerpted with modifications from *Our Prodigal Sun*, a pamphlet prepared by the National Aeronautics and Space Administration. This pamphlet (stock number 3300-00569) can be purchased from the Superintendent of Documents, Government Printing Office, Washington, DC 20402.

2. International Astronomical Union News Release - IAU0603: IAU 2006 General Assembly: Result of the IAU Resolution votes Aug 24, 2006, Prague. www.iau.org/. Downloaded (accessed 6-30-08).

3. Courtland, Rachel. June 2008. NewScientist news service. http://space.newscientist.com/article/dn14118-plutolike-objects-to-be-called-plutoids.html. Downloaded (accessed 6-30-08).

4. The discussion of the space shuttle was excerpted with minor modifications from *NASA Facts: The Space Shuttle*, prepared by the National Aeronautics and Space Administration. This publication (stock number 003-000-00679-9) is available for purchase from the Superintendent of Documents, Government Printing Office, Washington, DC 20402.

chapter 12

Earth/Space Science Lesson Ideas

Putting the Content into Action

Kelly's Gift

Kelly was in such a rush to get into the school that she bumped into the big, brown trash can by the front door and dropped her lunch box. She picked it up, walked through the doorway, and raced down the hallway to her classroom. The door was open and the lights were on, which meant that her teacher was somewhere in the building. She pulled a chair to the side of her teacher's desk, sat down holding her lunch box on her lap, and patiently waited.

In Kelly's lunch box was a present that Aunt Nicole had brought back from vacation. Kelly had wrapped it carefully in foil before putting it next to her sandwich. It was a very special rock, a rock filled with holes, a rock that would float!

"Good morning, Kelly. You certainly are an early bird today," her teacher said, entering the classroom.

"I've got a surprise for you," said Kelly, placing the shiny object at the front of the teacher's desk. "You can show it during science, but I wanted you to see it first."

"That's wonderful. I'll do that, but right now, I have to get the model volcano from Mr. Johnson's room." Kelly's teacher turned and hurried out the door.

Kelly went to her own desk and stared at the foil-wrapped rock. "Oh well," she thought to herself, "I guess it's OK if everybody sees it at the same time."

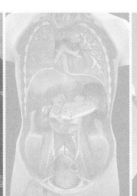

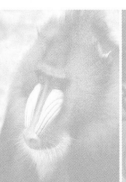

Science time was right after lunch. The lesson was about the earth's crust. Kelly's teacher forgot about the rock, and Kelly was too shy to mention it.

When Kelly got to school the next day, she went right to the teacher's desk, picked up the foil-wrapped object, looked at it, and without a word handed it to her teacher.

"Thanks, Kelly. I'm so sorry I forgot this yesterday. We'll unwrap it during science time today. I can't wait to see what it is."

Science time finally arrived, but just as the teacher was reaching for the foil-wrapped rock, the school fire alarm went off. There wasn't a fire, but everyone had to stay outside until someone fixed the alarm, which wouldn't stop ringing. By the time the children were able to enter the school, science time was over.

At the end of the day, Kelly quietly walked up to the teacher's desk, picked up the magic floating rock, and a minute later dropped it in the big, brown trash can just outside the school.

As you plan earth/space science and technology units and lessons, think about Kelly's magic floating rock and all of the children for whom rocks and oceans and outer space are sources of wonder. Once you have done this, begin to think of your plans as starting places, not ending places. You do need to plan well and to plan ahead, but you also need to be flexible enough to receive and incorporate the gifts that children bring. What are these gifts? They are the children's ideas about the natural world, their questions about things they observe that don't make sense—and, of course, the occasional foil-wrapped floating rock.

▶ Getting Started

Try the following true/false statements:

1. The earth is closest to the sun during winter in the Northern Hemisphere.
2. Ocean currents are caused by winds.
3. Thunder is a result of clouds colliding.
4. The metal roof of a car protects us from lightning strikes.
5. Dinosaurs and humans existed at the same time.
6. Moon phases result from the shadow of the earth cast on the moon.
7. The moon emits its own light.
8. The greenhouse effect and global warming are the same things.
9. Groundwater is water that flows in underground rivers.
10. Raindrops are tear-shaped.

How do you think you did? The answers are given at the end of the chapter on page 248. These statements address common misconceptions among children and adults about earth and space science. Often our explanations are well entrenched in our minds, and for good reason. Explanations often make sense based on our mental models of phenomena. However, good science requires a healthy dose of skepticism and openness to revisions of our mental models as we acquire insights through experience and reflection. Teaching often consists of re-educating by creating experiences and insights that challenge children's current understandings and force them to revise their mental models and explanations. The first step to re-teaching is to probe children's current understanding. Therefore, the beginning of a unit or lesson usually starts by assessing children's prior knowledge.

Probes for Assessing Earth and Space Science Prior Knowledge

"But we learned all that in Mr. Greeley's class last year."

So, as a teacher in the real world of schools and classrooms, how can you quickly get a sense of what the children know, what skills they possess, and what they believe? Part of the answer is to use *probes:* basic questions and simple activities that get children thinking and talking about particular topics. The answers children give will provide very direct guidance about what you should include in science units and lessons.

The probes and sample responses that follow come from informal interviews that I or my students have done with children. I think you'll be amazed at some of the responses and motivated to develop probes that you can use *before* planning units and lessons.

Probe	Responses That Reveal Prior Knowledge and Conceptions
• After giving a young child an assortment of rocks, leaves, and twigs: *Would you please put these into groups and then tell me how you made your choices.*	"I wanted to get three in each group." "I put the big rock with these because it was lonely."
• After showing a fossil: *How do you think this fossil was made?*	"The animal touched the mud and it hardened. Then the bones were left behind." "When the rock was made, the object was touching it."
• *Why is it light outside during the day and dark outside during the night?*	"Because a different part of the country faces the sun." "Because the sun isn't around during the nighttime. The moon is there instead."
• *How do you think the earth began?*	"The Big Bang. We learned about it last year." "I don't know. I wish Adam and Eve didn't take the apple of knowledge; then we wouldn't have to go to school."
• *Where do you think soil comes from?*	"It doesn't come from anything. It was always here." "Well, some of it comes from leaves." "I think it's from under the rocks and then the rocks get moved by the glaciers and the soil is left."

(continued)

Probe	Responses That Reveal Prior Knowledge and Conceptions
• *What are the stars?*	"They are reflections from the moon." "They are little balls of light."
• *Some people think we should send astronauts to explore Mars, and some people think doing that would be a waste of money. What do you think?*	"Well, it depends if it's safe or not. If it's safe to go, we should go to see what is there. But if it wasn't safe, we could just send more rockets with TV cameras." "We should send people there to see if anything there is alive. There might be some things there we could get, like metals and gold."

Unit, Lesson, and Enrichment Starter Ideas

Unit Plan Starter Ideas and Questions

That great idea for a science-teaching unit may come from deep within your brain, your school curriculum guide, a state science curriculum framework, a science resource book, a course, a workshop, a discussion you have with children, or some other source. Unfortunately, a great idea (like a friend, an umbrella, and a good restaurant with cheap food) is sometimes hard to find when you really need one.

To make it easier for you to come up with great ideas for science units, I have prepared two different sources of unit starter ideas:

1. The first is based on the National Science Education Standards (NSES) for science content. I created these starter ideas for standards related to grades K–4 and 5–8.

2. The second source of starter ideas is based on my study of earth/space science topics that commonly appear in school curriculum guides. These are shown by grade level.

I am certain that the unique compilation of starter ideas that follows will help you plan and create wonderful discovery-based teaching units.

Because science is about seeking explanations, each starter idea is accompanied by a big question. The question serves as the anchor for the unit. Each inquiry lesson of the unit should contribute to a deeper, more comprehensive answer to the unit question. At the conclusion of the unit, children should be able to provide an explanation of their answer to the question that reflects what was taught in the unit.

Ideas Based on the NSES K–8 Content Standards

> **NSES** **Content Standard K–4:** Earth and Space Sciences [ESS]
>
> As a result of their activities in grades K–4, all students should develop an understanding of:
>
> Properties of earth materials
>
> Objects in the sky
>
> Changes in earth and sky[1]

▶ STARTER IDEAS for the Properties of Earth Materials

UNIT TITLE: *My Rock Collection*

QUESTIONS: Could you pick your rock out of a group? What is the same and different about rocks?

UNIT OVERVIEW: Students gather rocks outdoors, observe them, learn that they are made of different substances, and classify them.

UNIT TITLE: *Soils Here/Soils There*

QUESTIONS: What is the dirt on dirt? What are properties of soils, and what do they tell us about where the soil comes from?

UNIT OVERVIEW: Students collect soil samples from various locations, observe them, and classify them on the basis of color, particle size, texture, and how they react with water.

▶ STARTER IDEAS for Objects in the Sky

UNIT TITLE: *Look to the Sky*

QUESTION: What do you see when you look in the sky?

UNIT OVERVIEW: Through observations of the sky during the day and at night, children describe the objects in the sky, near and far (clouds, stars, moon, sun [do not observe the sun directly], planes, birds). They identify the general properties, relationships in space, and movements of the objects.

UNIT TITLE: *The Planets and the Stars*

QUESTION: Where are the planets and the stars?

UNIT OVERVIEW: Children will learn the relative spatial relationships of the planets within our solar system and the visible stars.

▶ STARTER IDEAS for Changes in the Earth and Sky

UNIT TITLE: *Our Earth Changes*

QUESTION: Is the earth the same place today as it was yesterday, last year, when I was born, when dinosaurs roamed?

UNIT OVERVIEW: Using observations over a short period along with photographs, illustrations, and interviews for longer periods, children will recognize changes in the earth's landforms, weather, and climate.

UNIT TITLE: *The Sun, Moon, and Earth*

QUESTION: How do cycles of the Sun, moon, and Earth create years, months, and days?

UNIT OVERVIEW: Through actual observations, charts, diagrams, and simulations, children will learn that the earth revolves around the sun in approximately 365 days and rotates on an axis once per day. The moon revolves around the earth in approximately 30 days (1 month).

> **NSES** **Content Standard 5–8:** Earth and Space Sciences [ESS]
>
> As a result of the activities in grades 5–8, all students should develop an understanding of:
>
> Structure of the earth system
>
> Earth's history
>
> Earth in the solar system

▶ **STARTER IDEAS** for the Structure of the Earth's System

UNIT TITLE: *The Earth Is a System*

QUESTION: What is beneath the surface of the earth?

UNIT OVERVIEW: Students describe the layers of the earth, its core, and how the core and layers interact.

UNIT TITLE: *Solid or Not?*

QUESTION: What are the forces that shape the earth?

UNIT OVERVIEW: Students give descriptions of the evidence that supports the hypothesis that the solid earth beneath their feet is constantly changing. Their descriptions will include references to the movements of plates, constructive and destructive forces, and the rock cycle (i.e., the change of old rocks to particles and their eventual reformation into rocks).

▶ **STARTER IDEAS** for the Earth's History

UNIT TITLE: *Gradual Changes in the Earth*

QUESTION: How is the earth changing from day to day?

UNIT OVERVIEW: Students identify modern earth processes—such as plate movement, erosion, and atmospheric changes—and make hypotheses about whether these processes have also occurred in the past.

UNIT TITLE: *Earth-Shattering Events*

QUESTION: What causes earth-shattering events?

UNIT OVERVIEW: Students create written research reports using information from reference books and Internet searches that describe the characteristics of possible catastrophic events in the earth's history, including asteroid or comet collisions.

▶ **STARTER IDEAS** for the Earth in the Solar System

UNIT TITLE: *The Solar System*

QUESTION: Where are we, really?

UNIT OVERVIEW: Students create charts, graphs, and drawings that demonstrate their knowledge of the position of Earth in the solar system and the locations of the other seven planets, moons, asteroids, and comets.

UNIT TITLE: *The Sun Does It All*

QUESTION: How does the sun power the earth?

UNIT OVERVIEW: Students give evidence that supports the hypothesis that the sun is the major source of energy for phenomena such as plant growth, winds, ocean currents, and the water cycle.

NSES **Content Standards K–8 Related To:**

Science and Technology [S&T]

Science in Personal and Social Perspectives [SPSP]

History and Nature of Science [HNS][2]

UNIT TITLE: *Weather Prediction*

QUESTION: How do they know a storm is coming?

UNIT OVERVIEW: Students identify the forms of technology used by meteorologists and build a model of at least one instrument used to gather weather observations.

UNIT TITLE: *Protect Yourself*

QUESTION: How can an understanding of the earth's systems save lives?

UNIT OVERVIEW: Students identify natural hazards that might affect them or others, their frequency of occurrence, and the protective steps individuals can take when specific hazards such as violent storms and earthquakes occur.

UNIT TITLE: *Important People*

QUESTION: Who were some people with big ideas about the earth and its systems?

UNIT OVERVIEW: Students do library and Internet research to prepare brief biographies of Ptolemy, Tycho Brahe, Johannes Kepler, and Alfred Wegener that focus on their contributions to our understanding of the earth and its systems.

Lesson Plan Starter Ideas for Common Curriculum Topics

Sometimes, you will be responsible for teaching lessons that are part of units prepared by committees of teachers in your school district or units that are commercially available. You may wonder how to break these units into lessons. To help you come up with lesson ideas for the earth/space sciences, I have analyzed a variety of teaching units and prepared a list of lesson plan starter ideas based on topics usually covered in these units. The lesson descriptions are very specific, so each description may also be viewed as the lesson's principal objective.

Go to **MyEducationLab**, select the topic Earth and Space Science, view the artifact entitled "A Glacier's Life," and complete the questions that accompany it.

▶ **STARTER IDEAS** for Characteristics of the Earth, Its Atmosphere, and the Oceans

- Make a labeled drawing that shows that the earth consists of rock layers.
- Draw clouds children have observed, and then classify each cloud into one of the following categories: cumulus, cirrus, or stratus.
- Predict tomorrow's weather based on today's weather, write a script for a weather forecast, and videotape the forecast.
- Evaluate the accuracy of a television weather forecast.
- Use a stopwatch to find the time interval between lightning and thunder.
- Calculate the distance from a thunderstorm using the time interval between lightning and thunder.
- Judge how well children could follow safety precautions if they were playing outside and thought that a thunderstorm or tornado was coming.
- Prepare a weather chart that identifies temperature, wind speed, wind direction, cloud cover, and precipitation every day for one week.

▶ **STARTER IDEAS** for the Water Cycle

- Describe and diagram the water cycle, and then make a presentation to a class of children at an earlier grade level.
- Write a story that includes a prediction of how life in school would change if the water supply to the school was cut in half.
- Count the number of times a water fountain is used in an hour, and estimate the water usage for one day.
- Observe and collect data related to the impact of people on the water cycle.

- Evaluate local streams, rivers, ponds, lakes, or ocean beaches to decide which would pose the least pollution hazard for swimmers, using newspaper articles gathered by the teacher as the basis for their evaluations.
- Make a hypothesis about how weather affects daily life, and carry out a survey to test the hypothesis.
- Create labeled drawings that show the characteristics of three different climate zones.

▶ **STARTER IDEAS** for Rocks and Minerals and the Earth's Crust

- Compare and contrast the characteristics of the earth's crust, mantle, and core.
- Make a chart that compares the characteristics of rocks and minerals.
- Classify rocks by their characteristics and the processes by which they were formed.
- Make a cartoon in which each frame shows a stage in the process by which rock is broken down to produce soil.
- Analyze soil samples using a hand lens, and separate rock and mineral particles from organic matter.
- Describe how fossils are formed and how they are used to determine the relative ages of rocks.

▶ **STARTER IDEAS** for Space

- Identify the major objects seen in the sky—such as the sun, moon, stars, and planets—from pictures and through direct observation.
- Infer the relative positions of the sun, earth, and moon from a list of observations made during an annular eclipse.
- Write a poem that includes the idea that the sun is the source of the earth's energy.
- Make a chart that compares the sun and the earth in terms of size, shape, color, state of matter, and temperature.
- Use an orange and a flashlight to show how the rotation of the earth determines night and day and how the earth's revolution and tilt determine the seasons.
- Create a sequence of drawings that shows how the moon appears to change shape as it revolves around the earth.
- Make a labeled diagram that shows the relative positions of the eight planets of the solar system.
- Make a chart that compares the other seven planets with Earth in terms of physical characteristics.
- Create an illustration on chartpaper that shows the orbits of planets, moons, asteroids, and comets.
- Make a hypothesis to explain what motivated humans to view groupings of stars as constellations.
- Write a poem that includes the idea that a star changes size and color and goes through a life cycle.
- Describe the relative locations of the planets with respect to the sun and our solar system within the Milky Way.
- Predict what humankind will do to survive when the sun ceases to shine.

WebQuest Starter Ideas

Imagine the WebQuest possibilities for your students when you teach the earth/space sciences! They'll be able to use the vast resources of the Internet to discover fascinating information about the galaxies, the stars, the sun, the planets, and the earth, their home.

The starter ideas in this section will help you plan your own earth/space science WebQuests. As you study the ideas, please keep the following in mind:

1. The starter ideas follow the WebQuest format presented in detail in Chapter 8.
2. The WebQuests are correlated with the NSES for grades K–8 (which are reprinted inside the front cover).
3. In the WebQuest context, the term *reports* has a very broad meaning and includes poster preparation, skits, dance, video presentations, labeled diagrams, and, of course, traditional written reports, if and when appropriate.

NSES

▶ **STARTER IDEAS** for WebQuests

WEBQUEST TITLE: *Your Home on the Moon*

SUGGESTED GRADE LEVELS: 2, 3, 4

NSES CONTENT STANDARDS: ESS 3; S&T 1 and 3; SPSP 3

CHALLENGE—MOTIVATION: You wake from a deep sleep. Your mother enters your room and says, "Dear, pack your favorite things. Our neighborhood has been picked to move to the moon. You'll be able to bring . . ."

CHALLENGE—REPORTS: Do Internet research to discover what your *new* neighborhood will be like. Then write a letter to your grandmother that has drawings that show your home on the moon, breathing equipment, and even your pets.

KEY TERMS FOR SEARCH ENGINES: Moon, Moon Base, Moon Colony, Living on the Moon

WEBQUEST TITLE: *Learn About Volcanoes*

SUGGESTED GRADE LEVELS: 2, 3, 4

NSES CONTENT STANDARD: ESS 3

CHALLENGE—MOTIVATION: You and your family have won an all-expenses-paid trip to the "big island" of Hawaii.

CHALLENGE—REPORTS: Make a travel guide that your family can use when they visit Kilauea. The travel guide should include pictures, a map, and . . .

KEY TERMS FOR SEARCH ENGINES: Hawaiian Volcanoes, Eruptions, Lava, Volcano Model, Kilauea

WEBQUEST TITLE: *Your Trip Through the Solar System*

SUGGESTED GRADE LEVELS: 3, 4, 5

NSES CONTENT STANDARDS: ESS 5 and 6; SPSP 1

CHALLENGE—MOTIVATION: You have just won a contest that provides enough prize money to make a 20-minute film for children called *Your Solar System Neighbors*.

CHALLENGE—REPORTS: Plan the film, showing how much time you would spend on each object in our solar system, what you would tell about each, and . . .

KEY TERMS FOR SEARCH ENGINES: Astronaut, Cosmonaut, Solar System, Asteroid Belt

WEBQUEST TITLE: *The Dinosaur Discovery*

SUGGESTED GRADE LEVELS: 3, 4, 5

NSES CONTENT STANDARDS: ESS 1; SPSP 4; LS 8

CHALLENGE—MOTIVATION: You wake up perspiring with your hands shaking. You have had a bad dream about a dinosaur trying to get into your house. It had a very large head, small front legs, and . . .

CHALLENGE—REPORTS: Do Internet research to find out what dinosaurs lived near your house. Then make a poster that shows what they looked like, what they ate, and . . .

KEY TERMS FOR SEARCH ENGINES: Prehistoric, Dinosaur, Extinct, Fossil

WEBQUEST TITLE: *Tracking the "Twisters"*

SUGGESTED GRADE LEVELS: 3, 4, 5

NSES CONTENT STANDARDS: ESS 3; S&T 1 and 2

CHALLENGE—MOTIVATION: You were just given the job of "Chief Tornado Tracker." You must be able to tell where tornadoes will most likely strike this year and . . .

CHALLENGE—REPORTS: Prepare a pamphlet (a small booklet) for people to read that has a map, tornado danger zones, safety precautions, and . . .

KEY TERMS FOR SEARCH ENGINES: Tornadoes, Twisters, Tracking Tornadoes, Tornado Safety

WEBQUEST TITLE: *Rocks Under Your Feet*

SUGGESTED GRADE LEVELS: 3, 4, 5

NSES CONTENT STANDARDS: ESS 1 and 3; SPSP 3

CHALLENGE—MOTIVATION: Your teacher wants your group to make a presentation about the rocks in your state or province, but he or she wants you to do it in a very interesting way.

CHALLENGE—REPORTS: Write a skit (a short play) in which the characters are all different rocks that have entered a "Rock Beauty Contest." In the play, each rock must . . .

KEY TERMS FOR SEARCH ENGINES: (Your State or Province), Geology (Your State or Province), Rocks, U.S. Geological Survey

WEBQUEST TITLE: *The Message in the Bottle*

SUGGESTED GRADE LEVELS: 5, 6, 7

NSES CONTENT STANDARD: ESS 3

CHALLENGE—MOTIVATION: While walking along a beach on the eastern coast of North America, you see a bottle that has just been trapped against a rock. As you get closer, you can see that there is a message . . .

CHALLENGE—REPORTS: Write a two-page story that tells what the message said, where it was put in the ocean, and the path it probably took. Be sure to include . . .

KEY TERMS FOR SEARCH ENGINES: Gulf Stream, Ocean Currents, Atlantic Ocean

WEBQUEST TITLE: *The Ozone Layer—What Is It?*

SUGGESTED GRADE LEVELS: 5, 6, 7

NSES CONTENT STANDARDS: ESS 3; SPSP 1, 5, and 8

CHALLENGE—MOTIVATION: Here is a mystery: Having ozone in the stratosphere is a good thing, but it's dangerous at ground level. Why is there such a difference?

Make the Case *An Individual or Group Challenge*

● **The Problem**

Children need science experiences that range across the earth/space, life, and physical sciences. Teachers may tend to emphasize those topics they feel most comfortable with and thus inadvertently limit the scope of children's learning.

● **Assess Your Prior Knowledge and Beliefs**

1. When you compare your knowledge of the earth/space sciences to your knowledge of the life sciences and physical sciences, do you believe you have acquired more, less, or the same amount of basic science content in each?

	More	*Less*	*Same*
Physical sciences	_____	_____	_____
Life sciences	_____	_____	_____

2. When you were a student in grades K–8, were you exposed to more, less, or the same amount of earth/space science content as you were to life science content and physical science content?

	More	*Less*	*Same*
Life sciences	_____	_____	_____
Physical sciences	_____	_____	_____

3. Dinosaurs are an ever-popular earth/space science topic for children. Identify five discrete items of knowledge that you have about dinosaurs.

_____

_____

_____

_____

_____

4. Now identify five things about dinosaurs that you think you should know but do not.

_____

_____

_____

_____

_____

● **The Challenge**

You are part of a team of teachers planning a unit on dinosaurs. Give examples of earth/space science activities you might include.

FIELD TRIP TITLE: *Pollution Prevention Location!*

IDEA: Many factories have added pollution controls to smokestacks and have taken other measures to reduce air pollution. Contact the public relations officer of any large company in your region to arrange for a visit. Consider a visit to a garage to see automobile air pollution devices being repaired, cleaned, or installed. Finally, many states and cities have installed pollution-monitoring stations to measure air quality. If your state has a mobile monitoring station, you might arrange for it to be brought to your school.

Many of the factors that make the city an interesting and exciting place to live also make it a place that overflows with field trip possibilities. Here are additional starter ideas that should stimulate your thinking about field trips for children in city schools:

▶ **STARTER IDEAS** for Field Trips

FIELD TRIP TITLE: *What Cracks the Sidewalks?*

IDEA: Children survey the sidewalks on the school grounds to find large and small cracks and make hypotheses about what causes the cracks.

FIELD TRIP TITLE: *What Happens to the Rain (Snow)?*

IDEA: Children search for evidence that will tell how rain or melted snow is absorbed by the soil or carried off.

FIELD TRIP TITLE: *What Clouds Are Those?*

IDEA: Children go outside to draw clouds, classify them, and track their movements.

FIELD TRIP TITLE: *Which Way Is North?*

IDEA: Children use compasses to identify north, south, east, and west on their playground.

FIELD TRIP TITLE: *Map Our Block*

IDEA: Children estimate distances to key buildings, count steps between landmarks, and gather related information to create a map of their block.

FIELD TRIP TITLE: *Earth Resources in the School Building*

IDEA: Children walk through and around the school to locate earth resources that are part of their building.

FIELD TRIP TITLE: *Trash and Treasure*

IDEA: Children walk around the block on recycling day (i.e., the day in which households and businesses are to use special blue or green plastic boxes to dispose of materials that may be recycled) to determine the extent to which apartment houses, homes, and businesses participate in recycling.

Additional Field Trip Destinations

Archaeological dig

Astronomy department at a local college

Building site with foundation excavation

Geology department at a local college

Gravel or sand pit

Hot-air balloon festival or exposition

Lakeshore or seashore

Museum with geological display

Road cut where rock layers can be safely observed

Stone quarry

Water reservoir

Water treatment plant

Cooperative Learning Projects

As you consider the following starter ideas for cooperative learning projects, keep in mind the importance of stressing the three key aspects of cooperative learning (discussed in detail in Chapter 5):

1. Positive interdependence
2. Individual accountability
3. Development of group process skills

▶ STARTER IDEAS for Cooperative Learning Projects

PROJECT TITLE: *Planet X*

IDEA: Provide each cooperative learning group with access to resource books containing descriptive information about each planet in the solar system. After the students have had an opportunity to skim through the books, give each group an envelope with the words *Planet X* written on it. Inside each envelope will be an index card with the name of a planet. The groups are not to divulge the names of the planets. Provide all groups with art materials, including pâpier-maché, paint, and posterboard. Give each the goal of creating a model of the planet that fits the descriptive information in the resource books and a poster that lists important information. Instruct the groups not to include the name of their planet on the poster. After the groups have completed their work, organize the mystery planets and posters in a display. Encourage members of each learning group to work as a team as they study the other planets and posters and attempt to identify them.

PROJECT TITLE: *Mission Possible*

IDEA: Provide each learning group with resource materials describing the characteristics of the planets of the solar system. The materials should include some information on the distances of these planets from the sun. Also provide the groups with posterboard, drawing materials, and a pocket calculator. Challenge each group to select a planet, do additional library research, and prepare large drawings and charts that show the group's response to the following:

1. How far away is the planet from the earth?
2. Has the planet been explored with space probes?
3. How long would it take a spaceship to get to the planet?
4. What special features should a group of scientists exploring the planet be sure to observe?
5. Make a drawing showing the inside of an imagined spaceship sent to explore the planet. Be sure to include places for the crew to eat, exercise, rest, and so forth.

PROJECT TITLE: *Weather the Storm*

IDEA: Give each group the challenge of developing a skit about the approach of a violent storm and a group of people camping outdoors. The skit must include accurate scientific information about violent storms and the safety measures that should be taken. Write the name of a violent storm (e.g., blizzard, hurricane, thunderstorm, tornado) on an index card, and give each group a different storm. Warn the groups to do their work in a way that does not reveal the storm to other groups. Encourage the groups to make simple props out of art materials. Have each group present its skit to the class as a whole.

▶ **ADDITIONAL STARTER IDEAS for Learning Groups**

- Have groups create and update weather maps.
- Have each group make a weather forecast and broadcast it on the school public address system.
- Challenge groups to build model volcanoes.
- Have groups write and perform skits on earthquake safety.
- Have groups create displays of rocks found in the state or province.
- Have groups create a series of newsprint panels that illustrate the major events in a recent spaceflight.

Attention Getters, Discovery Activities, and Demonstrations for Earth's Surface, Atmosphere, and Weather

Attention Getters

For Young Learners [ESS 1]

How Are Rocks the Same and Different?

Materials	3 locally gathered rocks 1 large nail
	3 sheets of white paper

Motivating Questions
- Do any of the rocks look or feel like any of the other rocks?
- How can we tell if one rock is harder or softer than the others?

Directions
1. Bring to class or take the class outside to find three rocks that look and feel different.
2. Display one rock on each sheet of paper, and have children come forward to make observations. As they do, write their observations on the board.

Children can discover the similarities and differences among types of rocks by doing hands-on activities.

3. Scratch each rock with the nail, and have the children observe that some rocks are harder than others, that some rock particles scrape off, and that the scraped-off particles are of different sizes and colors.

**Explanation/
Science Content
for the Teacher**

The earth's crust is made of different types of rocks. Rocks are different because of the materials within them and the ways in which they are formed. Wind, water, and ice break rocks into smaller pieces. Soil is made of small particles of rock as well as other material.

▶ *For Young Learners* [ESS 1]

What Is in Soil?

Materials

1 cup of potting soil   3 sheets of white paper
1 cup of top soil from outdoors   3 hand lenses (magnifying glasses)
1 cup of sand (aquarium sand will do)

Place materials on a table so individual children can observe the soils.

**Motivating
Questions**

- Will these soils look the same or different when we examine them with a hand lens?
- What do you think we will find in the soils?

Directions

1. Write the following terms on the board: *sand, outdoor soil, potting soil*. Read and pronounce each term with the class.
2. Sprinkle a small amount of each type of soil on a sheet of paper, and have the children use hand lenses to examine the soils.
3. As the children make observations, write them on the board under the appropriate term. *Note:* You may wish to sprinkle some soil particles on an overhead transparency and project the image.

**Explanation/
Science Content
for the Teacher**

Over long periods of time, rocks are broken into tiny particles. These particles, mixed with other materials, make up soil. Although sand gathered from a shoreline will contain pieces of shell and other debris, soil is mostly rock particles. Top soil contains amounts of sand, water, air, and decayed organic material. Potting soil usually contains less sand and more organic material than top soil. The organic material allows it to retain water for long periods of time.

▶ *For Young Learners* [ESS 3]

How Does a Thermometer Change
on Hot and Cold Days?

Materials

1 outdoor thermometer containing red liquid   1 glass of cool water
3 rubber bands   1 glass of hot water

**Motivating
Questions**

Display the thermometer and ask:
- What do we call this?
- Where have you seen thermometers?

Directions

1. Wrap a rubber band around the thermometer at the level of the liquid.
2. Put the base of the thermometer in cool water, and have volunteers observe the new level of the liquid. Put a second rubber band at this level.

3. Have the children predict how the level will change when the thermometer is placed in warm water; then place the thermometer in warm water and mark the level of the liquid with the third rubber band.

4. Discuss how looking at an outdoor thermometer might help people decide what to wear on hot and cold days.

Explanation/ Science Content for the Teacher

A thermometer registers the temperature of its surroundings. The level of liquid rises or falls due to increases or decreases in its volume as a result of heating or cooling. The red liquid in a typical household thermometer is tinted alcohol. Some thermometers, however, contain mercury, a silvery liquid metal.

▶ *For Young Learners*   [HNS 2 and 3]

Weather Sayings: True or False?

Materials

Access to the Internet   Science resource books and encyclopedias
Posterpaper and markers

Motivating Questions

- What does the word *superstition* mean?
- What are some of the superstitions you know about?
- What are some examples of weather superstitions?

Directions

1. Have the class vote on whether each of the following statements is true or false. Then ask them to give their reasons for voting as they did and to explain how each statement could be tested.
   "Birds flying south means cold weather is coming."
   "Squirrels gathering nuts means cold weather is coming."
   "When the leaves on trees turn upside down, it's going to rain."
   "A sunny shower won't last half an hour."
   "If you wash your car, it's going to rain tomorrow."

2. Divide the class into cooperative groups and give them the task of discovering three weather sayings, deciding how each could be tested, and sharing their reasons for believing it to be true or false. Each group should write their sayings on posterpaper.

3. Bring the groups together, and ask for a class vote on whether each saying is true or false.

4. Finally, have the groups reveal the results of their research.

Explanation/ Science Content for the Teacher

Here are some additional weather sayings you may wish to share:
   "You can smell rain when it's coming."
   "When your joints give you pain, it's going to rain."
   "Red sky at night, sailor's delight. Red sky in the morning, sailors take warning."
   "When smoke descends, good weather ends."

▶ *For Middle-Level Learners*   [ESS 4]

What Crushed the Can?

Materials

2 empty soda cans
Tongs or heat-resistant potholder mitts
Ice cubes in a bowl of water
Access to an alcohol burner, stove top, or electric hot plate

Motivating Questions	• What do you think will happen if we put a little water in the can, heat the can, and plunge it into the ice water? • What do you think causes this to happen?
Directions	1. Add about one-fourth of a cup of tap water to the empty can. 2. Heat the can over the heat source until the water boils and steam is visible. 3. Using tongs or mitts, invert the can and insert the open end first into the ice water.
Explanation/ Science Content for the Teacher	The heated water changes to steam. The steam forces some of the air out of the can. When the can is dropped into ice water, the steam in the can condenses and the pressure within the can is reduced. Atmospheric pressure (the pressure of the air outside the can) crushes the can.

For Middle-Level Learners [ESS 4]

What Pushed the Egg into the Bottle?

Materials	1 cooled, peeled, hard-boiled egg Matches 1 sheet of paper about 8 cm square Tongs 1 glass gallon jug or old-fashioned milk bottle
Motivating Questions	• What do you think will happen if we put the egg on the empty bottle? • What do you think will happen if we put the egg on the bottle after we have burned some paper in the bottle?
Directions	1. Put the egg on the open bottle top with the narrow end down, and ask the second motivating question. 2. After listening to the predictions, remove the egg, light the paper with the match, drop it (using the tongs) into the bottle, and quickly replace the egg. The egg will be pushed into the bottle.
Explanation/ Science Content for the Teacher	The burning paper heats the air within the bottle, causing it to expand. The egg acts as a valve, allowing some but not all of the expanding air to leave the bottle around the narrow end of the egg. Thus, the air in the bottle is at a lower pressure than the air outside the bottle. The pressure of the air outside of the bottle (atmospheric pressure) slowly forces the egg into the bottle. *Safety Note:* Be sure to point out to the children the safety precautions you employ as you use a match and handle the burning paper. Explain that they should not try this activity at home without adult supervision.

For Middle-Level Learners [S&T 4]

Can We Make Fog?

Materials	2 resealable sandwich bags containing ice cubes 2 empty, clean plastic 2-liter soda bottles with labels removed 1 funnel 1 electric tea kettle or other source of very hot water 1 flashlight

Motivating Questions	• What do you think will happen when we put a bag of ice cubes on top of the bottle with cool water? • What do you think will happen when we put a bag of ice cubes on top of the bottle of hot water?
Directions	1. Add cold water to one bottle until it is about four-fifths full. Fill the second bottle with hot water to the same level. 2. Cover the top of each bottle with a sandwich bag containing ice cubes, and have the children predict the changes that will occur within the bottle. 3. Use the flashlight to illuminate the inside of each bottle. The children should be able to observe fog above the surface of the hot water. You may wish to darken the room for this part of the demonstration.
Explanation/ Science Content for the Teacher	Some of the hot water evaporates into the air above it. When that air is cooled by the bag of ice cubes, the water vapor condenses into tiny droplets. These droplets are in fact a cloud. When a cloud is formed at the earth's surface above land or water, it is called *fog*. Depending on the room's temperature and other factors, the children may be able to see some fog above the hot water even without the use of the sandwich bag with ice cubes.

Discovery Activities

For Young Learners [S&T 1]

How to Make a Fossil

Objectives	• The children will create fossils from samples of plant material. • The children will explain the process by which fossils are produced in nature.
Sciences Processes Emphasized	Hypothesizing Communicating Experimenting
Materials for Each Child or Group	Aluminum foil pie plate Water Plaster of paris Plastic spoon Petroleum jelly Assortment of plant materials, including portions of a carrot, a leaf, and a twig
Motivation	Be sure to have two or three real fossils on hand, if possible, or reference books with pictures of various fossils. Display the fossils or pictures of the fossils, and have children make observations about their characteristics. Encourage the children to discuss how the fossils may have been formed. Tell the children that they will create their own fossils during this activity.
Directions	1. Have the children coat each portion of the plants they are using with a thin layer of petroleum jelly. 2. Have the children mix the plaster of paris with water in the bottom of the pie plate until they obtain a thick, smooth mixture. 3. Have the children gently press the plant material into the upper surface of the plaster of paris and set the plaster aside to harden. 4. Bring the children together for a group discussion. Emphasize that what they have done represents *one* way in which fossils are formed; that is, plant or animal material falls into sediment, making an imprint. If the sediment then hardens into rock, the imprint will remain even though the organic matter decays.

5. When the plaster is dry and they have removed the plant material, the children will be able to observe a permanent imprint.
6. Establish a display of reference books showing pictures of fossils. Have the children look at pictures of fossils and hypothesize about how they were formed.

Key Discussion Questions

1. Have you ever found any fossils or seen any fossils on display? If so, what were they like and where did you see them? *Answers will vary.*
2. The fossils you made are known as *molds*. How could a scientist use a mold fossil to make something that looked like the object that formed the mold? *He or she could use something like clay to press against the mold fossil. The surface of the clay would take the shape of the original material.*

Science Content for the Teacher

A fossil is any preserved part or trace of something that lived in the past. Leaves, stems, bones, and even footprints have been preserved as fossils. Some fossils are formed when water passing over and through portions of animal or plant remains deposits minerals that replace the original materials. In other cases, animal and plant remains are buried in sediment. An imprint of the shape is left in mud even when the material decays, and if the mud hardens and turns to rock, the imprint is preserved. This type of impression, which the children have replicated in this activity, is known as a *mold*.

Extension

Science: You may wish to encourage some children to do an activity that will extend their knowledge of fossil molds to fossil casts. They can replicate the formation of a cast fossil by mixing plaster of paris outdoors and filling in animal tracks with it.

▶ *For Young Learners* **[ESS 3]**

Weather or Not

Objectives

- The children will observe and record daily weather conditions.
- The children will compare their observations with information on weather maps.

Go to **MyEducationLab**, select the topic Earth and Space Science, and read the lesson plan entitled "How Does a Weather Vane Work?"

Sciences Processes Emphasized

Observing   Comparing
Measuring

Materials for Each Child or Group

Outdoor thermometer marked in Celsius
Newspaper weather map for the days of the activity
Legend from weather map showing symbols and meanings

Motivation

On the chalkboard create a weather chart that has columns for temperature, cloud, wind, and precipitation data. While the children watch, fill the columns of the chart with your personal observations of the present weather, using the appropriate symbols from a weather map. Challenge the children to guess what is meant by each symbol. After some discussion, explain what each symbol represents, and indicate that the children will use these symbols on the charts they make.

Directions

1. After giving the children some time to practice drawing each weather symbol that you have explained, have them make blank charts.
2. For the next two to three days, have the groups take their charts to some location on the school grounds where they can make weather observations. They should use weather symbols to record their observations. *Safety Note:* Be sure that each group is visible to you in a safe location.
3. You can generate additional excitement if you have the children compare the observations from their weather charts with weather maps for the same days.

Key Discussion Questions

1. What kinds of measurements can we make of weather conditions outside? *Temperature, whether it's raining, how hard the wind is blowing, and whether there are clouds in the sky.*
2. How are clouds different from one another? *Some are white and puffy, some are flat and gray, some are high in the sky, and some you can see through.*

Science Content for the Teacher

There are three major types of clouds: *cirrus, cumulus,* and *stratus*. Clouds that are high in the sky and wispy are cirrus clouds. Cumulous clouds are often billowing with white tops. Stratus clouds are sheets of gray clouds that are close to the ground. Depending on your climate, precipitation may take the form of rain or snow. Temperature varies from place to place on a given day as well as from day to day.

Extension

Science/Art/Technology: Encourage some children to create a cloud display. After consulting reference books for pictures of various types of clouds, they can use cotton balls, cotton batting, and Styrofoam to create their displays. Challenge the children to make instruments to measure wind direction, wind speed, or precipitation.

For Middle-Level Learners [ESS 4]

How Do Layers of Sediment Form?

Objectives

- The children make a model and use it to discover the order in which particles of different sizes settle to the bottom.
- The children make drawings to document the results of their experimentation and discuss their results.

Sciences Processes Emphasized

Observing   Communicating
Experimenting

Materials for Each Child or Group

| Large glass jar with lid | Pebbles | Soil |
| Source of water | Gravel | Sand |

Motivation

This is a good activity to do before the children begin studying how various types of rocks are formed. Display at the front of the room or at a learning station all of the materials in the materials list. Ask the children to guess what this activity will be about. After some initial discussion, focus their attention on the soil, pebbles, gravel, and sand. Ask them to think about what would happen if a stream carrying these materials slowed down. Once the children have begun to think about the materials settling into layers on the bottom of a stream or river, begin the activity.

Directions

1. Have each group fill one-third of a large glass jar with equal amounts of soil, pebbles, gravel, and sand.
2. Have the groups fill the jars the rest of the way with water and screw on the lids.
3. Have the groups shake the jars so that all the materials are thoroughly stirred in the water.
4. Ask the groups to let the materials settle.
5. Have the groups observe the settling and then make drawings of the layers they observe.
6. Engage the class in a discussion of the results of the activity.

Key Discussion Questions	1. Which of the materials settled to the bottom of the jar first? *The gravel.*
	2. How can you explain the results in this activity? *The large pieces of gravel settled first because they were heavier than the other materials. The heaviest materials are at the bottom, and the lightest materials are at the top.*
	3. What type of rock is formed from layers of earth materials that settle out of water? *Sedimentary.*

Science Content for the Teacher

When water moves across the surface of the earth, it picks up tiny rocks, pebbles, grains of sand, and soil. This flow of water and materials eventually reaches streams, rivers, and the ocean, and the particles within the water become known as *sediment*. Whenever a flow of water is slowed, some of the sediment is deposited on the bottom of the flow. Layers of sediment pile up under the water. After hundreds of years have passed, the weight of these layers may have become so great that the bottom layers are turned into rock.

Extension

Science/Social Studies: Some children may be encouraged to do research on the effect of moving water on farmland. The loss of topsoil due to water erosion is a significant threat to agriculture. Through research, these children will find that there are many government agencies that assist farmers who are trying to protect their soil from erosion.

▶ *For Middle-Level Learners* [ESS 4]

Quakes and Shakes: An Earthquake Watch

Objectives

- The children will be able to locate those regions of the earth that have more earthquake activity than others.
- The children will study earthquake occurrence data and make hypotheses to explain any patterns they observe.

Sciences Processes Emphasized

Interpreting data
Making hypotheses

Materials for Each Child or Group

Note: This is a long-term activity in which children plot data from current government information on earthquakes. Thus, you will need to order the *Preliminary Determination of Epicenters: Monthly Listing* from the Superintendent of Documents, Government Printing Office, Washington, DC 20402 or go to http://earthquake.usgs.gov.eqcenter/.

Copies of the epicenter charts	Access to an atlas
Paper	Pencil
World map with latitude and longitude marked	

Motivation

Ask the children if they have ever been to a part of the country that has a lot of earthquake activity, such as San Francisco. If any of them have, encourage them to discuss anything they may have heard about earthquakes from persons who live there. If no one has, engage the children in a discussion about earthquakes. Stress their cause and possible hazards. Explain that scientists are able to study information about previous earthquakes to predict the general locations of future earthquakes. Tell the children that they will be working with some of the same information that scientists use. Then display the collection of epicenter charts and the world maps.

Directions

1. Give a map and copies of the epicenter charts to each child or group. Explain that the information on the charts shows where scientists believe the source of an earthquake was; then explain the information. Although there is a lot of information on

each chart, the children should work with only the date, time of eruption, latitude, longitude, region, depth, and *magnitude.* Explain that magnitude indicates the strength of the earthquake.

2. Have the children refer to an atlas to find the specific location of each earthquake and then mark their copy of the world map with a symbol for the earthquake. They should plot all earthquakes with a source from 0 to 69 kilometers deep with one symbol, 70 to 299 kilometers with another symbol, and more than 299 kilometers with a third symbol.

3. When they have recorded data from the epicenter chart, you may wish to have a discussion of the patterns they observe.

4. Have the children maintain their maps for a few months and repeat the activity each time you receive a monthly epicenter chart.

Key Discussion Questions

1. Do you see any pattern on your map that tells you what parts of the earth seem to have the most earthquakes? Where are those places? *Yes, along the western portion of the Pacific Ocean, from the Mediterranean Sea across Asia, and along the west coast of North and South America.*

2. What problems do you think are caused by earthquakes? *Answers will vary. Some may include comments such as the following: buildings may fall; earthquakes in the ocean may cause great waves.*

Science Content for the Teacher

An *earthquake* is the shaking of the ground caused by the shifting of the plates that make up the earth's surface and the release of pressure through faults in the earth's crust, which results in the movement of blocks of rocks past each other. The vibrations at ground level are sometimes strong enough to do structural damage to buildings and threaten life. The shaking of the ocean floor can produce gigantic waves that roll across the ocean. Scientists record the presence of an earthquake with an instrument known as a *seismograph.* To pinpoint the source of an earthquake's vibrations, scientists gather data from seismographs all over the world. The *epicenter* is thought to be directly above the place where the initial rock fractures occurred. When the locations of epicenters are plotted on a map, they roughly mark the places on the earth where crustal plates grind against each other.

Extension

Science/Social Studies: Some children may wish to research the effects of the San Francisco earthquake of 1906. They will be able to find pictures in encyclopedias showing how the city looked after the earthquake. Ask the children what effects the earthquake likely had on community life immediately after it occurred and its effect after a few years had passed.

▶ *For Middle-Level Learners* [ESS 4]

How to Find the Dew Point

Objectives

- The children will find the temperature at which water vapor in the air condenses.
- The children will analyze their data and offer an explanation of how changes in treatment of moisture in the air will affect dew point readings.

Sciences Processes Emphasized

Observing   Interpreting
Gathering data

Materials for Each Child or Group

Empty soup can with one end cut out	Supply of ice cubes
Outdoor thermometer that will fit into the soup can	Rag

Motivation

Begin a discussion with the children about the invisible water vapor present in the air. Ask them if they have ever observed any evidence of the presence of water vapor in the air. They will probably share such observations as the steaming up of mirrors in bathrooms and the steam that seems to come out of their mouths when they breathe on a cold day. Tell the children that water vapor in the air is usually not observed because the air temperature is sufficiently high to keep the water vapor a gas. As a gas, water vapor is invisible. Display the equipment that will be used for this activity, and tell the children that they will be using it to find the temperature at which the water vapor presently in the air will condense. Explain that this temperature is known as the *dew point*. The dew point is the point at which water vapor changes from a gas to a liquid.

Directions

1. Distribute the soup cans to the children and have them remove the labels, scrub the outside of the cans with soap and water, and polish the surfaces. (Be sure to remove sharp edge prior to distribution of the cans to children.)
2. Demonstrate the following procedure for the children: Fill the shiny can about two-thirds full of water at room temperature, and place a thermometer in it. Then add small amounts of ice, and stir the mixture until the ice melts. Have the children observe the outside of the can as you add small amounts of ice and stir. Eventually, the outside will begin to lose its shine, and a layer of moisture will be observable.
3. Have the children do this activity on their own. Ask them to keep track of the temperature on the thermometer and to pay close attention to the outside of the can as the temperature drops. Stress the importance of observing the precise temperature at which the film forms.
4. After the children have found the dew point inside the classroom, you may wish to have them find it outside. When the children have completed the activity, begin a class discussion of their results. Be sure the children understand that the drier the air, the lower the temperature must be in order for moisture to condense.

Science Content for the Teacher

The air's capacity to hold moisture is determined by its temperature. The temperature at which air can no longer hold water vapor is known as the *dew point*. *Condensation,* the change from water as a gas to water as a liquid, is usually observable in the atmosphere as dew, fog, or clouds. Condensation occurs when the air is saturated with water vapor. *Saturation* occurs when the temperature of the air reaches its dew point. In this activity, the air near the outside surface of the can is cooled to its dew point. The moisture in that layer of air condenses on the available surface—the outside of the can.

Key Discussion Questions

1. Why do you think we use a shiny can for this activity? *It makes it easy to tell when the moisture condenses. The moisture makes the shiny can look dull.*
2. Why do you think knowing the dew point might be important to weather forecasters? *If they know the dew point, they will know the temperature at which the moisture in the air will condense. Then they can more easily predict when fog, clouds, or rain will happen.*
3. Why do you think dew forms only at night? *During the night, the temperature of the air falls because the earth is not receiving sunlight. Sometimes the temperature falls so low that the dew point is reached. When this happens, the moisture condenses on grass and on the leaves and branches of plants.*

Extension

Science/Math: You may wish to have some children find the dew point with both Celsius and Fahrenheit thermometers. After they have done this, they can use conversion charts to be sure the dew point expressed in the number of degrees Celsius is equivalent to that expressed in the number of degrees Fahrenheit.

Demonstrations

Indoor Rainmaking[3]

Objectives	• The children will observe the production of rain. • The children will explain how the rainmaking model can be used to illustrate the water cycle.

Sciences Processes Emphasized

Observing	Explaining
Inferring	

Materials

Hot plate or stove	Large pot	Ice cubes
Tea kettle	Water	

Motivation Show the materials to the children, and ask how the materials could be used to make a model that shows how rain forms. After some discussion, they will be ready to observe the demonstration and follow the path of the water. You may wish to have a volunteer assist you.

Directions
1. Place water in the tea kettle and begin to heat it. As the water is heating, put the ice cubes in the pot.
2. When the water in the tea kettle is boiling, hold the pot with the ice cubes above the steam emerging from the tea kettle. Have children observe the formation of water droplets on the bottom of the pot.
3. Have the children note when the water droplets become large enough to fall.
4. Using the questions below, discuss the rainmaking process as a model illustrating the water cycle.

Key Discussion Questions
1. What do you think the tea kettle of boiling water stands for in the model? *Oceans and lakes.*
2. How does water from the oceans and lakes get into the atmosphere? *The sun heats the water and it evaporates.*
3. Where are the clouds in our model? *The steam stands for the clouds.*
4. Rainmaking is part of the water cycle. What do you think scientists mean when they talk about the water cycle? *Water is always moving. Water that leaves the lakes and oceans moves into the air. Water that is in the air forms clouds and sometimes falls to the earth. Rain, snow, sleet, and hail fall onto the land and oceans. Water that reaches the land flows back into the oceans and lakes.*

Science Content for the Teacher Water on the earth is continually recycled. The path that water takes in nature is known as the *water cycle*. Water that evaporates from oceans, lakes, and rivers enters the atmosphere. *Precipitation* forms when this water vapor accumulates around dust particles at low temperatures and high altitudes. The water then returns to the earth.

Extension *Science/Language Arts:* Some children may wish to use this demonstration as a starting point for writing poetry about the principal form of precipitation in their area. They could write their poetry on large sheets of paper suitable for display.

For Young Learners [ESS 3]

Whose Fault Is It?

Objectives
- The children will observe the occurrence of folds and faults in simulated rock layers.
- The children will infer the causes of changes in rock layers.

Sciences Processes Emphasized

Observing
Inferring

Materials

2 blocks of wood
4 sticks of modeling clay, each a different color

Motivation

Ask the children how you could use clay to make rock layers. Flatten each stick of clay into a strip that is about 1 centimeter (less than 1/2 inch) thick and 8 to 10 centimeters (about 3 to 4 inches) wide.

Directions

1. Place the clay strips on top of one another. Ask the children to guess whether the strips represent sedimentary, igneous, or metamorphic rocks.
2. Gently press the wood blocks against the ends of the clay layers, and have the children observe changes.
3. Eventually, small cracks will appear on the layers, and the layers will be forced into a hump. *Note:* If the clay is too soft or too warm, the fractures will not occur. You may wish to allow the layers to dry or cool for a day before performing this part of the demonstration.

Key Discussion Questions

1. If the clay layers were layers of rock, which layer would probably be the youngest? Why? *The top one. The material in it was deposited last.*
2. What causes the bends and breaks in real rock layers? *Answers will vary. Some children may be aware that the pushing together of the plates of the earth's crust produces great forces that change and fracture rock layers.*
3. Do you think that breaks in the rock layers might allow molten rock to move toward the earth's surface? Why? *Yes. The molten rock can flow up through the cracks because there is nothing to hold it back.*

Science Content for the Teacher

Layers of sedimentary rock provide important clues about the relative ages of rocks. Top layers are *usually* younger than lower layers. Sometimes, however, layers of rocks are turned upside down as a result of the collusion of the crustal plates and the movement of molten rock beneath the surface.

Extension

Science/Art: You may wish to have children construct detailed models of various types of faults described in reference books.

For Middle-Level Learners [ESS 4]

You've Heard of Rock Musicians, but Have You Heard of Rock Magicians?

Objectives
- The children will observe one unusual characteristic in each of five rocks.
- The children will describe each characteristic observed.
- The children will name each of the rocks used in the demonstration.

Sciences Processes Emphasized	Observing Communicating

Materials

Bowl of water	Matches
Sheet of paper	White vinegar or any dilute acid

Samples of the following rocks: pumice, anthracite, asbestos, calcite, willemite
(or any other rock that will fluoresce)

Any ultraviolet-light source (you may be able to borrow one from a high school earth
science teacher)

Optional: Bow tie, magic wand

Very optional: Top hat and/or cape

Motivation

Because of the nature of this demonstration, it will take little to get the children's attention. You may wish to be the rock magician yourself, or you may happen to have a child who would be perfect for the part! Be sure that all the children have a good view of what is to transpire. Be clear that science is not magic, although all magic is based on science.

Directions

1. The rock magician should use the materials in the list to demonstrate the following:
   a. The floating rock: Pumice will float in water.
   b. The writing rock: Anthracite will write on paper.
   c. The fizzing rock: A few drops of vinegar will cause calcite to fizz.
   d. The fluorescent rock: With the room darkened, the willemite will fluoresce when placed under ultraviolet light.
2. Before each demonstration, the magician should name the rock, spell it, and write its name on the chalkboard. The children will thereby learn the name of each rock displayed.
3. Have the children write down their observations.

Key Discussion Questions

1. Why do you think geologists are interested in the special characteristics of these rocks? *They can tell a lot about the rock from its properties.*
2. Why do you think the pumice floated? *It has a lot of air trapped in it.*
3. Do you think the material in your pencils might be something like the anthracite? Why? *Yes, both can make marks on paper.* Note: The material in pencils these days is not lead, but graphite. Graphite is essentially carbon. Anthracite is also carbon.

Science Content for the Teacher

Pumice is magma (molten rock) that trapped bubbles of steam or gas when it was thrown out of a volcano in liquid form. When magma solidifies, it is honeycombed with gas-bubble holes. This gives it the buoyancy to float on water. *Anthracite* is a type of coal that results from the partial decomposition of plants. The carbon in the plants is the primary constituent of anthracite and other forms of coal. *Calcite* is a mineral found in such rocks as limestone and marble. Geologists test for its presence by placing a few drops of a warm acid on the rock under study. If calcite is present, carbon dioxide gas will be released with a fizz by the chemical reaction. *Willemite* is a mineral that fluoresces; that is, it gives off light when exposed to ultraviolet light. Some other minerals, generally available from science supply companies, that can be used to demonstrate fluorescence are calcite, tremolite, fluorite, and scapolite.

Extension

Science/Social Studies: You may wish to follow this demonstration with a map or study exercise in which the children find out where the various rocks come from. They will need some earth science reference books and an atlas.

How to Find the Relative Humidity

Objectives
- The children will observe how to construct a wet/dry bulb hygrometer.
- The children will measure the relative humidity.

Sciences Processes Emphasized

Observing

Using numbers

Materials

2 identical Celsius thermometers
Small piece of gauze
Small rubber band

Baby food jar full of water at room temperature
Small board or piece of heavy cardboard
Relative humidity table (see page 236)

Motivation

Ask the children if they have ever heard the term *relative humidity*. After some discussion, indicate that the term represents a comparison of the amount of water in the air to the amount of water the air could hold at the present temperature. Tell the children that they are about to observe how to construct an instrument that will permit them to find the relative humidity.

Directions

1. With the help of a student volunteer, tape both thermometers about 6 centimeters (about 2.4 inches) apart on a piece of cardboard. The bulb end of one thermometer should extend 6 centimeters beyond the edge of the cardboard.
2. Wrap the extending end in gauze. Fasten the gauze with a rubber band, but leave a tail of gauze that can be inserted into the baby food jar.
3. Place the tail in the baby food jar filled with water, and moisten the gauze around the bulb. The tail will serve as a wick to keep the bulb moist.
4. Fan both thermometers vigorously. In a few minutes, the volunteer will observe that the thermometers display different temperatures. Use the wet/dry bulb table to find the relative humidity. (Example: If the dry bulb reading is 10°C and the difference between the wet bulb reading and dry bulb reading is 4°C, then the relative humidity is 55%.)

Relative humidity expressed as a percentage

Dry Bulb Reading (°C)	Difference between Wet Bulb Reading and Dry Bulb Reading (°C)									
	1	2	3	4	5	6	7	8	9	10
0	81	64	46	29	13					
2	84	68	52	37	22	7				
4	85	71	57	43	29	16				
6	86	73	60	48	35	24	11			
8	87	75	63	51	40	29	19	8		
10	88	77	66	55	44	34	24	15	6	
12	89	78	68	58	48	39	29	21	12	
14	90	79	70	60	51	42	34	26	18	10
16	90	81	71	63	54	46	38	30	23	15
18	91	82	73	65	57	49	41	34	27	20
20	91	83	74	66	59	51	44	38	31	24
22	92	83	76	68	61	54	47	41	34	28
24	92	84	77	69	62	56	49	44	37	31
26	92	85	78	71	64	58	51	47	40	34
28	93	85	78	72	65	59	53	48	42	37
30	93	86	79	73	67	61	55	50	44	39

Key Discussion Questions	1. Why do you think the wet bulb showed a lower reading than the dry bulb? *Water evaporated from the gauze and cooled the thermometer.*
	2. Would more or less water evaporate on a drier day? *More, because water enters the air faster if there is little water in the air to begin with.*

Science Content for the Teacher   Hygrometers are used to measure relative humidity. The evaporation of water lowers the wet bulb temperature. The amount of lowering depends on a variety of factors, including the amount of water vapor already in the air.

Extension   *Science/Social Studies:* Have the children interview adults to find out if they have lived in places where the relative humidity is high or low. The interviewers can find out how this affected the way of life in each place. Children can practice geography skills by locating various high and low humidity regions on a world map.

Attention Getters, Discovery Activities, and Demonstrations for the Cosmos

Attention Getters

For Young Learners [ESS 2]

Can You Move Like the Planets?

> Go to **MyEducationLab**, select Resources, and then Web Links. Then select "Planetary Fact Sheet."

Materials   8 sheets of $8\frac{1}{2} \times 11$ in. pastel paper, one sheet for each group
1 larger sheet of orange paper
Crayons or water-based markers for each group

Motivating Questions
- What are some of the things you see in the sky on a bright day?
- Display a globe and ask: Do you think our earth moves or stays still?

Directions
1. Write the planet names on the chalkboard, distribute the paper, and assign a planet name to each group.
2. Write the word *sun* on the orange sheet, and have each group write the name of its planet on the paper it received.
3. Have volunteers from each group join you at a central place in the room. Arrange the volunteers in proper sequence from the sun (the orange sheet that you are holding), and have the children circle around you.
4. Finally, indicate that the planets spin (rotate) as they move (revolve), and have the children do the same, slowly.

Science Content for the Teacher   Eight major planets travel around the sun in orbits. These planets do not emit light. They reflect the sun's light. The sun is a star whose apparent motion is due to the earth's rotation. Seasonal changes are due to the change in the relative position of the earth as it orbits around the sun.

For Young Learners [ESS 3]

Can You Move Like the Moon?

Materials   1 orange sheet of paper   1 blue sheet of paper
1 white sheet of paper   Crayons or water-based markers

Motivating Questions	• Do you think the earth moves around the sun, or do you think the sun moves around the earth? • Do you think the moon moves around the earth, or do you think the earth moves around the moon?
Directions	1. Write the word *sun* on the orange sheet of paper, the word *earth* on the blue sheet, and the word *moon* on the white sheet. (You may wish to have children copy the words from the board.) 2. Select one student to stand and hold the orange sheet to represent the sun. 3. Select another student to hold the blue sheet and move in orbit around the sun. 4. Finally, select a student to hold the white sheet and orbit the earth as it travels around the sun.
Science Content for the Teacher	The moon is a satellite of the earth. This means that the moon revolves around the earth as the earth rotates and revolves around the sun. The moon also rotates as it orbits the earth.

For Young Learners [ESS 1]

Why Is Earth Called the "Blue Planet"?

Materials	1 model car, plane, and doll 1 globe
Motivating Questions	• Is this a real car, plane, or person? • How are these the same or different from real cars, planes, and people?
Directions	1. Write the words *Sun* and *Earth* on the chalkboard. 2. Pronounce each word, and then display the toys. Discuss how models are different from real things. 3. Display the globe, and ask what it is a model of. Have children point out the locations of lands and oceans on the globe, and discuss the relative amounts of each. 4. Move the globe as far from the children as possible, and ask how astronauts in space might describe the earth.
Science Content for the Teacher	Scientists often use models. Just as toys stand for real things, a globe stands for, or is a model of, the earth.

For Middle-Level Learners [ESS 6]

Is Day Always as Long as Night?

Materials	1 tennis ball Chalk 1 steel knitting needle 1 m of string 1 small lamp without lampshade 1 marking pen
Motivating Questions	• If you didn't have to go to school, would you have more time to play outside in the summer months or in the winter months? • Are the lengths of the days and nights the same all through the year?

Directions

1. Before class, carefully push the knitting needle through the tennis ball from top to bottom. Use a marking pen to make a dot that stands for your city or town on the tennis ball.

Earth in orbit in the classroom

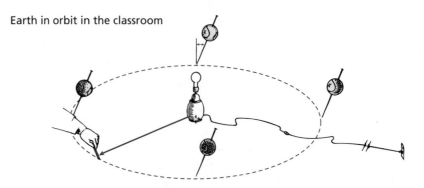

2. Use the string to make a circle on the classroom floor. Put the lamp at the center of the circle. Use the chalk to label the furthest-left part of the circle *June 21*. Label the furthest-right part of the circle *December 21*, the topmost point *March 21*, and the lowest point *September 21*.
3. At the start of class, have the children gather around the model. Explain that the circle *almost* represents the path of the earth.
4. Tell the children that the path is really a flattened-out circle called an *ellipse*. Convert the circle to an ellipse by using the original circle as a guideline and drawing an ellipse with chalk.
5. Incline the tennis ball approximately 23° from the vertical, and have a child hold it at the spot marked March 21 and slowly rotate it. The children will note that their town gets light for half the rotation (12 hours). When this procedure is repeated at June 21, the children will note that the town is lit for approximately two-thirds of a rotation (16 hours). At the December 21 spot, the children will note their town gets few hours of sunlight (8–10 hours). To make this more obvious, have a child sit at the sun's location and tell whether she or he sees the town for a long or short period of time on June 21 and December 21.

Science Content for the Teacher

Spring and fall are times when the earth's axis is not tilted toward or away from the sun. At these times, day and night are of equal length. During summer in the Northern Hemisphere, the earth's axis is tilted in the direction of the sun, so any location in the Northern Hemisphere has longer days.

▶ *For Middle-Level Learners* [ESS 6]

Can You Draw an Orbit?

Materials
1 m of string
1 large sheet of paper
1 pencil
2 pushpins or thumbtacks
1 sheet of cardboard about the same size as the paper
1 meter stick

Motivating Questions
- What shape is the earth's path around the sun?
- Do you think the shape is a circle?

Directions

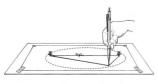

How to make an ellipse

1. Place the paper on the cardboard. Stick the pushpins through the paper and cardboard toward the center of the paper but about 20 centimeters apart.
2. Tie a knot in the string to make a closed loop, and put the loop around the pushpins.
3. Holding the pencil vertically inside the loop and pushed against the string, move it in a complete path around the pins. Be sure to keep the tension of the pencil against the loop constant.
4. Explain to the children that the figure you have drawn is an *ellipse* and that the planets travel in ellipses around the sun. If you wish, remove one of the pushpins after you have drawn the ellipse and explain that the remaining pushpin represents the sun.

Science Content for the Teacher

Although people often describe the orbits of the planets as circles, they are in fact ellipses. An ellipse has two foci. The sun is at the location of one of the foci for the earth's orbit.

> *For Middle-Level Learners* **[ESS 6]**

Where Does the Sun Rise and Set?

Materials

2 sheets of drawing paper for each child
Pencils, crayons, or markers

Motivating Questions

• Can you remember where the sun sets?
• Can you remember where the sun rises?

Directions

1. Have each child place the drawing paper so the long side runs from left to right in front of him or her.
2. On one sheet of paper, have each child draw some of the objects he or she would see while looking toward the east of where he or she lives: buildings, trees, fields, forests, parks, or whatever is toward the east of his or her home. On the other sheet, have each child do the same for the west.
3. Next, have each child draw a rising sun on the sheet at the place that represents where the sun rises and a setting sun at the place that they think represents where the sun sets.
4. Have the children take both papers home for a few days to correct, if they need to, the locations of their suns. *Safety Note:* Remind the children never to look directly at the sun.

Science Content for the Teacher

It seems to us that the sun is moving across our sky every day, rising in the east and setting in the west. However, the sunrise and sunset that we see are due to the earth's rotation. In this activity, the children simply compare their memories of where the sun rises and sets to the actualities.

> *For Middle-Level Learners* **[HNS 2 and 3]**

Earth Centered versus Sun Centered: The Great Debate

Note: To be successful, this Attention Getter will require a little acting on your part!

Materials

Access to the Internet
Science resource books and encyclopedias
Assorted art materials
Assorted fabric pieces

Motivating Questions

- Let's do some voting! How many of you agree with each of the following hypotheses, and how many disagree?
    "The sun moves around the earth."
    "The earth moves around the sun."
- If you agree with the first hypothesis, what evidence do you have to support it?
- If you agree with the second hypothesis, what evidence do you have to support it?

Directions

1. Have two volunteers stand at the front of the room. Ask the other students to shut their eyes for a moment. Say, "When I ask you to open your eyes, I will be *two* different scientists!"
2. Have the students open their eyes. Using your best acting voice, slowly walk around one student and say, "I am Ptolemy. *I* believe the sun moves around the earth." Then walk around the other student and say, "I am Copernicus. *I* believe the earth moves around the sun." Return to your normal voice and continue.
3. Have half of the cooperative groups focus on Ptolemy and half on Copernicus. Ask each group to research the life and beliefs of their scientist and to select one member to play the scientist. He or she must state his or her hypothesis and supporting evidence. The group must prepare any notes, drawings, props, and costuming.
4. After research time, have each "scientist" speak to the class. Then lead a discussion about what we know today about our solar system.

Explanation/ Science Content for the Teacher

Ptolemy proposed that the earth was at the center of the universe and that the sun moved around it. Everyday observations supported his hypothesis. Some 1,500 years later, Copernicus proposed that the earth moved around the sun and supported his hypothesis with careful observations of the planets' orbits.

Discovery Activities

For Young Learners [ESS 2]

Planets on Parade

Objective

- The children will place the planets in sequential order from the sun.

Science Processes Emphasized

Using numbers
Using space/time relationships

Materials for Each Child or Group

1 deck of 8 index cards, each labeled with a different planet name

Motivation

Tell the children that they are going to play a game that will help them learn about the planets. Display the eight index cards you will be distributing.

Directions

1. Before beginning this activity, create a set of clues for each planet, such as "I am Venus; I am closer to the sun than the Earth"; "I am Neptune; I am farther from the Sun than Mars."
2. Distribute a randomly sequenced deck of index cards to each group. Explain that each card represents a planet that is traveling around the sun but that the cards are not in the proper order. Challenge the groups to rearrange the cards based on the clues you give.
3. Read each clue, and encourage the children to rearrange the cards on the basis of the clues.

Key Discussion Questions	1. Which planet is closest to the sun? *Mercury*
	2. Which planet is farthest from the sun? *Neptune*
	3. Which planet is just before Earth, and which planet is right after Earth? *Venus, Mars*

Science Content for the Teacher   The eight known planets of our solar system in order from the sun are Mercury, Venus, Earth, Mars, Jupiter, Saturn, Uranus, and Neptune.

Extension   *Science/Math:* After the children have put their decks in order, have them turn the decks over and number each card sequentially from 1 to 8. Have pairs of children play a game in which one child removes one of the numbered cards and the other child has to guess the planet name that is on the reverse side.

▶ *For Young Learners* [ESS 3]

Making a Simple Sundial

Objectives
- The children will use numbers to write time measurements.
- The children will predict the actual time from the position of the shadow on a sundial.

Science Processes Emphasized
Using numbers
Predicting

Materials for Each Child or Group
Sheet of light cardboard 25 cm (10 in.) square
Masking tape
Straw

Motivation   Display the materials and tell the children that they are going to be making their own clocks. Indicate that they will be strange clocks because they will only work when the sun is shining.

Directions
1. Prior to class, make a 20-centimeter (about 8-inch) circle on each sheet of cardboard and punch a small hole at the center of each circle. Be sure to have a compass available for step 3.
2. Distribute a straw and a few strips of masking tape to each group. Have the groups insert one end of the straw into the hole and tape the straw so that it can stand upright. Tell them to write the letter *N* at any point along the edge of the circle.
3. On a sunny day, take the groups and their sundials outside. Using the compass, point north and have the children orient their sundials so that the *N*'s are pointed north. Have them mark the location of the straw's shadow, and then tell the children the actual time. Have them write the time on the cardboard at the end of the shadow.
4. After repeating this procedure at various times on consecutive days, have the children predict where the straw's shadow will be at a given time and take them outside at that time to check. As a final step, take the children outside and have them use their sundials to tell you the time.

Key Discussion Questions
1. There is one time in the day when the shadow is shortest or does not exist at all. What time is that? *When the sun is directly overhead.*
2. What are some of the problems with using sundials to tell time? *You can't tell the time on a cloudy day or at night.*

Science Content for the Teacher	Because Earth is constantly changing its position in relation to the sun, the sundials made in this activity will be fairly accurate for only a few days. Sundials in gardens or parks are constructed to compensate for Earth's changing position. They usually do not use a vertical object for the shadow but rather a rod that is inclined at the angle of the location's latitude and pointed toward the North Star.
Extension	*Science/Social Studies:* Do library research to locate pictures or drawings of various time-keeping devices used through the ages. Show the pictures to the children and ask them to suggest any problems, such as the size of the devices, that people might have had using these devices.

▶ *For Young Learners* [ESS 3]

Sunlight in Winter versus Summer

Objective	• The children will observe that light striking an inclined surface does not appear as bright as light striking a surface directly.
Science Process Emphasized	Measuring

Materials for Each Child or Group	Black construction paper	Book	Flashlight
	Chalk	Tape	

Motivation	Ask the children if they have ever wondered why it is colder in winter than in summer. Tell them that they will discover one of the reasons in this activity.
Directions	1. Be sure to have a globe available before beginning this activity. Darken the classroom and distribute a book, tape, chalk, paper, and flashlight to each child or group.
	2. Have each child or group tape the paper to the book and hold the book vertically on a flat surface. Ask them to shine the flashlight on the paper and use the chalk to draw a circle outlining the lit area.
	3. Next, tell the children to keep the flashlight at the same distance from the book but to move it so the light strikes a different part of the paper. Have them tilt the book away from the flashlight and outline the lit area.
	4. Turn the lights on and display the globe. Use a flashlight to represent the sun, and tilt the globe to show that the earth's tilt causes the Northern Hemisphere to be angled away from the sun during the winter months. Relate this to the light striking the paper that was tilted away from the light source.

Key Discussion Questions	1. How are the drawings you made different from one another? *The first was smaller.*
	2. Was the patch of light brighter the first or second time you had the light strike the paper? *The first.*

Science Content for the Teacher	Although many people believe that winter occurs because the earth is farther from the sun at that time of the year than it is in summer, the principal cause for winter is the earth's tilt, not its orbit. This tilt serves to spread out the sun's energy more in the Northern Hemisphere during the winter months. Sunlight strikes the Northern Hemisphere more directly in June than in December.

Extension   *Science/Social Studies:* Have the children look at the globe and consider how their lives would be different if they lived in an equatorial region, which receives a great deal of direct sunlight all through the year, or in a polar region, which receives much less sunlight.

▶ *For Young Learners* [ESS 2]

Make a Solar System Mobile

Objective
- The children will construct mobiles showing the eight planets of the solar system.

Science Processes Emphasized
Measuring
Using space/time relationships

Materials
1 wire coat hanger	3 or 4 straws
String	Scissors
Crayons	Tape

8 circles of oak tag 8 cm (about 3 in.) across

Motivation
Tell the children they are going to create an art project that illustrates some science knowledge they have. You may wish to display a sample planet mobile at this point.

Directions
1. Prior to class, create a mobile using a coat hanger as a base and an arrangement of strings and horizontal straws. Attach the eight oak tag circles to the strings that dangle from the straw ends.
2. Display the mobile, and explain that each circle represents one of the planets in the solar system. Write the names of the planets on the chalkboard, and distribute the materials. Tell the children to write the name of a planet on each circle.
3. Once the circles are labeled, have the children construct the mobiles. Be ready to assist those children who need help tying knots to attach string to straws or to oak tag circles. Some children may find it easier to tape the parts of their mobile together. You may wish to suggest that the children construct some of the subparts of the mobile first—for example, a straw with two or three planets hanging from it. If you are fortunate enough to have parent volunteers or assistants in the classroom, urge them to help those children who have limited psychomotor abilities.
4. When the children are done, have them hang their mobiles in the classroom.

Key Discussion Questions
Because this activity is focused on the construction of a mobile, the questions you raise should facilitate the children's use of psychomotor skills.
1. If you wanted to hang two planets from a straw, where would you tie them? *One at each end.*
2. If you hung one planet from each end of a straw, where would you tie the string that attaches the straw to the hanger? *At the center.*

Science Content for the Teacher
Be sure to remind the children that although their planets are all the same size, the real planets are of different sizes.

Extension
Science: Children with advanced reading and writing skills may be asked to use resource books to locate key descriptive words and write them on the planet circles. Challenge these children to find words that tell about the colors or temperatures of the planets.

▶ *For Middle-Level Learners* **[S&T 4]**

How to Build an Altitude Finder (Astrolabe)

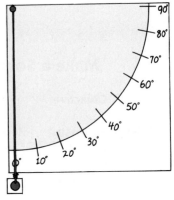

An altitude finder

Objectives
- The children will construct a simple device for measuring the heights of planets and stars above the horizon.
- The children will measure how many degrees an object is above the horizon.

Science Processes Emphasized
Observing Measuring
Using numbers

Materials for Each Child or Group
Piece of cardboard 25 × 25 cm (about 10 × 10 in.)
25 cm (10 in.) length of string
Small weight, such as a washer or nut
Protractor
Tape

Motivation
Tell the children that they will be building an instrument that the Greeks invented long ago to discover how far above the horizon the planets and stars are. Explain to the children that scientists call this instrument an *astrolabe* but that they can call it an *altitude finder* because it finds altitudes.

Directions
1. Distribute a protractor to each child or group. Show the children that the protractor scale can be used to measure angles from 0° to 180°.
2. Distribute a cardboard square to each group, and have the children place a 0° mark at the lower-left-hand corner of the cardboard. Have them place a 90° mark at the upper-right-hand corner.
3. Have the children attach one end of the string to the upper-left-hand corner of the cardboard with the tape and tie a pencil to the free end of the string. Now they can use the string and pencil as a compass to draw an arc from the lower-left-hand corner to the upper-right-hand corner.
4. Have the children divide the arc they have drawn into 10° intervals from 0° to 90°—that is, 0°, 10°, 20°, . . . , 90°. The protractor can be used to help mark these divisions.
5. The children should now untie the pencil and tie the nut or washer to the string. The string should cross the 0° mark when the upper edge of the cardboard is held horizontally. Tell the children that they will be sighting objects along the top of the cardboard with the string on the edge of the cardboard that is farthest away from them.
6. When the children have constructed their altitude finders, you may wish to take them outside to find how many degrees such things as chimneys, treetops, or lampposts are above the horizon. Be sure they do not try to sight the sun with their altitude finders.
7. Encourage the children to take their altitude finders home and measure the number of degrees the visible heavenly bodies are above the horizon.

Key Discussion Questions
1. Why do you think we attached a weight to the string? *To pull the string straight down.*
2. Sometimes people use the term *angle of elevation* when they use an astrolabe. What do you think the term means? *How many degrees the object is above the horizon.*
3. Does the altitude finder tell you anything about the direction the object is from you? *No.*
4. How could you find the direction? *Use a compass. Note:* The next activity in this chapter involves creating an instrument that measures the angle of a heavenly body from true north.

Science Content for the Teacher	The astrolabe was invented by the Greeks for observing heavenly bodies. It consisted of a movable rod that was pointed at a star or planet. The position of the rod against a circle indicated the altitude of the sun, moon, and stars. The astrolabe was eventually refined for use as a navigational tool. The sextant, a more accurate device that fulfills the same purpose, came into use in the eighteenth century. It uses a small telescope and a system of mirrors to compare the position of a heavenly body with the horizon.
Extension	*Science/Social Studies:* You may wish to have a group of children do some library research to find out more about the extent to which the ancient Greeks were involved in astronomy. This group can also research the importance of the astrolabe and sextant in the exploration of the world by seafaring countries.

For Middle-Level Learners [S&T 4]

How to Build an Azimuth Finder

Objective	• The children will construct a simple device that will tell them how many degrees from north, measured in a clockwise direction, a heavenly body is.
Science Processes Emphasized	Observing Measuring Using numbers
Materials for Each Child or Group	Magnetic compass 50 cm (20 in.) square of cardboard 25 cm (10 in.) length of string Pencil Protractor

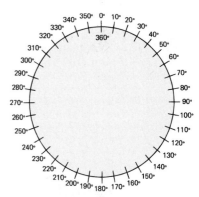

An azimuth finder

Motivation	Tell the children that astronomers usually keep track of both the positions of heavenly bodies above the horizon and their direction in relation to north. Write the word *azimuth* on the chalkboard, and explain that this term refers to how far an object is from north. Distribute the materials, and begin a discussion of how they can be used to make an azimuth finder.
Directions	1. Have the children use the protractor and pencil to draw a circle on the cardboard square. 2. Show the children that they can divide the circle into 10° units by placing the protractor so that its center measuring point is at the center of the circle. Have the children label any point on the circle 0° (north). Then have them mark off 10° positions from 0° to 360°, going in a clockwise direction. Once they have marked off the 10° units, they can use the bottom of the protractor as a straightedge. *Note:* Since the protractor goes from 0° to 180°, the children should simply turn it upside down in order to continue around the circle in 10° intervals from 180° to 360° (0°). 3. When the azimuth finders are complete, take the children outside to use them to find the azimuths of chimneys, treetops, and other tall objects. In order to do this, they must first rotate the case of the compass so the needle is pointing north. (You may wish to introduce the difference between true north and magnetic north at this point. Refer to Science Content for the Teacher for information on this subject.) Have each child align the azimuth finder so that the 0° mark is oriented to the north.

4. The children can find various azimuths by noting the number of degrees clockwise the object is from the 0° reading.

5. Encourage the children to take their azimuth finders home to make evening measurements of the positions of heavenly bodies. They will need flashlights to read the finders.

Key Discussion Questions

1. What would be the azimuth of a planet that was due east of you? *90°.*
2. What would be the azimuth of a planet that was due south of you? *180°.*
3. What would be the azimuth of a planet that was due west of you? *270°.*

Science Content for the Teacher

You can readily find the azimuth of a heavenly body by using true north as a reference point. Navigators generally label true north as 0° and describe the azimuth of an object in terms of the number of degrees, measured in a clockwise direction, by which its direction differs from true north. (Astronomers tend to use true south as 0°. However, for school use, the 0° north reading used by navigators is a perfectly acceptable method of measurement.)

One problem in the use of an azimuth finder is that the magnetic north measured by a compass is displaced from geographic north, except for a small portion of North America. The amounts of deviation for some representative cities are as follow:

Portland, Oregon	21°E
San Francisco	17°E
Denver	13°E
St. Paul	5°E
Atlanta	0°
Cleveland	5°W
Philadelphia	9°W
Portland, Maine	17°W

Extension

Science/Social Studies: You may wish to have some children do library research on the history of astronomy. The children can find information on Egyptian, Babylonian, Chinese, and Mayan astronomy in most reference books. They may also be interested in gathering pictures of Stonehenge to share with the rest of the class.

▶ *For Middle-Level Learners* **[S&T 4]**

Using Altitude and Azimuth Finders to Follow the Motion of a Planet

Objective

• The children will use simple altitude- and azimuth-measuring instruments to observe the motion of a planet.

Science Processes Emphasized

Observing   Communicating
Measuring

Materials for Each Child or Group

Altitude-measuring instrument (see first Discovery Activity for Middle-Level Learners, pages 234–235)
Azimuth-measuring instrument (see previous activity)
Chart with the following headings: *Observation, Date, Time, Altitude, Azimuth*
Paper and pencil

Motivation Ask the children if they have ever seen planets in the evening sky. They may have observed that planets do not twinkle and that some appear other than white in color. Discuss with the children the importance of making observations of planets over an extended time in order to see patterns of motion. Indicate that this activity is going to extend over a period of months and will require them to do their observations at home.

Directions 1. Review the use of the altitude and azimuth measurers described in the two previous activities. If the children have not constructed these instruments, they will need to do so before beginning this extended activity.
2. Have each child prepare an observation chart.
3. Explain to the children that they should attempt to locate one planet in the evening sky and record observations at the same time each day. To help them locate a planet, find one for yourself and determine its altitude and azimuth. (You can get help from any almanac that describes the locations of visible planets for your area at various times of the year.) Share the location of this planet with the class. The children can then try to find it on their own with their measuring devices.
4. Every few months, hold a class discussion of the observations that have been made as of that time.

Key Discussion Questions 1. What planet did you observe? How did you know what planet it was? *Answers will vary.*
2. What problems did you have during the activity? *Answers will vary but may include such problems as cloud cover obscuring the planets, precipitation making outdoor work difficult, misplacing instruments, and forgetting to make observations at the same time every day.*

Science Content for the Teacher See the content presented in the previous two activities.

Extensions *Science:* You may wish to encourage a group of children to carry out some long-term library research to coincide with this extended activity. Children can focus on such topics as the astronomers Tycho Brahe and Copernicus, the invention of the telescope, and the use of modern astronomical instruments, such as the radio telescope.

Science/Social Studies: You may wish to have some children explore the resistance of society to Copernicus's and Galileo's conclusion that the sun is the physical center of the solar system.

Demonstrations

For Young Learners [ESS 2]

Moon Watcher

Objectives • Using a model, the children will observe the phases of the moon.
• The children will explain why the moon seems to change in shape.

Science Processes Emphasized Observing
Communicating

Materials Small lamp with ordinary light bulb and removable shade
Orange
Paper and pencil
Signs with the labels *Earth, Moon,* and *Sun*

Motivation   Ask the children to describe and draw the various shapes that the moon seems to take. Have them show their drawings to the class. Ask if they think the moon really changes shape. After some discussion, display the materials for the demonstration, and tell the children that they will be observing a model of the moon in orbit around Earth that will help them understand the changes in its shape.

What phase of the moon is this?

Directions

1. Remove the lampshade, and place the sun label on the lamp. Place the sun at the center of the front of the room. Select one child, and affix the *Earth* label to him or her.

2. Darken the room by drawing the shades and shutting off the classroom lights.

3. Now have the child hold the orange (the moon) so that his or her hand is fully outstretched. Have the child first stand so that he or she is facing the sun and holding the moon directly in line with it. The child should be about 1 meter (a little more than 3 feet) from the sun.

4. The lamp should be turned on at this point. Have the child holding the orange describe how much of the orange's lit surface is seen. None of the lit surface should be seen; the moon is not visible in the sky.

5. Have the child turn sideways, and ask him or her how much of the lit surface of the orange he or she can see. Half the lit surface should be visible; the child sees a half-moon.

6. Have the child stand so that his or her back is to the lamp and the orange is about 30 centimeters (1 foot) away from his or her eyes and slightly to the left of the head. Ask how much of the lit surface of the moon can be seen. All of it should be visible; the child sees a full moon.

7. Repeat the demonstration so that the crescent moon and three-quarter moon can be seen.

Key Discussion Questions

1. Does the moon produce light? *No, it just reflects light from the sun.*
2. What name do we give to the shapes that the moon seems to take? *Phases.*
3. Does the moon really change in shape? Why? *No. The only thing that changes is the pattern of the light we can see bouncing off the moon.*

Science Content for the Teacher   The sun shines on only half the surface of the moon. This entire lit surface is not always visible from the earth. The apparent shape of the moon at any given time is really the portion of the lit surface that is visible. The different portions of the surface that are lit at different times are the phases of the moon. The *full moon* is that phase in which we see the entire lit surface. When full, the moon appears as a round disk in the sky. We refer to the phase in which we see half the lit surface as the *half-moon*. The *crescent moon* is a phase in which we see only a sliver of the lit surface. The *new moon* is the phase in which none of the lit surface can be seen.

Extensions   *Science:* You may wish to encourage a group of children to use the lamp, orange, and other round objects to demonstrate other astronomical phenomena, such as lunar and solar eclipses.

Science/Arts: A group of children may wish to draw a sequence of pictures to represent an imaginary incident that occurs as astronauts explore a mysterious crater on the moon.

▶ *For Young Learners* [ESS 3]

The Shoebox Planetarium

Objective
- The children will observe the Big Dipper constellation projected in the classroom and will be able to locate it in the night sky.

Science Processes Emphasized   Observing

Materials
Shoebox with lid   Electrical tape
Index card   Scissors
Flashlight

Motivation   Tell the children that they will observe something they can then ask a parent or other adult to help them find in the night sky.

Directions
1. Tape the lid to the shoebox. At one end, cut out a hole sufficiently large for you to insert the lamp end of a flashlight. Cut a rectangular window the size of a small index card in the other end.
2. Using the electrical tape, seal one end of the box around the flashlight so that the switch is not in the box.
3. Poke small holes in an index card in the shape of the Big Dipper. Attach the index card to the window in the shoe box. *Note:* For somewhat older children, you may wish to prepare additional index cards to use to project images of other constellations.
4. Darken the room, turn on the flashlight, and project the Big Dipper on a screen or wall. Have the children note the shape of the handle and the cup. Encourage the children to ask an adult to help them find it in the night sky.

Key Discussion Questions
1. Look at the sides of the Big Dipper. What do you notice about them? *Answers will vary. If no one mentions that sides of the dipper slope inward, do so.*
2. Look at the handle of the Big Dipper. What do you notice about it? *Answers will vary. If no one mentions that the handle is curved, do so.*

Science Content for the Teacher   We are able to observe thousands of stars with the naked eye. Groupings of stars that seem to move together in an apparent path around the North Star are known as *constellations*. The following is a sample of the many constellations visible from the northern latitudes at various times in the year: *spring,* Leo, the Lion; *summer,* Cygnus, the Swan; *fall,* Andromeda, the Maiden; *winter,* Orion, the Hunter. This demonstration focuses on the constellation known as the Big Dipper, which is visible throughout the year. The Big Dipper is part of another constellation known as Ursa Major, the Bear, with the tail of the bear made from the handle of the Big Dipper.

Extension   *Science/Math:* Have the children create their own connect-the-dots puzzles that include numbers representing the seven stars of the Big Dipper. Have the children exchange papers so each can complete a puzzle made by someone else.

▶ *For Middle-Level Learners* [ESS 6]

Space Journey

Note: Due to the unique nature of this demonstration, Motivation, Directions, Key Discussion Questions, and Extensions have been integrated under one heading.

Objectives

- Each child will take the role of a member of a space exploration team and describe his or her imaginary adventure.
- The children will explain the similarities and differences between their imaginary journeys and a possible real journey into outer space.

Materials

A classroom that can be darkened by shutting off the light and adjusting the blinds

Motivation, Directions, Key Discussion Questions, and Extensions

Through this simulation of a journey into outer space, children have an opportunity to use their knowledge of the solar system to form mental images of the planet their spaceship lands on. The experience encourages children to use their imagination, to communicate orally with the remainder of the class, and at a later time, to use their creative writing and artistic abilities.

Prior to the simulated space journey, divide the class into teams of space explorers. Each team will have four members: a pilot, a navigator, a scientist, and a medical officer. Allow group members to select their roles, and change the classroom seating arrangement so that team members can sit side by side. Have various team members explain what their jobs will be at the time of launch and during planetary exploration. You may, with the assistance of the class, redecorate the classroom so it looks like the interior of a spacecraft. To add realism to the experience, play a sound effects record of a rocket launch during blastoff.

Have each team prepare for the launch by sitting quietly in their seats for a few seconds. Indicate that you will soon begin the countdown for blastoff. Tell them that they should shut their eyes and listen to your words.

Begin the countdown. Tell the children that the rocket engines are beginning to work. When you reach 0, tell them that the rocket is lifting off the launchpad.

Use phrases such as the following to guide their thinking during the flight:

You are being pressed backward. . . . You are in the most dangerous part of the flight, a time when a group of astronauts once lost their lives. . . . Your journey will be a safe one. Imagine that you are looking back at the earth. . . . You are flying higher and higher. . . . The earth is getting smaller and smaller. . . . It is a tiny blue dot. Ahead of you is the blackness of space. . . . The stars are bright. Brighter than you have ever seen them before. . . . Way ahead you see a tiny reddish-colored dot. . . . The pilot puts the spacecraft on automatic pilot, and all the members of the crew go to special sleeping compartments, where they will sleep as the spacecraft approaches its target. . . . You are sleeping.

You awake to the sound of a buzzer. You return to your seats and see that the planet is now a large reddish ball directly ahead.

As the spacecraft gets closer, the pilot prepares for a landing. The spacecraft gently lands. You look out the windows and see the surface of the planet. . . . Think about the way it looks. Is it flat or bumpy? Does it have mountains? Don't answer. Just think about how it seems to you.

The science officer checks some instruments that tell about the planet's surface and atmosphere. The science officer says that it is safe to explore the planet if you wear spacesuits.

Imagine that you put the bulky spacesuits on. You check each other's suits to be sure they are working properly. Imagine that the pilot opens the door and you go down a ladder to the surface of the planet.

You look around and then look back at one another. You check to be sure that your radios are working. Now each of you starts out in a different direction. After you've walked for a few minutes, you stop and look around to see if you can still see the other crew members. You can see each of them. Keep walking and making observations. . . . You notice something very interesting at your feet. You bend down, pick it up, and gently place it in your collection bag. You reach a large boulder and walk behind it. There on the ground, you see something in the shadows. You are amazed at what you see. You try to move it but you can't. You pull and pull and finally get it free. Just as you are getting ready to call the other crew members to tell them what you have found, you hear the pilot's voice: "Emergency, get back to the ship immediately." You take what you discovered and race back to the ship. You and the other crew members are safely on board. Relax . . . the pilot makes a safe liftoff. You begin the long journey back to Earth. . . . A few months later, you see a tiny blue speck straight ahead. It gets larger and larger. . . . It is Earth, your home. The pilot makes a safe landing. . . . You may open your eyes. Welcome home!

When all the spacecraft have made safe landings, engage the participants in discussions of what they observed and how their observations compare with what they have learned about the solar system and planets. You may wish to have the children prepare illustrated written reports about their adventures.

Science Content for the Teacher

Prior to this demonstration, study the physical characteristics of the various planets in our solar system as well as the stars. This knowledge will enable you to assist the children when they discuss their experiences.

> *For Middle-Level Learners* [ESS 6]

What Is a Light-Year?

Objectives
- The children will interpret data given to them and calculate the distance light travels in one year.
- The children will interpret data given them and develop a strategy for finding the time it takes for light to reach the earth from the sun.

Science Processes Emphasized

Interpreting data
Using space/time relationships

Materials

Transparency and transparency pen
Flashlight

Clock with second hand
Globe

Motivation

Clap your hands, and ask the children how long they thought it took the sound waves to reach them. Write down their estimates. Then position yourself so that they can watch you clap and also see the clock. Tell them that you want them to try to time the travel of sound waves. Clap once again. The children will note that it was either impossible to time the sound waves or that it took less than a second. Explain that they have been trying to time the rate at which sound travels and that the speed of sound, although high (340 meters/second, 1,090 feet/second at 0° Celsius), is much less than the speed of light. Tell the children that they are going to discuss the speed of light.

Directions	1. Write *300,000 km/sec* on the transparency. Aim the flashlight toward the children, and turn it on briefly. Explain that light from the flashlight traveled to their eyes at the rate shown on the transparency. Tell them that at this speed, if light could travel around the earth, it would circle the earth seven times in 1 second. Hold up the globe and illustrate the seven trips by moving your finger around the equator as the children snap their fingers to represent 1 second. As you obviously cannot get your finger around a tiny globe seven times in 1 second, the children should appreciate the magnitude of the speed of light.
	2. Challenge the children to calculate the actual number of kilometers a beam of light can travel in a year. Begin by having them determine the number of seconds in a year (60 seconds/minute /60 minutes/hour/24 hours/day/365 days/year = 31,536,000 seconds/year).
	3. Again direct the flashlight toward the students, and flick it on and off. Tell them to imagine that the flashlight is the sun. Ask them how long it takes light to travel from the sun to the earth. Write *149,600,000 km* on the transparency. Indicate that this is the average distance that the earth is from the sun as it travels in orbit. Have the children invent a strategy for finding out how many seconds it takes for light to get to the earth. *Hint:* Round off the kilometer distance to 150,000,000 and divide it by 300,000 kilometers per second, which will equal 500 seconds. Remind the children that they did some rounding, so the actual number of seconds is somewhat less.
Key Discussion Questions	1. How far away from the flashlight would you have to be in order for the light to reach you in exactly 1 second? *300,000 kilometers.*
	2. If the sun were to stop shining right now, how long would it be before we would notice it? *Between 8 and 9 minutes.*
Science Content for the Teacher	Light waves travel at a speed of 300,000 kilometers per second (about 186,000 miles per second). Light does not require a medium and can travel through empty space. The speed of light is constant in the universe. Scientists use the distance that light can travel in one year, a *light-year,* as a standard measurement of distance.
Extension	*Science/Math:* Ask the children to determine how long it takes light to travel from the sun to the dwarf planet Pluto (about 5 hours) and from the sun to Proxima Centauri, the closest star to the sun (about 4 years). This extension requires library research, the ability to round numbers, and the use of a calculator.

Earth/Space Sciences Sample Lesson

Title:	The power to move continents: convection currents and plate tectonics
Articulation with NSES:	Grades 5–8 **Content Standard:** Earth and Space Science • Structure of the Earth System
Background for Teacher:	The movement of the continents is appropriately referred to as continental drift. Fundamental to the understanding of this incredible system we call Earth is an understanding of the powerful forces within the Earth that can move continents. As stated earlier, the Earth's crust, which consists of the ocean floors and continental land masses, sits on a mantle with a consistency similar to hot asphalt that acts like a slow moving fluid. The movement is caused by the heating and cooling in the mantle, which

creates a temperature differential of hot, molten rock near the liquid outer core and cooler rock material closer to the crust. The circulation created by hot, less dense rock material rising toward the crust that in turn cools, becomes denser and sinks toward the outer core is called a convection current. Imagine large chunks of crust that make up the oceanic and continental plates floating on this cyclical convection current. The slow, powerful force created by the convection current moves the plates sitting on top of them.

Materials

1 beaker (500 mL or 1 L)
glitter
colored ice cubes
clear plastic cups } for each student
1 thermometer for every 2 students
1 computer
LCD projector

Element 1: Content to be Taught

Content Analysis: Convection and Plate Tectonics

Elements	Properties	Rules of relationship (spatial)
Crustal plates	Solid granite, basalt	Floating on mantle
Upper mantle	Viscous, temperature ~871°C, more dense than upper mantle	Sinks toward lower mantle
Lower mantle	Viscous, temperature ~1200°C, less dense than upper mantle	Rises toward upper mantle
Convection currents	Circular flow between hotter and cooler rock material	Causes mantle to flow in a circular pattern
Rocks particles in mantle	Vary inversely in density with temperature	Cycle between upper and lower mantle
Emergent properties	Movement of crustal plates	

Students will learn that convection currents occur where there is a temperature difference in gases or liquids. Warm matter rises and cooler matter sinks. Convection currents in the mantle cause the crustal plates on the surface of the earth to move.

Element 2: Prior Knowledge and Misconceptions

Children may perceive of the earth as a solid rock, consisting of one giant, homogenous layer.

Element 3: Performance Objectives

1. Given a diagram of a cross section of the earth, students will use arrows to correctly indicate the movement of the mantle and crustal plates.
2. Given a diagram depicting hot air near the surface of the earth and cool air above the surface of the earth, children will predict in writing that the warm air will rise and the cool air will sink, resulting in convection currents.
3. Given a diagram of Pangea and the current location of the continents, students will explain in writing how convection currents are formed and move the continents. Acceptable answers will demonstrate achievement at the "Good Job" or "Well Done" level as indicated by the assessment rubric.

● Element 4: Concept Development

Engagement

As the children enter the room, project an animation depicting continental drift from the University of California Museum of Paleontology www.ucmp.berkeley.edu/geology/tecall1_4.mov.[4] Pause the animation at the beginning (740 million years ago) and ask the children what they think the picture represents. After the children express their ideas, run the animation. Ask them again what they think the animation represents. When they recognize the animation as a depiction of moving continents, tell them that many scientists have discovered evidence that the continents are indeed moving. Raise the essential question, "What force of nature could actually move continents?"

Exploration

Safety: Create a safety splash zone around the boiling water during the demonstration in part II of the exploration. Direct children to stand behind the zone boundary.

Set the zone boundary to prevent spillage of hot water on the children. Alternatively, use a plexiglass shield around the boiling water to prevent spillage.

Part I: Activity—Tell the students that the following activity[5] provides some information that might help them answer the essential question.

Fill your cup three-fourths full with tap water. Do **not** fill it to the very top. You will be adding something to the cup that will raise the water level.

Using the thermometer, measure the temperature of the water at the bottom, midway point, and top of the water level. Record the values in the chart, "Tap Water, No Ice."

Place a colored ice cube **gently** on the surface of the water. Once the ice cube is in the cup, do not shake the table. **Do not disturb** the ice cube or cup because this will prevent the demonstration from working properly.

Wait 5 minutes, then measure the temperature of the water again at the bottom, midway, and top.

As the ice melts, write down your observations of the colored water in your science notebook.

Once the ice is melted, measure the temperature of the water at the bottom, midway and the top. Record the temperatures in the chart.

Make a written descriptive model of the system that identifies the elements, properties of the elements, background, and rules of interaction among the elements.

Write your explanation for the movement that you observed in the cup.

Tap water, no ice	
Placement	Temperature °C
Bottom	
Midway	
Top	

Tap water, with ice after 5 min.	
Placement	Temperature °C
Bottom	
Midway	
Top	

Tap water, with ice melted	
Placement	Temperature °C
Bottom	
Midway	
Top	

Part II: Demonstration—Place a beaker of cool water on a hot plate. Sprinkle glitter into the water. Direct the children to make a descriptive model of the system that you have created. Ask the students to predict what will happen when the water is heated. Point out that the water will get warmer on the bottom of the beaker first.

Heat the water (but do not boil) until the glitter begins to move vertically. Ask the children to explain the movement of the glitter based on their observations of the colored ice cube in water. Encourage them to use diagrams and/or a graphic organizer.

Part III: Post a diagram of the earth's layers.[6] Based on prior lessons, review the properties of the mantle with the children: the mantle is viscous, like hot asphalt. The lower mantle is warmer (2200°C) than the upper mantle (871°C). Ask the children to predict the effect of the difference in temperature of the mantle.

Explanation

Ask the children to try to answer the essential question, "What force of nature could actually move continents?" Require the children individually to write their responses in their science notebooks. Next, ask them to share their responses with two other children. Have each group of three devise a way to record and share their group explanation. This is an opportunity to offer multiple means of expression: diagram, text, simulation, PowerPoint, or verbal report.

Allow the groups to present their answers to the essential question. Then go to http://education.sdsc.edu/optiputer/flash/convection.htm for an animation of convection currents in the context of plate tectonics. Use the animation to explain that the warmer lower mantle heats the rock, which rises to the upper mantle, where it cools and sinks back to the lower mantle. (If children understand density, you can explain that heat energy makes the particles in the rock move faster and expand, decreasing the density and making the rocks rise.) Identify this process as *convection*. Convection is the movement of particles with high heat energy to areas with less heat energy. The movement creates a circular motion in the mantle that moves the earth's crustal plates floating on top of the mantle.

Elaboration

Show children a weather map with warm fronts and cold fronts. Ask them to use their knowledge of convection to predict what will happen when the two fronts meet.

Element 5: Evaluation

Assessment I: Show the children a diagram of Pangaea (organization of the continents about 175 mya) and a picture of the continents today. Go to the United States Geological Survey website for good pictures http://pubs.usgs.gov/gip/dynamic/historical.html. Ask the children to explain in writing how the continents shifted position. Assess children based on the following rubric.

Well Done	Satisfactory	Needs Improvement
Children include all five relationships in their explanation:	Children include any three out of five relationships in their explanation:	Children include fewer than three relationships in their explanations:

Relationships

- The lower mantle is hotter than the upper mantle.
- The hotter lower mantle rocks rise and then cool in the upper mantle.
- The cooler upper mantle rocks sink to the lower mantle.
- The rising and sinking of rock particles causes a circular movement.
- The movement of the mantle moves crust floating on top.

Assessment II: Give the students a diagram depicting hot air near the surface of the earth and cool air farther above the surface of the earth. Ask the children to predict in writing and diagrams how the hot and cool air will interact.

Assessment III: Give the students a diagram of the cross-section of the earth. Instruct the children to indicate the convection currents in the mantle, using arrows to represent the currents.

Element 6: Accommodations

English Language Learner

1. The teacher will state directions and procedures verbally as well as in writing.
2. The teacher will create a word bank with definitions to remain posted in the room.

Attention Deficit/Hyperactivity Disorder

1. There are several coherent transitions to engage students and minimize the time spent on one particular task.
2. The students will be given a checklist for the activities to keep track of their progress and accomplishments.
3. The teacher will explicitly state the directions prior to each activity.

Emotional and Behavioral Disorder

1. Criteria for class participation and considerate group work (such as raising one's hand and giving everyone in the group an opportunity to participate) will be reviewed before the lesson.

1902   Walter Sutton discovers that chromosomes separate for reproduction, an idea that will become the foundation for other scientists' work as they attempt to fully understand inheritance.

1925   Tennessee schoolteacher John Thomas Scopes is brought to trial for teaching evolution. William Jennings Bryan is the lead prosecutor, and Clarence Darrow defends Scopes.

1938   Fishermen find a *coelacanth,* a fish that was thought to be extinct, off the coast of South Africa.

1953   James D. Watson and Francis H. C. Crick publish their paper on the molecular structure of deoxyribonucleic acid (DNA) in *Nature* magazine.

1959   In Africa, Mary Leakey, a paleontologist, finds a hominid skull belonging to *Australopithecus boisei.*

1971   Stephen Jay Gould and Niles Eldredge propose their theory of punctuated equilibrium, which states, essentially, that evolution often occurs in short bursts followed by longer periods in which no or only very modest changes occur in a species.

1974   Donald Johanson and others discover the fossils of a female fossil hominid, *Australopithecus afarensis.* The team names her *Lucy* and proposes that hominids walked upright before they developed large brains.

1974   Bob Bakker proclaims that birds are the descendants of dinosaurs.

1978   Mary Leakey discovers fossil footprints at Laetoli in Africa, which demonstrates that hominids walked upright 3.6 million years ago.

1990   Headed by James D. Watson, the 13-year Human Genome Project formally begins, representing an effort to "find all the genes on every chromosome in the body and to determine their biochemical nature."

1992   A yeast chromosome (*S. cerevisiae*) gene sequence is published.

1993   Biologist E. O. Wilson concludes that there may be as many as 30 million species of insects on Earth.

1995   The *Haemophilus influenzae* genetic sequence is published by Venter, Smith, Fraser, and others.

1996   The yeast genome sequence is investigated and published by an international consortium.

1997   The Roslin Institute, in Edinburgh, Scotland, successfully clones a sheep, producing Dolly the Lamb. She is the first mammal to be cloned from an adult.

1999   Gunter Blobel, a cell and molecular biologist at Rockefeller University, receives a Nobel Prize for identifying how and where proteins move in the cell. He shows that new proteins move to their correct locations by using a molecular "bar code" that the cell can read.

1999   The DNA of the first human chromosome, chromosome 22, is sequenced.

2000   A "draft" of the human genome is completed. Researchers essentially receive a road map that will result in the identification of the entire human genome DNA sequence.

2003   Sequencing of the human genome is finished, and researchers celebrate the completion of the Human Genome Project, begun in 1990.

2006   Craig Mello and Andrew Fire are awarded the Nobel Prize for their discovery of RNA interference-gene silencing by double-stranded RNA.

Women and Men Who Have Shaped the Development of the Life Sciences

ANDREAS VERSALIUS (1514–1564) secured corpses for the earliest scientific dissections. As a professor at the University of Padua in Italy, he conducted many of these dissections for the benefit of future medical students. He summarized and categorized his lifetime of work in *De humani corporis fabrica libri septem,* which, when translated from Latin, means "The Structure of the Human Body in Seven Volumes."

CARL VON LINNE (CAROLUS LINNAEUS) (1707–1778) was known for his careful study and classification of plants, animals, and minerals. Although he was a physician, he is most famous for his book *Systema Naturae,* which still provides the foundation for the methods used to observe and classify natural objects.

JEANNE VILLEPREUX-POWER (1794–1871), a French-born woman, was a self-taught naturalist who studied in Sicily. She was one of the first scientists to use aquariums for experimentation with living organisms. In honor of this and other scientific achievements, a crater on the planet Venus was named for her.

ELIZABETH BLACKWELL (1821–1910) received the first medical degree granted to a woman in the United States. She specialized in the treatment of women and children and established what came to be the New York Infirmary for Women and Children.

ALEXANDER FLEMING (1881–1955) spent much of his life searching for an effective antiseptic and ultimately discovered that a sample of mold from the *Penicillium* family was extraordinarily effective in killing microbes.

GEORGE WASHINGTON CARVER (1896–1943) experimented widely in the field of plant genetics. He crossed plants of various types to produce new flowers, fruits, and vegetables and was known as an expert in the study of molds and fungi. His work did much to speed the progress of agriculture in the United States.

PERCY LAVON JULIAN (1899–1975) received his bachelor's degree from DePauw University, his master's in chemistry from Harvard University, and his Ph.D. in chemistry from the University of Vienna. Although trained as a chemist, he devoted most of his life's work to the development and refinement of chemicals that could be used as medicines.

BARBARA MCCLINTOCK (1902–1992) was a biologist who specialized in the study of genetics. She received the Nobel Prize for medicine in 1983 for the analysis of mechanisms that affect genes and, in fact, evolution itself.

RITA LEVI-MONTALCINI (1909–   ), an Italian-born biologist, came to St. Louis, Missouri, where she studied cellular reproduction and growth in the human body at Washington University. Her research led to her sharing of the Nobel Prize for physiology and medicine in 1986.

FRANCIS HARRY COMPTON CRICK (1916–2004) was trained as a physicist but is known for his work with James D. Watson, in which they proposed that DNA has a double-helix structure and then explained how it is replicated. With Watson and Maurice Wilkins, Crick received the Nobel Prize for medicine and physiology in 1962.

JONAS SALK (1914–1995), as head of the Virus Research Laboratory at the University of Pittsburgh, worked to improve a previously developed influenza vaccine; his synthesis of data from other scientists led to strategies that would create a vaccine to stop the polio virus. His work led to the large-scale vaccination of schoolchildren and the reduction of polio as a threat to public health worldwide.

GERTRUDE BELLE ELION (1918–1999) focused her scientific research on the creation of drugs to treat cancer, malaria, leukemia, and other diseases. She shared the 1988 Nobel Prize for physiology.

JAMES DEWEY WATSON (1928–   ), who had earned a Ph.D. in genetics, joined Francis H. C. Crick, Maurice Wilkins, and Rosalind Franklin in the study of the structure of DNA. Watson, Crick, and Wilkins shared the Nobel Prize for medicine and physiology in 1962. The year 2003 marked the fiftieth anniversary of the Watson/Crick discovery and the successful completion of the Human Genome Project, of which Watson was the head.

▶ Personal and Social Implications of the Life Sciences

Go to **MyEducationLab**, select Resources, and then WebLinks. Then select "National Association of Biology Teachers."

No area of scientific exploration has clearer implications for our health and well-being than the life sciences. But along with progress comes certain risks and benefits. Let's consider a few areas of our personal and societal lives that are affected by developments in the life sciences.

Personal and Community Health

Many life scientists spend their careers in search of the causes and cures of illnesses and injuries. Some of that work has looked at the roles of proper nutrition and sanitation. And other research has led to the discovery that some illnesses and predispositions for particular illnesses may come from a person's genetic makeup. The discovery has led to enormous strides in biomedical research.

The study of the sources and effects of pollution is another area of study that has implications for personal and community health. The effects of water pollution, acid rain, and the depletion of ozone in the atmosphere are a few examples of topics that have drawn the attention of life scientists.

Hazards, Risks, and Benefits

The life sciences have brought us new knowledge about natural hazards in the environment, including the risks for becoming infected with sexually transmitted diseases (STDs), the effects of eating food containing parasitic organisms, and even ways for coexisting with large predators. How well we cope with these natural hazards is, to some extent, grounded in how well we understand the life sciences in all of its forms. Each of us must make careful decisions, assessing the risks and benefits associated with the choices we have about the kinds of food we eat, whether to smoke, and whether to use alcohol or potentially dangerous drugs.

We have enjoyed great benefits as the result of pharmaceutical technologies, surgical procedures, and even organ transplantation. But these benefits have sometimes been achieved through medical research that has used human subjects. Individuals who volunteer for treatment with new drugs and procedures must be made aware of the possible risks and benefits of doing so.

▶ Life Science Technology: Its Nature and Impact

You might not think of the life sciences as having a significant technological component, but they do! Moreover, that technology touches you in some very specific ways.

Modern health care—from making eyeglasses to performing cardiovascular surgery—overflows with instrumentation that has been brought to your health care provider (and ultimately to you) by engineers who have applied their expertise to the life sciences. Even something as banal as a visit to the dentist will give you a visual display of electromechanical devices to probe, unearth, and repair cavities; carry out root canal procedures; and even administer anesthetics.

Of course, biomedical research is only one aspect of the life sciences that receives the attention of engineers. Other engineering challenges include improving crop production, removing contaminants from water supplies, and designing facilities to help preserve endangered species.

The Design of Life Science Technology

Whether they work in environmental protection, criminal investigation, horticulture, or health care, life scientists require devices whose design meets the following criteria:

1. It does no harm or as little harm as possible to living things and the environment.

2. It addresses a problem that has been clearly identified and for which data can reasonably be expected to be obtained.

3. It presents data in a manner that is readily interpretable by life science researchers or health care providers, as appropriate.

4. If it is a tool, it can be easily used and safely operated.

5. It provides the users of life science technology with constant feedback about the accuracy of the data being represented and/or the health and welfare of the living things being treated.

Examples of Life Science Technology

A variety of technologies are used to gather information about living things and to improve their health and welfare:

Binoculars

Optical microscope

Electron microscope

Autoclave (sterilizing device)

Heart/lung machine

Blood pressure monitoring devices

Conventional pharmaceuticals

Genetically engineered pharmaceuticals

Prosthetic devices

Cardiac pacemaker

CAT (computerized axial tomography) scan devices

MRI (magnetic resonance imaging) devices

Safe capture traps (to study living things)

Technologies to convert biomass into biofuels

Long-Term Implications of Life Science Technology

The technology that has come from the wellspring of life science research has done much to improve the quality of our lives and our environment. We now have the tools to analyze and solve almost any problem imaginable.

But along with this capability comes concern about how to reduce the biological dangers new technology sometimes creates. This is truly a double-edged sword, as these examples point out:

- Oral contraceptives are widely available, but their use may have as an unintended consequence an increase in sexually transmitted diseases (STDs).

- X-ray technology permits exploration of the human body and the treatment of some cancers, but it may lead to increased health risks—including a risk for cancer.

- False-positive results on medical tests can lead to unnecessary treatment regimens.

- The biological control of some insects can result in the increased population of other more harmful insects who have lost their natural predators.

- The use of antibiotics to treat infections that do not have bacteria as a root cause may inadvertently result in increasing the number of species of bacteria that are resistant to antibiotics.

Finally, the increased use of technology in all fields of the life sciences traditionally brings increases in the costs of goods and services. The implications of these increases for the consumer—whether a farmer calculating the cost of the foods he or she produces or a patient dealing with increases in the costs of his or her health care—must be considered as new technologies are invented and applied.

chapter 13

Living Things

Content

Living or Nonliving? That's the Question

Dust from the surface of an African plain, dotted with grass and small plants, is kicked into clouds by the plodding feet of a rhinoceros. As the huge, lumbering beast moves along munching plants, it frightens insects into confused flight. Some of these insects land on the rhino's body and are carried to greener pastures as the rhino moves across the plain. Some of these insects become food for the tick birds that also ride on the rhino's back (see Figure 13.1). As the rhino feeds on grasses and weeds, the tick birds flutter about, feasting upon the newly arrived insects. The rhino, the insects, the tick birds, and the grass are all living things, but the dust, of course, is not.

What makes the dust fundamentally different from the rhino, insects, tick birds, and grass? When scientists make observations to determine whether something is living or nonliving, they search for these eight characteristics, or *functions,* of life:

1. All living things are composed of cells: The smallest structural unit of an organism that is capable of independently carrying out the processes listed below.
2. Living organisms use energy that they produce or acquire. They use this energy to carry out energy-requiring activities such as movement, growth, or transport.

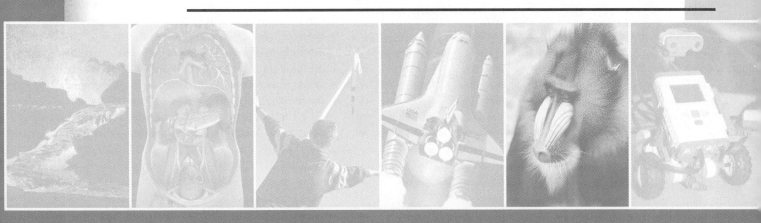

3. Living organisms get rid of the waste products of energy use.

4. All living organisms reproduce, either by sexual or asexual means.

5. Living organisms inherit traits from the parent organisms.

6. All living things respond to stimuli in their environment.

7. All living things maintain a state of internal balance called homeostasis.

8. Living organisms adapt to their environment and evolve as a species.

Scientists who study the characteristics of living things are known as *biologists*. Life on Earth is so complex that biologists can specialize in one or more parts of biology:

Zoology, the study of animals

Botany, the study of plants

Anatomy, the study of the structure of living things

Ecology, the study of the relationships among living things and their surroundings

Similarities in Living Things

Believe it or not, you have a lot in common with a cactus plant! This hopefully doesn't apply to your outward appearance, but it most definitely applies to your inside appearance. You, the cactus plant, and every other living thing are made up of one or more *cells*. Within every cell is a gelatinlike, colorless, semitransparent substance called *protoplasm*, which is made up of a variety of elements: carbon, hydrogen, oxygen, potassium, phosphorous, iodine, sulfur, nitrogen, calcium, iron, magnesium, sodium, chlorine, and traces of other elements.

In living things that contain more than one cell, any group of cells that performs a similar function is called a *tissue*. A group of tissues that function together is called an *organ*. And a group of organs that work together to perform a major function is known as a *system*. For instance, in plants, the various cells and tissues that enable the food made in the leaves to be transported to the stems and roots make up the vascular system. Plants contains many different systems that all perform different functions. So does the human body. In a human, those systems include the skeletal system, muscular system, respiratory system, nervous system, excretory system, and reproductive system.

Figure 13.1   The tick birds and the rhinoceros both benefit from their relationship.

Differences in Living Things

You and that cactus plant are also different in many ways. The protoplasm in the cells of a particular type of living thing is unique to that thing. The ptotoplasm of a cactus enables cactus cells to carry on the unique functions that permit the cactus to function as a cactus. So it is with the protoplasm of the human body and every other living thing.

The cells that make up living things also differ. Most have clearly defined nuclei, but some one-celled organisms do not. And although plants and animals have clearly defined nuclei in their cells, the cell walls of plants contain cellulose while the cells of animals are bound by membranes that do not contain cellulose. Plants and animals, of course, possess other characteristics that allow us to distinguish between them:

Plants	**Animals**
Organs are external to the plant's body—for example, leaves and flowers.	Most organs are internal to the animal's body—for instance, the heart and the stomach.
They produce their own food.	They cannot produce food internally.
They show little movement.	Most can move freely.
No organs have a specific excretory function.	They possess excretory organs.
They respond slowly to changes in the environment.	They can respond quickly to changes in the environment.

Even within any given multicellular living thing, the cells are not all similar to one another. For example, your skin cells, although they contain protoplasm and a nucleus, differ in many ways from the cells that make up the muscles of your heart. Similarly, every plant and every animal contains a variety of very specialized cells that make up its tissues and organs.

Classifying Living Things

Long ago, biologists classified all living things into just the two categories we've already discussed: plants and animals. With further study and more sophisticated equipment, biologists were surprised to discover living things that really didn't fit into either group.

The Five Kingdoms

Modern biologists use a classification system that includes five distinct kingdoms (see Figure 13.2):

1. *Monera*—This kingdom includes one-celled living things that don't have a membrane around the cell's genetic material. In other words, none of these things has a nucleus. Monerans include bacteria, which don't produce their own food, and blue-green algae, which can produce food through photosynthesis. Most of the earth's oxygen is produced by blue-green algae, also called cyanobacteria. A few species of bacteria live deep underwater near thermal vents and are able to manufacture food using chemical energy.

2. *Protista*—This group includes single-celled organisms that do have a membrane surrounding the cell's genetic material—for example, diatoms, protozoa, and euglena. Common amebas and paramecia are also protozoans. All protists are found in moist or aquatic habitats and get their nutrition in a variety of ways. Protists are believed to be early examples of the types of life forms that eventually became the fungi, plants, and animals that live on Earth today.

Figure 13.2 A five-kingdom classification system

Kingdom		Examples	
Monera	One celled, lack nuclear membranes and other cell structures with membranes, sometimes form groups or filaments, nutrition usually by absorption, reproduction usually by fission or budding	Bacteria Blue-green algae	
Protista	Includes one-celled and multicelled living things, have an organized nucleus and organelles with membranes, reproduction usually by fission	Ameba Paramecium	
Fungi	Some one celled, some multicelled, nutrition by absorption, cell walls made of chitin, sexual or asexual reproduction	Bread molds Mildews Yeasts Mushrooms	
Plantae	Multicellular, produce own food through photosynthesis, cells surrounded by cell wall, sexual and asexual reproduction	Mosses Ferns Trees Grasses Palms Roses	
Animalia	Multicellular, nutrition by ingestion, cells surrounded by cell membrane, have complex organ systems, mainly sexual reproduction	Sponges Flatworms Starfish Insects Amphibians Reptiles Mammals	

3. *Fungi*—This group of living things may be one celled or multicelled. They gain their nutrition by absorbing nutrients from their surroundings, and they store energy in the chemical compound glycogen, which makes them different from plants that store food as starch. Fungi can reproduce sexually or asexually. Asexual reproduction is carried out through the production and release of tiny spores that can be carried long distances through the air. Sexual reproduction occurs from the fusion of cell material from two types of fungi competing on the same food source.

4. *Plantae*—This kingdom includes living things that are multicellular and have true cell nuclei and cell walls. Most use photosynthesis to produce food. The green plants in this kingdom—mosses, ferns, grasses, trees, and so on—reproduce sexually or asexually.

5. *Animalia*—This group is made up of multicelled living things that are able to ingest food directly from their environments. Animal cells contain nuclei. Members of this kingdom reproduce sexually, with a few exceptions. Sponges, for example,

reproduce asexually by forming buds that can break free of the parent sponge and be carried to a place they can develop into a complete sponge. Although some animals, such as sponges, are sessile (i.e., they remain in one specific place during their life cycle), most are able to move freely from place to place.

How to Classify a Particular Living Thing

When biologists classify an organism, they must first decide which of the five kingdoms provides the best fit. Then, because kingdoms are divided into various categories and subcategories, biologists must identify the appropriate subcategory. They do so by looking at how other living things with the identical characteristics as the mystery organism have already been classified.

Every living thing is classified according to the following system, in order from the largest (most general) to the smallest (most specific) group:

Kingdom
Phylum
Class
Order
Family
Genus
Species

This means, of course, that every living thing actually has seven names that ultimately specify its exact place among all living things. Let's see how this would work for a relatively easy-to-find organism—the common grasshopper:

Kingdom	Animalia
Phylum	Arthropoda
Class	Insecta
Order	Orthoptera
Family	Acridiidae
Genus	*Schistocerca*
Species	*americana*

The grasshopper is an animal, so its kingdom is Animalia. And because the animal kingdom has so many members, it is further classified as a member of the Arthropoda phylum. There are thousands of other arthropods, so the grasshopper is placed in the class Insecta. The process continues until the grasshopper is identified by the series of seven names. Notice how the classification of a grasshopper and a human differ:

	Grasshopper	**Human**
Kingdom	Animalia	Animalia
Phylum	Arthropoda	Chordata
Class	Insecta	Mammalia
Order	Orthoptera	Primates
Family	Acridiidae	Hominidae
Genus	*Schistocerca*	*Homo*
Species	*americana*	*sapiens*

The use of a classification system helps biologists avoid confusion when they talk and write about living things.

The Plant Kingdom: A Closer Look

Recent classification systems have grouped the organisms of the plant kingdom into two major phyla: the Bryophytes (Bryophyta) and the Tracheophytes (Tracheophyta). *Bryophytes* are small plants that lack conducting vessels for transporting water and nutrients. This phylum includes mosses, liverworts, and hornworts. The phylum *Tracheophyta* includes all vascular plants—that is, plants that have vessels for transporting water and nutrients.

Table 13.1   The structure of flowering plants

Element	Characteristics	Function(s)
Roots	Roots grow downward and outward into the soil. Tiny root hairs behind the root tip absorb water and minerals.	Anchor the plant. Absorb water and minerals. May store food.
Stems	*Monocot* stems emerge from seeds with one cotyledon or seed leaf (such as corn, grasses). *Dicotyledonous* stems emerge from seeds with two cotyledons (such as tomatoes, roses). *Herbaceous* (soft and green) stems are found in short-lived plants (such as dandelions, tomatoes, grasses). *Woody* stems are found in longer-lived plants (such as forsythia, lilac, trees).	Serve as a pipeline, carrying produced foods downward and water with dissolved minerals upward. Display the leaves to sunlight.
Leaves	Leaves come in many shapes and sizes. *Monocot* leaves are narrow and have smooth edges and parallel veins. *Dicot* leaves are broad and have veins that spread out. Water vapor leaves the plant through leaf openings called *stomata.*	Carry out photosynthesis (food making) because they contain chlorophyll. Assist the plant in losing excess water through transpiration.
Reproductive organs	A typical flower has sepals, petals, stamens, and a pistil. *Sepals* form the leaf-like outer covering of the developing flower bud, which is usually green. *Petals* are usually bright colored, have an odor that's attractive to insects, and produce a sugary nectar (a food source for insects and birds). *Stamens* are male reproductive organs that produce pollen containing a sperm nucleus. At the top of each stamen is an *anther*, or pollen box, that releases pollen. The *pistil* is the female reproductive organ. At the top of the pistil is the *stigma,* to which pollen can stick.	Produce fruits containing seeds, which produce new plants.

Table 13.2   Sexual and asexual reproduction in flowering plants

Type of Reproduction	Characteristics
Sexual	The sperm and egg nucleus unite in the process known as *pollination.* Pollen grains are carried to the *stigma* and produce a tube that grows downward to the *ovary,* or enlarged bottom part of the pistil. The sperm nucleus travels down the tube and unites with egg cells in the ovary to eventually produce seeds.
Asexual	Parts of plants—such as leaves, stems, and roots—are used to produce new plants. Examples include "cuttings" (containing a stem with leaves) from begonias, bulbs (which have large, food-storing, underground stems) from lilies and tulips, and potato pieces that contain buds, or "eyes."

Ferns, conifers, and flowering plants are all tracheophytes. Ferns do not produce true seeds. Both conifers and flowering plants are seed-producing tracheophytes. These seed-producing plants are grouped into two classes: the gymnosperms and the angiosperms. Most gymnosperms do not produce flowers—they produce cones. Evergreen trees such as pines, redwoods, and spruces are all gymnosperms. Angiosperms produce flowers. Fruit trees, rose plants, and daisies are all examples of angiosperms.

● The Structure of Flowering Plants

Incredibly, there are over 250,000 species of flowering plants, or *angiosperms.* As the most advanced form of plant life on Earth, this class can survive and even thrive in a variety of climates and soil types. The structure of these plants is what enables them to survive (see Table 13.1, page 262).

● Sexual and Asexual Reproduction in Flowering Plants

Most flowering plants have both male and female organs, Thus, in angiosperms, reproduction is generally accomplished by the union of sperm and egg cells to form seeds. This is called *sexual reproduction.* However, fruit and vegetable growers are able to produce new plants without using seeds. *Asexual reproduction* can happen in the natural world when separated plant parts reach soil and moisture. They will grow into a new plant that has the exact genetic makeup of the original plant. Table 13.2 (above) presents key points about sexual and asexual reproduction in flowering plants.

The Animal Kingdom: A Closer Look

Animals are multicellular organisms that obtain food from their environments. Most have systems that allow them to move, and most reproduce sexually. Almost 1 million different kinds of animals inhabit the earth. In order to keep track of them, biologists have found it useful to classify them into two major groups: animals without backbones and animals with backbones. Animals without backbones are called *invertebrates.* They include sponges, jellyfishes, starfishes, worms, mollusks, lobsters, spiders, and insects.

Go to **MyEducationLab**, select the topic Life and Environmental Sciences, examine the artifact entitled "A Butterfly's Life," and complete the questions that accompany it.

The second major group, those with backbones, are called *vertebrates*. This group includes fishes, frogs, snakes, birds, and mammals. Vertebrates and invertebrates are divided into various phyla.

Vertebrates: Mammals

Mammals are vertebrates who nourish their young with milk produced by mammary glands. Their bodies are usually covered with hair or fur, although in some mammals, the hair takes the form of a few whiskers around the mouth. Although many mammals have four legs, some mammals—for example, whales, dolphins, and manatees—do not. In other mammals, the forelegs and rear legs are modified to perform particular functions. For instance, the forelimbs of kangaroos enable them to grasp food, whereas their strong, enlarged back legs enable them to hop.

The eggs of mammals are usually fertilized internally, and most mammals produce young by giving birth to them (although the duck-billed platypus, which is a monotreme mammal, does lay eggs). Female mammals suckle their young and care for them as they mature. The amount of time for a young mammal to mature into an adult varies greatly. Mammals seem able to teach their young to perform functions that will ensure their survival. Some mammals care for their young until they are fully grown and able to survive on their own.

Female opossums and kangaroos are marsupial mammals. They have pouches in which they place their young as soon as they are born. Although bats appear to be birds, they have hair rather than feathers. Bats can fly through the use of a leathery membrane stretching between their forelimbs and hind legs.

Although whales look like fish, they are really sea-living mammals. The hair on their bodies takes the form of whiskers around the mouth. The blue whale can reach almost 30 meters (about 100 feet) in length and weigh more than 140,000 kilograms (about 150 tons).

The primates, which include monkeys, apes, and humans are the most intelligent of the mammals. They have the best-developed brains of all animals, fingers that are able to grasp objects, opposable thumbs, and nails instead of claws. (An opposable thumb can be positioned opposite of the other fingers, making it possible to manipulate objects with one hand.) The largest of all apes is the gorilla, which can weigh as much as 180 kilograms (about 400 pounds). The gorilla is able to walk upright and to support itself by placing its hands on the ground. Except for humans, one of the most intelligent of all animals is probably the chimpanzee, though some people feel that a sea mammal, the dolphin, may be more intelligent than the chimpanzee and perhaps as intelligent as humans.

Biologists usually group the human species with the primates. The characteristics that have traditionally differentiated humans from other primates include the ability to reason, the use of complex communication systems, and the use of tools. In recent years, the observation of chimpanzees and gorillas in the wild, as well as laboratory research, has revealed that primates may have capabilities that challenge traditional views.

Sexual Reproduction in Vertebrates

Vertebrates reproduce in a variety of ways. Some lay eggs; others give birth to living young. Fertilization may occur externally or internally. The young may be born fully developed, or they may be born in a very immature condition. Table 13.3 provides an overview of vertebrate reproduction using three types of animals: frogs, birds, and mammals. (Human reproduction is discussed in Chapter 14.)

Table 13.3   Sexual reproduction in vertebrates

Type of Vertebrate	Method of Reproduction
Frog	Although the frog is an amphibian, its reproductive cycle occurs in the water. The male frog releases sperm cells over egg cells expelled into the water by the female. The many-celled embryo becomes a tadpole that's capable of absorbing oxygen through its gills. The tadpole changes with time: Its gills shrink, its lungs form, and it becomes reliant on air for oxygen. With these changes, it has become a young frog.
Bird	Birds reproduce as a result of internal fertilization. An ovary within the female bird produces eggs, which may be fertilized if sperm is deposited by a male. The fertilized egg becomes covered with a shell that protects it when it passes from the female's body and reaches the outside world. Nearly all birds sit on their eggs in a nest to provide the best temperature for the embryos within them to mature. The eggs are turned and moved by the incubating parent so that they are evenly warmed. Once hatched, most baby birds are completely dependent on their parents for food, nearly naked except for down feathers, and generally helpless. Baby birds mature quickly, however. They develop other kinds of feathers, learn to fly, and eventually leave the nest.
Mammal	Sperm cells enter the female reproductive system and internally fertilize an egg cell. The fertilized egg travels to the female's uterus, where it grows and develops. The time in the uterus is known as the *gestation period;* for a human, it is about 9 months. A few mammals, such as the spiny anteater and the duck-billed platypus, lay eggs in a manner similar to birds and reptiles. Marsupials, such as kangaroos and opossums, carry their young, who are very undeveloped at birth, in a pouch. Newborn mammals cannot survive on their own. They rely on their parents to provide food, warmth, and a secure place to sleep.

Bioterrorism: What Today's Teachers Must Know

The events of "9/11," along with prior and subsequent terrorist acts, have affected us all in countless ways. Perhaps the most insidious effect has been the *fear* that's been generated. Much of that is fear of the unknown—What else is going to happen? And one of the most frightening possibilities is *bioterrorism*, in which individuals and groups use biological agents to achieve terrorist goals.

By becoming a teacher, you have become part of your community's defense against present and future attacks. Your contact with children will enable you to teach them—in a prudent and age-appropriate manner—about diseases that may affect their present and future health and well-being.

Previous generations of teachers have assumed this responsibility in the context of *natural* disease threats. Now, with a new sense of urgency, you must teach children about diseases that may be *purposefully* introduced into a specific human population. Thus, the scientific knowledge that children learn in your classroom will lay the foundation for lives in which these individuals learn to take sensible precautions to preserve their health. Additionally, with this knowledge, perhaps a few of your students will become motivated to enter health care fields, in which they will make personal contributions to keeping us all safe from bioterrorism.

Although there are a variety of disease processes that you must consider as part of your science content, two are particularly important in light of recent events: anthrax and smallpox.

Anthrax

Imagine an assassin that can lie in wait for its victims for decades and is too tiny to see with the naked eye. Although the spore-forming bacterium *Bacillus anthrac* usually causes disease in grazing animals, we have sadly learned that it can be successfully targeted at humans, as well.

The disease, called *anthrax,* is purposefully spread by putting spores into the air, which are then inhaled by victims or come into contact with the skin. Although a person can be accidentally infected by eating the undercooked meat of an infected animal or by working with the hide or fur of such an animal, these infections are rare. Using the spores of the bacteria in an act of bioterrorism is a much more serious threat to us all.

Process and Symptoms   Whether an anthrax infection originates on the skin or through the respiratory system, the effect has been known to turn the body's natural immune system against the rest of the body. The toxins in the bacteria cause *macrophages*—natural disease-hunting and -killing cells—to overreact, summoning so many chemical agents that the blood vessels begin to leak and the organs begin to fail. If the person or animal dies, the bacteria consume the remaining nutrients. And when the bacteria run out of nutrients, they turn back into the spore state, in which they are dormant until they infect another animal or person.

The immediate symptoms of anthrax vary, depending on whether the person has inhaled spores or bacteria, ingested them, or had them enter the body through a cut or open area of the skin. Inhaled anthrax begins with symptoms that resemble those of the common cold or flu; these symptoms can lead to breathing problems. Ingested anthrax produces symptoms that include loss of appetite, vomiting, and fever. Eventually, the victim has abdominal pain, vomiting of blood, and severe diarrhea. When spores or bacteria enter the skin, they produce a sore that becomes a blister and then develops a black scab at its center.

All three types of anthrax can result in death.

Transmission and Treatment   There is some good news about anthrax: It can be successfully treated if detected at an early stage of infection. Antibiotics such as penicillin, doxycycline, and fluoroquinolones can all be effective. There is also a vaccine that can work against anthrax, but it isn't widely available.

Fortunately, anthrax is not a contagious disease—in other words, incidental contact between an infected and an uninfected person will not transmit the disease. To become infected, you must have direct contact with the bacterium or spores.

Smallpox

The virus has the scientific name *Orthopoxvirus,* and the most serious disease it causes in humans is *variola major.* In common language, it is *smallpox,* an extremely contagious disease and probably the largest bioterrorist hazard faced by the world today.

The virus itself is one of the smallest living organisms presently known. Given this small size, it can become an aerosol very easily, and once airborne, it can infect virtually everyone in a crowded area. The sneeze or cough of a person infected with smallpox will release millions of virus particles into the air, which will, in turn, infect anyone who inhales them.

Because smallpox is a virus, not a bacterium, antibiotics will not kill it. A vaccine against the virus does exist, but its use was discontinued in the 1970s. Large-scale vaccinations were discontinued because the risk of getting seriously ill from the vaccine had become much higher than from actually getting the disease, which had pretty much been wiped out. This means that today, there are enormous numbers of children and adults who have not been inoculated against smallpox. Thus, an outbreak of smallpox—resulting from either bioterrorism or natural causes—would devastate any population.

Process and Symptoms   The symptoms of smallpox include fever, headache, and a rash that starts on the face, arms, and mucous membranes of the mouth and throat and eventually spreads to the trunk of the body and the legs. The rash eventually becomes raised, infected bumps on the skin. The patient will likely die as a result of respiratory problems. The mortality rate may be as high as 30%. If the patient survives, he or she will be left with considerable scarring.

Transmission and Treatment   Smallpox is transmitted from person to person in a number of ways. As noted earlier, simply inhaling the air exhaled by an infected person is the most common means of transmission. Contact with secretions from the bumps of a smallpox rash can also result in transfer of the virus from one person to another and eventual inhalation of the virus. Even contact with the bedding or other materials that have been touched by the infected person can cause infection in others.

Because smallpox is so highly contagious, patients must be quarantined (or separated from others) for at least three weeks. The same is true for any unprotected person who has come in contact with a patient. In addition, bedding and other materials must be destroyed or sterilized.

Clearly, the best course of action is prior vaccination. Health care workers, first-responders to smallpox outbreaks, police, teachers, and others in direct contact with children will all be vaccinated over time. Additionally, the smallpox vaccine may once again become widely used for infants and children.

In short, the only effective long-term choice in addressing the threat of smallpox is to vaccinate entire populations. Early efforts to do so have been met with some resistance, however, as legitimate concerns have been raised over the possible side-effects that may occur during such a massive vaccination program. These concerns will have to be weighed against the threat of bioterrorism before a vaccination program will be started again.

Summary Outline

I. Living things can be distinguished from nonliving things on the basis of characteristics known as functions of life.

   A. All living things use energy, get rid of waste, reproduce, inherit traits, respond to stimuli, maintain homeostasis, adapt to their environment, and evolve as a species.

   B. *Biology* is the study of living things.

   C. All living things are made up of one or more cells. Plants have cellulose in their cell walls; animals do not.

II. Living things can be classified into groups based on their common characteristics.

   A. The major groupings are the five kingdoms: Monera, Protista, Fungi, Plantae, and Animalia.

   B. Living things can be further classified into the following categories: phylum, class, order, family, genus, and species.

III. The plant kingdom can be divided into several phyla and subdivided into several classes.

   A. Flowering plants, or angiosperms, are the most advanced form of plant life on Earth.

   B. Plants can reproduce through sexual or asexual reproduction.

IV. The animal kingdom includes the invertebrates and vertebrates.

   A. Invertebrates are animals with backbones, including hydra, jellyfishes, corals, worms, mollusks, and jointed-leg animals.

   B. Vertebrates are animals with backbones, including fish, frogs, birds, and mammals.

V. Bioterrorism is the use of biological agents to achieve a terroristic cause.

   A. Anthrax is an infectious disease that humans get most commonly through inhalation or direct skin contact with the spore-forming bacterium *Bacillus anthracis*.

   B. Smallpox is a highly contagious disease resulting from contact with the virus *Orthropoxvirus*.

chapter 14

The Human Body

Content

The Body's Systems

In the cold gray light of dawn, a runner moves briskly along the pavement. The row houses look quietly on as her footsteps echo off their walls. Her stride is steady and firm. Her breathing barely reflects the strain of four miles of running. Her gaze is clear and her ears are sensitive to the sounds of the neighborhood awakening. The blood courses through her arteries, bringing oxygen and nourishment to her body's cells and carrying away by-products produced by the cells. The runner's body systems are functioning well when she arrives home. Within minutes, her body has recovered from this morning's ritual run. She feels refreshed and alive.

The well-functioning systems of the runner's body enable her to concentrate on the things that matter in her life. The discipline of her body is matched by the discipline of her mind, which wills her to rise early each day to run. To understand fully how the human body is able to perform, we need to consider its basic systems. *Body systems* are groups of organs that work together to carry out a particular function. For example, the heart, arteries, and veins each perform specific tasks that together enable the bloodstream to transport oxygen, nutrients, and waste products. This system of heart, arteries, and veins is called the *circulatory system.* The other basic body systems are the *digestive, skeletal-muscular, respiratory, nervous, excretory,* and *reproductive systems.* To understand them, you need to know both their structures and their functions.

The Digestive System

Go to **MyEducationLab**, select Resources, and then Web Links. Then select "National Institutes of Health Office of Science Education."

Thinking a thought, blinking an eye, and taking a step are not possible without energy. The basic source of this energy is the food we eat. The process of digestion changes food from its original form to a fuel that can release energy when it reacts with oxygen. Digestion also releases and transforms proteins—the materials necessary for building new cells and repairing old ones. The hamburger, french fries, and ear of corn on your plate at a late-summer picnic are the raw materials for the conduct of life itself.

● Structure and Function

Digestion is the process through which the body breaks down the molecules that make up the food that has been eaten and prepares them to react with oxygen to produce energy. Digestion begins in your mouth. As you chew food, glands in your mouth secrete *saliva,* a digestive juice that mixes with the food particles. Saliva contains water, mucus, and an enzyme that begins the process of breaking down the food.

As food moves through the digestive system, *enzymes* continue to act on it. Each enzyme breaks down a particular material found in food. The seeds of certain fruits, the cellulose in vegetables, and some meat tissues are indigestible. Such material passes into the large intestine and is eventually excreted.

● Food and Nutrition

All food contains *nutrients,* specific substances that provide the energy and materials the body requires to function properly. The nutrients in the food we eat are used in one of two basic ways by the body. Some are converted into energy and used immediately. Others are

Figure 14.1
This food guide pyramid illustrates the recommended daily requirements for a well-balanced diet.

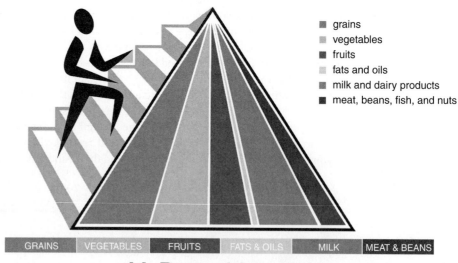

- grains
- vegetables
- fruits
- fats and oils
- milk and dairy products
- meat, beans, fish, and nuts

GRAINS   VEGETABLES   FRUITS   FATS & OILS   MILK   MEAT & BEANS

MyPyramid.gov*
STEPS TO A HEALTHIER YOU

*MyPyramid, released by the United States Department of Agriculture (USDA) on April 19, 2005, is an update on the previous U.S. food guide pyramid.

used to build new cells. Six specific nutrients are necessary for health and growth: carbohydrates (starches and sugars), fats, proteins, minerals, vitamins, and water. The foods we eat contain different amounts of these nutrients.

The United States Department of Agriculture recommends that we all eat more grains, fruits, and vegetables and less meat, fat, and sweets. To convey this view of appropriate nutrition, the Department of Agriculture has created a food guide pyramid that can help you make wise decisions about what you eat (see Figure 14.1).

The Skeletal-Muscular System

Bones: Structure and Function

Your bones and muscles work together to give your body its form and structure. The bones provide support, protection for vital organs, a place in which red blood cells and some white blood cells are produced, a storage area for minerals, and surfaces to which muscles are attached. Although many people think that bones are hard, dry objects within the body, they are really alive.

Bone tissue is composed of living bone cells (which require food and oxygen just as other body cells do), the products of bone-cell respiration, and deposits of minerals. Most bones in the human body originate from softer bone-like structures, or *cartilage*. As you age, the cartilage present in your body when you were very young becomes strong bone. This process continues until you are 20 to 25 years old.

A *joint* is a place where two bones meet. There are five types of joints in the human body: immovable, hinge, ball-and-socket, pivot, and gliding. Each provides flexibility of movement. In some joints—such as the one that connects the upper arm to the shoulder—bands of strong connective tissue, called *ligaments*, hold the bones of the joint together.

Muscles: Structure and Function

The muscles in your body provide you with the ability to move. This results from the ability of muscle cells to contract. There are three types of muscles in your body: smooth muscle, cardiac muscle, and skeletal muscle. *Smooth muscles* are those that act involuntarily. For example, the muscles that line the stomach and intestinal walls and the arteries are all involuntary muscles. This means they are able to operate quickly and without the direct control of the brain.

The involuntary muscle found in your heart is called *cardiac muscle*. When the fibers in this muscle contract, the chambers of the heart are squeezed and blood is forced out through blood vessels. If the cardiac muscle was not involuntary, your brain would have to tell your heart to beat each time blood needed to be pumped through your circulatory system.

Skeletal muscles are voluntary muscles. They work because the brain tells them to bend or flex or stretch. Skeletal muscles attach directly either to bones or to other muscles. *Tendons* are bands of connective tissue that attach the ends of some skeletal muscles to bones. When a skeletal muscle such as one in your upper arm contracts as a result of a message your brain gives it, it pulls on the muscles of your lower arm. The movement of the lower arm results from the contraction of the voluntary skeletal muscle.

The Respiratory System

Go to **MyEducationLab**, select the topic Life and Environmental Sciences, and read the lesson plan entitled "How Can You Measure Lung Capacity?"

The food you eat supplies your body with energy through a series of chemical reactions that take place in the body's cells and require oxygen. Without oxygen, the food molecules could not be broken down and energy would not be released. Although some of this energy is released as heat, much of it is stored in chemical form. Carbon dioxide and water are given off during this energy-producing process. The stored energy is used by body cells, tissues, nerves, and other body organs. This simple model shows the process by which energy is produced in your body cells:

$$\text{food} + \text{oxygen} \rightarrow \text{carbon dioxide} + \text{water} + \text{energy}$$

The Diaphragm, Windpipe, and Lungs: Structure and Function

The oxygen your body needs to produce energy from food is contained in the air you breathe. Air is about 21% oxygen and about 78% nitrogen. When you inhale, both oxygen and nitrogen enter your lungs. The nitrogen, however, is not used by the body. The in-and-out action of your lungs is controlled by the *diaphragm,* a large curved muscle that lies underneath them. As the diaphragm contracts, it moves downward. At the same time, the rib muscles separate the ribs and move them forward. These actions increase the amount of space in your chest and allow the lungs to expand.

After the air space in your chest has been enlarged, outside air pressure forces air through your nose and throat, down your windpipe, and into your lungs. After you have inhaled air, the action of your diaphragm and rib muscles increases the pressure within your chest and pushes air out through your windpipe, throat, and nose. This occurs each time you exhale.

The *windpipe* is a tube that stretches from your throat to your lungs. At your lungs it divides into two branches. Each of these branches subdivides into smaller and smaller branches within the lungs. These small branches end in tiny air sacs, each of which is surrounded by tiny blood vessels called *capillaries.* The air sacs have very thin walls that permit the oxygen to pass through them and into the capillaries.

Oxygen Transport

Once oxygen has entered the air sacs of the lungs and diffused into the capillaries, it is picked up by red blood cells and carried to all parts of the body, where it reacts chemically with food to produce energy, carbon dioxide, and water. Carbon dioxide produced in the cells enters the bloodstream and is carried back to the air sacs in the lungs. There it leaves the bloodstream, enters the lungs, and is exhaled. The paper-thin walls of the air sacs are continually allowing oxygen to pass from the lungs to the bloodstream and carbon dioxide to pass from the bloodstream to the lungs.

The Nervous System

A chirping bird catches your attention during a quiet morning walk along a wooded path. You stop and turn your head in an attempt to locate the source of this early morning joy. Your ears help focus your attention on the uppermost branch of a nearby tree. The song seems to come from somewhere behind a clump of leaves and twigs attached to the branch. Suddenly, your eyes pick out a slight movement and come to rest on a brownish head that pokes its way over the nest top and looks directly at you.

Your sight and hearing are precious gifts that, along with your other senses, gather information about the surrounding world. These sense organs are the farthest outposts of your nervous system. It is your nervous system that permits you to see, hear, touch, smell, taste, and, of course, become aware of and enjoy the existence of chirping birds on quiet morning walks through the woods.

Nerves: Structure and Function

The nervous system consists of the brain, the spinal cord, and many nerve cells. A *nerve cell* has three parts: a cell body; short, branchlike fibers that receive impulses from the brain; and long, thin fibers that carry impulses away from the cell body. Bundles of either short or long fibers are known as *nerves.* Nerves carry messages from the brain to other parts of the body and from other parts of the body to the brain. Messages are carried by nerve *impulses,* chemical changes that cause electrical charges to be transmitted through the nervous system.

Twelve pairs of nerves directly connect the brain to the eyes, ears, nose, and tongue. These nerves are called *cranial nerves.* Branches of some of these nerves leave the head and connect with the variety of muscles and other internal organs in other parts of your body.

The principal way in which messages are sent from the brain to the body is through the *spinal cord,* a column of nerves that extends from the base of the brain down through the backbone. Thirty-one pairs of nerves directly connect the spinal cord with such organs as the lungs, intestines, stomach, and kidneys. These organs usually function without voluntary control. Thus, the nerves that control these functions make up what is known as the *autonomic nervous system.* Actions over which the individual has some control or awareness of are controlled by the *somatic nervous system.*

A *reflex* is another type of automatic action controlled by the nervous system. A reflex, the simplest way in which your nervous system operates, occurs when some part of the body is stimulated. The knee-jerk reaction is a good example of a reflex. If a person taps the tendon below your kneecap with an object, your lower leg swings upward. The tapping of the tendon stimulates a nerve cell in your lower leg. The nerve impulse travels along nerves to the spinal cord. When the impulse reaches the spinal cord, a message is immediately sent to the leg muscle, which causes the jerking movement. In this and many other reflex reactions, the response is not controlled by the brain. Reflex reactions are completed well before the brain is aware of their occurrence. Other reflexes are coughing, blinking, and laughing when you're tickled.

The Senses

The sense organs, the farthest outposts of the human nervous system, contain specialized nerve cells that receive stimulation from the outside world and carry messages to the brain. Nerve cells that are capable of receiving information from the external environment are called *receptors.* Each of your sense organs has special receptors.

The Skin Sensors   Your skin is able to sense a variety of stimuli, including touch, pressure, pain, heat, and cold. Whenever a receptor is stimulated, an impulse, or nerve message, begins traveling along the nerve to which the receptor is connected and eventually arrives at the central nervous system. Receptors for the various skin senses are distributed at different locations and different depths in the skin. The touch receptors are close to the surface of the skin. Your fingertips contain many touch receptors. Pressure receptors are deeper in the skin.

Taste   Your ability to taste results from specialized nerve receptors on your tongue. The areas containing these receptors are called *taste buds*. There are specialized taste buds for each of the following flavors: sour, sweet, salt, and bitter. What you interpret as taste is actually a combination of taste and smell, for when you chew food, vapors from it reach your nose. Thus, you simultaneously taste and smell the food you're eating. You may have noticed that when you have a cold, food does not taste as good as usual. This is due to the fact that you cannot smell it as you eat it.

Smell   The principal nerve that carries information about smell to the brain is the *olfactory nerve*. Branches of this nerve are contained in a cavity in your nasal passage. Vapor from the food you eat enters your nasal cavity, is dissolved in a liquid, and stimulates the endings of the olfactory nerve.

Hearing   The ear is the principal organ through which sound waves enter the body. Sound waves enter the opening in your external ear and travel through a tube called the *auditory canal*. This canal ends at a membrane called the *eardrum*. The sound waves stimulate the eardrum, causing it to vibrate. On the other side of the eardrum a group of tiny bones—the hammer, the anvil, and the stirrup—transmit vibrations from the eardrum to the cochlea and the semicircular canals, located in the inner ear. These organs relay the vibrations to the sensitive receptors at the end of the auditory nerve, which carries them to the brain.

Sight   Your eyes receive information in the form of light from the external world (see Figure 14.2). Light passes through a transparent covering called the *cornea* and enters the *pupil*, a small opening at the front of the eyeball. The size of the pupil is controlled by the opening and closing of the *iris,* the colored portion of the eyeball. Directly behind the pupil is the *lens,* which focuses your sight. Focusing is achieved by a muscular contraction that changes the shape of the lens. Between the lens and the cornea is a watery liquid known as the *aqueous humor.* Within the eyeball is a thicker, transparent substance called the *vitreous humor.* The structures at the front of the eyeball all serve to focus light on the *retina*, the rear portion of the eyeball containing light receptors. These receptors are of two types: cones and rods. The cones are responsible for color vision; the rods

Figure 14.2
The human eye receives information from the external environment.

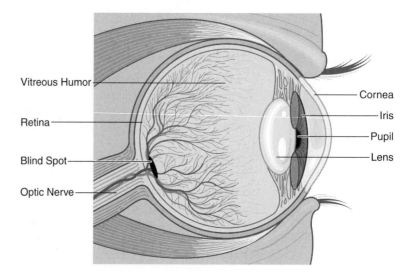

Vitreous Humor

Retina

Blind Spot

Optic Nerve

Cornea

Iris

Pupil

Lens

produce a material that helps you see in dim light. Focused light rays, or images, that reach the retina stimulate the receptors, which in turn transmit information about them to the brain via the optic nerve. In interpreting these messages, the brain gives us the sense we call sight.

The Excretory System

The process by which your body rids itself of wastes is called *excretion*. Virtually all forms of energy production create waste by-products. The human body produces both energy and an abundance of gaseous, liquid, and solid wastes. These wastes result from the production of energy and the process through which complex food materials are changed to simpler, more usable ones. If, for some reason, wastes cannot leave the body, sickness and death are certain to follow. The human body is able to rid itself of wastes by means of a very efficient group of organs.

The Kidneys: Structure and Function

Wastes from your body's cells enter the bloodstream and are carried to specific excretory organs. The major excretory organs are the kidneys and the skin. The kidneys lie on each side of the spine in the lower back. Each kidney is protected by a layer of fat. Waste-containing blood enters the kidneys and is divided into smaller and smaller amounts as the arteries transporting it branch into capillaries. From the capillaries, the blood flows through filters that separate the wastes from the blood and combine them into urine. *Urine* is a liquid that contains, in addition to the body's waste by-products, water and excess mineral salts that have also been filtered from the blood by the kidneys. Tubes called *urethras* carry the urine from the kidneys to the *urinary bladder*. This muscular organ then expels the urine from the body through the *urethra*. Meanwhile, the cleansed blood exits the kidneys through the renal veins.

The Skin and Lungs: Function

You may be surprised to learn that your skin is an important excretory organ. Its principal role is the removal of excess heat. When the body becomes too warm, blood vessels in the skin open wide, increasing the flow of blood to the capillaries, which allows heat to be given off to the air. Through pores in the skin exit water, salts, and small amounts of *urea*, a waste found principally in the urine. The liquid that contains these body wastes is *perspiration*. As perspiration evaporates, it helps cool the body. The lungs are considered part of the excretory system because they rid the body of carbon dioxide and excess water in the form of water vapor.

The Liver and Intestines: Function

Although the liver is principally a digestive organ, it is also able to form urea and secrete it into the bloodstream. Bacteria, some drugs, and hormones are removed from the blood in the liver and converted into less harmful substances. These substances are returned to the blood and eventually excreted from the body by the kidneys.

The large intestine performs an important excretory function by removing from the body food that has not been digested by the small intestine. Solid waste that moves through the large intestine is composed largely of undigested food and bacteria. It is eliminated from the body through the *anus*—the end of the digestive tract. The *rectum* is that portion of the large intestine that lies directly above the anus.

The Circulatory System

A complex system consisting of a pump and conducting vessels keeps you alive. This system, known as the *circulatory system,* operates efficiently whether you are sitting, standing, walking, running, or sleeping. The circulatory system is an extraordinarily complex system but so efficient and automatic that you are able to carry out the activities of living without even an awareness of its existence.

● The Heart and Blood Vessels: Structure and Function

The heart is the powerful pump that moves blood through your body's blood vessels. It has four chambers: a right atrium, a left atrium, a right ventricle, and a left ventricle. Blood enters this marvelous pump through the *atria* (the upper chambers) and is pumped out of the heart by the *ventricles* (the lower chambers). Between the atria and the ventricles are *valves* that prevent the blood from flowing backward. Once blood passes from the atria to the ventricles, it is impossible for it to return through these controlling valves. The opening and closing of the heart valves produce the sound that a physician hears when he or she uses a stethoscope to listen to your heart. The "lub-dub, lub-dub" is simply the opening and shutting of the valves. If the heart valves are damaged and blood is able to leak backward from the ventricles to the atria, a health problem results. Physicians can usually detect this problem by listening through their stethoscope for the sound produced by blood moving in the wrong direction. This sound is called a *heart murmur.*

The vessels that carry blood from the ventricles to various parts of the body are called *arteries.* The vessels that return blood to the heart are called *veins.* Within the body tissues the major arteries branch into smaller and smaller arteries and small veins merge to form large veins. A series of microscopic *capillaries* connect small arteries and veins and permit the exchange of dissolved nutrients, oxygen, wastes, and other substances.

The right side of the heart receives blood from the body and pumps it to the lungs. This blood contains the carbon dioxide produced by the cells as they converted nutrients to energy. In the lungs, the carbon dioxide is removed from the blood, and oxygen from inhaled air is added. The oxygen-rich blood is then carried to the left side of the heart, which pumps it to the remaining organs of your body (see Figure 14.3). To understand the circulatory system, you must remember that the heart seems to act like two pumps. On the right side, blood that contains carbon dioxide is pumped to the lungs. On the left side, blood that is rich in oxygen, as a result of having passed through the lungs, is pumped to all parts of the body.

● Blood

Human blood is made of a variety of materials. One such material is *plasma,* which is 90% water and 10% various dissolved substances. Among the most important of these substances are *antibodies,* which help your body fight diseases.

Red blood cells are another component of blood. They contain *hemoglobin,* the iron-rich substance that receives oxygen from the lungs and carries it to the tissue cells.

Another type of cell found in the bloodstream is the *white blood cell.* White blood cells do not contain hemoglobin. Rather, they are your body's first line of defense against infection. If you have an infection, the number of white cells in your blood increases very rapidly. White blood cells are able to surround disease-causing bacteria and kill them.

Fibrinogen, which makes possible the process of clotting, is found in plasma. If you cut yourself, substances called *platelets* release a chemical that causes fibrinogen to turn into needlelike fibers that trap blood cells and form a clot. It is this clotting process that allows the bloodstream to repair itself in the event of a cut. It simply restricts the flow of blood to an open cut or puncture.

Figure 14.3   The human heart consists of two pumps lying side by side to form a single organ. The right side of the heart sends oxygen-poor blood to the lungs; the left side of the heart sends oxygen-rich blood to the rest of the body.

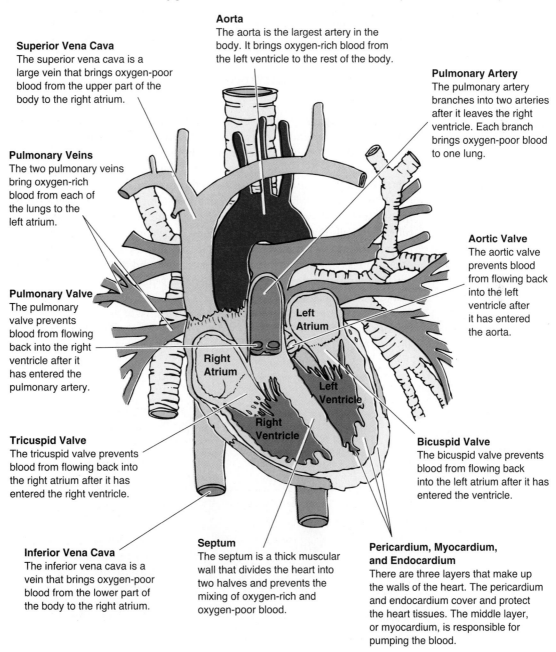

Aorta
The aorta is the largest artery in the body. It brings oxygen-rich blood from the left ventricle to the rest of the body.

Superior Vena Cava
The superior vena cava is a large vein that brings oxygen-poor blood from the upper part of the body to the right atrium.

Pulmonary Artery
The pulmonary artery branches into two arteries after it leaves the right ventricle. Each branch brings oxygen-poor blood to one lung.

Pulmonary Veins
The two pulmonary veins bring oxygen-rich blood from each of the lungs to the left atrium.

Aortic Valve
The aortic valve prevents blood from flowing back into the left ventricle after it has entered the aorta.

Pulmonary Valve
The pulmonary valve prevents blood from flowing back into the right ventricle after it has entered the pulmonary artery.

Tricuspid Valve
The tricuspid valve prevents blood from flowing back into the right atrium after it has entered the right ventricle.

Bicuspid Valve
The bicuspid valve prevents blood from flowing back into the left atrium after it has entered the ventricle.

Inferior Vena Cava
The inferior vena cava is a vein that brings oxygen-poor blood from the lower part of the body to the right atrium.

Septum
The septum is a thick muscular wall that divides the heart into two halves and prevents the mixing of oxygen-rich and oxygen-poor blood.

Pericardium, Myocardium, and Endocardium
There are three layers that make up the walls of the heart. The pericardium and endocardium cover and protect the heart tissues. The middle layer, or myocardium, is responsible for pumping the blood.

Left Atrium, Right Atrium, Left Ventricle, Right Ventricle

As blood passes through the body, it picks up many things. In the capillaries of the small intestine, it absorbs dissolved food, which it then carries to the liver, an organ that is able to store sugar. Other nutrients in the blood are carried to the various body cells, where, in combination with oxygen, they are converted to energy. This energy production results in carbon dioxide, water, and other waste by-products. These wastes leave the cells and are carried by the bloodstream to organs that are able to rid the body of them.

The Reproductive System

The egg or sperm cells within your body are so tiny that they can be seen only with a microscope, yet within each reposes half of a blueprint for a new human being, who may one day contribute one of its own reproductive cells to the process of creating a new person. We are bound backward in time to our parents, grandparents, and all those who have preceded us.

Structure and Function

The male reproductive organs produce *sperm,* or male reproductive cells. The female reproductive organs produce female reproductive cells, or *eggs.* Through sexual intercourse, a sperm cell and an egg cell may unite to form a human embryo. The embryo has the potential for becoming a new human being.

Sperm are produced in an organ called the *testis.* A pair of testes are contained in a pouch called the *scrotum.* Because this scrotum is outside the body wall, the temperature of the testes is somewhat lower than the body temperature. However, the production of healthy sperm cells requires this lower temperature. Within each testis are numerous coiled tubes. The cells that line the walls of these tubes produce sperm. These tubes merge to form a larger tube, the *sperm duct.* The sperm duct carries sperm and fluids produced by other glands (Cowper's gland, the prostate gland, and the seminal vesicles) into the body and then through the external sexual organ, the *penis.* The penis is used to fertilize egg cells in a female (see Figure 14.4).

Human egg cells are produced in a pair of *ovaries* in the female body. During a human female's lifetime, about 500 eggs, or *ova,* will mature and be released by the ovaries. Usually one ovum matures and is released at one time. A mature ovum leaves the ovary and

Figure 14.4
The human male reproductive system

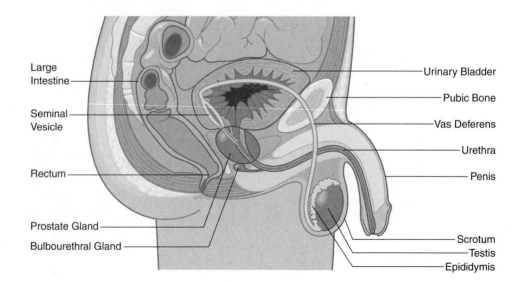

Large Intestine

Seminal Vesicle

Rectum

Prostate Gland

Bulbourethral Gland

Urinary Bladder

Pubic Bone

Vas Deferens

Urethra

Penis

Scrotum

Testis

Epididymis

Figure 14.5
The human female reproductive system

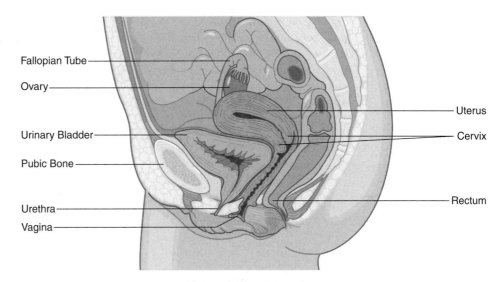

Fallopian Tube

Ovary

Urinary Bladder

Pubic Bone

Urethra

Vagina

Uterus

Cervix

Rectum

passes into a tubelike organ known as an *oviduct,* where it is pushed along by hairlike projections to a large muscle-lined tube called the *uterus.* If the egg is fertilized by a sperm, it will become attached to the uterus wall and develop into an embryo (see Figure 14.5).

The *vagina* is a tube that connects the uterus with the outside of the body. During intercourse, sperm cells placed here may swim through the uterus and reach the oviducts. If a healthy sperm cell reaches a healthy, mature egg cell, fertilization occurs. The nucleus of the female egg cell and the nucleus of the male sperm unite to form the beginning of a new human being.

Within one week of fertilization, the cell produced by the union of the sperm and egg will divide into about 100 cells. Nine months later, the embryo will consist of more than 200 billion cells, each designed to carry out a particular life function.

The developing embryo gets its food through a membrane called the *placenta.* Nutrients and oxygen in the mother's bloodstream pass from the uterus into the blood vessels of the placenta and from there into the embryo, by way of blood vessels in an umbilical cord. The belly button, or *navel,* marks the place where the umbilical cord entered the developing embryo's body. Wastes produced by the cells of the developing embryo enter the embryo's bloodstream and are eventually carried by the placenta to the mother's bloodstream. However, the blood of the mother and the embryo do not mix.

When the embryo reaches maturity, birth occurs. At birth, the embryo is forced through the vagina and out of the mother's body as a result of contractions of the uterine wall. The umbilical cord that had connected the embryo with its mother is cut. The baby is born.

Reproduction and Heredity

Heredity is the transmission of the physical traits of the parents to their offspring. Your physical traits result from the transmittal of hereditary information that occurred when a sperm and egg united to produce you. The nucleus of the sperm cell and the nucleus of the egg cell contain material that determines the embryo's physical traits. The part of the nucleus that contains hereditary information is the *gene.* Genes occupy distinct places on ribbon-like structures called *chromosomes.* The nuclei of all human cells contain chromosomes. Although the nuclei of most cells contain 46 chromosomes, the nucleus of a human sperm cell and the nucleus of a human egg cell contain only 23 chromosomes. When a sperm cell and an egg cell unite, the resulting cell has 46 chromosomes. Twenty-three carry genes from the male parent, and 23 carry genes from the female parent. The genes on the chromosomes of the first complete cell and the particular order in which they are located on the chromosome give the offspring its inherited traits.

Identical twins result when an embryo splits in two. The two halves develop into individuals who have the same physical traits. *Fraternal twins* are the result of two ova being fertilized by two sperm. They are simply siblings who happened to be conceived and born at the same time.

Summary Outline

    I. The digestive system converts food into energy or cell-building material.

    II. The skeletal-muscular system provides the body with its shape and structure and gives it the ability to move.

    III. The respiratory system secures the oxygen necessary for the conversion of food to energy and eliminates carbon dioxide.

    IV. The nervous system receives stimuli and carries them to the brain; it then transmits the brain's messages to various parts of the body by means of nerve impulses.

    V. The excretory system rids the body of gaseous, liquid, and solid wastes.

    VI. The circulatory system moves a variety of substances from place to place in the body.

    VII. The reproductive system of a male produces sperm cells capable of fertilizing an ovum, the reproductive cell of a female.

chapter **15**

Life Sciences Lesson Ideas

Putting the Content into Action

The Tapper

The sound of John Williams's footsteps bounced off the walls lining the dimly lit hallway and echoed after him as he counted down the classroom numbers. Room 12, 11, 10, 9, 8. And there it was—Room 7. With excitement and more than a little apprehension, he opened the door. His first quick look around the room brought a sinking feeling. Drab, drab, drab—25 desks with firmly attached chairs, an old wooden teacher's desk, green chalkboards, bookshelf after bookshelf filled with school books, and some bulletin boards swiss-cheesed with tack holes. No real tables or even counter space for science work or hands-on projects of any kind.

John walked to the front of the room and sat down behind the old wooden desk. The eerie silence and warmth of the last days of summer soothed him only slightly. What would it be like teaching in this school? Would the other teachers accept him? Where was he going to get the materials he was going to need? What would the children be like? That was his primary question: What would the children be like?

He didn't notice the tapping sound for a while. Finally, a particularly loud tap broke him from his reverie. He turned to his right and saw the concerned face of a child outside, tapping on the window pane with one hand to get his attention. He left his chair, walked to the window, and opened it wide.

"Hi, I'm Mr. Williams. I'm going to be the teacher in this room."

"I found this nest in the bushes. It was on the ground."

John asked, "What grade are you going to be in?"

"It's got some pieces of eggshell in it," the Tapper answered.

John tried again, "What's your name? Do you live near here?"

"The birds. What happened to the little birds?"

Children are concerned about life. They want to know what happens to baby birds, and they want to know the names for the colorful, creepy-crawly caterpillars they find on the way to school. In this chapter, you will find ideas and resources to assist you as you plan discovery-oriented life science experiences for children that will develop and extend their curiosity, knowledge, and concern for life in its multitude of forms.

► Getting Started

Try the following true/false statements:

1. We can see because light travels to our eyes and then from our eyes to the object.
2. Plants can respond to stimuli.
3. The two main categories of cells are plant and animal.
4. Plants feed by absorbing food through their roots.
5. Hibernating animals sleep throughout the entire hibernation period.
6. Respiration is synonymous with breathing.[1]
7. The brain uses less power than most light bulbs, about 20 watts of energy.
8. Stem cells are found in adults as well as embryos.
9. Your heart stops when you sneeze.
10. You can estimate the temperature by listening to the chirping of a cricket.

How do you think you did? The answers are given on page 335. These statements address common misconceptions among children and adults about the life sciences. Often our explanations are well entrenched in our minds, and for good reason. Explanations often make sense based on our mental models of phenomena. However, good science requires a healthy dose of skepticism and openness to revisions of our mental models as we acquire insights through experience and reflection. Teaching often consists of re-educating by creating experiences and insights that challenge children's current understandings and force them to revise their mental models and explanations. The first step to re-teaching is to probe children's current understanding. Therefore, the beginning of a unit or lesson usually starts by assessing children's prior knowledge.

Probes for Assessing Life Sciences Prior Knowledge and Conceptions

The probes and sample responses that follow come from informal interviews that I or my students have done with children. I think you'll be amazed at some of the responses and motivated to develop probes that you can use *before* planning units and lessons.

Probe	Responses That Reveal Prior Knowledge and Conceptions
• *Is the wind a living thing?*	"Yes. It moves things." "No. It just blows stuff around." "No. It's just cold." "No. You can't see it."
• *Is fire a living thing?*	"No. It burns things." "Yes. It makes smoke." "Yes. It's hot and red and moves." "No. I don't know why."
• *Is the sun a living thing?*	"Yes. If it wasn't, it couldn't make things hot." "No. It's like a star."
• After pointing out some clouds overhead: *Are those clouds living things?*	"Yes. They work by bringing the rain down." "No. They are just a bunch of rain." "No. They are just puffy and float." "No. They don't breathe or have babies."
• *What is a seed?*	"Something you stick in the ground." "A thing that makes flowers grow." "A plant grows out of them." "Little thing you put in the ground." "They get bigger to make a plant."
• After having the child observe a variety of seeds: *Where do seeds come from?*	"Plants. Some have things that make the air put it somewhere else. They have fuzz on them." "Other plants." "Flowers." "Pumpkins. Sometimes if you eat one, it will stay there and grow." "When someone plants two seeds and if one of them doesn't grow, then someone digs the other seed up." "Sometimes ants make them and lay them like eggs." "They come from big, big bags."
• *Do you eat any plants or parts of plants?*	"Yes. Raspberries." "Yes. I eat carrots." "We can eat berries and beans." "Corn. I eat the whole thing." "No. Brian eats clovers. He's bad." "No way. They are bad for you."

(continued)

Probe	Responses That Reveal Prior Knowledge and Conceptions
• After showing a collection of forest pictures: *What animals and plants live in a forest?*	"All of them except dogs and cats." "Spiders. Lots of spiders." "Trees and wolves." "Lions and bears." "People could, but they don't. I don't think anybody lives there now."
• After showing a child pictures of the desert: *What animals and plants do you think live in a desert like this one?*	"No dogs and cats." "Snakes." "Tigers." "Dinosaurs used to live there." "Some cows do." "Wolves . . . No, maybe no wolves."
• *What is pollution?*	"Dirty air." "Cars give pollution." "Big cities have pollution." "Garbage on the ground." "It comes from cars on the street." "Where the air gets dirty and mixes up with the bad stuff then we can't breathe." "When people litter with cars." "Air . . . disgusting air." "Stuff that flies around the world."

Unit, Lesson, and Enrichment Starter Ideas

Unit Plan Starter Ideas and Questions

That great idea for a science-teaching unit may come from deep within your brain, your school curriculum guide, a state science curriculum framework, a science resource book, a course, a workshop, a discussion you have with children, or some other source. Unfortunately, a great idea (like a friend, an umbrella, and a good restaurant with cheap food) is sometimes hard to find when you really need one.

To make it easier for you to come up with great ideas for science units, I have prepared two different sources of unit starter ideas:

1. The first is based on the National Science Education Standards (NSES) for science content. I created these starter ideas for standards related to grades K–4 and 5–8.

2. The second source of starter ideas is based on my study of life science topics that commonly appear in school curriculum guides. These are shown by grade level.

I am certain that the unique compilation of starter ideas that follows will help you plan and create wonderful discovery-based teaching units.

Because science is about seeking explanations, each starter idea is accompanied by a big question. The question serves as the anchor for the unit. Each inquiry lesson of the unit should contribute to a deeper, more comprehensive answer to the unit question. At the conclusion of the unit, children should be able to provide an explanation of their answer to the question that reflects what was taught in the unit.

Ideas Based on the NSES K–8 Content Standards

> **Content Standard K–4:** Life Sciences [LS]
>
> As a result of activities in grades K–4, all students should develop an understanding of:
>
> > The characteristics of organisms
> >
> > Life cycles of organisms
> >
> > Organisms and environments[2]

▶ STARTER IDEAS for the Characteristics of Organisms

UNIT TITLE: *Taking Care of Plants*

QUESTION: What conditions are needed to keep a plant alive and healthy?

UNIT OVERVIEW: Children care for classroom plants for a two-week period and then prepare charts and drawings to show how they helped the plants meet their requirements for life (e.g., air, water, nutrients, and light).

UNIT TITLE: *Taking Care of Animals*

QUESTION: What conditions are needed to keep an animal alive and healthy?

UNIT OVERVIEW: Children care for classroom chameleons, gerbils, and guinea pigs and identify through diagrams and written explanations how they have helped the animals meet their requirements for life (e.g., air, water, and food).

▶ STARTER IDEAS for Life Cycles of Organisms

UNIT TITLE: *Cycles in a Garden*

QUESTION: What are the changes a plant undergoes from seed to death?

UNIT OVERVIEW: Children maintain an outdoor garden, observe plants growing into adulthood from seeds, and maintain logs that show the changes that occur as the plants go through their life cycles.

UNIT TITLE: *Seed Cycles/Frog Cycles*

QUESTION: How are the life cycles of animals and plants similar and different?

UNIT OVERVIEW: After raising plants from seeds and frogs from eggs, children compare plant and animal life cycles, including attention to birth, adulthood, reproduction, and death.

▶ **STARTER IDEAS** for Organisms and Environments

UNIT TITLE: *Find the Chains*

QUESTION: What organisms does energy flow through in forest, desert, tundra, meadow, and ocean food chains?

UNIT OVERVIEW: Through library research, Internet research, and direct observations at a local nature area, children prepare diagrams to show a sample food chain that could be found in each of the following environments: forest, desert, tundra, meadow, and ocean.

UNIT TITLE: *The Incredible Life in the Lawn*

QUESTION: What is life like in the lawn?

UNIT OVERVIEW: Children are assigned a plot of lawn that is left unmowed. They make careful descriptive models of life in the lawn during the school year, recording their observations in their lab notebook, raising questions, and conducting experiments throughout the year.

NSES **Content Standard 5–8: Life Sciences [LS]**

As a result of the activities in grades 5–8, all students should develop an understanding of:

  Structure and function in living systems

  Reproduction and heredity

  Regulation and behavior

  Populations and ecosystems

  Diversity and adaptation of organisms

▶ **STARTER IDEAS** for Structure and Function
in Living Systems

UNIT TITLE: *Cells—The Basis of Life*

QUESTION: What makes a cell so special to life?

UNIT OVERVIEW: Each child or team of children is given a sample of cells that are easily observable using a microscope (paramecium, euglena, volvox, ameba). They will be charged with taking care of the cell culture for two weeks, periodically estimating the number of organisms in the culture, graphing the data, and figuring out how they survive based on observations and research. *Note:* A digital microscope can be used to help students visualize their cultures.

UNIT TITLE: *Body Systems*

QUESTION: What is a body system?

UNIT OVERVIEW: Use a WebQuest to assign each group a body system. They will prepare a report (i.e., written, PowerPoint, diagrammed, acted out, poster, or song) that describes the elements, rules of relationships, and emergent properties of the system.

▶ **STARTER IDEAS** for Reproduction and Heredity

UNIT TITLE: *You and Heredity*

QUESTION: What makes me unique?

UNIT OVERVIEW: Children describe how each new human being receives a "set of instructions" that specifies his or her inherited traits.

UNIT TITLE: *My Traits and My Environment*

QUESTION: How do my genes and my environment influence who I am?

UNIT OVERVIEW: Children identify five of their inherited traits and five traits that may have been acquired from their environment.

▶ **STARTER IDEAS** for Five Senses

UNIT TITLE: *Our Senses, Windows to the World*

QUESTION: How do we know the world around us?

UNIT OVERVIEW: Children will use each of their five senses to solve a mystery. Put a popcorn popper in a mystery box. Hand out popcorn kernels in a black bag so the children can touch but not see them. Turn on the popcorn popper and let the children try to describe what is in the box. They will need to use their sense of hearing and smell. Hand out popped corn for them to see. If you choose, let them taste the popcorn to use the final sense.

▶ **STARTER IDEAS** for Populations and Ecosystems

UNIT TITLE: *Nature's Incredible Solar Chefs*

QUESTION: What organisms can convert the sun's energy into food?

UNIT OVERVIEW: Children identify those organisms that capture the sun's energy in a desert, a woodland, a meadow, and an ocean ecosystem.

UNIT TITLE: *Eating Out . . . Naturally*

QUESTION: What organisms eat the food created by producers?

UNIT OVERVIEW: Children identify those organisms that use energy captured by others in a desert, a woodland, a meadow, and an ocean ecosystem.

▶ **STARTER IDEAS** for Diversity and Adaptation of Organisms

UNIT TITLE: *Special Species*

QUESTION: What is an adaptation?

UNIT OVERVIEW: Children identify the external adaptations and the related advantages possessed by five birds of prey, five land predators, and five ocean predators.

UNIT TITLE: *Life in a Log*

QUESTION: How many different forms of life can there be in a log?

UNIT OVERVIEW: Children explore a rotting log for all the different forms of life that they can find (review safety precautions: do not handle organisms, wear gloves, check logs for stinging organisms). This can be coordinated with "The Incredible Life in the Lawn."

NSES **Content Standards Related to:**
Science and Technology [S&T]
Science in Personal and Social Perspectives [SPSP]
History and Nature of Science [HNS][3]

UNIT TITLE: *Becoming an Earth Citizen*

QUESTION: How does my life affect the earth?

UNIT OVERVIEW: Each student will complete a carbon footprint based on his or her habits and energy use. There are several carbon footprint calculators available online.

UNIT TITLE: *Taking Action to Preserve the Earth*

QUESTION: What can I contribute to a healthy Earth?

UNIT OVERVIEW: Children decide what they can do to decrease their carbon footprint. They can use the carbon footprint calculator to predict how their actions will alter their footprint. Extend the idea to the school, and ask what their school community can do to contribute to a healthy Earth. This may lead to a schoolwide initiative to recycle, shut off computers, or install light sensors at your school.

Lesson Plan Starter Ideas for Common Curriculum Topics

Sometimes you will be responsible for teaching lessons that are part of units prepared by committees of teachers in your school district or units that are commercially available. You may wonder how to break these units into lessons. To help you come up with lesson ideas for the life sciences, I have analyzed a variety of teaching units and prepared a list of lesson plan starter ideas based on topics usually covered in these units. The lesson descriptions are very specific, so each description may also be viewed as the lesson's principal objective.

▶ **STARTER IDEAS** Characteristics of Living Things

- Observe and measure the growth and movement of living things that are kept in the classroom.
- Count the number of living things in the classroom, and prepare a bar graph that shows the number of each type of living thing.
- Orally describe the similarities and differences between plant and animal parts.
- Analyze the conditions under which animals at a local zoo are kept, and list the observed conditions on a chart.

▶ **STARTER IDEAS** Plant and Animal Life Processes

- Choose one plant and one animal from the school yard ecosystem, and explain how each addresses the fundamental life functions.
- Identify from a list of foods those that are the best sources of protein, fiber, carbohydrates, and fat, and locate each food in the nutrition food pyramid.

Go to **MyEducationLab**, select the topic Life and Environmental Sciences, and read the lesson plan entitled "When Do Green Plants Give Off Carbon Dioxide During Their Growing Cycle?"

- Explain orally how humans can prevent the spread of diseases, including sexually transmitted diseases (STDs).
- Explain orally the effects of tobacco, alcohol, and drug use on the human body.
- Explain how food is converted as it travels through the body.
- Recognize and identify different patterns of animal growth (continuous, molting, metamorphosis).
- Identify the functions of the principal organs of the human reproductive system for both males and females.

▶ STARTER IDEAS for Populations

- Identify factors that might cause a population of animals or plants to become extinct.
- Explain the factors that trigger the migration of a population from one place to another.
- After doing library and Internet research to evaluate explanations for successful migration to distant locations, select the two most likely explanations.
- Explain the similarities and differences in the survival needs of the following populations: bees, ants, deer, humans.
- Make a labeled diagram that shows the role decomposers play in returning water, minerals, and other nutrients to a population.

▶ STARTER IDEAS for the Environment

- Describe the meaning of the phrase *global climate change.*
- Explain what it means to be a good Earth citizen.
- Infer the requirements for keeping an ecosystem self-sustaining.
- Create a timeline for the last 100 years that shows the changes in the local environment described by senior citizens.
- Identify the human use of natural resources found in the environment.

Children's curiosity about plants makes this topic an excellent source of starter ideas.

Make the Case *An Individual or Group Challenge*

● **The Problem**

Children need science experiences that range across the earth/space, life, and physical sciences. Teachers may tend to emphasize those topics they feel most comfortable with and thus inadvertently limit the scope of children's learning.

● **Assess Your Prior Knowledge and Beliefs**

1. When you compare your knowledge of the life sciences to your knowledge of the earth/space sciences and physical sciences, do you believe you have acquired more, less, or the same amount of basic science content in each?

	More	*Less*	*Same*
Earth/space sciences	_____	_____	_____
Physical sciences	_____	_____	_____

2. When you were a student in grades K–8, were you exposed to more, less, or the same amount of life science content as you were to earth/space science content and physical science content?

	More	*Less*	*Same*
Earth/space sciences	_____	_____	_____
Physical sciences	_____	_____	_____

3. Whether life as we know it exists on other planets is an ever-popular life science topic for children. Identify five discrete items of knowledge that you have about the topic.

_____

_____

_____

_____

_____

4. Now identify five things about the requirements for life that you think you should know but do not.

_____

_____

_____

_____

_____

● **The Challenge**

You are part of a team of teachers planning a unit on the requirements for life. Give examples of life science activities you might include.

▶ **STARTER IDEAS for How Life Adapts and Changes**

- Evaluate how an animal's characteristics increase its chances for survival in its environment.
- Given illustrations of the ancient and modern forms of horses and dogs, infer any advantages the modern form would have over the ancient form in today's world.
- Create a timeline that shows when life began on Earth, the origin and extinction of dinosaurs, and the origin of humans.
- Identify the major changes that have occurred in the bodies and behaviors of humans over the past 3 million years.
- Predict changes that will occur in human bodies as the species adapts to increased water and air pollution.

▶ **STARTER IDEAS for Ecosystems**

- Explain how all animals depend on the food-making ability of green plants.
- Classify the members of a community as producers, consumers, and decomposers.
- Count the number of organisms found in a sample of water from a pond ecosystem.
- Explain that an ecosystem consists of the physical environment and a group of interacting living things that also interact with the environment.
- Infer how changes in the characteristics of an ecosystem can affect the balance among producers, consumers, and decomposers.
- Given specific information about the components of an ecosystem, infer how the introduction of a population of new producers changes the rest of the ecosystem.
- Describe an experiment that could test the effects of drastic changes in each of the following on an ecosystem: water, food, temperature, and availability of light.

WebQuest Starter Ideas

Imagine the WebQuest possibilities for your students when you teach the life sciences! They'll be able to use the vast resources of the Internet to discover fascinating information about animals, plants, their own bodies, and the incredible web of life of which they are a part.

The starter ideas in this section will help you plan your own life science WebQuests. As you study the ideas, please keep the following in mind:

1. The starter ideas follow the WebQuest format presented in detail in Chapter 8.

NSES

2. The WebQuests are correlated with the NSES for grades K–8 (which are printed inside the front cover).

3. In the WebQuest context, the term *reports* has a very broad meaning and includes poster preparation, skits, dance, video presentations, labeled diagrams, and, of course, traditional written reports, if and when appropriate.

▶ **STARTER IDEAS** for WebQuests

WEBQUEST TITLE: *Help the Polar Bears*

SUGGESTED GRADE LEVELS: K–1 (to be done with an adult)

NSES CONTENT STANDARDS: LS 1 and 3; SPSP 4

CHALLENGE—MOTIVATION: Have you ever seen a polar bear? Sometimes, young polar bears become orphans. What would a zoo need to raise polar bear orphans?

CHALLENGE—REPORTS: Pretend you are going to start a zoo for polar bear orphans. List what you will need to keep them healthy. Draw and label the parts of their new zoo home.

KEY TERMS FOR SEARCH ENGINES: Polar Bear, Arctic Animals, Alaskan Bears

WEBQUEST TITLE: *Save the Tigers*

SUGGESTED GRADE LEVELS: 2, 3

NSES CONTENT STANDARDS: LS 1, 2, and 3; SPSP 4

CHALLENGE—MOTIVATION: The sign outside a zoo says "Donate Money So We Can Raise Endangered Bengal Tigers." You ask the zoo manager what a Bengal tiger is and why they are in danger. She goes into her office and takes out a poster about the Bengal tiger to help answer your questions about . . .

CHALLENGE—REPORTS: What might be on the zoo manager's poster? Make a poster that you could use to tell others about Bengal tigers. Be sure to include . . .

KEY TERMS FOR SEARCH ENGINES: Bengal Tiger, Royal Bengal Tiger, Asian Tiger

WEBQUEST TITLE: *Rain Forest Animals*

SUGGESTED GRADE LEVELS: 4, 5

NSES CONTENT STANDARDS: LS 7 and 8; SPSP 10

CHALLENGE—MOTIVATION: You are getting ready to lead a team of scientists in exploring a South American rain forest. They will be all coming to your laboratory next week to learn about . . .

CHALLENGE—REPORTS: Prepare an outline for the speech you will give to your team. Tell them where they'll be going, what they should wear, which species they should look for, and . . .

KEY TERMS FOR SEARCH ENGINES: Rain Forest Animals, Costa Rica Rain Forests, Rain Forest Habitat, Amazon Rain Forest

WEBQUEST TITLE: *Your Healthy Heart and Lungs*

SUGGESTED GRADE LEVELS: 5, 6

NSES CONTENT STANDARDS: LS 4; SPSP 6

CHALLENGE—MOTIVATION: You've seen many signs and posters that tell people not to smoke. Have you ever wondered what health problems are caused by smoking?

CHALLENGE—REPORTS: Make two posters for your class that will help keep your friends from becoming smokers. Make one poster that shows how smoking affects the heart and another that shows . . .

KEY TERMS FOR SEARCH ENGINES: Secondhand Smoke, American Heart Association, American Lung Association

WEBQUEST TITLE: *Watch the Whales*

SUGGESTED GRADE LEVELS: 5, 6, 7

NSES CONTENT STANDARDS: LS 4, 6, 7, and 8; SPSP 10

CHALLENGE—MOTIVATION: Imagine that you are going on a whale-watching trip. You pack art supplies and very powerful binoculars for the adventure.

CHALLENGE—REPORTS: Select either the Pacific or Atlantic Ocean for your trip. Then make five labeled drawings that show the kinds of whales you expect to see. Be sure to show . . .

KEY TERMS FOR SEARCH ENGINES: Marine Mammals, Humpback Whales, Sea World, Shamu

WEBQUEST TITLE: *What's Your Biome?*

SUGGESTED GRADE LEVELS: 5, 6, 7

NSES CONTENT STANDARDS: LS 7 and 8; SPSP 7

CHALLENGE—MOTIVATION: You have just been given a scientific award from the Metropolis Museum that includes enough money to travel to and live in any biome you want to for one year. But there is a catch: . . .

CHALLENGE—REPORTS: To get the money, you must write a letter to the museum that tells what biome you have chosen, why you chose it, what animals and plants you expect to study, and . . .

KEY TERMS FOR SEARCH ENGINES: Biome, Plant Adaptation, Animal Adaptation

WEBQUEST TITLE: *Sense or Nonsense?*

SUGGESTED GRADE LEVELS: 5, 6, 7

NSES CONTENT STANDARDS: LS 6; SPSP 6

CHALLENGE—MOTIVATION: You have just been made president of the Ajax Advanced Robot Company. The owners have told you that they want you to produce a robot that has at least three human senses.

CHALLENGE—REPORTS: Select three senses, identify the organs that gather information for each sense, and explain how information travels to the brain. Draw a robot that has all three senses. Label all the parts that allow the robot to have the three senses. Be sure to . . .

KEY TERMS FOR SEARCH ENGINES: Five Senses, Nervous System, Sense Organs, Spinal Cord, Ganglia

WEBQUEST TITLE: *What Is a Human Population?*

SUGGESTED GRADE LEVELS: 6, 7, 8

NSES CONTENT STANDARDS: LS 7; SPSP 7 and 10

CHALLENGE—MOTIVATION: You have just been assigned the job of reporting to your country's leaders the size of the population and where the population is the most dense. This is important for future planning because . . .

CHALLENGE—REPORTS: The report must include a map showing where population is most and least dense, a chart showing resources that will be needed if the most dense areas keep growing, and . . .

KEY TERMS FOR SEARCH ENGINES: Population Map, Population Density, Overpopulation, World POPClock

Classroom Enrichment Starter Ideas

● In-Class Learning Centers

A well-prepared in-class learning center offers children many opportunities to make their own discoveries. In order to be well prepared, such a center must provide a wide range of materials that encourage hands-on, discovery-based learning, ranging from print and audiovisual resources to art supplies and games. In addition, the learning center must be located where children have ready access to it yet can also be somewhat removed from the larger classroom setting while doing independent activities.

NSES

The following starter ideas for in-class learning centers should get you thinking about how to create centers in your own classroom. Note that the relevant NSES is identified for each starter idea and that asterisks indicate those that are particularly suited for young children.

▶ STARTER IDEA for a Learning Center

CENTER TITLE: *The Wonder Machine*

NSES CONTENT STANDARD: LS 4

IDEA: A corner of your classroom would be a good location for this learning center. Allow enough floor space for children to make outlines of themselves by rolling out shelfpaper and tracing around their bodies. You may want to cover part of the floor with newspapers on which the children can work with clay and paste. If you have computer software or videos related to the human body, make them available in this center, too.

This in-class learning center—the Wonder Machine—holds a host of activities to interest children.

So that students will know what to do in the center, prepare activity cards or guide sheets that give directions for activities based on the following ideas:

- *Find Your Pulse* Children use a stopwatch or the second hand of a clock to count heartbeats, do mild exercise, and count heartbeats again. The children should graph their results.
- *Take a Breather** Children breathe on a mirror and record what they observe.
- *Bright Eyes* Children observe changes in their partners' eyes when they briefly shine a flashlight at them.
- *Different Bodies** Children trace each other while lying on shelfpaper and then, after referring to materials on the principal organs of the body and their locations, draw the organs on the shelfpaper. Some children may use a tape measure to gather data for a chart on foot sizes.
- *What's Inside?* Children use clay, construction paper, and other art materials to construct models of organ systems.

▶ **ADDITIONAL STARTER IDEAS** for Learning Centers

CENTER TITLE: *Rain Forest Adventure**

NSES CONTENT STANDARDS: LS 1 and 3

IDEA: Use art materials to draw pictures of and make models of living things unique to the rain forest; tell in which layer of the rain forest each is found.

CENTER TITLE: *Save a Species**

NSES CONTENT STANDARDS: LS 1 and 3

IDEA: Carry out research in books and the Internet to identify five endangered plants and animals, and locate on a world map where each species is found.

CENTER TITLE: *Worm Wonders*

NSES CONTENT STANDARD: LS 4

IDEA: Identify the body parts of an earthworm, describe the function(s) of each, and carry out resource book and Internet research to discover the nature of the earthworm's life cycle. If possible, also provide living earthworms at the center.

CENTER TITLE: *Something Fishy*

NSES CONTENT STANDARDS: LS 4 and 8

IDEA: Using a whole, dead (but refrigerated) fish, identify its body parts and adaptations that enable this species to swim efficiently, respire, capture prey, reproduce, and carry out its life cycle. If possible, also provide living fish at the center.

Bulletin Boards

Good bulletin boards have the potential to be something that children can both look at and learn from. There are many ways to use classroom bulletin boards to enhance life science units and extend your teaching to nonscience areas. The following list offers a few starter ideas for you. Again, asterisks indicate activities that may be particularly appropriate for young children.

▶ STARTER IDEAS for Bulletin Boards

BULLETIN BOARD TITLE: *Flower Power**

IDEA: Create vocabulary word cards for the words *stem, leaf, roots, petals, soil, air, sun,* and *water.* Make construction paper cutouts of a plant stem, leaves, petals, roots, the sun, clouds, soil, and raindrops, and display them on the bulletin board with the word cards. After the children have become familiar with the vocabulary on the word cards, provide an age-appropriate method for attaching the cards to the appropriate parts. Provide a self-correcting key.

BULLETIN BOARD TITLE: *I'm Lost**

IDEA: Divide a bulletin board into six areas, all of which can be reached by a young child. Each area should have one of the following labels and magazine pictures illustrating the label: *Insects, Fish, Amphibians, Reptiles, Birds, Mammals.* Place at the bottom of the bulletin board a folder or envelope containing a random assortment of pictures or drawings for each of the six categories. Provide some age-appropriate method for attaching the pictures to the areas, and encourage the children to spend free time at the bulletin board, placing each picture from the folder in the appropriate category.

BULLETIN BOARD TITLE: *Desert Animal Homes**

IDEA: Cover the bulletin board with easel paper, and use colored paper, crayons, pastels, paint, and other art supplies to create, with the children's assistance, a desert scene without animals. Include cactus, sand, rocks, blue sky, a shining sun, and so forth. Draw or cut out 10 magazine pictures of desert animals (e.g., a hawk, rattlesnake, scorpion, and lizard), and place these in a folder or envelope at the bottom of the bulletin board. Provide an age-appropriate method for children to attach the pictures to the bulletin board. Encourage children to use their free time to work on putting the animals in their proper places.

BULLETIN BOARD TITLE: *Plant Munchers**

IDEA: Create a large, generic plant that includes a flower, seed, fruits, leaves, stems, and roots. Add unlabeled arrows that point to each part. Put pictures of commonly eaten fruits and vegetables in a large envelope attached to the bulletin board. In their free time, have children attach the pictures to the appropriate arrows.

BULLETIN BOARD TITLE: *Producers, Consumers, and Decomposers*

IDEA: Cover the bulletin board with easel paper. Divide it into three equal-sized parts, and label each with one of these headings: *Producer, Consumer,* or *Decomposer.* As the children have free time, ask them individually or in groups to draw and label an example of each type of organism following this rule: "The three organisms must interact with one another."

BULLETIN BOARD TITLE: *Body Systems*

IDEA: Place a large drawing of the human body at one side of the bulletin board. Each week, place a large index card with the name of a body system (e.g., digestion, circulation, respiration) at the top of the other side of the bulletin board. Challenge children to attach smaller cards with labels to show the sequence of steps that occur in the identified system. For example, if the system was digestion, the children might attach cards under it that said "Food eaten," "Food enters stomach," and so on.

Field Trips

Field trips provide amazing opportunities for discovery learning, as they take children out of the classroom and immerse them in the real world. Whether you teach in a city, suburban, or small-town school, you can find ideas for field trips all around you. To understand just how true that is, think about how you could tailor each of these topics to the resources of the community in which you teach:

> Seasonal changes
> Local foods
> Area plants
> Area animals

The field trip may be to the regional aquarium or the pond down the street, but either way, children will be eager to see what the day will hold. After all, children *love* field trips! Also consider mini field trips to ecosystems in your own school yard.

Here are starter ideas for field trips for all schools. Note that asterisks indicate activities that may be particularly appropriate for young children.

▶ STARTER IDEAS for Field Trips

FIELD TRIP TITLE: *Animal Study**

IDEA: Visiting a zoological park, aquarium, or farm gives children the opportunity to observe some of the animals they have seen only in pictures, movies, and television shows. Consider having individual children or cooperative learning groups become "experts" on one animal they will see during the trip, and have them compare their research with what they actually observe during the trip. Any nearby stream, field, or park also can offer the children a chance to obtain firsthand knowledge about animal life. Because such trips can also provide opportunities for students to draw and write about interesting animals, art materials and notebooks should be available. If the location is easily accessible, visit it at different times in the year so variations in animal life can be observed.

FIELD TRIP TITLE: *Is It Alive?**

IDEA: A field trip on school grounds or to a nearby park or nature area will provide many opportunities for young children to differentiate between living and nonliving things. Prior to the trip, have children discuss the characteristics of living and nonliving things. You may wish to create a checklist that children can take along on the trip. They may discover that some objects do not easily fit into the two categories. Such an observation could prompt a good discussion of the problems that arise when objects are classified.

A field trip to an aquarium gives children the chance to see animals up close that they would otherwise see only in books or on television.

FIELD TRIP TITLE: *Searching for Changes*

IDEA: A walk through the school neighborhood can provide opportunities to observe how the environment has been modified to meet the needs of people. If farmland has been converted to a residential area, you may see some signs of previous farm use. Have the children look for evidence of resources being brought into the environment, such as electric poles, water pipes, and so forth. Also look for evidence of materials being taken out of the area, such as sewage pipes and trash bins. Emphasize that an environment may look stable, but, if we observe it for any length of time, we can see many changes occurring.

FIELD TRIP TITLE: *Plants on Parade*

IDEA: A nature walk focused on plants may reveal a great deal to children about the types and quantities of plants that live on or near the school grounds. Prior to the trip, have children predict the number of different plants they will see. During the trip, have them keep track of the kinds of plants they observe.

Many of the factors that make the city an interesting and exciting place to live also make it a place that overflows with field trip possibilities. Here are additional starter ideas that should stimulate your thinking about field trips for children in city schools:

▶ **STARTER IDEAS** for Field Trips

FIELD TRIP TITLE: *Mud Puddle Life*

IDEA: Children observe living things in and at the margins of a mud puddle after a rainstorm.

FIELD TRIP TITLE: *Dandelion Detectives*

IDEA: Children count dandelions, note where they are found, and observe their structures.

FIELD TRIP TITLE: *Squirrel Detectives*

IDEA: Children count the squirrels they see on a nature walk and note their behavior.

FIELD TRIP TITLE: *Bushes Change*

IDEA: Children study hedges and other plants growing on the school grounds to observe seasonal changes.

FIELD TRIP TITLE: *City Birds*

IDEA: Children study pigeons, sparrows, starlings, and other birds that live in the city.

FIELD TRIP TITLE: *Bug Business*

IDEA: Children go on a nature walk to locate (without touching) as many insects as they can and note what the insects are doing.

FIELD TRIP TITLE: *Is There Life in That Lot?*

IDEA: Under close supervision and at a vacant lot that is safe in every respect, children note the presence of such living things as ragweed and milkweed plants, fungi, moths, butterflies, and so forth.

FIELD TRIP TITLE: *Pyramid Power*

IDEA: Children visit restaurants and neighborhood grocery stores to learn what foods people from various cultures enjoy and then use the nutrition food pyramid to classify the foods.

Additional Field Trip Destinations

Aquarium	Food-processing facility
Botany or zoology department at local college	Forest preserve
	Natural history museum
Bird/wildlife sanctuary	Orchard
Commercial greenhouse	Pet store
Fish hatchery	Ranch, dairy, chicken, or vegetable farm
Flower or garden show	

Cooperative Learning Projects

As you consider the following starter ideas for cooperative learning projects, keep in mind the importance of stressing the three key aspects of cooperative learning (discussed in detail in Chapter 5):

1. Positive interdependence
2. Individual accountability
3. Development of group process skills

▶ STARTER IDEAS for Cooperative Learning Projects

PROJECT TITLE: *"Life's My Game, Amy's the Name"*

IDEA: Have each group research career options available to people interested in the life sciences. After the groups have finished their research, have each group select one career and train one person in the group to present the career to the remainder of the class. Emphasize that the group is responsible for getting the information needed, rehearsing the person, and providing constructive feedback. On the presentation day, the person trained should come to class dressed as a person in the career is dressed and prepared to describe what he or she does, the working conditions, the rewards, and the educational background required.

PROJECT TITLE: *We Are the . . .*

IDEA: Give each group a choice of an animal or plant phylum (you may wish to include protists), and have the groups prepare presentations that creatively teach the characteristics of the phyla. Groups should be encouraged to use music, dance, art, puppets, poetry, and other media for their presentations. Each group should build into the presentation a way of assessing whether the audience has learned the characteristics.

PROJECT TITLE: *Big as a Whale*

IDEA: Have each group prepare life-sized outlines of three animals on the school lawn, using lengths of clothesline pulled around popsicle sticks that have been placed at points marking the ends of the animal's tail, head, feet, and other body parts. In preparation for this project, each group should choose the three animals they will create and carry out library research to acquire the needed information. All the groups should create their animals on the lawn at the same time. This will permit the children to compare their own size to the sizes of various animals.

▶ **ADDITIONAL STARTER IDEAS for Learning Groups**

- Have each group select a human body system, research the system, and then present the system to the remainder of the class in a creative way.
- Challenge groups to raise popcorn plants to see which group can produce the healthiest and largest plants in the shortest period of time.
- Have groups prepare arguments for or against the operation of zoos. This can serve as the basis for a debate or discussion among groups.
- Have groups research and design a truly healthy breakfast that reflects knowledge of the nutrition food pyramid. Groups can be challenged to prepare portions of their proposed breakfasts that can be sampled by the rest of the class.

Attention Getters, Discovery Activities, and Demonstrations for Living Things

Attention Getters

For Young Learners [LS 1]

Is It a Plant or an Animal?

Materials for Each Child or Group	Scissors 3 mailing envelopes 10 colorful magazine pages that show plants, animals, and protists
Motivating Questions	• Do you see any living things in the pictures? • What is the same (different) about all the plants (animals)?
Directions	1. Distribute the materials, and ask the children to cut out all of the pictures they find of living things. 2. Write the words *animals* and *plants* on the board, pronounce them, and have the children write each word on one of the envelopes. Tell the children that there is another type of living thing called a *protist*. Make a protist envelope, and then explain that most protists are too small to see. 3. Have the children sort their pictures into the plant, animal, and protist envelopes.
Science Content for the Teacher	There are many different ways to group living things. A common classification system uses three categories: plants, animals, and protists. Plants have cell walls that have cellulose and make food through photosynthesis. Animal cells do not have cell walls. Their cells are bounded by cell membranes. Animals take food into their bodies. Protozoa and slime molds are classified as protists.

How Does Color Help Animals?

Materials for Each Child or Group	Sheet of green construction paper Sheet of brown construction paper	Scissors Paper leaf pattern

Motivating Questions
- What kinds of animals eat insects?
- What are some ways that insects can escape from other animals?

Directions

1. Distribute the materials, and have the children use the leaf pattern to draw and then cut out one brown leaf and one green leaf. Have them cut out a few small green and brown squares that are about 2.5 centimeters (1 inch) on edge.
2. Tell the children that they should pretend the squares are insects. Have them place the green insects on the brown leaf and the brown insects on the green leaf.
3. Ask them how hard they think it would be to find the insects if they were birds.
4. Have the children put the green insects on the green leaf, and ask the question again.

Science Content for the Teacher

Many animals have protective coloration that increases their chances of escaping predators. Insects that have the same color as their background stay still when predators are near and blend into their background, which increases their chances of survival.

Are You a Good Animal Detective?

Materials	Sheet of easel paper	Marking pen

Motivating Questions
- What animals do you think we will see outside?
- How many animals do you think we will see?

Directions

1. Take the children on a 10-minute nature walk around the school grounds to identify the animals that live around the school.
2. On your return to the classroom, prepare a three-column chart and list the children's recollections of the types and quantities of animals seen. Also note where the animals were seen—for example, under a rock.

Science Content for the Teacher

Life is both diverse and widespread. Any lawn, playground, or natural area on or near the school will have an abundance of animals. Depending on your locale and the season, expect to see squirrels, birds, cats, and dogs. Search for insects and other small creatures under rocks and near moist areas such as the ground near a water fountain or a mud puddle as well as on the bark of trees. Caution students not to handle insects and animals.

How Are Seeds the Same and Different?

Materials for Each Child or Group

One common fruit per group. (*Note:* Try to have a variety of fruits available, including oranges, apples, pears, grapefruit, peaches, and plums.)
Lightweight plastic serrated knives (if you are working with older children)
Paper towels
Drawing paper
Hand lens

Motivating Questions

- Do you think your fruit has a seed?
- Do you think your fruit has more than one seed?
- What do you think the seed or seeds in your fruit will look like?
- Do you think different fruits will have seeds that are the same or different?

Directions

1. Distribute the materials, and give each group one or more fruits. Before they cut open their fruits, have the groups predict the number, shape, size, and color of the seed or seeds and then draw what they think their seed or seeds will look like.
2. Have the groups cut open the fruits and examine the seeds. *Safety Note:* Cut open the fruit for younger children after the groups have completed their drawings.
3. Have the groups compare the seeds, and then discuss the variety in the number and types of seeds in fruits.

Science Content for the Teacher

Although there is great variety in the seeds of common fruits, fruits of the same type have the same type of seeds. An interesting addition to your discussion would be a consideration of the great size and variation in seeds, with the coconut as one of the largest seeds in the natural world. You may wish to point out to the children that many types of seeds are important to humans. Examples include corn, oats, and wheat.

Can You Grow a Sweet Potato Plant Indoors?

Materials

1 small sweet potato   6 toothpicks
1 glass that is wider than the potato's diameter   Water

Motivating Questions

- Do you think the sweet potato is a root or a stem?
- Where does a new potato plant get food?

Directions

1. Distribute the materials and have the children wash the sweet potatoes to remove any excess dirt.
2. Have each group of children stick the toothpicks into the potato so it can be suspended in the glass with the narrow end submerged in the water. (About one-fourth should be in the water.)
3. After each group has prepared its potato, put the potatoes in a warm, well-lit area of the room. Children will need to add water periodically to replace that used by the growing potato plant and lost through evaporation.

Science Content for the Teacher

Unlike the white potato, which is a tuber, or underground stem, the sweet potato is a root. The rapid root and leaf growth that will occur is partially due to the availability of starch in the fleshy material within the sweet potato root.

Do Insects Have the Same Kinds of Body Parts?

Materials   1 collection of common insects with different insects in different jars with net tops
(grasshoppers, crickets, butterflies, flies, ants)
Hand lens
Drawing paper

Motivating Questions
- Are all these animals insects?
- How are these animals alike? How are they different?

Directions
1. Have the groups observe the insect or insects in each jar. Provide a hand lens for those who want to make closer observations. Encourage the children to make a descriptive model and drawing of each insect.
2. After each group has made observations and drawings, begin a discussion of how the insects are the same and different.

Science Content for the Teacher   Although insects vary greatly in size, color, and the detailed shapes of their body parts, all insects have three main body parts: head, thorax, and abdomen. Unlike spiders and other arachnids that have eight legs, insects are six-legged creatures. Insects have two antennae and wings. They are invertebrates with *exoskeletons,* relatively hard exterior body coverings that protect the softer interior parts.

The Mystery of the 17-Year Locust

Materials   Access to the Internet
Science resource books and encyclopedias
Posterpaper and markers
Drawing or picture of an adult cicada (misnamed the *17-year locust*)

Motivating Questions
- What does this picture remind you of?
- How old do you think this creature is?
- What hypotheses can you make about its life cycle?

Directions
1. Have the groups do research to learn about the life cycle of the cicada, also known as the *17-year locust*. They should find out where and when it lays its eggs, where the nymph stage of the insect lives, when the nymph becomes an adult, and the effects the adult insect has on its surroundings when it lays its eggs.
2. Have the children make drawings of the cicada at the various stages of its life cycle.
3. Bring the groups back together to discuss what they have learned. In particular, why is the cicada sometimes called the *17-year locust?*

Science Content for the Teacher   The species of cicada that has a 17-year life cycle is commonly known as the *17-year locust.* It is a member of the grasshopper family and is not a locust. Its life cycle includes three stages: The adult female lays eggs in slits cut in young twigs, and then larvae develop. The larvae drop from the trees, burrow into the ground, and suck on juices from roots. After 13 or 17 years, depending on the species, nymphs emerge from the ground and become winged adults, which live for about a week.

Discovery Activities

How Is a Kitten Different from a Stone?

Objective	• Children will describe three ways in which a kitten (or other small animal) is different from a stone.

Science Processes Emphasized	Observing	Communicating
	Classifying	Inferring

Materials for Each Child or Group
Small animal (or a picture of a small animal)
Stone
One picture of a living thing and one picture of a nonliving thing

Motivation
Keep both the kitten and the stone out of sight at the beginning of the activity. Secretly pick up the stone and tell the class that you would like them to guess what is in your hand. After a few guesses, show the stone and tell them that today's activity will teach them how a stone is different from a living thing. Show them the kitten (or picture of a kitten), and begin the lesson.

Directions
1. Ask the children to make observations of both the kitten and the stone.
2. Make a list of their observations on the chalkboard.
3. Begin a discussion of their observations of the stone and the kitten, focusing on the differences between living and nonliving things.
4. Distribute one living thing and one nonliving thing to each child or group. Have them study the objects and think about the differences between the living and nonliving things.
5. Have the children summarize what they have learned about the differences between living and nonliving things.

Key Discussion Questions
1. What are some nonliving things you have noticed on your way to school? *Water. Sun. Wind.*
2. What are some living things you have noticed on your way to school? *Children. Plants. Animals.*
3. What are some of the living things in this classroom? *Children. Teachers. Plants.*
4. What are some of the nonliving things in this classroom? *Books. Desks. Pencils.*

Science Content for the Teacher
Living things differ in many ways from nonliving things. The characteristics of living things—the functions of life—include reproduction; energy production, acquisition, and/or use; homeostasis; internal transport of materials; responsiveness to stimuli; secretion and excretion of waste products; and respiration.

Extensions
Science: A field trip in conjunction with this activity will enable children to observe living and nonliving things in the environment and begin to differentiate one type of living thing, plants, from another type of living thing, animals. This would be an excellent time for children to begin thinking about the fact that a specific living thing (such as the kitten) more closely resembles its parents in appearance than it resembles other living things.

Social Studies: Some children may begin to think about the relationships of living things to nonliving things. Shelter and implements are among the uses of nonliving things that you can highlight. You may wish to have children begin to think about and discuss how nonliving things, such as volcanoes, violent weather, and landslides, affect the lives of humans.

For Young Learners [LS 2]

What Is a Seed?

Objective
- The children will be able to describe a seed as something capable of growth.

Science Processes Emphasized

Predicting   Interpreting data
Observing   Contrasting variables
Recording

Materials for Each Child or Group

Large cardboard box cut 2 to 4 inches tall and lined with plastic
Soil or starting mixture (vermiculite plus soil)
Collections of seeds and other small things ("red-hot" candy, marbles, pebbles)
Chartpaper
1 index card per student

Motivation

Ask the children to bring in seeds and other small items for some science experiments. When the candy comes in, tell them they will begin their study of seeds and discover whether the candy will grow.

Directions

1. Begin by setting out samples of the small things that have been brought in. Ask the students to describe the items while you list their observations on the chartpaper.
2. Have each group record in pictures and in words the appearance of each item at the start of the experiment. In addition, each group can glue an item to an index card and then use the index card to record observations from the activity.
3. Have each group decide how many of each item should be planted and the depth of planting. Explain that the amount of water, light, warmth, and so on should be the same for each item. These things will be easy to control if the samples are planted in the same box.
4. Have each group label each row with the name of the item planted. Then, set aside a short period of time each day for maintenance and data gathering. Encourage the children to keep a daily log of what they see.
5. Some children may want to peek at the items during the experiment. If they do this, they need to think about the number of each item that was planted and how they can make their inspection without disturbing the others. One way to observe germination without disturbing the seeds is to place moist paper toweling in a glass jar and "plant" the item between the toweling and the glass. Such a jar will allow students to see what is going on in the soil in the boxes, but perhaps it can be kept a secret until the students have had the pleasure of digging up a few of their own seeds.

Young children enjoy bringing in their own seeds and observing how they grow.

6. When the seeds have been growing for awhile, have the children dig up samples of each type of seed. They can make observations, record them, and compare their new observations with the observations they made at the start of the experiment.

7. After some items have sprouted, it would be useful to divide the original set of items into growers and nongrowers. With this set to examine, students should begin to investigate where the items come from and develop a general definition of a *true seed*.

Key Discussion Questions

1. In what ways are all these items alike? *They are all small.*
2. How many items of each type should be planted? *More than one or two, since some might die before they come up and can be seen.*
3. How deeply should they be planted? *Answers will vary based upon gardening experience, but common sense usually prevails.*
4. What should be done about the amount of water, sunlight, temperature, and so on that the items receive? *They should be kept the same so that all seeds have the same chance of living.*
5. What is the biggest difference among the items at the end of the experiment? *Some grow and some don't.*
6. What did some seeds become? *They grew into new plants.*

Science Content for the Teacher

Seeds come in all sizes, from those as small as the period at the end of a sentence to others as big as a coconut. Shape can also vary dramatically, from round and smooth to pyramidlike. Seeds have protective shells (seed coats) that keep the embryonic plant alive. Stored food will provide the energy for the seedling to reach the soil surface and begin producing food of its own.

In order to survive, some plants produce *great* numbers of seeds, and others produce seeds with structures (such as the hooks on burrs and the "wings" on maple seeds) that enable them to be dispersed. Some seeds even look like insects, which discourages seed-eating birds from consuming them.

Even with this great diversity, seeds differ significantly from all the nonseed items in this activity by being able to *grow* and reproduce their own kind (much to the despair of some candy lovers!).

Extensions

Science: You may wish to cut open some fruits and have the children find and describe the seeds. Some students may then wish to produce a poster or bulletin board with as many kinds of seeds as can be collected. The seeds can be grouped by size, shape, or color.

Math: Some students may be interested in collecting seeds to be used as "counters." These students can sort the seeds into sets and arrange them in order from smallest to largest.

▶ *For Young Learners* [LS 3]

Who Goes There?

Objective

• The children will be able to match pictures of common animals with the animals' footprints.

Science Processes Emphasized

Observing

Inferring

Materials for Each Child or Group

Set of pictures of the animals for which you have footprints
Set of pictures showing the various environments in which the animals live
Set of animal name cards
Construction paper headband
Paper feathers of various colors

Motivation

Hand out the animal pictures and a headband to each group. Suggest that they pretend they are teams of animal trackers, and explain that each team will be awarded one feather for each animal they successfully track.

Directions

1. Before beginning this activity, you will need a set of unlabeled animal footprints and a set of pictures illustrating environments in which the animals are likely to be found.
2. Hold up pictures of the animal track and its environment. After some discussion, have the children try to think of the animal being described. The group members can discuss the possibilities among themselves before the group suggests an animal. Each group should elect a chief to be their spokesperson.
3. When all the teams are ready, have each chief hold up the picture of the animal his or her group selected. Encourage each chief to tell why his or her group's choice is the correct one.
4. Staple a paper feather to the headband of each chief that is correct. The job of being chief is then rotated to the next person in each group, and the game continues.

Key Discussion Questions

1. Which of the tracks comes from the biggest animal? *Answers will depend on the tracks and the pictures you are using.*
2. Which of the tracks comes from the smallest animal? *Answers will vary.*
3. Which of the tracks comes from an animal with claws that stick out? *Answers will vary.*
4. Which of the tracks belongs to an animal that can climb trees? *Answers will vary.*
5. Hold up the pictures of various environments (e.g., a treetop for squirrels and an open plain with trees in Africa for elephants), and ask which of the animals might be found in them. Ask the students to try to guess which footprint might be found in most environments. (Be sure to have the teams explain why they decided on particular footprints.)

Science Content for the Teacher

Footprints hold clues about the lives and environments of the animals that made them. Very large footprints often belong to large animals or to animals that travel over soft terrain. For example, the relatively large feet of the snowshoe rabbit support its weight on snow, thus allowing it to travel well on terrain that hinders most other animals. Most animals that live on the open range have evolved smaller feet with hooves that allow them to run fast on fairly smooth, hard land. Some footprints show evidence of claws used for defense as well as climbing. Retractable claws are an obvious benefit to animals that must be able to run quickly and silently before catching their prey.

Extensions

Science: Obtain or reproduce pictures of various tracks showing something happening (e.g., animals walking and then running). Have the teams determine what happened.

Some students may wish to research the topic of fossils, especially fossilized tracks, and what scientists have learned about the animals that made them. Other students may enjoy making answer boards on which others try to match pictures of animals with pictures of their footprints.

Art: Students may want to make pictures from a set of linoleum printing blocks of footprints.

> *For Middle-Level Learners* [LS 5]

Male and Female Guppies: What's the Difference?

Objective	• The children will observe the physical characteristics of male and female guppies.
Science Processes Emphasized	Observing Classifying
Materials for Each Child or Group	Male and female guppies 2 clean liter- or quart-size jars filled with aquarium water Dry fish food Hand lens
Motivation	Ask the children if they know what a guppy is. If possible, have them describe guppies without the benefit of guppies to observe. Now display the guppies you will be using for the activity, and tell the children that they will have a chance to make careful observations of male and female guppies.

Directions

1. Distribute a jar containing aquarium water, a female guppy, and a hand lens to each child or group.
2. Ask each child or group to observe the external characteristics of the guppy and make a drawing of it, labeling the body parts. Encourage them to shade in parts of their drawing to show the guppy's markings.
3. Once the drawings are completed, distribute a jar containing aquarium water and a male guppy. Have the children observe the male guppy and then make a labeled drawing of it.
4. Allow the children to visit with one another to see if their male guppy resembles other male guppies and if their female guppy resembles other female guppies.
5. Circulate around the room, and sprinkle a small amount of dry fish food on the surface of each container. Ask the children to observe the feeding behavior of the guppy.

Key Discussion Questions

1. How can you tell the difference between a male and a female guppy? *The female is usually larger, with a gray color and a fan-shaped fin; the male is smaller, with patches of color and a tubelike part at the base of its tail.*
2. How does the location of the guppy's mouth make it easier and safer for the guppy to feed? *It's at the top of its head, which lets it feed on surface food without having to lift its head out of the water; this makes it easier for it to sneak up on food.*

Science Content for the Teacher

Guppies are tropical fish. The male is smaller than the female but has a larger tail. It is also more brightly colored. The female is usually a uniform gray. The female has a fan-shaped anal fin. The male's anal fin is pointed and tubelike.

Extensions   *Science:* The demonstration on the birth of guppies, described later in this chapter (pages 313–314), is an effective follow-up to this activity.

Art: Some children may wish to create larger drawings of the guppies they have observed. Drawing paper and a supply of pastels will assist them in such a project. Encourage the children to reproduce nature's coloration faithfully by using the appropriate colors and shades of pastels. You may wish to spray fixative on the children's finished drawings to preserve them.

For Middle-Level Learners [LS 6]

Do Mealworms Like or Dislike Light?

Objectives
- The children will set up and carry out an experiment to determine how a mealworm responds to light.
- The children will collect, summarize, and interpret the data they gather.

Science Processes Emphasized

Observing   Recording data
Interpreting data

Materials for Each Child or Group

Live mealworm (available in a pet store)
Small flashlight
20 cm (about 8 in.) circle of paper divided into 8 pie-shaped sections

Motivation   Ask the class how they can determine if people like something. The children will suggest that they can ask people or try something and see if people smile, frown, or become angry. Some children may suggest that the number of times a person does something could be used to determine what the person likes. Tell the children that they will be finding out how well mealworms like being in the dark and that because mealworms do not talk, the children will have to do an experiment to find the answer.

Directions
1. Display the mealworms, and discuss some strategies that the children could use to find out what a mealworm likes. Show the circle that has been divided into eight parts, and explain that it is the tool they will use to find out whether a mealworm likes light.
2. Have the children prepare their own circles and divide them into eight parts. They should number the sections from 1 to 8.
3. Place the flashlight about 30 centimeters from section 1 on the circle. Direct the light toward the center of the circle, darken the room, and have the children observe your setup.
4. Have the children place a light source near their section 8 and the mealworm in the center of the circle where all the lines intersect. The children should record the number of the section toward which the mealworm moves. This should be repeated 10 times.
5. Have the children develop charts or graphs to summarize their findings. Finally, have the class suggest a strategy for combining the results from all the groups so that conclusions can be drawn.

Science Content for the Teacher   Mealworms usually avoid lighted areas. They are frequently found in bins of old grain or meal, which provide dark, dry environments. A mealworm that enters a lit area will lose touch with its food supply and possibly fall prey to birds or other predators.

Key Discussion Questions	1. Why should you do this experiment many times before concluding that a mealworm likes or dislikes light? *Mealworms don't always move in the right direction. It takes several trials to determine a pattern of behavior.*
	2. What other things might make a mealworm respond by moving? *They might be afraid of us. They might not like the heat that comes from the light. They see light from other parts of the room.*
	3. Why might a mealworm avoid light? *It likes dark. The light may mean danger to the mealworm.*

Extensions	*Science:* Some children may wish to design and conduct experiments to see how mealworms respond to heat, cold, moisture, dryness, loud sounds, and different kinds of food.
	Language Arts: Have the children pretend that they are mealworms and write stories describing their adventures in a land of giants.

For Middle-Level Learners [LS 7]

How Does Light Affect the Growth of Plants?

Objectives	• The children will design and conduct an experiment to test the effect of light on the growth of grass.
	• The children will observe and record the color and length of grass grown under two conditions: light and dark.

Science Processes Emphasized	Formulating hypotheses Experimenting
	Interpreting data

Materials Needed	2 paper cups
	1/4 tsp. of grass seed
	Potting soil or synthetic plant-growing material
	Light source that can be placed about 25 cm (about 10 in.) above the cup (a fluorescent grow-light fixture would be best)
	Ruler
	Graph paper
	Easel paper for class data

Motivation	Tell the class that they are going to observe and measure the effect something has on plants. Display the grass seeds and related materials. Ask the children to guess what they will be investigating.

Directions	1. Distribute the materials, and have the children label one cup *light* and one cup *dark*. They should also record the date on each cup. Tell them to fill each cup two-thirds full of soil, scatter a pinch of seeds across the surface, and then lightly cover the seeds with more soil. Tell the children to punch a few holes into the bottom of the cup to allow excess water to drain.
	2. Ask each group to predict what will happen if one cup is placed in a dark location and one cup is placed in a light location for three days. Have the groups record their predictions. This would be a good time to have a class discussion about the range of predictions that are made.

3. Have the children add the same amount of water to each cup and then put their cups in the appropriate environments. *They should plan to observe the cups every three days.*
4. When the groups make their observations, they should record the appearance, color, and average length of plants. The determination of length will be challenging because the groups will need to invent a strategy that does not require the measurement of every plant. One strategy might be to measure five plants from different parts of the cup and average the measurements. Another would be to simply record the total height of the sample. The length measurements as well as other observations should be recorded on a data sheet, which should be maintained for about two weeks.

Key Discussion Questions

1. If we want to see if the seeds need light to grow, what must we do to the water and temperature of the plants? *We have to keep the water and temperature the same for both cups.*
2. Why did all the seeds start to grow equally well? *Seeds don't need light to sprout.*
3. Why did the plants in the dark stop growing and turn yellow after awhile? *They ran out of food. They needed light to grow.*

Science Content for the Teacher

Grass seeds contain a small amount of stored food in their cotyledons, which allows them to begin growing. When the food is used up, the plant must rely on sunlight for the energy required for further growth.

Extension

Science/Nutrition: Some students may wish to obtain seeds at a health food store that are appropriate for sprouting (mung beans, alfalfa, lettuce). Once the seeds have sprouted, the class can have a feast while discussing the nutrients found in the sprouts.

Demonstrations

For Young Learners [LS 3]

The Curious Gerbils

Note: This demonstration is a long-term classroom project that involves proper care of living organisms. You must face many questions if you embark upon it, not the least of which is what you will do with the gerbils that are born in the classroom. You will quickly run out of appropriate living space for these creatures, as they are capable of reproducing at an alarming rate. The children will undoubtedly volunteer to take excess gerbils. However, do not assume that every child who wants a gerbil will be able to provide appropriate care or that his or her family will want to have a new addition to the household. Also be aware that some of the children who may want gerbils may be allergic to them. *You should spend time thinking about both the benefits and problems associated with raising animals in the classroom before beginning this project.*

Objective

- The children will observe the characteristics of gerbils.
- The children will provide appropriate care for gerbils in the classroom.
- The children will observe the birth of gerbils in the classroom.

Science Processes Emphasized	Observing Inferring
Materials	Male gerbil Gerbil food Female gerbil Supply of lettuce Gerbil cage with exercise wheel, water bottle, nesting material (cedar shavings, newspaper, cloth, and so on)

Motivation Keep the presence of the gerbils and the cage supplies secret. Tell the children that they are going to have an opportunity to meet some classroom pets. Do not divulge what kind of animals the pets are. Ask the children if they think they can be responsible for the care of some pets in the classroom. Assuming the answer is yes, proceed with the demonstration.

Directions
1. Display all the materials and the male and female gerbils.
2. Place the nesting material, food, and exercise wheel in the cage and fill the water bottle. Have the children discuss the purpose of each object in the cage.
3. Before placing the male and female gerbils in the cage, allow the children to observe them.
4. Discuss the importance of proper care of the gerbils. Talk about the children's responsibilities and appropriate rules for the gerbils' care.
5. If you are fortunate, within a month or two you may have a litter of gerbils. In this event, have the children observe the changes that occur as the tiny creatures begin to appear more and more like their parents.

Key Discussion Questions
1. Are gerbils mammals? *Yes. They are alive, they drink their mother's milk, and their bodies are covered with hair/fur.*
2. What do you think gerbils need in order to survive and stay healthy in the classroom? *Answers will vary but may include food, water, nesting material, air, exercise, and some peace and quiet.*
3. Various other questions concerning the children's responsibilities for the continuing care and feeding of the gerbils should be asked. Such questions should focus upon what the responsibilities will be, how they should be carried out, and who will carry them out.

Science Content for the Teacher Gerbils are small animals that are easy to care for in the classroom. They are covered with hair, give birth, and suckle their young; they are true mammals. Young female gerbils may bear young every six to eight weeks.

Extensions *Science:* Students may be interested in learning about the care of puppies, cats, guinea pigs, hamsters, and other animals.

Art: The class may want to make drawings of both the male and female gerbil and any babies. The children can use commercially available crayon-like pastels to reproduce the coloring of the animals.

▶ *For Young Learners* [S&T 3]

Is It Alive?

Objective • The children will observe and describe the differences between living and nonliving things.

Science Processes Emphasized	Observing Communicating	Inferring

Materials   Living animal (fish, insect, mouse)
Living plant
Nonliving thing (shoe, pencil, book)
Wind-up toy that makes sounds (or nonelectric ticking clock with second hand)
Cardboard box with fitted top

Motivation   Prior to class, place the mechanical toy or ticking clock in a box with a fitted top. Do not tell the children what is in the box. Have volunteers come forward to listen to the toy or clock in the box. Tell the children that they are going to discover some things about the object in the box and how to tell the difference between things that are alive and things that are not.

Directions
1. Hold up for observation the animal, the plant, and the shoe, book, or pencil. Display each object one at a time so that the children can focus their observations.
2. On the chalkboard, create a chart on which to record the children's observations. Provide a space at the bottom of the chart to write their guesses about the object in the box and whether or not it is alive.
3. Once all the observations have been recorded, play a game of 20 questions with the children to help them refine their thinking. Suggest that they use their observation when asking questions. *Hint:* Actually peek into the box after each question. A little acting on your part will help maintain interest in the game.
4. Finally, display the object in the box and engage the children in a discussion of the differences between living and nonliving things.

Key Discussion Questions
1. In what ways are living and nonliving things the same? *Answers will vary and may include such observations as living and nonliving things can be the same color or size. They can both be soft or hard.*
2. In what ways are living things and nonliving things different? *Answers will vary and may include the idea that nonliving things stay the same, last a long time, don't change very much; living things like plants have seeds; animals have baby animals.*

Science Content for the Teacher   Living things and nonliving things may share some common characteristics. They both may move; they both may make noise; they may be the same color or weight. However, things that are alive grow, change, or develop from infant to adult and are able to reproduce their own kind.

Extension   *Health:* Discuss the special responsibilities involved in caring for living things that are different from the responsibilities involved in caring for nonliving things. Some children may want to make drawings or posters that show how to care for pets or other living things.

▶ *For Middle-Level Learners* **[LS 5]**

The Birth of Guppies

Note: This demonstration can be used as a follow-up to the discovery activity on male and female guppies described earlier in this chapter (pages 308–309).

Objectives
- The children will observe the construction of an aquarium.
- The children will describe the roles of male and female guppies in the reproductive process.

Science Processes Emphasized	Observing Inferring

Materials

Fish aquarium	Thermometer
Aged tapwater at room temperature	Small container with 2 male guppies
Aquarium sand and gravel	Small container with 4 female guppies
1 dip net	Light source (a reading lamp can be used)
2 or 3 nursery traps	Dry fish food
Assorted freshwater plants, including *Anarchis,* duckweed, and eelgrass	

Motivation

Ask the children if they have ever seen the birth of guppies. After a discussion of any observations they have made of guppies reproducing, tell them that within the next few weeks they may be able to see guppies being born. Display the aquarium and other materials.

Directions

1. Have the children observe all the materials that you have placed on display.
2. Begin assembling the aquarium by placing a 5-centimeter (2-inch) layer of sand on its floor. Plant eelgrass in the sand. Now add the aged tap water; do it gently so as to avoid stirring up the sand. Float the duckweed and *Anarchis* in the water.
3. Put the thermometer in the water and place the light source nearby. The light source will need to be moved back and forth during the demonstration so as to maintain the water temperature at 25°C (75°F).
4. Place the male and female guppies in the aquarium.
5. Float the nursery traps in the aquarium, and sprinkle some fish food on the water's surface.
6. Maintain the aquarium over a two- or three-week period, and encourage the children to make observations of any changes that occur in the shape of the female guppies. A pregnant female will develop a bulging abdomen. Use the dip net to place each pregnant female in its own nursery trap. This increases the chances that the soon-to-be-born babies will survive, for the traps will protect the new guppies from hungry adult fish.

Key Discussion Questions

1. Why did we plant eelgrass and other aquarium plants in the aquarium? *Answers will vary. They may include: So that some living things in the aquarium would have plants to eat.*
2. What does the male guppy do in the reproductive process? *Places sperm in the female guppy.*
3. What does the female guppy do in the reproductive process? *Produces the eggs that get fertilized; has a place inside her body where the new guppies begin to develop.*

Science Content for the Teacher

For this demonstration, you must know how to assemble and maintain a simple freshwater aquarium. The preceding directions provide some of the basic information. If you wish to increase the likelihood of maintaining a healthy aquarium for more than one or two weeks, it would be worthwhile to talk with a knowledgeable salesperson in a pet store to learn the details of raising and caring for tropical fish in general and guppies in particular. Additional materials—such as water heaters, pumps, and filters—are necessary if you wish to keep the aquarium functioning all through the year. This equipment is commonly available at pet shops.

For Middle-Level Learners [LS 7]

The Insect Aquarium

Note: This demonstration should be done in the spring.

Objectives	• The children will observe the construction of a freshwater insect aquarium. • Children will infer the reasons for the placement of various materials in the aquarium.
Science Processes Emphasized	Observing Inferring
Materials	4 liter wide-mouth jar (about a gallon) or a small plastic or glass aquarium Source of fresh pond or stream water Collection of live water plants and insects from a pond or stream Small twigs from the pond or stream Pebbles and rocks found at the water's edge Clean aquarium sand (available from a pet shop) Fine mesh screening to cover the top of the aquarium
Motivation	Tell the children that you have gathered a variety of materials to use to construct a freshwater aquarium. Discuss the difference between freshwater and saltwater. Tell the children that the aquarium you are going to build will not contain fish but may contain other interesting creatures. Their job will be to give you ideas as you construct it.

Directions

1. In the spring prior to the demonstration, gather freshwater and a variety of plants and aquatic insects from a local pond or stream. Keep the specimens fresh, and take them to class.
2. In the classroom, fill the bottom of the container with about 5 centimeters (about 2 inches) of sand, and root the water plants in the sand. Place a few large twigs at the side of the jar in a way that roots their ends in the sand, and put some rocks and pebbles on the surface of the sand.
3. Gently add freshwater until the water level is about 12 centimeters (about 5 inches) from the top. Float some twigs on the surface so that any insects emerging from the water have a place to stay. Cover the top with the mesh, and put the aquarium where it can receive sunlight and benefit from air circulation.
4. Encourage the children to create an initial descriptive model of the aquarium and its contents, make daily observations of the aquarium and to infer the reasons for some of the changes they observe.

Key Discussion Questions

1. Why do you think we are doing this demonstration in the spring? *Answers will vary and may include the idea that insects hatch in the spring.*
2. Why do you think we put the aquarium in the sunlight? *Answers will vary and may include the idea that the plants need sunlight to make food.*

Science Content for the Teacher

Insects you may be able to find in a pond are the nymphs of dragonflies, water boatmen, mosquito larvae, mayflies, and water beetles. Insects are easily found in the shallow water at the edge of a pond or stream.

Extension

Science/Language Arts: After about a week of observation, ask the children to write a poem entitled "Changes" that will include at least three observations they have made of the aquarium.

The Human Body

Attention Getters

▶ *For Young Learners* [S&T 1]

How Can We Help People See Us at Night?

Materials	1 sheet of dark construction paper Transparent tape
	1 small mirror 1 flashlight
	Silver glitter Bicycle reflector (optional)
	Glue

Motivating Questions
- Is it hard or easy to see people who are walking or riding bikes at night?
- What should people who are out at night do to keep themselves from being hit by a car?

Directions
1. Darken the room, and ask the children if it would be hard or easy to see a person on a bicycle at night wearing a shirt that is the color of the construction paper. *Note:* This would be an excellent time to have a brief discussion of bicycle safety.
2. Shine the flashlight near the paper, and have the children pretend that the light is an automobile headlight. Ask how visible the person would be if the children were in a car. Tape the mirror to one side of the paper, and repeat the demonstration. Be sure the children notice that mirrors do not help if the light beam does not shine directly on them.
3. Draw a circle on the paper, fill the circle with glue, and sprinkle it with silver glitter. Try to produce some layers of glitter so that not all the glitter is flat on the paper. Your intent is to replicate a bicycle reflector. Have the children compare the extent to which the paper is lit without anything on it, with the mirror on it, and with the glued-on glitter. If you are able to obtain a bicycle reflector, attach that to the paper, as well.

Science Content for the Teacher
How well we see something depends on how well light is reflected from the object. A bicycle reflector contains many tiny mirrorlike objects that reflect light from many directions, so it is easy to see at night.

▶ *For Young Learners* [SPSP 1]

What Things Do We Do That Keep Us Healthy and Strong, and When Do We Do Them?

Materials	1 large clock with hour and minute hands
	Easel paper and marker

Motivating Questions
- What things do you do before, during, and after school that help keep you healthy and strong?
- What things could you do that you are not doing now?

Directions	1. Begin by explaining to the children that they are going to discuss what an imaginary child named Pat might do to stay healthy and strong. Tell them that you are going to make a chart on which you will record their ideas.
	2. Set the hands of the clock to 7:00 A.M., review or teach time telling, and have the children give their ideas about what Pat might be doing. For example, 7:00 A.M. might be the time for washing, 7:15 A.M. might be the time that Pat eats a healthy breakfast, 7:30 A.M. might be the time that Pat brushes her or his teeth, and 7:45 A.M. might be the time that Pat puts on a seat belt for the bus ride to school. Carry this through the school day.

Science Content for the Teacher   Children do many things in the course of a day that contribute to their health and well-being. The sequence of activities is relatively constant. By thinking about what more they could do and by trying to fit new ideas into their sequence, they can improve their health.

> *For Young Learners* [LS 3]

How Do Your Ears Help You Recognize Things?

Materials	1 small rubber ball	1 empty glass
	1 sheet of newspaper	1 glass of water
	1 empty soda bottle	
	Movable room divider or other object to use as a visual screen	

Motivating Questions
- Which sounds are easy (hard) to guess?
- Why are some sounds easy to guess and some sounds hard to guess?

Directions	1. Keep all materials behind a screen for the duration of the demonstration. Ask for volunteers to sit in front of the screen facing the class.
	2. Use the newspaper, ball, soda bottle, and glass of water to produce various sounds—such as the crumpling of paper, the bounce of a ball, the noise of water poured from glass to glass, or the sound made blowing across the soda bottle—and have the volunteers try to identify them. Discuss what factors make it easy or difficulty to recognize the sources of sounds.

Science Content for the Teacher   The human senses are important because they allow us to take in information about our surroundings. The sense we make of the sounds we hear depends on a variety of factors, including our previous experience, whether the sound is clear or muffled, how loud the sound is, and the sensitivity of our ears.

> *For Middle-Level Learners* [LS 4]

How Does Light Affect Your Eyes?

Note: This Attention Getter can be done as a cooperative group activity, if you have a flashlight and drawing paper for each group.

Materials	1 flashlight	Drawing paper

Motivating Questions
- Why do people sometimes wear dark glasses?
- Does your vision change when you go from a well-lit room to a dark room?

Directions
1. Distribute the drawing paper to the children. Have the children carefully observe one another's eyes and make drawings that show the iris (the pigmented part of the eye) and the pupil (the entryway of light into the eye).
2. Darken the room somewhat so that the children can observe changes in the pupil, and have them note additional changes when the lights are turned on.
3. Ask for a volunteer to come to the front of the room, and then select two observers. Have the observers look into the volunteer's eyes and tell the rest of the class how large the pupils are.
4. While the observers are studying the volunteer's eyes, briefly shine the flashlight perpendicular to the volunteer's eyes. Have the observers describe any changes they see. *Safety Note:* Do not shine the light into the volunteer's eyes. Light coming from the side will be sufficient to cause the pupils to dilate.

Science Content for the Teacher
Our capacity to see depends on how much light enters the pupil and reaches the retina. It is difficult to see when too little light enters. Too much light can cause severe damage to the eyes. Muscles in the iris of the eye cause the pupil to become larger or smaller, depending on the availability of light. It is interesting to note that both eyes will react to changes in light intensity even if the changing light conditions occur for one eye.

▶ *For Middle-Level Learners* [SPSP 6]

What Is in That Cereal?

Materials
2 or 3 large cereal boxes, including at least one heavily sweetened cereal
1 small cereal box for each group
1 transparency made from a cereal nutrition label

Motivating Questions
• Which of these boxes of cereal do you think has the most calories per serving?
• Which of these boxes of cereal do you think has the most vitamins and minerals?

Directions
1. Project the cereal nutrition label, and review the categories of information on the label.
2. Distribute one cereal box to each group, and ask the groups to interpret the information on the nutrition labels. Be sure they note the number of calories per serving, the suggested serving size, and the percentage of sugars and fats in the cereal as well as the types and amounts of vitamins and minerals.

Science Content for the Teacher
Although cereal can provide some of the carbohydrates the body needs, many cereals have added sugar, which is not good for you. The nutrition information provided on a food label can be very helpful to consumers. As children study the labels, they should note the differences between various cereals and the contributions made by milk to the nutrient values of the cereals.

▶ *For Middle-Level Learners* [SPSP 6]

What Is in Cream?

Materials
1 pt. of pasteurized heavy whipping cream   1 mixing bowl
Electric hand mixer or eggbeater

Motivating Questions
• How is cream the same or different from milk?
• What do you predict will happen if we beat cream with a hand mixer?

Directions
1. Ask the children how cream differs from milk. Pour the cream into the bowl, and have children make observations about its consistency and color.
2. Ask for volunteers to take turns using the mixer or eggbeater to churn the cream. Have some children act as observers who describe to the class the changes they observe as the cream is beaten.
3. In time, butter will begin to form and the bowl will contain butter and buttermilk. Ask for volunteers to taste the buttermilk and butter.

Science Content for the Teacher
Cream has a very high fat content. When it is shaken vigorously, the fat begins to form granules. These granules gradually clump together, making butter. Although the color of butter we buy in the store is yellow, in some cases this color is due to the addition of food coloring. The actual color of butter varies greatly and depends on the type of cows that produced the milk and the type of food the cows consumed.

> *For Middle-Level Learners* [HNS 2, 3, and 4]

The Mystery of Galen, Harvey, and the Heart

Note: Use this Attention Getter to motivate interest for a unit on human body systems or the circulatory system, in particular.

Materials
Access to the Internet	Science resource books and encyclopedias
Posterpaper and markers	Assorted art materials
Assorted fabric pieces	

Motivating Questions
- Lightly touch your heart to feel it beating. People sometimes say your heart is like a pump. What do you think they mean by that?
- Do you think arteries and veins are similar?
- Do you think that people's ideas about how the heart works have stayed the same over the years?

Directions
1. Give half of the groups the task of researching the life and theories of Galen and the other half, the life and theories of William Harvey.
2. Once each group has the needed information, they should select and prepare one of the group members to play the role of its scientist: Galen or Harvey. That "scientist" will explain his theories about the heart and circulatory system to the class.
3. Have each "scientist" speak to the class for 3 or 4 minutes, telling about his life and theories.
4. Keep track of questions and comments that class members have, and use them to structure a later discussion on human body systems.

Science Content for the Teacher
The Greek physician Galen believed that the right side of the heart squeezed blood into the left side through tiny holes in the "wall" between the chambers. About 1,400 years later, William Harvey proposed a detailed theory about bloodflow, in which he specified the locations and functions of arteries and veins and identified one-way valves in veins. Harvey's theory serves as the basis for much of our present understanding of the circulatory system.

Discovery Activities

The Mystery Bag

Objectives	• Using their sense of touch, the children will name assorted objects. • The students will match objects that they see with ones that they feel.
Science Processes Emphasized	Observing Inferring
Materials for Each Child or Group	Assorted objects, including pencils, erasers, paper clips, rubber bands, wooden blocks, marshmallows, and coins of various sizes Boxes for the objects Large paper bags with two holes (large enough for a hand to fit through) cut near the bottom of each bag 2 paper clips to close the tops of the bags
Motivation	Before class begins, place one of the objects in a bag. Explain to the children that they are going to discover how their sense of touch can help them identify things. Begin the activity by placing your hand in one of the holes in the bag to feel the object inside. Describe the object to the children. Have various children come to the front of the room to feel the object in the bag. On the chalkboard or easel pad, record what they think the object is.

Directions

1. Form two-person cooperative learning teams, and give each team a box containing the objects listed for this activity. Have the teams decide who will go first in each team, and have that person close his or her eyes. At the front of the room, hold up the type of object for the other team member to place in the bag.
2. Have the children who have had their eyes closed put one hand through each hole and feel the mystery object.
3. Ask the children to identify the object. If they are unable to name the object, hold up an assortment of objects and have the children vote for the one they think is correct.

Key Discussion Questions

1. What part of the body do we use most to feel things? *The hands.*
2. What are some of the things that the hands can feel? *How hot or cold things are. Whether objects are sharp, smooth, rough, soft, hard, and so on.*
3. What are some things that hands can't tell? *What color an object is, how shiny or bright it is, and so on.*

Science Content for the Teacher

The skin has sense receptors that are sensitive to touch, warmth, cold, pain, and pressure. These sense receptors are not evenly distributed. Pressure is felt most accurately by the tip of the nose, the tongue, and the fingers. Sense receptors in our hands give us our awareness of heat, cold, pain, and pressure.

Extension

Math: You may want to place a set of rods of different lengths in the bags and ask the children to select the biggest rod, the smallest, the second biggest, and so on.

Art: Some children may want to build a "feely board" collage out of materials of various textures, shapes, and sizes.

Sniff, Snuff, and Sneeze

Objectives	• The students will use their sense of smell to determine the contents of closed paper bags. • The students will be able to identify various common odors (those of an onion, vinegar, an apple, and an orange).

Science Processes Emphasized

Observing
Inferring

Materials for Each Child or Group

Paper bags (lunch size)	Peppermint oil	Vinegar
25 cm (10 in.) of string for each bag	Wintergreen oil	Onion
Plastic sandwich bags	Camphor oil	Apple
Paper towels	Lemon extract	Orange

Motivation

Place a small amount of one of the odor-producing substances in one of the bags. Tie the bag loosely with string so that odors are able to escape but the students cannot see into it. Invite the students to identify the scent in the bag without looking in it and without using their hands.

Directions

1. Distribute the paper bags and string, and have the children write their names on the bags. Have them select one of the odor-producing foods (apple, orange, or onion), place a small piece of it on a small piece of paper toweling in the bag, and loosely tie the bag.
2. Divide the children into cooperative learning groups, and have the members of the groups try to identify what is in each bag without looking.
3. Have each group select one bag to share with another group. Each group should discuss their observations and reach some agreement about what is in the other group's bag.
4. Place one or two drops of each oil and the vinegar on a small piece of paper towel, and seal it in a plastic bag.
5. Give each group a set of bags. Tell them to smell all of the bags and then identify and classify the scents any way they can.

Key Discussion Questions

1. How can we tell what is in the bag without opening it or touching it? *By smell.*
2. What are some words that can be used to describe odors? *Good, bad, strong, sour, sweet, medicine-smelling, food-smelling.*
3. How does smelling help animals survive? *By helping them track prey. By helping them sense enemies.*

Science Content for the Teacher

When we smell something, we sample the air by inhaling it and having it move over receptors deep in our nasal cavity. These receptors analyze the chemicals in the air sample with great precision and transmit the findings to our brain for analysis and storage. Minute odors can trigger vivid memories.

Extension

Art: Some children may want to produce a collage of pictures of good- and bad-smelling things. The children may be able to scent portions of the collage, such as pictures of flowers.

Using Your Senses to Classify Things

Objective	• The children will use their senses of sight and touch to classify seeds.
Science Process Emphasized	Classifying
Materials for Each Child or Group	Paper plate Hand lens Small plastic bag containing a variety of dried seeds, including sunflower seeds, kidney beans, lima beans, lentils, and so forth
Motivation	Display a bag of seeds, and tell the children that they are going to see how well they can sort through such a bag. Explain to them that they are to sort the seeds into different groups on their paper plates.
Directions	1. Distribute a bag, paper plate, and hand lens to each group, and have the groups classify the seeds by placing them in like piles on a paper plate. *Safety Note:* If you are doing this activity with very young children, caution them not to eat any of the seeds or to put them in their nose, ears, or mouth. 2. After the groups have begun their work, display the hand lenses and ask how they could be used to help classify the seeds.
Key Discussion Questions	1. How did your sense of sight help you group the seeds? *Answers will vary but might include references to color or shape.* 2. If I asked you to group the seeds by how smooth or rough they were, what sense would you use? *Touch.* (After you ask this question, have the groups reclassify their seeds on the basis of smoothness and roughness.)
Science Content for the Teacher	Our senses provide us with detailed information about our surroundings. Even something as simple as calling a person by name requires us to first use our senses to identify the person and then to decide whether we know the person or not. We can identify the person by sight or by the sound of her or his voice.
Extension	*Science/Health:* You may want to bring in a variety of healthy foods and have the children group them according to taste: sweet, salty, sour, or bitter.

How Does Smell Affect Taste?

Objectives	• The children will predict the effect of the smell of a substance on its taste. • The children will observe how the ability to smell affects taste. • The children will infer the relationship between the senses of smell and taste.
Science Processes Emphasized	Observing Inferring Predicting

Materials for Each Child or Group

Onion slice in a closed container
Apple slice in a closed container
White potato slice in a closed container
5 packs of small hard candies, such as Lifesavers or Charms, each of a different flavor
2 glasses of water   2 blindfolds

Safety note: Confirm that students do not have food allergies or conditions that prohibit them from tasting the foods used.

Motivation

Keep the materials out of sight, and ask the children if they have ever noticed that they sometimes lose some of their ability to taste foods. Some children may note that food lost some of its taste when they had colds. Tell the children that in this activity, they will discover how the smell of a substance affects its taste.

Directions

Note: This activity has two parts. Begin by doing steps 1–5 as a demonstration. Then have the children work in groups to try the experiment using a volunteer from their group.

1. Tell the children that you need a volunteer for a taste test of hard candies. Blindfold the volunteer, and have the class predict how well the volunteer will do.
2. Give the volunteer one of the candies, and have him or her taste it and tell its flavor. Have the class record the accuracy of the result.
3. Have the volunteer take a drink of water to rinse the taste from his or her mouth, and repeat the taste test with a different flavor of candy. Continue repeating the taste test until all the flavors have been tested. Be sure the volunteer rinses his or her mouth after each test and that the class records the results of each test.
4. Blindfold the volunteer, hold an apple slice under his or her nose, and have him or her take a small bite of the potato slice. Ask the volunteer what kind of food was eaten.
5. Have the volunteer take a sip of water before beginning the second test. Place an onion slice in front of the child's nose, provide an apple slice for him or her to chew on, and ask him or her to identify the food.
6. Now have the class form cooperative learning groups to carry out steps 1–5 with a volunteer from each group.

Key Discussion Questions

1. Were you surprised at any of the things you observed during this activity? Why? *Answers will vary.*
2. How do you think the way something smells affects its taste? *When we taste something our brain also discovers how it smells. The taste of food depends in part on how it smells.*

Science Content for the Teacher

Substances must be dissolved in liquid before sensory nerves are able to detect their presence. The nerve endings in the taste buds are stimulated by the dissolved substances and send information about them to the brain. The nerve that carries information about smells to the brain branches into receptors

By observing how smell affects taste, middle-level learners can infer the relationship between these two senses.

that line the nasal cavities. Particles of food that enter the air as gases are dissolved in the liquids on the surface of the nasal cavities and stimulate the smell receptors. A cold or allergic reaction that produces large quantities of mucus in the lining of the nasal cavities limits the ability of the olfactory nerve to receive information.

Extension   *Art:* Have the children discover the relationship between what we see when we look at food and how we think the food is going to taste. Using food colorings, they can prepare cookies, bread, and fried eggs in different colors and investigate why some people may not wish to sample them.

For Middle-Level Learners [SPSP 6]

How Does Rest Affect Tired Muscles?

Objectives
- The children will gather data about the number of exercises they can do within a given period of time.
- The children will determine the effect of rest on the amount of exercise they can do.

Science Processes Emphasized   Observing and gathering data
Inferring

Materials for Each Child or Group

Pencil	Chart with 10 columns
Paper	Watch or clock with a second hand

Motivation   Ask the children if they remember that in the lower grades, their parents or teachers tried to make them rest or take naps. Have the children discuss why the adults wanted them to rest. You may wish to point out that young children are very active and tire quickly. Explain that rest gives muscles a chance to regain some strength. Tell the children that in this activity, they will find out how rest affects their muscles.

Directions
1. Divide the class into two-member teams. One member will perform the exercise while the other member records data. Have the member who is going to perform the exercise make a clenched fist with one hand and then extend his or her fingers. Have the other member count how many times this exercise can be completed within 15 seconds. He or she should then enter the number in the first column of the chart.
2. Have all teams repeat this procedure four times, with no rest between trials. After the first member has completed five trials, have him or her rest for 10 or 15 minutes. During this rest period, have the other member of the team do the exercise.
3. After the other member has completed five trials, have the teams repeat the activity but this time with a minute of rest between trials. Have the partners record the data as they did before.

Key Discussion Questions
1. How did resting for a minute between trials affect the results? *When I rested between trials, I was able to do more exercises during the trials.*
2. How can you use what you learned in this activity? *If I want to improve how well my muscles work when I play a sport or a game, I should rest as much as possible during time-outs or between innings.*

Science Content for the Teacher   Skeletal muscles are voluntary muscles. They contract because we tell them to do so. When they contract, they cause various body parts to move. The energy that produces this movement comes from food that is digested in our body. As the cells produce energy, wastes accumulate. When too much waste has accumulated in the muscle cells and tissues, the cells are no longer able to contract normally. If this occurs, we experience muscle fatigue. One way of dealing with muscle fatigue is to allow muscles to rest. This permits the bloodstream to remove excess wastes that have built up in the muscle tissue.

Extension   *Math:* You may wish to have some students synthesize all the data from this activity and prepare a classroom graph showing the average number of exercises performed during each trial for both the first part of the activity (exercises without rest periods) and the second part of the activity (exercises with intervening rest periods).

> *For Middle-Level Learners* [LS 7]

Are You Part of Any Food Chains?

Objectives
- The children will trace the locations of foods they have eaten in the food chain and discover their own location in the food chain.
- The children will communicate orally or in writing information about the factors that may affect the quantity and quality of the food that reaches them.

Science Processes Emphasized   Inferring
Communicating

Materials   Potato   Magazine picture of a hamburger

Motivation   After a brief discussion of what the children's favorite meals are, ask whether they have ever thought about how the food was produced. Hold up a potato and a picture of a hamburger, and tell the children that they are going to discover how they receive energy from the sun through each of these foods.

Directions
1. Distribute a small potato and a magazine picture to each group. Ask the groups to make food chain charts that relate the foods to them. The chart for the potato, for example, would simply show the potato and a human. The chart for the hamburger would identify grass or grain, beef cattle, and humans.
2. Challenge some of the students to create a food chain that includes a human and a great white shark. When they are done, ask them to look at their food chain to see if they have shown the complete sequence of events that leads from the sun's energy to the energy the shark needs to survive to their own needs for energy.

Key Discussion Questions
1. How would changes in temperature, water, air, or amount of sunlight affect the food you eat? *Answers will vary but should note that extreme temperature, limited water or sunlight, and air pollution can affect plant growth and thus affect animals that eat the plants and people who eat the plants and animals.*
2. If you are a vegetarian, is your food chain longer or shorter than the food chain of a person who is a meat eater? Why? *Shorter because the energy from the sun that is captured through photosynthesis goes directly from the fruits and vegetables to the person.*

Science Content for the Teacher   Photosynthesis, the process by which the sun's energy is captured by plants, depends on the temperature, water, sunlight, and air. Meat eaters as well as vegetarians require access to this captured energy in order to carry out life processes.

Extension   *Science/Social Studies:* Encourage the children to identify the specific geographic locales where some of their favorite foods are produced. Have them describe and illustrate the various modes of transportation used to move the food products to them.

Demonstrations

For Young Learners [SPSP 1]

What Can Change Bones?

Objectives
- The children will observe two changes in bones.
- The children will infer the presence of minerals and water in bones.

Science Processes Emphasized
Observing
Inferring

Materials
4 small chicken bones   Paper label
Jar of white vinegar

Motivation   Tell the children that this demonstration will help them understand what bones are made of. Display the bones and vinegar. Ask the children to guess how these materials could be used to discover some things about bones.

Directions
1. Place two of the bones in the jar of vinegar. Put a label on the jar, and write the date on the label. Tell the children that you are putting the jar aside and will remove the bones from the jar in about a week. Place one of the two remaining bones in a shallow pan to dry, also for one week. Encourage the children to make observations of the contents of the jar and pan each day during the week.
2. Compare the flexibility of the remaining bone by bending it slightly.
3. After the bone has been dried for a week try to bend it. If it has been thoroughly dried, it will break in two easily.
4. After a week has passed, also retrieve the bones that were placed in the vinegar. Show the children that these bones bend easily.

Key Discussion Questions
1. How did drying affect the bone? *It made the bone break easily.*
2. How were the bones that were placed in vinegar changed? *They could be bent very easily.*

Science Content for the Teacher   Vinegar is a weak acid that is able to react with the calcium in bones. Calcium gives bones the strength to support weight. Bones contain living cells as well as calcium and other minerals. Drying a bone eliminates the water contained in the cells. Without water, the bone becomes brittle.

Extension   *Art:* You may wish to have some of the children research how artists use their knowledge of bone structure in animals and humans in creating paintings and sculptures.

Your Nose Knows

Objectives
- The children will observe how long it takes for them to notice a substance introduced into the air in the classroom.
- The children will infer how the scent of a substance travels to their noses.

Science Processes Emphasized

Observing

Inferring

Materials

Perfume	Oil of citronella
Oil of peppermint	4 saucers

Motivation

Pinch your nostrils closed, and ask the children if they have ever done this. Tell them that they are going to discover how much their sense of smell tells them about their world.

Directions

1. Have the children sit around the room at various distances from the table you will use for the demonstration. Open one of the containers, and pour a few drops of one of the substances on a saucer. Tilt the saucer to spread the liquid over its surface.
2. Ask the children to raise their hands when they smell the substance.
3. After you have repeated the process for each substance, ask the children to try to explain how the smell got from the substance on the saucer to their noses. This is an opportunity for you to discuss the idea of particles entering the air from the substance and gradually spreading out, or *diffusing.*

Key Discussion Questions

1. Would opening a window or turning on a fan help us notice the smell more quickly or less quickly? *Answers will vary. If the movement of air directs molecules of the substance toward the children, they will smell the substances more quickly than they will if the window is closed or there is no fan.*
2. Do you think dogs have a better sense of smell than humans? *Answers will vary. Some children may have seen television programs or movies showing dogs used to track crime suspects.*

Science Content for the Teacher

Sense organs gather information about our surroundings and send the information to the brain. Our sense of smell, or olfactory sense, results from the stimulation of olfactory cells in the nose by odors in the air. Nerve impulses carry information from the olfactory cells to the brain. What we know as smell is in fact the brain's response to the information it receives.

Extension

Science/Health: Engage the children in a discussion of the possible safety advantages provided by the ability to smell odors. Ask: Does your nose help keep you safe? As the children respond, be sure to comment on how the smell of food going bad gives our brains important information.

What Is Your Lung Capacity?

Objectives	• The children will estimate the capacity of the teacher's lungs. • The children will measure the capacity of the teacher's lungs.

Science Processes Emphasized

Observing	Using numbers
Predicting	Measuring

Materials

4-liter (1 gallon) glass or translucent plastic jug
1 liter container of water
1 m (about 3 feet) of clear plastic tubing (available for purchase in any hobby store)
Bucket large enough for the jug to be totally immersed
Source of water
Reference book that has a diagram of the human lungs and upper torso

Motivation

Tell the children that this demonstration will give them an idea of the amount of air that can be contained by the lungs. Display the drawing of the lungs. Ask the children to estimate how many liters of air the lungs can hold. Have the children write down their predictions.

Directions

1. Involving the children as assistants, fill the bucket to a depth of 10 centimeters (about 4 inches) with water. Fill the jug completely with water.
2. Cover the mouth of the jug with your hand, invert the jug, and place it in the bucket. When the mouth of the jug is under water in the bucket, carefully remove your hand. The water in the jug will remain in place. Have a child hold the inverted jug in position.
3. Place one end of the tube inside the jug, at least 10 centimeters (about 4 inches) up from its mouth. Leave the other end of the tube free.
4. Take a deep breath and exhale as much of the air in your lungs as possible through the free end of the tube. This air will displace some of the water in the jug.
5. Cover the free end of the tube with your thumb, and have a child cover the inverted end of the jug with his or her hand. Now extract the tube and have the child completely seal the mouth of the jug.
6. Turn the jug upright. The jug will be partly empty. This empty region represents the amount of water displaced by your exhaled air and, therefore, represents your lung capacity.
7. Have the children determine the number of liters of air that were exhaled. To do this, have them pour water into the jug from the liter container and record the volume of water needed to refill the jug.
8. The children can compare the resulting figure with their predictions.

Key Discussion Questions

1. How could we make a jug that would tell us the amount of air that was exhaled? *Fill the jug with liters of water, and make a mark on the out side of the jug to show where the water level is for each liter of water. When the jug is turned upside down and used, measure the amount of air in it by seeing how many liters of water were pushed out.*
2. How did your prediction of lung capacity compare with the lung capacity we measured? *Answers will vary.*
3. What are some things that might shrink a person's lung capacity? *Answers will vary but may include any injury or disease that affects one or both lungs.*

Science Content for the Teacher

Each time you breathe, the diaphragm muscle (located under your lungs) contracts, enabling the rib cage to expand. This expansion allows the lungs to expand to full capacity. As this occurs, air is taken into the lungs. As the diaphragm returns to its normal state, the contents of the lungs are expelled. The capacity of the lungs depends on a variety of factors, including general body size, the condition of the diaphragm and lung tissues, and the health of the respiratory system in general.

Extension

Art: You may wish to encourage some children to make a series of large labeled drawings that show the location and size of the lungs in a variety of animals. These children will need access to reference books in order to carry out this activity.

> *For Middle-Level Learners* [LS 6]

How Fast Is Your Reaction Time?

Objectives

- The children will gather, graph, and interpret reaction time data.
- The children will suggest strategies for decreasing their reaction time.

Science Processes Emphasized

Interpreting data
Controlling variables

Materials

Penny   Meterstick

Motivation

Display the materials, and ask the children to guess how you will use them. Explain that the demonstration will deal with reaction time, and ask them to suggest techniques that you could use to assess reaction time with a penny and with a meterstick.

Directions

1. Ask for several volunteers. Have one volunteer extend his or her hand with the thumb and forefinger separated. Hold a meterstick by one end, and have the other end dangle between the volunteer's thumb and forefinger. Tell the volunteer that you are going to let go of your end of the meterstick, and ask him or her to catch it with his or her thumb and forefinger. The distance that the meterstick drops before it is caught is an indicator of reaction time. Repeat this exercise a number of times, and have the children create and interpret a graph of the data gathered.
2. Hold a penny above the outstretched hand of one of the volunteers. Tell the volunteer to try to move his or her hand away from the penny as it falls. Hold the penny at various distances above the child's hand. When the penny is close to the child's hand, it will be difficult for the child to move his or her hand away before the penny hits.
3. Ask the children what variables might affect reaction time. For example, a penny dropper might inadvertently signal a forthcoming drop with a facial gesture. Encourage them to invent ways to control some of the variables.

Key Discussion Questions

1. Can you think of an invention for a bicycle that might decrease the time between seeing a danger and braking? *Answers will vary. One example would be a radar-like device that would automatically engage the brakes when it sensed an object directly in the rider's path.*
2. What can an automobile driver do or avoid doing to improve his or her reaction time? *Answers will vary. Responses might include never driving while impaired by alcohol or drugs, keeping windshields clean, or playing the automobile radio at moderate volume levels so horns or sirens can be heard.*

Science Content for the Teacher

Reaction time is the time between the receipt of sense information by our brain and the movement of muscles in response to the information. In everyday life, this movement can have important safety consequences. Alcohol is one example of a substance that can increase reaction time.

Extension

Science/Language Arts: Have the children create a story about a superhero or -heroine whose principal advantage is the speed of his or her reaction time. Have the children focus on developing a central incident in which this advantage leads to the capture of a villain.

Life Sciences Sample Lesson

Title:

Looking for Life in Your Own School Yard

NSES

Articulation with NSES:

Grades K–4
Content Standard C: Life Sciences
• Organization and environments

Grades 5–8
Content Standard C: Life Sciences
• Diversity and Adaptations of environments

Background for Teacher:

In his book, *Last Child in the Woods,* Richard Louv addresses the growing distance of children from direct experiences with nature. This sample lesson is really a year-long activity that will provide a foundation for the exploration and discovery of many life science concepts while placing children in direct contact with the wonders of nature.

In this ongoing investigation, children will observe a 1-meter square plot in the school yard. It could be a woodland, meadow, or wetland (consider safety). If none of these are available, request that a portion of the school grounds be left unmowed throughout the year. I will mention a few of the concepts that you can develop with the children, but the list can easily be expanded and will grow throughout the year. Building on a familiar theme throughout the year will enable children to deepen their understanding by making connections in a meaningful context.

Biodiversity refers to the number and variety of living things in a particular region. Maintaining biodiversity is essential to the sustenance of *ecosystems,* which consists of all the living and nonliving elements that function together as a unit. This rather broad definition encompasses a wide spectrum of scale. A rain forest could be considered an ecosystem as well as a tide pool or puddle. When one element of an ecosystem is compromised, the other elements will also be affected. This leads to adaptations, migrations, or extinctions. Inherent in any ecosystem is the flow of energy through food chains and webs. Consider also the flow of energy through abiotic factors such as atmospheric heating, cooling, and running water.

This lesson will focus on establishing the concept of biodiversity and ecosystem while integrating math and language arts.

● Element 1: Content to be Taught

Note: Specific elements and their properties and relationships will vary with the ecosystem. Therefore, the content analysis is generic.

Elements	Properties	Rules of relationship
Plants	Green, sessile, varied	Planted in soil, eaten by animals
Animals	Vertebrates, invertebrates, varied	On plants, under plants, in soil, in water, eat plants, consume soil
Microorganisms	Invisible to the naked eye	On plants, on animals, in soil
Soil	Size, composition, water retention	Supports plants, used by animals, absorbs water
Water	Stagnant, flowing, surface, subterranean	Moistens soil, used by animals and plants
Emergent properties	Changing, growing, consistent	

Students will learn that biodiversity refers to the number and variety of types of living things in an ecosystem.

● Element 2: Prior Knowledge and Misconceptions

If students do not know how to make bar graphs, you will need to provide guidance during the lesson. They should be familiar with the meter as a unit of measurement and the properties of a square. Students may confuse biodiversity for the number of organisms rather than the number of different species of organisms.

● Element 3: Performance Objectives

1. Given a 1 m² unpaved quadrant on the school grounds, each student will create a bar graph that represents the number and type of at least five species of plant, animal, or microbe found in their quadrant.
2. Given an incorrect description of biodiversity, each student will rewrite the description correctly scoring a 3 on the rubric provided.

● Element 4: Concept Development

Engagement

Ask the children where they think they are likely to find many different forms of life. Use a Think-Pair-Share methodology to process the children's responses. Post responses on the board. Ask children how many forms of life they think that they could find in a 1 m² area of land in their school yard. Record the children's predictions. Tell the children that their challenge today is to find as many different forms of life as possible in a 1 m² plot of their school yard. The essential question can be posted on the board, "How many different forms of life can you find in your 1 m² school yard plot?"

Exploration

Materials needed per group: meterstick, 4 wooden stakes, colored tape, permanent markers, 5 meters of string, magnifying glasses, clear plastic collection jars, sieve nets, grid for graphing on overhead sheets.

Safety: *Reconnoiter the study site for stinging insects, potentially irritating plants such as poison ivy, oak, or sumac, thorn bushes, and anything else that may pose a hazard. Note any students with allergies to insect bites and plants, and prepare an appropriate response plan to exposure or bites. Instruct the children not to handle any insects. Students should wash their hands after handling soil, plants, and equipment. Encourage students to wear sunscreen and appropriate clothing (e.g., hat, long-sleeved shirt) to minimize the damaging effects of sun exposure.*

Assign children to research teams with the following roles:

- Group leader: Responsible for ensuring that the group knows its task and follows the instructions.
- Equipment manager: Ensures that the group has the proper equipment, and that the equipment is returned at the conclusion of the investigation.
- Data collector: Ensures that all data are recorded in appropriate tables.
- Safety officer: Ensures that safety regulations are followed.

Rotate the roles each time the group visits their site.

Designate a region where the children can establish their plots. Instruct the groups to measure a 1 m^2 plot in the designated region of the school yard and create a descriptive model of their quadrant in their science notebooks. Next, have them count the number of different life forms in their quadrant. Don't worry about names of organisms, but have them draw or describe in writing each organism. If you can supply a digital camera, allow the children to take pictures as well. You can provide a sieve net for them to sweep the quadrant and put the organisms in collection jars to observe. Instruct the children to return the organisms to the quadrant when they finish observing them.

Explanation

Return to the essential question. Ask the children, "How many different forms of life did you find in your 1 m^2 school yard quadrants?" Give each team an overhead sheet with a grid on it. Instruct each team to make a bar graph on the overhead representing the number of at least five different organisms that they found. Display each group's bar graph on the overhead and tally the different types of organisms that each group found. Ask the children to compare their predictions to their actual data.

Tell them that they measured the biodiversity of the school yard. Ask them which data tell them about the biodiversity, the number of different organisms (the number of bars), or the number of organisms (the height of the bars). Reinforce that biodiversity refers to the number of different types of organisms, not the total number of organisms in a region.

Elaboration

- There are many elaborations on this investigation that you can explore and develop throughout the year.
- Compare the quadrant to an artificial ecosystem such as a garden, mowed lawn, or landscaped wooded area.
- Collect soil samples and test them for their composition and water retention properties.
- Collect data on the biodiversity of soil organisms.
- Identify food chains and webs within the ecosystem.

- Place squares of untreated wood on different parts of the quadrant for extended periods of time to see what effects it has on the ecosystem's plants and animals. You will find that it attracts many organisms that live under the wood, while plants will be destroyed.
- Look for signs of life such as tunnels, nests, or droppings.
- Classify the organisms into kingdoms.
- Change elements in the quadrant and predict the results.

Element 5: Evaluation

Assessment 1:   Read the following letter from a child on vacation to the children. After the reading, provide a written copy as well.

> Dear Jill,
>
> I can't wait to show you the pictures that I took at the beach. It was wonderful. We spent the entire day at the beach where I counted 48 sea gulls. Some were white while others were gray. I guess that means that there is a lot of biodiversity at the beach, wouldn't you agree? Well, time to go fishing. On the last fishing trip we caught 25 flounder. That proves that the ocean has a lot of biodiversity too.
>
> See you soon,
> Aaron

Instruct the children to write a letter to Aaron and explain why they agree or disagree with Aaron's use of the term *biodiversity*.

Use the following rubric to assess the children's responses.

1	2	3
Agrees with Aaron's use of the term *biodiversity*.	Disagrees with Aaron's use of the term *biodiversity*, but does not explain why they disagree.	Disagrees with Aaron's use of the term *biodiversity*. Explains that biodiversity refers to the variation in types of different organisms, not the number of organisms.

Assessment 2:   Require each student to make bar graphs representing the number and type of five species found in his or her quadrant.

Element 6: Accommodations

English Language Learner (ELL)

1. The teacher will state directions and procedures verbally as well as in writing.
2. The teacher will create a word bank with definitions to remain posted in the room.
3. The teacher will group students proficient in English language usage with ELL students.

Learning Disabilities

1. Provide extra time for writing and assessment.
2. The students will be given a checklist for the activities to keep track of their progress and accomplishments.

Mobility Disabilities

1. If the child uses a wheelchair, situate him or her in a plot near a paved area that provides easy access for wheelchairs.

Resources for Discovery Learning

Internet Resources

 Websites for Life Science Units, Lessons, Activities, and Demonstrations

The Electronic Zoo
netvet.wustl.edu/pix.htm

**The Natural History Museum (London)
"The Life Galleries"**
www.nhm.ac.uk/museum

The Wild Ones
www.thewildones.org

Sea World: Science Information Content
www.seaworld.org/animal-info/index.htm

Sea World: Science Information Resources
www.seaworld.org/teacherguides/index.html

The Tree of Life
tolweb.org/tree/phylogeny.html

Science Education Partnership Award
www.ncrrsepa.org

NIH Office of Science Education
science.education.nih.gov

Backyard Biology
www.backyardbiology.net

Print Resources

Articles from Science and Children and Science Scope

Almeida, S., et al. "Involving School Children in the Establishment of an Urban Green Space: Long-Term Plant Biodiversity Study." *The American Biology Teacher* 68, no. 4 (April 2006): 213–220.

Aram, Robert J. "Habitat Sweet Habitat." *Science and Children* 38, no. 4 (January 2001): 23–27.

Bradway, Heather. "You Make the Diagnosis." *Science Scope* 24, no. 8 (May 2001): 23–25.

Coverdale, Gregory. "Science Is for the Birds: Promoting Standards-Based Learning through Backyard Bird-watching." *Science Scope* 26, no. 4 (January 2003): 32–37.

Fraser, W. J., et al. "Teaching Life Sciences to Blind and Visually Impaired Learners." *Journal of Biological Education* 42, no. 2 (Spring 2008): 84–89.

Galus, Pamela. "Snail Trails." *Science Scope* 25, no. 8 (May 2002):14–18.

Gates, Donna M. "Pond Life Magnified." *Science Scope* 25, no. 8 (May 2002): 10–13.

Giacalone, Valerie. "How to Plan, Survive, and Even Enjoy an Overnight Field Trip with 200 Students." *Science Scope* 26, no. 4 (January 2003): 22–26.

Hammrich, Penny L., and Fadigan, Kathleen. "Investigations in the Science of Sports." *Science Scope* 26, no. 5 (February 2003): 30–35.

Houtz, Lynne E., and Quinn, Thomas H. "Give Me Some Skin: A Hands-On Science Activity Integrating Racial Sensitivity." *Science Scope* 26, no. 5 (February 2003): 18–22.

Inman, D. "Magic School Bus Explores the Human Body [review]." *Science and Children* 33, (September 1995): 52.

Keena, Kelly, and Basile, Carole G. "An Environmental Journey." *Science and Children* 39, no. 8 (May 2002): 30–33.

Keteyian, Linda. "A Garden Story." *Science and Children* 39, no. 3 (November/December 2001): 22–25.

Koschmann, Mark, and Shepardson, Dan. "A Pond Investigation." *Science and Children* 39, no. 8 (May 2002): 20–23.

Lawry, Patricia K., and Hale McCrary, Judy. "Someone's in the Kitchen with Science." *Science and Children* 39, no. 2 (October 2001): 22–27.

Lebofsky, Nancy R., and Lebofsky, Larry A. "Modeling Olympus Mons from the Earth." *Science Scope* 25, no. 7 (April 2002): 36–39.

Lener, C., et al. "Learning with Loggerheads." *Science and Children* 45, no. 1 (September 2007): 24–28.

Mannesto, Jean. "The Truth about Wolves." *Science and Children* 39, no. 8 (May 2002): 24–29.

McGinnis, Patricia. "Dissect Your Squid and Eat It Too." *Science Scope* 24, no. 7 (April 2001): 12–17.

McWilliams, Susan. "Journey into the Five Senses." *Science and Children* 40, no. 5 (February 2003): 38–43.

Mitchell, Melissa, and Mitchell, James K. "A Microbial Murder Mystery." *Science Scope* 25, no. 5 (February 2002): 24–30.

Morrison, Geraldine, and Uslick, JoAnn. "Summer Science Camp, Anyone? *Science and Children* 39, no. 7 (April 2002): 34–37.

Moseley, C., et al. "Elementary Teachers' Progressive Understanding of Inquiry through the Process of Reflection." *School Science and Mathematics* 108, no. 2 (February 2008): 49–57.

Norrell, Mark A. "Science 101: What Is a Fossil?" *Science and Children* 40, no. 5 (February 2003): 20.

Rowlands, M. "What Do Children Think Happens to the Food They Eat?" *Journal of Biological Education* 38, no. 4 (Autumn 2004): 167–171.

Rule, Audrey, and Cynthia Rust. "A Bat Is Like a . . ." *Science and Children* 39, no. 3 (November/December 2001): 26–31.

Science Scope 26, no. 4 (January 2003) (Entire issue emphasizes addressing science misconceptions)

Sitzman, Daniel. "Bread Making: Classic Biotechnology and Experimental Design." *Science Scope* 26, no. 4 (January 2003): 27–31.

Stein, M., et al. "The Elementary Students' Science Beliefs Test." *Science and Children* 45, no. 8 (April/May 2008): 27–31.

Thompson, S. L. "Inquiry in the Life Sciences: The Plant-in-a-Jar as a Catalyst for Learning." *Science Activities* 43, no. 4 (Winter 2007): 27–33.

Notes

1. Statements 1, 3, 4, and 6 from B. Berthelsen, "Students' Naïve Conceptions in Life Science," *MSTA Journal* 44, no. 1 (Spring 1999): 13–19. www.msta-mich.org. (accessed 07-11-08).
2. This standard, as well as the others identified in later sections, are excerpted with permission from the National Research Council, *National Science Education Standards* (Washington, DC: National Academy Press, 1996), pp. 104–171. Note that the bracketed symbol to the right of each standard was prepared by this author. See also the list of all the K–8 content standards inside the front cover of this book.
3. Note that I have related this sampling of NSES E, F, and G to the life sciences.

▶ **Answers:** 1. F, 2. T, 3. F, 4. F, 5. F, 6. F, 7. T, 8. T, 9. F, 10. T.

part **four**

The Physical Sciences

► History and Nature of the Physical Sciences

What makes that arching band of colors appear from nowhere in the distant sky and then, in the blink of an eye, disappear? What are *you* really made of? How can I speak to someone in Hong Kong, half a world away, and not be connected by a telephone wire? How can a cardiac surgeon tell exactly where my elderly uncle has a blocked coronary artery?

The answers to these questions and more come from the most fundamental of the sciences: the physical sciences. In fact, *all* science emerges from our knowledge of matter and energy. These topics are at the center of physics and chemistry.

Careers in the Physical Sciences

A range of career paths are open to those women and men who have the required knowledge, skills, and motivation to explore the nature of matter and energy. Here are a few of the possibilities:

- *Chemist.* The chemist's work, in general, involves assembling atoms to form new molecules or breaking down complex molecules to explore the numbers and types of atoms they contain. The results of this work include improved processed food products, cosmetics, fuels, household products, industrial chemicals, pollution control, weapons systems, and drugs.

- *Physicist.* Through careful experimentation, the physicist tries to find explanations for natural phenomena such as the action of forces on matter, as well as for the behavior of energy in all its diverse forms. *Theoretical physicists* explore phenomena that are impossible to represent on Earth, such as the nature of space and time, the formation of black holes, and the interactions that occur as stars pass through their life cycles.

● *Engineer.* Engineers apply the knowledge produced by physicists and chemists to the development of products and procedures that solve human problems. The subspecialties of engineering include the development of electronic circuits on chips; the creation of machines to fabricate products; the design of bridges, aircraft, and satellites; and the creation of new drugs to improve our health and well-being.

Key Events in the Development of the Physical Sciences

500 B.C.E. Sometime during the fifth century B.C.E., Empedocles proposes that everything comes from four *elements:* earth, air, fire, and water.

440 B.C.E. Democritus observes and reflects upon the matter around him and concludes that it is made of fundamental particles he calls *atoms.*

260 B.C.E. Archimedes uses mathematics to propose the principle of the lever. He also discovers the principle of buoyancy, which states that the upward force on an object in water is equal to the weight of the volume of water displaced by that object.

1490 Leonardo da Vinci observes and then describes capillary action in detail.

1581 Galileo Galilei observes that the movement of pendulums displays a time-keeping property.

1589 By observing rolling balls on an inclined plane, Galileo Galilei shows that objects of different masses fall with the same acceleration.

1687 Isaac Newton publishes *Principia Mathematica.*

1781 Joseph Priestly creates molecules of water by combining hydrogen and oxygen and igniting them.

1786 Luigi Galvani discovers what he refers to as *animal electricity* and concludes that the bodies of living animals contain electricity.

1808 John Dalton proposes the theory that each element has its own type of atom and that every compound is made of a particular combination of atoms.

1820 Hans Oersted observes that a current in a wire can affect a compass needle.

1852 James Joule and Lord Kelvin show that a gas that expands rapidly cools while it does so.

1862 Dmitri Mendeleyev summarizes his research about the properties of elements by creating a chart known as the *periodic table,* which places elements into groups and rows. The elements of each group have similar properties.

1873 James Clerk Maxwell concludes that light is an electromagnetic phenomenon.

1895 Wilhelm Roentgen discovers X-rays.

1897 Joseph Thomson discovers electrons and calls the particles *corpuscles.*

1897 Marie Curie begins research on so-called uranium rays, which eventually leads to the discovery of radioactivity.

1905 Albert Einstein explains the photoelectric effect.

1905 Albert Einstein states the theory of special relativity as well as the law of mass/energy conservation.

1907   Albert Einstein states that gravitation and inertia are the same and uses this to predict the gravitational red shift of starlight.

1907   Albert Einstein infers from his studies that time is slowed in a gravitational field.

1911   Ernest Rutherford conducts experiments that indicate that particular types of atoms radiate particles and discovers that alpha particles are helium atoms without electrons and beta particles are high-speed electrons.

1912   Albert Einstein concludes that the space/time continuum is curved and that gravity is caused by that curvature.

1913   Niels Bohr proposes that when electrons move from a high energy level to a lower energy level around an atom, photons ("packets") of light are released. He also states that the movement of electrons from a low energy level to a higher energy level is the result of photons being absorbed.

1915   Albert Einstein puts forth his complete theory of general relativity and also proves that the excess precession of the planet Mercury is a result of general relativity.

1932   The first atom is split with a particle accelerator.

1934   Irene Joliot-Curie and Frederick Joliot-Curie bombard aluminum atoms with alpha particles and create artificially radioactive phosphorus-30.

1934   Leo Szilard concludes that nuclear chain reactions may be possible.

1939   Lise Meitner and her nephew, Otto Hahn, reveal that uranium nuclei can disintegrate through a process called *fission.*

1943   The first all-electronic calculating device (computer) is developed by a team led by Alan Turing and used to crack German codes during World War II.

1945   On July 16, the first atomic bomb is successfully tested in the United States.

1949   William Bradford Shockley and his research team invent the transistor.

1952   The first hydrogen bomb is tested.

1969   Murray Gell-Mann wins the Nobel Prize for physics for his work on classifying elementary particles.

1994   Kyriacos Nicolau and Robert Holton create a synthetic molecular form of the naturally occurring cancer treatment compound Taxol.

1997   Steven Chu, Claude Cohen-Tannoudji, and William D. Phillips win a Nobel Prize for developing a way to trap and study individual atoms using laser technology.

1998   Robert B. Laughlin, Horst L. Stormer, and Daniel C. Tsui win a Nobel Prize for discovering a new form of matter known as *quantum fluid.*

2001   Carl E. Wieman, Wolfgang Ketterle, and Eric A. Cornell win the Nobel Prize in physics for work on an exotic state of matter that results from cooling down an alkali gas to 0.00000002° above absolute zero.

2002   Raymond Davis, Jr., Mastoshi Koshiba, and Riccardo Giacconi win a Nobel Prize for their study of the nearly undetectable cosmic radiation that reaches Earth.

2005   Roy J. Glauber, John L. Hall, and Theodor W. Hänsch receive the Nobel Laureate in Physics for their contributions to the development of laser-based precision spectroscopy, including the optical frequency comb technique.

2006   Nobel laureate, Carl E. Wieman, renowned for his leadership in science education, joins The University of British Columbia to boost science education.

2007   The Nobel Prize in physics is awarded to two European scientists—Albert Fert and Peter Grünberg—for their discovery of a physical effect, known today as Giant Magnetoresistance or GMR.

Women and Men Who Have Shaped the Development of the Physical Sciences

ISAAC NEWTON (1642–1727) is known as the founder of modern physics and mathematics. His studies of the natural world led to the laws of inertia, action and reaction, and the acceleration of a mass being proportional to force applied. He also proposed the universal law of gravitation and is considered to be the inventor of calculus.

COUNT ALESSANDRO VOLTA (1745–1827) was an Italian nobleman who conducted research into the nature of electricity. The unit of electricity known as the *volt* is derived from his name.

MICHAEL FARADAY (1791–1867) was a bookbinder whose intense curiosity led him to read every book that he bound, particularly those that dealt with energy. Later in life, he became a chemist and a physicist. His accomplishments included the separation of benzene from petroleum and experiments with electromagnetic induction (the production of current in wires moved through a magnetic field).

LADY AUGUSTA ADA BYRON, COUNTESS OF LOVELACE (1815–1851) wrote in 1843 what we now refer to as the *code,* or the program to operate the first mechanical computer. The U.S. Navy named the computer language *Ada* in her honor.

THOMAS ALVA EDISON (1847–1931) was perhaps the greatest inventor in history. His patents led to development of the phonograph, the motion picture camera, electric lights, and power plants to produce electricity. He received over 1,000 patents in his lifetime.

LEWIS H. LATIMER (1848–1928) invented, among other things, a method for producing the carbon filaments used in the electric lamps of his time. He was an engineer at the Edison Electric Light Company and the only African American in Edison's engineering and invention group. Latimer authored *Incandescent Electric Lighting,* the first book describing the installation and operation of lighting systems.

GRANVILLE WOODS (1856–1910) was an African American whose early work as a fireman/engineer on railroads provided a foundation for his later studies of electrical and mechanical engineering. His inventions included devices that could send telegraph messages between moving trains and an automatic airbrake system.

MARIE CURIE (1867–1934) was a Polish-born scientist whose work touched both physics and chemistry. An indication of her extraordinary contribution to the sciences is the fact that she won the Nobel Prize twice! She and her husband, Pierre, shared the Nobel Prize in 1903 for their discovery of radium and polonium, and in 1911, she won it by herself for the research that led to the isolation of pure radium.

ERNEST RUTHERFORD (1871–1937) was known for his exploration of many phenomena related to atomic structure, energy release, and the nature of particles, including alpha, beta, and gamma radiation and the proton and neutron. He is credited with discovering the nucleus of an atom and with proposing a model of the atom in which electrons orbited the central nucleus.

ALBERT EINSTEIN (1879–1955) stands as one of the true geniuses in the history of civilization. His theories shaped the development of modern science and have had profound implications on science and society. Among his many accomplishments, he explained Brownian motion and the photoelectric effect, and he developed both the special and general theories of relativity. Born in Germany, he emigrated to the United States while in his fifties. He joined the Institute for Advanced Study in Princeton, New Jersey.

NIELS BOHR (1885–1962), a Danish physicist, provided an explanation for the structure of the atom that included a description of how electrons absorb and lose energy. His theory provided the best explanation for experimental results gathered by atomic physicists from around the world. Bohr received the Nobel Prize for physics in 1922.

GRACE HOPPER (1906–1992) was an active-duty U.S. Navy lieutenant who was key in developing computer programs. Her programming skills were used in one of the earliest computers, the Univac I. She is credited with invention of the term *computer bug.*

CHIEN-SHIUNG WU (1912–1997) received her Ph.D. in physics from the University of California, Berkeley. She is most well known for her work in developing an experiment that confirmed a theory related to particle physics proposed by T. D. Lee and C. N. Yang. Lee and Yang received the Nobel Prize for their work on the theory but Wu did not. She did receive the Comstock Award from the National Academy of Sciences in 1964 and was the first woman to do so.

RICHARD FEYNMAN (1918–1988) won the Nobel Prize in Physics in 1965 for his work on quantum electrodynamics, or QED. In 1986 he served on the presidential commission investigating the explosion of the space shuttle *Challenger*. He is known for his 1985 memoir, *Surely You're Joking, Mr. Feynman*, which portrayed him as whimsical character. He earned a bachelor's degree at MIT in 1939 and a doctorate from Princeton in 1942. During World War II he worked at the Army research center at Los Alamos, New Mexico, helping design the first atomic bomb. *The Feynman Lectures on Physics*, a collection of his lectures to CalTech freshmen, remains a popular text in the field.

ROSALIND FRANKLIN (1920–1958) received her doctorate in physics from Cambridge University in 1941 and developed great expertise in the study of crystals. She analyzed the behavior of fine beams of X-rays through DNA (deoxyribonucleic acid).

ROSALYN SUSSMAN YALOW (1921–   ) shared the Nobel Prize for medicine in 1977, which was awarded for development of a method to detect minute traces of substances in blood and other body fluids.

MURRAY GELL-MANN (1929–   ) is most famous for proposing a theory that grouped atomic particles into eight "families." This grouping was grounded in his belief that all particles are composed of smaller particles that he called *quarks.* He won the Nobel Prize for physics in 1969.

STEVEN WEINBERG (1933–   ) is known as one of the twentieth century's most talented theoretical physicists. He is best known for his work on a unified field theory, or a single explanation that ties together the laws of physics dealing with gravity, electromagnetism, the strong force holding the atom's nucleus together, and the weak force (which results in the breaking apart of the nucleus). He shared the Nobel Prize for physics in 1979 with Sheldon Glashow and Abdus Salam.

▶ Personal and Social Implications of the Physical Sciences

Personal and Community Health

Maintaining your personal health depends, in large part, on the work of physicists and chemists. Does that sound a bit surprising? Just think about it for a moment. Every medication was most likely created by chemists, any instrument used to fix broken bones or repair other body parts uses metals and plastics that came from a physical scientist's laboratory, and many of the diagnostic procedures used to identify the causes of illnesses emerged from the laboratories of physical scientists. To be sure, scientists from other disciplines are obviously also heavily involved in the development and delivery of personal health care, but in many ways, chemists and physicists carry out the fundamental research upon which health-related work is done.

Your health, and that of those around you, also depends a great deal on the environment in which you live. And knowledge about that environment emerges, in part, from the work of physicists and chemists. The quality of land surfaces, oceans, and atmosphere is constantly being assessed (and hopefully improved) as a result of the basic research done by physical scientists and the engineering of diagnostic instruments and remedial equipment done by engineers.

Hazards, Risks, and Benefits

The degradation of natural resources—whether the land, water, or atmosphere—poses a severe threat to the health and well-being of *all* populations of living things. Many scientists work to acquire knowledge that will serve as the basis for inventing devices and systems to measure changes in environmental quality and to use chemical agents and physical processes to retard or correct problems that affect life in its many forms.

One example of work in this area is that done to stop or at least slow down depletion of the ozone layer, which is a part of the atmosphere that shields us from certain radiant energy. The free movement of ultraviolet radiation through the atmosphere and to the skin surfaces of living things can cause serious harm. The instrumentation for monitoring the ozone layer, the modification of industrial processes to slow down ozone depletion, and even the creation of chemicals to retard sunburn have all emerged from work done in the physical sciences.

Personal safety for workers as well as travelers can be increased by the use of certain technologies, such as air pollution measurement devices, built-in sprinkler systems, and procedures and equipment that permit the rapid exiting of individuals from factories, businesses, homes, automobiles, trains, and airplanes. Technology has also brought us increased surveillance techniques that can be used to safeguard our personal and societal well-being. Of course, with these surveillance techniques comes the potential for risk to our privacy. As with any technology, we must carefully weigh the benefits against the risks.

Physical Science Technology: Its Nature and Impact

If you've eaten a slice of toast today or traveled in a car or turned on a light, you have used technology that came from the physical sciences. The study of matter and energy has not only revealed some of the deepest secrets of our natural world but has also provided the basis for most of the world's technology. Engineers have used the principles of physics and chemistry to produce items as varied as disposable diapers, long-lasting lipstick, palm-sized computers, and nuclear bombs.

Even your personal recreation possibilities have been affected by the technology that's rooted in the physical sciences. Plastic kayak hulls, indoor ice rinks, roller coasters, snowboards, specialized shoes, and, of course, the aluminum softball bat have all come from work in the physical sciences.

The Design of Physical Science Technology

The engineers who create technology based on the findings of the physical sciences develop measuring devices, materials, and tools whose design usually meets the following criteria:

1. It addresses a problem that has been clearly identified and for which data can reasonably be expected to be gathered.
2. It serves as a data-gathering tool to assist in physical science exploration or as a device to be used in the fabrication of a material or product.
3. It can withstand a wide range of external environmental conditions.
4. It presents data in a manner that is readily interpretable by chemists or physicists, as appropriate.
5. If it is a tool, it can be readily used.
6. It preserves the safety and health of individuals who use it.
7. It provides constant feedback about the accuracy of the data being represented or the efficiency of the tool.

Examples of Physical Science Technology

Many devices have been developed from the foundation of knowledge produced from work in physics and chemistry, and they can be used to produce further knowledge about the physical world or to improve the quality of life:

Radiation-measuring devices   Wind tunnels

Computers   Lasers

Circuit testers   Solar energy collectors

Particle accelerators

Chemical reagents (molecules that can split or combine other molecules)

Oscilloscopes (convert sound waves to electrical signals that can be viewed on a screen)

Spectrophotometers (measure the intensity of light absorbed at different wavelengths)

Chemical indicators (for example, a solution that can identify the presence of hemoglobin)

Calorimeters (can measure the amount of energy released during a chemical reaction)

Long-Term Implications of Physical Science Technology

The technological implications of the physical sciences are profound. In the area of medicine, knowledge of the behavior of elements, including how they may be combined to form molecules, has led to the development of pharmaceutical agents that have done much to reduce pain and suffering. In the area of food production, the application of scientific techniques to the measurement of trace amounts of substances has provided government and other agencies with the capability of analyzing food products to determine if they meet certain standards of purity.

Technology has led to the creation of an amazing array of brand-new materials. In addition to some rather extraordinary synthetic materials—including plastic, nylon, and rayon—there are some very specialized materials used to construct recreational boats and automobiles, replacement devices for joints and organs, and even aircraft that are invisible to radar.

In this early part of the twenty-first century, we have seen how discoveries related to digital electronics have been used to develop widespread use of the Internet, computerized manufacturing, computing for personal and business uses, and the ubiquitous cellular phone. Looking ahead, we can see truly extraordinary technology emerging, including miniature robotic devices, made of only a few hundred or thousand molecules, that can be injected into the bloodstream and travel to specific sites, where they will repair damaged tissues or organs! And while this may sound like science fiction, is it really that hard to foresee?

Before you answer that question, consider all of the technological innovations that seemed like utter fantasy at one time but have become real—very real. It seems that what the human mind can imagine, the physical sciences can create!

chapter 16

Matter and Motion

Content

From Atoms to Rockets and Other Technological Wonders

Imagine the thrill of driving in the Indy 500. Now imagine doing so in a fuel cell vehicle, like that shown in Figure 16.1. In the not-too-distant future, we may all be trading in our gas-guzzling cars for newer models powered by other forms of energy, such as fuel cell, solar energy, or electricity.

Our ability to accomplish such amazing things as faxing a document across the world or microwaving a meal in only a matter of minutes is the result of the technology available to us. We can have full-color photographs in a minute; we have drugs that can prevent or cure illnesses; we have automobiles, airplanes, unbelievable weapons of destruction, and, wonder of wonders, sonic toothbrushes. The rapid pace of technological development is a direct result of our increased knowledge of the nature of matter, our ability to release energy from it, and our ability to predict and control the motion of objects.

Figure 16.1
This fuel cell vehicle may seem an oddity today, but it's quite likely the car of the future.

Matter

Go to **MyEducationLab**, select the topic Physical Science, view the artifact entitled "Materials Cannot Occupy the Same Space," and complete the questions that accompany it.

Silly Putty, a chicken, and pistachio ice cream all have something in common. They are all *matter*. Anything that occupies space and has mass is matter. The earth, the planets, the sun, and everything else in our universe that has mass and occupies space are composed of matter. This definition allows us to distinguish matter from energy. *Energy* is defined as the capacity to do work or to produce change. Electricity, light, sound, heat, and magnetism are all considered forms of energy. Matter and energy are related. Under very special circumstances, matter can be changed into energy, and energy can be changed into matter.

Scientists have found that all matter in the universe exerts an attractive force on all other matter in the universe. The matter in this book is exerting an attractive force on you, and you are exerting an attractive force on the matter in the book. This attractive force is called *gravitation,* and it exists regardless of the location of the matter. The strength of the force depends on the amount of matter in both you and the book, for example, and your distance from the book. The force that the earth exerts on matter is called *weight.* The weight of an object is a measurement of the extent to which the earth pulls on the object and the object pulls on the earth.

There are many different types of matter. The earth is itself a vast storehouse of matter. Here is a list of some of the common types of matter found in the earth's crust (and next to each is the symbol that scientists use to refer to it):

	Symbol	Percent by Weight
Oxygen	O	47.3
Silicon	Si	27.7
Aluminum	Al	7.9
Iron	Fe	4.5
Calcium	Ca	3.5
Sodium	Na	2.5
Potassium	K	2.5
Magnesium	Mg	2.2
Hydrogen	H	0.2
Carbon	C	0.2
All others		1.5

The Physical Properties of Matter

We usually describe matter by its physical properties. We say various types of matter are *solids, liquids,* or *gases.* These forms of matter are known as *states,* or phases, of matter. Rocks and soils are solids. Water may be found as a solid, a liquid, or a gas. The state that matter is in can be determined by observation. A solid has a definite shape. A liquid takes the shape of its container. Both solids and liquids have a definite volume: They occupy a certain amount of space. A gas takes the shape of its container, but it also expands to fill all of the container. Thus, gases do not have a definite volume: Their volume is the volume of the container.

We can also describe matter by describing its color, how hard or soft it is, the extent to which it dissolves in liquid, and whether it is easily stretched or broken. Another specific physical property of matter is its *density.* Unlike units of weight, which represent a gravitational attraction for that matter, units of mass, such as grams and kilograms, represent the amount of matter in something. Density is commonly measured as mass per unit of volume and is expressed in grams per cubic centimeter. To find the density of something, we can simply divide its mass by its volume. Density may also be found by dividing weight by volume.

Kinetic Molecular Theory

Matter can be changed from one state to another. A cold, crystal-clear icicle receives morning light from the sun and begins to change—to melt into water. A child wanting to draw a "happy face" without paper and pencil breathes on a cold mirror, creating a thin film on which to draw. All these changes in matter are *physical changes.* The matter has undergone a change, but the original substance remains. Some of the water in the solid icicle has changed to a liquid; the water vapor exhaled by the child has become the tiny droplets of water that formed the "canvas" for the drawing. No new substances were produced in any of these cases. They were all physical changes. This can happen, scientists have concluded, for several reasons:

1. Matter is made up of small particles called *molecules.*
2. Spaces exist among the molecules.
3. The molecules of matter are in constant motion.

Changes in the state of matter, then, can be explained by the motion of molecules. A solid has a definite shape because its molecules are arranged in a pattern. Although the molecules hold this pattern, they also vibrate. If heat is applied to a solid, the rate at which its molecules vibrate becomes so fast that they break away from one another in the pattern. If we add sufficient heat, the solid melts and becomes a liquid. If we add even more heat, the molecules in the liquid may move fast enough to escape from the surface of the liquid and enter the air. These molecules have gone from the liquid state to the gaseous state—the process known as *evaporation.*

If we reverse this process, if we take the heat from gas, its molecules may slow down sufficiently to form a liquid. If we take away more heat, the molecules may begin forming the patterns in which they exist in their solid state. These types of changes in matter are physical changes. No new matter is created.

The kinetic molecular theory of matter can be used to explain the expansion and contraction of matter. When the speed of the molecules in matter increases, they bump into one another more and tend to spread apart. *Expansion* of matter thereby occurs. If heat is removed, the molecules move more slowly and tend to come closer to one another. When this occurs, matter *contracts.*

Chemical Changes in Matter

Some types of matter are capable of uniting with one another to form very different types of matter. This characteristic is known as a *chemical property of matter*. A chemistry teacher holds a piece of magnesium with tongs and places it in the flame of a Bunsen burner. Bright light is produced, and the metallic magnesium changes to a white powder: magnesium oxide. Changes resulting in substances that differ from the original substance are known as *chemical changes*. The rusting of iron and the burning of wood or paper are other examples of matter changing and combining to produce new forms of matter.

Although we can describe these changes in many ways, to fully understand the chemical properties of matter it will be helpful to think about specific chemical changes. The roasting of a marshmallow and the phenomenon of fire are two good examples.

The Roasting of a Marshmallow   A marshmallow is made of sugar. Sugar contains carbon, hydrogen, and oxygen. You've probably noticed that when you heat a marshmallow over an open flame, the surface of the marshmallow darkens. It does so because the sugar undergoes a chemical change. The heat added to the sugar breaks the sugar into carbon, hydrogen, and oxygen. The dark material on the outside of the marshmallow is carbon. Hydrogen and oxygen leave the heated marshmallow in the form of water.

Fire   The flickering candles atop a birthday cake, the ring of blue flame on a gas stovetop, and a raging forest fire are all examples of matter that is undergoing a rapid chemical change that gives off both light and heat. In each case, three things are present: (1) a material that will burn (a fuel), (2) oxygen, and (3) something that heats the fuel to a temperature at which it will burn. The temperature at which a fuel will begin to burn is known as its *kindling temperature.*

All common fuels contain carbon. When these fuels burn, they undergo various chemical changes. The carbon within them combines with oxygen to form the gas carbon dioxide. If there is insufficient oxygen, however, carbon monoxide, a very dangerous gas, is released. If the fuel contains hydrogen as well as carbon, during *combustion* (another word for "burning"), oxygen in the air also combines with the hydrogen in the fuel to form water vapor. In each of these examples, matter undergoes chemical changes to become a new type of matter, and in each example, it is the presence of oxygen that allows the changes to occur quickly.

Elements, Compounds, and Mixtures

An *element* is a substance that cannot be separated into simpler substances by chemical changes. Carbon, hydrogen, and oxygen are elements and the basic building blocks of all matter. Through chemical changes, elements can be combined into *compounds*. Table salt is a compound composed of the elements sodium and chlorine. Its chemical name is *sodium chloride*. Elements and compounds can be represented as *formulas*. The formula for table salt, for example, is NaCl. This combination of symbols indicates that there is one part sodium (Na) and one part chlorine (Cl) in salt. The formula H_2O stands for a combination of two parts of hydrogen and one part of oxygen.

If we break down a molecule of water or a molecule of salt, we will produce hydrogen and oxygen or sodium and chloride. These parts of a molecule are called *atoms*. When we write the chemical formula H_2O, we are indicating that a molecule of water contains two atoms of hydrogen and one atom of oxygen. When we write CO_2, we are saying that one molecule of carbon dioxide contains one atom of carbon and two atoms of oxygen. The number written below the line in the formula tells us how many atoms (if more than one) of the preceding element are present in the molecule.

Chemists use chemical equations to describe chemical changes in matter. Let's see how this is done. If we place a clean iron nail in a solution of copper sulfate, a chemical change will occur: The iron nail will become coated with a reddish covering, which is copper. As this occurs, the blue color of the copper-sulfate solution becomes less intense. In the chemical change that occurs, iron in the nail changes places with some of the copper in the copper sulfate. The equation that describes this reaction is as follows:

$$Fe + CuSO_4 \rightarrow FeSO_4 + Cu$$

Fe represents iron. $CuSO_4$ represents copper sulfate. The arrow means "forms" or "yields." On the right side of the arrow are the products of the chemical change: $FeSO_4$ (iron sulfate) and Cu (copper). Notice that the number of atoms on each side of the arrow is the same. No atoms are gained or lost during a chemical change.

Not all combinations of elements form compounds. The principal test is whether the various substances can be separated from one another. For example, if you were to mix a small amount of sand with a small amount of salt, no chemical change would occur. If you had patience and a strong lens, you could probably separate the two materials. It would take time, but it could be done, because the salt and sand do not chemically unite with each other. Any combination of materials that can be separated from one another is known as a *mixture*. The air we breathe is a mixture of various gases. The soil we walk on is a mixture of various rocks and minerals.

The Parts of an Atom

Scientists know a great deal about the way in which atoms interact with one another as well as the way in which they absorb and release energy. With this knowledge, scientists have constructed a model of what they believe an atom to be. Keep in mind that the protons, neutrons, and electrons that make up an atom are not really the round objects they are depicted to be in diagrams. Even so, diagrams can help us understand atomic interaction. Figure 16.2 illustrates six different atoms. The electrons in these atoms exist in the outer rings, or shells. Electrons are negative electrical charges that orbit around the atom's nucleus. A *shell* is an energy level on which an electron exists.

The center of an atom is called the *nucleus*. This is the place where *protons*, heavy particles having a positive electrical charge, and *neutrons*, heavy particles having no electrical charge, are found. It is the protons and neutrons that make up most of the atom's mass. An *electron* has only $\frac{1}{1837}$ the mass of a proton. Atoms are electrically neutral. That is, an atom contains as many positive charges (protons) in its nucleus as there are negative charges (electrons) around the nucleus. Some atoms do not have neutrons. The hydrogen atom, for example, has one proton and one electron but no neutrons. The helium atom consists of two protons and two neutrons in the nucleus surrounded by two orbiting electrons.

The *atomic number* of an element is the number of protons it contains. The *atomic weight* of an element is the weight of its protons plus the weight of its neutrons. An element's atomic weight is also determined in relation to the weight of a carbon atom, which is 12 units. A hydrogen atom has about $\frac{1}{12}$ the weight of a carbon atom. Therefore, hydro-

Figure 16.2 Models like these are used to keep track of the number and placement of protons, neutrons, and electrons in atoms.

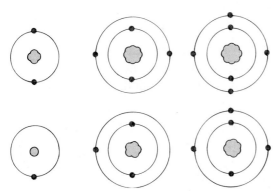

gen has an atomic weight of about 1. Magnesium is about twice as heavy as carbon; its atomic weight is 24. Here are the atomic weights of some elements:

Aluminum	27.0
Carbon	12.0
Chlorine	35.5
Copper	63.5
Gold	196.9
Hydrogen	1.0
Lead	207.2
Oxygen	16.0
Silver	107.0
Sulfur	32.1

Some atoms of an element are slightly heavier than most atoms of the same element. These atoms are known as *isotopes*. Isotopes differ in atomic weight because they have a different number of neutrons. For example, the most common sulfur atom has an atomic weight of 32. However, some sulfur atoms have a weight of 36. Both types of atom are sulfur atoms, since they have an atomic number of 16. The average atomic weight of sulfur atoms is about 32.1. The 0.1 results from the atoms that have slightly different atomic weights. These isotopes of sulfur have the exact chemical properties of the element sulfur. Their physical properties, however, may differ from those of the predominant sulfur atoms. There are at least three isotopes of hydrogen in nature: hydrogen 1, hydrogen 2, and hydrogen 3. Study Figure 16.3 and note that most hydrogen atoms have one proton and one electron. However, hydrogen isotopes may have one proton, one electron, and one neutron (hydrogen 2) or one proton, one electron, and two neutrons (hydrogen 3). The atomic weight of hydrogen represents the average weight of all hydrogen atoms, including the isotopes.

Quarks and Other More Fundamental Parts of Matter

The preceding discussion of the fundamental parts of matter is intended to provide you with background knowledge for teaching the science content commonly covered in elementary and middle school materials. Although these materials seldom carry their descriptions much further, you should be aware that there are even more fundamental particles than protons and neutrons. Scientists have hypothesized the existence of these particles as a result of experiments carried out with powerful atom-smashing devices. Two of the many laboratories involved in this type of work are the Stanford Linear Accelerator Center in California and the European Laboratory for Particle Physics in Geneva, Switzerland.

Figure 16.3   The nuclei of these hydrogen isotopes have the same number of protons but not the same number of neutrons. Because the number of neutrons is different, each isotope has slightly different physical properties.

Hydrogen 1	Hydrogen 2	Hydrogen 3
Atomic weight 1.008	Atomic weight 2.014	Atomic weight 3.020

At the present time, it is believed that the most fundamental particle of matter is the *quark*. There are six kinds, or *flavors*, of quarks that are known as *up, down, strange, charm, bottom,* and *top*. Each kind of quark has three varieties, or *colors: red, blue,* and *green*. (The terms *flavor* and *color*, of course, bear no relationship to our everyday use of these words.) Scientists believe that protons and neutrons are composed of quarks.

Obviously, a discussion of quarks is not likely to occur in elementary school. However, you should be aware of the term, as your students will undoubtedly come across it. You may want to encourage some children to pursue independent reading on this and other more advanced subjects.

Nuclear Energy

When matter undergoes chemical change, some of the electrons of the various atoms involved may be exchanged or shared. In doing this, energy is released. Energy can also be released through the nucleus of the atom. Such release of energy is brought about not by an ordinary chemical change but by a change in the nucleus of the atom. Atoms of some elements, such as radium and uranium-235, are naturally unstable: They have the potential to break up spontaneously. When they break up, they throw off some of their particles and a great amount of energy. The energy that is given off is known as *radiation*. Radioactive materials are too dangerous to be handled directly, because they may discharge rays that can damage human cells. This special property of radioactive materials is used by doctors to treat cancer patients. Focused radiation can destroy cancer cells; unfortunately, healthy cells also may be destroyed in the process.

Some uranium isotopes break down spontaneously, releasing energy and particles of matter that form radium. The nucleus of the radium atom can break down further to form a stable atom of lead. The breakdown of the nucleus of an atom is called *fission*. The amount of energy released in this process can be calculated by multiplying the amount of matter that is seemingly destroyed (actually it's converted to energy) by c (the speed of light) squared. If one gram of matter is changed directly to energy, the amount of that energy is equal to the amount produced by the burning of about 3,000 tons of coal. When scientists control these reactions, they harness great amounts of energy. A controlled flow of chain reactions occurs in nuclear power plants. In detonated atomic bombs, on the other hand, uncontrolled chain reactions take place.

Matter can also be changed by a different type of nuclear reaction: *fusion*. In this process, atoms combine to create an atom that has a smaller mass than the sum of the original atoms combined. The change in mass releases energy. Hydrogen bombs operate as a result of fusion. The sunlight that reaches you each day, as well as the light from the other stars in the universe, is all produced by nuclear fusion. At present, controlled fusion has been accomplished only in the laboratory.

Motion

Go to **MyEducationLab**, select the topic Physical Science, watch the video entitled "Physics at an Amusement Park," and complete the questions that accompany it.

"How long till we get there?"

This question commonly punctuates long family drives to distant destinations, regardless of the frequency of the parents' response. The driver, if he or she is patient enough, will try to give the child a response that is based on the speed of the automobile, its present location, and the location of the destination.

The *speed* of an automobile is determined by the distance it travels in a given unit of time. The units commonly used to express the speed of automobiles are *kilometers per hour* and *miles per hour*. We can use our knowledge of speed to answer the child's question about how long it will take to reach a destination fairly easily. Because speed is the distance divided by the time, we can multiply the speed of the object by the time available to find how far we will travel in that time. If you know the destination is 100 kilometers (about 60 miles) away and the average speed during the journey will be 50 kilometers (about 30 miles) per hour, you can divide the speed into the distance and remark calmly that the journey will take about 2 hours.

If you specify the speed of an object and the direction in which it is traveling, you are talking about an object's *velocity*. We call changes in velocity *acceleration*. An automobile speeding up is accelerating. The rate of acceleration is equal to the change in velocity divided by the time it took for the change. If your car stops at a red light during your trip and then gains a speed of 50 kilometers per hour (about 30 miles per hour) in 10 seconds, traveling in a straight line, the change in velocity is 50 kilometers per hour and it occurs in 10 seconds. Therefore, the rate of acceleration of the car is 5 kilometers per hour per second (about 3 miles per hour per second).

Because scientists define velocity as both speed and direction, an object that moves with constant speed yet changes direction is accelerating. For example, a racing car traveling around a track at a constant speed is accelerating because its direction is constantly changing.

With this information in mind, we can now consider objects in motion. To understand why objects in motion behave as they do, we need to understand the laws that govern them.

Newton's Laws of Motion

Have you ever blown up a balloon, held its end shut, and then released it to watch it rocket around the room? You may not have realized it, but you were demonstrating a phenomenon described about 300 years ago by Isaac Newton. Newton's observations of the motion of objects led him to reach conclusions that we now refer to as *laws of motion*. Newton's three laws of motion help us explain the motion of objects that are subjected to forces.

Newton's first law of motion, sometimes called the *law of inertia*, states that an object at rest will remain at rest and a body moving with a constant velocity in a straight line will maintain its motion unless acted upon by an unbalanced external force. This law tells us that in order to change the position of an object at rest, we must apply a force to it. Similarly, if we wish to change the velocity of an object, we must apply a force. To move a golf ball from the grass of a putting green to the hole, we apply a force with the putter. To increase the speed of an automobile, we cause the engine to increase the forces that turn the wheels. To slow down a bicycle that is moving along at a constant velocity, we apply frictional forces by using the brakes.

Newton's second law of motion states that the amount of acceleration produced by a force acting on an object varies with the magnitude of the force and the mass of the object. If the force on an object is increased and no mass is added to or taken away from the object, the object's acceleration will increase. Specifically, this law tells us that an object will accelerate in the direction in which an applied force is acting and that the acceleration will be proportional to the applied force. For example, when we begin to push or pull a child in a wagon that was stationary, the wagon moves in the direction of the push or pull and increases its acceleration as the force we apply increases.

Newton's third law of motion states that for every action, there is an equal and opposite reaction. The air escaping from the blown-up balloon mentioned earlier moves in one direction; it is the action force. The balloon moves in the opposite direction as a reaction to the action force.

Gravity and Motion

Whether you live in Beijing, China, or Paramus, New Jersey, you know that what goes up must come down, and the downward path is always the same: All objects fall toward the center of the earth. After studying the behavior of falling objects, Newton concluded that the cause for the path of a falling object was the attractive force that exists between masses. This force of attraction depends on two variables: the mass of each attracting object and the distance between them.

Very precise scientific instruments have revealed that Newton was correct in his conclusion that all masses exert attractive forces. Newton's conclusion is called the *law of universal gravitation,* and it is a fundamental law of the universe. Every mass in the universe attracts every other mass with a force that varies directly with the product of the masses of the objects and inversely with the square of the distance between them. This law can be written as an equation:

$$F = G \, m_1 m_2 / r^2$$

Although it may not look it, this is actually an easy equation to understand. The m's represent the masses of the two objects. The r is the distance between the centers of the objects. The G is a constant. In other words, the same value of G is used every time the equation is solved. F stands for the actual force of attraction between objects. As noted earlier, the force of attraction between an object and the earth is the object's weight.

The earth's gravitational pull causes falling objects to accelerate at the rate of 9.8 meters per second per second (32 feet per second per second). This means that an object increases its speed 9.8 meters per second (32 feet per second) during each second it falls. Strictly speaking, this rate applies to objects falling through a vacuum, because the presence of air retards the acceleration of objects that have a large surface area compared with their mass.

Jet and Rocket Engines

Rockets and jet airplanes are designed to capitalize on Newton's third law of motion. Both utilize engines that discharge hot gases in one direction (an action force) so as to produce thrust (a reaction force). In both engines, chemical energy is changed to the energy of motion.

The jet engine uses kerosene fuel to heat air that is taken into the engine. The products of the combustion of kerosene reach a high temperature and pressure and leave through the rear of the engine. This produces the reaction force, or *thrust.* In the turbojet, turning compressor blades take in air through the front of the engine and force it into the combustion chamber. At this point, kerosene is sprayed into the air and ignited. The hot exhaust gases expand and move out the back of the engine, turning the turbine blades in the process. The turbine blades are connected to the compressor blades and cause them to turn and bring in more air.

The engine of a rocket is designed to operate in outer space in the absence of oxygen. To provide the fuel that is burned with the oxygen needed for burning, tanks of liquid oxygen are carried near the engine. Some rocket fuels do not require oxygen. Instead, they use a chemical known as an *oxidizer.*

Flight

> *"Just pull the yellow oxygen mask toward you.*
> *Now cover your mouth and breathe normally."*

Each time a flight attendant says that prior to takeoff, I begin to wonder: How exactly do you breathe *normally* when an aircraft is having a serious problem that may soon give it the aerodynamic characteristics of a rock? I understand the physics of flight, but I am always astonished that masses of metal can become airborne. It is most amazing!

What causes an airplane to rise? The answer is a force called *lift.* A plane's wings are shaped so that air going across the upper surface moves at a higher velocity than the air going across the bottom surface. This causes a region of low pressure to form above the

Figure 16.4   Each of these controls can change an airplane's direction.

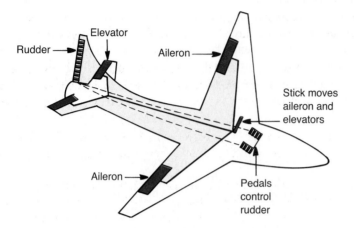

wing. The air pressure below the wing is greater than the air pressure above the wing, causing an unbalanced upward force.

The lifting force on a wing can be varied in several ways. For example, the faster a plane moves, the more lift is created. The angle that the front of the wing makes with the oncoming air also affects lift. This angle is known as the *angle of attack.* In fixed-wing aircraft, the pilot varies the angle of attack by using movable portions of the wing called *wing flaps,* or ailerons. Extending the wing flaps also increases the surface area of the wing. A larger surface produces more lift than a smaller surface.

While the forward motion, or thrust, of a jet is a reaction force to hot exhaust gases expelled from the rear of the engine, propeller-driven planes move forward because of the propeller, which is designed very much like a miniature wing. The pressure on the rear surface of the propeller pushes the plane forward. Pilots use the term *drag* to describe a force that retards the forward motion of an aircraft. It results from the friction between the air and the surfaces of the aircraft.

The direction in which an airplane moves is controlled by the pilot's use of the ailerons, elevator, and rudder (see Figure 16.4). The *elevator* (the movable flap on the horizontal part of the tail) causes the aircraft's nose to move up or down. The *rudder* (the movable flap on the vertical portion of the tail) causes the nose of the aircraft to move left or right. The *ailerons* change the lift on the wing surfaces. The pilot uses all these surfaces in combination to turn the plane.

Summary Outline

    I. Anything that occupies space and has mass is matter.

        A. A change in matter from one state, or phase, to another is a physical change.

        B. Kinetic molecular theory is used to explain a variety of changes in matter.

        C. A change in matter that produces a new substance is a chemical change.

        D. Matter exists as elements, compounds, and mixtures.

        E. Atoms are composed of smaller particles.

        F. Under special conditions, portions of the matter in an atomic nucleus can be converted to energy.

    II. Matter can be caused to move from place to place.

        A. Newton's laws of motion describe how the motion of an object will change as a result of the application of a force.

        B. The law of universal gravitation states that all masses are attracted to all other masses by a force that varies directly with the product of the masses and inversely with the square of the distance between them.

        C. The motion of jet planes and rockets can be explained by Newton's third law of motion, which states that for every action there is an equal and opposite reaction.

        D. Airplanes fly as a result of the action of two forces: lift and thrust.

chapter 17

Energies and Machines

Content

How Energy Is Transferred

"Pssst. Drop your pencil at exactly 9:15. Pass it on."

A little mischief is about to take place, and a substitute's teaching day is about to take a turn for the worse. It's an old prank, but it will work once again. At precisely 9:15, 25 pencils fall from desktops to the floor, and innocent faces gaze about, waiting for the substitute's reaction.

I'll bet that the conspirators in the old drop-the-pencils-on-the-floor routine don't realize that they are demonstrating an important scientific phenomenon: the process of energy change. Imagine that the substitute teacher outsmarted the class by not reacting to the tap, tap, tap of the pencils, and the class decided to try a repeat performance. Follow the energy changes as the prank is recycled.

When you pick up the pencil from the floor and place it on your desk, you do work and use energy. Your body uses some of the energy created by the chemical breakdown of the food you eat. This energy enables you to move, grasp, and lift. It may surprise you to learn that when you pick up the pencil, some of the energy that you use increases the pencil's potential energy. The pencil resting on the desk has some potential energy. When it is lifted above the desktop, it has even more. It is higher above the earth than

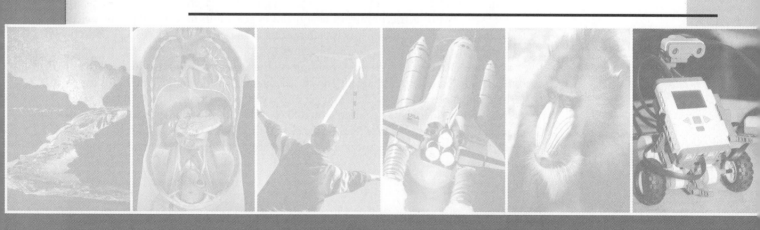

it was before, and if you drop it again, you will hear a sound when it hits the floor. That sound is produced when the potential energy of the falling pencil is converted to the energy of motion.

Energy of motion is called *kinetic energy*. The amount of kinetic energy of an object is equal to $\frac{1}{2}mv^2$ (one-half the object's mass times its velocity squared). As the pencil falls, it moves faster and faster, continually gaining kinetic energy. When it hits the floor, its acquired kinetic energy causes the floor and itself to vibrate, producing a sound wave (a vibration that moves through the air). The pencil and the floor also heat up slightly. The original potential energy of the pencil was transformed into sound energy and heat energy.

The Conservation of Energy

The ability of energy to change its form is the basis of the *law of conservation of energy*. This important law simply states that energy is neither created nor destroyed. Whenever we use energy, we change its form, but we do not use it up. The energy we use may be changed to a less useful form, but it still exists. In the example of the pencil being picked up, placed on a table, and dropped again, some of the sun's energy was stored in food. Your digestive and cellular-respiration processes released some of this energy, and you used this energy to lift the pencil. In the process, you transferred some of this energy to the pencil in the form of heat. The pencil acquired potential energy from its new position, and as it fell, it displayed increasing kinetic energy. The kinetic energy was changed to heat and sound. It is at least theoretically possible, if difficult in practice, to recapture this heat and sound energy and reuse it. All the energy you used to pick up the pencil still exists. It has just changed to other forms of energy.

According to Albert Einstein, energy and matter are related. In fact, they can be considered one and the same, because each can be converted to the other. Einstein's equation $E = mc^2$ does not contradict the law of conservation of energy because mass can be viewed as stored energy. Scientists no longer say that energy is never used up; instead, they say that the total amount of energy and mass in the universe is never used up. The interchangeability of mass and energy has resulted in the use of a more general law than either the law of conservation of energy or the law of conservation of mass. Now it is generally agreed that we should think in terms of a *law of conservation of mass and energy*.

Energy Transfer in Action: The Segway

For an extraordinary example of how cutting-edge technology is able to transfer energy from one source to another, just consider the *Segway Human Transporter (HT)* (see Figure 17.1). This personal transportation vehicle, invented by a group of scientists led by Dean Kamen, can "read" the minute changes in muscle pressure transmitted by its rider and move accordingly: forward, backward, left, right, and so on.

In terms of energy transfer, the process begins at an electricity-generating plant, where fossil, hydroelectric, or nuclear energy causes generators to turn and produce electrical energy. That electrical energy is then sent through power wires to a variety of destinations: homes, factories, schools, and businesses.

At one such destination—say, your home—the Segway is connected to an electrical outlet and its batteries are charged. The stored chemical energy in the batteries is transformed into electrical energy once you get onboard and direct the Segway. In fact, based on what other riders have reported, you'll likely find that the Segway is so sensitive to changes in your body position that it will seem as though it's reading your mind! In any event, the wheels turn as electrical energy is converted to kinetic energy, and the Segway rolls along.

Figure 17.1
The Segway Human Transporter (HT) converts electrical energy to kinetic energy.

Structural components are thoroughly analyzed, fatigue and strength tested, and subjected to long-term durability testing.

Segway HT's on-board processors (10 in total) monitor balance and system health 100 times a second, responding instantly to the rider's movements.

Segway HT's electrical system meets or exceeds industry standards for electrical safety and interference.

Fully redundant electrical design can continue to balance and gracefully come to a stop after a component failure.

The Segway HT's design puts the weight low, resulting in a center of gravity only 10 inches above the ground.

Electrical Energy

The bright flash of lightning jumping across the night sky and the subdued light coming from a desk lamp are both produced by electrical energy. They are similar to each other in that the source of their energy is electrons. They are different, however, in that lightning is a form of static electricity and the light from a desk lamp is a form of current electricity.

Static Electricity

Lightning, a spark jumping from your fingertip to a metal doorknob, and the clinging together of articles of clothing when they are removed from a clothes dryer are all forms of *static electricity*. In order to understand them, you will need to review your knowledge of atoms. An atom consists of protons, neutrons, and electrons. Each proton has a positive charge—one unit of positive energy. Each electron has a negative charge—one unit of negative energy. Neutrons have no charge. Because atoms normally have the same number of electrons as protons, the positive and negative charges cancel each other out. As a result, atoms usually have no charge; they are considered neutral.

If, however, an electron is removed from a neutral atom, the atom is left with a positive charge. If an electron is added to a neutral atom, the atom acquires a negative charge. When certain materials are rubbed together, electrons are transferred from one surface to the other. In other words, one surface gains electrons and acquires a negative charge. The other surface, having lost electrons, is left with a positive charge. When a surface has acquired a strong negative charge, the extra electrons may jump to a neutral or positive object. You see this jump of electrons when you see a spark. A spark is a rapid movement of a number of electrons through the air.

You may have had the exciting adolescent experience of kissing a boyfriend or girl-friend with braces and being shocked by a spark. The excitement may have come from the kiss, but the shock was the result of static electricity. Electrons were probably inadvertently rubbed from the fibers of a rug or other floor covering by the soles of the "kisser" or "kissee," giving that person's body a surplus negative charge. The extra charge was removed by the spark jumping from the negatively charged person to the neutrally charged person.

Lightning is a giant spark that sometimes occurs when clouds that have acquired a charge suddenly discharge electrons. The rapid outward movement of the air heated by the lightning causes the sound wave that reaches our ears as thunder.

Current Electricity

Sometimes it seems that my doorbell never stops ringing, and, if I am busy, I get grumpier each time it rings. If I get grumpy enough, sometimes I curse Benjamin Franklin, Thomas Edison, and my local electric company all in one breath for bringing electrical energy to my home. Even so, I know we are living at a time when electricity is a necessity, not a luxury. Occasional electrical blackouts bring activities to a grinding halt: Traffic lights don't work; elevators stop wherever they happen to be; heating and cooling equipment stops functioning; lights go out; and food in refrigerators begins to rot. Electricity has become a necessity for us because it is an excellent and convenient form of energy. It can be converted to heat, to light, and to sound. It can also be used to operate electric motors that cause objects to move.

Current electricity comes from a stream of electrons moving through a conductor. The rate at which the electrons move through the conductor is called *current*. So many electrons flow through a given point in a conductor in a short time that scientists have found it useful to have a unit to represent a large number of electrons flowing through a current. The unit for measuring electrical current is the *ampere*. It is equal to the flow of 6.25×10^{18} electrons past a point in a conductor in 1 second. Electron current that moves in just one direction is termed *direct current*. Electricity from dry cells (batteries) is direct current. Current that changes direction is known as *alternating current*. Electricity for home or industrial use is alternating current.

A *conductor* is any material that electrons can move though easily. Such a material offers little *resistance* to the flow of electrons. The amount of resistance to the flow of electrical energy is measured in *ohms*. Examples of materials that are good conductors include copper, silver, gold, and aluminum. Energy is transferred through a conductor by a process that includes high-energy electrons imparting their energy to the outermost electrons of adjacent atoms of the conductor.

Not all substances are good electrical conductors. Wood, rubber, plastic, and dry air are examples of substances that do not carry electrical energy very well. Because these materials are poor conductors, they offer high resistance to the flow of electrons and are called *insulators*.

Some substances—for example, germanium, silicon, and selenium—are neither conductors nor insulators. They are *semiconductors* that can be used to make tiny electrical devices to control the flow of electrons. Semiconductors are widely used in the fabrication of computer chips.

Electrical Circuits   Figure 17.2 (page 359) illustrates a simple electrical circuit. In an electrical circuit, electrons with a great deal of energy leave a source (in this case, a dry cell), move through a conductor (a wire), lose some energy in a load or resistance (a light bulb), and return to the source. As long as the switch is closed (the wires are connected), energy is transmitted through the circuit. The light bulb—the resistance—converts some of the electrical energy to light energy.

Figure 17.2 In this electric circuit, the lamps are wired in series.

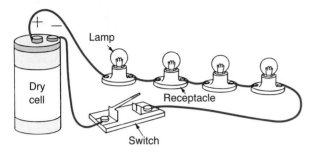

Figure 17.3 When lamps are wired in parallel, as shown here, the bulbs will remain lit even if one goes out.

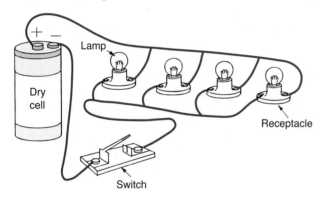

In the type of electrical circuits illustrated in Figure 17.2 and Figure 17.3, chemical reactions in the dry cell provide the push that starts and keeps high-energy electrons flowing into the conductor. The electrons leave the negative pole, or port, and return to the dry cell at the positive pole, or port. The amount of push that causes the electrons to move through a circuit is called the *voltage*. The voltage that a dry cell can produce can be measured by determining the amount of work that the electrons do in the circuit. The unit of measurement for voltage is *volts*.

Although there are many ways to attach sources of high-energy electrons, conductors, and loads to each other, we usually concern ourselves with two basic circuits: series circuits and parallel circuits. A *series circuit* has only one path for electrons. A circuit that has more than one path for electrons is a *parallel circuit*. Figure 17.2 shows a series circuit. Figure 17.3 shows a parallel circuit.

Because there is only one path, the current is the same throughout a series circuit. In a parallel circuit, however, the current is divided among many paths. If one light bulb in a series circuit burns out, all the light bulbs will go out because only one path for electrons exists. If a light bulb in one branch of a parallel circuit burns out, the bulbs in the other branches will remain lit.

Magnets, Generators, and Motor Although chemical reactions in dry cells can start a flow of electrons through a conductor, moving a conductor through a magnetic field or moving a magnet so that the lines of force in the magnetic field cut through the conductor can also start a flow of electrons. Metals that have the ability to attract iron, steel, and some other metals are said to have a property called *magnetism*. Magnetite, or lodestone, is a naturally occurring iron ore that has such magnetic properties. Alnico—a material that contains aluminum, nickel, cobalt, and iron—can be used to make a permanent magnet, even though aluminum, nickel, cobalt, and iron are not naturally magnetic. When these substances are brought near a strong magnet, they become magnetic.

All magnets have two poles: a north pole and a south pole. A bar magnet suspended at its center by a string will rotate until one end points north. The magnet end that points north is known as the *north-seeking pole*. The other end of the magnet is the *south-seeking pole*. If two **N** poles or two **S** poles are brought near each other, they will repel. When unlike poles are brought near each other, they attract. The rotation of a freely suspended bar magnet until it is oriented north and south is evidence that the earth itself is a magnet. The earth's magnetic pole attracts the pole of a magnet.

Around all magnets is a region that we call a *magnetic field*. If we move a conductor through a magnetic field so that it cuts through the lines of force in the field, an electric current will be produced in the conductor. An electrical generator produces electrical energy either by spinning a coiled conductor between the poles of a magnet or by rotating a magnet or series of magnets around a coiled conductor. Of course, a source of energy is needed to spin the coiled conductor or rotate the magnets. For commercial electrical generators that source may be moving water; fossil fuels such as coal, gas, and oil; or nuclear fission.

An electrical generator permits us to produce electricity. An electric motor permits us to put electricity to work moving objects. A simple electric motor converts electrical energy into the energy of motion by means of a coil of wire wrapped around a metal core. This wire-wrapped core is suspended between the magnetic poles of a permanent magnet. When a current flows through the coil, it becomes a magnet. The coil's **N** and **S** poles are repelled by the **N** and **S** poles of the permanent magnet. As a result of this repulsion, the coil turns. If we change the direction of flow of electricity through the coil, the location of its **N** and **S** poles will change. The coil will continue to spin as its ends are continually repelled by the poles of the permanent magnet.

Sound Energy

Sounds affect us in many different ways. The purring of a kitten brushing against your leg may make you feel wanted. The chirping of baby birds may make you feel joyful. The uproarious and chaotic sounds of sanitation workers waking up your neighborhood with an early morning symphony of bangs, crunches, screeches, and shouts may annoy you immensely. But what causes the sounds that bring you pleasure or irritation?

What Causes Sound?

All sounds, whether they come from a garbage-can orchestra or a kitten, are produced by vibrating matter. A vibrating object receives energy from a source (a kitten or a dropped garbage can) and transfers energy to a *medium,* such as air. The medium carries the energy away from the vibrating object. Sound travels in all directions from its source. In other words, you can hear a sound whether your ears are above it, to the side of it, or below it.

A vibrating tuning fork is a good example of a source of sound. When a tuning fork is struck, its prongs move back and forth rapidly. When a prong moves in one direction, it presses together the modules in the air ahead of it. This pressed-together air is known as a *compression.* As the tuning fork moves in the opposite direction, it causes a portion of air to pull apart. This area is known as a *rarefaction.* The movement of each prong back and forth alternately produces compression and rarefaction.

The molecules in the air disturbed by the vibration of the tuning fork during compression transfer energy to adjacent molecules before returning to their original positions during rarefaction. The newly disturbed molecules pass some of their energy on to still other molecules, and the process is repeated. If you could see the molecules being disturbed, you would see areas of compression and rarefaction, or *sound waves,* being continuously created and moving away from the source of the vibration. A full sound wave consists of one compression and one rarefaction.

Sound waves require a medium for transmission. They cannot travel through a vacuum, so, if you are wondering how astronauts communicate with one another in the vacuum of space, they do so using radio transmissions. Radio waves do not require a medium. Sound waves travel most rapidly through solids and least rapidly through gases. At a temperature of 0°C, sound travels at a speed of 340 meters per second (about 1,090 feet per second) in air. In water, sound travels at about 1,420 meters a second (about 4,686 feet a second).

The *wavelength* of a sound wave is the distance between the centers of two rarefactions. The amount of energy contained in a wave is interpreted by our ears as the loudness or softness of a sound. The loudness, or *intensity,* of a sound is measured in decibels. The *pitch* of a sound—how high or low the sound is—depends on the number of complete vibrations that the vibrating object makes in one second. This rate of vibration is known as the *frequency.*

● Sound Can Be Absorbed or Reflected

Sound waves that strike a surface may be so strong that they travel through the object struck. However, some surfaces absorb little sound and cause the sound wave being received to bounce off the surface, or be reflected. Reflected sound waves that can be distinguished from the original sound are known as *echoes.* Although echoes are interesting to hear, they can be distracting. Therefore, many classrooms are fitted with sound-absorbing tiles or draperies.

Some of the energy carried by a sound wave causes the surface of the object it strikes to heat up slightly. Usually, the amount of heat produced cannot be detected without the use of special instruments.

Light Energy

Light energy, like sound energy, travels in waves, but a light wave is very different from a sound wave. Light waves travel at the speed of 300,000 kilometers per second (about 186,000 miles per second) and do not require a medium. Thus, light waves, unlike sound waves, can travel through a vacuum.

Light energy is produced from other types of energy. If we burn a substance, one of the products of combustion is light energy. The light is released as a result of the electrons in the substance changing energy levels as new compounds are formed. Electric light bulbs change electrical energy to light energy. The light energy that reaches us from the sun and other stars is the result of nuclear explosions. On stars, huge amounts of matter are converted to energy as a result of nuclear fusion. In nuclear fusion, hydrogen atoms are fused together to form helium atoms, a process accompanied by the release of light energy as well as other types of energy.

Light energy can be transformed into other forms of energy, such as heat or electricity. If you've ever had a sunburn, you've experienced both the conversion of light energy into heat (as your skin became warm) and the effect of light energy on the molecules of substances that make up your skin (as it turned red or blistered).

● The Reflection and Refraction of Light

Light is able to pass through some materials, such as clear plastic or glass. A material that light can pass through is called *transparent.* Materials that light cannot pass through are called *opaque.* Materials that permit some, but not all, light to pass through are called *translucent.* Windows made of frosted glass are translucent.

As light passes from one medium to another, it is bent, or *refracted.* Light traveling through air bends as it enters water, glass, or clear plastic. This bending, or refraction, of light waves can be put to good use. A lens, for example, changes the appearance of objects because the image we see through the lens is produced by rays of light that have been bent. Eyeglasses, microscopes, hand lenses, and telescopes all provide images formed by light rays that have been refracted.

A *convex* lens is thicker in the middle than it is at its edges. Such a lens pulls light rays together. The point at which rays of light are brought together by the lens is called the *focal point.* The distance from the focal point to the center of the lens is the lens's *focal length.* When light is reflected from an object through a convex lens, the rays of light are brought together at the focal point, and an image is formed. The size, position, and type of image formed depend on the distance of the object from the lens. If the object is more than one focal length from the lens, the image is inverted and formed on the opposite side of the lens. This type of image is called a *real image,* and it can be projected onto a screen. If the image is two focal lengths away, the image is the same size as the object.

Figure 17.4

These ray diagrams for convex lenses illustrate how a convex lens focuses light. Light passing through the lens converges to form an image that can be seen on a screen when the object is more than one focal length from the lens. When the object is less than one focal length from the lens, a virtual image is formed. It cannot be projected on a screen.

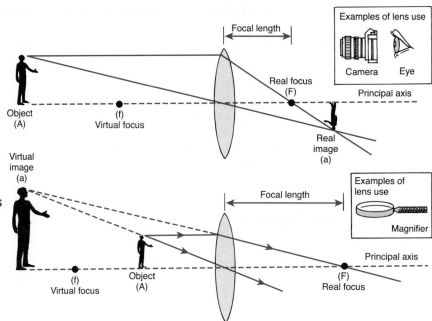

If the object is less than one focal length from the lens, the image formed is magnified and rightside up. This type of image is called a *virtual image*. It is formed on the same side of the lens as the object and can be seen by looking through the lens toward the object, but it cannot be placed on a screen. When you use a convex lens as a magnifier, the image you see is a virtual image.

The refraction of light through a lens can be illustrated with a *ray diagram*. Look at the ray diagrams in Figure 17.4. As you study them, note that the *principal axis* is an imaginary line passing perpendicular to the lens through its center. The *virtual focus* is the point on the axis at which the light would converge if you passed the light through the lens to the object, rather than from the object to the lens.

A lens that is thicker at its edges than at its center is a *concave lens*. A concave lens causes light rays to bend toward its edges. This type of lens can produce only virtual images that are smaller than the real objects (see Figure 17.5).

Figure 17.5 As this ray diagram for a concave lens illustrates, the lens disperses light, and the image produced cannot be seen on a screen.

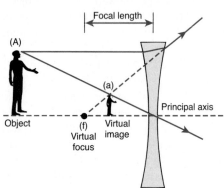

● Light, Prisms, and Color

Have you ever been surprised to see an array of colors projected on a wall or ceiling as a result of sunlight passing through a crystal glass? This band of colors is called a *spectrum*. Some pieces of glass are made to separate sunlight or artificial light into a spectrum. A triangle-shaped piece of such glass is called a *prism*.

The colors of a spectrum represent the components of a light wave that enters a prism. As the light wave is refracted by the prism, the light is separated according to wave lengths. Each wavelength corresponds to a different color. The colors of a spectrum caused by the refraction of light by a prism are red, orange, yellow, green, blue, indigo, and violet.

The color of an object we see is a property of the wave length reflected from the object. *Pigments*—the chemical substances that we usually think of as the sources of color—actually produce their effects because they absorb some light waves and reflect others. Grass is green to our eyes because pigments in grass absorb the red, orange, yellow, blue, indigo, and violet waves and reflect the green.

Heat Energy

Suppose that one hot summer afternoon, you decide to buy a double-dip chocolate ice cream cone and sit in the park while you eat it. As you walk toward the park clutching your cone, you will certainly notice the effect of heat on ice cream. Heat from the hot surrounding air will flow to the colder ice cream, causing an increase in the temperature of the ice cream, a lowering of the temperature of the surrounding air, and the immediate need for a napkin as the change in the temperature of the ice cream results in a change in the ice cream's state—from solid to liquid. The phenomenon of melting can be a good starting point for understanding heat and how it brings about change.

What Is Heat?

Heat is energy that travels from a warm substance to a cool substance. Keep in mind that all substances are made of molecules, and molecules, even in solids, are in constant motion. The motion and positions of these molecules determines the internal energy of (the energy within) a substance. If the molecules in a substance move slowly, the substance has a low level of internal energy. If the molecules move rapidly, the substance has a high level of internal energy. *Temperature* is an indication of the internal energy of a substance. The higher the temperature of a substance, the greater its internal energy and the more heat it releases to a cool substance. The temperature of a substance is measured in *degrees*. There are two temperature scales in wide use: the Celsius, or centigrade, scale and the Fahrenheit scale.

A *thermometer,* which measures temperature, consists of a narrow column of mercury or tinted alcohol sealed in a glass tube. Changes in temperature cause the liquid in a thermometer to expand or contract. Because the mercury or alcohol within the thermometer expands and contracts more than the surrounding glass with each degree of temperature change, we can see changes in the mercury or alcohol level.

Two important markings on all thermometers are the freezing and boiling points of water. The Celsius thermometer shows the temperature at which water freezes as 0° and the temperature at which water boils as 100°. The Fahrenheit scale shows the temperature at which water freezes as 32° and the boiling temperature as 212°. Wherever possible, use a Celsius thermometer and Celsius measurements in the classroom.

How Is Heat Measured?

Because it is virtually impossible to add up the individual energies possessed by the millions of individual molecules found in even a very small amount of a substance, heat energy must be measured indirectly. This is done by measuring its effect on a substance. The standard unit of heat is the *calorie,* the heat required to raise the temperature of 1 gram of water 1° Celsius. Because this is a very small amount of heat, the *kilocalorie,* which equals 1,000 calories, is a more practical unit. The energy contained in foods is expressed in kilocalories.

In the English system of measurement, the British Thermal Unit (BTU) is the standard unit of heat. This is the amount of heat required to raise the temperature of 1 pound of water 1° Fahrenheit.

How Do Changes in State Occur?

When you knock on a door or kick a tire, your hand does not go through the door and your foot does not go through the tire, even though each object is made of millions of molecules that vibrate. Therefore, there must be some force that holds the molecules together. The forces that hold molecules together are known as *cohesive forces*. By adding heat to an object, we cause the individual molecules of the object to move more freely. If we add sufficient heat, the molecules of a solid will move out of their fixed positions, and the solid will melt to form a liquid. The addition of even more heat can cause the molecules in the liquid to break free of the cohesive forces. At this point, the liquid becomes a gas. These transformations are called *changes of state*.

Machines

It is our ability to harness the various types of energy discussed in the previous sections that permits us to use machines to do work. To understand how machines operate, you need to understand what a force is. In its simplest terms, a *force* is a push or a pull. Machines enable us to increase a force, increase the speed of an object, change the direction in which a force is acting, or change the place where a force is acting. Machines work by changing one form of energy to another.

Regardless of the type of machine we study, we are always concerned with two forces: the effort and the resistance. The *effort* is the force we apply. The *resistance* is the force we overcome. We are also concerned with the amount of resistance that can be overcome by the application of a given effort. In scientific terms, this quantity is known as the *mechanical advantage*. There are various ways of calculating the mechanical advantage of a machine. In many cases, we can simply divide the resistance by the effort.

When we use a machine, we put energy into it. But not all of this energy goes into moving the resistance; some is lost to friction. The *efficiency* of a machine is a comparison of the work done by the machine (the energy put out by the machine) with the work (energy) put into it.

In Chapter 16, Newton's laws were discussed. You will recall that they are used to explain how forces can change the motion of objects. Humans discovered, through the invention of simple machines, that they could multiply the force they could apply to an object or change the direction in which an effort force is applied.

Figure 17.6   There are three classes of levers. In a first-class lever, the fulcrum falls between the resistance and the effort. In a second-class lever, the fulcrum is at one end, the effort at the other end, and the resistance at some point between the two. In a third-class lever, the effort is applied between the fulcrum and the resistance.

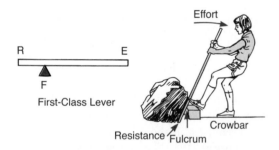

First-Class Lever

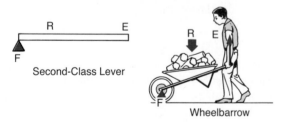

Second-Class Lever

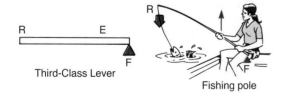

Third-Class Lever

Simple Machines

You may not realize it, but the school yard seesaw is a simple machine: a *lever*. Wheelbarrows and fishing poles are also levers, as are crowbars, shovels, hammers, and oars. All levers, regardless of shape, have three parts: *a fulcrum, an effort arm,* and *a resistance arm*. As shown in Figure 17.6, there are three types, or classes, of levers. Note the location of the effort, resistance, and fulcrum in each type. It is the position of the fulcrum that determines the type of lever.

Levers are not the only simple machines. Others are the wheel and axle, the pulley, the inclined plane, the screw, and the wedge.

Figure 17.7 A fixed pulley remains stationary, while a movable pulley travels with the object.

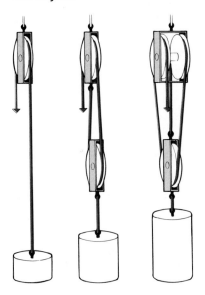

All other machines (which are known as *compound machines*) combine at least two simple machines.

The *wheel and axle* can be thought of as two circular objects, one larger than the other. The larger one is the wheel; the smaller one is the axle. Think of the wheel as a lever that can be moved in a complete circle around its fulcrum. The axle is the wheel's fulcrum and is at the center of the wheel. Examples of the wheel and axle are the windlass, water wheel, doorknob, pencil sharpener, screwdriver, windmill, and potter's wheel. A wheel and axle increase the effort force applied to it. When an effort force is applied to the wheel, a larger force is produced at the axle. However, the wheel moves slowly because of the resistance the effort must overcome. When effort is applied to the axle, there is less resistance, and the increased force moves the wheel more quickly. To find the ideal mechanical advantage of a wheel and axle, divide the radius of the wheel by the radius of the axle.

A *pulley* is a grooved wheel that turns loosely on an axle. The grooved wheel and axle do not have to turn together. The grooved wheel is called a *sheave*. The frame in which it rotates is called the *block*. Pulleys may be either fixed or movable. Figure 17.7 shows examples of each. A fixed pulley does not travel with the resistance, or *load;* a movable pulley does. A block and tackle is a combination of a fixed pulley and a movable pulley. The mechanical advantage of a pulley can be calculated by dividing the effort distance (the distance the load moves) by the resistance distance (the distance the rope you pull moves) or by dividing the resistance by the effort. The ideal mechanical advantage of a pulley system can be determined simply by counting the number of supporting ropes. Figure 17.7 shows how mechanical advantage can be achieved through an increase in the number of supporting ropes and pulleys in the system. Assuming the same effort is applied in each pulley system shown and that the pulley systems are frictionless, the three-pulley system can lift three times the weight that a single-pulley system can.

An *inclined plane* is a flat surface that is raised at one end. Ramps, slopes, and stairs are inclined planes. A resistance can be moved up an inclined plane to a desired height with less effort than it can be lifted directly to the same height. The ideal mechanical advantage of an inclined plane can be found by dividing the length of the inclined plane (the effort distance) by its height (the resistance distance).

A *screw* is a twisted or rolled-up inclined plane. Some common screws are a wood screw, a bolt, a screw jack, a brace and bit, and an auger. Screws are used to lift objects, to hold objects together, and to carry things from place to place. The rotary motion of a turning screw is changed into a straight-line motion by a lever, which is needed to turn the screw. The ideal mechanical advantage of a screw is the distance the effort moves divided by the distance the resistance moves (the distance between the threads of the screw, or its *pitch*).

A *wedge* is a double inclined plane. Some common wedges are knives, needles, axes, can openers, and cold chisels. Wedges are used to pierce, split, cut, and push apart things. Effort is needed to move the wedge into the resisting object. The ideal mechanical advantage of a wedge can be calculated by dividing its length by the thickness of its widest end.

● Friction

To work, every machine, whether simple or complex, must overcome friction. *Friction* is the resistance that an object meets when the surface of the object rubs against another surface. Friction retards motion and generates heat. It is the result of the irregularities that exist in every surface. Even surfaces that seem smooth to our touch consist of bumps and grooves. To overcome the attraction of particles of the surfaces to one another and the retardation of motion caused when a bump hits a groove, some of the energy used to move an object is changed to heat where surfaces are in contact.

There are many ways to reduce friction. Ball bearings, oils, and other lubricants permit surfaces to slide across one another more easily. If you drive a car, you should know that both the condition of bearings at the junction of the axle and wheels and the quality and quantity of lubricating oil in the engine must be checked periodically. If this is not done, the metal parts that are in contact will wear excessively or break.

Although we usually think of friction as a phenomenon that must be overcome, friction also has many positive benefits. Our ability to walk, for example, is a direct result of the friction between the bottoms of our shoes and the floor. Without friction, shoes would simply slide across floors and we would not be able to move forward.

Summary Outline

I. Energy is never destroyed. It is changed from one form to another.

II. Electricity is a form of energy that results from the storage or movement of electrons.

   A. Static electricity is produced by an imbalance between the positive and negative charges on the surface of an object.

   B. Current electricity is produced when electrons flow through a conductor.

      1. A source of current, a conductor, and a load (a device that converts electricity to some other form of energy) can be combined to form an electrical circuit.

      2. Generators produce electricity by moving a conductor across a magnetic field or vice versa.

      3. Motors convert electrical energy to kinetic energy.

III. A sound wave is produced in a medium by the vibration of an object.

IV. Light travels in waves that are refracted, or bent, as they pass from one medium to another.

V. The heat energy contained by a substance is the total kinetic energy possessed by the atoms or molecules of the substance.

VI. Machines are devices that enable us to increase a force, increase the speed of an object, change the direction of a force, or change the location of a force.

chapter 18

Physical Science Lesson Ideas

Putting the Content into Action

The Letter

Her throat was hoarse, her eyes itched, and her feet ached. It had been one of those long, long school days. On her way out of the building, she stopped in the main office to check her mailbox. A pink envelope, which signified interoffice mail, was tucked in the back of the box. Fishing it out, she opened it and began to read:

Dear Elizabeth:

You will recall that last year, our elementary science curriculum committee recommended that we revise our entire elementary science curriculum this year. In order to accomplish this, each teacher will be a member of a subcommittee responsible for making recommendations about various parts of the curriculum. I would like to ask you to serve on the subcommittee that will review the physical science units that are presently in the curriculum. Part of that review should include assessing the extent to which the units are correlated to the NSES.

Each subcommittee should be prepared to make recommendations concerning the appropriateness of various units, activities, and materials to the full elementary science curriculum review committee within three months. I would like to thank you in advance for your contribution to this very important effort.

Cordially,

Margaret Stephanson

Margaret Stephanson
Elementary School Curriculum Coordinator

At the bottom of the page, there was a handwritten note: "P.S. Beth, would you mind being the chairperson for the subcommittee? Your principal and I both feel that you would be terrific for the job. Thanks. Margaret." A wry smile crossed Beth's face as she thought about her consistent avoidance of, and lack of interest in, physical science in high school and college and the irony of being appointed chairperson of a subcommittee that was going to focus on physical science units. She shook her head, tucked the letter in the pile of papers under her arm, and walked out the door.

Regardless of whether you enjoy learning about atoms, molecules, and energy, physical science topics make up a substantial portion of any curriculum or textbook series that you are likely to work with. If you enjoyed working with magnets, pushing on levers, playing with tuning forks, and making light bulbs light, you are going to have a lot of fun observing children's involvement in these activities. If you didn't enjoy physical science, you will discover how interesting it can be when approached with a child's sense of wonder.

▶ Getting Started

Try the following true/false statements:

1. Gases do not have mass.
2. Simple machines make work easier by decreasing the force and increasing the distance needed to do work.
3. An object's speed is the same as its velocity.
4. Matter retains its identity during physical changes.
5. If an object is at rest, no forces are acting on the object.
6. Atoms in a solid can be in motion.
7. Work and force are the same.
8. Grass is green because its pigment does not absorb the wavelength of green light.
9. Mass, volume, and weight all describe the same property.
10. The total amount of matter and energy in the universe is constant.

How do you think you did? The answers are given on page 420. These statements address common misconceptions among children and adults about the physical sciences. Often our explanations are well entrenched in our minds, and for good reason. Explanations often make sense based on our mental models of phenomena. However, good science requires a healthy dose of skepticism and openness to revisions of our mental models as we acquire insights through experience and reflection. Teaching often consists of re-educating by creating experiences and insights that challenge children's current understandings and that force them to revise their mental models and explanations. The first step to re-teaching is to probe children's current understanding. Therefore, the beginning of a unit or lesson usually starts by assessing children's prior knowledge.

▶ Probes for Assessing Prior Physical Science Knowledge and Conceptions

The probes and sample responses that follow come from informal interviews that I or my students have done with children. I think you'll be amazed at some of the responses and motivated to develop probes that you can use *before* planning units and lessons.

Probe	Responses That Reveal Prior Knowledge and Conceptions
• After showing a child an ice cube and a glass of water: *What is the difference between these two things?*	"Ice is frozen and water is plain." "One's colder, it's been frozen. Oh, and how fast the molecules are moving."
• After putting a magnet on a metal file cabinet: *Why do you think the magnet sticks?*	"Because the drawer is metal and the magnet is a different kind of metal that sticks." "Because it's a magnet." "Because one has got negative charges and one has got positive—or something like that."
• After showing some eyeglasses: *How do eyeglasses work?*	"I'm not sure. I think it has something to do with the shape and the way that they carved it."
• *Why is it easier to bike down a hill than up a hill?*	"The gravity pulls on the bicycle when you are going down the hill."
• *What are some ways that people could save energy?*	"Turn off the lights, radio, and TV. "Wear a sweater instead of turning up the heat." "Be careful of what you throw away."
• After turning a desk lamp on for a minute: *Slowly move your hand toward the bulb, but don't touch it. How is it possible for you to feel the warmth from a fire, the sun, or a light bulb when you are not touching it?*	"Because they are so hot that it comes on so strong. It comes all the way down to the earth from the sun or comes to your hand from the light bulb."
• *How is an airplane able to stay in the air?*	"The pressure from the air keeps it up somehow—it can dip up or down—I really don't know."

Unit, Lesson, and Enrichment Starter Ideas

Unit Plan Starter Ideas and Questions

That great idea for a science-teaching unit may come from deep within your brain, your school curriculum guide, a state science curriculum framework, a science resource book, a course, a workshop, a discussion you have with children, or some other source. Unfortunately, a great idea (like a friend, an umbrella, and a good restaurant with cheap food) is sometimes hard to find when you really need one.

To make it easier for you to come up with great ideas for science units, I have prepared two different sources of unit starter ideas, which are presented as three lists:

1. The first is based on the National Science Education Standards (NSES) for science content. I created these starter ideas for standards related to grades K–4 and 5–8.

2. The second source of starter ideas is based on my study of physical science topics that commonly appear in school curriculum guides. These are shown by grade level.

I am certain that the unique compilation of starter ideas that follows will help you plan and create wonderful discovery-based teaching units.

Because science is about seeking explanations, each starter idea based on the NSES is accompanied by a big question. The question serves as the anchor for the unit. Each inquiry lesson of the unit should contribute to a deeper, more comprehensive answer to the unit question. At the conclusion of the unit, children should be able to provide an explanation of their answer to the question that reflects what was taught in the unit.

 Ideas Based on the NSES K–8 Content Standards

> NSES **Content Standard K–4:** Physical Sciences [PS]
>
> As a result of activities in grades K–4, all students should develop an understanding of:
>
>   Properties of objects and materials
>
>   Position and motion of objects
>
>   Light, heat, electricity and magnetism[1]

▶ **STARTER IDEAS** for Objects and Materials

UNIT TITLE: *Observe, Think, Sort*

QUESTION: What are some properties of matter?

UNIT OVERVIEW: Children classify the objects in collections of marbles, blocks, small tiles, and pebbles into categories based on weight, shape, color, and size.

UNIT TITLE: *Tell Me About It*

QUESTION: How can properties of matter be measured?

UNIT OVERVIEW: Children use tools such as rulers, balances, and thermometers to take, record, and describe measurements they make about the items in a collection of solid objects and containers of liquids.

UNIT TITLE: *Water Changes*

QUESTION: What makes water change from solid to liquid to gas?

UNIT OVERVIEW: Children observe and explain why water and other substances can be changed from a solid to a liquid to a gas and from a gas to a liquid to a solid.

▶ STARTER IDEAS for Position and Motion of Objects

UNIT TITLE: *Spatial Relationships*

QUESTION: Where is it?

UNIT OVERVIEW: Using three objects labeled "a," "b," and "c," children describe their relative positions using the terms *in back of, in front of, above, below,* and *beside.*

UNIT TITLE: *Forces Cause Changes*

QUESTION: How did it get there?

UNIT OVERVIEW: Children demonstrate to their peers how an object's change in position is related to the strength and direction of the applied force.

UNIT TITLE: *Vibrations Cause Changes*

QUESTION: How do sounds change?

UNIT OVERVIEW: Using a variety of objects, children demonstrate that sound is produced by vibrating objects and that pitch can be changed by changing the object's rate of vibration.

▶ STARTER IDEAS for Light, Heat, Electricity, and Magnetism

UNIT TITLE: *Paths of Light*

QUESTION: How can light be directed?

UNIT OVERVIEW: Using mirrors, lenses, focused-beam flashlights, and pins to mark path positions, children compare the actual paths of beams of light to predicted paths of light through a maze.

UNIT TITLE: *Electrical Energy*

QUESTION: What is the path of electricity through a circuit?

UNIT OVERVIEW: Children identify the characteristics of a simple series circuit, build a circuit, and use it to produce light, heat, sound, or magnetic effects.

UNIT TITLE: *Magnets*

QUESTION: What are the properties of magnets?

UNIT OVERVIEW: Children use permanent magnets to demonstrate attraction, repulsion, the presence of poles, and the existence of magnetic fields.

> **NSES** **Content Standard 5–8:** Physical Sciences [PS]
> As a result of the activities in grades 5–8, all students should
> develop an understanding of:
>
> Properties and changes of properties in matter
> Motion and forces
> Transfer of energy

▶ **STARTER IDEAS** for Properties and Changes
of Properties in Matter

UNIT TITLE: *It's Dense*

QUESTION: How dense is it?

UNIT OVERVIEW: Students calculate the densities of regular and irregular objects
using tools such as a ruler, graduated cylinder, overflow container, and balance.

UNIT TITLE: *Matter Changes*

QUESTION: What properties identify the mystery powders?

UNIT OVERVIEW: Students gather, organize, and chart data about the changes in
characteristics of sugar, cornstarch, baking soda, and flour as a result of testing
each by heating, adding water, and adding vinegar.

UNIT TITLE: *Physical and Chemical Changes*

QUESTIONS: Is the change physical or chemical? How can you tell?

UNIT OVERVIEW: Students observe teacher demonstrations of physical and chemical changes, make observations, and correctly group the demonstrations into
those that show physical changes and those that show chemical changes.

▶ **STARTER IDEAS** for Motion and Forces

UNIT TITLE: *Observe the Motion*

QUESTION: Where is it going, and how does it get there?

UNIT OVERVIEW: Children gather and record data about the positions, directions
of motion, and speeds of battery-powered toy cars moving across the classroom
floor.

UNIT TITLE: *Graph the Motion*

QUESTION: Where is it now?

UNIT OVERVIEW: Children graph the positions, directions of motion, and speeds
of battery-powered toy cars moving across the classroom floor.

UNIT TITLE: *Predicting Motion*

QUESTION: Where is it going?

UNIT OVERVIEW: Children predict the motions of objects acted upon by
unbalanced forces that cause changes in speed or direction.

▶ **STARTER IDEAS** for Transfer of Energy

UNIT TITLE: *Generators Small and Large*

QUESTION: How are the energy transfers from the hand generator and power station the same and different?

UNIT OVERVIEW: After classroom science activities and field work at a power station, children make labeled diagrams that compare the initial energy sources and the energy transfers that occur in a classroom hand-operated generator and at the power station.

UNIT TITLE: *Energy Changes*

QUESTION: What happens to the electrical energy that comes into the school?

UNIT OVERVIEW: Children construct hands-on displays for a school science fair that demonstrate the transfer of electrical energy into heat, light, and sound.

UNIT TITLE: *Energy—The Space Traveler*

QUESTION: What happens to the energy from the sun?

UNIT OVERVIEW: After library research work and class discussions, children explain how energy is produced by the sun, transmitted through space, and captured by green plants.

NSES **Content Standards Related to:**

Science and Technology [S&T]

Science in Personal and Social Perspectives [SPSP]

History and Nature of Science [HNS][2]

UNIT TITLE: *Egg Saver*

QUESTION: How can energy be absorbed?

UNIT OVERVIEW: Using everyday materials, children design containers that can protect an uncooked egg dropped from the height of a stepladder to a school sidewalk.

UNIT TITLE: *Safest, Cleanest, Cheapest*

QUESTION: What are the safest, cleanest, cheapest ways to generate energy?

UNIT OVERVIEW: After library research work, Internet research, field work, and classroom discussions, children compare three alternate forms of energy with respect to safety, pollution, and economy.

UNIT TITLE: *Who Are They?*

QUESTION: Who are five women physicists, and what are their contributions to science?

UNIT OVERVIEW: After library research work, Internet research, and classroom discussions, children identify and write brief biographies of five women scientists who have had made significant contributions to the physical sciences.

Lesson Plan Starter Ideas
for Common Curriculum Topics

Sometimes, you will be responsible for teaching lessons that are part of units prepared by committees of teachers in your school district or units that are commercially available. You may wonder how to break these units into lessons. To help you come up with lesson ideas for the physical sciences, I have analyzed a variety of teaching units and prepared a list of lesson plan starter ideas based on topics usually covered in these units. The lesson descriptions are very specific, so each description may also be viewed as the lesson's principal objective.

▶ **STARTER IDEAS** for Characteristics of Matter

- Identify, compare, and classify objects on the basis of touch, taste, smell, and emitted sounds.
- Describe objects using the characteristics of size, shape, and color.
- Infer the characteristics of a small object in a closed box without looking in the box.
- Name three forms of matter (gas, liquid, and solid), and give an example of each.
- Illustrate how the movement of molecules in solids, liquids, and gases differs using body movements.
- Create a diagram illustrating an imaginary experiment that shows that air expands when it is heated and contracts when it is cooled.

▶ **STARTER IDEAS** for Energy and Its Changes

- Observe that sound waves are produced by objects vibrating in a medium.
- Use a stopwatch correctly during an outdoor activity to calculate the speed of sound.
- Identify light, heat, electricity, and magnetism as forms of energy, and prepare a two-column chart that shows a human use for each form.
- Evaluate three different light bulbs to determine which will provide the most light, which will last the longest, and which will be the best value for the money.
- Given appropriate safe materials, construct a simple electromagnet.
- Make a graph that compares the speed of sound with the speed of light.
- Make a hypothesis about the ability of light waves to travel without the presence of a medium, and invent an experiment to test the hypothesis.
- Make a hypothesis to explain the formation of rainbows using the knowledge that water droplets can act as prisms.
- Make a labeled diagram that shows how convex and concave lenses differ in shape.

▶ **STARTER IDEAS** for Forces and Motion

- Observe the operation of various machines, and then identify the effort, force, and resistance.
- Create an illustrated chart identifying the characteristics of six simple machines.
- Draw an imaginary "wake-me-up-and-get-me-out-of-bed" machine that uses at least six different simple machines.

- Make a labeled drawing of one frequently used object that is made up of at least two simple machines.
- Using simple instruments, measure direction, distance, mass, and force of gravity (weight).
- Describe the position of an object relative to another object using the terms *north, south, east,* and *west*.
- Construct a simple machine, and use it to do work.
- Make a hypothesis to explain how a pulley system is able to multiply force, and invent an experiment to test the hypothesis.

▶ **STARTER IDEAS** for Airplane, Jet, and Rocket Motion

- Make a diagram of an airplane in flight, and label the forces of gravity, lift, thrust, and drag.
- Explain how a jet engine takes advantage of the law of action and reaction.
- Explain how gravity affects large objects and that the strength of attraction between objects depends on their masses and distance apart.
- Write a story about a boy or girl who lives on an imaginary planet that does not have gravity.
- Make a diagram of a rocket in flight, and label the action and reaction forces.
- After doing library research on the exploration of Mars, evaluate the likelihood of humans reaching the planet by the year 2020.

WebQuest Starter Ideas

Imagine the WebQuest possibilities for your students when you teach the physical sciences! They'll be able to use the vast resources of the Internet to discover fascinating information about the atoms and molecules that make up everything they see around them—including themselves, how matter and energy interact, and how the sun produces and releases the energy on which every living thing depends.

The starter ideas in this section will help you plan your own physical science WebQuests. As you study the ideas, please keep the following in mind:

1. The starter ideas follow the WebQuest format presented in detail in Chapter 8.
2. The WebQuests are correlated with the NSES for grades K–8 (which are printed inside the front cover).

NSES

3. In the WebQuest context, the term *reports* has a very broad meaning and includes poster preparation, skits, dance, video presentations, labeled diagrams, and, of course, traditional written reports, when and if appropriate.

▶ **STARTER IDEAS** for WebQuests

WEBQUEST TITLE: *The Best Bubble-Making Recipe*

SUGGESTED GRADE LEVELS: 1, 2, 3 (to be done with an adult)

NSES CONTENT STANDARDS: PS 1 and 4; S& T 1

CHALLENGE—MOTIVATION: The King of Bubbledom has asked you to be his "Bubble Maker." He is going to have a birthday party next week and wants everyone there to make bubbles as part of the fun.

Make the Case *An Individual or Group Challenge*

● **The Problem**

Children need science experiences that range across the earth/space, life, and physical sciences. Teachers may tend to include those topics they feel most comfortable with and thus inadvertently limit the scope of the children's learning.

● **Assess Your Prior Knowledge and Beliefs**

1. When comparing your knowledge of the physical sciences to your knowledge of the earth/space sciences and life sciences, do you believe you have acquired more, less, or the same amount of basic science content in each?

	More	*Less*	*Same*
Earth/space sciences	_____	_____	_____
Life sciences	_____	_____	_____

2. When you were a student in grades K–8, would you say you were exposed to more, less, or the same amount of physical science content as you were to life science content and earth/space content?

	More	*Less*	*Same*
Earth/space sciences	_____	_____	_____
Life sciences	_____	_____	_____

3. Gravity is a common physical science topic for children. Identify five discrete items of knowledge that you now have about gravity.

_____

_____

_____

_____

_____

_____

4. Now identify five things about gravity that you think you should know but do not.

_____

_____

_____

_____

_____

_____

● **The Challenge**

You are part of a team of teachers planning a unit on gravity. Give examples of physical science activities you might include.

CHALLENGE—REPORTS: Go on the Internet and find three recipes for making bubble liquid. Try each recipe and list your observations about the bubbles it makes. Then . . .

KEY TERMS FOR SEARCH ENGINES: Bubble Recipe, "Bubbleology," Bubble Making

WEBQUEST TITLE: *How Can the Sun Help Heat Our School?*

SUGGESTED GRADE LEVELS: 2, 3

NSES CONTENT STANDARDS: PS 3; S&T 1 and 2

CHALLENGE—MOTIVATION: The fuel used to heat your school and to make hot water is too expensive. Your principal wants your ideas on how to use the sun's energy to heat the school.

CHALLENGE—REPORTS: Make a sketch of the outside of your school. Then use the Internet to find out how the sun's energy could be used for heating. Now make a new sketch of your school that shows . . .

KEY TERMS FOR SEARCH ENGINES: Solar Homes, Solar Energy, Home Greenhouse

WEBQUEST TITLE: *Simple Machines in a Bicycle*

SUGGESTED GRADE LEVELS: 4, 5, 6

NSES CONTENT STANDARDS: PS 1, 2, 5, and 6; S&T 1, 2, 4, and 5

CHALLENGE—MOTIVATION: Your teacher has asked you to do a science demonstration on the topic of simple machines. To keep the other students' attention, you bring your bicycle to school for it.

CHALLENGE—REPORTS: Make a poster that has a labeled picture of a bicycle and the simple machines it contains. Show your classmates where each machine is on the bicycle. Also . . .

KEY TERMS FOR SEARCH ENGINES: Bicycle Physics, Wheel and Axle, Simple Machines

WEBQUEST TITLE: *What Is an Atom?*

SUGGESTED GRADE LEVELS: 4, 5, 6

NSES CONTENT STANDARDS: PS 1 and 4

CHALLENGE—MOTIVATION: Kelly just told you that atoms are small bits of matter. Kelly also said that there is nothing smaller than an atom. Do you think Kelly is right?

CHALLENGE—REPORTS: Find out if Kelly is right or not. Then write a short poem that tells whether atoms have parts. If they do, tell what they are called . . .

KEY TERMS FOR SEARCH ENGINES: Atom Parts, Atom Model, Proton, Neutron, Electron

WEBQUEST TITLE: *Famous African American Inventors*

SUGGESTED GRADE LEVELS: 4, 5, 6

NSES CONTENT STANDARDS: S&T 1 and 2; HNS 1, 2, 3, and 4

CHALLENGE—MOTIVATION: Do you know who these people are? Dr. Charles Richard Drew, Percy Julian, Lewis Latimer. Do research to find how who they are and what they did as . . .

CHALLENGE—REPORTS: Select any three African American scientists or inventors and study their lives. Then write a one-minute speech that each might give if he or she could visit your class.

KEY TERMS FOR SEARCH ENGINES: African American Scientists, African American Inventors, Science Biographies

WEBQUEST TITLE: *How Do Birds Fly?*

SUGGESTED GRADE LEVELS: 4, 5, 6

NSES CONTENT STANDARDS: PS 5 and 6; LS 4

CHALLENGE—MOTIVATION: Isn't it strange that birds can fly but people can't? You can wave your arms really fast, but you'll never get off the ground!

CHALLENGE—REPORTS: Find out how a bird's body and wings are adapted to make flying possible. Then make two or three labeled drawings of a bird in flight to show . . .

KEY TERMS FOR SEARCH ENGINES: Bird Flight, Bird Wings, Flight Feathers

WEBQUEST TITLE: *How Does a Light Stick Work?*

SUGGESTED GRADE LEVELS: 4, 5, and 6

NSES CONTENT STANDARDS: PS 4, 5, and 6; S&T 4 and 5

CHALLENGE—MOTIVATION: Have you ever had a light stick—one of those plastic tubes that produces light after you bend it? Sometimes, children have them at celebrations and sporting events. Have you ever wondered how light can come from a plastic tube?

CHALLENGE—REPORTS: Get a light stick at a toy store and do research on the Internet to find out how it works. Demonstrate and explain how a light stick works to your class. Make a diagram that includes the part of the light stick that has the chemicals and . . .

KEY TERMS FOR SEARCH ENGINES: Light Stick, Fluorescent, Chemiluminescence

WEBQUEST TITLE: *How Does a Battery Work?*

SUGGESTED GRADE LEVELS: 4, 5, 6

NSES CONTENT STANDARDS: PS 4, 5, and 6; ST 4 and 5

CHALLENGE—MOTIVATION: Your hand-held computer game has batteries, CD players have batteries, and so do many other things you use. Have you ever wondered how a battery produces electricity?

CHALLENGE—REPORTS: Make a collection of small batteries to show your class. Then make a labeled overhead transparency that shows how all of the battery parts make electricity. Use the transparency and battery to explain how a battery works to your class. Also, . . .

KEY TERMS FOR SEARCH ENGINES: Battery Chemistry, Battery Technology, Dry Cell Chemistry

Classroom Enrichment Starter Ideas

In-Class Learning Centers

A well-prepared in-class learning center offers children many opportunities to make their own discoveries. In order to be well prepared, such a center must provide a wide range of materials that encourage hands-on, discovery-based learning, ranging from print and audiovisual resources to art supplies and games. In addition, the learning center must be located where children have ready access to it yet can also be somewhat removed from the larger classroom setting while doing independent activities.

The following starter ideas for in-class learning centers should get you thinking about how to create centers in your own classroom. Note that the relevant NSES is identified for each starter idea and that asterisks indicate those that are particularly suited for young children.

An in-class learning center like this one, called Energy Savers, can encourage students to discover more about the physical sciences.

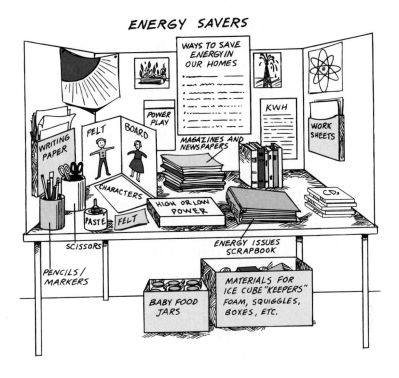

ENERGY SAVERS

▶ **STARTER IDEA** for a Learning Center

CENTER TITLE: *Energy Savers*

NSES CONTENT STANDARD: PS 6

IDEA: Try to locate the center in an area that has enough space for writing, game-playing, dramatizing, and constructing activities. Be sure to provide construction paper, cardboard boxes of various sizes, foam packing peanuts, ice cream buckets, and a scrapbook. Have the children sign up to work for a half-hour on one activity per day in the center. If you have computer software or videos related to energy, make them available in this center, too.

So that students will know what to do in the center, prepare activity cards (cards that give directions for activities you develop) based on the following ideas:

• *Feltboard** Have the children make figures out of paper or cardboard. Glue strips of felt to the backs of the figures, and give them names such as "Walter Waste Energy," "Conni the Conserver," and so forth. Have the children invent and dramatize the adventures of these characters and their friends.

• *Ice Cube Race* Challenge the children to build ice cube "keepers." Provide foam packing peanuts, ice cream buckets, cardboard, tape, and small cardboard boxes. Have the children use baby food jars to hold ice cubes that are allowed to melt at room temperature to get data for a control.

• *Energy Scrapbook** Have the children cut out pictures and articles from newspapers and magazines on such energy issues as nuclear power and solar energy. Then have them prepare scrapbook pages for an energy scrapbook that will be kept in the center.

• *Power Play* Have the children invent and construct a board game that employs a die, tokens, and a set of "chance" cards that say such things as "You left the TV on; go back two spaces" and "You took a 30-minute shower; go back four spaces" and "You put on a sweater instead of turning up the heat; go ahead ten spaces." The children can use file folders or construction paper to make the board.

▶ **ADDITIONAL STARTER IDEAS** for Learning Centers

CENTER TITLE: *Matter Can Change**

NSES CONTENT STANDARD: PS 1

IDEA: Carry out activities that reveal properties of matter, such as melting, freezing, and evaporating.

CENTER TITLE: *Pushes and Pulls**

NSES CONTENT STANDARDS: PS 1 and 2

IDEA: Use a toy car to show how pushes and pulls can affect the positions and motions of objects, such as starting, stopping, moving with constant speed, speeding up, and slowing down.

CENTER TITLE: *Magnet Time**

NSES CONTENT STANDARDS: PS 2 and 3

IDEA: Using bar and horseshoe magnets, do activities to identify the poles and show attraction and repulsion.

CENTER TITLE: *Conductors and Insulators*

NSES CONTENT STANDARD: PS 6

IDEA: Build a working simple series circuit with batteries, wire, a bulb, and a switch; then test a variety of materials to determine how much each is an electrical insulator or conductor.

Bulletin Boards

Good bulletin boards have the potential to be something that children can both look at and learn from. There are many ways to use classroom bulletin boards to enhance physical science units and extend your teaching to nonscience areas. The following list offers a few starter ideas for you. Again, asterisks indicate activities that may be particularly appropriate for young children.

▶ **STARTER IDEAS** for Bulletin Boards

BULLETIN BOARD TITLE: *Matter and Its Composition*

IDEA: Divide the bulletin board into 16 squares: four rows going down and four columns going across. Leave the top of the first column blank, but label the next three columns *Solid, Liquid,* and *Gas.* Label the four rows going down *Object, Molecules, Characteristics,* and *Container.* Set aside three cards and draw a rock on one, a vial filled with colored water on another, and an inflated balloon on the third. Create three cards illustrating the organization of molecules in solids, liquids, and gases; three cards illustrating a solid, a liquid, and a gas in flasks; and six cards listing the characteristics of solids, liquids, and gases. Place the cards in manila envelopes labeled *Object, Molecules, Characteristics,* and *Container.* After discussing the characteristics of solids, liquids, and gases and demonstrating how matter can change from one state to another by melting ice and boiling water, have the children take the cards from the envelopes and arrange them in the appropriate rows and columns, using pushpins to hold the cards in place. Children should do this in their free time; they can check their work using an answer key that you provide.

This bulletin board, Matter and Its Composition, invites students to apply what they have learned.

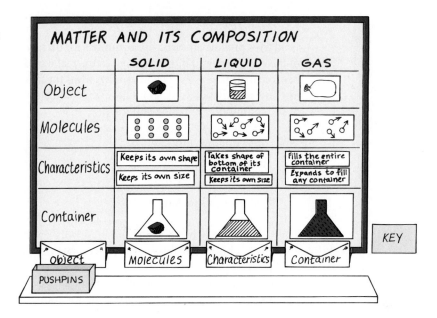

BULLETIN BOARD TITLE: *Sound and Light**

IDEA: Divide the bulletin board into three sections, and label each *Light, Heat,* or *Sound.* Subdivide each section allowing space for children to attach pictures, and add the following subtitles: *Where does it come from? How does it move? How do we use it?* Provide magazines, scissors, drawing paper, and markers so children can locate or create pictures to place in each subsection.

BULLETIN BOARD TITLE: *Find the Forces**

IDEA: Place the title "Find the Forces" across the top of the bulletin board. Have children locate magazine pictures of people actively participating in gymnastics, dancing, or sports. Each week, place one of the pictures on the bulletin board; have children attach index cards with the words *push* and *pull* near the pictures to identify where forces are acting.

BULLETIN BOARD TITLE: *Temperature and You**

IDEA: Draw three large thermometers on the bulletin board showing the following temperatures: 0°C (32°F), 20°C (68°F), 35°C (95°F). Challenge the children to attach magazine pictures or their own drawings depicting outdoor activities that could be done at each temperature.

BULLETIN BOARD TITLE: *The Simple Circuit*

IDEA: Create a three-dimensional bulletin board that is, in fact, a working circuit. Temporarily mount and hook up a dry cell, wires, switch, and bulb holder with bulb. Have children create a label for each item. (*Safety Note:* You must use insulated wire and make sure that neither the bulb nor any bare ends of wire touch any surface. Also be sure that the circuit is switched off after each use.)

BULLETIN BOARD TITLE: *Find the Machine*

IDEA: Create a three-dimensional bulletin board to display items such as a scissors, doorknob, wood chisel, nutcracker, wood screw, clay hammer, and hand-operated egg beater. Encourage children to attach a label on or near each object that identifies the type of simple machine the item is or the name and location of a simple machine within the item.

● Field Trips

Field trips provide amazing opportunities for discovery learning, as they take children out of the classroom and immerse them in the real world. Whether you teach in a city, suburban, or small-town school, you can find ideas for field trips all around you. To understand just how true that is, think about how you could tailor each of these topics to the resources of the community in which you teach:

Forces and machines
The electric company
The telephone company
Types of transportation

The field trip may be to the regional airport or the train depot down the street, but either way, children will be eager to see what the day will hold. After all, children *love* field trips!

Here are starter ideas for field trips for all schools. Note that asterisks indicate activities that may be particularly appropriate for young children:

▶ STARTER IDEAS for Field Trips

FIELD TRIP TITLE: *The Telephone Company**

IDEA: A trip to the local telephone company will be a memorable science lesson that has many language arts, geography, and art applications. When you make the initial contact, find out what the facility contains; repair services are often in a different location and could be considered for a separate field trip. During the actual visit, children can discover how long-distance and overseas calls are made, how records of calls are kept, the many styles of phones, and the latest advances in communication technology.

FIELD TRIP TITLE: *Force, Motion, and Machines*

IDEA: The study of friction can be the basis for various field trips. Contact the showroom of a car, boat, airplane, or snowmobile dealership or the repair facility at a bus station, garage, or airport to arrange the excursion. Alert the individual who will serve as your tour guide that the children will be interested in how the design of the vehicle minimizes air and surface friction, how it's propelled, and what type of energy it uses. As a follow-up to the trip, have children draw diagrams and then build models of what they have seen. They can also invent modifications to the vehicle that would further reduce friction.

FIELD TRIP TITLE: *Energy-Conserving Home**

IDEA: Look around the community for a building or home that was constructed or retrofitted to save energy. One with an active or passive solar system, windmill, off-peak power storage system, or underground design would be especially interesting. Installers of alternative energy systems and building contractors are good sources of information on energy-efficient building techniques and places to visit. After the visit, children can study the school and their homes for energy-efficient features as well as improvements needed.

Many of the factors that make the city an interesting and exciting place to live also make it a place that overflows with field trip possibilities. Here are some additional ideas that should stimulate your thinking about field trips for children in city schools:

▶ STARTER IDEAS for Field Trips

FIELD TRIP TITLE: *Shadow Study*

IDEA: Children track changes in the shadows they see on a sunny day.

FIELD TRIP TITLE: *Simple Machines on the Playground*

IDEA: Children locate and classify playground equipment according to the simple machines incorporated in them.

FIELD TRIP TITLE: *Temperature Here, Temperature There*

IDEA: Children use thermometers to discover if the temperatures at various places on the school grounds are the same.

FIELD TRIP TITLE: *Getting from Here to There*

IDEA: During a walk around the block, children gather data about the numbers of cars, trucks, buses, and bicycles observed traveling on a street. On returning to the classroom, children graph the data they have collected.

FIELD TRIP TITLE: *Count the Passengers*

IDEA: After observing and gathering data about the number of people riding buses, children draw inferences regarding energy savings brought about by the use of public transportation.

FIELD TRIP TITLE: *Harbor Machines*

IDEA: If your city is on an ocean, lake, or river, children can observe machines at work in the harbor.

FIELD TRIP TITLE: *Building Going Up*

IDEA: From a safe distance, children can observe the machines in use at a building construction site to identify the sources of energy for the machines and the simple machines that make up the more complex machines at work.

Additional Field Trip Destinations

Airport control tower

Cellular phone service provider

Chemistry or physics department at a local college

Computer repair facility

Electrical power station (hydroelectric)

Electrical power station (fossil fuel or nuclear powered)

Electronics company

Eyeglass preparation facility

Internet service provider

Oil refinery

Photographic film-processing plant

Radio station

Television station

● Cooperative Learning Projects

As you consider the following starter ideas for cooperative learning projects, keep in mind the importance of stressing the three key aspects of cooperative learning (discussed in detail in Chapter 5):

1. Positive interdependence
2. Individual accountability
3. Development of group process skills

▶ STARTER IDEAS for Cooperative Learning Projects

PROJECT TITLE: *The Living Machine*

IDEA: After doing activities or observing demonstrations related to the three types of simple machines, challenge groups to use their bodies to demonstrate each type. Various members of each group can represent resistance, fulcrum, and effort. Groups can also use their bodies to create and demonstrate a complex machine that uses all three types of simple machines. After the groups have practiced, they should present their machines and have the rest of the class identify the simple machines and locations of the resistance, fulcrum, and effort.

PROJECT TITLE: *Fancy Flyers*

IDEA: This project should occur over a period of days. Provide the groups with a wide assortment of materials (e.g., plastic wrap, paper of different weights, cardboard, strips of balsa wood, glue) that can be used to build model gliders. Have the groups do research to learn about various designs for gliders. After they have studied the topic, encourage each group to prepare three gliders for display and demonstration. If weather permits, have the groups display and demonstrate their gliders outdoors. If this is not possible, the gym or cafeteria might serve as an acceptable environment.

PROJECT TITLE: *Density Detectives*

IDEA: After discussing the concept of density (density = mass/volume), have each group develop a way to find the density of an irregular object and explain its method to the class. (*Hint:* The volume of an irregular solid can be found by determining the volume of water it displaces when it is submerged.)

PROJECT TITLE: *School Energy Survey*

IDEA: Have each group evaluate how the school building loses heat to the outside environment or how heat from the outside environment enters the school. Have groups observe such things as how fast the front doors close, how airtight the windows are, and how well weather stripping seals around door jambs. After organizing their observations, groups should report the results of their studies and their recommendations for slowing down heat loss or heat gain to the class and, if appropriate, to the school principal.

▶ **ADDITIONAL STARTER IDEAS** for Learning Groups

- Provide groups with flashlights, cardboard tubes, wire, "C" or "D" batteries, flashlight bulbs, and other materials, and encourage them to create their own working flashlights.
- Challenge groups to use cardboard tubes, straws, rubber bands, balloons, tape, and so forth to create air-powered rockets that will move along a length of fishing line stretched across the room.
- Challenge groups to use straws, paper, cardboard, and tape to create bridges that will support one or more school books. If you use this idea, be sure that each group gets the same amount of each material you provide and that the bridges must all span a fixed distance, such as 25 centimeters (about 10 inches).

Attention Getters, Discovery Activities, and Demonstrations for Matter and Motion

Attention Getters

For Young Learners [PS 2; SPSP 9]

Why Do We Need to Wear Safety Belts?

Materials
1 small toy wagon or truck
1 doll that can ride in or on top of toy wagon or truck
2 large rubber bands

Motivating Questions
- What direction will the doll move when the wagon suddenly stops?
- If the doll were wearing a safety belt, would it still move?

Directions
1. Display the wagon or truck without the doll. Gently roll it into the wall.
2. Put the doll in the wagon, gently push the wagon, and have the children predict in what direction the doll will move when the wagon strikes the wall.
3. After they have observed the wagon striking the wall, relate the wagon and doll to a car and passenger. Discuss the likelihood of the passenger's striking or going through the windshield if the car hits something or stops suddenly.
4. Use the rubber band to restrain the doll, and repeat the demonstration. Ask the children for their observations.

Science Content for the Teacher
A fundamental law of motion is that an object at rest or in uniform motion tends to continue in that condition. An unrestrained passenger in a forward-moving automobile continues to move forward if the car stops, since he or she is not connected to the car.

For Young Learners [PS 1]

Where Does the Water Go?

Materials	1 sponge	Bowl of water
	Paper towels	3 dishes
	1 clean, dry dishcloth	Pan balance (optional)

Motivating Questions

- How will the sponge (paper towel, cloth) change when we dip it in water?
- Where do you think the water goes when something dries?

Directions

1. In this demonstration, the children will observe a sponge, paper towel, and cloth when dry and when wet. The children will already know that when they dry themselves after a bath or shower, the towels they use become wet, but they may not have connected this knowledge with the concept that some materials can absorb water.
2. Dip the sponge, paper towel, and dishcloth in the bowl of water. Have the children make observations that you record on the board.
3. After wringing out the objects, place them on plates so that further observations can be made. If a pan balance is available, the children can check changes in mass as the objects dry.

Science Content for the Teacher

Many materials are capable of absorbing water. They retain this water as a liquid. The liquid that is in contact with the surrounding air evaporates and enters the air as water vapor.

For Young Learners [PS 2]

Where Are Wheels?

Materials	Easel paper and markers
	Pack of index cards

Motivating Questions

- Is it easier to pull something with wheels or something without wheels?
- Do wheels all have the same shape or size?

Directions

1. Take the children for a walk around the school, both inside and outside the building. Challenge them to find as many wheeled vehicles as they can. As they search, model how a scientist keeps track of information by writing notes on an index card about each wheeled vehicle observed. Use a different index card for each vehicle. Look for such things as automobiles, bicycles, cafeteria and custodial carts, wagons, and trucks. Don't miss the wheels under audiovisual carts and movable chalkboards or room dividers.
2. When you return to the room, prepare a three-column chart that includes a drawing of each vehicle and the number of wheels on it. Have the children discuss how wheels help move objects.

Science Content for the Teacher

Friction is a force that acts against the forward-moving wagon. If the force is large enough, it can slow down or stop the wagon. Wheels reduce the friction between objects and the ground. As a wheel turns, only a small amount of it touches the ground, which reduces the friction between the object and the ground and makes the object easier to move.

Why Do Mothballs Rise and Fall?

Materials
1 unopened 2-liter bottle of club soda
6 mothballs

Motivating Questions
- Where do the bubbles in soda come from?
- What is in the bubbles?
- Why do the mothballs go up and down?

Directions
1. Have the children make some observations of the club soda before you open the cap.
2. Open the cap, have the children observe the bubbles that form throughout the soda, and then display the mothballs.
3. Drop the mothballs into the club soda, and have the children make observations about the motion of the mothballs.

Science Content for the Teacher
Club soda is water to which carbon dioxide has been added under pressure. Mothballs have a density that is close to the density of water. Thus, they will almost but not quite float. The carbon dioxide bubbles coat the surface of the mothballs, increasing the volume of the mothballs but only minimally increasing their mass. The mothballs and attached bubbles move toward the surface of the soda. When they reach the surface, the bubbles burst and the mothballs sink. This process continues as long as carbon dioxide gas is released in the soda.

Can You Separate Sugar and Sand?

Materials
1 empty, clear 2-liter soda bottle   1/4 cup of sugar
1/4 cup of sand   1 saucer

Motivating Questions
- When you mix sugar and sand, are you making a physical or chemical change?
- How could we separate the sugar and sand?

Directions
1. Fill the bottle half full of water, and keep it out of sight. Display the sand and sugar. Mix both together on the saucer, and challenge the children to invent a way to separate them.
2. After a discussion of alternative strategies, show the bottle containing water. Ask the children if they have any ideas on how the bottle could be used to separate the mixture.
3. Add the mixture to the bottle, and shake it vigorously. The sand will settle to the bottom, and the water will dissolve the sugar. Challenge the children to think of a way to get the sugar back.

Science Content for the Teacher
Sugar, sand, and water do not chemically react to produce a new substance. The dissolving of sugar in water is a physical change, because the sugar can be recovered by evaporating the water.

▶ *For Middle-Level Learners* [PS 5]

What Causes Lift?

Materials	2 textbooks of equal thickness 1 sheet of notebook paper

Motivating Questions
- What do you think will happen if we blow under the paper?
- What does the movement of the paper tell us about how an airplane is able to fly?

Directions
1. Align the books on a table top so they are about 10 centimeters (about 4 inches) apart. Lay the notebook paper across the tops of the books.
2. Ask the children to predict what will happen if you blow under the paper. Blow under the paper, and then ask the children for their observations.

Science Content for the Teacher

According to Bernoulli's principle, if we cause a fluid to move, the pressure in the fluid is reduced. Think of air as a fluid. By causing the air under the paper to move, you reduce the air pressure under the paper. Because the air pressure under the paper is slightly lower than the air pressure above the paper, the paper moves down. An airplane wing has a shape that forces air to move faster across the top than across the bottom. This lowers air pressure at the top and causes the wing to rise. The unbalanced force that moves the wing up is called *lift*.

▶ *For Middle-Level Learners* [HNS 2, 3, and 4]

Marie Curie: Scientist and Humanitarian

Materials	Access to the Internet Science resource books and encyclopedias
	Assorted art materials Assorted fabric pieces

Motivating Questions
- What do you think the word *humanitarian* means?
- Have you ever heard of Marie Curie and what she discovered?

Directions
1. Ask each group to research one of the following sets of questions (but more than one group can work on a given set):
   a. Where and when was Marie Curie born? What was her home life like? Where did she go to school? What subjects did she study? What research did she and Pierre Curie do? What was dangerous about it?
   b. What prize did Marie Curie win? What prize did she and Pierre win?
   c. How did the Curies' scientific work eventually help others? What other work did Marie Curie do to help people?
2. Each group should select and prepare someone to play Marie Curie. She will speak to the class for 2 or 3 minutes and answer questions about her group's research information. "Marie Curie" may wear some primitive costuming and use props.

Science Content for the Teacher

Marya Sklodowska, later known as Marie Curie, was an extraordinary physicist who, with her husband Pierre, received the Nobel Prize for discovering natural radioactivity. Marie received another Nobel Prize on her own for her study of radium. The Curies' work led to the development of X-ray technology and the use of radiation to treat cancer. In addition to Marie Curie's scientific achievements, she devoted much of her attention to ways of relieving human suffering.

Discovery Activities

Matter and Changes[3]

Objectives	• The children will identify a substance as a solid or a liquid. • The children will describe changes in the color, shape, size, and state of samples of matter.
Science Processes Emphasized	Observing Communicating
Materials for Each Child or Group	1 ice cube Paper and pencil 3 saucers Source of hot water 1 cube of butter the same size as the cube of clay 1 cube of modeling clay 2.5 cm × 2.5 cm × 2.5 cm (about 1 inch on edge)
Motivation	Put an ice cube in a glass, and tell the children that you are thirsty. Pretend to drink from the glass, and ask the children why you are having trouble getting a drink. The children will indicate that the ice cube must melt before you can have water to drink. Have the children discuss whether an ice cube is really water. Suggest that ice cubes might be made of "smush," a clear solid that changes to water. After some discussion of ways in which they could check to see if there is such a thing as "smush," begin the activity.
Directions	1. Have the children compare the size, shape, and color of the butter, clay, and ice cubes. 2. When this is done, have the children heat the plates in the hot water and then place the cube of butter on one plate, the cube of clay on another plate, and the ice cube on the third plate. 3. Have the children keep a record of the changes they observe. 4. After the butter and ice cubes have changed in form, discuss the states of matter, using the following questions to focus the children's thinking.
Key Discussion Questions	1. Which cubes were solid when you started the activity? What changes did you observe? *All three. The butter and the ice cubes started to melt.* 2. Did the color or shape of the cubes change? *The color didn't but the shape did.* 3. What would happen if we put the saucers in a freezer before the activity? How would the changes have been different? *The butter and ice cubes would not have melted as fast.* 4. What do you think caused the changes? *Heat.*
Science Content for the Teacher	Matter is commonly found in one of three forms or states: solid, liquid, or gas. In this activity, three substances that display the essential observable characteristics of solids are observed as heat from the air in the room and preheated sources cause a change in state. The flow of energy from these sources causes the molecules in the substances to increase their motion. In the case of the butter cube and the ice cube, this increased energy causes the molecules to begin to flow past each other, and melting is observed. The change is a physical change because the substance remains the same but changes in form.

Extensions   *Science/Art:* Have some children make drawings of various changes, such as an icicle melting, water in a pond freezing, and a pond drying up during the summer.

Science/Physical Education: Some children may wish to make drawings of various sports that utilize water or ice. The children can discuss their drawings with the class and consider what would happen if the water depicted in them changed to ice or the ice changed to water.

For Young Learners [PS 3]

From Gas to Liquid

Objective
- The children will observe the result of water changing from gas to liquid.
- The children will infer the source of the water that condenses on the outside of a can.

Science Processes Emphasized
Observing
Inferring

Materials for Each Child or Group
1 shiny metal can or container   Paper towel
Supply of crushed ice

Motivation
Display an ice cube and a glass of water, and ask the children if they think that the ice is water. After some discussion of the possibility that water can be in a liquid form or in a solid form, explain to the children that water can be in still another form: a gas. Tell them that in this activity, they will make the invisible water in air become visible.

Directions
1. Distribute a can and paper towel to each group, and ask the children to polish the outside of the can with the towel. Have the children describe what they observe when they examine the outside of the can.
2. Have each group add crushed ice to the can.
3. Have the children again observe the outside of the can. In a short time, a thin film of water will appear on the can.

Key Discussion Questions
1. Where do you think the water that formed on the outside of the can came from? *The air.*
2. How could we get the water that formed on the outside of the can to go back into the air? *Answers will vary. Some children will suggest that they remove the ice from the can and add hot water.*

Science Content for the Teacher
Air contains water vapor, which is water in a gaseous state. The amount of water vapor that air can hold depends on various factors, including its temperature. If the temperature of air is lowered sufficiently, the water vapor in it will condense on any available surface. The temperature at which this occurs is called the *dew point*. The cold can causes air near its surface to condense and form a film of liquid water.

Extension
Science/Health: Ask the children to breathe on a mirror or windowpane and observe the surface. The film of water they see on the surface results from the condensation of the water vapor that is contained in the breath they exhale. The water is a by-product of the process by which food is converted to energy in the body.

For Young Learners [PS 1]

What Is Your Squeezing Force?

Objective	• The children will measure the amount of squeezing force they can apply.
Science Processes Emphasized	Measuring Interpreting data
Materials for Each Child or Group	1 bathroom scale thin enough for children to grip
Motivation	Display the bathroom scale, and explain that it provides a measurement of the amount of pull the earth exerts on our bodies. Tell the children that they will use the scale to see how much pushing force they can exert with their hands.
Directions	1. Divide the class into groups, and have each group member squeeze the top and bottom of a bathroom scale together. The children should use both hands. As each child concentrates on squeezing the scale, another member of the group should write down the reading on the scale's weight display. 2. Have each group make a graph that shows the name of the person and the squeezing force he or she applied.
Key Discussion Questions	1. Is the force you used to squeeze the scale a push or a pull? *The children should realize they are exerting two pushes with each hand. They are pushing the top of the scale down and the bottom of the scale up.* 2. When we weigh ourselves, what is pulling us down on the scale? *The earth is pulling on us.*
Science Content for the Teacher	A bathroom scale has a spring system that reacts in response to the pull of gravity on any mass placed on the scale. Some scales include electrical devices that convert the movement of the springs to electrical information that is displayed in the form of a digital display.
Extension	*Science/Health:* Since young children experience rather steady growth in their skeletal/muscular system, they may find it interesting to measure their squeezing force at the beginning, middle, and end of the school year and prepare a simple graph of the results.

For Middle-Level Learners [PS 1]

Secret Messages and Chemical Changes

Objectives	• The children will observe physical and chemical changes. • The children will describe the characteristics of physical and chemical changes.	
Science Processes Emphasized	Observing Communicating	Making a hypothesis

Materials for Each Child or Group	Cotton swab

Materials for Each Child or Group

Cotton swab   Roll of masking tape
Sheet of white paper   Plastic container of water
Iron nail   A few sheets of paper toweling
Desk lamp with incandescent 100-watt light bulbs
Access to a small container of freshly squeezed lemon juice
Small, clear plastic containers (such as disposable glasses) containing copper-sulfate solution. *Safety Note:* The containers of copper sulfate should remain under your supervision in a central location. The groups will place their iron nail in the container and simply observe the changes. At the end of the activity, you are responsible for disposing of the solutions. *At no time should the children handle copper sulfate.*

Motivation

This activity should be done following activities or discussion on physical changes. Ask the children to review the characteristics of a physical change with you, and discuss the possibility that some changes may result in the production of new substances. Tell the children that they will be doing some activities that may help them think about such changes.

Directions

1. Distribute the lemon juice, cotton swabs, and paper. Have the children write secret messages on their paper, using the swabs and lemon juice.
2. Have the children allow the paper to dry. While it is drying, have them record their observations of the lemon juice patterns on the paper.
3. Under your supervision, have the children exchange messages and take turns heating them over the desk lamps.
4. Ask the children whether they think a physical or a chemical change has occurred.
5. Distribute an iron nail to each group. Have the children clean the nails with paper towels.
6. Tell each group to make a small identifying tag out of masking tape for its nail and affix it to the top of the nail.
7. Have each group place its nail in one of the containers of copper sulfate and make observations every few hours (if this is convenient) or every time science class begins.
8. After some changes have occurred, discuss whether the changes observed are physical changes or something else.

Key Discussion Questions

1. When the secret writing became visible, do you think that there was a physical change in the lemon juice? *No, the lemon juice changed to something else. It got darker; we probably couldn't make it turn back into lemon juice.*
2. What were some changes you observed after the iron nail was placed in the blue liquid? *The blue color of the liquid got less; red stuff started to cover the nail.*
3. Do you think you saw a physical change? *No. Some new things formed. The color of the liquid changed, and the red stuff wasn't there when we started.*

Science Content for the Teacher

When matter undergoes a physical change, it changes in form but remains the same substance. Physical changes are usually easy to reverse. In contrast, this activity shows two chemical changes. In the first case, heat added to the lemon juice caused the formation of molecules that absorb light, giving the juice a dark color. In the second case, the copper that was part of the solution left the solution and accumulated on the surface of the nail as iron from the nail entered the liquid. The iron reacted with the copper sulfate to form a new substance: iron sulfate. The copper atoms that left the solution were observed in their metallic form on the surface of the nail.

Extensions *Science:* You may wish to have some children observe an additional chemical change. Have them wedge some steel wool into a small glass, moisten it, and invert it in a pan of water. There should be an air space between the steel wool in the inverted glass and the water. Within a few days, the children will be able to observe the formation of rust on the steel wool—a chemical change.

Science/Language Arts: Activities such as this one can make children more sensitive to the concept of change. Recognizing changes in the environment can serve as an important first step in writing experiences that focus on change. You may wish to have the children write poetry about the changes they observe in the world around them.

For Middle-Level Learners [PS 2]

Pendulums

Objectives
- The children will predict how changing the string length and mass of a pendulum bob affect the motion of the pendulum.
- The children will measure the effect of changing the string length and mass of the bob on the motion of the pendulum.

Science Processes Emphasized Observing   Measuring
Predicting

Materials for Each Child or Group
Horizontal wooden support at least 1 m (about 40 in.) long
4 screw eyes fastened along the length of the support
Spool of heavy-duty twine
4 sticks of modeling clay
Stopwatch
Metric ruler

Motivation Display the materials, and ask the children to guess what they will be learning about in this activity. Tell them that they will be making some predictions and then doing an activity to check their predictions.

Directions
1. Have one member of each group be responsible for making the pendulum bob from the clay and attaching it to string. Have another member be responsible for using the stopwatch. The children should switch roles during the activity.
2. Begin by having the children predict how changing the length of the string will affect the time it takes for the pendulum to make one complete forward-and-backward movement. Use the term *period* to represent this amount of time.

Working with pendulums gives children opportunities to make predictions and form hypotheses.

3. Explain that any object hanging from a pendulum string is call a *bob*, and ask the children to make a bob from half a stick of clay.

4. Have the children start with a 1 meter length of string and shorten it by 10 centimeters (about 4 inches) during each of the five trials. In starting the pendulum movement, always move the bob 10 centimeters (4 inches) to the left of its stationary position before releasing it.

5. The children should find the time of one back-and-forth movement by completing five such movements and then dividing by five. Once they have found the time, have them check it against their predictions.

6. Now have the children repeat this procedure using three different bobs made of one-quarter, one-half, and three-quarters of a stick of clay. Maintain the string lengths at 1 meter (about 40 inches). Each time the bob is changed, the children should predict the period and then check their predictions against their observations.

Key Discussion Questions

1. Did you predict that the length of the string would affect the period of the pendulum? *Answers will vary.*

2. What did you observe when just the length of the string was changed? *The length of the string affects the period. The longer the string, the longer the period.*

3. Did you predict that the mass of the bob would affect the period of the pendulum? *Answers will vary.*

4. What did you observe when just the mass of the bob was changed? *Changing the mass of the bob does not change the period of the pendulum.*

Science Content for the Teacher

A pendulum is a weight, or bob, suspended from a fixed point that is able to swing back and forth freely. The period of a pendulum is the time it takes for the bob to make one complete back-and-forth swing. Galileo discovered that the period of a pendulum is independent of the mass of the bob and depends only on the pendulum's length.

Extensions

Science: Ask the children if they think that the period of a pendulum depends on how far the bob is released from the point at which it is hanging straight down. They can then conduct an activity to check their ideas. (The period remains the same regardless of the position from which the bob is released.)

Science/Social Studies: This activity provides an excellent opportunity for children to become aware of Galileo. Read a brief biography of Galileo in a reference book, and then have children do some social studies activities that focus on him. For example, they can make a timeline and mark on it the time of Galileo's life as well as such events as the discovery of America, the American Revolution, the launching of the first space satellite, and the first moon walk. The children could also locate Italy on a world map and find the town of Pisa, where Galileo made his observations of the swinging pendulum.

For Middle-Level Learners [PS 3]

Heat and the Fizzer

Objective

• The children will experiment to discover the relationship between temperature and the speed of a chemical reaction.

Science Processes Emphasized

Experimenting

Materials for Each Child or Group	3 Alka Seltzer tablets 3 clear plastic cups 1 ice cube Access to cool and hot water

Motivation   Review the difference between physical and chemical changes with the children. Tell the children that in this activity, they will observe the results of a chemical change and discover how heat affects chemical changes.

Directions

1. Distribute three cups and three tablets to each group. Provide access to ice cubes as well as to hot and cold water.
2. Tell the children that they are going to use their senses of sight and hearing to gauge the speed of the reaction of the tablet with water.
3. Have the children prepare the three cups of water and arrange them from cold (tap water plus an ice cube) to cool to hot. Tell the children to write their observations of bubble production and fizzing after they have dropped one tablet in each cup.

Key Discussion Questions

1. How did the temperature of the water affect the speed of each reaction? *The hotter water produced more bubbles faster.*
2. Does this experiment prove that heat speeds up a chemical reaction? *No. It only shows that more heat seems to speed up this reaction. There may be reactions that slow down if heat is added.*

Science Content for the Teacher   One of the products of the reaction of Alka Seltzer with water is carbon dioxide gas. The rate of production of carbon dioxide bubbles is one indicator of the rate at which this reaction takes place.

Extension   *Science/Health:* Have the students compare the ingredients in a variety of over-the-counter stomach upset remedies. After they have done this, have them research the common causes of an upset stomach and the preventive steps people can take to reduce their dependence on over-the-counter remedies.

Demonstrations

For Young Learners [PS 2]

The Toy Car in the Wagon: Pushes and Pulls

Objectives

- The children will identify one type of force as a push and another as a pull.
- The children will observe the tendency of an object to remain in one place or to remain in uniform motion.

Science Processes Emphasized   Observing
Making hypotheses

Materials	Child's wagon	Large toy car with functioning wheels

Motivation   Display the wagon, but keep the car out of sight. Tell the children that you are going to use the wagon to help them learn some interesting things about how objects move. Ask for a volunteer to assist you.

Directions   *Note:* Because this demonstration requires ongoing discussion, Key Discussion Questions are included in each step.

1. Ask the children why the wagon is not floating in the air. Use their responses to help them understand that the earth is pulling the wagon downward. Explain that this pull is called a *force*. Then pick up the wagon, and ask the children if you used a force. Put the wagon down, and ask your volunteer to use a force to pull the wagon. Have the volunteer demonstrate a push. Summarize by explaining that forces can be pushes or pulls.
2. Ask the children if the wagon moves in the same direction as the force. *Yes.*
3. Place the toy car in the back of the wagon so the back of the car is touching the back of the wagon. Have the children make guesses (hypotheses) about what will happen to the wagon and car if the volunteer pulls the wagon forward at a steady but high speed. Before the volunteer demonstrates this, ask how the toy car in the wagon will move during the journey and at the stop. Have the children watch the demonstration closely. They will observe that the toy car continues to move forward after an abrupt stop. Repeat this with the toy car at the front of the wagon.

Key Discussion Questions   See Directions.

Science Content for the Teacher   When the wagon is stationary, all forces acting on it balance each other. The earth's pulling force is balanced by a reacting force: the earth pushing on the cart in the opposite direction. The wagon displays forward motion if an unbalanced force acts on it. Although the term is not used, the toy car placed at the back of the wagon is used to demonstrate *inertia*. In other words, an object set in motion tends to keep moving.

Extension   *Science/Physical Education:* Bring a variety of athletic equipment to class, such as a baseball, baseball bat, football, field hockey stick, field hockey ball, jump rope, and so forth. Have various children demonstrate how forces are involved in using these objects.

> *For Young Learners* [PS 2]

How Does an Earth Satellite Get Placed in Orbit?

Objectives
- The children will observe a model of the launching of a rocket and the placement of a satellite in orbit.
- The children will identify the forces at work during the launching process.
- The children will infer the causes of the forces.

Science Processes Emphasized   Observing
Inferring

Materials

Tennis ball	Globe
1 m (1 yd.) length of string	Small model rocketship
Magazine pictures of various satellites that have been placed in orbit	

Motivation   Before class, firmly attach the tennis ball to the string. When class begins, display the magazine pictures of the satellites and engage the children in a discussion of how satellites are placed in orbit. Solicit their ideas about why satellites remain in orbit after they are launched. Now display the materials, and explain to the children that you are going to use these materials to illustrate the process of launching and orbiting a satellite.

Directions

1. Hold the rocket so the children can see it. Place it on the surface of the globe. Indicate that a satellite is usually placed in the nose cone of the rocket that will launch it into orbit. Show the satellite being launched by lifting the rocket from the earth's surface. Explain that the exhaust gases are expelled from the back of the rocket and that this causes the rocket to move forward.
2. Explain that as the rocket moves upward, it must counteract the force of gravity pulling on it. Show the rocket turning as it places the satellite in orbit.
3. Use the tennis ball on the string to show how the satellite stays in orbit. Whirl the ball around your head by the string that is attached to it, and explain that the string represents the earth's pull on the satellite. The reaction force that is produced on the forward-moving satellite acts outward and counteracts the effect of gravity. Because the inward force is counterbalanced by the outside force, the satellite is weightless.

Key Discussion Questions

1. Have you ever seen a satellite launch on television? What were some of the things you noticed? *Answers will vary.*
2. Does the rocket stay attached to the satellite when the satellite is put into orbit? *No. It falls to the earth, and the satellite keeps moving ahead.*
3. What keeps pulling the satellite downward? *Gravity.*
4. Why does the satellite keep moving forward? *If you start an object moving, it keeps moving unless something slows it down. In space, there are no air particles to slow the satellite down.*

Science Content for the Teacher

A ball thrown in a perfect horizontal line from the top of a tall building follows a curved path as it falls to the earth. How far it travels from the building before it strikes the earth depends on how fast it was thrown and how high the building is. An object thrown forward at a speed of 7,800 meters per second (about 25,600 feet per second) at a height of 160 kilometers (about 100 miles) would not return to the earth. Instead, it would follow a curved path around the earth. Inertia would carry it forward, and the attraction of the earth's gravitational field would keep it continually bending toward the earth's surface.

Satellites remain in orbit as a result of a balance between the pull of gravity inward and a reaction force outward. The scientific names for these forces are *centripetal* (inward) and *centrifugal* (outward). The satellite orbits the earth because the inward and outward forces produce a balance.

Extensions

Science: This demonstration provides a good starting point for a somewhat more extensive study of rockets and space exploration. You may wish to obtain age-appropriate books from your learning center to place in your classroom. Encourage children to look for pictures of rocket launches, actual satellites, and descriptions of each satellite's use.

Science/Social Studies: Talk to the children about the financial cost of space exploration. Are the costs justified when compared with the short-term and long-term benefits? The risks involved in space travel could also be part of this discussion, given the potential for loss of lives as well as costly resources. Children can be made aware of the fact that a society's resources are limited and that difficult decisions must be made to ensure that they are used wisely.

Teacher on Wheels: Action and Reaction Forces

Objectives

- The children will observe that an action force applied in one direction produces a reaction force in the opposite direction.
- The children will predict the direction and magnitude of reaction forces.

Science Processes Emphasized

Observing
Predicting

Materials

A pair of inline skates or a skateboard
Length of board 25 cm × 3 cm × 50 cm (about 10 in. × 1 in. × 20 in.)
12 large marbles
Old textbooks of assorted sizes (or large beanbags)

Motivation

Tell the children that you intend to get on inline skates or a skateboard to demonstrate action and reaction forces. That should be sufficient motivation!

Directions

1. Place the board on the floor. Stand on the board, and have the children predict what will happen to it when you jump off one end of it. Jump and then explain to the children that although they didn't observe anything happening to the board, your action caused a reaction force to be applied to it. The board didn't move because of the friction between the floor and the board.
2. Ask the children to predict what will happen if you repeat your jump but reduce the friction between the floor and the board. Place all of the marbles under the board. Spread them out so that they support all parts of the board. Step on the board gently so that you do not disturb the marbles under it, and jump off one end. The children will see the board move in the opposite direction.
3. Put on the skates or step on the skateboard. Have a volunteer hand you some old textbooks or beanbags. Ask the children to predict what will happen if you throw a textbook or beanbag from your perch on wheels. Execute a rapid underhand throw of the textbook or beanbag to an awaiting container.
4. Vary the number of books or beanbags and the direction and speed with which they are thrown. Have children make predictions prior to each demonstration of action and reaction.

Key Discussion Questions

1. When I threw the book while I was standing on the skateboard (skates), what was the reaction and what was the action? *The action was the book being thrown. The reaction was your movement in the other direction.*
2. What happened when I threw the book faster? *You moved in the other direction faster.*
3. Jet and rocket engines work because of action and reaction. What is the action and what is the reaction when these engines operate? *The hot gases going out the back of the engine is the action. The plane or rocket moving forward is the reaction.*

Science Content for the Teacher

This demonstration illustrates Newton's third law of motion, although it is unnecessary to refer to it as such. This law states that for every action, there is an equal and opposite reaction. For example, when we apply a force to the earth as we try to take a step, a reaction force pushes our body forward. Similarly, any time we apply a force to an object, a reaction force is produced. This law of nature can be taken advantage of to produce motion in any direction. A jet engine causes an airplane to move forward as a reaction to the action force produced when hot gases are expelled from the rear of the engine.

Extensions *Science:* Have a group of children follow up this demonstration by attempting to build a device that will launch small objects in one direction and display a reaction force in the other direction.

   Many toy stores sell plastic rockets that are launched as a result of the rearward movement of water out the back end. A small pump is used to fill the rocket with water. A small group of children might wish to demonstrate (under your close supervision) the launching of such a rocket on the playground.

Science/Physical Education: Some children may wish to extend their knowledge of action and reaction forces by identifying athletic events that depend on these forces. For example, the downward jump on the diving board by a diver is the action force; the reactive force is the upward propelling of the diver.

Attention Getters, Discovery Activities, and Demonstrations for Energies and Machines

Attention Getters

For Young Learners [PS 2]

How Do Instruments Make Sounds?

Materials 1 ruler
Assortment of musical instruments: cymbals, bells, small drum, triangle, guitar, clarinet, and so on

Motivating Questions Point to each instrument and ask:
   • Do you think this instrument will make a high or low sound?
   • What part of this instrument does the musician vibrate?

Directions 1. Ask the children what happens when you tap on your desk. Walk around the room tapping on various objects.
2. Indicate that tapping on an object causes it to move back and forth very quickly, or vibrate. Explain that there are many ways to make things vibrate.
3. Display each instrument, and have the children suggest what parts vibrate.

Science Content for the Teacher All sounds are the result of vibrating objects. High-pitched sounds come from objects that vibrate very fast. Each musical instrument produces a sound because the musician causes some part of it to vibrate.

For Young Learners [PS 3]

Do Magnets Pull on All Objects?

Materials Assortment of objects such as a rubber band, a metal tack, a piece of chalk, paper clips
Magnet

Motivating Questions • Which of these objects do you think will be pulled toward the magnet?
   • How are the objects that are pulled to the magnet different from objects that are not pulled?

Directions	1. Write the names of the objects on the board.
	2. Display the magnet, and have the children predict which objects will be pulled toward it. Note their predictions under the names of the objects you have written on the board.
	3. Have the children touch each object with the magnet. Record the results in another row on the chart, and explain that the objects that are attracted are those that contain iron (steel).

Science Content for the Teacher	A magnet has the ability to attract objects that contain iron, nickel, cobalt, and their alloys. Most common objects that are attracted to a magnet contain iron in the form of steel.

▶ *For Young Learners* [PS 2]

Why Do Some Machines Need Oil?

Materials	1 ice cube	Sandpaper	1 wooden block
	1 saucer	1/4 cup of sand	1 can of motor oil

Motivating Questions	• Which will move more easily: the ice cube on the plate or the block on the sandpaper?
	• Why do you think a car needs oil?

Directions	1. Show the children how easily the ice cube slides across the plate, and then show them how difficult it is to move the wooden block across the sandpaper. Explain that it is difficult for car tires to stop or move forward on roads that are covered with snow or ice.
	2. Ask the children for ideas about what could be done to make it easier for tires to start and stop in ice and snow.
	3. Demonstrate how friction can be increased by sprinkling some sand on the plate and sliding the ice cube across the sand. Display the can of oil, and discuss its use as a liquid that permits the metal parts of an engine to slide over one another easily.

Science Content for the Teacher	The ice cube on the plate melts slightly, producing a layer of water that reduces the friction between the ice cube and the plate. Reducing the friction makes it easier to move one surface over another surface. The presence of friction converts some of the energy used to operate a machine into heat. Oil is frequently used to reduce this energy loss. The oil fills in some of the roughness on the metal surfaces so the parts ride on an oil film.

▶ *For Middle-Level Learners* [PS 6]

Can Sound Travel through a Solid Object?

Materials for Each Group	Meterstick

Motivating Questions	• Have you ever heard sounds while you were swimming underwater?
	• Have you ever heard sounds through a wall?
	• Do you think sound can travel through a meterstick?

Directions

1. Have the children work in pairs. One child will stand, and one child, the listener, will be seated. The child standing will hold one end of the meterstick, and the listener will hold the other. The meterstick should be parallel to the floor and 50 centimeters (about 20 inches) away from the listener's ear.
2. Have the child who is standing gently scratch his or her end of the meterstick. The listener should say whether he or she heard the scratches.
3. Repeat the procedure with the meterstick 25 centimeters (about 10 inches) away from the listener's ear.
4. Finally, have the listener position the meterstick so that it is gently touching the jawbone joint in front of his or her ear, and have the standing student gently scratch the meterstick. The listener should hear the sounds clearly.

Science Content for the Teacher

Sound waves are disturbances that move through a medium. The medium may be a solid, liquid, or gas. A dense solid, such as the hardwood in a meterstick, carries sound waves very well. When the standing child scratches the meterstick, the sound waves travel through the meterstick and into the tissues and bones near the listener's ear, eventually reaching his or her eardrum.

> *For Middle-Level Learners* [PS 6]

What Type of Cup Loses Heat the Fastest?

Materials

Plastic cup   Ceramic cup
Styrofoam cup   Source of hot water
Metal cup or empty soup can with label removed

Motivating Questions

- If you were going to have a cup of hot chocolate on a cold day, which of these cups do you think would keep it hot for the longest time?
- If you were going to have a cup of cold chocolate milk on a hot day, which of these cups would keep it cold for the longest time?

Directions

1. Display the cups, and have the children make predictions about their heat-retaining abilities. You may wish to have the children arrange the cups in order of their ability to retain heat.
2. Fill each cup half full of hot water. *Safety Note:* Alert the children to the dangers of working with hot water.
3. Have the children gently touch the outside of each cup as soon as the water is added and then gently touch the cup again after 1 minute and after 2 minutes.
4. Have the children discuss how their predictions matched or differed from their experiences.

Science Content for the Teacher

All solids conduct heat; however, some conduct heat better than others. Metals tend to be good conductors of heat. Thus, a cup made of metal will permit heat to pass through it easily, resulting in the cooling down of the liquid within the cup. Ceramic materials, on the other hand, are good insulators, so most china cups will retain heat. The Styrofoam cup is an excellent insulator because bubbles of air are part of the materials that make up the cup.

Can You Move a Stream of Water Without Touching It?

Materials	Access to a water faucet	Inflated balloon
	Plastic or hard rubber comb	Piece of wool fabric

Motivating Question
- Do you think it is possible to move a stream of water without touching it or blowing on it?

Directions
1. Keep the comb and balloon out of sight as you begin this activity. Turn the water faucet on so that it produces a thin stream of water, and ask the children how the stream could be moved without touching it.
2. Display the comb and the balloon. Run the comb through your hair or over the wool fabric a few times, and then move it near the stream of water. The water will bend toward the comb.
3. Repeat the demonstration using the balloon rubbed across the wool fabric.

Science Content for the Teacher
The water has a neutral charge. The comb picks up a negative charge after it has been run through hair or over a sweater. When the comb is positioned near the water, negative ends of neutral water molecules move away from the negatively charged comb, leaving the positive ends on the portion of the molecules closest to the comb. These ends are attracted to the comb, causing the stream to bend toward the comb. The same phenomenon can be observed if you use a charged balloon in place of the comb.

"I Am Alfred Nobel"

Materials	Access to the Internet	Science resource books and encyclopedias
	Posterpaper and markers	Assorted art materials
	Assorted fabric pieces	

Motivating Questions
- How would you feel if you invented something to blast apart rocks and help make roads, tunnels, and foundation holes for schools and hospitals and the invention was also used to make bombs?
- What would you do with your money if you became rich because of your invention?

Directions
1. Have the children form cooperative groups, and give each group the same challenge:
   a. Research the life and scientific work of Alfred Nobel. Find out what he did and what he invented.
   b. Discover what is meant by the term *Nobel Prize.*
   c. Find out who won the most recent Nobel Prizes for science, literature, peace, and other topics.
2. Have each group write a script in which "Alfred Nobel" tells about his life and work in a 3- or 4-minute presentation. Each group should select and prepare one of its members to play Nobel, and he or she may use primitive costume pieces and simple props. The presentation must begin with "I am Alfred Nobel."

Science Content for the Teacher

Alfred Bernhard Nobel (1833–1896) was a Swedish scientist who experimented with nitroglycerin and eventually invented dynamite. His sale of explosives made him wealthy. Some of his fortune was used to create a fund for prizes that are awarded each year for outstanding work in fields that benefit humanity, such as medicine and literature.

Discovery Activities

> *For Young Learners* [PS 2]

Move Those Loads: Making and Using a Simple Lever

Objectives

- The children will identify the effort force, load, and fulcrum of a lever.
- The children will construct a lever and make and test hypotheses about the effect of changing the fulcrum's position.

Science Processes Emphasized

Making hypotheses
Experimenting

Materials for Each Child or Group

30 cm (12 in.) wooden ruler   Masking tape
Flat-sided pencil   Marking pen
2 paper cups
8 to 10 objects of equal mass, such as washers
Small objects to serve as loads: chalk sticks, boxes of paper clips, chunks of clay

Motivation

On the day of the activity, take to class a block of wood with a nail partially embedded in it and a claw hammer. Before beginning the activity, demonstrate how to remove the nail using the claw end of the hammer. Tell the children that the hammer is a lever. Without pointing to the apparatus, review the meaning of effort force, load, and fulcrum (turning point). Then ask if they can locate the effort force, load, and fulcrum. Leave this as an open question, and begin the activity.

Directions

1. Distribute the cups, rulers, tape, flat-sided pencil, washers, and objects used as loads to each group.
2. Have the children make one label reading *Effort Force* and attach it to one cup. Have them make another label reading *Load* and attach it to the second cup. Have them tape a cup to each end of the ruler.
3. Tell the children to place a load in the Load cup and center the ruler on the flat-sided pencil. Have them determine how much effort force is needed to move the load by adding washers to the Effort Force cup.
4. Have the children make and test hypotheses about the effect of moving the fulcrum closer to or farther from the load.

Key Discussion Questions

1. Where is the load, fulcrum, and effort force in your lever? *The load is the weight of the objects in the Load cup, the fulcrum is the top of the pencil, and the effort force is the weight of the washers in the Effort Force cup.*
2. When did you use the least amount of force to move the load? The most? *The least force was needed when the fulcrum was near the Load cup. The most was needed when the fulcrum was close to the Effort Force cup.*
3. When you moved the load with a small force, what moved the greatest distance— the load or the effort force? *The effort force.*

Science Content for the Teacher	The lever constructed by the children is a lever of the first class. This lever multiplies the effect of an effort force. A small effort force moving a large distance can move a large load a small distance.
Extension	*Science/Art:* Some children may enjoy discovering that mobiles are really levers. They can use thread, plastic straws, paper cutouts of birds, and other objects to assemble mobiles.

For Young Learners [S&T 1]

Can You Build a No-Frills Telephone?

Objectives	• The children will construct a telephone-like device that allows them to communicate with one another. • From their experimentation, the children will infer that a vibration moving through a thread is the basis for how their devices work.
Science Processes Emphasized	Communicating Inferring
Materials for Each Child or Group	2 paper cups 2 toothpicks or buttons 2 m (about 7 ft.) or longer length of strong sewing thread or dental floss Additional thread, buttons, and cups for those children who wish to invent more complicated phone circuits
Motivation	Display the materials. Ask the children if they can guess what they will be making with them. After they have made some guesses, tell them that they will be making telephones that will actually work.
Directions	1. Before distributing the cups, punch a small hole in the center of the bottom of each one. You can use scissors or a pencil to make the holes. 2. Distribute two toothpicks or buttons, two cups, and a length of thread to each group. Have the children thread the string through the prepunched hole in the bottom of the cup and knot one end of the thread around the center of the toothpick or through the button. You may need to assist some children with this. They should then do the same with the other cup. 3. When the thread between the cups is stretched, the toothpick will keep the thread end in the cup. If the thread is taut, the sound of one child speaking directly into a cup will be transmitted along the thread to the cup held to a listener's ear. 4. Encourage the children to try their telephones. Some groups may want to construct more complicated telephone circuits.
Key Discussion Questions	1. Which cup is used like the bottom part of a telephone? *The speaker's cup.* 2. Which cup is used like the top part of a telephone? *The listener's cup.* 3. How could you make a telephone that will let one person speak and two people listen? *Answers will vary. Have children try an experiment to test out their ideas. Some will find that tying a second cup somewhere along the string will permit the second listener to hear the sounds made by the speaker.*

Science Content for the Teacher	When we speak, our vocal cords vibrate and produce sound waves that travel through the air. When the children use their string telephones, sound waves vibrate the bottom of the speaker's cup. These vibrations move through the string and cause the bottom of the listener's cup to vibrate and reproduce the sound waves in the air inside the listener's cup. These sound waves strike the listener's eardrum and cause it to vibrate. In a real telephone, the vibrations produced by the speaker are converted to variations in electrical impulses that travel through wires.
Extension	*Science/Art:* Have the children design and then draw various arrangements of thread and cups for more complex telephone systems prior to further experimentation.

For Middle-Level Learners [S&T 4]

Simple Circuits

Objectives	• The children will assemble a simple series circuit and a simple parallel circuit. • The children will describe the similarities and differences between a series circuit and a parallel circuit.

Science Processes Emphasized	Observing Experimenting	Communicating

Materials for Each Child or Group	3 bulbs 3 bulb sockets	2 dry cells, size "D" Switch

8 pieces of insulated bell wire, each 2.5 cm (about 1 in.) long and stripped at the ends

Motivation	This activity should follow a class discussion about the nature of simple circuits and the functions of various circuit components. Display the materials, and make schematic drawings on the chalkboard of a three-lamp series circuit and a three-lamp parallel circuit (like the ones shown on the next page). Have a general discussion of how the circuit diagrams are alike and different. Keep the discussion open ended, and begin the activity at an appropriate point in the discussion.

Directions	1. You may wish to have half of the groups construct series circuits, and the other half construct parallel circuits. If you happen to have double the amount of equipment listed, each group can construct both circuits. 2. Have the children light the bulbs to demonstrate how their circuits operate. Suggest that they make observations of what occurs when one bulb is removed from each type of circuit. 3. Allow the children time to make observations, and then have a class discussion about how the circuits are the same and different.

Key Discussion Questions	1. What do the symbols in the circuit diagrams stand for? 2. How is the path of the electrons different in the two circuits? *In the series circuit, all the electrons go through all the bulbs. In the parallel circuit, they split up; some go to each bulb.* 3. What happened when you took one lamp out of each type of circuit? Why? *In the series circuit, the other bulbs went out. In the parallel circuit, the other bulbs got a little brighter. The series circuit bulbs went out because there was a gap (a break) in the circuit, so the current stopped. In the parallel circuit, the electrons stopped going through one path and joined the electrons going through the other paths. The bulbs got brighter because they had extra current going through them.*

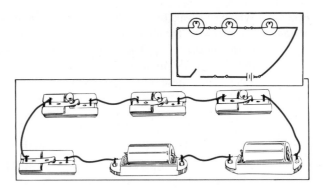

A series circuit

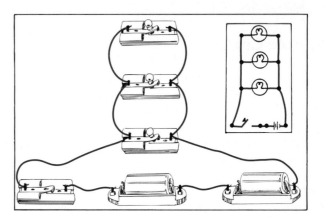

A parallel circuit

Science Content for the Teacher   Circuits can be represented by diagrams and symbols like those shown above. In a series circuit, all the electrons go through all the bulbs (or other resistances) in the circuit. A gap, or break, at any place in the circuit will stop the flow of current through the entire circuit. A defective bulb, a loose connection, or a break in the wire will stop the flow of current. If the voltage is large enough, electrons may jump across gaps in the circuit, a phenomenon evidenced as a spark. In a parallel circuit, the current divides. Some of it flows through each resistance. If a resistance is removed from a parallel circuit, the current that would normally have flowed through it is distributed to the remaining resistances.

Extensions   *Science:* If you have access to a small electric motor, have a group substitute it for a bulb in the series circuit and in the parallel circuit to determine the effect of a running motor on the brightness of the bulbs.

You may wish to challenge one or two groups to combine their resources and make a circuit that is partly parallel and partly series.

Science/Social Studies: Some children might enjoy studying one of the bulbs more closely to see if they can find the path that the electrons take. This could be the beginning of some library research on the scientist who invented the incandescent bulb: Thomas Edison. Have the children focus their attention on how everyday life has been affected by Edison's many inventions.

Electrical Conductors and Nonconductors

Objectives	• The children will distinguish between materials that conduct electricity and materials that do not. • The children will make hypotheses about characteristics of conductors.
Science Processes Emphasized	Experimenting Making hypotheses

Materials for Each Child or Group

Dry cell, size "D"	Box of paper clips
Dry-cell holder	Sharpened pencils
Flashlight bulb	Box of toothpicks
Flashlight-bulb holder	Box of crayons
Strips of aluminum foil	Box of steel nails

3 pieces of insulated bell wire, each about 25 cm (10 in.) long and stripped at the ends
Assortment of 2.5 cm (1 in.) lengths of bell wire of various thicknesses

Motivation

This activity should follow activities or class discussions about the characteristics of simple circuits. Ask the children to describe the function of the wire used in circuits. They will indicate that the wire serves as the path for electrons. Then display the materials, and indicate that the children will be finding out whether the electrons can pass through them.

Directions

1. Have each child or group assemble a simple circuit using two of the pieces of wire, a dry cell, and a bulb. After the bulb lights, detach the wire attached to the negative end of the battery and attach the third wire in its place. The exposed ends of the two wires (one from the dry cell and one from the bulb holder) will serve as probes to be touched to the materials tested.
2. Ask the children to check that their testers work by briefly touching the exposed ends together. If the dry cell is fresh, the bulb is in working condition, and all the connections have been properly made, the bulb will light.
3. When all the circuits are working, have the children test the various materials by touching both exposed wires to the materials at the same time. If the material is a conductor, the circuit will be completed and the bulb will light. Have the children note which materials are good conductors of electricity. They should manipulate each material to see if those that are conductors share similar characteristics.
4. When this has been accomplished, have the children make hypotheses that distinguish electrical conductors from nonconductors.

Key Discussion Questions

1. Which of the materials were good conductors of electricity? *Aluminum foil, paper clips, wire pieces.*
2. Which of the materials did not conduct electricity? *Toothpicks, crayons.*
3. Was there anything that conducted electricity but conducted it poorly? *The lead (graphite) in the pencil.*
4. What are some hypotheses that you made? *Metals conduct electricity.*
5. What other activities could you do to test your hypotheses? *Answers will vary.*

Science Content for the Teacher

Substances that allow the movement of electrons with relatively little resistance are known as *conductors*. Materials that do not allow electrons to pass through them are *insulators*. There are no perfect conductors, since all materials offer some resistance to the flow of charges. Metals are better conductors than nonmetals. Metals differ in conductivity. The following metals are arranged from highest to lowest conductivity:

Silver
Copper
Aluminum
Tungsten
Platinum
Tin
Steel
Lead

Extensions

Science: Some children may wish to invent activities that will reveal whether good electrical conductors are also good conductors of heat. Others may wish to modify their tester circuit so that the entire apparatus can be packaged in a small cardboard box. The tester should have two probes extending from the side and the light bulb extending from the top.

Science/Social Studies: Some children may be interested in discovering what areas of the world are sources of the various metals used in this activity. To identify these regions, the children can use an encyclopedia or search on the Internet and look under headings such as "Copper" and "Aluminum."

▶ *For Middle-Level Learners* [PS 6]

The Ink-Lined Plane

Objectives

- The children will construct a simple device that can be used to measure forces.
- The children will use their force measurer to find how an inclined plane makes work easier.

Science Processes Emphasized

Experimenting
Measuring

Materials for Each Child or Group

Piece of cardboard 25 × 12 cm
   (about 10 × 5 in.)
3 paper clips
Rubber band
1 m (40 in.) length of board
String
Small box of paper clips, crayons, or chalk
5 books
Wood wax and cloth for polishing the
   board

Motivation

Start this activity with some humorous wordplay. Do not display any of the materials. Tell the children that today they are going to work with an "ink-lined plane." When you say the phrase, space the words as shown and do not write the words on the chalkboard. Tell the children that one

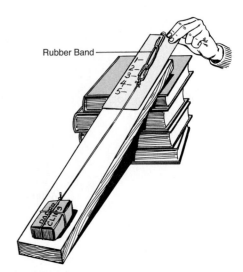

Rubber Band

How to use a force measurer

year you had a student who thought you wanted him to build an "ink-lined plane" (say it exactly as you said it before). The children should be a little puzzled. Now show the children what the imaginary child built by making a paper airplane and drawing some lines across it. Explain that the child was really confused until you wrote the phrase on the chalkboard. Ask the children to guess what you wrote on the board.

When they have done this, write the words *inclined plane* on the chalkboard, bring out the materials, and discuss the characteristics of an inclined plane. Tell the children that in this activity, they are going to make a device that measures forces and then use it to see how an inclined plane makes work easier.

Directions

1. Have each child or group of children make a force measurer by clipping one paper clip to the cardboard, attaching a rubber band to the paper clip, and clipping another paper clip to the end of the rubber band. Now have the children make their own scale divisions on the cardboard. The scale divisions shown in the illustration above are arbitrary, but the first division should began at the bottom of the rubber band.

2. Tell the children to assemble the inclined plane by elevating one end of the board and placing three books under it. The children should wax the board until its surface is smooth.

3. Have the children determine how much force is needed to lift the box of paper clips from the tabletop straight up to the high end of the board using their force measurers. To do this, they will need to tie a string around the box and attach the string to the paper clip hanging from the bottom of the rubber band on the force measurer. Have them note the amount of force required.

4. Now have them measure the force needed to move the paper-clip box to the same height by means of the inclined plane. They should pull the box up the length of the board, parallel to the surface of the board.

5. Have the children compare the amounts of force required and experiment with various loads and inclined-plane heights. Then hold a class discussion of the results.

Key Discussion Questions

1. Which required less force, pulling the load straight up or moving it along the sloping board? *Moving it along the board.*

2. Why do you think people use inclined planes? *You can move heavy objects up without applying a lot of force.*

3. Show the children that the distance the load moves vertically is the *load distance,* or *resistance distance,* and that the distance along the sloping board is the *effort distance.* Now ask the children how the effort distance compares with the load distance. *The effort distance is longer.* (This question helps the children see that inclined planes require that the small effort force moves over a long distance.)

Science Content for the Teacher

The inclined plane is a simple machine used to move heavy objects to heights. Ramps used to load boxes on a truck and roads that slope upward are inclined planes. An inclined plane multiplies force at the expense of distance, since the effort force must move farther than the distance the load is raised. Steep inclined planes require more effort force than less steep planes.

Extensions

Science: Have two or three groups of children assemble inclined planes of various slopes and move the same load up all of them to observe the increased force needed on the steeper machines. If possible, secure a toy truck with wheels that roll easily and have the groups compare the effort forces required to move it up the various slopes.

Science/Math: Have some children measure the effort distance and load distance of an inclined plane and compare them. Then have the children make the inclined plane steeper and repeat their measurements of effort and load distance. They can then repeat their measurements with the inclined plane in steeper, and less steep positions.

Demonstrations

How Do Heating and Cooling Change a Balloon?

Objective	• The children will predict and then observe how balloons are affected by heating and cooling.

Science Processes Emphasized	Observing Predicting	Communicating

Materials	2 or 3 round balloons Hot plate	Saucepan 1/4 full of water Access to a refrigerator

Motivation   Display the balloons. Then inflate each one to about one-half its capacity and tie a knot in the neck. If the balloons are new, stretch them a few times before inflating to make them more elastic. Ask the children to predict what will happen to the sizes of the balloons as they are heated and cooled.

Directions
1. Have a volunteer draw the balloons at their exact sizes on the chalkboard.
2. Place one balloon on the saucepan so it is held above the surface of the water by the sides of the pan. Have another volunteer take the other balloon to the school kitchen to be stored in a refrigerator. Turn on the hot plate, and set the heat indicator to low or warm.
3. Have the children note changes in each balloon every half hour for the next 2 hours. After they have made their observations, have them try to explain what caused the changes.

Key Discussion Questions
1. Why do you think the heated balloon became larger? *The molecules of the gases in the air in the heated balloon started to move faster. They started to bounce into each other and the sides of the balloon more.*
2. Why do you think the cooled balloon became smaller? *It lost energy. The molecules of the gas slowed down and didn't bounce into each other or the sides as much. They moved closer together.*

Science Content for the Teacher   The heat energy of an object is the total energy of motion of all atoms the object has. An object gains energy if it is placed in an environment that has more heat energy than it and loses heat energy if it is placed in an environment that has less heat energy than it.

Extension   *Science/Health:* Discuss how the loss of heat from an object can be diminished. This will offer the children an opportunity to talk about the need to wear particular types of clothing to decrease or increase heat loss.

Tuning Forks Feed Food for Thought

Objectives	• The children will observe that the source of the sound produced by a tuning fork is the vibration of the tines. • The children will predict various effects that will occur when the tuning fork is struck vigorously.

Science Processes Emphasized	Observing Predicting

Materials 2 tuning forks that produce sounds of different pitches
Rubber striker (rubber tuning fork hammer)

Motivation Display the tuning forks, and ask the children if they have ever seen any objects like them before. Ask the children if they have any ideas about what these objects are used for.

Directions
1. Without striking the fork, have the children sit quietly and listen to the natural sounds of the classroom and school. After a minute or two, gently strike one of the forks with the rubber hammer and have the children listen to the sound produced. Ask volunteers to touch, very gently, one of the tines after you have struck the fork. Have them tell the class what they feel.
2. Strike the tuning fork harder, and have the children listen to the change in the sound.
3. Ask the children to predict how the sounds produced by the two forks will differ. Strike one fork, stop its vibration, strike the other fork, and ask the children how correct their predictions were. If you happen to have a larger selection of tuning forks available, ask the children to place them in order from the highest pitch to lowest pitch. Check the children's ideas by striking each fork in turn.

Key Discussion Questions
1. Can you guess why the tuning fork is called a *fork? Answers will vary. Some children will note the resemblance between a tuning fork and a fork used for eating.*
2. How do you think the sound will change if I hit the tuning fork harder? *Answers will vary. Some children will say that the sound will be louder.*
3. How can you explain the different sounds made by the two forks? *Answers will vary. Some children will say the forks differ in size.*

Science Content for the Teacher When you strike a tuning fork, the tines vibrate back and forth. This vibration produces sound waves in the air. Although tuning forks are used for experimentations with sound, they are also used by piano tuners and others who need to hear sounds at exact pitches.

Extension *Science/Music:* Some children may be interested in how musical instruments amplify sounds. Display various musical instruments, and for each, have the children identify the part that vibrates and the part or parts that make sounds louder—for example, the wooden structure of the guitar amplifies the sound of the vibrating string.

▶ *For Middle-Level Learners* [PS 6]

You Could Hear a Pin Drop: The Conduction of Heat[4]

Objectives
• The children will observe the ability of various materials to conduct heat.
• The children will make a hypothesis concerning the nature of objects that conduct heat.
• The children will predict which of three objects will conduct heat the fastest.

Science Processes Emphasized	Observing Making hypotheses	Predicting

Materials	Candle	5 steel pins
	Safety matches	Chalk stick
	Old metal fork	Long, narrow chip of pottery
	Support stamp and burette clamp	Watch with second hand
	Container of water to extinguish matches	
	Glass, steel, and brass (or aluminum) rods of equal thickness	

Motivation

This demonstration should follow a class discussion about energy and heat as a form of energy. *Safety Note:* The demonstration requires the lighting of a candle by you and manipulation of the candle flame by you. Appropriate safety measures should be observed.

Display all the materials, and indicate that you are going to do a demonstration that will help the children discover how well various materials conduct heat. Explain that you are going to attach a pin near one end of each rod with a dab of wax, heat the end of each rod, and measure the time for the wax to melt and the pin to fall. Select a responsible child to measure the length of time it takes the wax to melt.

Directions

1. Fasten a steel pin to a dab of wax placed 4 centimeters (about 1.5 inches) from the end of each of the three rods. Do this by lighting the candle, allowing it to burn for 2 minutes, and then rolling the rod in the pool of wax beneath the candle flame. Briefly heat the head of a pin in the flame and press it into the wax. Repeat this procedure for the fork, the piece of pottery, and the chalk.
2. Place one of the rods in the burette clamp, and lower the clamp so that the end of the rod is about 1 centimeter from the tip of the flame.
3. Ask your assistant to time how long it takes for the pin to drop.
4. Repeat steps 2 and 3 for the other two rods, and ask the class to make a hypothesis about the type of material that is a good conductor of heat.
5. Display the test objects, and have the children use their hypothesis to predict which will be the best heat conductor. Repeat steps 2 and 3 with each object.

Key Discussion Questions

1. Which rod was the poorest conductor? *Glass.*
2. What conclusion can you make about heat conducting? *Metals are good conductors of heat.*
3. What are some objects that are good conductors of heat? *Pots and pans.*
4. What test object did you predict to be the best conductor of heat? *The metal fork.*

Science Content for the Teacher

The carrying of heat by a solid is called *conduction*. Heat energy is transferred through a conductor as a result of the increased movement of molecules at the point on the object where heat is applied. The increased motion of these molecules causes adjacent molecules to increase their energy.

In this activity, the glass rod will be the poorest conductor. The best heat conductor among the metal rods will be the aluminum one, followed by the brass, and then the steel.

Extensions

Science: Have some children find out how the transfer of heat takes place in air. They should focus their investigation on the term *convection*.

Have some children bring in samples of kitchen utensils that are both conductors and insulators (e.g., a stirring spoon with a metal end and a wooden handle).

Science/Math: You can extend this demonstration by fastening pins at regular intervals along each rod. The children can time how long it takes the heat to travel down the rods to release each pin. This data can then be graphed, with "Time for Pin to Drop" on the vertical axis and "Distance from Heat Source" on the horizontal axis.

Making Work Easier: Using Fixed and Movable Pulleys

Objectives
- The children will predict how a fixed pulley and a movable pulley can be used to make work easier.
- The children will observe the effect of using various pulley arrangements to move loads.
- The children will compare the required effort force and the direction of the effort force used in various pulley arrangements.

Science Processes Emphasized
Observing
Measuring
Predicting

Materials
Spring scale
String
Rock that has about 100 grams of mass
Single fixed pulley
Single movable pulley
2 screw hooks
Supported horizontal wooden board

Motivation
Prior to the demonstration, insert the screw hooks into the wooden support. Display the pulleys, and ask the children if they have ever seen one being used. Discuss various uses of pulleys, and then display the rock. Tell the children that pulleys make work easier and that they will observe this during the demonstration. Have a volunteer come forward to assist you.

Directions
1. Have your assistant weigh the rock by tying a piece of string around it and attaching it to the spring scale. Write the weight on the board. Be sure that the children understand that the rock is the load to be moved with the pulleys. Attach the fixed pulley to the screw hook on the horizontal board, tie one end of a piece of string around the rock, and run the string through the pulley.
2. Ask the children to predict what the effect of using a fixed pulley will be. Have your volunteer carry out the demonstration by gently pulling on the string with the spring scale until the rock is lifted. Ask the children to compare their predictions with the actual result.
3. Attach a string to the other screw hook, run one end of it through the pulley, and attach the rock to the pulley with another piece of string. Have your volunteer carry out the demonstration.
4. Now use the fixed pulley and the movable pulley together. Attach the string to he eye of the fixed pulley, and run the string through the bottom of the sheave of the movable pulley and up through the top of the sheave of the fixed pulley. Have your assistant repeat the demonstration.
5. Have the children compare the distance moved by the effort in step 4 with the distance moved by the load.

Key Discussion Questions
1. How does using a fixed pulley make work easier? *You can apply the effort force in a different location.*
2. How does using a movable pulley make work easier? *You use less force to move the load.*
3. About how much less effort do you need to raise a load with a movable pulley? Why? *You need about half as much. The load is held up by the hook and by the person holding the other end of the string.*
4. How does using a movable pulley and a fixed pulley together make work easier? *You use less force than the load's weight. The fixed pulley lets you change the direction of the effort force.*

**Science Content
for the Teacher**

Pulleys are simple machines that enable us to multiply the effect of an effort force or change the direction in which the effort force is applied. A fixed pulley performs the latter function. For example, a fixed pulley at the top of a flagpole makes it possible to move a flag upward by pulling down on the rope attached to the flag. A movable pulley attached to a load can ideally halve the effort needed to move the load. Friction, of course, diminishes the pulley's efficiency. When a movable pulley is used to lift a load, the effort force must move farther than the distance the load is lifted.

Extensions

Science: If you can acquire additional pulleys, children may enjoy assembling more elaborate machines. A movable-and-fixed pulley arrangement (block and tackle) can be used to show how loads can be moved by quite small effort forces.

Science/Math: You can help children understand the amount of energy lost to overcoming of friction by comparing the actual mechanical advantage of the pulley (found by dividing the load by the effort) with the ideal mechanical advantage (found by dividing the load by the number of strands supporting the movable pulley).

Physical Sciences Sample Lesson

Title: The Path of Light

**Articulation
with NSES**

Grades K–4
Content Standard B: Physical Sciences
- Light, heat, electricity, and magnetism
- Light travels in a straight line until it strikes an object. Light can be reflected by a mirror, refracted by a lens, or absorbed by the object. (PS 3)

Grades 5–8—Transfer of Energy
- Light interacts with matter by transmission (including refraction), absorption, or scattering (including reflection). To see an object, light from that object—emitted by or scattered from it—must enter the eye. (PS 6)

**Background
for Teacher**

Light is energy that can be described as behaving as a wave or as a particle. Light seems to travel in waves similar to the way water travels in waves. It also seems to travel in energy packets called *photons*, which have no mass. Unlike sound waves, light does not need a medium through which to travel. Light can be reflected, refracted, diffracted, or transmitted. When light is reflected, the angle at which it is reflected is equal to the angle at which it hits the mirror. That is, the *angle of reflection* is equal to the *angle of incidence.* The angles referred to are the angles formed between the light ray and an imaginary normal line (the line perpendicular to the mirror, see diagram). Light also travels in a straight line. This lesson addresses these two properties of light: 1. reflection and 2. light travels in a straight line.

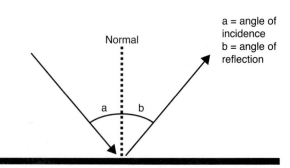

An image is formed in a mirror because the light reflected from the object hits the mirror and is reflected according to the law of reflection. If the reflected rays enter the eye, the individual can see the image. The image appears to be located where the lines of reflection would meet if they were extended beyond the mirror.

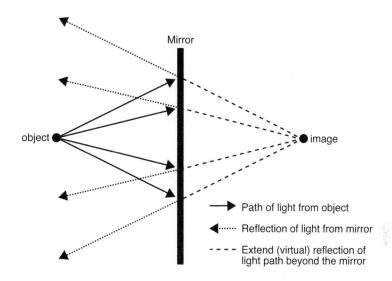

Element 1: Content to be Taught

Elements	Properties	Rules of relationship (spatial)
Light	Travels in a straight line Can be reflected A point source radiates light rays in all directions	Reflects at the same angle it hits a surface (angle of incidence = angle of reflection)
Mirror	Reflective, flat, shiny	Reflects light rays
Objects	Reflect light	Light reflected from objects enters our eyes
Emergent properties	Light travels in a straight line, light reflects, the angle of incidence = the angle of reflection	

Students will learn that light travels in a straight line and that the angle of reflection equals the angle of incidence. An image can be seen in a mirror only if the reflected rays intersect with the eyes of the viewer.

Element 2: Prior Knowledge and Misconceptions

Students should know that they can see their reflection in a mirror. They also should understand the image we see is created by light that reflects off an object and enters our eyes. Our eyes do not generate light. The students will need to know how to use a protractor to measure angles, or you can use this lesson as an opportunity to instruct them on the use of a protractor. (Alternatively, students can carefully color in the angles, label each one, and cut them out to compare sizes.)

Some possible misconceptions students may have about light are as follows:

- Light can bend around corners.
- Objects generate their own image that bounces off mirrors.

Element 3: Performance Objectives

Given a diagram of two people at different locations in front of a mirror, each student will explain why each person can or cannot see images placed in front of the mirror. They will support their answer by drawing a ray diagram that illustrates the law of reflection. Acceptable responses will score at least a 2 on the accompanying rubric.

Element 4: Concept Development

Engagement

Hang a mirror on the wall. Make sure it is vertical to the floor. Make sure that the class is seated in front of the mirror. Ask each student to note the boundaries of the image they see in the mirror. Children on the left side of the room will see children on the far right, but not on the far left. Children on the right side of the room will see children on the far left, but not on the far right. Ask the children to describe the range of the images reflected in the mirror. Ask the essential question, "Why can you see some classmates reflections and not others?"

Exploration 1

Materials needed per group: 4 mirrors, one light box with a slit that is capable of projecting a beam that can be tracked horizontally on a table (If a light box is not available, cut a slit about 2 mm wide in the side of a box and cover a flashlight with the box so that the light shines through the slit and onto the paper.), newsprint paper, ruler, protractor

Safety: Do not use laser lights with young children

Assign children to teams of three with the following roles:

- Measurer: Responsible for measuring distances and angles
- Manager: Ensures that the procedure is being followed correctly
- Lab technician: Sets up the mirrors and holds the flashlight
- Recorder: Ensures that all data are recorded in appropriate tables

Rotate the roles for each trial. Instruct the students as follows:

1. Place the light box so that it projects a beam of light that can be seen on the table top.
2. Place the mirror upright (perpendicular) on the paper.
3. Trace the location of the mirror on the paper.
4. Shine the light beam on the mirror. Be sure that you can see the light beam on the paper.
5. Use a ruler to trace the path of the light rays to and from each mirror.
6. Label the angles between the light rays and the mirror as projected and reflected.

7. Measure the angle between the light rays and the mirror. (*Note:* The angles measured will not be angles of incidence and reflection strictly speaking because they were not made relative to the normal. For younger children, the discovery that the angles at which the light hits and reflects off the mirror are equal meets the goals of this lesson. You may opt to introduce the concept of the normal to students now or during a later lesson.)

8. Record the measurements of the projected and reflected angles in your science notebooks. Use a table like the one below to record your angle measurements. Repeat the process two more times using different angles.

Trial	Measurement of light beam angle in degrees	
	Projected	
	Reflected	
	Projected	
	Reflected	
	Projected	
	Reflected	

Explanation 1

Ask the children what they discovered about the way light behaves. Specifically, "How do light rays reflect off a mirror?" Clarify the light travels in a straight line and that the angle at which it hits the mirror is the same as the angle at which it reflects off the mirror. This property of light is called the *law of reflection*. The angle at which light hits the mirror is called the *angle of incidence*. The angle at which the light reflects off the mirror is called the *angle of reflection*.

Exploration 2

Ask the children to answer the essential question "Why can you see some classmates reflections and not others?" Project the diagram below on the board and distribute the same diagram to each child.

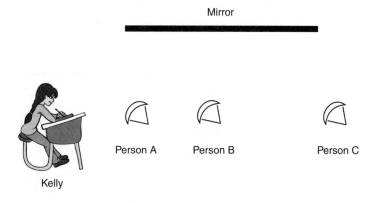

Ask the children to use the law of reflection to draw the light rays from Kelly to each person and determine who can see Kelly's reflection in the mirror.

Explanation 2

Solicit responses to the question. Person A will not see Kelly, whereas person B and person C will see Kelly. There is no light ray from Kelly with an angle of reflection that intersects person A. The mirror would have to be extended to the left for person A to see Kelly's reflection.

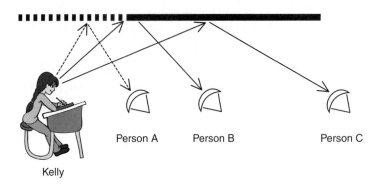

Elaboration

Challenge the children to simulate a light ray emanating from them to the outside edges of the mirror in the classroom using string. Working in teams of three, two children can hold the string and one can measure the angle of incidence. Using the string to simulate the angle of reflection, have the children determine the range of the images they can see in the mirror.

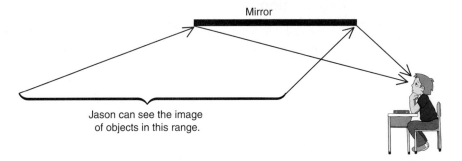

● Element 5: Evaluation

Draw light rays using a protractor and ruler to determine the images that Jason and Kelly can see in the mirror. Label the measurement of each angle in the diagram.

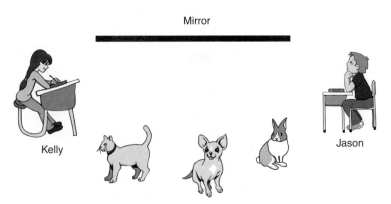

Use the following rubric to assess the children's responses.

3	2	1
Writes that Jason can see the cat and dog but not the rabbit. Kelly can see the rabbit and dog but not the cat. The reason either can see an image is because the light beam from the object reflects in the mirror at an angle that directs the rays to the viewer's eyes. The ray diagram clearly indicates that the angle of incidence equals the angle of reflection.	Writes that Jason can see the cat and dog but not the rabbit. Kelly can see the rabbit and dog but not the cat. The ray diagram does not clearly support that the reasoning is based on knowledge that the angle of incidence equals the angle of reflection.	Student expresses uncertainty about the images that Jason and Kelly will see and does not explain correctly why they will or will not see the images.

Element 6: Accommodations

Learning Disabilities

The use of diagrams, simulations with strings, written instructions, and verbal instructions will provide multiple modes of presentation.

Visual Disabilities

Create diagrams using glue to raise the lines of the ray diagrams. If the child has some visual ability, provide seating near the mirror. Using strings to represent the rays that the child can feel may also provide additional assistance.

Resources for Discovery Learning

Internet Resources

 Websites for Physical Science Units, Lessons, Activities, and Demonstrations

- **Bill Nye Demo of the Day**
  www.nyelabs.com

- **The Atoms Family**
  www.miamisci.org/af/sln/

- **The Science Explorer**
  www.exploratorium.edu

- **Kids Web: Science**
  www.npac.syr.edu/textbook/newkidsweb

- **PhET Interactive Simulations University of Colorado at Boulder**
  www.phet.colorado.edu/index.php

Print Resources

Articles from Science and Children and Science Scope

Burns, John, et al. "Solving Solutions." *Science Scope* 24, no. 2 (October 2000): 30–33.

Cavallo, Ann M. L. "Convection Connections." *Science and Children* 38, no. 8 (May 2001): 20–25.

Chessin, Debby. "Simple Machine Science Centers." *Science and Children* (February 2007): 36–41.

Cox, Carole. "Isaac Newton Olympics." *Science Scope* 24, no. 8 (May 2001): 18–22.

Frazier, Richard. "Rethinking Models." *Science Scope* 26, no. 4 (January 2003): 29–33.

Galus, Pamela. "Reactions to Atomic Structure." *Science Scope* 26, no. 4 (January 2003): 38–41.

Hammrich, Penny L., and Fadigan, Kathleen. "Investigations in the Science of Sports." *Science Scope* 26, no. 5 (February 2003): 30–35.

Harris, Mary E. "Slurper Balls." *Science Scope* 25, no. 4 (January 2002): 22–27.

Hechtman, Judith. "The Science of Invention." *Science and Children* 40, no. 5 (February 2003): 16–18.

Lucking, Robert A., and Edwin P. Christmann. "Tech Trek: Technology in the Classroom." *Science Scope* 26, no. 4 (January 2003): 54–57.

Proto, Christopher, and Edmund A. Marek. "Disecting Light." *Science Scope* 23, no. 7 (April 2000): 14–16.

Radhe, Sue Ellen, and Cole, Lynn. "Star Trek Physics." *Science Scope* 25, no. 6 (March 2002): 52–57.

Roy, Ken. "Safety Is for Everyone." *Science Scope* 26, no. 5 (February 2003): 16–17.

Sarow, Gina A. "Miniature Sleds, Go, Go, Go." *Science and Children* 39, no. 3 (November/December 2001): 16–21.

Shaw, Mike. "A Dastardly Density Deed." *Science Scope* 26, no. 4 (January 2003): 18–21.

Stroup, Diana. "Balloons and Newton's Third Law." *Science Scope* 26, no. 5 (February 2003): 54–55.

Villano, Diane D. "Classroom Catapults." *Science Scope* 24, no. 5 (February 2001): 24–29.

Weimann, Kimberly. "Blue Solids, Red Liquids, and Yellow Gases." *Science Scope* 23, no. 5 (February 2000): 17–19.

Wetzel, David R. "Fan Car Physics." *Science Scope* 23, no. 4 (January 2000): 29–31.

Notes

1. This standard, as well as the others identified in later sections, are excerpted with permission from the National Research Council, *National Science Education Standards* (Washington, DC: National Academy Press, 1996), pp. 104–171. Note that the bracketed symbol to the right of each standard was prepared by this author. See also the list of all the K–8 content standards inside the front cover of this book.
2. Note that I have related this sampling of NSES E, F, and G to the physical sciences.
3. This was adapted from "Change," Module 17, in *Science: A Process Approach II* (Lexington, MA: Ginn).
4. This demonstration is an adaptation of a portion of "Conduction and Non-Conduction," Module 70, *Science: A Process Approach II* (Lexington, MA: Ginn).

▶ **Answers:** 1. F, 2. T, 3. F, 4. T, 5. F, 6. T, 7. F, 8. T, 9. F, 10. T.

For the
Teacher's Desk

Your Classroom Enrichment Handbook

Position Statements of the National Science Teachers Association (NSTA)
- Women in Science Education
- Multicultural Science Education
- Substance Use and Abuse
- Science Competitions

Keeping Living Things . . . Alive
- Living Materials in the Classroom
- The Plant Picker

Safety Management Helper
- Safety Checklist

Materials to Keep in Your Science Closet
- Primary Grades
- Middle Grades

The Metric Helper

Content Coverage Checklists
- The Earth/Space Sciences
- The Life Sciences
- The Physical Sciences

Your Science Survival Bookshelf
- The Bookshelf
- The Magazine Rack

Your Science Source Address Book

Free and Inexpensive Materials

The "Wish Book" Companies

Bilingual Child Resources

Special-Needs Resources

Science Teachers Associations

NASA Teacher Resource Centers

Position Statements of the National Science Teachers Association (NSTA)*

Women in Science Education

The continuing policy within NSTA is, and has been, to involve and encourage all teachers and members of the scientific community, regardless of sex, to participate in all organizational activities.

As teachers, however, our responsibility for contributing to the development of the science skills and interests of women lies principally in the classroom. Three elements within the educational system have subtle but significant roles in supporting or negating our efforts in this regard. They are (1) the development and use of criteria for the selection of student-used materials, e.g., textbooks, films, filmstrips, to ensure the equitable portrayal of girls and boys, women and men involved in science; (2) the support of guidance departments that encourage students to develop to their full potential and to advise them of the course options available to them in school and the career options available to them after school; (3) the encouragement and guidance provided by the teacher regarding student achievement and careers in science; and (4) the inclusion of appropriate role models.

Because of the importance of these three elements, NSTA takes the following positions:

I. Any teacher whose charge includes the responsibility of evaluating or selecting instructional materials should demand that the materials (a) eliminate sex role stereotyping and (b) reflect a realistic female/male ratio in relation to the total number of people portrayed. Materials should be rejected by the teacher if they do not meet the above two criteria.

II. Science teachers must exert their influence to encourage guidance counselors to treat female students identically to male students relative to career opportunities and program planning. Science teachers can assist guidance counselors in this endeavor by providing them with detailed updated information and data on the interests and abilities of specific female students.

III. Science teachers must consciously strive to overcome the barriers created by society which discourage women from pursuing science for its career opportunities and for the enjoyment it brings to involved students.

—Adopted by the NSTA Board of Directors, July 1985

Multicultural Science Education

Science educators value the contributions and uniqueness of children from all backgrounds. Members of the National Science Teachers Association (NSTA) are aware that a country's welfare is ultimately dependent upon the productivity of all of its people.

*The position statements on pages 422–424 are reprinted courtesy of the National Science Teachers Association, Arlington, VA www.nsta.org/position.

Many institutions and organizations in our global, multicultural society play major roles in establishing environments in which unity in diversity flourishes. Members of the NSTA believe science literacy must be a major goal of science education institutions and agencies. We believe that ALL children can learn and be successful in science and our nation must cultivate and harvest the minds of all children and provide the resources to do so.

Rationale

If our nation is to maintain a position of international leadership in science education, NSTA must work with other professional organizations, institutions, corporations, and agencies to seek the resources required to ensure science teaching for all learners.

Declarations

For this to be achieved, NSTA adheres to the following tenets:

- Schools are to provide science education programs that nurture all children academically, physically, and in development of a positive self-concept;
- Children from all cultures are to have equitable access to quality science education experiences that enhance success and provide the knowledge and opportunities required for them to become successful participants in our democratic society;
- Curricular content must incorporate the contributions of many cultures to our knowledge of science;
- Science teachers are knowledgeable about and use culturally-related ways of learning and instructional practices;
- Science teachers have the responsibility to involve culturally diverse children in science, technology and engineering career opportunities; and
- Instructional strategies selected for use with all children must recognize and respect differences students bring based on their cultures.

—Adopted by the NSTA Board of Directors, July 2000

Substance Use and Abuse

Rationale

There is abundant evidence that the general public considers substance abuse a major problem. Students have revealed the same concern in surveys conducted nationwide. NSTA endorses the efforts of many school systems to conduct programs to help students understand the problem.

NSTA proposes the following guidelines for the development and implementation of such programs:

- The science education curriculum should include information about the effects of substance use and abuse.
- The thrust of such programs should be to promote healthful living.
- The programs should include information to help students make rational judgments regarding the consumption of commonly accepted over-the-counter drugs such as nicotine, alcohol, caffeine, and aspirin.
- The fact that the use of tobacco or tobacco products in any form is harmful to good health should be clearly documented.

- Student should be informed of the research which demonstrates clearly that marijuana, cocaine, and other illegal substances does cause physiological harm.

- Facts concerning the effects of the use of substances that may be abused should be presented, rather than counter-productive detailed discussion and explanation of the substances themselves.

- The programs should make available to students medical evidence that will help them to understand the inherent dangers of substance use and abuse.

- The ultimate goal of substance use/abuse awareness programs should be to eliminate substance abuse by giving students the up-to-date scientific knowledge they must have in order to make informed decisions.

—Adopted by the NSTA Board of Directors, January 2000

Science Competitions

The NSTA recognizes that many kinds of learning experiences, including science competitions, can contribute significantly to the education of students of science. With respect to science competitions such as science fairs, science leagues, symposia, Olympiads, and talent searches, the Association takes the position that participation should be guided by the following principles:

I. Student and staff participation in science competition should be voluntary.

II. Emphasis should be placed on the learning experience rather than on the competition.

III. Science competitions should supplement and enhance other educational experiences.

IV. The emphasis should be on scientific process, content, and/or application.

V. Projects and presentations must be the work of the student with proper credit to others for their contributions.

—Adopted by the NSTA Board of Directors, July 1986

Keeping Living Things . . . Alive

Living Materials in the Classroom*

Animals

Before introducing animals into the classroom, check the policy of your local school district. When animals are in the classroom, care should be taken to ensure that neither the students nor the animals are harmed. Mammals protect themselves and their young by biting, scratching, and kicking. Pets such as cats, dogs, rabbits, and guinea pigs should be handled properly and should not be disturbed when eating. Consider the following guidelines for possible adoption in your science classroom.

1. Do not allow students to bring live or deceased wild animals, snapping turtles, snakes, insects, or arachnids (ticks, mites) into the classroom, as they are capable of carrying disease.

2. Provide proper living quarters. Animals are to be kept clean and free from contamination. They must remain in a securely closed cage. Provision for their care during weekends and holidays must be made.

3. Obtain all animals from a reputable supply house. Fish should be purchased from tanks in which all fish appear healthy.

4. Discourage students from bringing personal pets into school. If pets are brought into the classroom, they should be handled only by their owners. Provision should be made for their care during the day—give them plenty of fresh water and a place to rest.

5. When observing unfamiliar animals, students should avoid picking them up or touching them.

6. Caution students never to tease animals or insert fingers, pens, or pencils into wire mesh cages. Report animal bites and scratches to the school's medical authority immediately. Provide basic first aid.

7. Rats, rabbits, hamsters, and mice are best picked up by the scruff of the neck, with a hand placed under the body for support. If young are to be handled, the mother should be removed to another cage—by nature she will be fiercely protective.

8. Use heavy gloves for handling animals; have students wash their hands before and after they handle animals.

9. Personnel at the local humane society or zoo can help teachers create a wholesome animal environment in the classroom.

Plants

Create a classroom environment where there are plants for students to observe, compare, and possibly classify as a part of their understanding of the plant world. Plants that are used for such purposes should be well-known to you. Plants that produce harmful substances should not be used.

*From "Living Materials in the Classroom," *Science Scope* 13, no. 3 (November/December 1989): p. 517. Used with permission of the National Science Teachers Association.

Because many plants have not been thoroughly researched for their toxicity, it is important for students and teachers to keep in mind some common-sense rules:

1. Never place any part of a plant in your mouth. (*Note:* Emphasize the distinction between nonedible plants and edible plants, fruits, and vegetables.)
2. Never allow any sap or fruit juice to set into your skin.
3. Never inhale or expose your skin or eyes to the smoke of any burning plant.
4. Never pick any unfamiliar wildflowers, seeds, berries, or cultivated plants.
5. Never eat food after handling plants without first scrubbing your hands.

The reason for these precautions is that any part of a plant can be relatively toxic, even to the point of fatality. Following is a list of some specific examples of toxic plants. This list is only partial; include additional poisonous (toxic) plants for your specific geographical area.

A. Plants that are poisonous to the touch due to exuded oils are:

Poison ivy (often found on school grounds)	Poison oak
Poison sumac	(other)

B. Plants that are poisonous when eaten include:

Many fungi (mushrooms)	Belladonna	Pokeweed	Indian tobacco
	Wake robin	Tansy	Jimson weed
Aconite	Henbane	Foxglove	(other)

C. The saps of the following plants are toxic:

Oleander	Trumpet vine	Poinsettia	(other)

Note: Also be aware that many common houseplants are toxic.

The Plant Picker

Plants That Will Survive with Little Sunlight

African Violet	Corn Plant	Peperomia	Spider Plant
Asparagus Fern	English Ivy	Philodendron	Spiderwort
Begonia	Ficus	Piggyback (Tolmeia)	(Tradescantia)
Boston Fern	Hen and Chickens	Snake Plant	Staghorn Fern
Chinese Evergreen	Parlor Palm		

Plants That Need a Great Deal of Sunlight

Agave	Echeveria	Mimosa (Acacia)	Spirea
Aloe	Geranium	Oxalis	Swedish Ivy
Blood Leaf	Hibiscus	Sedum	(filtered sunlight)
Cactus	Jade Plant		Yucca
Coleus	(filtered sunlight)		

Safety Management Helper

Safety Checklist*

The following general safety practices should be followed in your science teaching situation:

_____ Obtain a copy of the federal, state, and local regulations which relate to school safety, as well as a copy of your school district's policies and procedures. Pay special attention to guidelines for overcrowding, goggle legislation, and "right to know" legislation.

_____ Know your school's policy and procedure in case of accidents.

_____ Check your classroom on a regular basis to ensure that all possible safety precautions are being taken. Equipment and materials should be properly stored; hazardous materials should not be left exposed in the classroom.

_____ Before handling equipment and materials, familiarize yourself with their possible hazards.

_____ Be extra cautious when dealing with fire, and instruct your students to take appropriate precautions. Be certain fire extinguishers and fire blankets are nearby.

_____ Be familiar with your school's fire regulations, evacuation procedures, and the location and use of fire-fighting equipment.

_____ At the start of each science activity, instruct students regarding potential hazards and the precautions to be taken.

_____ The group size of students working on an experiment should be limited to a number that can safely perform the experiment without confusion and accidents.

_____ Plan enough time for students to perform the experiments, then clean up and properly store the equipment and materials.

_____ Students should be instructed never to taste or touch substances in the science classroom without first obtaining specific instructions from the teacher.

_____ Instruct students that all accidents or injuries—no matter how small—should be reported to you immediately.

_____ Instruct students that it is unsafe to touch their faces, mouths, eyes, and other parts of their bodies while they are working with plants, animals, or chemical substances and afterwards, until they have washed their hands and cleaned their nails.

When working with chemicals:

_____ Teach students that chemicals must not be mixed just to see what happens.

_____ Students should be instructed never to taste chemicals and to wash their hands after using chemicals.

_____ Elementary school students should not be allowed to mix acid and water.

_____ Keep combustible materials in a metal cabinet equipped with a lock.

_____ Chemicals should be stored under separate lock in a cool, dry place, but not in a refrigerator.

_____ Only minimum amounts of chemicals should be stored in the classroom. Any materials not used in a given period should be carefully discarded, particularly if they could become unstable.

*Reprinted with permission from *Safety in the Elementary Science Classroom.* Copyright © 1978, 1993 by the National Science Teachers Association, 1840 Wilson Boulevard, Arlington, VA 22201-3000.

Glassware is dangerous. Whenever possible, plastic should be substituted. However, when glassware is used, follow these precautions:

_____ Hard glass test tubes should not be heated from the bottom. They should be tipped slightly, but not in the direction of another student.

_____ Sharp edges on mirrors or glassware should be reported to the teacher. A whisk broom and dustpan should be available for sweeping up pieces of broken glass.

_____ Warn students not to drink from glassware used for science experiments.

_____ Thermometers for use in the elementary classroom should be filled with alcohol, not mercury.

Teachers and students should be constantly alert to the following safety precautions while working with electricity:

_____ Students should be taught to use electricity safely in everyday situations.

_____ At the start of any unit on electricity, students should be told not to experiment with the electric current of home circuits.

_____ Check your school building code about temporary wiring for devices to be used continuously in one location.

_____ Electrical cords should be short, in good condition, and plugged in at the nearest outlet.

_____ Tap water is a conductor of electricity. Students' hands should be dry when touching electrical cords, switches, or appliances.

Materials to Keep in Your Science Closet

Primary Grades

Depending on the maturity of your students, you may wish to keep some or most of these items in a secure location in the room:

aluminum foil
aluminum foil pie plates
aquarium
baking soda
balance and standard
  masses
basic rock and mineral
  collection
beans, lima
camera and supplies
cardboard tubes from
  paper towel rolls
clipboard
cooking oil
corks
dishes, paper

dishes, plastic
egg cartons
feathers
first aid kit
flashlight
food coloring
globe
hand lenses
hot plate
iron filings
latex gloves
lemon juice
lunch bags, paper
magnets, various sizes
  and shapes
masking tape

measuring cups
measuring spoons
meterstick
microscope
mirrors
modeling clay
peas, dried
plastic bucket
plastic jugs
plastic spoons
plastic wrap
potholder
potting soil
rain gauge
rubber balls of various
  sizes

salt
sandwich bags, plastic
scales and masses
seeds, assorted
shell collection
shoe boxes
small plastic animals
small plastic trays
sponges
string
sugar
tape measure
terrarium
vinegar
yeast, dry

Middle Grades

Depending on the maturity of your students, you may wish to keep some or most of these items in a secure location in the room:

aluminum foil
assorted nuts and bolts
balance and standard
  masses
balloons
barometer
batteries
beakers
binoculars
cafeteria trays
calculator
candles
cans, clean, assorted,
  empty
cellophane, various
  colors
chart of regional birds
chart of regional rocks
  and minerals
clothespins, spring-
  variety

compass, directional
compass, drawing
desk lamp
extensive rock and
  mineral collection
eyedroppers
first aid kit
flashlight
flashlight bulbs
forceps or tweezers
glass jars
graduated cylinders
graph paper
hammer
hand lenses
hot glue gun*
hot plate*
hydrogen peroxide (3%)*
incubator
iron filings
isopropyl alcohol*

latex gloves
lenses
litmus paper
map of region, with
  contour lines
map of country, with
  climate regions
map of world
marbles
microscope slides and
  coverslips
mirrors
net for scooping material
  from streams and/or
  ponds
petroleum jelly
plastic bucket
plastic containers,
  wide-mouth, 1- and 2-L
plastic straws
plastic tubing

plastic wrap
pliers
prisms
pulleys
safety goggles
screwdriver
seeds, assorted vegetable
sponge, natural
steel wool
stop watch
sugar cubes
switches for circuits
tape, electrical
telescope
test tubes (Pyrex or
  equivalent)
thermometers
toothpicks
washers, assorted
wire for making circuits
wood scraps

*Keep these items in a locked closet.

The Metric Helper

Length

1 centimeter (cm) = 10 millimeters (mm)

1 decimeter (dm) = 10 centimeters

1 meter (m) = 10 decimeters

1 kilometer (km) = 1,000 meters

Liquid Volume

1,000 (mL) = 1 liter (L)

Dry Volume

1,000 cubic millimeters (mm^3) = 1 cubic centimeter (cm^3)

Mass

1,000 milligrams (mg) = 1 gram (g)

1,000 grams (g) = 1 kilogram (kg)

Some Important Metric Prefixes

kilo = one thousand

deci = one-tenth

centi = one-hundredth

milli = one-thousandth

micro = one-millionth

Temperature

Water freezes at 0° Celsius

Normal body temperature is 37° Celsius

Water boils at 100° Celsius

Approximate Sizes

millimeter = diameter of the wire in a paper clip

centimeter = slightly more than the width of a paper clip at its narrowest point

meter = slightly more than 1 yard

kilometer = slightly more than ½ mile

gram = slightly more than the mass of a paper clip

kilogram = slightly more than 2 pounds

milliliter = 5 milliters equal 1 teaspoon

liter = slightly more than 1 quart

Content Coverage Checklists

The following content checklists can be used to evaluate various elementary science textbooks, curriculum materials, audiovisual materials, software packages, and other resource materials for use in your classroom. Obviously, these lists do not include every concept, but they will provide a framework for analysis.

The Earth/Space Sciences

_____ The universe is 8 to 20 billion years old.

_____ The earth is about 5 billion years old.

_____ The earth is composed of rocks and minerals.

_____ Evidence of the many physical changes that have occurred over the earth's history is found in rocks and rock layers.

_____ The study of fossils can tell us a great deal about the life forms that have existed on the earth.

_____ Many species of animals and plants have become extinct.

_____ Our knowledge of earlier life forms comes from the study of fossils.

_____ Such forces as weathering, erosion, volcanic upheavals, and the shifting of crustal plates, as well as human activity, change the earth's surface.

_____ Natural phenomena and human activity also affect the earth's atmosphere and oceans.

_____ The climate of the earth has changed many times over its history.

_____ *Weather* is a description of the conditions of our atmosphere at any given time.

_____ The energy we receive from the sun affects our weather and is the primary source of energy for life on earth.

_____ The water cycle, a continuous change in the form and location of water, affects the weather and life on our planet.

_____ Weather instruments are used to assess and predict the weather.

_____ The natural resources of our planet are limited.

_____ The quality of the earth's water, air, and soil is affected by human activity.

_____ Water, air, and soil must be conserved, or life as we know it will not be able to continue on the earth.

_____ The responsibility for preserving the environment rests with individuals, governments, and industries.

_____ Our solar system includes the sun, the moon, and eight planets.

_____ The sun is one of many billions of stars in the Milky Way galaxy.

_____ Rockets, artificial satellites, and space shuttles are devices that enable humans to explore the characteristics of planets in our solar system.

_____ Data gathered about the earth, oceans, atmosphere, solar system, and universe may be expressed in the form of words, numbers, charts, or graphs.

The Life Sciences

_____ Living things are different from nonliving things.

_____ Plants and animals are living things.

_____ Living things can be classified according to their unique characteristics.

_____ The basic structural unit of all living things is the cell.

_____ All living things proceed through stages of development and maturation.

_____ Living things reproduce in a number of different ways.

_____ Animals and plants inherit and transmit the characteristics of their ancestors.

_____ Species of living things adapt and change over long periods of time or become extinct.

_____ Living things depend upon the earth, its atmosphere, and the sun for their existence.

_____ Living things affect their environment, and their environment affects living things.

_____ Different areas of the earth support different life forms, which are adapted to the unique characteristics of the area in which they live.

_____ Animals and plants affect one another.

_____ Plants are food producers.

_____ Animals are food consumers.

_____ Animals get their food by eating plants or other animals that eat plants.

_____ The human body consists of groups of organs (systems) that work together to perform a particular function.

_____ The human body can be affected by a variety of diseases, including sexually transmitted diseases.

_____ Human life processes are affected by food, exercise, drugs, air quality, and water quality.

_____ Medical technologies can be used to enhance the functioning of the human body and to diagnose, monitor, and treat diseases.

The Physical Sciences

_____ *Matter* is anything that takes up space and has weight.

_____ Matter is found in three forms: solid, liquid, and gas.

_____ All matter in the universe attracts all other matter in the universe with a force that depends on the mass of the objects and the distance between them.

_____ Matter can be classified on the basis of readily observable characteristics, such as color, odor, taste, and solubility. These characteristics are known as *physical properties of matter*.

_____ Matter can undergo chemical change to form new substances.

_____ Substances consist of small particles known as *molecules*.

_____ Molecules are made of smaller particles known as *atoms*.

_____ Atoms are composed of three smaller particles called *protons*, *neutrons*, and *electrons*. (Protons and neutrons are composed of yet smaller particles known as *quarks*.)

_____ Atoms differ from one another in the number of protons, neutrons, and electrons they have.

_____ Some substances are composed of only one type of atom. These substances are known as *elements*.

_____ In chemical reactions between substances, matter is neither created nor destroyed but only changed in form. This is the law of conservation of matter.

_____ An object at rest or moving at a constant speed will remain in that state unless acted upon by an unbalanced external force.

_____ *Acceleration* is the rate at which an object's velocity changes.

_____ The amount of acceleration that an object displays varies with the force acting on the object and its mass.

_____ Whenever a force acts on an object, an equal and opposite reacting force occurs.

_____ The flight of an airplane results from the interaction of four forces: weight, lift, thrust, and drag.

_____ *Energy*—the capacity to do work—manifests itself in a variety of forms, including light, heat, sound, electricity, motion, and nuclear energy.

_____ Energy may be stored in matter by virtue of an object's position or condition. Such energy is known as *potential energy*.

_____ Under ordinary circumstances, energy can neither be created nor destroyed. This is the law of conservation of energy.

_____ The law of conservation of matter and the law of conservation of energy have been combined to form the law of conservation of matter plus energy, which states that under certain conditions, matter can be changed into energy and energy can be changed into matter.

_____ The basic concepts of matter, energy, force, and motion can be used to explain natural phenomena in the life, earth/space, and physical sciences.

_____ The diminishing supply of fossil fuels may be compensated for by the increased utilization of alternate energy sources, including wind, water, and synthetic fuels, and by energy-conservation measures.

Your Science Survival Bookshelf

The Bookshelf

Abruscato, Joseph. *Whizbangers and Wonderments: Science Activities for Young People.* Boston: Allyn and Bacon, 2000.

Abruscato, Joseph, and Jack Hassard. *The Whole Cosmos Catalog of Science Activities.* Glenview, IL: Scott Foresman/Goodyear Publishers, 1991.

Adelman, Benjamin. *The Space Science.* Teaching Hand book, Silver Springs, MD: 1962.

American Chemical Society. *The Best of Wonder Science.* Florence, KY: Wordsworth, 2000.

Blough, Glenn, and Julius Schwartz. *Elementary School Science and How to Teach It.* Fort Worth, TX: Holt Rinehart & Winston, 1990.

Carin, Arthur A. *Teaching Science through Discovery.* Columbus, OH: Merrill, 1996.

Esler, William K., and Esler, Mary K. *Teaching Elementary School Science.* Belmont, CA: Wadsworth, 1996.

Friedl, Alfred E. *Teaching Science to Children.* New York: Random House, 1991.

Hassard, Jack. *Science Experiences: Cooperative Learning and the Teaching of Science.* Menlo Park, CA: Addison-Wesley, 1990.

Jacobson, Willard J., and Bergman, Abby B. *Science for Children.* Englewood Cliffs, NJ: Prentice-Hall, 1991.

Lorbeer, George C., and Nelson, Leslie W. *Science Activities for Children.* Dubuque, IA: W. C. Brown,1996.

Martin, Ralph, and Sexton, Colleen, and Franklin, Teresa. *Teaching Science for All Children: an Inquiry Approach.* Boston: Allyn and Bacon, 2008.

Mitchell, John, and Morrison, Gordon. *The Curious Naturalist.* Amherst, MA: University of Massachusetts Press, 1996.

Neuman, Donald B. *Experiencing Elementary Science.* Belmont, CA: Wadsworth, 1993.

Tolman, Marvin H., and Hardy, Gary R. *Discovering Elementary Science.* Boston: Allyn and Bacon, 1999.

Van Cleave, Janice Pratt. *Chemistry for Every Kid.* New York: Wiley, 1989.

Victor, Edward, and Kellough, Richard E. *Science for the Elementary School.* New York: Macmillan, 1997.

The Magazine Rack

For Teachers

Audubon Magazine
National Audubon Society
225 Varick St.
New York, NY 10014

Natural History
The American Museum of Natural History
Central Park West at Seventy-Ninth Street
New York, NY 10024

Science Activities
Heldref Publications
1319 Eighteenth Street, NW
Washington, DC 20036

Science and Children
National Science Teachers Association
1840 Wilson Boulevard
Arlington, VA 22201-3000

Science Scope
National Science Teachers Association
1840 Wilson Boulevard
Arlington, VA 22201-3000

Science Teacher
National Science Teachers Association
National Education Association
1840 Wilson Blvd.
Arlington, VA 22201-3000

For Children

Chickadee
Young Naturalist Foundation
P.O. Box 11314
Des Moines, IA 50340

Current Science
Xerox Education Publications
5555 Parkcenter Circle Suite 300
Dublin, OH 43017

Junior Astronomer
Benjamin Adelman
4211 Colie Drive
Silver Springs, MD 20906

Ladybug
Cricket Country Lane
Box 50284
Boulder, CO 80321-0284

National Geographic Kids Magazine
National Geographic Society
Seventeenth and M Streets, NW
Washington, DC 20036

Owl Kids
Maple Tree Press
10 Lower Spadina Avenue
Toronto Ontario
MSV 22 Canada

Ranger Rick
National Wildlife Federation
1412 Sixteenth Street, NW
Washington, DC 20036-2266

Science Weekly
CAM Publishing Group
Subscription Department
P.O. Box 70638
Chevy Chase, MD 208B-0638

Science World
Scholastic Magazines, Inc.
557 Broadway
New York, NY 10012

SuperScience
Scholastic Magazines, Inc.
557 Broadway
New York, NY 10012

Your Science Source Address Book

Free and Inexpensive Materials

American Solar Energy Society
2400 Central Avenue, Suite G–1
Boulder, CO 80301

American Wind Energy Association
777 North Capitol Street, NE, Suite 805
Washington, DC 20002

Environmental Protection Agency Public Information
Center and Library
401 M Street, SW
Washington, DC 20460

Environmental Sciences Services Administration
Office of Public Information
Washington Science Center, Building 5
Rockville, MD 20852

Fish and Wildlife Service
U.S. Department of the Interior
1849 C Street, NW
Mail Stop 304 Web Building
Washington, DC 20240

Jet Propulsion Laboratory (JPL)
Teacher Resource Center
4900 Oak Grove Drive
Mail Stop CS–530
Pasadena, CA 91109

National Aeronautics and Space Administration (NASA)
NASA Education Division
NASA Headquarters
300 E Street, SW
Washington, DC 20546

National Institutes of Health
Office of Science Education
6100 Executive Blud.,
Suite 3E01
MSC 7520
Bethesda, MD 20892-7520

National Park Service
U.S. Department of the Interior
1849 C Street, NW
Washington, DC 20240

National Science Foundation
Division of Pre-College Education
1800 G Street, NW
Washington, DC 20550

National Wildlife Federation
8925 Leesburg Pike
Vienna, VA 22184-0001

Superintendent of Documents
U.S. Government Printing Office
732 North Capital Street, NW
Washington, D.C. 20401

U.S. Bureau of Mines
Office of Mineral Information
U.S. Department of the Interior
1849 C Street, NW
Washington, DC 20240

U.S. Department of Education
555 New Jersey Avenue, NW
Washington, DC 20208

U.S. Department of Energy
Conservation and Renewable Energy Inquiry
and Referral Service
P.O. Box 8900
Silver Spring, MD 20907

U.S. Department of the Interior
Earth Science Information Center
1849 C Street, NW, Room 2650
Washington, DC 20240

U.S. Forest Service
Division of Information and Education
Fourteenth Street and Independence Avenue, SW
Washington, DC 20250

U.S. Geological Survey
Public Inquiries Office
U.S. Department of the Interior
Eighteenth and F Streets, NW
Washington, DC 20240

U.S. Public Health Service
Department of Health and Human Services
66 Canal Center Plaza, Suite 200
Alexandria, VA 22314

The "Wish Book" Companies

AIMS Education Foundation
P.O. Box 7766
Fresno, CA 93747

Carolina Biological Supply Co.
2700 York Road
Burlington, NC 27215

Central Scientific Company (CENCO)
3300 CENCO Parkway
Franklin, Park, IL 60131

Connecticut Valley Biological Supply Co., Inc.
82 Valley Road
Southhampton, MA 01073

Delta Education, Inc.
P.O. Box 915
Hudson, NH 03051-0915

Exploratorium Store
3601 Lyon Street
San Francisco, CA 94123

Flinn Scientific, Inc.
131 Flinn Street
P.O. Box 291
Batavia, IL 60510

Frey Scientific
905 Hickory Lane
Mansfield, OH 44905

Hubbard Scientific
3101 Iris Avenue, Suite 215
Boulder, CO 80301

Learning Things, Inc.
68A Broadway
P.O. Box 436
Arlington, MA 02174

LEGO Systems, Inc.
555 Taylor Road
Enfield, CT 06802

NASCO West, Inc.
P.O. Box 3837
Modesto, CA 95352

Ohaus Scale Corp.
29 Hanover Road
Florham Park, NJ 07932

Science Kit and Boreal Labs
777 East Park Drive
Tonawanda, NY 14150

Ward's Natural Science Establishment, Inc.
5100 West Henrietta Road
P.O. Box 92912
Rochester, NY 14692

Wind and Weather
P.O. Box 2320-ST
Mendocino, CA 95460

Young Naturalist Co.
614 East Fifth Street
Newton, KN 67114

Bilingual Child Resources

Alabama, Florida, Georgia, Kentucky, Mississippi, South Carolina, Tennessee

Bilingual Education South Eastern Support Center [BESES]
Florida International University
Tamiami Campus, TRM03
Miami, FL 33199

Alaska, Idaho, Montana, Oregon, Washington, Wyoming

Interface Education Network
7080 SW Fir Loop, Suite 200
Portland, OR 97223

American Samoa, Hawaii

Hawaii/American Samoa Multifunctional Support Center
1150 South King Street, #203
Honolulu, HI 97814

Arizona, California (Imperial, Orange, Riverside, San Bernardino, San Diego Counties)

SDSU-Multifunctional Support Center
6363 Alvarado Court, Suite 200
San Diego, CA 92120

Arkansas, Louisiana, Oklahoma, Texas Education Service Regions V–XIX

Bilingual Education Training and Technical Assistance Network [BETTA]
University of Texas at El Paso
College of Education
El Paso, TX 79968

California (all counties north of and including San Luis Obispo, Kern, and Inyo), Nevada

Bilingual Education Multifunctional Support Center
National Hispanic University
255 East Fourteenth Street
Oakland, CA 94606

California (Los Angeles, Santa Barbara, Ventura Counties), Nevada

Bilingual Education Multifunctional Support Center
California State University at Los Angeles School of Education
5151 State University Drive
Los Angeles, CA 90032

Colorado, Kansas, Nebraska, New Mexico, Utah

BUENO Bilingual Education Multifunctional Support Center
University of Colorado
Bueno Center of Multicultural Education
Campus Box 249
Boulder, CO 80309

Commonwealth of Northern Mariana Islands, Guam, Trust Territory of the Pacific Islands

Project BEAM [Bilingual Education Assistance in Micronesia]
University of Guam
College of Education
UOG Station,
Mangilao, GU 96923

Commonwealth of Puerto Rico, Virgin Islands

Bilingual Education Multifunctional Support Center
Colegio Universitario Metropolitano
P.O. Box CUM
Rio Piedras, PR 00928

Connecticut, Maine, Massachusetts, New Hampshire, Rhode Island, Vermont

New England Bilingual Education Multifunctional Center
Brown University, Weld Building
345 Blackstone Boulevard
Providence, RI 02906

Delaware, District of Columbia, Maryland, New Jersey, North Carolina, Ohio, Pennsylvania, Virginia, West Virginia

Georgetown University Bilingual Education Service Center
Georgetown University
2139 Wisconsin Avenue, NW, Suite 100
Washington, DC 20007

Illinois, Indiana, Iowa, Michigan, Minnesota, Missouri, North Dakota, South Dakota, Wisconsin

Midwest Bilingual Educational Multifunctional Resource Center
2360 East Devon Avenue, Suite 3011
Campus Box 136
Des Plaines, IL 60018

New York

New York State Bilingual Education Multifunctional Support Center
Hunter College of CUNY
695 Park Avenue, Box 367
New York, NY 10021

Texas Education Service Center, Regions I through IV, XX

Region Multifunctional Support Center
Texas A&I University
Kingsville, TX 78363
Native American Programs

Alaska, Arizona, California, Michigan, Minnesota, Montana, New Mexico, North Carolina, Oklahoma, South Dakota, Utah, Washington, Wyoming

National Indian Bilingual Center
Arizona State University
Community Services Building
Tempe, AZ 85287

Special-Needs Resources

Alexander Graham Bell Association for the Deaf
3417 Volta Place, NW
Washington, D.C. 20007

American Foundation for the Blind
15 West Sixteenth Street
New York, NY 10011

American Printing House for the Blind
1839 Frankforth Avenue, Box A
Louisville, KY 40206

American Speech, Language, and Hearing Association
10801 Rockville Pike
Rockville, MD 20852

Center for Multisensory Learning
University of California at Berkeley
Lawrence Hall of Science
Berkeley, CA 94720

Council for Exceptional Children
1920 Association Drive
Reston, VA 22091

ERIC Clearinghouse on Handicapped and Gifted Children
1920 Association Drive
Reston, VA 22091

The Lighthouse for the Blind and Visually Impaired
1155 Mission Street
San Francisco, CA 94103

National Technical Institute for the Deaf
One Lomb Memorial Drive
Rochester, NY 14623

The Project on the Handicapped in Science
American Association for the Advancement of Science
1776 Massachusetts Avenue, NW
Washington, DC 20036

Recording for the Blind
20 Roszel Road
Princeton, NJ 08540

Sensory Aids Foundation
399 Sherman Avenue
Palo Alto, CA 94304

Science Teachers Associations

The major association for teachers with an interest in science is the National Science Teachers Association (NSTA). For information on membership, write to this address:

National Science Teachers Association
1840 Wilson Boulevard
Arlington, VA 22201-3000

This affiliated organization may also be reached through the NSTA address:

Council for Elementary Science International

Other science-related associations that may be of interest include the following:

American Association of Physics Teachers
c/o American Institute of Physics
335 E. 45th Street
New York, NY 10017

American Chemical Society
1155 Sixteenth Street, NW
Washington, DC 20006

National Association of Biology Teachers
1420 N. Street, NW
Washington, DC 20005

National Earth Science Teachers Association
P.O. Box 2194
Liverpool, NY 13089-2194

School Science and Mathematics Association
16734 Hamilton Court
Strongsville, OH 44149-5701

NASA Teacher Resource Centers

NASA Teacher Resource Centers provide teachers with NASA-related materials for use in classrooms. Contact the center that serves your state for materials or additional information.

Alabama, Arkansas, Iowa, Louisiana, Missouri, Tennessee

NASA Marshall Space Flight Center
Teacher Resource Center at the U.S. Space
   and Rocket Center
P.O. Box 070015
Huntsville, AL 35807

Alaska, Arizona, California, Hawaii, Idaho, Montana, Nevada, Oregon, Utah, Washington, Wyoming

NASA Ames Research Center
Teacher Resource Center
Mail Stop 253-2
Moffett Field, CA 94035

California (cities near Dryden Flight Research Facility)

NASA Dryden Flight Research Facility
Teacher Resource Center
Lancaster, CA 93535

Colorado, Kansas, Nebraska, New Mexico, North Dakota, Oklahoma, South Dakota, Texas

NASA Johnson Space Center
Education Resource Center
1601 NASA Road #1
Houston, TX 77058

Connecticut, Delaware, District of Columbia, Maine, Maryland, Massachusetts, New Hampshire, New Jersey, New York, Pennsylvania, Rhode Island, Vermont

NASA Goddard Space Flight Center
Teacher Resource Laboratory
Mail Code 130.3
Greenbelt, MD 20771

Florida, Georgia, Puerto Rico, Virgin Islands

NASA Kennedy Space Center
Educators Resource Laboratory
Mail Code ERL
Kennedy Space Center, FL 32899

Kentucky, North Carolina, South Carolina, Virginia, West Virginia

NASA Langley Research Center
Teacher Resource Center at the Virginia Air
   and Space Center
600 Settlers Landing Road
Hampton, VA 23669

Illinois, Indiana, Michigan, Minnesota, Ohio, Wisconsin

NASA Lewis Research Center
Teacher Resource Center
21000 Brookpark Road
Mail Stop 8-1
Cleveland, OH 44135

Mississippi

NASA Stennis Space Center
Teacher Resource Center
Building 1200
Stennis Space Center, MS 39529-6000

Virginia and Maryland Eastern Shore

NASA Wallops Flight Facility
Education Complex-Visitor Center
Building J-17
Wallops Island, VA 23337

General inquiries related to space science and planetary exploration may be addressed to:

Jet Propulsion Laboratory
NASA Teacher Resource Center
Attn: JPL Educational Outreach
Mail Stop CS-530
Pasadena, CA 91109

For catalogue and order forms for audiovisual material, send request on school letterhead to:

NASA CORE
Lorain County Joint Vocational School
15181 Route 58 South
Oberlin, OH 44074

Index

Note: Page numbers in **bold** type indicate activities/demonstrations.

Photo, Figure, and Text Credits